HINDU CASTES AND SECTS

HINDU CASTES AND SECTS

AN EXPOSITION OF THE ORIGIN OF THE HINDU CASTE SYSTEM AND THE BEARING OF THE SECTS TOWARDS EACH OTHER AND TOWARDS OTHER RELIGIOUS SYSTEMS.

BY

JOGENDRA NATH BHATTACHARYA, M.A., D.L.,

President of the College of Pandits, Nadiya

Author of "Commentaries on Hindu Law,"

" Vyavastha Kalpadruma,"&c

KALPAZ

ISBN: 978-93-5128-473-4(HB)

First Published in 1896
Indian Reprint in 2017

Published by

Kalpaz Publications
C-30, Satyawati Nagar,
Delhi – 110052
E-mail: kalpaz@hotmail.com
Website: kalpazpublications.com
Ph.: +91-9212142040

PREFACE.

In the last edition of my "Commentaries on Hindu Law" I devoted a chapter to the Hindu Caste System which attracted the attention of the Publishers, and they suggested that the subject might well be expanded so as to be brought out as a separate volume. They suggested also that, in order to make the book complete, I should give an account not only of the Castes, but also of the important Hindu Sects, some of which are practically so many new Castes.

As I had been already engaged in writing a book about the history and philosophy of religions, the proposal, so far as the sects were concerned, was welcome indeed. About the Castes I felt very considerable diffidence; but it seemed to me that, in a town like Calcutta, where there are men from every part of India, it might not be quite impossible to collect the necessary information. When, however, I actually commenced my enquiries, then I fully realised the difficulty of my task. The original information contained in this work has been derived from a very large number of Hindu gentlemen hailing from different parts of India. I here gratefully acknowledge the kindness that they have shown in according to me their assistance. I feel very strongly inclined to insert in this book a list of their names. But the publication of such a list is not desirable for more reasons than one. To begin with, such a list would be necessarily too long to be conveniently included. Then, again, the subject of castes and sects is, in some of its aspects, a very irritating one, and if I were to give publicity to the names of the persons who have assisted me, it might place them in a very false position. So I thank them generally without mentioning any names.

In connection also with this part of the work, I must acknowledge my obligations to the works of Risley, Wilson and Sherring, and to Mr. Narsimayangar's Report of the last Census of Mysore. As to the last of these, which is compiled by an educated native of the country, it is hardly necessary to observe that it is very reliable, though not very complete. Mr. Risley's "Tribes and Castes of Bengal" is an exhaustive treatise, and is, generally speaking, reliable also. If there had been similar works for the other provinces, then the task of taking a bird's-eye view of the whole would not have been quite so arduous to me as it has actually been.

With regard to the part of the book devoted to the Hindu Sects, I may mention that the greater portion of it had been written originally for my promised work on the philosophy of religion which I hope to bring out before long. For the sake of many of my friends and relations near and dear to me I hesitated to give publicity to my views before ; but it seems to me high time now that I should speak out and do what lies in me to set forth the true character of the cults that the majority of those who profess to be Hindus believe and practise.

The religions of those who are not regarded as Hindus do not come within the scope of this work. But the position which I assign to Christianity, Mahomedanism, Zoroastrianism, &c., must appear clear enough from what I have said in the Introduction to my account of the Hindu Sects, about the evolution of human faiths, and about the different principles on which they may be classified. I have tried my best throughout to avoid irreverence and offensive expressions, and the reader, who is not altogether blinded by orthodoxy, will, I hope, admit that, even with regard to the worst of the abomination-worshipping sects, I have nowhere been harsher than the nature of the case absolutely required. Reverence ought to be by all means shown to persons and institutions that have a just claim to it. But nothing can, in my opinion, be more sinful than to speak respectfully of persons who are enemies of mankind, and to whitewash rotten institutions by esoteric explanations and fine phrases.

It is no doubt extremely difficult to get rid of the effect of early training and associations. But those who claim to be educated and enlightened will, I trust, give me an impartial and patient hearing. However strong their faith in Saivism, Saktaism and Radha worship may be, they cannot be altogether blind to the real character of these creeds. One of the greatest thinkers of modern times has, in connection with certain questions of political economy, said :—

> It often happens that the universal belief of one age of mankind—a belief from which no one *was*, nor, without any extraordinary effort of genius and courage, *could*, at that time be free—becomes to a subsequent age so palpable an absurdity, that the only difficulty then is to imagine how such a thing can ever have appeared credible.

This, I am sure, will before long be the feeling of every honest Hindu with regard to some of the most important features of his so-called religions, and I shall feel I have performed an almost sacred duty if this work promotes in some degree that end.

JOGENDRA NATH BHATTACHARYA.

CALCUTTA, *May* 1896.

CONTENTS.

HINDU CASTES.

PART I.

INTRODUCTION.

PART II.

THE BRAHMANS GENERALLY.

PART III.

The Brahmans of Northern India.

PART IV.

The Brahmans of Southern India.

PART V.

The Semi-Brahmanical Castes.

PART VI.

The Degraded Brahmans.

PART X.

The Mercantile Castes.

PART XI.

The Artisan Castes Generally Recognised as Clean Sudras.

PART XII.

The Manufacturing and Artisan Castes that are Regarded as Unclean Sudras.

PART XIII.

The Clean Agricultural Castes.

PART XIV.

The Cowherds and Shepherds.

PART XV.

The Clean and the Unclean Castes Employed in Personal and Domestic Service.

PART XVI.

MISCELLANEOUS CASTES.

HINDU SECTS.

PART I.

INTRODUCTION.

PART II.

THE SIVITE AND THE SEMI-SIVITE SECTS.

PART III.

The Saktas.

PART IV.

The Vishnuvite Sects.

PART V.

The Semi-Vishnuvite and Guru-Worshipping Sects.

PART VI.

Modern Religions intended to bring about Union between the Hindus and the Mahomedans.

PART VII.

Buddhism.

PART VIII.

The Jains.

HINDU CASTES AND SECTS.

—:o:—

PART I.

INTRODUCTION.

CHAP. I.—THE NATURE AND ORIGIN OF THE HINDU CASTE SYSTEM.

THE institution of caste is a unique feature of Hindu society, and, as nothing exactly like it is to be found in any other part of the world, the manner in which it grew up in India cannot but be regarded as a question of the highest importance by the student of social phenomena. The subject has, therefore, attracted a large share of the attention of many erudite scholars, both European and Indian. The mass of information contained in their works, though not free from errors and inaccuracies, is of very great value. But the usefulness of their writings is marred, to a considerable extent, by the more or less superficial views which they take of the origin and nature of caste as a system. In speaking of it Mr. Sherring, who may be regarded as one of the chief authorities on the subject, characterises our social mechanism as "a monstrous engine of pride, dissension and shame,"* and generally has not one good word to say with reference to it or to its authors, the Brahmans. Dr. Wilson also condemns the caste system *in toto*, though in milder terms. He says that "among the Hindus the imagination of natural and positive distinction in humanity has been brought to the most fearful and pernicious development." In his dissertations on "the natural history of caste" Mr. Sherring gives, first of all, what he calls an analysis of the Brahman's character in which he finds nothing but arrogance, selfishness and ambition, and then goes on to observe :—

"To speak of the Brahmans as though they were one and the same people, with the same characteristics is delusive. For thousands of years they have been a disunited people, with mutual antipathies and non-resemblances, instead of mutual likenesses and concord. The Brahmans themselves, and none others, are responsible for this. Their monstrous arrogance, selfishness and assumption have proved the bane of their race. In the cultivation of these vicious qualities they are at one, but in all other respects they are the most inharmonious and discordant people on the face of the earth.

The spread of caste, and the multiplication of separate, mutually exclusive, and inimical tribes among the lower Hindu grades, also lies at their door. The detestable example they set could not but be followed by an imitative people without brains of their own. These Hindu tribes would never have dared to establish an infinity of castes among themselves without the direct sanction and assistance of the Brahmans. Moreover, when the Brahmans perceived that castes were increasing beyond decent limits, until the whole country was threatened with an endless number of caste sub-divisions, all for the most part mutually destructive, they might have peremptorily stopped their further multiplication. But they did not. On the contrary, it is plain that they looked on with the utmost satisfaction, pleased at the alienation of tribe from tribe."—Sherring's *Hindu Tribes and Castes*, Vol. III, pp. 234-35.

The inconsistencies and the fallacies abounding in these extracts are too obvious to require any critical exposition. The author's views with regard to our religion and our social polity were evidently more influenced by his zeal for his own faith of which he was a missionary, than by his sober judgment. In his lifetime he had a large number of Hindu friends who still cherish his memory with affection, and he had much better opportunities for studying the peculiarities of our

* See Mr. Sherring's Preface to his *Hindu Tribes and Castes*.

social fabric than most of his countrymen in India. At any rate, he may certainly be credited with having possessed sufficient knowledge of history to be aware of the shortcomings which existed in past generations, and still exist, among the priestly classes in other countries, and there can be no justification whatever for the severe censure that he has passed on the Brahmans. Yet the same views have been blindly accepted by some of the foremost of modern Hindu scholars. After stating his views regarding the probable origin of the caste system, Mr. R. C. Dutt, in his *History of India*, says :—

"It was unknown to the Hindus in the Vedic age, and was first developed in the Epic age. It divided and disunited the compact body of Aryan Hindus into three hereditary bodies, *viz.*, the priests, the soldiers, and the people. And it permanently placed the people under the priestly and military castes; and thereby hindered popular progress and the growth of popular freedom in India.

It should be remembered, however, that with the exception of the priests and soldiers, the mass of the Hindu people still formed one united caste, the Vaishya in the Epic and succeeding ages. And the mass of the people were still entitled, like the Kshatriyas and the Brahmans, to perform sacrifices, to acquire religious knowledge, and study the Vedas. But with the loss of their independence, the Hindus have become more disunited in modern times."

The great living poet of Bengal, Babu Hem Chandra Banerji, gives countenance to similarly erroneous views, when he calls upon his countrymen to cause a clean sweep of all caste distinctions, in order that they may, by united action, recover their ancient greatness.

I am no out-and-out admirer of caste, as it exists now, and I think that, in the state of things now arising, its discipline might be relaxed in certain directions with advantage. But I believe that, generally speaking, there does not exist that antipathy between the several castes which the world at large has been led to believe. A little hitch is caused sometimes when a man of a superior caste refuses to allow one of an inferior caste to sit on the same carpet, or when the use of his waterpot is disallowed by the former to the latter. For purposes of business, not the several castes only, but even Hindus and Mahomedans can and do mix on the most friendly terms. There is, upon the whole, no more animosity between a Rajput and a Brahman than between a Rajput and a Rajput, or between a Brahman and a Brahman. If the Brahman refuses to eat in the house of a Rajput on the ground that there are no true Ksatriyas in this age of sin, the Rajput also refuses to partake of the Brahman's hospitality on the plea, afforded by the Brahmanical Shastras, that a Brahman's property should not be appropriated by a man of any caste on any account. For purposes of marriage and interchange of hospitality each caste is an independent and exclusive body, and all the classes are placed on a coequal footing. Such being the case, the so-called inferior castes show no more eagerness to be enrolled among the higher, than the latter do to be reduced to the level of the former. It is open to the lower castes to practise any profession, excepting that of a priest, and as every Hindu has a recognized position within his own caste, which does not vary with any viscissitude of fortune, no one can feel inclined to crush out that system, and run the risk of losing its certain advantages, for the uncertain prospect of acquiring a better social footing by working as it were upon a *tabula rasa*. A few low caste parvenus there may be, who, in their innermost hearts, feel ashamed of even their own parents and brothers. But the aspirations of these men certainly do not deserve much sympathy. Generally speaking, the Hindus look upon the several divisions in their society as the necessary component parts of their social mechanism, and there can be no occasion for jealousy or bitter feelings.

Caste has had its origin, no doubt, in Brahmanical legislation. But there is no ground whatever for the doctrine that it is the outcome of the policy embodied in the Machiavelian maxim *Divide and Rule*. A very little reflection ought to show that the caste system, introduced and enforced by the Brahminical Shastras, could not possibly be the cause of any social split. On the contrary, it provided bonds of union between races and clans that had nothing in common before its introduction. There is no ground whatever for the supposition that in primitive India all classes of people were united as one man, and that the "unnatural and pernicious caste system" was forced on them by the Brahmans with the diabolical object of sowing dissensions among them. The more correct view seems to be that the legislation of the Rishis was calculated not only to bring about union between the isolated clans that lived in primitive India, but to render it possible to assimilate within each group the foreign hordes that were expected to pour into the country from time to time. If those Englishmen who have permanently settled in this country recognized the sacredness of the Shastras, and refrained from eating forbidden food, they might be admitted into the Ksatriya clan under the name of Sakya Seni Rajputs. The authors of such legislation deserve certainly to be admired for their large-hearted statesmanship, instead of being censured for selfish ambition and narrowness.

The ambition that led the Hindu lawgivers to place their own class above the rest of mankind, has, no doubt, an appearance of selfishness. But if self-aggrandisement had been, as is alleged, their sole motive, then there was nothing to prevent them from laying down the law that the proper men to enjoy the kingly office and the various loaves and fishes of the public service, were the Brahmans. The highest secular ambition of the Brahman was to be the unpaid adviser of the Crown, and, as a matter of actual practice, the entire civil service was left by them in the hands of the Kāyasthas. Such professions, accompanied by such conduct, do not betray selfishness. It was only in respect of matters relating to religion that the Brahmans kept in their hands the monopoly of power. But they could not have taken any other course without upsetting altogether the fabric which they had built up.

Circumstanced as India, presumably, was in ancient times, there could not possibly have been in that state of things, any great attraction either for military service or for intellectual pursuits. The resources of the country were then too limited for adequately rewarding either the soldier or the scholar, and as any able-bodied man could, in those times, earn his living without any difficulty, either in agricultural pursuits or by breeding cattle, the only way to induce any class of men to adopt a more ambitious or risky career, lay in giving them a superior status by hereditary right. The importance of the service which caste has done to India may be realized, to some extent, from the fact that when, in a party of Hindus, comments are made about an illiterate Brahman, an unbusiness like Kāyastha or a cowardly Ksatriya, they not unfrequently express their doubt as to his very legitimacy. Such being the case, no Kshatriya can refuse to fight, when there is occasion, without laying himself open to the most galling of reproaches. His ancestors never shrank from legitimate fighting, and so he has no choice left.

"He too would rather die than shame."

It is feeling of this kind that urged the ancient Ksatriyas to desperate deeds for the defence of their country, and though long since fallen, yet modern history is not altogether wanting in testimony as to the greatness of that mighty race. The name of Babu Kumāra Sing, the last great Rajput hero, is not likely to be soon forgotten, though English historians may not do him justice. Goaded on to rebellion by the ungenerous suspicions entertained against him by a local official, and by the attempt made by that official to insult and imprison him, he besought his friends, relatives and adherents, to remain loyal to the British Government, and to leave him to shift for himself. But he was the idol of the Bhojpuriās, and they gathered round him, like one man, to fight under his banner. At their head the octogenarian hero fought bravely to the last, and displayed throughout far better generalship and valour than the cowards who took the leading part in bringing about the conflagration. The old Rajput baron knew well that he had no chance of ultimate success. But as a Ksatriya, claiming the blood of the great Vikramaditya in his veins, he could not submit to die like a traitor on the scaffold. Had the Government of Bengal reposed that confidence in him which he certainly deserved, the whole province of Behar would probably have remained as quiet as Bengal, and the operations of the mutineers would have been confined to the North-West Provinces and Oude only.

In their fourfold division of caste, the Rishis placed their own class, *i.e.*, the descendants of the Vedic singers and their comrades, above all the others. To the fighting classes the Brahmanical codes assigned the second rank, and the process, by which they were reconciled to accept the position that was given them, is replete with interest. With regard to the superiority of the Brahmans, Manu says :—

> "Since the Brahman sprang from the most excellent part, since he was the first born, and since he possesses the Veda, he is by right the chief of this whole creation."—Manu, I, 93.

But while thus glorifying the Brahmans, the Rishis made great concessions to the Ksatriyas by declaring that the office of the king was their birthright, and also by enjoining on all classes the duty of implicit obedience to the king.

Brahmanical legislation has been very successful in organising the Brahman and the Ksatriya castes. To a very great extent, the descendants of the Vedic singers and their comrades have become one race under the name of Brahmans. To a still greater extent have the several fighting clans recognized each other as members of one great family, under the name of Ksatriyas or Rajputs. The Vaishya caste was, in all probability, never successfully formed, and, so far as this class is concerned, Brahmanical legislation failed to attain its very noble object. The Baniyas who practise trade and are, generally speaking, a wealthy class, claim in some places to be Vaishyas. But, in all probability, the majority of the traders, artisans, and agriculturists never cared for the honour of being invested with the sacred thread, or for the privilege of reading the Vedas. And when such was the case, the Brahmans themselves could not be too anxious to force these honours and privileges upon them. The chief concern of the Brahmans, in the efforts they made to realise their ideal of social polity, was to keep the fighting clans in good humour, so that even if the Vaishyas sought for the honour of the thread, the Brahmans could not have given it to them without depriving it of thevalue which it came to acquire in the eyes of the Ksatriyas.

Caste is often described by European scholars as an iron chain which has fettered each class to the profession of their ancestors, and has rendered any improvement on their part impossible. This view may, to some extent, be regarded as correct so far as the lower classes are concerned. But with regard to the higher classes, caste is a golden chain which they have willingly placed around their necks, and which has fixed them to only that which is noble and praiseworthy. Any little split that is caused by caste now and then is far outweighed by the union of races and clans which it has promoted and fostered, and there is no justification whatever for the abuse which has been heaped upon its authors.

CHAP. II.—WHETHER CASTE IS A SOCIAL, OR A RELIGIOUS DISTINCTION?

THE question has been hotly discussed, whether caste is a social or a religious distinction? As shown in the last chapter, it is mainly a social distinction. But as many of the ordinances of our Shastras are based upon it, it has a religious aspect also. The religious rights and duties of the Hindus do in fact vary, to a considerable extent, according to their caste. For instance, on the death of an agnate within seven degrees, a Brahman has to observe mourning for ten days only, while a man of the fighting caste has to wear the "weeds of woe" for twelve days, a man of the mercantile caste for fifteen days, and a Sudra for one full month. Then, again, the Vedic rites and prayers which the three higher castes are required to perform every day are all prohibited to the Sudra. The latter can be taught to repeat only those prayers that are prescribed by what may be called the new testaments of the Hindus, *i.e.*, the Purāns and the Tāntras. But the Brahman who enlists even a good Sudra among his disciples is lowered for ever in the estimation of the people, while by ministering to a Sudra of a low class he is degraded altogether.

CHAP. III.—THE REGULATIONS BY WHICH THE CASTES HAVE BEEN MADE EXCLUSIVE.

The rules defining the proper avocations of the several castes are not imperative, it being laid down in the Shastras that a person, unable to earn his livelihood otherwise, may take to a profession which is ordinarily prohibited to his class. Manu says :—

80. "Among the several occupations *for gaining a livelihood* the most commendable respectively for the sacerdotal, military, and mercantile classes, are teaching the Veda, defending, and commerce or keeping herds and flocks.

81. Yet a Brahman unable to subsist by his duties just mentioned may live by the duty of a soldier, for that is the next in rank.

82. If it be asked, how he must live, should he be unable to get a subsistence by either of these employments, *the answer is*, he may subsist as a mercantile man, applying himself *in person* to tillage and attendance on cattle.

95. A military man in distress may subsist by all these means, but at no time must he have recourse to the highest, *or sacerdotal* function.

98. A mercantile man, unable to subsist by his own duties, may descend even to the servile acts of a Sudra, taking care never to do what ought never to be done ; but, when he has gained a competence, let him depart from service.

99. A man of the fourth class, not finding employment by waiting on the twice-born, while his wife and son are tormented with hunger, may subsist by handicrafts.—Manu, *Chap. X.*"

Such being the precepts of the Shastras, it is very often found that a Hindu of one class is engaged in a profession which is the speciality of another, and the tendency of English education is to make all the castes more and more regardless about strict compliance with Shastric rules on the subject. The Hindu legislators made the castes exclusive, not so much by prescribing particular professions for each, as by prohibiting intermarriage and interchange of hospitality on a footing of equality. In the beginning intermarriage was allowed so far that a man of a superior caste could lawfully take in marriage a girl of an inferior caste. But, by what may be called the Hindu new testaments, intermarriage between the different castes is prohibited altogether. As to interchange of hospitality, the Shastras lay down that a Brahman must avoid, if possible, the eating of any kind of food in the house of a Sudra, and that under no circumstances is he to eat any food cooked with water and salt by a Sudra, or touched by a Sudra after being so cooked. In practice the lower classes of Brahmans are sometimes compelled by indigence to honour the Sudras by accepting their hospitality—of course, eating only uncooked food or such food as is cooked by Brahmans with materials supplied by the host. The prejudice against eating cooked food that has been touched by a man of an inferior caste is so strong that, although the Shastras do not prohibit the eating of food cooked by a Ksatriya or Vaishya, yet the Brahmans, in most parts of the country, would not eat such food. For these reasons, every Hindu household—whether Brahman, Ksatriya or Sudra—that can afford to keep a paid cook generally entertains the services of a Brahman for the performance of its *cuisine*—the result being that, in the larger towns, the very name of Brahman has suffered a strange degradation of late, so as to mean only a cook.

The most important regulations by which the castes have been made exclusive are those which relate to marriage. In fact, as Mr. Risley in his valuable work on the *Castes and Tribes of Bengal* rightly observes, "caste is a matter mainly relating to marriage." Matrimonial alliances out of caste is prevented by the seclusion of the females, their early marriage, and the social etiquette which requires that even the marriages of boys should be arranged for them by their parents or other guardians. The Hindu youth has to maintain an attitude of utter indifference about every proposal regarding his marriage, and when any arrangement in that respect is made by his parents, grand-parents, uncles or elder brothers, he has to go through the ceremony out of his sense of duty to obey or oblige them. The selection being, in all cases, made by the guardian in accordance with his sober judgment, and never by the parties themselves in accordance with their impulses for the time being, marriage out of caste is almost impossible in Hindu society, and is never known to take place except among the very lowest.

CHAP. IV.—THE ORIGIN OF THE ADDITIONAL CASTES AND THE SUB-CASTES.

THE sentiments which Brahmanical legislation engendered and fostered have led to the formation or recognition of a vast number of extra castes and subcastes. In all probability the laws of the Shastras failed to bring about a complete fusion of all the clans and races that had been intended to be included within the same group, and their recognition, as distinct subdivisions, was inevitable from the very beginning. New sub-divisions have also been formed in later times by the operation of one or other of the following causes :—

1. By migration to different parts of the country.
2. By different sections being devoted to the practice of distinct professions.
3. By any section being elevated above or degraded below the level of the others.
4. By quarrels between the different sections of the same caste as to their relative status.
5. By becoming the followers of one of the modern religious teachers.
6. By the multiplication of the illegitimate progeny of religious mendicants.

The Brahmanical sub-classes like the Rādhis, Bārendras and the Kanojias are so-called on account of their being the inhabitants of Rādh, Bārendra, and Kanoj, though they all belong to the same stock. The Vaidikas are evidently so-called on account of their devoting themselves exclusively to the study and the teaching of the Vedas. If so, then it is not difficult to see why they kept themselves aloof from those who pursued secular avocations. The Husainis, Kalankis Mahā-Brahmans, Agradānis, Sanicharis, Gangāputras, &c., have become more or less exclusive by being degraded and debarred from association with the other classes of Brahmans on a footing of equality. When one section of a caste affect a superior status and refuse to give their daughters to another section, the latter may for a time admit their inferiority by betraying an eagerness to marry their daughters in the superior caste without having the compliment reciprocated. But sooner or later the connection between them is cut off altogether, and they become distinct sub-castes. With regard to the additional castes, it is stated in the Shastras that they are due to intermarriage and miscegenation between the primary castes. This explanation is necessitated by the theory that originally there were only four castes, and has been of great use to the Brahmans for enforcing marriage within caste, and for humiliating such classes as the Vaidyas and the Acharyas who, being by the nature of their profession, very important factors in every native court, might otherwise have become too powerful.

To me it seems that most of the so-called "mixed castes" owe their exclusiveness to either Brahmanical policy, or to the impossibility of including them within any of the four primary groups; while there are some among the additional castes whose formation is clearly traceable to their being the followers of some revolutionary teacher of modern times.

The Brahmanical explanation of the origin of the additional castes has been accepted by some of the English writers on the subject. But to me it seems utterly impossible that any new caste could be formed in the manner described by Manu or any other Hindu lawgiver. In order to accept the theory it is necessary to assume that a careful record was kept of every case of irregular marriage and illicit sexual intercourse, and that the progeny of the parties were listed and included under separate groups by royal edicts. What seems much more probable is, that in order to make the primary divisions into four castes practically acceptable, most of the sub-divisions in each of them had to be recognized at the very beginning, and the tendency which was thus generated received further expansion by the recognition of the additional castes on account of the circumstances and reasons mentioned already. The motives that led the Brahmans to declare that the astrologer was the son of a shoemaker, and that the medical men were the offspring of irregular marriage between a Brahman and a Vaishya woman, ought to be clear enough to every one who has any idea of the intrigues that usually prevailed in the courts of the Hindu kings.

CHAP. V.—THE AUTHORITIES BY WHOM CASTE RULES ARE ENFORCED.

UNDER the Hindu kings, the rules relating to caste were enforced by the officers of the crown in accordance with the advice of the great Pandits who generally acted as ministers. During the period of Moslem ascendancy, the Hindu barons and chiefs exercised the prerogative where they could. But in Northern India, the Hindus have now no recognised spiritual head. In cases of serious violations of Shastric injunctions, the Pandits are consulted as to the nature of the expiation required. But their power to impose any penalty on the delinquent is not very considerable. In extreme cases they may, as a body, refuse to accept any gift from the offender, and keep aloof from the religious ceremonies celebrated in his house. But except where public opinion is too strong to be disregarded, they are very seldom sufficiently united to visit anyone with the punishment of excommunication in such manner.

In Southern India the case is somewhat different. There the non-Vishnuvite Hindus are completely under the spiritual authority of the Superiors of the Sankarite monasteries. In fact, the head of the Sringeri monastery, at the source of the Toonga Bhadra in Mysore, has the same power over the Smarta Hindus of Southern India that the Pope has over the Roman Catholic population of Europe. See *The Queen* v. *Sri Sankara*, I. L. R., 6 Madras, p. 381.

The main agency by which caste discipline is still maintained to some extent is the religious sentimentalism of the Hindus as a nation. But in this respect there is no consistency to be found in them. For instance, there are lots of men who almost openly eat forbidden food and drink forbidden liquors, and yet their fellow-castemen do not usually hesitate to dine in their houses, or to have connections with them by marriage. But if a man goes to Europe he loses his caste, even though he be a strict vegetarian and teetotaler. Then, again, if a man marry a widow he loses caste, though such marriage is not in any way against Shastric injunctions, while the keeping of a Mahomedan mistress, which is a serious and almost inexpiable offence, is not visited with any kind of punishment by castemen. Similarly, a man may become a Brahmo or agnostic and yet remain in caste; but if he espouse Christianity or Mahomedanism, his own parents would exclude him from their house, and disallow every kind of intercourse, except on the most distant terms. He cannot have even a drink of water under his parental roof, except in an earthen pot, which would not be touched afterwards by even the servants of the house, and which he would have to throw away with his own hands, if no scavenger be available.

The only acts which now lead to exclusion from caste are the following :—

1. Embracing Christianity or Mahomedanism.
2. Going to Europe or America.
3. Marrying a widow.
4. Publicly throwing away the sacred thread.
5. Publicly eating beef, pork or fowl.
6. Publicly eating *kachi* food cooked by a Mahomedan, Christian or low caste Hindu.
7. Officiating as a priest in the house of a very low class Sudra.
8. By a female going away from home for an immoral purpose.
9. By a widow becoming pregnant.

In the villages, the friendless and the poor people are sometimes excluded from caste for other offences as, for instance :—adultery, incest, eating forbidden food and drinking forbidden liquors. But when the offender is an influential personage or is influentially connected, no one thinks of visiting him with such punishment.

CHAP. VI.—NATURE OF THE PENALTY OF EXCLUSION FROM CASTE.

WHEN a Hindu is excluded from caste—

1. His friends, relatives and fellow-townsmen refuse to partake of his hospitality.
2. He is not invited to entertainments in their houses.
3. He cannot obtain brides or bridegrooms for his children.
4. Even his own married daughters cannot visit him without running the risk of being excluded from caste.
5. His priest and even his barber and washerman refuse to serve him.
6. His fellow-castemen sever their connection with him so completely that they refuse to assist him even at the funeral of a member of his household.
7. In some cases the man excluded from caste is debarred access to the public temples.

To deprive a man of the services of his barber and washerman is becoming more and more difficult in these days. But the other penalties are (enforced on excluded persons) with more or less rigour, according to circumstances.

In the mofussil the penalties are most severely felt. Even in the towns such persons find great difficulty in marrying their children, and are therefore sometimes obliged to go through very humiliating expiatory ceremonies, and to pay heavy fees to the learned Pandits for winning their good graces.

PART II.

THE BRAHMANS GENERALLY.

CHAP. I.—THE POSITION OF THE BRAHMANS IN HINDU SOCIETY.

THE most remarkable feature in the mechanism of Hindu society is the high position occupied in it by the Brahmans. They not only claim almost divine honours as their birthright, but, generally speaking, the other classes, including the great Ksatriya princes, and the rich Vaishya merchants readily submit to their pretensions as a matter of course. A Brahman never bows his head to make a *pranam* to one who is not a Brahman. When saluted by a man of any other class, he only pronounces a benediction saying, "Victory be unto you." In some cases when the party saluting is a prince or a man of exalted position in society, the Brahman, in pronouncing his benediction, stretches out the palm of his right hand, in a horizontal direction, to indicate that he has been propitiated. The form of salutation by the inferior castes to Brahmans varies according to circumstances. When the Brahman to be saluted has a very high position, temporal or spiritual, and the man saluting desires to honour him to the utmost degree possible, he falls prostrate at the feet of the object of his reverence, and, after touching them with his hand applies his fingers to his lips and his forehead. In ordinary cases a man, of any of the three inferior castes, salutes a Brahman by either joining his palms and raising them to his forehead, in the form of a double military salute, or by simply pronouncing such words as *pranam* or *paunlagi*. Thus the amount of veneration shown to a Brahman may vary under different conditions. But no member of the other castes can, consistently with Hindu social etiquette and religious beliefs, refuse altogether to bow to a Brahman. Even the Chaitanites and the other classes of modern Vaishnavas, who do not profess to have any veneration for the Brahmans as such, and speak of them as heretics in their own circle, cannot do without bowing to Brahmans and accepting their benedictions in public.

The more orthodox Sudras carry their veneration for the priestly class to such an extent, that they will not cross the shadow of a Brahman, and it is not unusual for them to be under a vow not to eat any food in the morning, before drinking Bipracharanāmrita, *i.e.*, water in which the toe of a Brahman has been dipped. On the other hand, the pride of the Brahman is such that they do not bow to even the images of the gods worshipped in a Sudra's house by Brahman priests.

The Brahman asserts his superiority in various other ways. His Shastras declare that on certain occasions, Brahmans must be fed and gifts must be made to them by members of all classes. But the Brahman can accept such hospitality and gifts without hesitation only where the host or donor is a member of one of the three superior castes. The position of the Sudras is, according to the theory of the Shastras and the practice of Hindu society such, that a Brahman cannot accept their presents without lowering himself for ever, while by eating any kind of food cooked by a Sudra he loses his Brahmanism and his sanctity altogether. In the house of a Sudra, a Brahman may eat uncooked food, or such food as is cooked by a Brahman. But the Brahman who does so, while not sojourning in a foreign place, is lowered for ever in public estimation. For all these reasons, a Brahman who accepts a Sudra's gifts and hospitality at a religious ceremony, is able to pose as a person who makes a great sacrifice to oblige the host and donor.

When a Brahman invites a Sudra, the latter is usually asked to partake of the host's *prasāda*, or favour, in the shape of the leavings of his plate. Orthodox Sudras actually take offence, if invited by the use of any other formula. No Sudra is allowed to eat in the same room or at the same time with Brahmans. While the Brahman guests eat, the Sudras have to wait in a different part of the house. It is not, however, to be supposed that the Sudras take any offence at such treatment. On the contrary, they not only wait patiently, but, in some places, insist upon eating the leavings of the Brahmans, and refuse to eat anything from clean plates. Such orthodoxy is against nature, and is happily somewhat rare. Ordinarily, the pious Sudra takes a pinch from the leavings of a Brahman's plate, and after eating the same with due reverence, begins to eat from a clean plate.

The high caste and well-to-do Sudras never eat in the house of a Brahman without paying for the honour a *pranami*, or salutation fee, of at least one rupee. The Brahman host never insists on such payment, and in fact it is usually forced upon him. But when a Brahman eats in the house of a Sudra on a ceremonial occasion, the payment of a fee by the host to the guest is a *sine qua non*. This fee is called *bhojan dakshina*, and ordinarily varies from one anna to one rupee. In special cases the Sudra host has to pay much heavier fees.

When a Sudra writes a letter to a Brahman, it must begin by declaring that the writer makes a hundred million obeisances at the lotus feet of the addressee. When a Brahman writes a letter to a man of any other caste, the style of his communication is that of a superior being, and he commences it by pouring "heaps of assurances of future bliss."

If the amount of honour which is shewn by any community to its female members is an indication of the degree of civilization attained by it, then, the Brahmans are, the most advanced race of men on earth. They never mention the names of their ladies without the affix *devi* (goddess). But while thus upholding the dignity of the female members of their own class, they have taught the Sudras to use the word *dasi* (slave) as an affix to the names of Sudra females.

For conversational purposes the proper form of address by Sudras to Brahmans is Thākoor Mahasaya or Thākoorji which means "venerable god." In the same way Brahman ladies have to be addressed by Sudras as Ma Thākoorain or mother goddess. Formerly, even the Brahman kings of the country preferred the address of Thākoor to any other honorific expression. But of late years the word has suffered a strange degradation, and though it means "god" it is now very often taken to denote a cook.* For this reason the Brahmans who have received an English education, and are engaged in secular pursuits, saw no objection at one time to be addressed as Babus. But the epithet, Babu itself, has suffered of late a similar degradation. Before the commencement of British rule, it was applied only to the collateral relatives of the great royal families of India. But Englishmen in India applied it indiscriminately to every untitled Hindu, and specially to their Hindu clerks in Bengal. The title is, therefore, now usually taken to be the equivalent of the English words, "clerk" and "accountant," and the higher classes of educated Hindus now consider it an insult to be called Babus. In the absence of any other Indian word for honorific address, some Hindu gentlemen now prefer to be addressed as "Mr." and "Esquire," and for this they

* See p. 11, *ante*.

are found fault with and ridiculed, both by their countrymen and foreigners. But the fact is that the Hindu titles have suffered such degradation of late, that the untitled aristocracy of the country are compelled by sheer necessity to assume other epithets. If the word Thākoor retained its original signification, surely no Brahman, however exalted his secular position might be, would feel ashamed of that glorious honorific, or prefer the foreign epithets "Mr" and "Esquire."

CHAP. II.—THE BRAHMAN'S PROPER PROFESSIONS.

According to the commandments of his religion, the proper avocations of Brahmans are the following :—

1. Studying the Shastras.
2. Teaching the Shastras.
3. Performance of religious rites for the three superior classes.
4. Acceptance of gifts from the three superior classes.

Until recently the teaching of the Shastras was considered as the most honourable profession for a Brahman. The great Pandits of the country are still honoured and subsidized by the well-to-do classes. But their pretensions to superior learning are not admitted by those who have received an English education, and as their vaunted lore does not open the doors to any kind of service under Government, or to the liberal professions, they are fast sinking to a very inferior position. There was a time when the first Pandit in the country was the first man in the country. The people believed in the Pandits and, under the Hindu kings, the entire administration was very often left in their hands. But under British rule, the Pandits are nowhere. They still exercise very considerable influence over the uneducated classes. But the dignity of their profession is gone, and the class itself is fast becoming extinct in consequence of the superior attractions of English education.

As to the priestly profession, it is to be observed that the ordinance which recommends it as a proper one for a Brahman, is subject to very important limitations. Those who officiate as priests for Sudras, and those who perform the service of idols in public or private shrines, are, according to the dogmas of the Hindu scriptures, degraded persons. The performance of priestly functions for the superior castes is nowhere condemned in the sacred codes, and is, in fact, recommended as a proper avocation for a Brahman. But, according to Hindu notions, a priest is a very inferior person, and no Brahman, who can live otherwise, would willingly perform the work of a priest. The duties of the Brahman pastor involve long fastings, and, in respect of the worship of idols, almost menial service. Further, the men who actually perform the function of priests are, in the majority of cases, ignorant persons with just the amount of the knowledge of rituals that is necessary for discharging their duties. The Pandits, who study the original works that regulate these rituals, can find fault with the priest at every step, and reserve for themselves the higher functions of the critic and superintendent.

Whatever be the reason, the priest has a very inferior position in Hindu society. The relative status of Brahman families depends partly upon the hereditary rank of its members, as determined by the records of Indian heraldry. But, apart from aristocratic lineage, the highest position among the Brahmans is, according to orthodox notions, occupied by the Pandits and the Gurus who have only Brahman disciples. The Gurus are principally of two classes—namely, Tāntric and Vaishnava. The Tāntric Gurus inculcate mainly the worship of Siva's consorts; while the Vaishnava Gurus or Gossains insist upon the worship of one of the incarnations of Vishnu. The disciples of the Gossains are men of very low castes, including vintners, oilmen, and even the "unfortunates" of the towns. Having such followers, the Gossains are a very well-to-do class, but are held in very low esteem, and very few good Brahmans eat in their houses.

Among the Tāntric Gurus there are a great many who have only Brahman disciples. They are generally very learned men, and are not like the Vaishnava Gossains, who are usually so illiterate that the few among them who can barely recite the Sri Bhāgavat are reckoned by their followers as prodigies of Sanskrit scholarship.

CHAP. III.—THE MODERN HINDU GURUS.

A FEW words about the probable origin of the modern Guru's profession may not be out of place here. There is no mention of it in the ancient scriptures of the Hindus, and it is recognized and regulated only by their new testaments. The word Guru or Acharya originally meant a teacher of the Vedas. The ancient legal and moral codes of the Hindus gave a very high position to the Vedic teachers. Manu says:—

> "Of him who gives natural birth, and him who gives knowledge of the whole Veda, the giver of sacred knowledge is the more venerable father, since the second or divine birth ensures life to the twice-born, both in this world and hereafter eternally."—Manu II, 146.

When, by such teachings, the position of the Guru became associated in the Hindu mind with the tenderest sentiments of regard and affection, the Brahmanical theologians began to think of devising ways to exact that reverence even from persons who have never been Vedic pupils, and who have not even the right to read our holy scriptures. The Vedic mantras are too voluminous and prosaic to attract any considerable number of pupils. Females and Sudras are not allowed to study them at all. For these reasons, no actual teacher of the Vedas could at any time hope to attract round him any considerable number of actual Vedic students. But the position of a Guru having a large number of pupils is a desirable one, and the Tāntrics invented a short cut to that position. They gave the name mantra to some mystic and meaningless syllables which might be communicated and learnt at one sitting. Sudras and females were made eligible for these mantras, and every Brahman with a little tact and show of piety was enabled to gather round him an army of *chellas* bound by their vow to worship him as a god and to pay a yearly tax to him and his descendants from generation to generation. The *chellas* are regarded by the Guru as his property, and when the sons of a deceased Guru make a partition of his estate and effects, the *chellas* are partitioned and distributed among them in the same manner as any other property inherited by them.

The simple method invented by the Tāntrics for acquiring the power and position of a Guru over a large number of disciples, has been remarkably successful. Looked at *à priori* such mystic syllables as *hoong*, *doong*, *kling* or *hring* are an outrage on common sense. But the gullibility of man has no limit, and the Guru who whispers these meaningless expressions in the ears of his disciple is worshipped and paid by him as the bestower of untold benefits. He is not allowed to reveal its nature to any one. The matter is certainly not such as to be capable of bearing the daylight of intelligent criticism. The Guru, therefore, acts wisely in insisting that the communication should be treated as strictly confidential.

The Gossains discard the mystic syllables more or less, and inculcate that in this age of sin the only way to attain salvation lies in constantly repeating the name of *Hari!* Their doctrine may not at first sight seem to be consistent with their professional policy. A Tāntric mantra is a mystic syllable which must necessarily be received from a Guru by those who may value it. But if, as the Vishnuvites say, a man can save his soul by merely repeating the name of some deity a certain number of times, surely he cannot be absolutely in need of a spiritual teacher to initiate him in the adoption of that method. But logic or reason has very little connection with faith, and as Gurus of all classes, including both the Tāntric and the Vaishnava; insist upon the necessity of a spiritual teacher for every human being, the idea has become too firmly implanted in the Hindu mind to be eradicated by any occasional gleam of common sense.

The abominations worshipped by the Tāntrics are eschewed altogether by the Vaishnavas. But the latter by reciting stories or singing songs about the illicit amours of Krishna, gives perhaps greater encouragement to immorality than any Tāntric the nature of whose phallic emblems is understood by very few of those who worship them. So there is very little to choose between the morality of the one or the other. But the Vaishnavas can perform their operations openly, while the Tāntrics require a shroud of mysticism to envelop them. Anyhow, the Vaishnavas are very fast extending the sphere of their influence, and many of the Tāntrics are now espousing Vaishnava tenets in order to have the advantage of enlisting among their followers the low classes that are becoming rich under British rule.

CHAP. IV.—ENQUIRIES BY WHICH THE CASTE STATUS OF A HINDU MAY BE ASCERTAINED.

CANNOT a man of one caste pass * as a member of another caste? This is a question which must occur to every foreigner interesting himself in the subject. But, as explained already, there cannot be any strong motive for such false impersonation, and the checks which are provided by Hindu social etiquette, are powerful enough to repress any such attempts. The unwritten law of Indian society requires that every Hindu, when asked, must mention not only the names of his paternal and maternal ancestors, but give also every information that he can about such queries as the following :—

1. **What is your caste?**
2. **What is your clan?**
3. **What is your Gotra?**
4. **What are your Pravaras?**
5. **What is your Veda?**
6. **What is your Sākha?**
7. **What is your Sutra?**

---

* I once heard a story about an attempt made by a shoemaker to pass as a Brahman. With a view to have a share of the nice eatables provided for the Brahman guests of a local Dives, he equipped himself like a Brahman with his sacred thread, and quietly joined the company when they assembled in the evening. As usual on such occasions, one of the party asked him what his name and his father's name were. He said, in reply, that his own name was Ram Chatterjea, and that his father's name was Kasi Lahiri. Being thus found out, he was hustled out of the place. His low position in caste saved him from kicks and blows, and while effecting his exit he gave expression to the sad moral of his adventure by muttering "a shoemaker cannot conceal his caste even under cover of night."

There are also special enquiries for each caste and clan, and these go into such details that it must be quite impossible for an outsider to answer them. I shall refer to some of those details further on, but it seems to me absolutely necessary to give some information about Gotra, Pravara, &c., in this place.

Gotra.—The Gotra of a Brahman is the name of the Rishi or Vedic poet from whom he and his agnates are supposed to be descended. The Gotra of a man of any other caste is the name of the Rishi who and whose descendants were entitled to officiate as priests in the family of his ancestors. The original meaning of the word was, in all probability, a place for keeping cattle. But, with the highest possible respect for the authority of Professor Max Müller, I see no reason whatever to suppose that the Brahmans, Rajputs and Vaishyas, who now profess to be of the same Gotra, have this tradition, because their ancestors lived within the same cow-pen. In the vernacular languages of India, the word *got* means simply a company of men, and the authority of the Shastras is distinctly in favour of the view that the men who profess to be of the same Gotra, are either the actual descendants, or the progeny of the spiritual sons of the same primitive priest. The origin of the Gotra is to be traced not to actual residence within the same cow-pen, but to a metaphorical use of the word similar to that which is made of the term 'flock' by the priests of the Christian Church.

Pravara.—The word literally means a person duly appointed. On the view which I take of the *Gotra*, the Pravaras of a Hindu are the Rishis who were entitled to be appointed as assistant priests for the performance of the religious ceremonies of his ancestors. On any other view the *Pravaras* can have no meaning whatever.

Vedas and Sākha.—Every Brahman is supposed to be a reader of one of the four Vedas, and though the study has, for various reasons, been suppressed long since, yet every member of the priestly caste is expected to know by tradition the name of the Veda, and the rescension of it of which his family profess to be students. Hence, when any enquiry is made about the lineage of any member of the twice-born castes, he is asked to mention the name of his Veda.

Sutra.—The Sutras are ritualistic works, and the Sutra of a Brahman is the name of the Rishi whose manual of rituals regulates the religious ceremonies of his family. Every Brahman in the country is supposed to know his Gotra, Pravara and Veda, and is expected to mention them whenever asked. But the Sākha and the Sutra are known only to the learned, and it is not very usual to make any enquiry about them even on formal occasions.

A difference of Gotra, Pravara, Vedas or Sākha does not usually imply any difference of caste or clan ; nor does any identity in these respects imply an identity of class. There is a saying in Bengali according to which there are only five Gotras in the world. As a matter of fact there are more than 100 different Gotras, and each one of these is to be found in almost all the primary castes. The Gotra is not only something very different from caste, but involves very opposite incidents. The most important feature of caste is that no Hindu can contract a marital alliance outside its limits. But as to Gotra the rule among the higher castes is that marriage can only be valid between persons of different Gotra.

CHAP. V.—THE SUB-DIVISIONS AMONG THE BRAHMANS.

ACCORDING to some authoritative texts of the Shastras, and according to popular belief also, the Brahmans of India are divided into two main classes, each of them being sub-divided into five sub-classes as shown in the following table :—

1. Panch Gaur or the five classes of Northern India.	1. Sarswata. 2. Kanya Kubja. 3. Gaudra. 4. Utkala. 5. Maithila.
2. Panch Dravira or the five classes of Southern India.	1. Maharashtra. 2. Andra. 3. Dravira. 4. Carnata. 5. Guzrat.

As a matter of fact the divisions among the Brahmans are so numerous that it is exceedingly difficult, if not actually impossible, to frame an exhaustive and accurate list thereof. For the purpose of giving an account of the Brahmans of Northern India alone, each of the following provinces and districts must be taken into consideration separately: (1) Bengal Proper ; (2) Tirhoot ; (3) South Behar ; (4) N.-W. Provinces and Oudh ; (5) Kurukshetra ; (6) Punjab ; (7) Kashmir ; (8) Sind ; (9) Rajputana ; (10) Central India ; (11) Assam ; (12) Orissa.

Even within the limits of each of the above-mentioned territorial divisions, the Brahmanical population are not, in any case, of the same class. In Bengal proper alone, there are, besides the degraded and the semi-degraded Brahmans, about half-a-dozen different divisions in the sacerdotal population which are, for all practical purposes, different castes altogether. The case is no better in any of the other provinces. On the contrary, among the Sarswatas of the Punjab, what were merely hypergamous groups formerly, now threaten to be separate castes, and when this transformation becomes complete, it will be quite as impossible to count their sub-divisions as those of the Guzratis.

PART III.

THE BRAHMANS OF NORTHERN INDIA.

CHAP. I.—THE BRAHMANS OF BENGAL.

EXCEPTING the recent immigrants from other provinces, the Brahmans of Bengal proper are divided into the following classes :—

1. **Paschatya Vaidikas** (Lit. Vedic Brahmans of Western India).
2. **Radhiyas** (Lit. Brahmans of Rādh or Western Bengal).
3. **Barendras** (Lit. Brahmans of Bārendra country, the name given to the northern part of Bengal).
4. **Dākshinatya Vaidikas** (Lit. Vedic Brahmans of Southern India).
5. **Madhya Sreni** (Lit. Brahmans of the midland country *i.e.*, of the district of Midnapore which forms the border land between Orissa and Bengal Proper).

It is said that there is, besides these, another class in Bengal called the Sapta Satis, or the Seven Hundred, who were the only Brahmans in Bengal before the colonisation of the five priests invited by King Adisur in the 9th century of the Christian era. I have never met with any Sapta Sati Brahmans ; but, so far as my information goes, members of this class may be found in some parts of East Bengal, and especially in Maheshpore in the eastern part of the Nadiya district. They usually intermarry with the Rādhiyas, and, for all practical purposes, may be regarded as a section of that class.

§ 1.—*The Pāschātya Vaidikas.*

The numerical strength of the Pāschātya Vaidikas is not very considerable. Their name indicates that they came from the west, and according to the traditions in their families, they are of the Kanojia stock, their ancestors having, at the commencement of Mahomedan rule, migrated from their original habitat to Tirhoot, and subsequently from Tirhoot to Bengal. Most of the Vaidika immigrants were specially invited by one or other of the many Hindu Rajas, who ruled over the country as semi-independent chiefs, during almost the entire period of Moslem ascendancy. The ancestor of the leading Vaidikas of Nadiya was a reader of the *Mahābhārat* who could recite it from memory, and was made to settle in Bengal by a Raja Kāshinath, who was the ruler of the Nadiya district before it was given by the Emperor Jehangir to Bhava Nanda, the ancestor of the present Raja of Nadiya. The founder of the Vaidika family of Kotālipāhār was invited from Kanoj by a Hindu prince who ruled over the district of Bākergunge in the thirteenth century, and was led to celebrate at an immense cost a religious ceremony for avoiding an evil that was foreboded by the fall of a dead vulture on the roof of his palace. The lucky priest secured for himself, by way of remuneration for his services, a valuable zemindari which is now in the possession of his descendants. The most important colonies of the Vaidikas are to be found now in the districts of Nadiya, Burdwan, 24-Pergunnahs, Malda, Rajshahi, Jessore, Bākergunge, Dacca and Faridpore.

The majority of the other classes of Bengali Brahmans are the spiritual disciples of the Vaidikas of Nadiya and Bhātpārā. A Vaidika never enlists himself as a disciple of a Brahman of any other class. Some Vaidikas have Sudra disciples, and have even stooped so far as to officiate as priests for Sudras and in public temples. But, generally speaking, their Brahmanical pride is such that the poorest among them would rather die than do any kind of manual work. Till recently they kept themselves aloof from English education and Government service. But their disciples do not submit now-a-days to be taxed by them to the same extent as in former times, and stern necessity has been compelling the Gurus of Nadiya and Bhātpārā to pocket their pride, and to qualify themselves for Government service and the liberal professions, by English education.

The usual surname of the Vaidikas is Bhattacharya. There are some in the class who have other family names such as Chackravarti, Roy and Chowdry ; but all these are honorific titles, and are not peculiar to the class. For the meanings of these titles, see Glossary.

§ 2.—*The Rārhiya Brahmans of Bengal.*

The Rārhiya and the Bārendra Brahmans of Bengal trace their descent from the five priests brought from Kanoj, in the 9th century, by King Adisur of East Bengal, for the purpose evidently of performing one of those Vedic sacrifices for which competent priests could be had only in the capitals of the great Hindu kings. The Rārhiyas and Bārendras are very proud of their descent. But even on the supposition that King Adisur was a Ksatriya, and not a Vaidya, it cannot be said that, according to Hindu notions, the five priests imported by him were entitled to be regarded as very high class Brahmans. The very title of Upādhya, which their patron gave them, shows that they were regarded as middle class, and not first class, Pandits. The Rārhiyas and the Bārendras may, with much better reason, boast of having had in their clans such great men as Raghunnāth, Gadādhar, Kulluka and Raghunandan, the last being by way of pre-eminence known throughout India as Smarta Bhattacharya, or the great professor of jurisprudence and theology.

The Rarhis derive their clan name from that of the tract of country which now forms the northern portion of the Burdwan division. Brahmans of this class are to be found in every part of Bengal proper, and their numerical strength is perhaps greater than that of all the other classes of Bengali Brahmans taken together. They are divided into about one hundred sub-classes, and grouped under the four main heads mentioned below:—

1. **Kulin (families of high lineage).**
2. **Bansaja.**
3. **Sudha Srotriya (pure Vedic scholars).**
4. **Kashta Srotriya (impure Vedic scholars.)**

A Rārhiya Kulin can give his daughter only to a Kulin. If he gives his daughter to a Bansaja or Srotriya his Kulinism is destroyed forever. A Kulin can marry the daughter of a Kulin or that of a Sudha Srotriya. If he marry the daughter of a Kashta Srotriya, he is lowered at once in rank. If he marry into a Bansaja family, his Kulinism lasts for some generations in a decaying condition, and his descendant in the eighth degree becomes a regular Bansaj. A Kulin who first marries into a Bansaj family generally gets a very high premium. The Kulins who have kept their Kulinism intact, generally find great difficulty in marrying their daughters, and are obliged to keep them unmarried, notwithstanding the Shastric injunctions that require every Hindu to give his female children in marriage before puberty. A Srotriya can give his daughter to a Bansaj as well as to a Kulin. A Bansaj cannot give his daughter to a Srotriya.

The usual and peculiar titles of the Rārhiyas are:—

1. **Mukhopādhya.**
2. **Bandyopādhya.**
3. **Chattopādhya.**
4. **Gangopādhya.**
5. **Ghosāl.**

Each of the first four of these titles consists of two words joined together. The first word is the name of the village* granted to the ancestor of the holder by

* This is in accordance with the explanation of the above-mentioned names given by Rārhiya Gattaks or College of Heralds. But Banodh being the ancient name of the tract of country, including the modern districts of Unao and Rai Bareilly in the vicinity of Kanoj, it is quite possible that Bandyopādhya means an Upādhaya of Banodh. Similar explanations seem to be possible regarding Mukhopādhya, Chattāpādhya and Gangopādhya.

King Ballalal Sen, and the last word is Upādhya, which means an assistant teacher or priest. The Rādhis have also other titles such as Putitunda, Kanji Lal, Pakrasi, &c., which are peculiar to their class; but an exhaustive enumeration of these is unnecessary in a book like this. Among the Rādhiyas, there are also Bhattacharyas, Majumdars, Roys, Chowdries, &c., but these titles are not peculiar to their class.

Formerly the Rādhiyas of the eastern and central districts of Bengal devoted themselves generally to the cultivation of Sanskrit, and abstained from all such pursuits as are considered to be derogatory to the dignity of a Brahman. But even under the Mahomedan rulers some of them accepted service as, for instance, Bhabananda Majumdar of Nadiya, and the unfortunate Raja Nand Kumār who, according to Macaulay himself, "had been great and powerful before the British Empire in India began to exist, and to whom in the old times Governors and Members of Council, then mere commercial factors, had paid court for protection."*

---

* Macaulay describes Nand Kumār as a "Brahman of Brahmans," and, at the same time, as the blackest monster in human form. Whether morally he was a worse or a better man than the Judge who convicted him "in order to gratify the Governor-General," or the Governor-General who, according to Macaulay's own showing, was the real prosecutor, is a question which does not fall within the scope of this work. But it may be mentioned here that Nand Kumār was not a high caste Brahman, and was very far from being the head of the Brahman community as Macaulay has represented him to have been for artistic colouring of the picture. Nand Kumār was in fact a middle class Rādhiya Brahman, whose family had once been outcasted, and regained their status partly by a humiliating and expensive ceremony of expiation, and partly by forming connections with families of a higher status. The inaccuracy in the description of his caste status given by a foreign historian is pardonable, but it is impossible to give him credit for impartiality. Apart from the trumpery charges on which Nand Kumār was convicted of felony, the head and front of his offending was that he had intrigued against Hastings for thwarting his ambition to be the Deputy of the East India Company in the place of Mahomed Reza Khan. The Nabob of Moorshedabad had recommended him for the office, and the Court of Directors, in a manner, ordered that he should be appointed to it. But Hastings "bore no goodwill to Nand Kumār. Many years before they had known each other at Moorshedabad, and then a quarrel had arisen which all the authority of their superiors could

Under British rule the Rādhiyas, and especially their outcasted Pirāli section, have been the first to adapt themselves to the exigencies of the new *régime*, and to take advantage of such opportunities for advancement as it offered to the people of the country. Dwarka Nath Tagore and Prasanna Kumar Tagore were Pirālis. Ram Mohan Roy and Ishwar Chandra Vidyāsagār were Brahmans of a better class, but even they did not hold a very high position in their caste. In fact until recently

---

hardly compose." Such being the attitude of Hastings towards Nand Kumār, it is no wonder that he carried out the orders of the Court of Directors only so far that he dismissed Mahomed Reza Khan, and removed the exchequer from Moorshedabad to Calcutta. But the office of Naib Dewan was abolished, and Nand Kumār was subjected to a cruel disappointment. So "it was natural," according to Macaulay himself, "that the Governor should from that time be an object of the most intense hatred to the Brahman." When the Councillors appointed by the Regulating Act arrived, and, possibly in accordance with instructions from the Ministers of the Crown, tried to upset the power of Hastings and indirectly that of the East India Company, Nand Kumār by a natural process became associated with the enemies of the Governor-General. Hastings had mortally offended Nand Kumār. When the latter saw his opportunity he tried to have his enemy disgraced. The enemy retaliated by having the Brahman *murdered* under colour of legal proceedings.

According to Brahmanical ideas of morality Nand Kumār deserves to be condemned in the strongest terms possible for the vices of office-seeking and vindictiveness which he betrayed. But the impartial historian cannot condemn him without condemning also in severer terms the conduct of a man in the position of Hastings, who retaliated insult by murder. If the rules of political morality be different from those of ordinary morality, and if the exigencies of the situation in which Hastings was placed justified the "sharp antidote" that he used, surely the conduct of Nand Kumār towards him ought to be judged by the same standard. But while the great English historian showers every kind of vituperation not only on Nand Kumār, but on the nation itself to which he belonged, he exculpates Hastings with an amiability that is not often found in the old parents of a spoilt only son. After observing that it is impossible to speak too severely of Impey's conduct, the great historian goes on to add :—

"But we look on the conduct of Hastings in a somewhat different light. He was struggling for fortune, honour, liberty, all that makes life valuable. He was beset by rancorous and unprincipled enemies. From his colleagues he could expect no justice. He cannot be blamed for wishing to crush his accusers."

Certainly the defence embodied in the above applies quite as much to Nand Kumār as to Hastings, yet, according to the verdict of the great English historian, Hastings was a politician to whom the ordinary rules of morality do not apply, while Nand Kumār and the nation to which he belonged are villains.

the high class Rādhiyas were usually quite illiterate. Their hereditary rank made them highly prized as bridegrooms for the daughters of their well-to-do clansmen, and many of them lived in former times by making marriage their sole profession. A Kulin of a high class might then marry more than a hundred wives without any difficulty, and there are still some who have such large numbers of wives as to necessitate their keeping regular registers for refreshing their memory, about the names and residences of their spouses. Not only each marriage, but each visit by a Kulin to his wife brought him valuable presents, and as his wives and children were supported by his fathers-in-law, he could pass his days in comfort without being qualified for any kind of service or profession. The Kulin's sons sometimes became rich by inheriting the property of their maternal relatives. But it was until lately very rare for a Kulin to be the architect of his own fortune. The state of things in Hindu society is, however, undergoing great changes. Most of the Kulins have become lowered in rank by marrying into inferior families, and Kulinism, even where it is preserved intact, is not now-a-days valued in the matrimonial market to the same extent that it used to be in former times. Wealth, university degrees and official position command a much higher premium at present than an ancient pedigree. The Kulins themselves have been taught, by the bitter experience of their ancestors, to be not too eager for polygamy. And the *coup de grace* to the practice has been given by a decision of the Bengal High Court declaring that, according to the law of the Shastras applicable to all Hindus, even the Kulins are bound to give maintenance to their wives. Whatever be the cause, monogamy is now becoming the rule among the Kulins, and they are fast on the way towards again taking their proper place among the most refined and cultured classes of the country. A Kulin of the highest rank has just retired on pension after having served the Government of Bengal for several years as Head Assistant in the Judicial Department. Even among the greatest of the living celebrities of Bengal there are at present some Kulins of a more or less high position in the Rādhiya peerage, the foremost among them being Mr. W. C. Bonnerjee, Advocate, Bengal High Court ; Dr. Guru Das Banerjee, Judge, Bengal High Court ; Mr. Pramada Charan Banerjee, Judge, N.-W. P. High Court ; Mr. Pratul Chandra Chatterji, Judge, Panjab Chief Court.

The late Mr. Justice Anookul Chandra Mookerji was also a Rādhiya Kulin. Mr. W. C. Bonnerjee is a member of the clan called *Pandit Ratni* or "the jewel of Pandits," and is lineally descended on his mother's side from the great Jagannāth, the author of the Digest translated by Mr. Colebrooke. Babu Pratul Chandra is of the Kharda clan. His grandfather made a fortune by marrying the daughter of Gokool Ghosal, one of the chief fiscal officers in the early days of the East India Company, and the founder of the Raj family of Bhu Kailas.

§ 3.—*Bārendras.*

The Bārendras trace their origin from the same stock as the Rādhis, *i.e.*, from the five priests invited by King Adisur from Kanoj. The Bārendras derive their class name from the ancient name of North Bengal. Their numerical strength is less than that of the Rādhis, but greater than that of the Vaidikas.

The usual family names of the Bārendras are the following :—

1. **Lāhiri.**
2. **Bhādari.**
3. **Sānyal.**
4. **Maitra.**
5. **Bagchi.**

These surnames are peculiar to the Bārendras. They have also among them Bhattacharyas, Majumdars, Joadars, Roys, and Chowdries. There are some high caste Bārendras who have the Mahomedan title of Khan. The Bārendras, like the Vaidikas, never do any kind of menial work, and the only class of Bengali Brahmanas who serve as cooks are the Rarhis of West Burdwan. The Rarhis of the eastern districts of Bengal, *i.e.*, of the districts to the east of the river Hooghly, are quite as aristocratic as the Bārendras and the Vaidikas.

The hypergamous divisions among the Bārendras are similar to those of the Rarhis in certain respects, the only important difference being that the Bārendras have a section among them called Cāp* who have a somewhat unique position, though resembling to some extent the Bansaj among the Rarhis.

Polygamy is rare among the Bārendras; but the marriage of a daughter among their higher classes is quite as expensive as among the Rarhis. There are many big Bārendra landholders, the most noted among

* With regard to the origin of the Cāps it is said that they are the descendants of a great Kulin named Madhu Moitra by his first wife. Madhu was an inhabitant of a village on the river Atrai, situated near the place where it is now crossed by the North Bengal State Railway. An inferior member of the clan, being treated at a dinner party of his castemen with great contumely, determined to form a matrimonial alliance with the great Kulin at any cost, and with that object hired a boat to take him to the vicinity of Madhu's residence and was careful to have with him on board of the vessel his wife, an unmarried daughter and a cow. On reaching the neighbourhood of Madhu's village, he inquired of a Brahman, who was saying his prayers after performing his ablutions on the banks of the river, whether he knew where the great head of the Bārendra clan lived. The Brahman, who was interrogated, was himself the person about whom the enquiry was addressed. When the fact was made known to the Brahman on board the boat, he produced a hammer and a chisel threatening to sink the boat with all its inmates unless Madhu agreed to marry the Brahman's daughter. The old man was too far advanced in life to be quite ready for complying with any request of the kind. But, as an orthodox Hindu, he could not take upon himself any share of the three great crimes, namely, the killing of a female, the killing of a Brahman, and the killing of a cow—which were threatened to be perpetrated in his presence. So he reluctantly gave his consent. But when his sons came to know what he was going to do they were very much annoyed, and they separated from their father at once. The old man was supported by his sister's husband, who was then the other great Kulin of the caste, and the sons who separated became Cāps. The position of their descendants is superior to that of the Srotriyas, but inferior to that of the Kulins. Matrimonial alliance between a Kulin and a Cāp reduces the former to the position of the latter.

them being the great house of Nattore that held possession of more than one-third of Bengal proper, at the time of the conquest of the country by the East India Company. Next in importance to the Nattore Rajas, but more ancient than their family, is that of the Putia zemindars. The late Maharani Sharat Sundari, whose name is venerated throughout India for her extensive charities, and for her character as a model Hindu widow, was a member of the Putia house. Among the other great Bārendra landholders of Bengal are the zemindars of Susang and Muktagacha in the district of Mymensing. Babu Mohini Mohan Roy, who is one of the most successful pleaders of the Bengal High Court, and who has lately been made an Additional Member of the Supreme Legislative Council of India, is a Bārendra.

The majority of the Vaidikas, Rarhis and Bārendras are moderate Saktas. They worship all the ancient deities of the Hindu pantheon; but Durgā, Kāli and Siva have the largest share of their devotion. Many of them sacrifice goats and buffaloes before the deities they worship; but among such of their orthodox members as are not affected by English education, and the temptations of modern town life, the drinking of spirituous liquors is still practically unknown.

§ 4.—*The Dākshinatya Vaidikas.*

The name of this class indicates that they originally came from the south. They are found chiefly in the district of Midnapore, and seem to have been originally Brahmans of Orissa. A few small colonies of the Dākshinatyas are to be found in the southern portion of the metropolitan district of 24-Pergunnahs. They are a separate caste altogether, and there can be neither intermarriage nor interchange of hospitality between them and the Pāschātya Vaidikas. Pandit Siva Nath Sastri, of the Sadharan Brahmo Samaj, is a Dākshinatya Vaidika.

§ 5.—*The Madhya Sreni Brahmans of the district of Midnapore.*

The Madhya Srenis are a very backward class of Brahmans, to be found only in the district of Midnapore. As they have the very same surnames and Gotras as the Rādhis of Bengal, they are evidently a section of the Rādhis. They themselves profess to be so, and account for their want of connection with the Rādhis properly so-called, by saying that as they refused to acknowledge the authority of the Ghataks to determine their status, the Rādhi College of Heralds refused to recognise their very existence. The true cause of their forming a separate caste seems, however, to be that they accepted the gifts of the Kaibartas, and lived in an out-of-the-way district. The Madhya Srenis are generally very poor and without any literary culture beyond what is necessary for doing the work of a priest.

The distinction between Kulins and Srotriyas is not recognised by the Madhya Srenis. The descendants of those who, at one time or other, became famous as Sanskrit scholars, enjoyed, until lately, a higher position than the secular Brahmans. But at present, the status of a party for matrimonial purposes depends chiefly upon the amount of wealth possessed by him. The Madhya Srenis partake of the hospitality of the Kaibartas, and minister to them as priests in all ceremonies except Shradhs.* The Shradhs of the Kaibartas are performed by a class of Brahmans called Vyasokta.

---

* Mr. Risley in his account of the Madhya Srenis says that they have eight Gotras, and that the Madhya Srenis of Mayna and certain other places have a higher position than the rest. But his account seems to be based upon erroneous information.

CHAP. II.—THE BRAHMANS OF MITHILA AND BEHAR.

§ 1.—*Maithilas.*

THE Brahmans of Mithila or Tirhoot are called Maithila Brahmans. They form one of the five leading classses of North Indian Brahmans called Panch Gaur. They have no sub-castes, though they are divided into many groups which are of importance for the purpose of arranging marriages among them. The following are the names of these hypergamous groups :—

1. Srotriya or Sote (Lit. A reader of the Vedas).
2. Jog (A family of an inferior class that has attained a superior status by marriage connections with Srotriyas).
3. Panji Badh (Recognized by the local College of Heralds).
4. Nagar.
5. Jaiwar.

A man of a higher group may take in marriage a girl from a lower group. But a girl of a higher group is never given to a bridegroom of a lower class, except where the parents of the former are too poor to marry her to a boy of the same or a superior group.

The Maithila Brahmans have a special kind of headdress. Their usual surnames are the following :—

1. Misra (A reader of the two Mimansas).
2. Ojha or Jha* (Both are corrupted forms of the Sanskrit word Upādhya, which means an assistant teacher or priest).
3. Thākoor (God.)
4. Pāthak (A reader of the Mahābhārat and the Purāns).
5. Pura.
6. Padri.
7. Chowdry.
8. Roy.

* Persons who profess to exorcise evil spirits or cure snake-bites are usually called Ojhas, or, by a further corruption of the word, 'Roja.' They do not belong to any particular caste, and are generally low class men.

The Maithilas are very conservative, and still think that it is beneath their dignity to accept service under the British Government, though such feeling has died out completely even among the highest classes of Bengali Brahmans.

The head of the Maithila Brahmans is the Maharaja of Darbhanga. The founder of the family, Mahesh Thākoor, bore a Brahmanical surname. But whether on account of the degradation of that highly honorific title, or on account of their belonging to a royal family, his descendants at present use the Ksatriya surname of Sing. The transformation is exactly the opposite of what has taken place in many Ksatriya families, though the ambition of a Rajput to be elevated from the rank of a Sing (lion) to that of Thākoor (god) is certainly more intelligible, than the desire on the part of any royal family to be degraded from the rank of a god to that of a lion.

Besides the Maharaja of Darbhanga, there are many other families of big landholders among the Maithila Brahmans. One of the most conspicuous of these is the Raja of Banaili, who is the owner of the extensive estate of Kharakpore in the district of Monghyr, but is about to be ruined by family quarrels, mismanagement and litigation. The Purnea Zemindars of Srinagar, who are also big landholders, are a branch of the Banaili family. The Banaili family belong to that division which is called Jog.

From very early times Mithila has been famous for the cultivation of Sanskrit. It has given birth to some of the greatest authorities in Hindu jurisprudence, and in the branch of Hindu philosophy called Nya. The great lawgiver Yajnavalkya is described in the opening lines of his work as a native of Mithila, and tradition still points to a place near the junction of the Ghogra with the Ganges, which is believed to have been the residence of the sage Gautama, the founder of the Nya philosophy. Of the mediæval and modern

Maithila authors, the names of Gangesha Upâdhya, Pakshadhar Misra, Udayanacharya, Chandeshwar and Bachaspati Misra will continue to be honoured so long as Hindu law and philosophy remain in existence. Among the Maithila Sanskritists of recent times, the late Pandit Bapu Jan Jha attained great eminence, and his son, Chumba Jha, is fully sustaining the reputation of the family. The other two great living Pandits of Mithila are Halli Jha and Vishwa Nath Jha.

The majority of the Maithila Brahmans are Sakti worshippers. They offer sacrifices before the deities they worship, and eat flesh and fish, but are not known to be in the habit of drinking spirituous liquors, as the extreme Saktas are required to do by their Shastras. The Maithila Brahmans do not smoke tobacco.

§ 2.—*Sakaldipi Brahmans of South Behar.*

There is a class of Brahmans in South Behar who call themselves Sakaldipis or Sakadipis. The majority of them live either by ministering to the other castes as priests, or by the practice of medicine. There are, however, a few Pandits and landholders among them. One peculiar custom in the community is that, like the Sarswat Brahmans of the Panjab, a Sakaldipi may marry within his Gotra, though such marriage is strictly prohibited among the three superior castes by Hindu law. The Sakaldipis are divided into a certain number of Purs or sections, and marriage is impossible only within the Pur.

CHAP. III.—THE BRAHMANS OF THE NORTH-WESTERN PROVINCES AND OUDH.

THE most important classes of Brahmans in the North-Western Provinces and Oudh are the following :—

1. Kanojia. | 2. Sarujuparia. | 3. Sanadhya.

Kanojia.—The Kanojias hold a very high position among the Brahmans of Northern India. They form one of the five divisions called Panch Gaur, and the Brahmans of Bengal take a great pride in claiming to have been originally Kanojias. The name is derived from the ancient Hindu city of Kanoj, at the confluence of the Ganges and the Kalinadi, in the district of Farrakkabad. The Kanojia Brahmans are to be found in almost every part of Northern India. But their original home is the tract of country which, before the time of Wellesley, formed the western half of the kingdom of Oudh, including the modern districts of Philibit, Bareilly, Shajehanpore Farakkabad, Cawnpore, Fatehapur, Hamirpur, Banda and Allahabad. The usual surnames of the Kanojia Brahmans are the following :—

1. Awasti.
2. Misra.
3. Dikshit.
4. Sukul.
5. Dobey or Dwivedi.
6. Tewari or Trivedi.
7. Chaube or Chaturvedi.
8. Pande.
9. Bajpai.
10. Pathak.

In each of these there are many sub-sections, having different positions for matrimonial purposes.

The Kanojias, notwithstanding their high position from the point of view of caste, freely enlist in the army as sepoys, and do not consider it beneath their dignity to serve even as orderlies, peons and gatekeepers. The title Pānde has a very bad odour with Englishmen since the Mutiny of 1857. But as a class the Kanojia Brahmans are very remarkable for their aristocratic demeanour and manners, and for their quiet and inoffensive nature. They seldom give way to bad temper, and the practice of any kind of cruelty seems to be quite inconsistent with their general character. They acted no doubt like fiends in some of the episodes of the sepoy revolt. But "the greased cartridge" was a matter serious enough to lead any Hindu to the perpetration of things far worse. Would the British soldiers willingly obey their officers if ordered to bite the dead bodies of their enemies in a battle field? And if they disobeyed the order, and in doing so subjected their officers to any kind of insult or ill-treatment, would any reasonable man find fault with them? The whole world would be horrified at any coercive measure for enforcing such a perverse order. The situation of the sepoys with respect to the "greased cartridge" was exactly the same, and yet it is thought that they have not sufficiently expiated by either being hanged in batches from the boughs of trees, or by being blown away from guns.

There are learned Sanskritists as well as good English scholars among the Kanojias. Many of them practise agriculture, and it is said some till the soil with their own hands. The majority of them are Sivites. There are among them a few Saktas and Srivaishnavas also. The Sivites and Srivaishnavas are strict vegetarians. There are some ganja-smokers and bhang-eaters among the Kanojias, but very few that would even touch any kind of spirituous liquor.

The late Pandit Sheodin, who was prime minister of Jaipore for several years, was a Kanojia Brahman of Moradabad.

Sarujuparia.—The Sarujuparias derive their name from the river Saruju which flows past the city of Ayodhya. They are most numerous in the vicinity of the river Ghogra. They are said to be a branch of the Kanojias. But whatever may have been their original connection there can be no marriage at present between the two classes, and they must be held to be independent castes. The usual family names of the Sarujeeans are the same as those of the Kanojians. There are good Sanskritists among the Sarorias. They never till the soil with their own hands.

Sanadhya.—The Sanadhyas are also said to be a branch of the Kanojia tribe. They are very numerous in the central districts of the Doab, between Mathura to the south-west and Kanoj on the north-east. They live chiefly, as shopkeepers and pedlars. The number of educated men among them is very small. The following are their usual surnames:—

1. Misr.
2. Pānde.
3. Dube or Dwivedi.
4. Tewari or Trivedi.
5. Choube or Chatervedi.
6. Upādhya or Ojha.
7. Pāthak.
8. Boidya.
9. Dikshit.
10. Parasar.
11. Devalya.
12. Goswami.
13. Katori.
14. Khenoriya.
15. Tripoti.
16. Choturdhuri or Chowdry.
17. Samadiya.
18. Monas.
19. Bratahari.
20. Chainpuria.
21. Bhotiya.
22. Modaya.
23. Sandaya.
24. Udenya.
25. Chushondiya.
26. Barsya.

The late Guru of the Maharaja of Jaipore, who was believed to have the power of working miracles, and who was venerated as a saint by most of the great Hindu potentates of Central India and Rajputana, was a Sanadhya.

CHAP. IV.—THE BRAHMANS OF THE KURUKSHETRA COUNTRY.

Gaur Brahmans.—The original home of the Gaur Brahmans is the Kurukshetra country. The Gaurs say that the other four main divisions of North Indian Brahmans were originally Gaurs, and have acquired their present designations of Sarswat, Kanya-kubja, Maithila and Utkal by immigrating to the provinces where they are now domiciled. The name Adi Gaur adopted by the Kurukshetra Brahmans is in consonance with this view. In Sir George Campbell's *Ethnology of India*, it is suggested that the Gaurs may have derived their name from the river Ghagar, which, in ancient times, was a tributary of the Sarswati, and which now discharges its water into the Sutlej near Ferozepore. According to popular usage the word Gaur means a priest, and it is not impossible that the name of Gaur Brahmans was given to those who served as priests to the ancient kings of Kurukshetra. The Adi Gaurs practise agriculture and till the soil with their own hands. But there are many good Sanskritists* among them, and they are the only Brahmans whom the Agarwala Baniyas would employ as their priests. There is a class of Gaur Brahmans called the Taga Gaur. These

---

* One of the greatest of these is Pandit Laksman Sastri, of Patiala, now residing in Calcutta, from whom I have derived the greater part of the information contained in this chapter. The late Pandit Gauraswami, who was the first Pandit in his time in the holy city of Benares, was also a Gaur.

are so designated because they have only the Brahmanical Taga or sacred thread. They are all addicted to agriculture, and are quite ignorant of the Brahmanical prayers and religious rites. They neither study the Shastras nor perform the work of a priest. The other castes do not make to them the kind of humble salutation (*pranam*) due to Brahmans, but accost them as they would a Rajput or Baniya by simply saying "*Ram Ram.*" Some of the Adi Gaurs are now receiving English education. The general surname of the Gaurs is Misra. Their special surnames are the following :—

1. Dikshit.	9. Mota.	17. Gandharwal.	25. Nagarwal.
2. Tiwari.	10. Indouria.	18. Randyana.	26. Sathya.
3. Chaube.	11. Haritwal.	19. Pantya.	27. Vajare.
4. Nirmal.	12. Bhanchaki.	20. Jhundiya.	28. Simanant.
5. Nagwan.	13. Mrichya.	21. Kanodiya.	29. Durgawal.
6. Chahanwal.	14. Ghagaun.	22. Gautama.	30. Khernal.
7. Marhota.	15. Vidhata.	23. Gugwal.	31. Surahya.
8. Lata.	16. Phoratwal.	24. Mudhalwan.	

The majority of the Gaurs are Sivites. Like the other high caste Brahmans of Northern India they worship also the Salagram ammonite as an emblem of Vishnu, and a triangular piece of Phallic stone representing the Devi or the consort of Siva. There are a few Ballabhachari Vaishnavas among the Gaurs. The majority of the Gaurs are strict abstainers from animal food and intoxicating drinks. Some of the Gaurs keep the sacred fire, and occasionally celebrate some of the Vedic sacrifices.

CHAP. V.—THE BRAHMANS OF KASHMIR, THE PANJAB AND SINDH.

§ 1.—*Bramhans of Kashmir.*

Kashmiri Brahmans. — The usual surnames of the Kashmir Brahmans is Pandit. The following observations in Sir George Campbell's *Ethnology of India* give an exact description of their ethnology and character :—

> The Kashmiri Brahmans are quite High Aryan in the type of their features, very fair and handsome, with high chiselled features, and no trace of intermixture of the blood of any lower race * * * * The Kashmiri Pandits are known all over Northern India as a very clever and energetic race of office-seekers. As a body they excel the same number of any other race with whom they come in contact.—*Ethnology of India*, pp. 57-59.

The late Mr. Justice Sambhu Nath Pandit of the Bengal High Court was a member of this class. So was also the late Pandit Ayodhya Nath, who was one of the ablest advocates of the Allahabad High Court, and also one of the principal leaders of the Congress. Babu Gobind Prasad Pandit, who was one of the pioneers of the coal mining industry of Bengal, was also a Kashmiri. He amassed such wealth by the success of his enterprise, that he became known as one of the richest men in the country in his lifetime, and, after his death, his descendants obtained the title of Maharaja from the Government of India.

Dogra Brahmans.—As there are Dogra Rajputs and Dogra Baniyas, so there is a class of Brahmans. called

Dogra Brahmans. The name is said to be derived from that of a mountain or valley in Kashmir. According to a Dogra student of Nya philosophy at Nadiya, whom I consulted, the name is derived from the Sanskrit compound Dwau Gartau, which means the "two valleys."

§ 2.—*The Brahmans of the Panjab.*

Sarswats.—The Brahmans of the Panjab are chiefly of this class. They derive their name from that of the sacred river Sarswati, which at a very remote period of antiquity was a noble river, and the course of which may still be traced from its source near the sanitarium of Simla to Thaneshur in the Kurukshetra. The Sarswats form one of the five primary classes of North Indian Brahmans, called Panch Gaur. A great many of the Sarswats practise agriculture, and freely partake of the hospitality of the Baniyas and the Kshetris. There are, however, many among them who are very erudite Sanskritists* and who, in point of culture and Brahmanical purity, are not inferior to the Brahmans of any other class. The majority of the Sarswats are Sakti worshippers, but very few of them eat flesh. They minister to the Kshetris of the Panjab as priests, and there is, in many respects, a close connection between the two castes. Until recently the Sarswats were divided into only two sub-castes, namely, the Banjais † and the Mohyals. The Banjais

---

* One of the greatest of these is Pandit Sadanand Misra of Calcutta, from whom I have derived a considerable part of the information contained in this chapter. In respect of personal appearance, obliging nature, and refined manners, it is hard to find a superior specimen of humanity.

† The word Banjai seems to be a corrupted form of the Sanskrit compound *Bahu Yaji*, which means a Brahman who ministers to many men. But the Sarswats say that their common name Banjai is a corrupted form of *Bayanna Jayi*, which means the fifty-two victorious clans, and to account for the origin of this name they add that they obtained this name by setting at defiance an order of an Emperor of Delhi directing them to allow the re-marriage of a widow.

minister to the Kshetris, but the Mohyals never serve as priests. There are many hypergamous groups among the Banjais, which are on the way towards becoming separate castes. So long as the lower of these classes gave their daughters in marriage to the higher, they could not be regarded as independent castes. But, in very recent times, the lower classes have resolved not to give their daughters to the higher classes, unless they choose to reciprocate the compliment. The result is that marriage alliances between the different classes are now extremely rare, and they are fast on the way towards becoming independent castes. The general surname of a Sarswat is Misr. But each clan has a special surname. The names of the several hypergamous groups among the Banjai Sarswats together with the special surnames of each class are given below :—

Names of Groups.	Titles.
1. Panjajati Adrai Ghar and Char Ghar ...	1. Morlhe. 2. Tekha. 3. Jhingan. 4. Jeteli. 5. Kumoria.
2. Inferior Panjajati	1. Kaliya. 2. Maliya. 3. Kupuria. 4. Madhuria. 5. Bagge.
3. Ashta Bans ...	1. Pathak. 2. Sori. 3. Tiwari. 4. Tasraj. 5. Jotashi. 6. Shand. 7. Kurla. 8. Bharadwaj
4. Barhi ...	1. Kaliya. 2. Prabhakar. 3. Lakhan Pal. 4. Airi. 5. Nabh. 6. Chitrachot. 7. Narad. 8. Sarad. 9. Jalpatra. 10. Bhamvi 11. Paranoty. 12. Manar.
5. Inferior Banjais not coming within the above groups...	1. Basude. 2. Bijora. 3. Raude. 4. Mehra. 5. Muslol. 6. Sudan. 7. Sutrak. 8. Teri. 9. Angul. 10. Haster.

A Sarswat cannot marry within his clan. But a marriage may take place among them within the Gotrā, though such matrimony is strictly prohibited by the Shastras.

The Mohyals are found chiefly in the western districts of the Panjab and in Kabul. Intermarriage between them and the other Sarswats is possible, but not very usual.

§ 3.—*The Brahmans of Sindh.*

The Brahmans of Sindh are mainly Sarswats. They are divided there into the following classes :—

1. Srikara.
2. Bari (Twelve families).
3. Bavanjahi (Fifty-two families).
4. Shetapalas.
5. Kuvachandas.

All these classes eat animal food, though some of them are Vaishnavas of the Vallabhachari sect. Like the Sarswats of the Panjab proper, those of Sindh also eat cooked food from the hands of Kshetris and Roda Baniyas. The Bavanajahis are Sakti worshippers of the extreme class, and not only eat flesh but drink wine. Some of the Shetapalas are also Sakti worshippers of the same type.

In speaking of the several classes of Sindh Brahmans Dr. Wilson says :—

> All these classes of Sarswats are Sukla Yajur Vedis. In using animal food they abstain from that of the cow and tame fowls, but eat sheep, goats, deer, wild birds of most species, and fish killed for them by others They also eat onions and other vegetables forbidden in the Smritis. They are generally inattentive to sectarian marks. They dress like the Hindu merchants and Amins of Sindh, though using white turbans. They shave the crown of their heads, but have two tufts of hair above their ears. They are the priests of the mercantile Lohanas or Lowanas. They have many small pagodas dedicated to the worship of the ocean, or rather the river Indus. Their fees are derived principally from their services at the marriages, births and deaths of their followers. They are partial to popular astrology, as far as easy prognostication is concerned. They pretend to know where lost articles are to be found. They also cultivate land, and sometimes act as petty shopkeepers.—Wilson's *Hindu Castes*, Vol. II, pp. 137-138.

CHAP. VI.—THE BRAHMANS OF ASSAM.

THE majority of the Brahmans of Assam profess to be Vaidakas, though, in fact, they practise either the Tāntric or the Vishnuvite cult. The inferior families among them appear to be of the Mongolian race, while even among their most aristocratic classes there appears to have been a copious admixture of Mongolian with Aryan blood. In Upper Assam, including the districts of Sibsāgar and Lakhimpur, which, before its annexation to British India, was for several centuries under the rule of the Ahang dynasty of Sibsāgar, a great many of the Brahman families profess to be descended from seven Kanojia priests imported into the country about the middle of the seventeenth century by the Ahang King Chutumala *alias* Jayadhwaja. The Aryan features of most of the members of these families, and the genealogies preserved by them, give very strong support to their claim; but, at the same time, it is equally certain that there has been a large infusion of non-Aryan blood among them. The fact is conclusively proved by their ethnology, and also by their traditions and customs. They themselves entertain the suspicion that many of the families with whom they now intermarry were originally Sudras, and were made Brahmans only by the edicts of their former kings. That their suspicions are not groundless is proved almost conclusively by some of the curious customs which still prevail among them as to interdining. In other parts of the country, the most puritanic Brahmans do not hesitate to partake of the hospitality of their fathers-in-law or maternal uncles. But among the aristocratic Brahmans of Upper Assam claiming to be descended from the Kanojian stock, no one will eat any kind of food in the house of either his father-in-law or his maternal uncle. It is said that even the daughter of a low class Brahman will not, after being married to a Kanojia of pure descent, eat in her father's house any *kachi* food though cooked by her own mother. The daughter's sons will eat in their maternal grandfather's house till their initiation with the sacred thread, but not afterwards. It seems that in practice, the alleged custom, so far as the daughter and the daughter's sons are concerned, is more honoured in the breach than in the observance. But the very recognition of such rules, if only for theoretical purposes, and the existence of Mongolian and Aryan types in the same families, clearly establish that the higher Brahmans are of the Aryan stock, and that they intermarried with local Brahmans of the Mongolian race, though with a very considerable degree of reluctance.

CHAP. VII.—THE BRAHMANS OF ORISSA.

AMONG the superior Brahmans of Orissa there are two main divisions which rest on territorial bases, and which are as follows :—

1. **Dākshinatya or Southern clan.**
2. **Jajpuria or Northern clan.**

There can be no intermarriage between these two divisions, and they have nothing in common between them except the status of being Brahmans.

§ 1.—*The Dākshinatya Brahmans of Cuttack and Puri.*

The Dākshinatya Brahmans of Southern Orissa are subdivided as follows :—

Surnames.

- **1. Vaidikas or Brahmans devoted to ecclesiastical pursuits which are not held degrading according to the Shastras.**
  - **1. Kulins or Vaidikas of the highest class, who are mostly residents of one of the sixteen Shasan or of the thirty-two Kotbar villages.** — **1. Samanta. 2. Misra. 3. Nanda. 4. Pati. 5. Kar. 6. Acharya. 7. Satapati. 8. Bedi. 9. Senapati. 10. Parnagrahi. 11. Nishank. 12. Bainipati.**
  - **2. Srotriyas or ordinary Vaidikas.** — **1. Bhatta Misra. 2. Upadhya. 3. Misra. 4. Rauth. 5. Ota. 6. Tewari. 7. Das. 8. Pati. 9. Satapasti.**
- **2. Pujari, Adhikari or Vaishnava Brahmans.** — **Forming one caste, found in every part of Orissa. Same titles as the above.**
- **3. Secular Brahmans divided into two classes designated as follows :—**
  - **1. Mahajanpanthi or Panigri.**
  - **2. Masthan.**

  — **1. Mahapatra. 2. Panda. 3. Shaubth. 4. Senapati. 5. Nekab. 6. Mekab. 7. Pathi. 8. Panni. 9. Shathera. 10. Pashupaloke. 11. Baru. 12. Mudhirath. 13. Doytha. 14. Poryari. 15. Khuntea. 16. GoraBaru. 17. Nahaka.**

The sub-classes that have the highest status among the Dākshinatya Brahmans of Orissa are the Kulins and Srotriyars of the sixteen Shashan and the thirty-two Kotbar villages. The Shashanis evidently derive their name from the fact of their obtaining, from some ancient Hindu king of the country, grants of land attested by Shashanas or royal firmans. The name Kotbar seems to be a corruption of Krobar and to be the proper designation of the suburban population of the Shasanas. The Shashan villages are inhabited only by the Kulin and Srotriya Brahmans of the ecclesiastic class. In the Kotbars there are other castes also.

The Shashani Kulins have a higher status than all the other classes of Orissa Brahmanas. There are a few good Pandits among the Shashanis, and the majority of them acquire a sufficient knowledge of Sanskrit to be able to discharge the duties of a priest. The following observations are made with regard to the class in Hunter's *Gazetteer of India* :—

They live on lands granted by former Rajas, or by teaching private students, or as spiritual guides, or more rarely as temple priests. They are few in number, for the most part in tolerable circumstances, though often poor, but held in such high estimation that a Srotriya Brahman will give a large dower in order to get his daughter married to one of them. But the Kulin who thus intermarries with a Srotriya loses somewhat of his position among his own people. The pure Brahman rarely stoops below the Srotriya, the class immediately next to him, for a wife.—*The Imperial Gazetteer of India*, Vol. X, p. 434.

The majority of the Srotriyas earn their living in the very same manner as the Kulins. All the Vaidikas are very aristocratic according to Brahmanical ideas of respectability, and a Shashani Kulin or a Srotriya Brahman will rather live by begging than be engaged in any menial occupation. In fact, there are among them, and especially among the landless Srotriyas, a great many who are regular beggars. But it would be hard to find any one of them tilling the soil, or employed as a domestic servant.

The Adhikari Brahmans are mainly followers of Chaitanya, and have the same position in Orissa that the Gossami and the Adhikari Brahmans have in Bengal. It is said that many of the Oriya Pujaris were originally men of low castes. They have generally many low caste disciples, and are employed as priests in the temples. The Adhikari Brahmans are known by the necklace of basil beads which they wear in addition to their sacred thread. They are not all the followers of one teacher, and the disciples of each individual Guru form a distinct subdivision.

Of the several classes of secular Brahmans the Mahajan Panthis or Panigiris have a high position; but the Masthans are regarded as a low class, and their very touch is regarded by some as contaminating.

With regard to the Masthan Brahmans, Mr. Stirling in his *Description of Orissa Proper* says:—

> There is another class known commonly in Orissa by the name of Mahasthan or Masthan Brahmans, who form a very considerable and important class of the rural population. Besides cultivating with their own hands gardens of the Kachu (*Arum Indicum*) cocoanut and areca, and the piper betel or pan, they very frequently follow the plough, from which circumstance they are called Halia Brahmans, and they are found everywhere in great numbers in the situation of Mukadams and Sarbarakars, or hereditary renters of villages. Those who handle the plough glory in their occupation, and affect to despise the Bed or Veda Brahmans who live upon alms. Though held in no estimation whatever by the pious Hindu, they are unquestionably the most enterprising, intelligent, and industrious of all the Company's ryots or renters of malguzari land in Orissa. *Asiatic Researches*, Vol. XV., p. 199.

The Pandas who serve as priests and cooks in the public temples receive in their official capacity some homage from other people. But irrespective of their connection with the holy shrines, they are regarded as a very low class everywhere; and throughout the greater part of India they form separate castes with a very inferior status. In Calcutta there are many Panda

Brahmans of Orissa who serve as cooks in the houses of the rich Sudras. The Pandas who tout* for pilgrims are not all of the Panda caste.

§ 2.—*Jajpuria Brahmans.*

Jajpur is one of the sixteen Shasana towns of Orissa, but, as intermarriage cannot take place between the Jajpuria Shasanis, and the Brahmans of the Shashans in Southern Orissa, the Jajpurias form a distinct class, They are said to be divided into thirteen Houses with the following six Gotras :—

1. Kaphala.	4. Krishnatriya.
2. Kumara.	5. Kamakayan.
3. Kausika.	6. Katyaana.

Their usual surnames are Pati, Panda, Das, Misra, Nondkar, Satapati, &c. There are Adhikari and Mahajanpanthi Brahmans in the northern parts of Orissa as in its southern parts. These do not form separate castes, but intermarriage can take place between them, and the corresponding sections of the Brahmanical caste of southern Orissa. The Jajpuria Adhikari are to be found in large numbers in Calcutta, a great many of them being keepers of stalls on the banks of the

* The tours of these Oriya touts are so organised that during their campaigning season, which commences in November and is finished by the approach of the car festival at the beginning of the rainy season, very few villages in any of the adjoining provinces of India can escape their visit and taxation. The very appearance of one of them causes a serious disturbance in the even tenor of every Hindu household in the neighbourhood. Those who have already visited the "Lord of the World" at Puri are called upon to pay an instalment towards the debt contracted by them while at the sacred shrine, and which debt, though paid many times over, is never completely satisfied. That is, however, a small matter compared with the misery and distraction caused by the "Jagannath mania," which is excited by the Pandas' preachings and pictures. A fresh batch of old ladies become determined to visit the shrine, and neither the wailings and protestations of the children, nor the prospect of a long and toilsome journey can dissuade them. The arrangements of the family are, for the time being, upset altogether, and the grief of those left behind is heightened by the fact that they look upon the pilgrims as persons going to meet almost certain death. The railway about to be constructed between Calcutta and Puri may make a visit to Jaggannath a less serious affair.

holy Bhagirathi, supplying the bathers with oil for anointing their persons before ablution, and materials for painting their foreheads with holy figures and names after bathing. In the town of Jajpur there are some families who have been keeping the sacred fire from generation to generation.

Besides the good Srotriyas and Mahajanpanthis there are in Orissa, as in every other part of the country, some classes of inferior Brahmans who are regarded as more or less degraded. One of these classes is called Atharva Vedi.* There may be intermarriage between the followers of Rik, Sham and Yajus, but not between these and the Atharva Vedis. The other classes of degraded Brahmans will be noticed in their proper place.

* Some say that the Atharva Vedis are the same as the Masthanis. But the result of my enquiries tends to establish that there are other Atharva Vedis besides the Masthanis.

CHAP. VIII.—THE BRAHMANS OF RAJPUTANA.

To make the description of the Brahmans of Rajputana intelligible, it is necessary to say something about the geography of the province. Broadly speaking, it is that portion of India which lies between the river Chambal on the east, and the valley of the Indus on the west. The greater part of this vast tract of country is ruled still by semi-independent Rajput chiefs, and hence it is called Rajasthan, Raithana or Rajputana. The number of chiefs whose territories collectively go by these names is not less than twenty, and the only British possession within the circuit is the district of Ajmere-Merwara, which lies in the centre of the province. The country of the "Kings' children" is, however, not endowed with much of nature's gifts. It is divided into two parts by the Aravali hills, which extend from Abu on the south to the historic ridge in the suburbs of Delhi. The western half of Rajputana comprising the territories of Marwar, Jesalmere and Bikanir, consists mainly of sandy deserts utterly unfit for growing any kind of food-grains. Of the eastern half which is more fertile, the southern portion is included within the dominion of Udeypur ; the central portion is ruled by the chiefs of Kota, Boondi and Jaipore ; while the northern portion is taken up by Dholepore, Bhurtpore and Alwar.

Though, according to its very name, Rajputana is the country of the Rajputs, and though the military Ksatriyas are the ruling caste almost throughout its length and breadth, yet its Brahmanical population is twice as large as that of the fighting clans, and the influence of the sacerdotal caste in the province is exactly as it is in other parts of India. There are in Rajputana large colonies of Sarswat, Gaur, Sanadhya and Kanojia Brahmans whose connection with the members of their respective races in their original homes, has not yet been completely severed. Of the several classes of Brahmans whose proper home is Rajputana, the following are the most important :—

1.	Srimali	... A numerous clan found in every part of Rajputana as well as in Gujarat.
2.	Mewad	... Found chiefly in Mewad.
3.	Pallivala	... Most numerous in Western and Northern Rajputana. Found also in Bombay and Gujarat.
4.	Pokarana	.. Most numerous in the Northern and Western parts of Rajputana. Found in considerable numbers also in Sindh and Gujarat.
5.	Sanchora	... Original home Sanchora in Sirohi.
6.	Dahima	... Found chiefly in Marwar and Bundi.
7.	Divas	... Found chiefly in Bikanir, Marwar and Nathadwara.
8.	Parik	... Found chiefly in Marwar and Bundi.
9.	Khandelwal	Found chiefly in Marwar and Jaipore.
10.	Nandwani Bora.	Found chiefly in Marwar and Kesouli.
11.	Sikhawal	... Found in Jaipore.
12.	Asopa	... Found in Marwar.
13.	Rajgor	... Found in every part of Rajputana.
14.	Gujar Gor	... In every part of Rajputana.
15.	Bhojaks	... Low class Brahmans who minister to the Jains.

The Bhats and the Charanas, who are the hereditary bards and genealogists of Rajputana, claim to have the rank of Brahmans, but as they are not regarded as such by Hindu society, I shall speak of them in the part of this work which is devoted to the semi-Brahmanical castes. I conclude this chapter with a few details of the more important sections of the Rajputana Brahmans, collected chiefly from English authorities.

§ 1.—*The Srimalis.*

The Srimalis have a very high position whether regarded from a religious or secular point of view.

They minister as priests not only to the Srimali Banyas, but to all the higher castes including the Brahmans of the other classes. They hold also very high offices in the service of the local chiefs.

The following account of the Srimalis is taken from Wilson's *Indian Castes* :—

The Srimalis derive their designation from the town of Srimal, now called Bhinmal, lying to the north-west of Abu and intermediate between that mountain and the river Loni. Their first representatives are said to have been collected by a local prince from no fewer than forty-five of the most sacred places of the north, west, south and east of India ; but to the traditions to this effect little importance is to be ascribed. The Aryan physiognomy is perhaps more distinctly marked in them than in any other class of Brahmans in India. In fact, they do not appear to differ much from the type of some of the European nations, especially of those who have claims to Roman descent. Their costume is generally of a simple but not unbecoming character. Their turbans are on the whole of a graceful form, though not so large as those of many of the other natives of India. On their brows they wear the sectarial marks of the Vaishnavas, Vishnu being their favourite deity. The Srimalis are now scattered not only through several of the provinces of Rajputana, but through Gujarat and Kacha, Central India, the countries bordering on the Indus, and the island of Bombay. In consequence of this dispersion of their body, they have been broken into several distinct castes, most of which now neither eat nor intermarry with one another. They are also divided into two castes, founded on the Vedas which they profess : the Yajur Vedi (White and Black), and the Sama Vedi of the Kauthumi Sākha. In the former there are seven gotras or lines of family lineage : the Gautama, Sandilya, the Chandras, Laudravon, Maudralas, Kapinjalas. In the latter there are also seven gotras, the Shaunakas, Bharadvaj, Parasara, Kausika, Vatsa, Aupamanya, and Kashyapa. Most of all their classes are either mendicants or officiating priests, though secular service appears to be on the increase among them. They act as gurus and ceremonial Brahmans to the Srimali, Poraval, and Patolya and Urvala Vanyas (merchants) and Sonis or goldsmiths ; and about 5,000 of them, now apart from their brethren, act as gurus to the Oswalas, a class of mercantile Jainas, and are called Oswala Brahmans. A favourite Kuladevi or family goddess among them is that of Mahalaksmi, the spouse of Vishnu, a celebrated image of whom was transferred from Bhimmal to Auhilpur, or Pattan in the times of the Gujarat kings. The celebrated Sanskrit poet Magh, who is said to have lived in the time of Bhoja Raja, belonged to their fraternity. Their greatest living ornament is Dalpatram Daya, the Kaviraj, or Poet Laureate of Gujarat, who is also distinguished for his historical research, and sincere aims at social reform. This stirring author and singer supposes that there are 500 Srimali houses in Kacha and Kattiwar; 5,000 in Gujarat ; and 35,000 in Marwad and Mewad, exclusive of 50 of impure birth called *Daskori* near Ahmedabad, 1,500 of them being in Jodhpur (the capital of Marwad) alone.—Wilson's *Indian Castes*, *Vol. II*, pp. 109—111.

§ 2.—*Pallivals.*

The Pallivals are numerous in Jesalmere, Bikanir, Marwad, Jaipur and Kishangarh. Very few of the clan are to be found in Ajmere. The following account of the Pallival Brahmans of Rajputana is also taken from Dr. Wilson's *Indian Castes* :—

The Pallival Brahmans receive their name from the town of *Palli, the commercial capital of Marwad in Rajputana. They have twelve gotras. They are shrafs, merchants, and cultivators, but serve only in their own caste. They don't eat or intermarry with other Brahmans. They are found in Jodhpur, Bikanir and Jesalmere, and some others of the Rajput States. A few of them are at Delhi, Agra, and in the Panjab, Gujarat and Mewad. Only one or two of them are in Bombay. They are Smartas and do not use animal food. They do not drink the water of the houses of their own daughters † or any persons not belonging to their own castes. They don't eat with those of their own caste, who have got isolated from them as with the Gurjas and Mewad Pallivalas. They belong to the Kanya Kubja division of the Brahmans. "The Nandavana and Pallivala Brahmans are traders; were formerly located at Nandavana and Palli, and were there chiefly robbers, conducting their excursions on horseback. They subsequently became traders. They are said still to worship a bridle on the Dasara in memory of their former state."‡ They are scattered throughout the north of India, as Bohras or middlemen between the cultivators and Government.—Wilson's *Indian Castes*, Vol. II, p. 119.

The following account of the Pallivals of Jesalmere is from Tod's *Annals of Rajasthan* :—

Next to the lordly Rajputs, equalling them in numbers and far surpassing them in wealth, are the Pallivals. They are Brahmans, and denominated Pallivals from having been temporal proprietors of *Palli* and all its lands, long before the Rathores colonized Marwar. Tradition is silent as to the manner in which they became possessed of this domain; but it is connected with the history of the Palli, or pastoral tribes, who from the town of Palli to Pallitana, in Saurashtra, have left traces of their existence; and I am much mistaken if it will not one day be demonstrated that all the ramifications of the races figuratively denominated *Agnicula* were Palli

---

* "PALLI."—Town in Jodhpur State, Rajputana situated on the route from Nasirabad to Disa, 108 miles to the south-west of the former cantonment. An ancient place acquired by the Rahtors of Kanoj in 1156 A.D. It is the chief mart of Western Rajputana, being placed at the intersection of the great commercial road from Mandavi in Cutch to the Northern States, and from Malwa to Bahalpur and Sind.—Hunter's *Imperial Gazetteer*, Vol. XI, p. 1.

† Here Dr. Wilson has evidently misunderstood the information given to him. The custom spoken of here is not the speciality of the Pallivals, but is a common one to all the orthodox Hindus throughout India. It is based not on any aristocratic feeling on the part of the father, but to too much obedience to the injunction of the Shastras forbidding the acceptance of any kind of gift from a son-in-law.

‡ Irving's *Topography of Ajmere.*

in origin: more especially the Chohans, whose princes and chiefs for ages retained the distinctive affix of *Pal.*

These Brahmans, the Pallivals, as appears by the Annals of Marwar, held the domain of Palli when Seoji, at the end of the twelfth century invaded that land from Kanoj, and by an act of treachery first established his power. It is evident, however, that he did not extirpate them, for the cause of their migration to the desert of Jesalmere is attributed to a period of a Mahomedan invasion of Marwar, when a general war contribution (*dind*) being imposed on the inhabitants, the Pallivals pleaded caste and refused. This exasperated the Raja, for as their habits were almost exclusively mercantile, their stake was greater than that of the rest of the community, and he threw their principal men into prison. In order to avenge this they had recourse to a grand *chandi* or act of suicide; but instead of gaining their object, he issued a manifesto of banishment to every Pallival in his dominions. The greater part took refuge in Jesalmere, though many settled in Bikanir, Dhat and the valley of Sind. At one time, their number in Jesalmere was calculated to equal that of the Rajputs. Almost all the internal trade of the country passes through their hands, and it is chiefly with their capital that its merchants trade in foreign parts. They are the *Metayers* of the desert, advancing money to the cultivators, taking the security of the crop; and they buy up all the wool and ghi (clarified butter) which they transport to foreign parts. They also rear and keep flocks. The Pallivals never marry out of their own tribe; and directly contrary to the laws of Manu the bridegroom gives a sum of money to the father of the bride. It will be deemed a curious incident in the history of superstition, that a tribe, Brahman by name, at least, should worship the bridle of a horse. When to this is added the fact that the most ancient coins discovered in these regions bear the Palli character and the effigy of the horse, it aids to prove the Scythic character of the early colonists of these regions, who, although nomadic, were equestrian. There is little doubt that the Pallival Brahmans are the remains of the priests of the Palli race, who, in their pastoral and commercial pursuits, have lost their spiritual power.—Tod's *Rajasthan*, Vol. II, pp. 318—320.

§ 3.—*The Pokaranas.*

The Pokaranas are very numerous not only in every part of Rajputana, but in Gujarat and Sind also. They derive their designation from the town of Pokarana, which lies midway between Jodhpore and Jesalmere. The priests at Pushkar are called Pushkar Sevakas or the "worshippers of the lake." The Pokarana Brahmans have no connection whatever with the holy lake called Pushkara near Ajmere. They are devoted chiefly to secular pursuits. They are also the priests of the Bhatyas, and there are a few among them who are good Sanskritists and astrologers. They do not eat any kind of animal food. Their physiognomy is distinctively Aryan.

CHAP. IX.—THE BRAHMANS OF CENTRAL INDIA.

By Central India is meant the part of Northern India enclosed by the river Chambal on the west, the river Narmada on the south, the upper half of the Sone on the east, and the valley of the Jumna on the north. The majority of the Brahmans settled in this tract are foreign immigrants belonging chiefly to the Maharashtrya, Gujrati and Kanojia stocks. The only classes of Brahmans whose original home can be said to be Central India are the following :—

1. **Malavis** ... **Found chiefly in Malwa.**
2. **Narmadis** ... **Found chiefly on the banks of the Narmada.**
3. **Jijhotia** ... **Found chiefly in and near Bundelkhand.**

The Jijhotias derive their designation from the old name* of Bundelkhand. As there are Jijhotia Brahmans so there are Jijhotia Banyas and Rajputs also. The usual surnames of the Jijhotia Brahmans are the same as those of the Kanojias. It deserves to be noted here that among the Jijhotia Brahmans there is a Mauna Gotra apparently derived from the name of the great Hindu legislator.

* The name of Jijhota is mentioned in Huen Tsiang's *Travels*.

PART IV.

THE BRAHMANS OF SOUTHERN INDIA.

CHAP. I.—PRELIMINARY REMARKS.

It has been already observed that both according to the Shastras and the popular belief of the people of this country, the Brahmans of India are divided into ten classes, of which five are natives of Northern India, and the remaining five have their habitat in the Deccan. The majority of the Deccani or Panch Dravira Brahmans are Sivites. The number of Vishnuvites among them is also very considerable. But there are very few Sakti worshippers among them, and they are strict abstainers from every kind of animal food and intoxicating drink. The Sivites paint three horizontal lines of white colour on their forehead. The Vishnuvites have perpendicular lines of red, black or yellow colour painted on their foreheads between the upper part of the nose and the scalp. The colour and the form of the lines differ in the different sects, of which a full description is given in a subsequent part of this work. Some of the Vishnuvites of the Deccan are regularly branded like cattle, either only once when they are first initiated in the privilege of the mantra, or from time to time whenever they are visited by their spiritual preceptors. Among the South Indian Brahmans the line of demarcation between the ecclesiastics and the laity is maintained with much greater strictness than in Northern India. In Bengal and Hindustan proper, a Brahman devoted to secular pursuits is not deemed to be altogether incapable of performing the functions of a Guru or priest, or of receiving religious gifts. For the discharge of clerical functions, those who do not stoop to any kind of secular employment are generally deemed to be best qualified. But in the North religious donations are very often given to, and received by, the secular Brahmans, and cases are known in Bengal in which the privilege of even administering the mantra has been allowed to be exercised by graduates of the Calcutta University, and by persons in the service of Government. The case, however, in Southern India is different. There the laity cannot accept religious gifts, and are debarred altogether from the performance of clerical work. Throughout the greater part of the Deccan, a Bhikshu may at any time become a member of the secular order, and intermarriages take place usually between the ecclesiastics and the laity. But in the Andhra country the distinction is carried to a far greater extent than anywhere else. There the laity form a different caste called Niyogis, and there cannot possibly be any intermarriage between them and the Vaidikas. Throughout the Deccan the laity are called *Laukika* Brahmans; and the ecclesiastics have the designation of *Bhikshus*. Another peculiar feature, common to the several classes of South Indian Brahmans, is the fact of their being all subject to the spiritual authority of the Sankarite monasteries. This fact has been noticed already. *See* p. 16, *ante*.

CHAP. II.—THE BRAHMANS OF GUJARAT.

THOUGH Gujarat is situated to the north of the river Narmada, yet, according to Shastric texts, the Gujarat Brahmans form one of the main divisions of the Panch Dravira or the sacerdotal class of Southern India. The majority of them are either Sivites or Vishnuites. But it is said that there are a few Saktas among them of an extreme type not to be found in Bengal. The profession of the Guru is said to be unknown among them. It may be so among the followers of the ancient Sivite cult, the actual nature of which is by very few clearly understood or thought of. But, considering the character of the rites said to be practised by the Gujarati Saktas and Vaishnavas, it does not seem likely that the Guru is less active among them than in other parts of the country.

Every Gujarati's name consists of two parts: the first part being his own name, and the second that of his father. The usual surnames of the Gujarati Brahmans are Bhatta, Yani, Sukkul, Upādhya and Vyas.

The number of separate clans among the Gujarati Brahmans is very large. They generally say that there are not less than 84 different sections among them. The list given in Wilson's *Hindu Castes* includes 160 independent clans among them. However that may be, the following are the most important:—

1. Andichya
2. Nagar
3. Raikwar.
4. Bhargava.
5. Srimalis.
6. Girnar.

These are the most aristocratic clans among the Gujarati Brahmans. There are very few among them who live by begging or manual work. But a great many of them have a high secular position, and the majority of them are in well-to-do circumstances. Of the other clans, the Sanchoras usually serve as cooks. The Valodras are, generally speaking, very well-to-do people, a great many of them being money-lenders on a large scale. But they all go about the country begging for alms. They usually perform their tours on horseback.

§ 1.—*Audichyas.*

The Audichyas, as their name indicates, profess to have come from the north. According to their traditions and the *Audichya Prakas*, a reputed section of the Skanda Purana, their origin is stated to be as follows :—

Mulraj, King of Anhilwara Pattana, the Hindu capital of Gujarat, collected the following numbers of Brahmans from the different sacred places mentioned :—From the junction of the Ganga and Yamuna 105; from the Chyavanasrama 100; Samavedis, from the country of Kanya Kubja 200; from Kashi 100; from Kuru Kshetra 272; from Gangadvara 100; from Naimisha forest and from Kuru Kshetra, an additional supply of 132, making a total of 1,109. He conferred upon them as a Krishnarpan, the town of Sihor, with 150 adjoining villages, and the town of Sidhapura, with 100 adjoining villages. By this liberality he did what satisfied those Brahmans denominated the Sahasra (thousand) Audichyas. But other intelligent Audichyas did not accept his dana (largesses) but forming a *toli* of their own, became the Talakya Audichya, who acquired for themselves Khambhat (Cambay) and twelve other villages; while of the others 500 were of Siddhapara and 500 of Sihor.—Wilson's *Indian Castes*, Vol. II, p. 94.

According to the above account, the Audichyas ought to be divided into the following three classes only :—

1. Tolakya Audichyas.
2. Siddhapuria Audichyas.
3. Sihor Audichyas.

According to the Audichya Brahmans of Gujarat whom I have been able to consult, there are many independent sections among them, of which the following are the most important :—

1. Tolakya.
2. Siddhapuria.
3. Sihoria.
4. Sahasra ... 1. Jhalwari.; 2. Kharuiri.; 3. Gohelwari.
5. Kherwar.
6. Unawar.
7. Gharia.

There can be no intermarriage between these sections, and, for all practical purposes, they are separate castes though they may eat together without violating any rule of caste.

Siddhapur is an ancient town and a place of pilgrimage within the territories of the Baroda Raj. Sihor is within the Bhaunagar State, Kathiwar, about 13 miles west of the Bhaunagar town. Its ancient names were Sinhapur and Sarswatpur. It formed the capital of the Gohel Rajputs until Bhaunagar town was founded.

The Jhallwaris take their name from the district of Jhallwar in Kathiwar. Kherali is a petty State in the Jhallwar division of Kathiwar. Gohelwar is a tract of country to the south-east of Kathiwar, and forms one of its four main divisions. Kheral is a petty State in Mahi Kantha, a province of Gujarat. Una was an ancient town in Junagarh State, ruled at one time by the Unawar Brahmans. Its modern name is Dalawar. Garh is the name of a petty State in Rewah Kanth, Gujarat.

The majority of the Audichyas are devoted to secular pursuits. But there are many among them who are regular beggars. There are a few Vedic Pandits in the class. But the number of these is not very considerable. Wilson says that some of the Audichyas act as domestic servants in the capacity of water carriers. Considering how proud the Brahmans usually are, that may seem as quite impossible. But the existence of the practice among the Gujrati Brahmans is borne out by the result of my own enquiries. The Siddhapurias like, many other classes of Brahmans, may be found to be engaged as cooks ; and the Siddhapuria cooks are said to be very expert in their line.

§ 2.—*Nagar Brahmans of Gujarat.*

The Nagar Brahmans are the priests of the Nagar Banyas. There are very few Sanskrit scholars among them. But they count among their numbers many who hold and have held high secular positions. The main divisions among them are the following :—

1. Vadnagara.	4. Prasnora.
2. Vishalnagora.	5. Kishnora.
3. Sathodra.	6. Chitroda.

The information which I have been able to collect regarding these several classes of the Nagara Brahmans coincides in all material points with what is given about them in Wilson's book. I therefore cite from it *in extenso* the following account of them :—

The *Vadnagora Brahmans* receive their designation from the city of *Vadnagora* lying to the east of Aunhilavada Pattana. They are mostly found in the Peninsula of Gujarat, formerly Saurashtra, now Kathiwar, where the business of the native estates is principally in their hands; but individuals of them are scattered over nearly the whole of the province of Gujarat, being found at Nadiyad, Ahmedabad, Baroda, Surat, &c. Most of them are Rig-Vedis, following the Sankhyana Sutras; but some of them profess the other three Vedas, particularly the White Yajur Veda. The majority of them are Smartas; but an inconsiderable number of them are Vaishnavas of the sects of Swami Narain and Vallabhacharya. None of them are practical cultivators, but a few of them act as Desais. The mendicants among them are few in number. They do not eat even with the Nagars of other denomination's.

The Vishalnagora Brahmans receive their name from the town of Vishal. founded by Vishal, the first king of the Vaghela dynasty of Gujarat, sometimes called Visaldeva (said by Colonel Tod to have been installed in Sumvat 1249, A.D. 1192) and which lies a little to the south-west of Vadanagora. They are principally Rig-Vedis, and are either Smartas or Vaishnavas of the sect of Swami Narain. They are mainly either public servants or agriculturists.

The Sathodra Brahmans get their name from the town of Sathod on the Narmada. There are some Rig-Vedis among them ; but they are principally of the Madhyandina Sâkha of the White Yajur Veda. They are found at Anand, Nadiyad, Ahmedabad, Dabboi and other places. Some of them are in public service, or engaged in buying and selling ; but a good many of them are still Bhikshus, or act as *Gurus*. They are principally if not wholly Smartas.

The Prasnoras are said to belong to Prasnora. They are Rig-Vedis, and of the Vallabhacharya sect, their chief residence being in Kathiwar. They are principally mendicants.

The Krishnoras of Krishnapura are of the Rig, Sama, and Yajur Vedas. Most of them are Bhikshukas of a "kind respectable for learning."

The Chitrodas are of the town of Chitrod. They are found at Bhaunagar and Baroda. They say that they have among themselves professors of each of the Vedas. They are not a numerous body.

The present Dewan of Baroda, Mr. Muni Bhai, is a Vadnagora Brahman. So was also Mr. Gouri Shankar, Udaya Shankar, C.S.I., formerly Dewan of Bhaunagar, whose portrait is given in Sir Monier Williams's recent work on *Brahmanism and Hinduism*.

§ 3.—*The Raikwar Brahmans of Gujarat.*

The Raikwars are to be found chiefly in Kach and in the district of Kheḍa in Gujarat. There are many Sanskritists and English scholars among them. The spiritual guide of the Rao of Kach is a Raikwar; so is the eminent Pandit Badri Nath Trimbak Nath. Mr. Bhai Sankar, who is one of the leading attorneys of the Bombay High Court, is also a Raikwar.

§ 4.—*The Bhargava Brahmans.*

The chief habitat of the Bhargavas is the district of Broach at the mouth of the Narmada. The name of the tract inhabited by them is evidently a corrupted form of the Sanskrit Bhrigu Kshettra, the territory of Bhrigu. The Bhargavas were formerly one of the poorest and most ignorant of all the classes of Gujarati Brahmans. In Wilson's book it is stated that, under the British Government, they were certainly rising. The correctness of his forecast is demonstrated by the fact that there are now many learned men and high officials among them.

§ 5.—*The Srimalis.*

The Srimalis are, properly speaking, Brahmans of Rajputana, and an account of them has been given in the chapter on Rajputana Brahmans in Part III, Chapter VIII, p. 66, *ante*.

Mr. Dalpatram Daya, C.I.E., the celebrated poet of Gujarat, and the author of the work on caste entitled "Gnati Nibandha," is a Srimali of Ahmedabad. The great Sanskrit poet Mâgha. is also said to have been a Srimali.

The Srimali Brahmans of Gujarat have the following sub-divisions among them :—

1. Kachi Srimali.	4. Ahmedabadi Srimali.
2. Kathiwadi Srimali.	5. Surati Srimali.
3. Gujarathi Srimali.	6. Khambhati Srimali.

§ 6.—*Girnars.*

Wilson gives the following account of the Girnar Brahmans :—

The Girnars derive their name from the ancient mountain city of *Girinagar*, now represented by Junagadh, the old fort at the root of the celebrated Girnara mountain. In this locality they are principally to be found. They are also met with in other towns of the peninsula of Gujarat. A few of them are in Bombay. They are divided into the following castes.

(1) The *Junagadhya Girnaras.*

(2) The *Chorvada Girnars* of the town of Chorvad on the coast of the peninsula of Gujarat between Pattana Somnath and Mangrol.

(3) The *Ajakyas*, so called from the village of *Ajak.*

These three castes readily eat together, but do not intermarry. They now rank low in the Brahmanhood, from their acting as *Gurus* to Kolis, and having a variety of occupations as those of administrators to native chiefs, clerks, astrologers, cultivators and mendicants. They are of various sects as suits them for the time being. They are said to professall the Vedas but the Sama, but are principally of the White Yajur Veda. They must be a very ancient confederation of Brahmans.—Wilson, Vol. II, p. 101.

§ 7.—*The other Classes of Gujarati Brahmans.*

The other classes of Gujarati Brahmans are mentioned in the following list with brief descriptive notices :—

1. *Anavalas or Bhatelas.*—Found chiefly in the tract of country between Broach and Daman. The Bhatelas are secular Brahmans, the majority of them being devoted to agriculture and trade. Some of them are employed as Government servants and mercantile assistants.

2. *The Borasidhas.*—These derive their name from the town of Borsad in the Kaira district, Bombay Presidency.

3. *The Chovishas.*—This tribe has representatives at Baroda, and at Sinor and Janor near the Narmada.

4. *The Dadhichis.*—Numerically a small body. Found chiefly on the Mahi. There are beggars, cultivators and ecclesiastics among them.

5. *The Dashaharas.*—Said to be found near Aunilwara Pattan. They are Sakti worshippers.

6. *The Deswali.*—Literally, the people of the country. They are found chiefly in the district of Kheḍa.

7. *The Jambus.*—The Jambus are the Brahmans of the town of Jambusara in the district of Broach. There are cultivators as well as mendicants and astrologers among them.

8. *The Khadayatas.*—The Khadayatas are chiefly of the ecclesiastical profession, acting both as priests and *Gurus.* They are to be found in the districts of Khedra, Ahmedabad and Broach.

9. *The Masthanas.*—The Masthanas are found in large numbers in the vicinity of Siddhapura. Like the Masthanas of Orissa, those of Gujarat also are chiefly cultivators.

10. *The Modhas.*—The Modha Brahmans are to be found chiefly in the districts of Ahmedabad and Kheda. They are the *Gurus* or spiritual preceptors of the Modha Banyas.

11. *The Nandodras.*—So named from Nandod, the capital of the Rajpipla State, situated about 32 miles east by north from Surat in a bend of the Korjan river. The *Gurus* of the Rajas of Rajpipla and Dharmpore are said to be Nandod Brahmans. There are both mendicants and cultivators among the Nandods.

13. *The Naradikas.*—The Naradikas are to be found chiefly in Cambay and its neighbourhood. They are a small body. There are cultivators as well as mendicants among them.

14. *The Narsiparas.*—The Narsiparas are followers of Vallabhacharya. The priests of the shrine of Krishna at Dakor, in the Thasra sub-division of the Kaira district, are Brahmans of this class.

15. *The Parasaryas.*—The Parasaryas are said to be found in the south-east of Kathiwar.

16. *The Sachora.*—The Sachoras are followers of Vallabhacharya. A great many of them serve as cooks.

17. *The Sajhodras.*—So named from the town of Sajodh near Broach. Like that of the Bhatelas the chief employment of the Sajhods is cultivation.

18. *The Somparas.*—The Somparas are the Brahmans who have charge of the temple of Siva at Somenath. They have a somewhat higher position than is usually assigned in the caste system to the priests of other shrines. The Somparas are all Smartas. After the destruction of the great temple at Somenath by Mahmud Ghazni a new one was erected by Bhima Deva I. This new temple was destroyed by the renegade Hindu, Sultan Muzaffer I. The present temple was erected by Rani Ahalya Bai.

19. *The Sorathiyas.*—The Sorathiyas derive their name from Saurashtra, modern Surat. They are found chiefly in Junagadha.

20. *The Talajyas.*—The Talajyas derive their name from the town of Talaja in the Bhaunagar State, situated about 31 miles south of Bhaunagar town. The Talajyas are now mainly shopkeepers, and are to be found at Jambusar, Surat, Bombay, Nasik and other towns of Western India.

21. *The Tapodhanas.*—The Tapodhanas derive their name from the river Tapti on the banks of which they are to be found. Some of them are priests in the local temples of Siva. But the majority of them are cultivators.

22. *The Valadras.*—The Valadras seem to derive their name from Wala, the capital of the Wala State in

the Gobelwar division of Kathiwar. The ancient name of Wala was Walabhipur. Some of the Valadras are very rich, being money-lenders on a large scale. But the majority of them are mendicants and beggars. Some of the latter class perform their tours on horseback. The Valadras are Smartas and Sakti worshippers.

23. *The Valmikis.*—The Valmikis are to be found in Kheḍa, Cambay and Idar. There are both beggars and cultivators among them.

24. *The Vayadas.*—The Vayadas are the spiritual preceptors of the Vayada Vanyas. The Vayada Brahmans are a very small body.

The other classes usually included in lists of Guzrati Brahmanas are either foreigners, or degraded and semi-degraded Brahmans, corresponding to the Agradānis, Mahá-Brahmanas and Barna Brahmanas of Northern India. The following are like Barna Brahmans :—

1. *Abhira* Brahmans—Brahmans who minister to the Abhira cowherds as priests.
2. *Muchigor*—Brahmans who minister to the Mochis.
3. *Kunbigor*—Brahmans who minister to the Kunbis.
4. *Darjigors*—Brahmans who minister to the darjis or tailors.
5. *Gandharp Gors*—Brahmans who minister to the Gandharps or musicians.
6. *Gurjara Gors*—Brahmans who minister to the Gurjaras.

CHAP. III.—THE BRAHMANS OF MAHA-RASHTRA AND KANKAN.

THE most important classes of Brahmans in Maharashtra and the Kankan are the following :—

1. Deshastha.
2. Kankanastha.
3. White Yajurvedi.
4. Karhade.
5. Shenavi.

It was on Brahmans of the first four of these classes that the Peshwas bestowed religious gifts, and donations in acknowledgment of literary merit. The last have great secular importance.

§ 1.—*The Deshastha Brahmans of Maharashtra.*

The word *Deshastha* literally means "residents of the country," and, in Maharashtra, the name is given to the Brahmans of the country round Poona, which was the metropolis of the Maharashtra empire. Most of the Deshasthas pursue secular professions as writers, accountants, merchants, &c. However, there were, and still are, among them great Pandits in almost every branch of Sanskrit learning. As among the other classes of South Indian Brahmans, the laity among the Deshasthas are called *Laukikas* (worldly men) or *Grihasthas* (householders). The *Bhikshus* or ecclesiastics are also householders, as every Brahman is required to be in his youth; but as they devote themselves entirely to the study of the Shastras, they alone are held entitled to receive religious donations, and are called *Bhikshus* or beggars. The secular Deshasthas have such secular surnames as Desai, Despande, Desmukha, Kulkarni and Patil. The Bhikshus are sub-divided into several classes, according to the branch of learning which they cultivate. Those who study the Vedas are called Vaidika; those who expound the law are called Shastri; those who make astrology their speciality are called Jotishi or Joshi; the votaries of the medical science are called Vaidyas; and the reciters of the Purāns are called Purānikas. These distinctions, however, do not affect their caste status. In fact the son of a Laukika Brahman may be a Bhikshu, and a Bhikshu himself may, at any time, by accepting secular employment, cease to be of the ecclesiastical order. The usual surnames of the Bhikshus are Bhatta, Shastri and Joshi.

The Deshasthas are followers of the Rik and the Krishna Yajus. There are some Vishnuvites among them of the Madhwa sect. But the majority are Sivites. There is, however, nothing to prevent intermarriage between the Sivites and the Madhwas. There is a large colony of the Deshasthas in Mysore. There are a great many Brahmans of this class in Benares also. Pandit Govinda Shastri, of the Government Sanskrit College of Calcutta, is a Deshastha. The great Sanskrit jurists, Nilkanta and Kamalakar were Deshasthas. The celebrated Tantia Topi of the Sepoy war was a Brahman of the same class. He was born in a village called Gowala, in the district of Nasik. His proper name was Raghu Nath Rao. Tantia Topi was the name of his boyhood. The late Sir T. Madhava Rao was of the same class.

§ 2.—*The Kankanastha Brahmans.*

As their name indicates, the original home of the Kankanasthas is the Kankan, or the narrow strip of country extending from Broach on the north, to Ratnagiri on the south, and bounded on the west by the Arabian Sea, and on the east by the Western Ghats. The Kankanasthas are also called Chitpavana, a word which evidently means a "purifier or curer of the soul." But on the authority of the Sahyadrikhanda of the Skanda Purāna, which seems to be the composition of a Deshastha, the other classes of Maharatta Brahmans say that Chitpavana is not a corrupted form of Chitta Pāvana, but of Chitāpāvana, which means a purifier of a funeral pyre. According to the Skanda Purāna, the Kankanasthas are so-called because the Brahminical hero and incarnation, Parushuram, created them out of a *chita* or funeral pyre. Leaving aside legends, the name of Chitpavan given to the Kankanastha Brahmans seems to be derived from the town of Chiplun in the Ratnagiri district, situated near the head of the Kumbharli pass, which is one of the easiest routes from the Deccan to the sea-board. The Peshwas, who very nearly succeeded in establishing Hindu supremacy in India during the last century, were Kankanastha Brahmans. Of the same class also were many of the high officials of the Mahratta empire—the Patvardhanas, the Gokales, the Rastyas, &c. Raja Dinkar Rao, who was Prime Minister of Scindia at the time of the Sepoy war, and who was regarded as one of the greatest administrators of his time, was a Kankanastha. Mr. Justice Ranade, of the Bombay High Court, is a Brahman of the same tribe. So was the late Rao Saheb Vishwanath Narayan Mandalika, who was one of the ablest advocates of the Bombay High Court, and was also a Member of the Legislative Council of India.

As among the Deshasthas, so among the Kankani Brahmans, the majority are devoted to secular pursuits. They are the persons who generally fill "offices of every kind, including the village and perganah accountantships all over the country."* A great many of them are *khotes* or landholders, who enjoy valuable proprietary over the Kankan villages. Though mainly secular, the Kankanasthas do not keep themselves quite aloof

* Campbell's *Ethnology of India*, p. 73.

from the cultivation of letters. On the contrary, they have had among them some of the best scholars in every department of learning. One of the greatest of these in recent times was the late Pandit Bapu Deva Sastri of the Government Sanskrit College, Benares. The following is from the appreciative notice of his life in Mr. Sherring's *Hindu Tribes and Castes* :—

Bapu Deva Sastri has greatly distinguished himself as a scholar, and has, by his works, shed a lustre on the Sanskrit College, in which for many years he has been a Professor of Mathematics and Astronomy, and on the city in which he lives. The titles of some of his numerous works are as follows: On Trigonometry in Sanskrit; Translation of the Surya Siddhanta into English; On Algebra in Hindi; On Geography in Hindi; On Arithmetic in Sanskrit; Symbolical Euclid in Sanskrit. * * * *

In consideration of the great services rendered to science and education in India, the Sastri has been made an Honorary Member of the Royal Asiatic Society of Great Britain, and also of the Asiatic Society of Bengal.—Sherring's *Hindu Tribes and Castes*, Vol. I, p. 90.

Like the Deshasthas, the Kankanis are followers of the Rik and the Krishna Yajus. The Rig Vedis are of the Ashwalayana Sākha, and the Yajur Vedis of the Taittiriya Sākha. The following are sub-classes of the Kankanasthas :—

1. Nirvankor.
2. Keloskar.

The Kankanis have more than three hundred surnames peculiar to their class.

§ 3.—*The Yajurvedis.*

The Yajurvedis among the Deshasthas are followers of the Black Yajus. The class of Maharatta Brahmans called Yajurvedi are followers of the White Yajus. They have two branches, namely,—

1. The Kanvas.
2. The Madhyandinas.

The Kanvas are so called on account of their adopting the Kanva rescension of the White Yajus. The Madhyandinas derive their name in the same manner from the Madhyandina Sākha of the White Yajus. Both the

Kanvas and the Madhyandinas follow the Shatapatha Brahmana, and the Srauta Sutras of Katyana. The Madhyandinas* attach great importance to the performance of the Sandhya prayer at noon, *i.e.*, after 11 A.M. But the Rig Vedis might perform the mid-day prayer even at 7 o'clock in the morning. The Madhyandinas cannot celebrate any Sradh except at noon, whereas the Rig Vedis can perform such a ceremony any time during the day. The Yajurvedis are to be found in every part of the Maharatta country, properly so-called, from Nasik on the north to Kolhapur on the south. They enjoy a very high position among the Brahmans of the country. The majority of them keep themselves aloof from secular pursuits, and devote themselves entirely to the study of the sacred literature and to the practice of the Vedic rites. During the reign of the Peshwas, they had perhaps the largest share of the religious gifts made by the State as well as in those made by private individuals. The families of the Guru of the Maharaja of Kolahpur, and of the titular Pratinidhi of Sattara are Yajurvedis of the Madhyandina Sākha.

§ 4.—*The Karhades.*

The Karhades derive their name from the town of Karhad near the junction of the Krishna and the Koina rivers, about fifteen miles to the south of Sattara. While the Deshasthas are Sivites, and the Yajurvedis are observers of the Vedic rites, the Karhades are the extreme Saktas of the Maharashtra country. In Northern India, Sivites, Saktas, Vishnuvites, and Vedists are to be found within the same class; and a difference of cult, though giving rise to great animosity, has very seldom brought about the formation of subdivisions in any caste. But in the Deccan, which has been

* The name of the Madhyandina Sākha of the White Yajus seems to be derived from that of the Madhyandina School of Hindu astronomers according to whom the day is regarded as beginning at noon, and not at sunrise or midnight.

ruled by great Hindu kings down to recent times, the case is naturally otherwise. The Peshwas were Sivite Brahmans, and, during their ascendancy, the Vishnuvites never could flourish in their country. The only cults, besides that of the Sivite, which then found a congenial soil in the country round Poona, were Sakti worship, which is only the counterpart of Saivism, and the Vedic rites which, though rendered obsolete by more effective and less wasteful forms of worship invented in later times, have still a great charm for the Hindu mind. The Sivite, the Sakta and the Vedic forms of worship have flourished side by side in the Maharashtra country, and naturally there was great bitterness between the professors of these forms of faith. Wherever there are two or more competitors for favour from the same quarter, and each tries to rise in the estimation of the common patron, at the expense of his rivals, sectarian hatred and bigotry must necessarily be rampant.

In the Sahyadri Khanda of the Skanda Purāna, which bears evidences of being the production of a Desastha Brahman, the Karhades are charged with the practice of offering human sacrifices, and of even murdering Brahmans to propitiate their deities. The charge being preferred by an infallible authority, the Karhades admit its truth, though with the usual qualification that the practice has been given up by them long since. As a matter of fact, perhaps, the practice never existed on a large scale among any class of Brahmans. The Tāntras recommending human sacrifice are accepted as authorities by the Brahmans of almost all the classes throughout India. Yet, in practice, the only animals that are usually sacrificed by the Sakti worshippers in Northern India are the goat and the sheep, *i.e.*, the animals, the flesh of which the Brahmans eat. The flesh of the buffalo is eaten by some of the low castes, and sometimes buffaloes are sacrificed by the Saktas. But human sacrifice, though recommended by one set of texts, is prohibited by others, and as it must be naturally revolting to every one excepting a few depraved fanatics, and as actual instances of it are extremely rare, if not quite unknown, in modern times, the case was apparently never very different in mediæval or ancient India. In the Mahābhārt, which is undoubtedly a very ancient work, Krishna himself is made to observe* that the slaughter of human beings for sacrificial purposes was unknown in practice. Coming down to historical times there is nothing in the early records of British rule, or in the Mahomedan chronicles to warrant the conclusion that the practice prevailed very extensively during the last seven centuries. The injunctions about it in the Tāntras were, it seems, meant only to excite awe on the minds of the common people, and to enable the priest to make the votaries more ready to offer as a substitute a goat or a sheep than they would otherwise be. The case is only that of an application of the maxim of priestly politics which the Brahmanical clerics formulate by saying that they must ask for a Kashmere shawl in order to get a bathing towel.

Whatever room there may be for comment on the religion of the Karhades, they are equal to the Kankanasthas and the Deshasthas in every other respect. The great Maharatta poet Moropant was a Karhade. So was the late Bala Gangadhar Shastri Jambhekor, who was a professor in the Elphinstone Institution.

The Karhades distinguished themselves sometimes in secular service also. Govinda Pandit, a Karhade Brahman, was sent by the Peshwa as his agent to Saugor, and the Pandit succeeded in taking possession of the district for his master, from Chattra Sal, in 1753. Sheo Ram Bhao was the Sir Soobah or Governor of the province of Jhansi at the time of the conquest of Northern India by the English. His descendants ruled the province as semi-independent kings, till the annexation of the State by Lord Dalhousie. The Karhade dynasty of

* See *Mahābhārt*, Sava Parva, Chapter XXII.

Jhansi has been rendered particularly famous by the name of the great Rani whose political genius and ability as a military commander have elicited the admiration of even English historians and generals. There is still a large colony of Karhade Brahmans in Saugor and Damoh who trace their descent from the companions-in-arms of their great clansmen who first conquered the country. There are many Karhades among the officers of the Mysore Raj, the majority of them being connected with its Revenue Survey Department.

§ 5.—*The Shenavi Brahmans of the Kankan.*

The Shenavis are believed to be a branch of the Sarswat Brahmans of the Panjab. They are found chiefly in the Kankan, Goa, and Bombay. There are a few among them who are of the priestly profession. But the majority of them are devoted to secular pursuits in which they are now generally far more successful than perhaps any other class of Brahmans. Like the Sarswatas, the Shenavis are in the habit of eating fish and such flesh as is not prohibited by the Shastras.

The Shenavis are not all of the same religion. There are Sankarites and Madhwa Vishnuvites among them. The late Dr. Bhau Daji, the late Mr. Justice Telang, and the late Pandit Shankar Pandurang were all Shenavis. So is also Mr. Bhandarkar, the present Vice-Chancellor of the Bombay University.

CHAP. IV.—MIDDLE CLASS AND INFERIOR BRAHMANS OF THE MAHARASHTRA.

§ 1.—*Middle Class Secular Brahmans.*

THE following are the middle class Brahmans of the Maharashtra country :—

1. Deva Ruke.
2. Savashe.
3. Kirvantas.

Deva Ruke.—The Deo Rukes are found chiefly in the Kankan. They are generally very poor. They are devoted mainly to agriculture. The Deshasthas will eat with them ; but the Kankanasthas generally refuse to do them that honour.

Savashe.—The Savashes are found chiefly in the Southern Maharatta country. They engage in trade, and are a prosperous class. The name is evidently derived from the Sanskrit word Sahavasi which means an "associate." The origin of the application of this designation to them is explained as follows :—

In remote times, a certain Brahman came upon a hidden treasure ; but to his amazement, the contents appeared in his eyes to be all live scorpions. Out of curiosity, he hung one of them outside his house. A little while after, a woman of inferior caste, who was passing by the house, noticed it to be gold, and upon her questioning him about it, the Brahman espoused her and, by her means, was able to enjoy the treasure. He gave a feast in honour of his acquisition of wealth. He was subsequently outcasted for his *mésalliance* with the low-caste female, while those who were with him were put under a ban, and thus acquired the nickname.—*Mysore Census Report*, p. 235.

Kirvantas.—The Kirvantas are found chiefly in the Kankan. Many of them are cultivators. But some of them are very rich, and there are good Sanskrit scholars too among them. They are now being recognized as good Brahmanas by the Kankanasthas.

§ 2.—*Yajaka Brahmans.*

The following classes of Maharashtra Brahmans minister to the Sudras as priests, and have consequently a very inferior position :—

1. Palashe. | 2. Abhira.

Palashe.—The Palashes are found chiefly in Bombay and its neighbourhood. They act as priests, astrologers and physicians to the Prabhus, Sutars, Bhandaris, Sonars, and other Sudra castes in Bombay. The high caste Maharatta Brahman say that the Palashes are no Brahmans. But as they are accepted as priests by the many Sudra castes mentioned above, they are certainly entitled to be regarded as one of the sacerdotal clans, however low their status may be.

Abhiras.—The Abhiras are found chiefly in Kandeish. They act as priests to the cowherd caste called Abhira.

§ 3.—*Javala Brahmans.*

The Javala Brahmans have a low status on account of their serving as cooks, and their habit of eating fish. They are found chiefly in the Kankan.

§ 4.—*Agricultural Brahmans.*

The following classes of Maharashtra Brahmans are mainly agricultural, and have a very low status :—

1. Kastas—found in Poona and Kandeish.
2. Trigulas—found on the banks of the Krishna.
3. Sopara—found chiefly in Bassin.

§ 5.—*The Degraded and Outcaste Brahmans.*

The following are the classes of Brahmans that in Maharashtra are regarded more or less as outcastes :—

1. The Hoseini. | 3. Kunda Golaka.
2. The Kalanki. | 4. Randa Golaka.
5. Brahman Jai.

An account of some of these will be given in a subsequent part of this work. See p. 118, *post.*

CHAP. V.—THE BRAHMANS OF KARNATA.

In English works on the history and the geography of India, the name Karnatic is usually applied to the tract of country on the east coast of the Deccan between Arcot and Madras. But the name of Karnat is properly applicable only to the tract where Kanarese is the prevailing language. It embraces almost the whole of Mysore with the British districts of North Kanara, Dharwar, and Belgaum of the Bombay Presidency. In external appearance, the Karnat Brahmans differ but little from the Deshasthas of Maharashtra.

The following classes are regarded as the indigenous Brahmans of Karnat:—

1.	Babburu Kamme	Derive their name from the Kamme country situated to the east of modern Mysore.
2.	Kannada Kamme	
3.	Ulach Kamme ...	
4.	Haisaniga ...	Very numerous in the Hassan division of Mysore. The great Madhavacharya, it is said, was a member of this caste.
5.	Arvatta Vakkalu	Secular Brahmans; followers of Madhava.
6.	Hale Karnataka...	Very numerous in Mysore, but have a low caste status.
7.	Karnataka.	
8.	Vaduganadu ...	(Lit. from the north).
9.	Sirnadu ...	
10.	Havika ...	From Haiga, the ancient name of North Kanara.
11.	Hubu—Found chiefly in North Kanara.	

Of these, the first seven classes are found chiefly in Mysore, and the last in North Kanara. The Havikas or Haigas have their principal home in North Kanara and the Shimog division of the Mysore territories. They claim to derive their name from the Sanskrit word Havya, which means "oblation." Their usual occupation is the cultivation of the supari or areca-nut gardens. But there are among them many who are of the priestly order. The Hubus of North Kanara are a degraded class. A great many of them live either by the practice of astrology, or by serving as priests in the public temples. The Hale Karnatikas of Mysore are considered as a still more degraded class. Their very Brahmanhood is not generally admitted, in spite of their having lately secured a Srimukh from the Sringeri monastery recognising them as a class of the sacerdotal caste. Their chief occupations are agriculture and Government service, as Shanbhogs or village accountants. By way of reproach they are called Maraka, which literally means slaughterer or destroyer. The following account is given of them in the *Mysore Gazetteer* :—

"A caste claiming to be Brahmans, but not recognised as such. They worship the Hindu triad, but are chiefly Vishnuvites and wear the trident mark on their foreheads. They are most numerous in the south of the Mysore district, which contains five-sixths of the whole number. The great majority of the remainder are in Hassan district. They call themselves Hale Kannadiga or Hale Karnataka, the name Maraka being considered as one of reproach. They are said to be descendants of some disciples of Sankaracharya, and the following legend is related of the cause of their expulsion from the Brahman caste to which their ancestors belonged—

One day Sankaracharya, wishing to test his disciples, drank some tadi in their presence, and the latter thinking it could be no sin to follow their master's example indulged freely in the same beverage. Soon after, when passing a butcher's shop, Sankaracharya asked for alms; the butcher had nothing but meat to give, which the guru and his disciples ate. According to the Hindu Shastras, red hot iron alone can purify a person who has eaten flesh and drunk tadi. Sankaracharya went to a blacksmith's furnace, and begged from him some red hot iron, which he swallowed and was purified. The disciples were unable to imitate their master in the matter of the red hot iron, and besought him to forgive their presumption in having dared to imitate him in partaking of forbidden food. Sankaracharya refused to give absolution, and cursed them as unfit to associate with the six sects of Brahmans.—*Mysore Gazetteer*, Vol. I, p. 341.

CHAP. VI.—THE BRAHMANS OF DRAVIRA.

DRAVIRA is the name given to the southernmost part of the Indian Peninsula, including the districts of Trichinopoli, Tanjore, Arcot, Tinnevelly, Kambakonam, and Madura. This tract of country being inhabited by the Tamil-speaking tribes is roughly distinguishable from the provinces of Karnat and Andhra towards its north, the prevailing languages of which are respectively Kanarese and Telugu.

The Brahmans of Dravira are divided into two main classes according to their religion. The followers of Sankaracharya are called Smartas, and those of Ramanuja and Madhava are called Vaishnavas. All the Dravira Brahmans are strict vegetarians and teetotalers.

§ 1.—*The Smarta Brahmans.*

The majority of the Smarta Brahmans are Sivites, and there are very few Saktas or Vishnu worshippers among them. They are all followers of Sankaracharya, and regard the Superior of the Sankarite monastery at Sringeri as their spiritual head. Those among the Smartas who devote themselves entirely to Vedic study and to the practice of Vedic rites are called Vaidikas, and those who earn their living by secular pursuits are called Laukikas. The Vaidikas alone are entitled to religious gifts, and the Laukikas cannot lay claim to largesses for pious purposes. But in other respects the distinction is of no importance whatever, as intermarriage is freely allowed between them.

The usual surname of the Smartas is Ayar. The Sanskritists among them use the title of Shastri while the title of Dikshit is similarly used by those in whose family any of the great Vedic sacrifices has ever been celebrated.

The following are the most important classes of Dravira Brahmans of the Smarta order:—

1. Warma.
2. Brihatcharana.
3. Ashta Sahasra.
4. Sanket.

Warma Brahmans.—The Warma Brahmans are very numerous in and near Tanjore. They are divided into the following classes :—

1. Chola Des.
2. Warma Des.
3. Sabayar.
4. Javali.
5. Eanjeay.

These may eat together, but there can be no intermarriage between them. The late Sir Muttuswami Ayar, of the Madras High Court, was a Warma Des Warma of the Tanjore district. Mr. Subramhanya Ayar, who has been appointed to succeed him on the Bench of the Madras High Court, is also a Warma Des Warma. Sir Muttuswami was not only an able Judge, but a great man in every sense of the term. Upon his death, which occurred in January last, the Chief Justice said of him :—

"We are assembled here to express our very great regret at the loss we have sustained by the death of Sir T. Muttuswami Ayar. His death is undoubtedly a loss to the whole country and the Crown. A profound Hindu jurist, a man with very excellent knowledge of English law, with very great strength of mind possessing that most useful quality in a Judge, common sense; he was undoubtedly a great Judge, very unassuming in manners, he had great strength of mind and independence of character, his judgments were carefully considered, and the decisions he ultimately arrived at were, in a great majority of instances, upheld in the final Court of Appeal. His advice was often asked for by the Judges of the Court, and—I can speak from experience—was always freely given and was most valuable. He was a man who did honour to the great profession of law, an upright Judge who administered justice without distinction of race or creed, a well read scholar and a gentleman in the best and truest acceptation of the word. The High Court by his death has sustained a heavy loss, a loss which undoubtedly it can ill bear."

The Warma Brahmans paint their foreheads in two different ways. Some have transverse lines of sandal or sacred ashes; while others have a perpendicular line of sandal or Gopichandana.*

Brihat Charana.—Among the Dravira Brahmans the Brihat Charanas are next in importance only to the Warmas. The Brihat Charanas paint their forehead with a round mark of Gopichandana in the centre, in addition to transverse lines of white sandal. Sir Sheshadri Ayar, K.C.S.I., the present Dewan of Mysore, is a Brihat Charana. So is also Mr. Sundar Ayar, Advocate, Madras High Court.

Ashta Sahasra.—The Ashta Sahasras are, generally speaking, more handsome than the other classes of Draviri Brahmans. Like the moderate Sakti worshippers of Bengal, the Ashta Sahasras paint between their eyebrows a round mark which is either of white sandal or of a black colouring material formed by powdered charcoal.

Sanket.—The Sankets are Dravidians, but are found also in Mysore. The Mysore Sankets cannot speak pure Tamil. There are two sub-divisions among them, namely, the Kausika Sanketis and the Bettadapara Sanketis. Their religion and their social customs are the same, but there can be no intermarriage between them.

The following remarks are made with reference to the Sanketis by Mr. Narsimmayangar in his report on the last Census of Mysore :—

> The Sanketis are proverbially a hardy, intensely conservative, and industrious Brahman community. They are referred to as models for simultaneously securing the twofold object of preserving the study of the Vedas, while securing a worldly competence by cultivating their gardens, and short of actually ploughing the land, they are pre-eminently the only fraction of the Brahman brotherhood, who turn their lands to the best advantage.—*Mysore Census Report*, 1891, p. 236.

* A kind of calcareous clay, said to be obtainable only from a tank near Somnath, where the wives of Krishna drowned themselves after his death.

§ 2.—*The Vishnuvite Brahmans of Dravira.*

The Vishnuvite Brahmans of Dravira are followers of Ramanuja. They are divided into two classes, namely, the Vadagala and the Tengala. An account of these sects will be given in a subsequent part of this work.

The late Mr. Rangacharlu, who was Prime Minister of the Mysore Raj, was a Vadagala Vaishnava. Mr. Bhasyam Ayangar and Rai Bahadur Anandacharlu, who are now the leading advocates of the Madras High Court, and have lately been appointed as Members of the Legislative Council of India, are also Vadagala Vaishnavas of the Tamil country.

CHAP. VII.—THE BRAHMANS OF TELINGANA.

TELINGANA is one of the names of that part of the Deccan where Telugu is the prevailing language. In ancient times this tract of country was included in the kingdoms then called Andhra and Kalinga. At the present time Telingana includes the eastern districts of the Nizam's dominions, in addition to the British districts of Ganjam, Vizigapatam, Godavari Krishna, Nellore, North Arcot, Bellary, Cudapa, Karnoul, and Anantpore. The Brahmans of this part of the Deccan are known by the general name of Tailangi Brahmans. They are mainly followers of the Apastamba Săkha of the Yajur Veda. There are also Rig Vedis among them. Nearly a third of them are Vishnuvites of the Ramanuja and Madhava sects, the rest being Smartas. There are very few Sakti worshippers among them even of the moderate type. Like most of the other classes of the Deccani Brahmans, the Tailangis are strict vegetarians and abstainers from spirituous liquors. The orthodox Tailangi does not smoke tobacco.

The Brahmans of Telingana are sub-divided into several distinct sections. On account of difference of cults there are among them the following three main sub-classes :—

1. Smartas.	2. Sri Vaishnavas.	3. Madhavas.

The followers of Madhava form a single caste. The Sri Vaishnavas among the Telingana Brahmans form a distinct caste called Andhra Vaishnava. They are not sub-divided as Vadgala and Tengala like their co-religionists of Dravira. The Smartas are sub-divided into two classes, namely, Niyogi and Vaidik. The Niyogis profess to value *Yoga* or religious contemplation more than Vedic sacrifices. In practice the Niyogis devote themselves mainly to secular pursuits, while the Vaidiks constitute the priestly class. The Niyogis are considered to be eligible for priestly service. But they will never either accept a religious gift, or partake of Shradha food. The several divisions and sub-sections among the Tailangi Brahmans are shown in the following table :—

- 1. SMARTA
  - 1. VAIDIKA ...
    - 1. *Velnad.*
    - 2. *Vengi Nadu.*
    - 3. *Kasal Nadu.*
    - 4. *Mulki Nadu.*
    - 5. *Telaga Nadu.*
    - 6. *Yajnavalkya Vaidika.*
      - 1. Kanva.
      - 2. Madhyandiva.
    - 7. *Kanara Kamma Vaidika.* Originally Karnata Brahmans now naturalised in the Andhra country.
  - 2. NIYOGI ...
    - 1. *Arvelu Varu* (Lit., "the six thousand").
    - 2. *Telingana Niyogi or Telgiana.*
    - 3. *Nanda Varika Niyogi.*
    - 4. *Pakul Moti Niyogi.*
    - 5. *Yajnyavalkya Niyogi.*
    - 6. *Karnata Kama Niyogi.* Originally of Karnata.
- 2. RAMANUJITES
  - 1. ANDHRA VAISHNAVAS.
  - 2. SRI VAISHNAVA—IMMIGRANTS FROM DRAVIRA.
    - 1. *Vadagala.*
    - 2. *Tengala.*
- 3. MADHAVA—FOLLOWERS OF MADHAVA.

Velnadu.—The Velnadus are the most numerous class of Tailangi Brahmans. Vallabhachari, who in the 15th century attained great success as a prophet with very little sacrifice of personal ease, and whose descendants are worshipped almost as gods still in Rajputana,

Gujrat and Bombay, was a member of this tribe. According to the Hindustani account of Ballava's "conquests" his father was a native of Kankarkom, but his birth took place at a place named Champa near Raipore, while his parents were on their way from their native village to Benares. A full account of Ballava is given in the part of this book dealing with the Indian sects. The Velnadus are most numerous in the Godavari and Krishna districts. Colonies of the tribe are found also in every part of Mysore except Kadur.

Venginadu.—The Venginadus are next in importance to the Velnadu, and are found chiefly in the British districts of Godavari and Vizigapatam, formerly called the Vengi country.

Kasalnadu.—The Kasalnadus derive their name from Kosala, the ancient name of Oude, from whence they profess to have emigrated to the Kalinga country where they are now found.

Murakanadu.—Brahmans of this class are found chiefly in the tract of country to the south of the Krishna. They are pretty numerous in Mysore. There are among them both priests and men devoted to secular pursuits. The present Superior of the chief Sankarite monastery at Sringeri is a Murakanadu.

Telaganadu.—The Telaganadus are quite as numerous as the Velnadus. The former are found chiefly in the north-eastern part of the Nizam's dominions.

Yajnavalkya.—This name is given in the Telugu country to the followers of the Kanwa Sākha of the White Yajur Veda. They are called also Pratham Sakhi as in the Mahratta country.

Niyogis.—The Niyogis are secular Brahmans. They derive their name from the word *Yoga*, which means religious contemplation, as opposed to *Yaga*, which means religious sacrifice. As the word *Niyoga* in Sanskrit means "employment," it is more probable that the Niyogis are so-called because they accept secular employment. The Komatis and the Sudras bow to them, but the ecclesiastical Brahmans address them with a benediction. From a secular point of view they have great importance. They are usually employed as writers and village accountants.

Aradhyas.—The word Aradhya signifies "deserving to be worshipped." The Aradhyas do not form a separate caste, as intermarriages take place between them and the Smartas. The Aradhyas of the Telugu country profess to be Brahmans, but are, in fact, semi-converted Lingaits, and are not regarded as good Brahmans. Though following Basava in attaching great importance to Linga worship, they adhere to caste and repeat the Gayatri prayers. They act as Gurus or spiritual preceptors to the higher classes of lay Lingaits, while the lower classes among the followers of Basava are left to the guidance of the Jangamas or the priestly Sudras of the sect.

CHAP. VIII.—THE BRAHMANS OF THE CENTRAL PROVINCES.

As a considerable portion of the territories included in what is now called the Central Province was formerly ruled by kings of the Gond tribe, and as there is still a large Gond population in the districts round Nagpore and Jubbulpore, the tract of country inhabited by them is popularly called Gondwana, and the Brahmans settled within it receive the designation of Gond Brahmans. They are called also Jhara Brahmans from the fact of their country being still, to a very large extent, covered by forest. Like some of the Mahratta Brahmans, the Gond Brahmans are divided into distinct sections on account of the differences in the Vedas and the Sākhas which they profess. The majority of them are followers of the Yajur Veda. There are also Rig Vedis among them, but very few followers of any of the other Vedas. The Yajur Vedis are divided into various Sākhas, the Madhyandinas, Kanvas, and the Apastambis being the most numerous. There cannot be intermarriage between these. But marriage alliances are possible between the Rig Vedis and the Apastambi section of the Yajur Vedis. All the Rig Vedis are of the Ashwalayana Sākha.

All the Gond Brahmans are vegetarians and abstainers from intoxicating drink. The Yajur Vedis are chiefly Sivites. There are a few Bhagabats and moderate Saktas among them. The Bhagabats are moderate Vishnuvites, paying reverence to Siva also.

Among the Rig Vedis the majority are Bhagabats and Sivites. There are a few extreme Vishnuvites among them. There may be intermarriage between the Sivites, Bhagabats, Vaishnavas and Saktas of the same class. Intermarriage is possible also between the Bhikshus and the Laukikas.

There are very few wealthy men among the Gond Brahmans. But they have in their community many learned Sanskritists and English scholars. There is in Gondwana a class of Brahmans called Charaki. There are also colonies of the Malwi and the Narmadi.

CHAP. IX.—BRAHMANS OF TULAVA, SOUTH KANARA AND COORG.

Tulava Brahmans.—Tulava is a small tract of country embracing only the British District of South Kanara and a part of Coorg. Udipi, the chief centre of the Madhava sect, is in Tulava, and is regarded by its members as a very holy place.

Dr. Wilson gives the following account of the Tulava Brahmans :—

"The Brahmans taking to themselves the designation of Tulavas are scattered not merely through this province but through some of the territories above the Ghats where they have nearly forgotten their original language. Mr. Stokes mentions the following local varieties of them as found in the Nagara districts :—

1. Shiwali.	3. Kota.
2. Panchagramadavuru.	4. Kandavaru.

"These are all varieties," he adds, "of Tulava Brahmans, and appear to be almost aboriginal (in a certain sense). They are very numerous in the South of Nagara, Kauladurga, Koppa and Lakavali, where they hold the greatest portion of the betel-nut gardens. They are mostly of Smarta sect, and disciples of the Shringeri and its subordinate Mathas of Tirtha, Muthar, Hariharpura, Bandigadra, Mulavagal, &c. They speak Kanaresе only, but their books are partly in the Grantha and partly in the Bal Bodha character. Some sign their names in the Tulava character. They are indifferently educated except a few who are either brokers or in public employ."

The Tulava Brahmans do not intermarry with the other Brahmans on the Malabar Coast. In the regulations, attributed to Sankaracharya, possessed by the Namburi Brahmans, "it is decreed that intermarriages among the Brahmans north of Parampol, forming thirty-two Gramas of Tulanad with the Brahmans of thirty-two Gramas to the south called Malaylam are forbidden.* A synonym of the Tula Brahmans is *Imbran* or rather *Tambaran*.

The Tulava Brahmans resemble the Namburis, and consider themselves as the proper lords of the country, pretending that it was

* MS. of Col. Mackenzie, quoted in *South Indian Christ. Repository*, Vol. II, p. 408.

created expressly for their use by Parashurama. They are polygamists. They cohabit, too, Dr. F. Buchanan tells us, with the daughters of the Rajas. Speaking of the Kumali Raja, a professed Ksatriya, he says: "The eldest daughter in the female line cohabits with a Tulava Brahman; her sons become Rajas, and her eldest daughter continues the line of the family. Whenever she pleases, she changes her Brahman."* They prevent widow re-marriage, but promote widow prostitution in the name of religion; and with widows and women who have forsaken their husbands and become "Moylar" and attached to the temples, they hold intercourse. They burn their dead. They abstain from animal food and spirituous liquors.

The Tulava Brahmans are equally divided between the sects of Sankaracharya and Madhavacharya.

In Mysore there are some Brahmanic colonists who call themselves Kavarga and Shishyavarga and who are believed to have been originally inhabitants of Tulava. The word Kavarga literally means the first five letters of the Sanskrit alphabet. The reason why the designation is applied to the tribe of Brahmans bearing the name is explained as follows in the report on the last Census of Mysore :—

The name is said to have a reproachful allusion to a legend, according to which a brother and sister of this tribe deceitfully received a gift by representing themselves as husband and wife at a Brahmanical ceremony. By the patriarchal law of visiting the sins of the fathers on the children, the tribe is to this day distinguished by the name of Kavarga (of the Ka class), Ka being the initial syllable of the Kanarese word Kullu (= thief).—*Mysore Census Report*, p. 235.

In Coorg there is a priestly class called Amma Kodaga or Kaveri Brahmans; but as they do not profess to follow any particular Veda, they are, properly speaking, no Brahmans. They are a very small community. With regard to them, Richter says :—

The Amma Kodagas live principally in the S.-W. parts of Coorg, and are the indigenous priesthood devoted to the worship of Amma the Kaveri goddess. They are of a quite unobtrusive character; do not intermarry with the other Coorgs, and are, generally speaking, inferior to them in personal appearance and strength of body. Their number is about 50, they are unlettered and devoid of Brahmanical lore. Their diet is vegetable food only, and they abstain from drinking liquor. Their complexion is rather fair, their eyes dark-brown, and their hair black and straight.—*Ethnological Compendium of the Castes and Tribes of Coorg*, by the Rev. G. Richter, p. 1.

---

* *Buchanan's Journey*, Vol. III, pp. 31, 16.

CHAP. X.—THE BRAHMANS OF KERALA, MALABAR, COCHIN AND TRAVANCORE.

THE part of the western coast of the Deccan which extends from Cannanore and the Chandra Giri river on the north to Cape Comorin on the south, and which embraces at present the British district of Malabar, and the principalities of Cochin and Travancore, is, in many respects, a homogeneous tract distinguishable from every other part of India. This strip of country was called in ancient times Kerala or Chera, and governed by its own king. The language spoken by its people is Malaylan which, though allied to the Tamil, is a quite distinct dialect. The Nairs and the Namburi Brahmans, who form the chief elements in the population of Kerala, are not to be found in considerable numbers even in the adjoining districts of Coimbatore, Trichinopoly, Madura or Tinnevely. It is, however, the peculiar laws and customs of Kerala that distinguish it most from other parts of India. The very family type among the Nairs is so different from what is found in other countries, that it is very difficult for an outsider to form an idea of it. Among most of the nations throughout the world, each male member when he marries, becomes an unit of the society. During the lifetime of his father he may, with his wife, and in some cases with his children also, live under the parental roof. But each of the male members of the society is, in the eye of law, the centre of an independent group actual or possible. After his death, the usual rule is that his sons succeed to his property and his status, and every one traces his lineage in the male line, *i.e.*, in the line of his father, grandfather, great-grandfather, &c. The case among the Nairs is very different. Among them every girl is married formally when a child with a Brahman. But the titular husband can never claim her as his wife, and when she grows up she may choose any one, either of her own or of the Brahman caste, provided he is not a member of the same *tarwad* (the common residence of the children of the same maternal ancestor). A female member of a wealthy *tarwad* never leaves her maternal home, but is visited there by her husband. In the case of less wealthy *tarwads*, the women generally live with the husbands chosen by them. But in all cases the children succeed to the property and status of their mother's *tarwad*, and not to their male ancestors.

The marriage customs of the Namburi Brahmans of Malabar are not the same as those of the Nairs; nor are they quite identical with those of the Brahmans in other parts of India. In a Namburi family, it is only the eldest brother who is ordinarily allowed to take a wife by a regular marriage. If no male children be born to the eldest, then the brother next in rank may marry in the regular way, but not otherwise. The younger brothers, who are forbidden marriage, are allowed to form connexions with Ksatriya and Nair women.

The Namburis exact greater deference from the Sudras than the Brahmans in other parts of the country. A *Nair*, who is a high caste Sudra, may approach, but must not touch, a Namburi. A Tir, who is a cultivator by caste, has to remain thirty-six steps off from one; a Malayaer hillman three or four steps further. A member of the degraded Puliyar caste has to keep himself at a distance of ninety-six steps. If a Puliyar touch a Brahman, the latter must make expiation by immediate bathing, and change of his Brahmanical thread.

The Namburis are, like most of the other classes of Deccani Brahmans, strict vegetarians. Their male members are allowed to eat with the Ksatriyas. The most striking peculiarity in a Namburi is the tuft of hair grown near the forehead, instead of the usual Brahmanical Sikha at the central part of the head. There are both Sivites and Vishnuvites among the Namburis. The former are called Chovar, the latter Panyon. The Namburi Brahmans seldom go abroad without holding a *chatra* or large umbrella. Their women also screen themselves with a *chatra* when they go out, which they do very seldom. The foreign Brahmans residing in Malabar are called Pattara. The Ambalvashis, who are the employés of the public shrines, are Namburis by descent, but degraded by their avocation.

The great Sankaracharya, whose name stands most conspicuous in the struggle for rooting out Buddhism from India, and who is regarded by Brahmans in every part of the country as an incarnation of Siva, was a Namburi.

PART V.

THE SEMI-BRAHMANICAL CASTES.

CHAP. I.—THE BHUINHAR BRAHMANS OF BEHAR AND BENARES.

THERE are various legends regarding the origin of this caste. The Bhuinhar Brahmans themselves claim to be true Brahmans descended from the rulers whom Parusu Ram set up in the place of the Ksatriya kings slain by him. The good Brahmans and the Ksatriyas of the country, however, look down upon them, and insinuate that they are of a mixed breed, the offspring of Brahman men and Ksatriya women. It is even said that the class was formed by the promotion of low caste men under the orders of a minister to a Raja who wanted a very large number of Brahmans to celebrate a religious ceremony, but for whom his minister could not procure the required number of true Brahmans. But this legendary theory is very strongly contradicted by the Aryan physiognomy of the Bhuinhars who, in respect of personal appearance, are in no way inferior to the Brahmans and the Rajputs. One of the most important points of difference between the Bhuinhar Brahmans, and the majority of the ordinary Brahmans is, that while the latter are divided into only those exogamous clans called Gotra, the former have among them, like the Rajputs, a twofold division based upon both Gotra and tribe. From this circumstance Mr. Risley* has been led to conclude that the Bhuinhar Brahmans are an offshoot of the Rajputs, and not true Brahmans. But as there are similar tribal divisions among the Maithila Brahmans of Tirhoot and the Saraswat Brahmans of the Panjab, it might, on the same ground, be said that the Saraswats and the Maithilas are offshoots of the Rajputs.

The theory that Bhuinhar Brahmans are an offshoot of the Rajputs, involves the utterly unfounded assumption that any of the military clans could have reason to be ashamed of their caste status. The 'royal race' had very good reasons to be proud of such surnames as Sinha, Roy and Thākoor, and it seems very unlikely that any of their clans could at any time be so foolish as to

* The grounds on which Mr. Risley rests his view will appear clear from the following extract:—

"An examination of the sections or exogamous groups into which the Babhans are divided appear, however, to tell strongly against the hypothesis that they are degraded Brahmans. These groups are usually the oldest and most durable element in the internal organization of a caste or tribe, and may therefore be expected to offer the clearest indications as to its origin. Now we find among the Babhans section names of two distinct types, the one territorial referring either to some very early settlement of the section, or to the birthplace of its founder, and the other eponymous, the eponym being in most cases a Vedic Rishi or inspired sage. The names of the former class correspond to or closely resemble those current among Rajputs; the names of the latter are those of the standard Brahmanical Gotras. Where the matrimonial prohibitions based on these two classes of sections conflict, as must obviously often happen where every member of the caste necessarily belongs to both sets, the authority of the territorial class overrides that of the eponymous or Brahmanical class. Suppose, for instance, that a man of the Koronch territorial section and of the Sandilya eponymous section wishes to marry a woman of the Sakanwar territorial section, the fact that she also belongs to the Sandilya eponymous section will not operate as a bar to the marriage. Whatever may be the theory of the *purohits* of the caste, the Brahmanical Gotra is disregarded in practice. This circumstance seems to indicate that the territorial sections are the older of the two, and are probably the original sections of the caste, while the eponymous sections have been borrowed from the Brahmans in comparatively recent times. It would follow that the Babhans are an offshoot, not from the Brahmans, but from the Rajputs."—Risley's *Tribes and Castes*, Vol. I, Introduction.

club together for the purpose of assuming the Brahmanic surnames of Dobe, Tewari, Chobe and Upādhya. On the theory that the Bhuinhar Brahmans are an offshoot of the Rajputs, the clans that now profess to be Bhuinhar Rajputs are the residue that have stuck to their original status, and have never aspired to a higher one. But on this supposition it would be difficult to find any reason for the distinction between Bhuinhar Rajputs and the ordinary Rajputs.

The clue to the exact status of the Bhuinhar Brahmans is afforded by their very name. The word literally means a landholder. In the language of the Indian feudal system, *Bhuṁ* is the name given to a kind of tenure similar to the *Inams* and *Jaigirs* of Mahomedan times. By a *Bhum*, according to the *Rajputana Gazetteer*, an hereditary, non-resumable and inalienable property in the soil was inseparably bound up with a revenue-free title. *Bhum* was given as compensation for bloodshed, in order to quell a feud, for distinguished services in the field, for protection of a border, or for the watch and ward of a village.* The tenure is very highly esteemed by Rajputs of all classes. The Maharajah of Kishengarh, the Thākoor of Fategarh, the Thākoor of Gunia, the Thākoor of Bandanwara, and the Thākoor of Tantoti are among the Bhumias of Ajmere. In Bengal the fact of the frontier districts of the east having been at one time under twelve Bhumia Kings is well known still by tradition.

The meaning of the designation Bhuinhar being as stated above, the Bhuinhar Brahmans are evidently those Brahmans who held grants of land for secular services. Whoever held a secular fief was a Bhuinhar. Where a Brahman held such a tenure he was called a Bhuinhar Brahman. Where the holder was a Ksatriya he was called a Bhuinhar Ksatriya. Bhuinhar Brah-

---

* The Assamese Bhuinhars do not wear the sacred thread, and do not claim to be either Brahmans or Ksatriyas.

mans are sometimes called simply Bhuinhars, just as the masons, whose class name in Bengali is *Raj mistri* (royal architect), are generally called *Raj*, which means a king.

In Assam the Bhuinhars hold their lands on very favourable terms; but no exceptional indulgence is shown to the Bhuinhars of Behar or Benares by the local zemindars. As may be expected the Bhuinhars are now chiefly an agricultural class; but like the good Brahmans, they never touch the plough. They will, however, do any kind of manual work except personal service. They serve not only as soldiers, constables, orderlies and gate-keepers, but also as porters, cartmen, and cutters of wood. Many of the Hindu cartmen and porters in Calcutta are Bhuinhars. Some of them are very proud and cantankerous. The fact that the Bhuinhars readily enlist in the army and in the police may be taken to show, to some extent, what their caste profession must have been in former times.

The Bhuinhars observe all their religious ceremonies in the same manner as the good Brahmans; but as they practise secular avocations they, like the Laukika Brahmans of Southern India, are not entitled to accept religious gifts, or to minister to any one as priests. The best Brahmans officiate as priests for the Bhuinhars, and it is not considered that they are degraded by doing so.

On the view that the Bhuinhars were anciently a fighting caste, it is not at all a matter for wonder that there are among them, as among the Rajputs, many big landholders. The Rajas named below are of the Bhuinhar caste :—

1. Raja of Benares.
2. Raja of Bettia in Champaran, North Behar.
3. Raja of Tikari in Gaya.
4. Raja of Hatwa in Saran, North Behar.
5. Raja of Tamakhi in Gorakpore.
6. Raja of Sheohar.
7. Raja of Maisadal in Midnapore, Bengal.
8. Raja of Pakour in Sonthal Pergunnahs, Bengal.
9. Raja of Moheshpore in Sonthal Pergunnahs, Bengal.

Like the Rajputs the Bhuinhar Brahmans form one great caste, and there are no sub-castes among them. They are divided into a large number of clans which, for purposes of marriage, are, with very few exceptions, all equal. The usual surnames of the Bhuinhar Brahmans are the same as those of the other Brahmans of Northern India. Being a fighting caste, a few of them have Rajput surnames.

CHAP. II.—THE BHATS AND THE CHARANAS.

THE Bhats and the Charanas are very important castes in Rajputana and the adjoining provinces. They are the minstrels, historians and genealogists of the Rajput chiefs, and are very much feared by their constituents, as it is in their power to lower any family by distorting history. They all take the holy thread, and as their persons are considered to be sacred by all classes, they seem to have been originally Brahmans. The very name of Bhatta points also to the same conclusion, as it means a learned man, and is an honorific surname of many of the best families of Brahmanas in every part of the country. In all probability the Bhats are the caste who were usually employed by the Rajput princes in diplomatic service, while the Charanas, as their very name indicates, were the spies. At any rate this view not only explains the fact that the Bhats have a higher caste status than the Charanas, but is supported also by the custom which still prevails among the Rajputs of employing the Bhats to conduct negotiations for marriage alliances.

Sir John Malcolm gives the following account of the Bhats :—

> The Bhats or Raos seldom sacrifice themselves; but as chroniclers or bards, they share power, and sometimes office with the Charanas. Among the Bhilalas and lower tribes they enjoy great and exclusive influence; they give praise and fame in their songs to those who are liberal to them, while they visit those who neglect or injure them, with satires, in which they usually reproach them with spurious birth and inherent meanness. Sometimes the Bhat, if very seriously offended, fixes the figure of the person he desires to degrade on a

long pole, and appends to it a slipper as a mark of disgrace. In such cases the song of the Bhat records the infamy of the object of his revenge. This image usually travels the country till the party or his friends purchase the cessation of the ridicule and curses thus entailed. It is not deemed in these countries in the power of a prince, much less any other person, to stop a Bhat, or even punish him for such a proceeding: he is protected by the superstitious and religious awe which, when general among a people, controls even despotism.—Malcolm's *Central India*, Vol. II, Chap. XIV, pp. 113-114.

The poetic castes in fact performed the functions of the *tiers-état* in Rajasthan, and the privilege of commenting on the actions of their Kings, which they possessed and very often abused, was very nearly unlimited. In Rajputana there are many big landholders and men of influence among the Bhats and the Charanas; but there are very few Sanskritists among them. The usual surname of the Bhats is Rao. They are divided into two classes, namely, the Brahma Bhats and the Yoga Bhats. The former are poets and minstrels who recount, in verse, the history of the great Rajput heroes, ancient and modern. The Yoga Bhats are the genealogists. The Bhats of Bengal are mere beggars, without regular constituents, and without the slightest pretension of poetic capacity. On the occasions of Pujas and Shradhas in the houses of the rich, they present themselves uninvited, and make such a horrid uproar by shouting and singing, that the master of the house besieged by them is glad to pay something to get rid of them. If refused, they will get to the top of a tree or wall, and threaten to commit suicide by falling headlong on the ground. Being thus terrorised the ladies of the house insist upon their immediate dismissal anyhow, and it is therefore quite impossible to avoid submitting to their exactions on ceremonial occasions. With regard to the Charanas Sir John Malcolm gives the following account:—

They are divided into two tribes, the Kachili who are merchants, and the Maru who are bards. These again branch out into one hundred and twenty other tribes, many of whom are the descendants in the female line of Brahmans and Rajputs. They are taught to read and write, and the class who traffic (generally in camels and horses) are shrewd men of business; while the Maru Charanas apply their skill to the genealogy of tribes, and to the recital of numerous legends (usually in verse), celebrating the praises of former heroes, which it is their duty to chant, to gratify the pride and rouse the emulation of their descendants. The Charana's chief power is derived from an impression that it is certain ruin and destruction to shed his blood, or that of any of his family, or to be the cause of its being shed. They obtain a high rank in society, and a certain livelihood, from the superstitious belief which they are educated to inculcate, and which they teach their children to consider as their chief object in life to maintain. A Charana becomes the safeguard of travellers and security for merchants, and his bond is often preferred among the Rajputs, when rents and property are concerned, to that of the wealthiest bankers. When he trades himself, he alone is trusted and trusts among the community to which he belongs. The Charana who accompanies travellers likely to be attacked by Rajput robbers, when he sees the latter approach, warns them off by holding a dagger in his hand, and if they do not attend to him, he stabs himself in a place that is not mortal, and taking the blood from the wound, throws it at the assailants with imprecations of future woe and ruin. If this has not the desired effect, the wounds are repeated, and in extreme cases one of the Charana's relations, commonly a female child or an old woman, is made a sacrifice. The same process is adopted to enforce the payment of a debt to himself or a claim for which he has become security. It is not unusual, as the next step, to slay himself; and the catastrophe has been known to close in the voluntary death of his wives and children. The females of the Charanas are distinct from all the other population, both in dress and manners. They often reside in separate villages, and the traveller is surprised to see them come out in their long robes, and attend him for some space, chanting his welcome to their abode. The Charanas are not only treated by the Rajputs with great respect (the highest rulers of that race rising when one of this class enters or leaves an assembly), but they have more substantial marks of regard. When they engage in trade, lighter duties are collected from them than others. They receive at all feasts and marriages presents that are only limited by the ability of the parties. The evil consequences of a Charana being driven to undergo a violent death, can be alone averted by grants of land and costly gifts to surviving relations; and the Rajput chief, whose guilt is recorded (for all these sacrifices are subjects of rude poems), as the cause of such sacred blood being shed, is fortunate when he can by any means have his repentance and generosity made part of the legend.—Malcolm's *Central India*, Vol. II, Chap. XIV, p. 108 *et seq.*

About the peregrinations of the Bhats and the Charanas, and the periodical visits paid by them to their constituents, a graphic account is to be found in the following extract :—

When the rainy season closes, and travelling becomes practicable, the bard sets off on his yearly tour from his residence in the Bhatwara of some city or town. One by one he visits each of the Rajput chiefs who are his patrons, and from whom he has received portions of land, or annual grants of money, timing his arrival, if possible,

to suit occasions of marriage or other domestic festival. After he has received the usual courtesies, he produces the 'Bahi,' a book written in his own crabbed hieroglyphics, or in those of his fathers, which contains the descent of the house; if the chief be the Tilayet or head of the family, from the founder of the tribe; if he be a Phatayo, or cadet, from the immediate ancestor of the branch, interspersed with many a verse or ballad, the dark sayings contained in which are chanted forth in musical cadence to a delighted audience, and are then orally interpreted by the bard, with many an illustrative anecdote or tale. The 'Bahi' is not, however, merely a source for the gratification of family pride, or even of love of song; it is also a record of authority by which questions of consanguinity are determined when marriage is on the *tapis*, and disputes relating to the division of ancestral property are decided. It is the duty of a bard at each periodical visit to register the births, marriages and deaths which have taken place in the family since his last circuit, as well as to chronicle all other events worthy of remark which have occurred to affect the fortunes of his patron; nor have we ever heard even a doubt suggested regarding the accurate, much less the honest, fulfilment of this duty by the bard.—Forbes's *Ras Mala*, Vol. II, pp. 263-64.

PART VI.

THE DEGRADED BRAHMANS.

PRELIMINARY REMARKS.

THERE are various classes of degraded Brahmans who now form, more or less completely, separate castes. Their social ostracism is due to one or other of the following causes :—

1. Alleged intercourse with Mahomedans at some by-gone period.
2. Ministering to the low castes as priests.
3. Being connected with the great public shrines.
4. Accepting forbidden gifts.
5. Ministering as priests at a cremation.
6. Being suspected to be of spurious birth.
7. By being tillers of the soil.
8. By menial service.

CHAP. I.—THE HOSAINIS AND KUVACHANDAS.

Hosainis.—These are a class of Brahmans to be found in many parts of Western India, and especially near Ahmednagar. They have actually adopted to some extent the Mahomedan faith and its observances, though they retain some of the Brahmanic practices too, and generally intermarry only among themselves. As a class they have no importance. They are chiefly beggars.

Kuvachandas—Found in Sind, and they generally resemble the Mussalmans in their habits.

CHAP. II.—THE PIRALI TAGORES OF CALCUTTA.

Of the several classes degraded by alleged intercourse with Mahomedans, the Pirālis of Bengal are the most important from many points of view. They claim to be a section of the Radriya Brahmans of the country with whom alone they intermarry, though such alliance is always very expensive to them. The good Radriya who marries into a Pirāli family is himself reduced to the rank of a Pirāli, and always demands a heavy premium as a *sine quâ non*. With the exception of the family of Babu Debendra Nath Tagore who are Brahmos, the Pirālis are very orthodox Hindus. The following account relating to the degradation of Purushottama, the ancestor of the clan, is given by one of their leading members, the late Honorable Prasanna Kumar Tagore, C.S.I.:—

Purushottama was called Pirāli for having married the daughter of a person blemished in caste. According to the books of the Ghattaks, Janaki Ballabha and Kamdeva Roy Chowdri, inhabitants of Gurgain, in Pergana Chengutia, brought a suit against an ancestor of Sri Kanta Roy, of Jessore. An Amin, named *Pirāli Khan*, was deputed by the zemindar for the purpose of holding an investigation into the case. There was an altercation between the Amin and some of the inhabitants of the place as to whether the smell of a thing was tantamount to half-eating it. Some time after the said Pirāli Khan invited several persons all of whom lost their caste, as he made them smell forbidden food. *Janaki Ballabha* and *Kamadeva* having sat near the Amin and been reported to have eaten the food, became Mahomedans, under the names of *Jamal Khan* and *Kamal Khan*, pursuant to the decision of the Pandits of those times. Their descendants, *Arjuna Khan*, *Dinanath Khan*, &c., live like Mahomedans up to this day in Magura and Basundia,

Pergana *Chengutia*, zillah Jessore. They form their connections by marriage with the Khan Chowdries of Broome, but not with any other Mahomedans. The remaining persons present on the occasion were called Pirâli. Purushottama was one of the latter. Others give a different account. They say that when Purushottama was in Jessore, on his way to bathe in the Ganges, the Chowdries of that place, who became polluted in the above mentioned way, forcibly took him to their house with a view to give him a daughter of theirs in marriage. Seeing that the bride was very beautiful, Purushottama agreed to marry her. After this marriage, Purushottama left the original seat of his family and settled in Jessore. Purushottama had a son named Balarama. Panchanana, the fifth in descent from Balarama left Jessore and came to *Govindpore*, the site of Fort William, where he purchased land, and built thereon a dwelling-house and a temple. His son Jairam was employed as an Amin in the settlement of the 24-Pergunnahs and discharged his duties with considerable credit. At the capture of Calcutta he is said to have lost all his property with the exception of Rs. 13,000 in cash.

Jairam's house was taken by the English for the purpose of building Fort William. He received some money and land as compensation, and removed himself to Pathuriaghata. He died in the year 1762, leaving four sons, named Ananda Ram, Nilmani, Darpa Narayan and Govinda. The eldest, Ananda Ram, was the first who received a liberal English education. His family and that of his youngest brother, who superintended the building of the Fort William, have become extinct. Nilmani was the grandfather of Dwarkanath Tagore, who occupied a foremost rank in the society of his day. See S. C. Bose's *Hindus as they are*, pp. 171—74.

With reference to the above, it may be observed here that the alleged enjoyment of the smell of a Mahomedan's savoury meat, cannot, by itself, explain the perpetual degradation of Purushottama, or of any of the other guests of Pirâli. The sin of even voluntary and actual eating of such food is not an inexpiable one, and there is not within the four corners of the Shastras, any such utterly unreasonable and Draconian law as would visit a man with eternal degradation for involuntarily inhaling the smell of forbidden food. There are also other inherent improbabilities in the story as narrated above. Unless the Amin, and the inhabitants of the locality where he was conducting his investigations, were quite demented, there could not possibly be an occasion for any altercation between the parties as to a question of the Hindu's religion. Then, again, if the habits and prejudices of the Hindus in those times be taken into consideration, it would seem quite impossible that Pirāli would have invited any number of them to his house, or that they would have responded to the invitation so far as to enter his dining-room. Hindus and Mahomedans very often exchange visits for ceremonial and official purposes. But even when they are on the most friendly terms, a man professing the one religion will not ask a votary of the other to sit by his table while he is at dinner. The orthodox Hindu's prejudices are such that after sitting on the same carpet with a Mahomedan or a Christian friend, or shaking hands with such a person, he has to put off his clothes, and to bathe or sprinkle his person with the holy water of the Ganges. The Mahomedan gentleman of the country who know well of these prejudices on the part of their Hindu fellow-countrymen, therefore, never ask them to mix too familiarly, and the Hindus also keep themselves at a sufficient distance to avoid that they must regard as contaminations. The dwelling-house of every native of India, be he a Hindu or a Mahomedan, consists of two parts, namely, the *zenana* and the *boytakhana*. The *zenana* apartments are reserved for the ladies, and the dining-rooms for the members of the house are always within the *zenana*. The *boytakhana* is the outer part of the house where visitors are received. The Mussalmans do sometimes entertain their co-religionists in the *boytakhana;* but no orthodox Hindu would enter such a place while the plates are in it, or would remain there a moment after any sign of preparations for introducing any kind of cooked eatables.

From what is stated above, it would appear that the causes assigned by the Pirālis themselves for their degradation cannot satisfactorily account for their status in the Hindu caste system. From the general tenor of their story, it seems more probable that Purushottama was an officer in the staff of the surveyor, Pirāli, and that, as Amins and their underlings usually do, he made himself very unpopular among his co-religionists by attempting to invade the titles to their patrimony, so as to lead them to club together for ostracising him on the allegation that he had tasted or smelt forbidden food.

The reason why the Pirālis left their original habitat, and settled in Calcutta, is not far to seek. Purushottama who was first outcasted had evidently made his native village too hot for him. He removed to Jessore; but even at Jessore he could not have, in his degraded condition, found many friends. His descendant, Panchanana, therefore removed to Calcutta in search of employment, and a place where he could live in peace. Calcutta was then practically ruled by the East India Company, who had no reason whatever to pay any regard to any rule or decree of caste discipline. The majority of the well-to-do population of Calcutta were then of the weaver caste, with a sprinkling of Sonar Banyas and Kāyasthas. Good Brahmans visited the towns sometimes for ministering to their disciples or collecting the donations of the rich Sudras to their *toles* or Sanskrit schools. But those were days when the orthodox and respectable Brahmans of Bengal considered it beneath their dignity to engage in secular pursuits, and even to those who were inclined to pocket their pride for the sake of pelf, the service of the East India Company could not then have much attraction. Whatever the cause might have been, the Brahmanic population of Calcutta was not very large in its early days. When such was the state of things Panchanana settled in it. A Brahman is a Brahman though outcasted by his clansmen. The Sonar Banyas of Calcutta were themselves outcastes, and as for the Tantis and Kāyasthas, they could have neither the motive nor the power to subject the outcaste Panchanana to any kind of persecution. The Setts and the Malliks actually befriended his family, though apparently without recognizing their status as Brahmans so far as to accept their hospitality in any shape. In Prasanna Kumar Tagore's account of his family history it is stated that Ram Krishna Mallik exchanged turbans with his ancestor Darpa Narain. That was no doubt a sign of friendship, but not of the kind of veneration which Banyas must have for good Brahmans. It is said however that for nearly half a century after the arrival of their ancestor, Panchanana, in Calcutta, the Pirālis were recognized as good Brahman. But when they became wealthy and influential, the late Babu Durga Charan Mukerji, of Bag Bazar, formed a party for degrading them. Perhaps some of the Kāyastha magnates of Calcutta secretly supported Durga Charan in persecuting the Pirālis.

The way in which the Tagores of the last century attained their wealth is not well known. Panchanana's son Jairam, by serving as an Amin for the survey and settlement of the villages acquired by the East India Company under the charter of Emperor Ferokshere, apparently laid a substantial foundation. His youngest son Govinda, who superintended the building of Fort William, presumably improved the patrimony materially. Darpa Narain, the third son of Jairam and the great-grandfather of Sir Maharaja Jotindra Mohan, held for some time a high office in the service of the French East India Company. Nilmoni, the second son of Jairam and the grandfather of the celebrated Dwarka Nath Tagore, did not inherit any share of the family estate. But he was befriended by one of the Sonar Banaiya millionaires of his time, and was enabled by his friend to build a separate house for his residence on the site now occupied by the palatial mansion belonging to his descendants. Nilmoni's second son, Ram Moni, served as a clerk in the Police Court. Dwarka Nath, the second son of Ram Moni, made himself wealthy and famous in various ways. He began his career by entering the service of the Government of Bengal in the Salt Department.

About the beginning of the present century when the estates of most of the great zemindars of Bengal were brought to sale, for arrears of revenue, the Pirāli Tagores bought many valuable properties, and became themselves great zemindars. The total income of the several branches of the Tagore family must at present be more than £100,000. The leading members of the clan in the last generation were Dwarka Nath Tagore, Prasunna Kumar Tagore and Ramanath Tagore. Among the living celebrities of the family, Maharaja Sir Jotindra Mohun Tagore is deservedly esteemed as one of its brightest ornaments. He was a member of the Legislative Council of India for several years, and the British Government ofIndia has conferred upon him every possible title of honour at its disposal. His brother Maharaja Sourendra Mohan Tagore is a votary of the science of music, but at the same time has been steadily improving his estate by efficient management like his illustrious brother. Dwarka Nath's son Devendra Nath is now in "sear and yellow leaf" of life. On account of his devotion to religion he is usually called a Maharshi or Saint. His son Satyendra Nath is the first Hindu member of the Indian Civil Service, and is now employed as a District Judge in the Bombay Presidency. Babu Kali Krishna Tagore, who represents another branch, does not move much in Calcutta society; but next to Sir J. M. Tagore, he is perhaps the richest member of the family.

From a long time the Tagores have been struggling hard to be restored to caste. Ward says that Raja Krishna Chundra of Nadiya was promised one lac of rupees by a Pirāli, if he would only honour him with a visit for a few minutes, but he refused. Similar offers, though of smaller amounts, have been again and again made to the great Pandits of Nadiya, but have been similarly declined. But the Tagores are now fast rising in the scale of caste. Poor Brahmans now more or less openly accept their gifts, and sometimes even their hospitality; and Sir J. M. Tagore is on the way towards acquiring an influence on the Pandits which may one day enable him to re-establish his family completely in caste.

CHAP. III.—THE BARNA BRAHMANS.

THE Brahmans that minister to the low Sudra castes and outcastes, are looked upon as degraded persons, and they generally form separate castes. The good Brahmans will not take even a drink of water from their hands, and intermarriage between them is quite out of the question. In Bengal the following classes of Sudras and outcastes have special priests :—

1. Sonar Vaniya—Gold merchants.
2. Goala—Cowherds.
3. Kalu—Oilmen.
4. Dhopa—Washermen.
5. Bagdi—Aboriginal tribe of woodcutters and fishermen.
6. Kaibarta.

The priests of each of these classes form independent castes, without the right of intermarriage or dining together with any other section of the Brahmanic caste. With the exception of a few of the Sonar Vaniya Brahmans, these Barna Brahmans, as they are called, are mostly very poor, and utterly without any kind of social position. The priests of the Kaibartas are in some places called Vyasokta Brahmans.

§ 2.—*Barna Brahmans of Mithila.*

The following castes of Mithila have special Brahmans :—

Tatwa—Weaver.
Teli—Oilman.
Kasara—Brazier.
Sonar—Goldsmith.

§ 3.—*Barna Brahmans of Gujrat and Rajputana.*

The following are regarded as Barna Brahmans in Gujrat, and have a low caste status :—

Abhira Brahmans—Priests of the cowherd caste.
Kunbi Gour—Priests of the Kunbis.
Gujara Gour—Priests of the Gujars.
Machi Gour—Priests of the Machi or fishermen.
Gandharpa Gour—Priests of the musicians.
Koli Gour—Priests of the Kolis.
Garudyas—Priests of the Chamhars and Dheds.

§ 4.—*Barna Brahmans of Telingana.*

The following are the names of the classes of Tailangi Brahmans that minister to the low castes :—

1. Ganda Dravidras.
2. Nambi Varlu.

§ 5.—*Barna Brahmans of Malabar.*

1. Eledus—Priests of the Nairs.

CHAP. IV.—THE BRAHMANS CONNECTED WITH THE GREAT PUBLIC SHRINES.

Of the Brahmans who are considered as having a very low status on account of their being connected with the great public shrines, the following classes are the most important :—

1. Gayalis of Gaya.
2. Chowbays of Muttra.
3. Pukar Sevaks of Pushkar.
4. Ganga Putras of Benares.
5. Pandas of Orissa.
6. Pandarams of Southern India.
7. Prayagwalas of Prayag or Allahabad.
8. Divas—connected with the Ballavachari shrines of Western India.
9. Moylars—connected with the Madhava temples of Tulava; said to be of spurious birth.
10. Ambalavasis—connected with the shrines in Malabar.
11. Numbi Brahmans—connected with the public shrines of Karnata.

Most of these classes are very rich, but utterly illiterate. Mere residence in a place of pilgrimage, for a few generations, tends to lower the status of a family. The Bengali Brahmans settled at Benares are called by their clansmen Kashials, and looked down upon as men whose birth is spurious, or as being in the habit of earning their livelihood by accepting forbidden gifts. The Brahmans of Southern India also look down upon their clansmen permanently residing in Benares, without any connection with their native country.*

*The reader may have some idea of this feeling from the following passage in Mr. Wilkin's *Modern Hinduism* :—

A few months ago, when travelling on the East India Railway,

The Somparas connected with the shrine of Somnath seem to have a higher position than the priests of the public shrines usually have. There is a class of Brahmans in the Doab who call themselves Chowbays of Mathura, but have nothing to do with priestly work. These are very high class Brahmans. There are many learned Sanskritists and English scholars among them. Some of them hold high offices in the service of Government and also of the Native States. One of the greatest of these is Kumar Jwala Prasad, who is at present the District Judge of Azimgarh. His father, Raja Jai Kishen, rendered eminent services to the Government at the time of the Sepoy Mutiny, and is still employed as a Deputy Collector. Another member of the Chowbay caste, named Raghu Nath Das, is the Prime Minister of Kota.

I met with two Brahmans from Mysore. They are educated men; one of them was expecting to appear in the following B. A. Examination of the Madras University. When we were leaving Benares, it occurred to me to ask if they had any friends in that holy city. They said,—"No, but we soon found some Brahmans from our part of the country." I said "oh, then you were well received and hospitably entertained by them of course?" I shall never forget the look of infinite disdain with which one of them replied: "Do you think we would eat with men who live in such a city as Benares, and associate with Brahmans of this district? No, we contented ourselves whilst there with one meal a day, which we cooked for ourselves." My question appeared to them about as reasonable as if I had asked a nobleman in England if he had dined with scavenger.—Wilkin's *Modern Hinduism*, pp. 163 164.

CHAP. V—THE BRAHMANS DEGRADED BY ACCEPTING FORBIDDEN GIFTS, AND OFFICIATING AS PAID PRIESTS AT CREMATIONS.

By the religious codes of the Hindus, the acceptance of certain kinds of movables, such as elephants, horses, etc., is strictly forbidden. But in actual practice even high caste Brahmans are sometimes led by poverty to accept such gifts, especially where the transaction takes place in a distant part of the country, and under circumstances that may render it possible for the donee to keep his act of sin unknown to his clansmen. If the fact becomes known to them he is outcasted, and his descendants remain in the same condition, so long as the nature of the original cause of their degradation is remembered by their fellow-castemen. But in almost every such case the family recovers its lost position after a few generations, and no separate caste is formed. There are, however, certain kinds of gifts which good Brahmans never accept, and which only certain classes of degraded Brahmans are held to be entitled to. These Brahmans are called Mahā-Brahman in Northern India, Agradāni in Bengal, Agra Bhikshu in Orissa, and Acharya in Western India. The Mahā-Brahmans or Great Brahmans are so-called by way of irony. Their caste status is so low that good Hindus consider their very touch to be contaminating, and actually bathe if accidentally affected by such pollution. Almost all the classes mentioned above take a part in the ceremonies which have to be performed within the first ten days after a man's death. A great many of them claim also the wearing apparel of the deceased and his bedding, as their perquisites.

There is a class of Brahmans in and near Benares called Sawalakhi. They are considered as degraded on account of their being in the habit of accepting gifts from pilgrims within the holy city of Benares. The Sawalakhis are not treated as an unclean class, and a good Brahman will take a drink of water from their hands.

There is a class of Brahmans in the N.-W. Provinces called Bhattas who minister as priests in ceremonies for the expiation of the sin of cow-killing. They are regarded as very unclean.

The Maruiporas who officiate in some public burning-ghâts as paid priests have a lower position than that of even the Mahā-Brhmans and the Agradānis. Generally the function is performed by the ordinary family priests without fee of any kind. But in some burning-ghâts certain families claim an exclusive right to administer the sacrament to the dead, and claim heavy fees in the most heartless manner. These are in Bengal called Maruiporas, literally, dead burners. In Western India they are called Acharyas.

In Rajputana and the neighbouring districts there is a kind of Brahman called Dakot and also Sanichar, who accept gifts of oil and sesamum made for propitiating the planet Saturn. They are, therefore, regarded as degraded Brahmans.

CHAP. VI.—THE CLASSES DEGRADED BY MENIAL SERVICE, AND THE PRACTICE OF AGRICULTURE.

THE Bhuinhars are now chiefly tillers of the soil; but apparently the original cause of their being lowered in the scale of caste was the adoption of the military profession, and their subsequent practice of agriculture has served only to degrade them a little further. Of the sections of the Brahmanical caste which are held to be more or less degraded on account of their being agriculturists, the following may be mentioned here :—

1. Tagas—Kurukshetra country.
2. Trigulas—found on the banks of the Krishna in the Southern Maharatta country.
3. Soparas—found in Bassein.
4. Sajhodra—found in Gujrat.
5. Bhatelas—found near Broach.
6. Mastanis—found in Orissa and Gujrat.

Among the classes degraded by menial service may be mentioned the following :—

1. Javala—cooks in the Maharatta country.
2. Gugali—servants of the Vallabhachari Maharajas.
3. Sanchora—cooks, found chiefly in Gujrat.

PART VII.

THE MILITARY CASTES.

CHAP. I.—THE RAJPUTS.

THE political importance of the Rajputs in India is well known, and I need not, in this book, say anything as to what their position had been until the country became subject to Moslem rule. Their past history is a glorious one; and although it is long since they have been shorn of their ancient greatness, yet it cannot be said even now that they have no importance whatever. From time immemorial, they looked upon war and politics as their only proper sphere, and although the Brahmans allowed to them the privilege of studying the Shastras, yet they never devoted their attention to the cultivation of letters. The traditions of their families, and the hereditary aptitude for the art of warfare developed in them, made them the perfect type of good soldiers. But their want of literary culture made their great generals incapable of recording their own experiences in such manner as to be available for the benefit of their successors. The Bhats who served as their genealogists lavished praises on their ancestors, and excited them to feats of bravery, but could never give them anything like a good history. The Brahmanical Purāns distorted the facts so as to suit the policy of their authors, and gave greater importance to the good or bad wishes of a Brahman, than to either military or diplomatic skill. On the other hand, the Rajputs themselves were too illiterate to profit by even the little authentic history that was in the Purāns. The result was that, with all their natural talents and personal bravery, they could not secure to the country a sufficient number of good generals and political ministers. A genius shone at times. But in no country and in no community are Chandra Guptas and Vikramadityas born every day. A natural genius like that of Sivaji or Ranjit may do without any kind of education ; but the majority of even the best men in every country require training in order to develop their capacities, and the necessary means for that training was sadly wanting among the Rajputs. Thus, in spite of all their soldier-like virtues, they failed to cope with the early Mahomedan invaders. But the greatest of the Mahomedan rulers—not even Akbar or Alaudin—could break their power completely. The wrecks which they preserve still of their former greatness are not at all inconsiderable. The majority of the leading Hindu chiefs of India are still of their tribe. A great many of the Hindu landholders, big and small in every part of India, are also of the same caste. The Rajputs are still generally quite as averse to education as their ancestors ever were. But already some members of the class have shaken off their old prejudices, and have received the benefits of English education. And the time seems to be fast coming when the scions of the Ksatriya aristocracy will prove to be formidable rivals to the Brahmans and the Kāyasthas, in the race for high offices, and for distinction in the liberal professions. Some noble examples of such departure have already been set in Bengal. The well-known Vakils, Babus Prasanna Chandra Roy and Saligram Sing, of the Bengal High Court, are Rajputs by caste. The former is a Rajput zemindar of Nadiya. In the early years of the Calcutta University he attained its highest honours, and for a time, practised with great success in the Bar of the Allahabad High Court. If he had continued in the profession, he might have been one of its recognized leaders ; but the exigencies of his patrimony and his indigo plantations compelled him to keep himself unconnected with the Bar for nearly twenty years. He has lately resumed his profession as a Vakil of the Bengal High Court, and is fast rising in eminence. In the Judicial Service of Bengal there are at present two gentlemen who are of the Rajput caste. They are the grandsons of the celebrated Babu Kesava Roy of Nakasipara, who was the terror of his district in his time, and who with his army of Goala clubmen successfully set at defiance the authority of the police and the magistracy.

The Rajputs are to be found in every part of India, and the total population of the tribe exceeds ten millions. The following table shows their numerical strength in each of the several Provinces where they are most numerous :—

N.-W. Provinces	3,793,433
Panjab	1,790,359
Bengal	1,519,354
Rajputana	785,227
Central India	713,683
Bombay	566,942
Central Provinces	379,297
Madras	171,244
Kashmir	402,918

There are no sub-castes among the Rajputs properly so-called. They are divided into a large number of clans, the rules among them relating to marriage being as follows :—

1. No one can marry within his tribe.
2. A girl should be given in marriage to a bridegroom of a higher tribe.
3. A male member of a Rajput tribe may take in marriage any Rajput girl though of a lower class.

Like the Sarswats, the Rajputs are said to marry within their Gotra provided the clan is different.

The principal clans of the Rajputs are the following:—

1. **Suryavansi** (Solar race).
2. **Somvansi or Chandravansi** (Lunar race).
3. **Yaduvansi.**
4. **Pramara.**
5. **Prarihara.**
6. **Chalukya or Solanki.**
7. **Chauhan.**

(Nos. 4–7: Born out of the sacred fire in accordance with the prayer of Brahmans.)

8. **Tuar.**
9. **Rathor.**
10. **Katchwa.**
11. **Grahilot.**
12. **Bais.**

Besides these, there are twenty-four other principal clans, and each of these is divided into numerous sub-clans. The usual surnames of the Rajputs are: Sing, Barman, Thākoor, Raut, Roy, &c.

In respect to diet the Rajputs do not strictly conform to the practice of high caste Hindus. There are many among them who eat both fish and such flesh as is not forbidden by the Shastras. Some eat even pork. There are, however, some among them who are very puritanic, and who do not eat any kind of animal food. Their caste vanity is such that it is very rare to find two Rajputs of different families who will eat together, and hence there is a common saying in the country that a "dozen Rajputs cannot do without at least thirteen kitchens." The Rajputs of Bengal eat *kachi* food, *i.e.*, rice, *dal*, fish, or flesh cooked in water by a Brahman. In other parts of the country the practice is not uniform, and some Rajputs refuse to take *kachi* food even from a good Brahman of their country, unless such person is the spiritual guide of the family. As to *pakki* food, *i.e.*, such as is prepared by frying flour or vegetables in *ghi*, the Rajputs have not much prejudice, and like the modern Brahmans of Bengal they will take it from any of the clean Sudra castes such as the Dhanuk, Kurmi, Kahar, Lohar, Barhi, Kumhar, Goala, Napit, Mali, Sonar and the Kaseri, provided that no salt or turmeric has been used in the making. These the Rajput will add himself before eating.

The Rajput is the best person from whom a Brahman can accept a gift. A Brahman may also officiate as a priest in a Rajput household without lowering himself in the estimation of his castemen. There is nothing in the Shastras to prevent a Brahman from eating even *kachi* food from the hands of a Rajput. But in actual practice the Brahmans do not eat such rice, *dal*, fish or flesh as is cooked, or touched after cooking, by a Rajput. The *ghi* cakes and sweetmeats made by the Rajputs are, however, eaten by the best Brahmans, with the exception of only a few of the over puritanic Pandits. The Brahmans will eat also *kachi*, food in the house of a Rajput, if cooked by a Brahman, and untouched by the host after cooking. The following is a list of the leading Rajput chiefs of India together with the names of the clans to which they belong :—

Rana of Udaipur ...	Sisodya branch of the Grahilot clan of Suryavansi Rajputs.
Maharaja of Jodhpur ...	Rathor clan of Suryavansi Rajputs.
Maharaja of Bikaneer ...	Rathor clan of Suryavansi Rajputs.
Maharaja of Kishengarh ...	Rathor clan of Suryavansi Rajputs.
Maharaja of Jaipore ...	Kachawa clan of Suryavansi Rajputs.
Maharao Raja of Alwar ...	Naruka clan.
Maharaja of Jaisalmir ...	Yadu Bhati clan.
Maharaja of Jhalwar ...	Jhala clan.
Maharaja of Karauli ...	Jadun clan of Yaduvansi Rajputs.
Maharaja of Kota ...	Chauhan.
Maharao Raja of Bundi ...	Hara sept of Chauhans.
Maharaja of Vizianagram ...	Of the same clan as the Rana of Udaipur.*

The number of minor chiefs and landholders who are of the Rajput caste is so large that a complete list

* The Maharaja of Vizianagram, in the Vizigapatam district, represents the royal house of the ancient Kalinga country. According to the local traditions, one of his remote ancestors, named Madhava Varma, came to the Telugu country from the north, and having conquered it, settled there with all his followers, who are divided into five classes. Intermarriage still takes place between these Rajputs and those of Northern India. But there is in Kalinga another class of the military caste who are called Khond Rajus (Lit., hill Chattris). The Gajapati Rajas are Khond Rajus, and intermarriage cannot take place between them and the Rajputs properly so-called.

of them cannot possibly be given in this book. The Maharaja of Domraon, near Arrah, one of the biggest landlords in Behar, is a high caste Rajput, represening, it is said, the line of the great Vikramaditya.

The Rajputs are admitted by all to be true Ksatriyas and are not to be confounded with the Kshettris of the Punjab who are usually regarded as Buniyas, and an account of whom is given in the next chapter. The inferior Rajputs of Bengal are call Pukuria, or "Tonk-men." They wear the sacred thread, but some of them are to be found employed as domestic servants and tillers of the soil.

CHAP. II.—THE KSHETTRIS.

THERE is very considerable difference of opinion as to the exact position of the Kshettris in the Hindu caste system. Some authorities take them to be the same as the bastard caste *Kshâtri*, spoken of by Manu as the offspring of a Sudra father by a Ksatriya mother.* The people of this country include the Kshettris among the Baniya castes, and do not admit that they have the same position as the military Rajputs. The Kshettris themselves claim to be Ksatriyas, and observe the religious rites and duties prescribed by the Shastras for the military castes. But the majority of them live either by trade or by service as clerks and accountants, and their caste status ought, it seems, to be intermediate between that of the Rajputs on the one hand, and the Baniyas and the Kāyasthas on the other.

In their outward appearance the Kshettris lack the manly vigour of the Rajput and the broad forehead of the Brahman. But they are generally very handsome, and with their slender figures, their blue sparkling eyes, and their aquiline nose, some of them look exactly like the Jews whom they resemble also in their character. In trading as well as in service, they generally display great shrewdness. But there is not found among them either the enterprise of the Parsis, or the literary industry

* See Manu X, 12, 13; see also Shyama Charan's *Vyavastha Darpan*, p. 659.

of the Brahmans and the Kāyasthas. What they want in real ability is, however, more than made up by their power of ingratiating themselves in the favour of their masters at any cost. They possess in great abundance all the virtues and vices of courtiers. But while these form the most conspicuous features in their character, they combine in it a great deal of what is good and noble in the Brahman, the Rajput, the Baniya and the Kāyastha. In Campbell's *Ethnology of India* is to be found the following account of the Kshetri caste :—

"Trade is their main occupation; but in fact they have broader and more distinguishing features. Besides monopolising the trade of the Panjab and the greater part of Afghanistan, and doing a good deal beyond these limits, they are in the Panjab the chief civil administrators, and have almost all literate work in their hands. So far as the Sikhs have a priesthood they are, moreover, the priests or Gurus of Sikhs. Both Nanak and Govind were, and the Sodis and Bedis of the present day are, Kshetris. Thus, then, they are in fact in the Panjab, so far as a more energetic race will permit them, all that the Maharatta Brahmans are in the Maharatta country, besides engrossing the trade which the Maharatta Brahmans have not. They are not usually military in their character, but are quite capable of using the sword when necessary. Dewan Sawan Mull, Governor of Mooltan, and his notorious successor Mulraj, and very many of Ranjit Sing's chief functionaries, were Kshetris. Even under Mahomedan rulers in the west they have risen to high administrative posts. There is a record of a Kshetri Dewan of Badakshan or Kunduz; and, I believe, of a Kshetri Governor of Peshwar under the Afghans. The Emperor Akbar's famous minister, Todar Mull, was a Kshetri; and a relative of that man of undoubted energy, the great commissariat contractor of Agra, Jotee Prasad, lately informed me that he also is a Kshetri. Altogether, there can be no doubt that these Kshetris are one of the most acute, energetic, and remarkable races of India. The Kshetris are staunch Hindus, and it is somewhat singular* that, while giving a religion and priests to the Sikhs, they themselves are comparatively seldom Sikhs. The Kshetris are a fine, fair, handsome race, and, as may be gathered from what I have already said, they are very generally educated.

"No village can get on without the Kshetri, who keeps the accounts, does the banking business, and buys and sells the grain. They seem, too, to get on with the people better than most traders and usurers of this kind. In Afghanistan, among a rough and alien people, the Kshetris are, as a rule, confined to the position of

---

* I cannot understand why Sir George Campbell considered this circumstance a singular one. It only illustrates the common saying that a prophet is never honoured in his own country. Christ is not honoured by the Jews; nor is Chaitanya honoured by the Brahmans of Nadiya.

humble dealers, shopkeepers, and money-lenders; but in that capacity the Pathans seem to look at them as a kind of valuable animal; and a Pathan will steal another man's Kshetri, not only for the sake of ransom, but also as he might steal a milch cow, or as Jews might, I daresay, be carried off in the Middle Ages, with a view to render them profitable."—Campbell's *Ethnology of India*, pp. 108—112.

Many of the Kshettris now go to England, and those who do so are not very harshly treated by their castemen, as in other provinces. Some of the Kshettris have qualified to practise as barristers.

There are four main divisions among the Kshettris. The name of their first and most important division is *Banjai*, which is probably a corrupted form of the Sanskrit word Bānijik meaning a "trader." Their second division, the *Sereens*, are probably so-called on account of their being, or having been at one time, *Sirinas*, i.e., ploughmen or cultivators. With regard to their third division, the *Kukkurs*,* it is said that they derive their name from that of a district near the town of Pind Dadan Khan on the Jhelum. The fourth division called *Rorhas* or *Arorhas* claim to be Kshetris, but are not regarded as such by any one except their own class.

§ 1.—*Sereens*.

The Sereens are to be found only in the Panjab. They have four main divisions among them, each of these having a large number of exogamous sections, as shown in the following table :—

Class No. 1.

1. Nagar. 2. Koshe. 3. Kupani.
4. *Bhalle*. 5. Munoaya.

Class No. 2.

1. Kuher.	5. Moorgahi.	9. *Sodi*.
2. *Tihan*.	6. Koondra.	10. Khoole.
3. Buhb.	7. Kumra.	11. Pooree.
4. Bhubhote.	8. Ouse.	12. Jeoor.

* The name of the Kukkur tribe is mentioned in the *Mahábhárat*. See *Udyoga Parva*, Chap. XXVII.

Class No. 3.

1. Sohni.	6. Jummoo.	11. Muhlhan.
2. Juyee.	7. Ghyee.	12. Buzaz.
3. Dasan.	8. Joolki.	13. Rera.
4. Awut.	9. Sooshi.	14. Subhikhi.
5. Dhoosa.	10. Mynra.	15. Suchur.
	16. Boochur.	

Class No. 4.

1. Kousai.	10. Sing race.	19. Chum.
2. Bisambhu.	11. Kudd.	20. Kulsia.
3. Choodu.	12. Kesor.	21. Khotbe.
4. Ural.	13. Umat.	22. Ghooman.
5. Kureer.	14. Lumbe.	23. Bulleat.
6. Bussee.	15. Lumb.	24. Surpal.
7. Vassesse.	16. Kupace.	25. Chiske.
8. Ubhee.	17. Pathri.	26. Mulhee.
9. Basantraee.	18. Hudd.	27. Myndra.

The above lists, taken from Sherring, were referred to Baba Sumera Singh, the Chief of the Sodi Gurus, now in charge of the Sikh Temple at Patna, and have been pronounced by him to be substantially correct. The third Guru of the Sikhs, Ummer Das, was of the Bhalle clan, included in class No. 1, of the Sereen Kshettris. The second Guru, Ungat, was of the Tihan clan, included in class No. 2. The last seven Gurus were all of the Sodi clan included within the same group. Guru Nanak, the founder of the sect, was not a Sereen, but a Banji of the inferior Bedi clan. His descendants are called Bedis. The last Guru left no descendants living, and the Sodis, who are now venerated by the Sikhs as his representatives, are the descendants of the following :—

1. Prithvi Chand (Elder brother of Guru Arjoon.)
2. Har Govind.

The Bhalles and Tihans form small communities. The Sodis and Bedis are very numerous. The chief of the Bedis is now the Hon'ble Baba Khem Sing, of Rawal Pindi, who has lately been made a member of the Legislative Council of India. The chief of the Sodis is, as stated above, Sumera Singh, the High Priest of the Sikh Temple at Patna. These gentlemen do not possess any knowledge of English. But they are both very intelligent, and there is an air of dignity and greatness in their very appearance which cannot fail to command notice and admiration.

It has been already stated that the Bedis, who are descendants of Guru Nanak, belong to the Banjai division of the Kshettri caste, and that the Sodis belong to the division called Sereen. Intermarriages, however, are now taking place between the Bedis and the Sodis.

§ 2.—*The Kukkurs.*

The Kukkurs are found chiefly on the banks of the Indus and the Jhelum, near the towns of Pind-Dadan Khan, Peshawar, and Nowshera. Their usual surnames are—

1. Anand.	4. Chude.	7. Kolee.
2. Bhuseen.	5. Sooree.	8. Sabhurwal.
3. Sohnee.	6. Sother.	9. Ussee.

Mr. Sherring says that there are some Kukkurs in Benares. In Calcutta there may be some of the class, but I have never met with any one claiming to be so.

§ 3.—*Rorha or Arorha.*

These are, properly speaking, Baniyas. But as they take the sacred thread and claim to be Kshettris, they are included in the group dealt with in this chapter. They are found chiefly in the Panjab. Their total number is 673,695. The majority of them are shopkeepers and brokers. The sweatmeat makers of Panjab are mostly Rorhas. The other classes of Kshettris neither eat with the Rorhas nor intermarry with them.

§ 4.—*Banjai Kshettris.*

The Banjai Kshettris are to be found throughout the greater part of Northern India. The total population of the class in each province is given in the following table :—

Panjab	447.933
Kashmir	52,392
N.-W. Provinces	46,650
Bengal	121,071

In Bengal proper the Kshettri population is very small. The only places in it where any considerable number of them are found to be settled are Calcutta and Burdwan. The Calcutta Kshettris live here for trade; the Burdwan Kshettris have been made to colonise there by the Maharajas of Burdwan, whose family are Kshettris of the Adrai Ghar clan. The Soni Kshettris of Behar who do the work of goldsmiths seem to have been enumerated as Kshettris in the last Census. But the Sonis are a distinct caste altogether, between whom and the good Kshettris there can neither be intermarriage nor intercharge of hospitality on a footing of equality. The Kshettri weavers of Gujrat are also a distinct caste.

The Banjai Kshettris are divided into many hypergamous and exogamous groups which, with their titles, are shown in the following table :—

Names of groups.	*Names of clans and titles.*
1.—{1. Adrai Ghar ... ... / 2. Char Ghar ... ...}	1. Khanna. 2. Mehra. 3. Kapoor. 4. Seth.
2.—Chazati or "the sex clans" ...	1. Bahel. 2. Dhouwan. 3. Beri. 4. Vij. 5. Saigol. 6. Chopra.
0.—Bora Ghor or "the twelve clans"	1. Upal. 2. Dugal. 3. Puri. 4. Kochar. 5. Nande. 6. Mahipe. 7. Hande. 8. Bhalle. 9. Mangal. 10. Badahre. 11. Sowti. 12. Kulhar.

Besides the above there are many other Kshettri clans which have a very low status. The Adrai Ghar Kshettris have the highest position in the caste, and though they may take in marriage a girl from a family of a lower group, they will never give a daughter of their own family to a bridegroom of a lower status. The Maharaja of Burdwan is of the Adrai Ghar clan. Guru Nanak, the founder of the Sikh religion, was a Banjai Kshettri of the inferior class called Bedi. The other Sikh Gurus were all of the Sereen tribe.

The Sarswat Brahmans of the Panjab usually officiate as priests in Kshettri households. It is said that the Sarswats will eat even *kachi* food cooked by a Kshettri. If they do so, they are quite within the law of the Shastras. The Brahmans of the other parts of the country do not honour the Kshettris by accepting their hospitality in the shape of *kachi* food cooked by them. But no Brahman will hesitate to accept their gifts, or to take a drink of water from them. Those Brahmans of Bengal and N.-W. Provinces whose religious scruples are not very strong, will take from the hand of a Kshettri *pakki* food unmixed with water or salt. They will eat also *kachi* food in the house of a Kshettri, if cooked by a Brahman, and untouched by the host after cooking.

The bastard descendants of the Kshettris are called *Puriwal*, a name which literally means a person belonging to a town. The *Puriwals* form a distinct caste, and the Sahu Kshettris or Kshettris of pure blood do not intermarry with them.

CHAP. III.—THE JATS.

THE Jats are the most important element in the rural population of the Panjab and the western districts of the North-Western Provinces. The last Census gives the following figures as the population of the Jats in the several provinces of India where they are found :—

Panjab	4,625,523
Rajputana	1,056,160
N.-W. Provinces	701,259
Kashmir	142,595
Central India	56,530
Sind	45,526

The Jats do not wear the sacred thread ; and have among them certain customs which are more like those of the Sudras than of the twice-born castes. But in every other respect they are like the Rajputs. Ordinarily, the majority of both the Jats and the Rajputs live by practising agriculture. But when the occasion arises, the Jat can wield the sword as well as the most aristocratic of the military castes. The late Lion of the Panjab and many of his leading generals were of the Jat tribe. To the same clan belongs also the Maharaja of Bhurtpur, whose ancestors, from the beginning of the last century, played an important part in the politics of Northern India, and at the time of the conquest of the Doab by Lord Lake compelled that great general to raise the siege of Bhurtpur which he had undertaken. The present reigning family of Dholepore are also Jats. The Jats themselves claim to be Ksatriyas. But as they do not wear the holy thread, they are usually looked upon as having the status of only clean Sudras. There cannot therefore be intermarriage between the Jats and the Rajputs. The Jats are, like the Rajputs, divided into a large number of exogamous groups, and, among them, as among the superior Ksatriyas, marriage is impossible between parties who are members of the same clan. The Jats have been supposed, by some of the best authorities on Indian ethnology and antiquities, to be a Scythic tribe. General Cunningham identifies them with the *Zanthii* of Strabo and the Jatii of Pliny and Ptolemy, and fixes their parent country on the banks of the Oxus between Bactria, Hyrkania, and Khorasmia. But the sufficiency of the grounds on which this view rests has been questioned, Prichard remarks:—

> "The supposition that the *Jats* of the Indus are descendants of the *Yuetschi* does not appear altogether preposterous, but it is supported by no proof except the very trifling one of a slight resemblance of names. The physical characters of the *Jats* are extremely different from those attributed to the *Yuetschi* and the kindred tribes by the writers cited by Klaproth and Abel Remusat who say they are of sanguine complexions with blue eyes.—*Researches* IV, 132.

The question cannot possibly be answered in a satisfactory manner so long as the ethnology and history of Russia and Central Asia are not carefully investigated by scholars. There are certainly historical works in Russia and Central Asia which might throw a flood of light on many an obscure passage of Indian history. But the necessary facilities for such study are sadly wanting at present, and the state of things is not likely to improve, until Russian scholars come forward to take their proper share in the field of Oriental research. In India itself a great deal yet remains to be done to provide the necessary basis of the ethnological sciences. A beginning has been made by Messrs. Dalton, Risley and Ibbetson. But the work must be prosecuted more vigorously before it can be expected to yield any important results.

CHAP. IV.—THE KHANDAITS OF ORISSA.

THE word Khandait literally means a "swordsman." The Khandaits are to be found chiefly in Orissa and in the adjoining districts of Chutia Nagpore. They were the fighting class of Orissa under the Hindu kings of the province. They are divided into two main sub-classes called the Mahanayaka or the Sreshta Khandaits, and the Paik or Chasa Khandaits. These names indicate that the former represent the ancient military commanders, and the latter the rank and file who are now mainly agriculturists, and are therefore called Chasa Khandaits. Intermarriage between these sub-classes is not impossible, but is very rare in practice. Intermarriage takes place sometimes between the Khandaits and the Karans of the Nulia clan.

Whatever their origin may have been, the Khandaits have now very nearly the same position as the Rajputs. The best Brahmans do not hesitate to accept their gifts, or to minister to them as priests. The Khandaits do not take the sacred thread at the time prescribed for the Ksatriyas. But they all go through the ceremony at the time of their marriage, and their higher classes retain the thread for ever as the twice-born castes are required by the Shastras to do. With regard to the Chasa Khandait, it is said that they throw away the *janeo* on the fourth day after marriage. There is a class of Khandaits in Chutia Nagpore who are called Chota Khandaits. They are in the habit of eating fowls and drinking spirits. The Brahmans regard them therefore as an unclean caste, and will not take even a drink of water from their hands. The usual titles of the Khandaits of Orissa are as stated below :—

1. Bagha, *Tiger.*
2. Bahubalendra, *Like the god Indra in strength of arm.*
3. Dakhin Kabat, *South gate.*
4. Daubarik, *Sentinel at the gate.*
5. Garh Nayaka, *Commander of the fort.*
6. Hati, *Elephant.*
7. Jena.
8. Maharath or Maharathi, *Great Charioteer.*
9. Malla, *Wrestler.*
10. Mangaraj.
11. Nayaka, *Leader.*
12. Paschim Kabat, *West gate.*
13. Praharaj.
14. Rana Sinha, *Lion of the fight.*
15. Rout.
16. Rui.
17. Samanta, *Officer.*
18. Samara Sinha, *Lion of the fight.*
19. Senapati, *General.*
20. Sinha, *Lion.*
21. Uttara Kabat, *North gate.*

CHAP. V.—THE MARATTA.

THE *Marattas* are the military caste of the Maharatta country. Their position in the Hindu caste system was originally not a very high one, and even now it is not exactly the same as that of the Rajputs of Northern India. But the political importance acquired by them, since the time of Sivaji, who was a member of their community, has enabled them to form connection by marriage with many of the superior Rajput families, and they may be now regarded as an inferior clan of the Rajput caste. The lower classes of the Marattas do not go through the ceremony of the Upanayana, or investiture with the thread. But they take it it at the time of their marriage, and are not held to be altogether debarred from its use. Their right to be reckoned as Ksatriyas is recognised by the Brahmans in various other ways. Even the most orthodox Brahmans do not hesitate to accept their gifts, or to minister to them as priests. The only ground on which they may be regarded as an inferior caste is the fact that they eat fowls. But in no part of the country are the military castes very puritanic in their diet.

The Marattas have two main divisions among them. The branch called the "seven families" has a superior status. The great Sivaji, and the Rajas of Nagpore and Tanjore were members of this division. The "seven families" are—

1. Bhonslay.
2. Mohita.
3. Sirkhe.
4. Ahin Roo.
5. Gujar (not the same as those of Gujrat.)
6. Nimbalkoar.
7. Ghorepore.

There is another division among the Marattas called the "ninety-six families." These have an inferior status. The Maharajas of Gwalior and Baroda are of this class. The inferior Marattas are usually employed by the superior castes as domestic servants. The Maratta tribe is not to be confounded with the tribe called Mahars who serve as village watchmen and also practise the art of weaving. The Mahars are an unclean tribe, while the Marattas are certainly a clean caste. The name of the Maratta country seems to be derived from that of the Maratta tribe.

CHAP. VI.—THE NAIRS OF MALABAR TRAVANCORE AND COCHIN.

THE Nairs of Malabar and Travancore are more a tribe than a caste. They are generally said to be all Sudras, and they have among them a large number of sections pursuing different avocations, from that of the soldier to the most degrading forms of menial service. The last Census includes them among the military and dominant castes, and as the Maharaja of Travancore is a Nair, I do not see any strong reason to give the tribe a different place in the caste system. The Nairs have among them many who are well educated, and who hold very high positions in the service of Government and in the liberal professions. The caste status of these is similar to that of the Kāyasthas of Northern India. But there are some sections among the Nairs whose usual occupation is menial work, and the status of the entire body of the Nairs cannot be said to be the same as that of the writer castes. The following are the names of the different sections of the Nairs :—

1. Valaima. First in rank.
2. Kerathi.
3. Ilakara.
4. Shrubakara.
5. Panda Mangolam.
6. Tamilipaudam.
7. Palicham, Bearers or servants to the Namburi Brahmans.
8. Shakaular or Velakaudu. Oilmen.
9. Pulikai or Audam Nairs. Potters.
10. Velathadam or Erinkulai. Washermen for Brahmans and Nairs.

11. **Pariari or Velakathara. Barbers for Brahmans and Nairs.**
12. **Agatacharnavar. Menial servants to Brahmans and Nairs.**
13. **Yedachairai or Yorma. Cowherds.**
14. **Kulata or Velur.**
15. **Yahbari. Merchants.**
16. **Udatu. Boatmen.**

The peculiarities in the social constitution and in the marriage laws of the Nairs have been described already. See p. 107, *ante*. Their unique customs and laws are the outcome of the undue advantage taken upon them by their priests, the Numburi Brahmans. The nominal marriage which every Nair girl has to go through with a Brahman is a source of profit to the titular husband. The freedom which is subsequently given to the girl to choose her male associate from an equal or a superior tribe is also advantageous to the Numburis. But the Nairs are being roused to the necessity of better laws, and they have of late been demanding for special legislation in order to get rid of their ancient customs, and to have the benefit of such laws as are recognised by the Hindu Shastras.

CHAP. VII.—THE MARAVANS, AHAMDIANS AND KALLANS OF SOUTHERN INDIA.

In the extreme south of India the most important military caste is that of the Maravans. The Rajas of Ramnad, and Sivaganga are of this caste. The head of the Maravans is the Raja of Ramnad who assumes the surname of Setupati or "Master of the Bridge," though it has been decided by the Privy Council that the shrine of Rameshwar belongs to its priest, and not to the Raja of Ramnad. The Raja of Ramnad is, however, entitled to great honor from the other Rajas and noblemen of his caste. "The Raja Tondiman, of Puthukottei, the Raja of Sivaganga, and the eighteen chiefs of the Tanjore country must stand before him with the palms of their hands joined together. The chiefs of Tinnevelly, such as Kataboma Nayakkan, of Panjala Kureichi, Serumali Nayakkan, of Kudal Kundei, and the Tokala Totiyans being all of inferior caste, should prostrate themselves at full length before the Setupati, and after rising must stand and not be seated."*

The Maravans are said to be in the habit of eating flesh and drinking wine. But they are regarded as a clean caste, and the Brahmans evince no hesitation to accept their gifts. The Maravans allow their hair to grow without limit, and both sexes wear such heavy ornaments on their ears as to make the lobe reach the

* Nelson's *Manual of Madura*, Part II, p. 41.

shoulders. Unlike the other races of the locality the Maravans are tall, well built and handsome.

The Ahamdians cannot be regarded as a separate caste. They are rather an inferior branch of the Maravans. Intermarriage is allowed between the two classes. The total population of the Maravans is more than three hundred thousand.

The Kallans have a very bad reputation. Their very name implies that they are a criminal tribe. They have some big men among them. Mr. Nelson, in speaking of the Kallans, says :—

"The bovhood of every Kallan is supposed to be passed in acquiring the rudiments of the only profession he can be naturally adapted, namely, that of a thief and robbery. At fifteen he is usually entitled to be considered as proficient, and from that time forth, he is allowed to grow his hair as long as he pleases, a privilege denied to younger boys. At the same time, he is often rewarded for his experience as a thief by the hand of one of his female relations.

"The Kallans worship Shiva, but practise the rite of circumcision like the Mahomedans."

CHAP. VIII.—THE PALIYAS AND THE KOCH OF NORTH BENGAL.

THE Poliyas and the Koch of North Bengal seem from their physiognomy to be a Mongolian race. They are now purely agricultural. But they may come within the class Poundraca enumerated by Manu* among the Ksatriya clans reduced to the condition of Sudras by not practising the rites prescribed for them. The Poliyas themselves derive their class name from the Sanskrit word *Palayita* which means a "fugitive," and claim to be fugitive Ksatriyas degraded to the rank of Sudras for the cowardice betrayed by them in a great battle which took place at some remote period of antiquity. The Koch were at one time a very powerful tribe, and their kingdom extended over a large portion of North Bengal. The Koch Rajas of Koch Behar and Bijni are believed by the Hindus to be the progeny of the great God Siva, and to have three eyes like their divine ancestor. The notion is so deep-rooted that it has not been eradicated even by the constant appearance of the present Maharaja of Koch Behar before the public.

* See Manu X, 44.

CHAP. IX.—AGURIS OF BENGAL.

THE Aguris of Bengal claim to be the Ugra Ksatriya caste spoken of in Manu's Code X, 9. In Mr. Oldham's recent work on the *Ethnology of Burdwan*, the right of the Aguri to be reckoned as identical with the Ugra Ksatriyas has been questioned. But Mr. Oldham's theory that the Aguris are the product of illicit unions between the Kshettris and the Shodgopas, has been shown to be utterly unfounded.* It can with

---

* See the following extract from a review of Mr. Oldham's work which appeared in a recent issue of the *Reis and Rayyet*.

The theory that the Aguris are the product of unions between the Kshettris of the Burdwan Raj family, and the Sadgopas of the Gopbhum dynasty, does not appear to be supported by any kind of proof, historical or ethnological. Mr. Oldham says that his theory is based upon admissions made by the Aguris themselves. But knowing what we do of them, it seems to us impossible that any of them would have given such a humiliating account of their origin. At any rate, according to the principles of the law of evidence recognised by almost every system of jurisprudence, an admission cannot be necessarily conclusive. In the case under consideration, there are very strong reasons why, in spite of Mr. Oldham's certifying it as properly recorded, the so-called admission should be rejected altogether. The ground on which we base this view is that there are among the Aguris many families whose history is well known to extend to a far earlier period than the time of even Abu Roy and Babu Roy, the founders of the Burdwan Raj. Then again, the ethnic and moral characteristics of the Aguris clearly mark them out as a separate community, unlike any other caste to be found in Bengal. They are by nature, hot tempered, and incapable of bearing subordination, while the Kshettris and Sadgopas, whom Mr. Oldham supposes to be their progenitors, are endowed by qualities the very opposite of these. A Kshettri would do anything to secure the good graces of his master. But a single word of comment or censure, though reasonable and proceeding from a person in authority, would cause the Aguris' blood to boil and urge him to desperate deeds. The supposed admixture of Sadgopa blood

more reason be said that the Aguris are connected with the Aghari tribe found in Chutia Nagpore and Central Provinces. With regard to the origin and character of the Ugra Ksatriyas, Manu gives the following account:—

> From a Ksatriya by a Sudra girl is born a creature called an Ugra which has a nature partaking both of Ksatriya and of Sudra, and finds its pleasure in savage conduct—Manu X. 9.

The word Ugra means 'hot tempered,' and it is said that to this day the Aguris' character fully justifies both the name and the description given of the Ugras in Manu's Code. The Aguris are now to be found chiefly in the district of Burdwan in Bengal. The majority of the Bengali Aguris practise agriculture. But some of them are more or less educated, and hold important offices in the service of Government, as well as of the local landholders. Some of the Aguris are themselves holders of estates and tenures of various grades. There are many successful advocates of the Aguri caste practising in the District Court of Burdwan.

The Burdwan Aguris appear to have a higher caste status than those of other parts of the country. In the eastern districts of Bengal, Aguris are classed with the hunting and fishing castes. In Burdwan the local Brahmans, who are mostly of a low class, not only accept their gifts, but even partake of such food in their houses as is cooked by Brahmans. As to taking a

---

with that of the Kshettri cannot account for these peculiarities in the moral character of their alleged progeny, except on the theory that when both the father and the mother are of a mild nature, the child, by some law of physiological chemistry, must be fierce and hot tempered. The strongest argument against Mr. Oldham's theory is afforded by the fact that, unlike the other leading castes, the Kshettris recognise, to some extent, their connection with the bastard, members of their class. The illegitimate sons of the Brahmans, Rajputs and of even the superior Sudra castes, have no recognised position whatever. The only alternative of the mother and the child in such cases is to adopt the faith of one of the latter day prophets, and to be members of the casteless Vaishnava community. Among the Kshettris the practice is very different. Their illegitimate progeny have a recognised though a lower status. They are called Puriwals and certainly not Aguris. See *Reis and Rayyet*, Feb. 16, 1895.

drink of water from the hands of the Aguris, the practice is not uniform. Some Brahmans regard them as clean castes, but many do not. Although the Aguris claim to be Ksatriyas, yet as they are the offspring of a Sudra woman, they have to perform their religious rites in the same manner as the Sudras. In practice also they perform the *Adya Shradh*, or the first ceremony for the benefit of the soul of a deceased person, on the thirty-first day after death, and not on the thirteenth day as the true Ksatriyas.

The Aguris are divided into two main classes, namely, the Suta and the Jana. The Janas take the sacred thread at the time of their marriage. There can be no intermarriage between the Suta and the Jana. The Sutas are sub-divided into several sub-classes, as, for instance, the Bardamaniya, the Kasipuri,* the Chagramis, the Baragramis, &c. Intermarriage is well-nigh impossible between these sub-castes, and they may be regarded as separate castes.

The surname of the Kulins, or the noblest families among the Aguris, is Chowdry. The surnames of the other Suta Aguris are Santra, Panja, Ta, Hati, Ghosh, Bose, Dutta, Hajra, Kower, Samanta. The surname of the Jana Aguris is usually Jana. There are among them also many families having the same surnames as the Sutas. The late Babu Pratapa Chandra Ray, who made a great name by the translation and publication of the great Sanskrit epic, *Mahabharat*, was a Suta Aguri. He was not only an enterprising publisher, but a man of rare tact and grace of manners. The actual work of translating the *Mahabharat* was done by a young but gifted scholar named Kishori Mohan Ganguli, a Brahman of the Rādhiya class.

---

* The Bardhamaniyas derive their name from the town of Burdwan, and the Kasipurias from the country of the Raja of Panchkote. I do not know where Chagram and Baragram are.

PART VIII.

THE SCIENTIFIC CASTES.

CHAP. I.—THE VAIDYAS OR THE MEDICAL CASTE OF BENGAL.

In Bengal the practice of Hindu medicine is the speciality of the caste called Vaidyas. In Assam there is a similar caste, called the Bez, who have the same privilege. But no such caste is to be found in any other part of India, and, in the other provinces, the Hindu medical science is studied and practised by the local Brahmans. In Bengal also there are a few Brahmans who are Vaidyas by profession. One of the greatest of these is Hari Nath Vidyaratna of Calcutta. He has not only established a large practice by his marvellous skill in the healing art, but his mastery of Sanskrit medical literature has attracted round him a crowd of admiring pupils such as very few of those, who are Vaidyas by birth, can boast of.

The Vaidyas of Bengal are supposed to be of the caste of mixed descent called Ambastha in Manu's Code. Though this account of their origin is accepted by most of the Vaidyas themselves, yet, for practical purposes, their position in the caste system is inferior to only that of the Brahmans and the Rajputs. A good Brahman will not minister to a Vaidya as a priest, but even among the Brahmans of the highest class there are very few who will hesitate to accept a Vaidya's gifts, or to enrol a member of the caste among his spiritual disciples. When there is a feast in a Brahman's house, the Vaidya guests are made to sit at their dinner in a separate room, but almost at the same time as the Brahman guests. The Kāyasthas neither expect nor claim such honor. On the contrary, the Dākshina Rarhi Kāyasthas of Bengal insist that, as they are the servants to the Brahmans, they cannot commence until their masters, the Brahmans, have finished. The Rajputs do not usually eat in the house of any Bengali Brahman, but when they do, they receive generally the same attention as the Vaidyas. The only reason why the caste status of a Rajput must be said to be superior to that of the Vaidya is that while a Brahman may, without any hesitation, accept a gift from a Rajput and officiate as his priest, he cannot so honour a Vaidya without lowering his own status to some extent.

The Vaidyas are, as a class, very intelligent, and in respect of culture and refinement stand on almost the same level as the Brahmans and the superior Kāyasthas. The majority of the Vaidyas, wear the sacred thread, and perform *pujas* and prayers in the same manner as the Brahmans. From these circumstances it might be contended that they are degraded Brahmans, but their non-Brahmanic surnames negative that supposition. In all probability, they are Ambastha Kāyasthas of South Behar. This view is supported by the fact that they themselves profess to be Ambasthas, and also by the circumstance that, like the Kāyasthas of Upper India, the Vaidyas of East Bengal consider the taking of the thread as more or less optional, instead of regarding it as obligatory. The Vaidyas of the eastern districts do not take it even now, and as to those of Dacca and the adjoining districts it is said that they are taking it only since the time of the famous Raj Ballava, who was one of the most powerful ministers in the Court of Suraj-Dowla, and whose ambition materially paved the way of the East India Company to the sovereignty of Bengal.

The numerical strength of the Vaidya caste is not very considerable. In the last Census their total number is given as amounting to 82,932. The computation of their number seems to be correct enough; but they have been most improperly placed in the same group with the astrologers, exorcisors and herbalists, implying an insult which is quite unmerited, and against which every one, knowing anything about the importance and usefulness of the class, must feel inclined to protest. If the Vaidyas themselves have not expressed any dissatisfaction at the wanton attempt to humiliate them, made by the authors of the Census Reports, it is perhaps the consciousness that the Hindu caste system, which gives them a position next only to that of the Brahmans, is not likely, for a long time, to be affected by the *fiat* of a foreign power, however great it may be.

The three main divisions among the Vaidyas are the following :—

1. Rarhi Vaidyas. 2. Bangaja or Bārenda Vaidyas. 3. Sylheti Vaidyas.

There is a class of Vaidyas in West Bengal called Panchakoti Vaidyas, who derive their name from the district of Panch Kote or Pachete now called Purulia or Manbhoom. But intermarriages take place sometimes between them and the Rarhi Vaidyas, and they may be regarded as a sub-class of the Rarhis. The Sylheti Vaidyas form a distinct class, not only by their omission to take the sacred thread, but also by intermarriage with Kāyasths and even low class Sudras.

The following are the usual surnames of the Vaidyas :—

1. Gupta.
2. Sen Gupta.
3. Barat.
4. Sen.
5. Das.
6. Datta
7. Kar.
8. Rakshit.

(4–8) These titles are common among the Kāyasthas also.

9. Chowdry.
10. Roy.
11. Sircar.
} Hindu titles of honour common among the rich of every caste.

12. Khan.
13. Mallik.
14. Majumdar.
} Mahomedan titles of honour.

Like the learned Brahmans, some of the eminent Vaidyas use as their surnames such academical titles as Kabi Ratna, Kabi Bhusana, Kantha Bharana, &c. The Vaidyas are the only non-Brahmanic caste who are admitted into the Sanskrit Grammar schools of Bengal for studying grammar and *belles lettres.* Not being Brahmans, they are not allowed to study the Vedas and the Smritis. But in respect of general scholarship in Sanskrit, some of the Vaidyas attain great eminence. The name of Bharat Mallik,* who was a Vaidya of Dhatrigram near Kalna, is well-known to every Sanskritist in Bengal as a commentator on the *Mugdhalbodha Vyakarana* and as the author of a series of excellent annotations, read by Brahmans themselves as a part of their curriculum, in order to be able to study and enjoy the leading Sanskrit poems. The late Kaviraj Gangadhar of Berhampore was perhaps one of the greatest Sanskritists of his time. He was the author of a large number of valuable works on different subjects, and even the greatest Pandits of the country used to consider him as a foeman worthy of their steel.

For professional eminence and skill the Vaidya names now best known are the following :—

1. Paresh Nath Roy (Benares).
2. Govinda Chandra Sen (Moorshedabad).
3. Mani Mohan Sen (Calcutta).
4. Dwarka Nath Sen (Calcutta).
5. Bijoy Ratna Sen (Calcutta).

Of these Paresh Nath, Govind Chandra and Dwarka Nath are the pupils of the late Kaviraj Gangadhar. Paresh Nath is perhaps the ablest and the most learned among them, though his devotion to study and certain

* Bharat Mallik has left no descendants. His brother's descendants are now living at Patilpara near Kalna.

eccentricities which prepossess men against him, have prevented him from being able to establish a large practice. Among the Kavirajes of the Vaidya caste, Bijaya Ratna and Dwarka Nath have the largest practice in Calcutta. Govinda Chandra is a descendant of the physician to the historical Raja Raj Ballava, and is himself employed in a similar relation to the present titular Nabob of Moorshedabad. Mani Mohan is a younger brother of Govinda. He is a young man, but is well grounded in Kaviraji learning, as well as English medical science ; and he is fast rising in eminence. He has perhaps the largest number of pupils next to the Brahmanic Kaviraj Hari Nath.

In spite of the laudable efforts made by these and other gentlemen, belonging to the profession, to revive the cultivation of our ancient medical lore, Kaviraji must be regarded, to a great extent, as a lost art. A great many of the leading Sanskrit text-books on the subject are still extant. But the necessary incentives and facilities for studying them are sadly wanting. In the absence of museums and botanical gardens adapted to the requirements of the Kaviraji student, the difficulties in his way are great. Until recently he could not get even a printed copy of *Charak* or *Susrata*, either for love or money. That difficulty has been removed by the enterprise of our publishing firms. But even now the only way to acquire a mastery of our ancient medical science lies in being apprenticed to some leading Kaviraj, and to be in his good graces for a great many years. This is necessarily well-nigh impossible except for a few of the friends and relatives of the teachers. There are no doubt a good many Kavirajes who, in accordance with the time-honored custom of the country, consider it their duty to devote their leisure hours, and their surplus income for the benefit of their pupils. But in the absence of regular colleges and museums it becomes very often impossible for them to give the student an exact idea of a great many of the drugs and plants mentioned in their books. In practice, the Kaviraji student very seldom studies the works of the best authorities on the subject. He reads a Manual of Therapeutics by some latter-day compiler, and then begins his practice. It is this system that has brought discredit on the Kaviraji science. There are splendid works on anatomy and surgery in Sanskrit. But these are neglected altogether. The Kaviraje's therapeutics no doubt supersedes the necessity of surgery even in such cases as dropsy, stone and carbuncle. But the practice of therapeutics itself is impossible without a supply of such drugs as very few Kavirajes can procure, or their patients can pay for. The majority of those who are known as Kavirajes are therefore quite incapable of vindicating the value of their lore, and the votaries of the English medical science have succeeded in securing the public confidence to a much greater extent. But the great Kavirajes, who have the necessary learning and stock of drugs, are known to have achieved success in cases which the best English physicians had pronounced to be quite hopeless. The very quacks among the Kavirajes often display very remarkable skill, in making diagnosis and prognosis, by simply feeling the pulse, and without the help of any scientific appliance, such as the watch, the thermometer, and the stethescope.

The Vaidya seldom fails to achieve success in any line that he adopts. The name of Raja Raj Ballava, who from a very humble station became the virtual Governor of Dacca under Suraj Dowla, has been already referred to. Under British rule no native of the country can have any scope for the display of similar ability. But, even under the present *régime*, many Vaidyas have distinguished themselves outside their own proper sphere. The late Babu Ram Kamal Sen, who was the friend and *collaborateur* of Professor H. H. Wilson, held with great credit the post of the Dewan or Treasurer of the Bank of Bengal. His son,

Hari Mohan Sen, not only held that post after his father's death, but subsequently became the Prime Minister of the Jaipur Raj. Babu Hari Mohan's son is the well-known publicist and patriot, Norendra Nath Sen, the proprietor and editor of the *Indian Mirror*.

The most gifted and the best known among the descendants of Ram Kamal Sen was the late Babu Keshav Chandra Sen. Whatever difference of opinion there many be as to his claaims to be regarded as a religious reformer or as to his capacity as a thinker, there cannot be the least doubt that India has not given birth to a more gifted orator. Wherever he spoke, and whether in English or in Bengali, he simply charmed the audience, and kept them spell-bound as it were. In the beginning of his career, he rendered a great service to the cause of Hinduism by counteracting the influence of the late Dr. Duff, and the army of native missionaries trained up by him. Babu Keshav Chandra was then the idol of the people, as he was the *bête noire* of the Christian propagandists. He was, however, too practical a man not to value the friendship of the ruling caste, and when Lord Lawrence, who was a man of prayer, became the Viceroy of India, he developed predilections *for* Christianity which found expression in his splendid oration on "*Jesus Christ, Europe and Asia.*" By this move, he softened the bitterness of the missionaries, and at the same time secured the friendship of the Saviour of the Punjab. Thenceforward his leaning towards Christianity increased, until it was actually apprehended that he was in fact a follower of Christ. Lord Lawrence left India in 1868, and in the next year Keshav Chandra visited England. He there professed such doctrines that he was allowed to preach from the pulpits of many Dissenting churches. The influence of Lord Lawrence, and his splendid oratorical powers, introduced him into the highest society. Her Gracious Majesty herself granted him the honour of an interview. Before his departure a farewell meeting was convened at the

Hanover Square Rooms, at which no less than eleven denominations of Christians were represented. While in England he spoke at upwards of seventy different public meetings to upwards of forty thousand people, and created the impression that his religion was only a form of Christianity. This attitude he maintained with consistency till 1879, the year of Lord Lawrence's death. On the 9th of April in that year he spoke about Christ as follows in the course of an oration delivered at the Town Hall:—

> Gentlemen, you cannot deny that your hearts have been touched, conquered and subjugated by a superior power. That power, need I tell you? is Christ. It is Christ who rules British India, and not the British Government. England has sent out a tremendous moral force in the life and character of that mighty prophet to conquer and hold this vast empire. None but Jesus, none but Jesus, none but Jesus, ever deserved this bright, this precious diadem—India, and Jesus shall have it.

At this time the political situation of Keshav was apparently very embarrassing. On the one hand, so long as Lord Lawrence was living, he could not, without gross inconsistency and forfeiture of the esteem of the ex-Viceroy, betray any leaning towards the religion of his forefathers. On the other hand, he had in the previous year married his daughter to the Maharaja of Kooch Behar, and, as by doing so and countenancing the celebration of the wedding in the Hindu form, he had exposed himself to the charge of inconsistency and ambitiousness for secular aggrandisement, he could not but feel inclined to profess a liking for those forms. From the point of view of one who did not believe in caste, and desired nothing more than to destroy it altogether, the marriage could be held to be objectionable on the only ground that the parties had not arrived at the marriageable age, according to the standard fixed by Keshav himself. But if the parties themselves desired the marriage, as they certainly did, Keshav could not, consistently with his principles, throw any obstacle in their way. Nor could he object to the form of the marriage which was also a matter entirely between the bridegroom and the bride. But popular voice, in awarding its praise or blame to public men, is seldom very reasonable. The pro-Christian doctrines which Keshav had been professing from the year 1866, and the church-like form of his prayer-house, had made him very unpopular among his countrymen. So the Kooch Behar marriage not only provoked open comments of a very strong character, but actually led to the secession of the majority of his followers. Keshav might perhaps have prevented the split by the line of defence, which, as stated above, was clearly open to him. But he made things worse by declaring that what he had done was in accordance with the order of God, communicated to him in some mysterious way. He said :—

"Men have attempted to prove that I have been guided by my own imagination, reason and intellect. Under this conviction they have from time to time protested against my proceedings. They should remember that to protest against the cause I uphold is to protest against the dispensations of God Almighty, the God of all Truth and Holiness.

"In doing this work I am confident I have not done anything that is wrong. I have ever tried to do the Lord's will, not mine. Surely I am not to blame for anything which I may have done under Heaven's injunction. Dare you impeach Heaven's Majesty? Would you have me reject God and Providence, and listen to your dictates in preference to his inspiration? Keshav Chandra Sen cannot do it, will not do it."

Such defence as is contained in the above might serve its purpose in the case of the leader of a set of uneducated rustics. But in the case of Keshav Chandra, who had some of the most cultured men of the metropolis of British India among his followers, it served only to shake their confidence in him all the more. The party that he had organised by years of hard work melted away in the course of a few days. He could hope to organise another party only by the more or less complete adoption of one of the faiths of his ancestors. But so long as Lord Lawrence was living that was impossible. And even so late as April 1879, he spoke as a devout Christian in public, as would appear from the passages cited at p. 165, *ante*. Lord Lawrence died in 1879, and the very next year Keshav gave the following certificate of good character to the Hindu religion :—

"Hindu idolatry is not to be altogether overlooked or rejected. As we explained some time ago, it represents millions of broken fragments of God, collect them together and you get the individual Divinity. To believe in an undivided deity without reference to those aspects of his nature is to believe in an abstract God, and it would lead us to practical rationalism and infidelity. If we are to worship Him in all His manifestation we shall name one attribute—Sarswatee, another Lakshmi, another Mahadeva, another Jagadhatri, &c., and worship God each day under a new name, that is to say, in a new aspect."—*Sunday Mirror*, 1880.

This is clearly inculcating idolatry to its fullest extent, though the author of it is careful enough not to enjoin expressly the worship of Siva's Linga, Kali's obscenities, or Krishna's battalions of sweethearts. The passage cited above appeared in a newspaper, and was apparently meant only to prepare men's mind for the *coup détat* that followed in 1881 under the name of New Dispensation. Ever since the Kooch Behar marriage, which certainly required something like a Papal Dispensation under which an unlawful marriage might take place among the Roman Catholics, the word "dispensation" had evidently taken a firm hold on Keshav's mind. At least, that is the only explanation which can be suggested of the name which he gave to his new cult. Its manifesto was in form addressed to all the great nations of the world, the chief burden of the document being an exhortation that they should learn to practise toleration. Taking into consideration, however, the events that immediately preceded it in the life of the author, there cannot be any doubt that it was meant only to cover his retreat to the fold of Hinduism, or rather to a position where he could organise a new party, without much inconsistency, and without losing the wrecks of his former party. My review of Keshav's life has already been carried to a far greater length than what may be deemed proper in this book. I cannot carry the notice further. But what I have said will, I hope, suffice to form a just estimate of his character and powers. His capacity or solicitude to achieve any real good for mankind may be doubted; but there can be no question as to his power to dazzle them in a manner which is rare indeed, and the Vaidya community to which he belonged might certainly be proud of him.

Although the profession of the Vaidayas enables them to acquire both money and power in a fair and noble way, yet the Brahmanical ambition of playing the *rôle* of a prophet is rather too common among them, and Keshav Chandra's case is not the only instance of such craving. Babu Pratap Chandra Majumdar, who was his colleague in his lifetime, and who is, or at least ought to be, regarded as his spiritual successor, is also a Vaidya, and possesses very nearly the same gifts as his late chief. Narhari Thākoor, who was one of the leading disciples of Chaitanya, and whose descendants are, as a result of that connection, now able to live like princes at Srikhand near Katwa, was also a Vaidya. So is also the living prophet "Kumar" Krishna Prasanna Sen, who, by his advocacy of Hinduism and his charming eloquence, has made himself almost an object of regular worship among certain classes of Hindus throughout the greater part of the Hindi-speaking districts between Bhagulpur and Allahabad. His want of sufficient command over the English language has prevented him from attracting much of the notice of the Englishmen residing in this country; but the influence which he has acquired among the half-educated classes in Behar and Upper India is very great. The higher classes, and especially the Brahmans, are somewhat prepossessed against him on account of his caste, and the usual shallow philosophy of a stumper. The parade which he makes of the fact of his being unmarried, by the use of the designation of "Kumar" serves to make him sometimes an object of ridicule.

Though the Vaidya population of the country is, as already stated, very small compared with the other leading castes, yet persons belonging to the medical clan are to be found in high positions in almost all the departments that can attract the intellectual classes. Among high officials, the names of Messrs. B. L. Gupta and K. G. Gupta of the Bengal Civil Service stand conspicuous. In the legal profession, the late Babus Mahesh Chandra Chowdry and Kali Mohan Das, who were among the ablest advocates of the Bengal High Court in their time, were Vaidyas by caste. So was also the late Babu Mritunjoy Roy, who was the leading pleader of the District Court of Nadiya. Among the living Vaidya vakils of the Bengal High Court, the names best known are those of Doorga Mohan Das, Girija Sankar Majumdar and Akhil Chandra Sen. Babu Girija Sankar is a zemindar also. Babu Akhil is a Vaidya of Chittagong. Among District Court practitioners the most conspicuous Vaidyas are Guru Prosad Sen, Ambika Chandra Majumdar and Baikant Nath Barat. Babu Guru Prosad practises in the District Court of Patna, Babu Ambika Chandra at Faridpore, and Babu Baikant Nath at Moorshedabad. The latter not only enjoys great professional eminence, but is the friend, philosopher and guide of the local zemindars.

In connection with the Press of Bengal, the name of Babu Narendra Nath Sen, Editor of the daily called the *Indian Mirror*, has been mentioned already. The weekly paper called *Hope* is also edited by a Vaidya named Amrita Lal Roy, who passed many years of his life in Europe and America, and served his apprenticeship in the art of journalism in connection with one of the leading newspapers of New York.

The Vaidyas are very clannish, and, wherever a Vaidya manages to get into a high office, he is sure to introduce as many of his castemen as he can into the department. Babu Ram Kamal Sen, who, as mentioned already, was the Dewan of the Bank of Bengal, introduced at one time a very large number of his clansmen there. The East Indian Railway office at Jamalpore is perhaps still similarly full of Vaidyas, introduced through the influence of its late head clerk, Babu Madhu Sudan Roy, the father of Babu Amrita Lal Roy, of the *Hope*.

The Vaidyas are a fast money-making, and a fast money-spending, class. Even the poorest among them are usually quite above want, while a great many of them are in very easy circumstances, either by the practice of their profession, or by their success in other lines of business. But a Vaidya has very seldom a long purse. He spends whatever he earns in feeding his relatives and his pupils. The descendants of Raj Ballava were at one time big landholders. But they have been ruined, and the only Vaidya zemindars to be now found in the country are those of Teota, Bani Bau, Rajbari, Meherpore, and Agradwipa. Among the traders and shopkeepers there is perhaps not a single man of the Vaidya caste.

CHAP. II.—THE BEZ OF ASSAM.

THE word Bez seems to be an Assamese corruption of the Sanskrit word "Vaidya." At any rate, the Bez caste of Assam have the same position and the same functions as the Vaidyas have in Bengal. Like the Vaidyas, the Bez are an aristocratic and cultured class. Some of the Bez practise Hindu medicine in their native country, while a great many of them are now receiving English education, and adopting one or other of the different professions which are open to the higher classes of Hindus under the present *régime*. The late Mr. Andi Ram Barua, of the Bengal Civil Service, was a Bez. So is also Dr. Golap Chandra Bez Barua, who holds at present the charge of a public hospital in British Guiana in South America.

The Bez wear the sacred thread.

CHAP III.—THE ASTROLOGER CASTES OF BENGAL AND ASSAM.

In Bengal, the astrologers form a separate caste which has a very low position. In Assam and Orissa the Ganakas and Nakshatra Brahmans, as they are called, are regarded as an inferior section of the sacerdotal caste, and not as an unclean non-Brahmanic caste as in Bengal. In other parts of India astrology is practised by the Joshis who are regarded as good Brahmans. The astrologer castes of Bengal are variously called Acharya Brahmans, Graha Bipras, Daivagnas, Grahacharyas, and Ganakas. In all probability they were Brahmans at one time, but have been degraded to a very low position by the policy of the superior Brahmans. According to a text cited as authoritative by the Pandits of Bengal, the astrologers are shoemakers by caste, and good Brahmans sometimes refuse to take even a drink of water from their hands. But, with an inconsistency which is quite unaccountable, the most orthodox Brahmans accept their gifts without the least hesitation, and one of the greatest Pandits of Nadiya enlisted the Acharyas of the place among his disciples—the connection thus formed being still in existence between their descendants.

The numerical strength of the Acharyas is very small. In the last Census, they were, it seems, included among the Jotishis or Joshis, and the total number of the Joshis in each province is given as follows :—

1.	N.-W. Provinces	...	35,266
2.	Bengal ...	...	18,360
3.	Bombay ...	...	10,147
4.	Central India	...	12,204

Very few of the Acharya caste of Bengal have yet been able to distinguish themselves, either by Western learning or by service under the British Government of India.

Ganaks of Assam.—The Ganaks of Assam have a somewhat higher position in their province than the Acharyas have in Bengal. The usual surnames of the Ganaks are Dalai and Bara Dalai and their total number 23,739. Compared with the total population of the province, their numerical strength is not very inconsiderable.

PART IX.

THE WRITER CASTES.

CHAP. I.—THE KAYASTHAS.

THE Kāyasthas are found in almost every part of India. They are a very large body ; the last Census gives the following figures regarding their numerical strength :—

Bengal ...	1,466,748
Assam ...	92,395
N.-W. Provinces	521,812
Central India	74,471
Rajputana	26,913
Total	2,239,810

The Kāyasthas are described in some of the sacred books of the Hindus as Ksatriyas ; but the majority of the Kāyastha clans do not wear the sacred thread, and admit their status as Sudras, also by the observance of mourning for a period of thirty days. But, whether Ksatriyas or Sudras, they belong to the upper layer of Hindu society, and though the higher classes of Brahmans neither perform their religious ceremonies nor enlist them among their disciples, yet the gifts of the Kāyasthas are usually accepted by the great Pandits of the country without any hesitation.

The literal meaning of the word "Kāyastha" is 'standing on the body'. According to the Purāns, the Kāyasthas are so-called, because being Ksatriyas, they must be regarded as having their origin in the arms of the great god Brahma. The real derivation of the word is, perhaps, to be traced to the idea that the Brahmans must be regarded as the head ornaments of the king, and the Kāyasthas as ornaments for the arms. However that may be, the Kāyasths have, from a very remote period of antiquity, been recognized as the class whose proper avocation is to serve as clerks and accountants.* The Brahmans excluded them from the study of the Sanskrit language and literature. But they learned the three R's with great care, and, during the period of Moslem rule, mastered the Persian language with such assiduity as to make it almost their mother-tongue. At the present time, the honours and distinctions conferred by the Indian Universities are as eagerly and as successfully sought by them as by the Brahmans and the Vaidyas. As authors, journalists and public speakers they do not now lag behind any other caste, and, in fact, in some of the departments of English scholarship they almost surpass the Brahmans themselves. In the field of journalism, India has not yet had better men than the two Mukerjis—Harish Chandra and Sambhu Chandra. But among public speakers the first to distinguish himself by his orations in English was the late Kāyastha Babu Ram Gopal Ghose, while amongst the living batch of orators, the field is equally divided between Kāyasthas and Brahmans. The case is the same in the legal profession. Of the two best native Advocates of the Bengal High Court one is a Brahman, and the other is a Kāyastha ; while of the eight Hindu Judges appointed to the Bench of the High Court of Bengal, since its creation, exactly half the number have been Kāyasthas.

During the time of the Hindu kings, the Brahmans refrained from entering the public service, and the

* See *Yajnavalkaya*, I, 335. From the manner in which the word Kāyastha is used in the ancient Sanskrit works, it seems that originally it meant a secretary, clerk or scribe.

Kāyasthas had almost the monopoly of the subordinate appointments. Even under the Mahomedan kings, some of them attained very high positions, as, for instance, the Bangadhikaris, who had charge of the revenue department under the Nababs of Moorshedabad, and Rai Durlav Ram,* the Prime Minister of Ali Verdi Khan. Rajas Shitab Roy and Ram Narayan, who were Governors of Behar, in the period of double government or interregnum which intervened between the battle of Plassey and the removal of the Exchequer to Calcutta, were also Kāyasthas. Under British rule the Kāyastha element has been predominating in all the departments of the public service. In the United Provinces, Bengal and Behar, the number of Kāyastha officials exceeds perhaps those of all the other castes taken together. The Kāyasthas are said to be the writer caste. But their experience of the ways of transacting public business has qualified them for the very highest offices connected with the civil government of the country. They generally prove equal to any position in which they are placed. They have been successful not only as clerks, but in the very highest executive and judicial offices that have yet been thrown open to the natives of this country. The names of the Kāyastha Judges, Dwarka Nath Mitra, Ramesh Chandra Mitra and Chandra Madhava Ghosh, are well known and respected by all. In the Executive service the Kāyasthas have attained the same kind of success. One of them, Mr. R. C. Dutt, is now the Commissioner or chief Executive Officer of one of the most important divisions of Bengal. Another named Kalika Das Datta has been for several years employed as Prime Minister of the Kooch Behar Raj, giving signal proofs of his ability as an administrator by the success with which he has been managing the affairs of the principality in his charge.

* Babu Gopal Lal Mitra, the able Vice-Chairman of the Calcutta Municipal Corporation, is, on his mother's side, descended from Rai Durlav.

CHAP. II.—THE KAYASTHAS OF BENGAL.

THE Kāyasthas of Bengal are divided into the following classes :—

1. Dākshina Rarhi.
2. Uttara Rarhi.
3. Bangaja.
4. Bārendra.
5. Sylheti.
6. Golam or slave Kāyasthas.

For all practical purposes these are separate castes, and intermarriage between them is, generally speaking, quite impossible.

§ 1.—*The Dākshina Rarhis of Bengal.*

The Dākshina Rarhis, or the Kāyasthas of the southern part of Burdwan, affect the greatest veneration for the Brahmans, and profess to believe in the legend that traces their descent from the five menial servants that are said to have accompanied the five Brahmans invited by King Adisur.* The Dākshina Rarhis are divided into three main groups, namely :—

1. Kulin.
2. Maulik.
3. The seventy-two houses.

The Kulins have the highest status, and they again are subdivided into several hypergamous sections that have different positions for matrimonial purposes. The

* See page 37, *ante*.

usual surnames of the several sections of the Dākshina Rarhi Kāyasthas are as stated below :—

1. Surnames of the Kulins among the Dākshina Rarhi Kāyasthas.	1. Ghose. 2. Basu. 3. Mittra.
2. Surnames of the Maulikas or middle class Dākshina Rarhis.	1. Dey. 2. Datta. 3. Kar. 4. Palit. 5. Sen. 6. Sinha. 7. Das. 8. Guha.
3. Surnames of the important classes among the seventy-two families of the Dākshina Rarhis.	1. Nag. 2. Som. 3. Rudra. 4. Aditya. 5. Aich. 6. Raha. 7. Bhanja. 8. Horh. 9. Bramha. 10. Nandi. 11. Rakshit. 12. Chandra. 13. Bardhan. 14. Bhadra. 15. Dhar. 16. Jas. 17. Sāin. 18. Rahut. 19. Manna.

The rules which regulate and determine the elegibility of a Kāyastha boy or girl for matrimonial purposes, are quite as complicated as those of the Rarhi Brahmans. But while the status of a Kulin Rarhi Brahman depends on his being able to marry his daughters with Kulin bridegrooms, the position of a Dākshina Rarhi Kāyastha remains intact only if he is able to marry his eldest son into the family of a Kulin of similar rank. A Kāyastha can give his daughter to any one whether he is a Kulin or a Maulika.

Among the Babus of Calcutta, the number of Dākshina Rarhi Kāyasthas is far larger than that of any other caste. The majority of the Dākshina Rarhis are Sakti worshippers of a moderate type. The deities they worship most generally are Durgā and Kāli. But their orthodox members follow the discipline imposed upon them by their Brahman Gurus, and they neither drink any kind of spirituous liquor, nor eat any kind of flesh excepting that of goats offered in sacrifice to some god or goddess. Of all the classes of Kāyasthas in Bengal, the Dākshina Rarhis have, under British rule, made the greatest progress in education, and in securing official positions.

§ 2.—*The Uttara Rarhi Kāyasthas.*

The caste position of the Uttara Rarhis, or the Kāyasthas of the northern portion of the Burdwan Division, is the same as that of the Dākshina Rarhis. But the northerners do not profess the same veneration for the Brahmans as the southerners. The former openly deny the authenticity of the legend which traces the descent of the Bengali Kāyasthas from the five menial servants of the five Brahmans brought by King Adisur from Kanouj in the ninth century of the era of Christ. An Uttara Rarhi very seldom falls prostrate at the feet of a Brahman, and usually salutes the priestly caste by a curt *pranam*, which does not imply much reverence.

The Uttara Rarhis are most numerous in the district called Birbhoom, and in the adjoining portions of the Moorshedabad District. Some families of the same clan are to be found also in the towns of Patna, Bhagalpur, Dinajpur and Jessore. Many of the leading zemindars of Bengal, as, for instance, the Rajas of Dinajpur, Paikpara and Jessore are Uttara Rarhis. There was formerly an Uttara Rarhi family of zemindars in the district of Malda who, for several generations, were in possession of the barony of Bhatia Gopalpore, including a portion of the city of Gour. No member of the community has risen very high in the service of Government in recent times. But under the Mahomedan rulers of Bengal, the Uttara Rarhis held some of the highest offices. The charge of the revenue department was then almost entirely in the hands of the Bangadhicary Mahasaya family of Dahpara near Moorshedabad; and so great was their influence that when Hastings removed the Khalsa or Exchequer to Calcutta, he was obliged to place it in the hands of one of their clansmen, who was also one of their quondam clerks. This man, whose name was Ganga Govind Sing, became, by virtue of his office, the arbiter of the destinies of the Bengal zemindars, and by taking advantage of his opportunities made himself one of the richest landlords in the country. His master was perhaps too shrewd to negociate directly with the zemindars, like Sir Thomas Rumbold of Madras. He required an intermediary, and as Ganga Govinda was his chief fiscal officer, he was deemed the best man for the office. Perhaps he acquired a great hold over Hastings by helping him in the prosecution and conviction of Nand Kumār. Whatever was the cause of the undue favour shown to him by his master, his power was great. Though serving under the immediate supervision of one of the greatest satraps that England has ever sent out to India, his confidence in the strength of his own position was such that he compelled the zemindars, whose revenue he had to assess, to give him not only money which could be easily concealed, but also substantial slices of their estates which conclusively proved his corrupt practices. The Raja of Dinajpur, who was his casteman, was, out of jealousy, absolutely ruined by him. The proud Brahman Raja Krishna Chandra of Nadiya was reduced by him to such straits as to be obliged to beg for his favour in the most humiliating terms;* and at a later time Raja Krishna Chandra's heir, Raja Sib Chandra, was compelled to be present at the funeral ceremony of Ganga Govind's mother. When Hastings was hauled up before the

* The original of this letter or rather memorandum is given in Dewan Kartika Chandra Roy's history of the Nadiya Rajas. The following is a translation of it:—

"My son is disobedient, the Exchequer Court is impracticable, I depend upon Ganga Govind."

British Parliament to answer the charges of maladministration and corruption that were brought against him, Ganga Govinda, as his right-hand man, naturally came in for a large share of the vituperative phrases that the genius of Burke could invent. The great orator characterized him as the "captain-general of iniquity" "and the broker-in-chief of bribery." Nothing, however, was ever done to compel him to disgorge the properties he had acquired, and they are still in the possession of his descendants by adoption, now called the Paikpara Rajas.*

Since Ganga Govinda's time no Uttara Rarhi has attained a high position in the service of Government. The highest officials in their class are at present not above the rank of Subordinate Magistrates. In the legal profession also the Uttara Rarhis are as meagrely represented as in the various departments of the public service. The only members of the clan who have any considerable amount of legal practice are Babu Surja Narain Sing, of the District court of Bhagalpur, Babu Purnendu Narain, of the District court of Patna, and Mr. S. P. Sinha, who is a barrister-at-law, and practises in the High Court of Calcutta.

Among the Uttara Rarhis Kulinism, or high caste status, is the result of having been originally residents of some particular villages in the Kandi Sub-division of the Moorshedabad District. The names of these villages are Rasorah, Panchthupi, Jajan, &c. An Uttara Rarhi Ghosh or Sinha is not necessarily a Kulin. It is only a Ghosh of Rasorah or Panchthupi that can claim a high position in the caste.

---

* The original home of Ganga Govinda was the town of Kandi, now the head-quarters of a sub-division in the district of Moorshedabad. When he became the Dewan of Hastings, he built, for his residence, a palatial mansion in Calcutta, on the site now occupied by the warehouses on the southern side of Beadon Square. His descendants used formerly to be called the Rajas of Kandi. But as they now usually reside at Paikpara, in the suburbs of Calcutta, they are also called Rajas of Paikpara.

The usual surnames of the Uttara Rarhis are as stated below:—

1. Surnames of the Kulins	1. Ghosh. 2. Sinha.
2. Surnames of the second class called Sanmoulik.	1. Das. 2. Datta. 3. Mittra.
3. Surnames of the third class called *Ekpoua* or one-fourth house.	1. Das. 2. Ghosh. 3. Kar. 4. Sinha.

§ 3.—*The Bangaja Kāyasthas.*

The importance of this clan is not less than that of any other class of Bengali Kāyasthas. The great Pratapaditya, whose father had been the prime minister of the last Patan King of Bengal, and who at the time of the conquest of the province by the Moguls carved out an independent kingdom in its seaboard, was a Bangaja. For a time Pratapaditya defied the great Akbar, and the conquest of his kingdom was ultimately effected by Raja Man Sing, chiefly through the treachery of Bhava Nand Majumdār, who had been in the service of Pratapaditya as a pet Brahman boy, and who subsequently became the founder of the Nadiya Raj family through the favour of the imperial general whom he had helped. The descendants of Pratapaditya are still to be found in the neighbourhood of his ruined capital in the Sundarbans. Though shorn of their greatness, they are to this day locally called Rajas, and possess very considerable influence among their castemen. The zemindars of Taki, who still possess some property, are the descendants of Pratapaditya's uncle, Basanta Roy. The ancient Rajas of Bakla, which covered nearly the whole of the modern district of Bākergunge, were also Bangajas. So, too, were the ancient zemindars of Noakhali and Edilpore. Perganah Edilpore in Fureedpore is now in the possession of Babu Kali Krishna Tagore of Calcutta.

The Bangajas are to be found chiefly in the eastern districts of Bengal. In Calcutta they are not numerically strong; but are represented by such leading men as Mr. Justice Chandra Madhava Ghosh, who is now one of the Judges of the Bengal High Court, and Mr. M. Ghosh, who is now one of its leading Advocates.

The usual surnames of the Bangaja Kāyasthas of the different grades are as mentioned below :—

Surnames of the highest class of Bangaja Kāyasthas.	1. Basu. 2. Ghosh. 3. Guha. 4. Mittra.
Surnames of the second class of Bangaja Kāyasthas.	1. Datta. 2. Nag. 3. Nath.
Surnames of the third class of Bangaja Kāyasthas.	1. Adhya. 2. Aukur. 3. Bhadra. 4. Bishnu. 5. Chandra. 6. Das. 7. Deb. 8. Dhar. 9. Kar. 10. Kundu. 11. Nanda. 12. Nandi. 13. Pal. 14. Palit. 15. Raha. 16. Rakshit. 17. Sen. 18. Sinha. 19. Som.

§ 4.—*The Bārendra Kāyasthas.*

The Bārendra Kāyasthas do not differ from the other classes of Bengali Kāyasthas either in culture or in respect of caste status. The usual surnames of the several grades of Bārendras are as stated below :—

First class	1. Chaki. 2. Das. 3. Nandi.
Second class	1. Datta. 2. Deb. 3. Nag. 4. Sinha.
Third class	1. Dam. 2. Dhar. 3. Gun. 4. Kar.

§ 5.—*The Golam Kāyasthas of East Bengal.*

There are many Kāyasthas in East Bengal who are called Golams or slaves. Some of them are still attached as domestic servants to the families of the local Brahmans, Vaidyas, and aristocratic Kāyasthas. Even those who have been completely emancipated, and are in the position of well-to-do and independent citizens, are obliged by local custom to render on ceremonial occasions certain menial services for the glorification of their ancient patrons and masters. Some of the Golams have in recent times become rich landholders, and it is said that one of them has got the title of Rai Bahadoor from Government. The marriage of a Golam generally takes place in his own class ; but instances of Golams marrying into aristocratic Kāyastha families are at present not very rare. The Golams are treated by all the high caste Hindus as a clean caste. The Brahmans who minister to the ordinary Kāyasthas as priests, evince no hesitation to perform similar rites for the Golams. The Golams of the Vaidyas serve also the Brahmans and the Kāyasthas ; but the Golams of the Brahmans and the Kāyasthas do not serve the Vaidyas.

CHAP. III.—THE LALA KAYASTHAS OF NORTH-WESTERN PROVINCES, BEHAR AND OUDH.

THE Lala Kāyasthas have the same position in Behar, N.-W. Provinces and Oudh that the several classes of Kāyasthas, spoken of in the last chapter, have in Bengal. The Lalas are, however, very much addicted to drinking and gambling, and in these respects they differ very materially from the Bengali Kāyasthas who, as moderate Saktas or bigoted Vishnuvites, are mostly teetotalers. The Kāyasthas of Hindustan proper are divided into the following classes :—

1. **Srivastas.**	7. **Mathuri.**
2. **Karana.**	8. **Surya Dhaja.**
3. **Ambasta.**	9. **Balmiki.**
4. **Sakya Seni.**	10. **Astama.**
5. **Kula Sreshti.**	11. **Nigama.**
6. **Bhatnagari.**	12. **Gour.**

13. **Unai.**

Members of these different clans may eat together and smoke from the same pipe. But intermarriage between them is impossible, and they must be regarded as separate castes having only a similar status. The usual surnames of the Lala Kāyasthas are : Das, Lal, Rai, Sahaya and Sing.

§ 1.—*The Srivasta Kāyasthas.*

The Srivastis derive their name from the ancient city of Srivasta, which was the capital of the kingdom of Uttara Koshala, and which has been identified with a place called at present Sahet Mahet * in the district of Gonda. The Srivasta Kāyasthas are a very numerous body, and are to be found in every part of the United Provinces, Behar and Oudh. Some of the Srivastis take the sacred thread, and some do not. Those who take the thread are teetotalers and vegetarians. The rest indulge in flesh meat and strong drink. It is said that the Srivastis are all of the Kasyapa Gotra. But if they are Sudras then they do not violate any rule of the Shastras by marrying within their Gotra as they are necessarily obliged to do. There are, however, some other peculiarities in the marriage customs of the Srivastis which cannot but be held to be inconsistent with the law of the Hindu Shastras on the subject. For instance, it is said that, as among some of the Rajputs and Kalwars, so among the Srivasta Kāyasthas, a marriage may take place between a boy and a girl even where the bride is older in age. The following surnames are assumed by some of the Srivastis :—

1. Akhori (literally "a man of letters").
2. Amodha.
3. Qanongo (a lawyer).
4. Muhtavi.
5. Bhowri.

Among the Kāyasthas of Upper India, the caste status of a family depends usually upon the official position held by their ancestors in the service of the former rulers of the country. The descendants of the Patwaris or village accountants have generally the lowest position. The four leading Srivasti families of Behar are the following :—

1. The family of the Rajas of Tillothu in the District of Arrah.
2. The family of Raja Rajesri Prosad of Surajpore in Arrah.
3. The family of the Rajas of Sedisapore near Dinapore.
4. The family of the Sudder Kanaregos of Bakhra† in the District of Mozufferpore.

---

* For a full account of the ruins of Sahet Mahet, and the grounds on which they are held to be the remains of the ancient city of Srivasta, see Hunter's *Imperial Gazetteer*, Vol. XII, p. 126.

† Bakhra is in the vicinity of the site of the ancient free city of Vaisah, of Buddhistic history.

The ancestors of these families held very high offices in the service of the Mogal Emperors, and also under the East India Company, in the early days of its political supremacy. The Sedisapore family rendered very important services to the British Government at the time of the Sepoy Mutiny. The four families mentioned above still possess considerable local influence, and among their castemen their supremacy is undisputed. The Srivasta zemindars of Sahebganj in the District of Chapra have also considerable influence among their castemen. The late Hon'ble Har Bans Sahoy of Arrah was a Srivasti. So also is Raj Jai Prokash Lal, the present factotum of the Raja of Domraon.

§ 2.—*The Ambastha Kāyasthas.*

Manu gives the name Ambasth to the progeny of a Brahman father and Vaishya mother, and lays down that their proper profession is the practice of medicine.* But there is a class of Kāyasthas in Behar, and in the eastern districts of the N.-W. Provinces, who alone use that name to designate their caste. Its derivation is not definitely known. It is quite possible that it is derived from the name of a Perganah in Oudh called Ameth. The Ambastha Kāyasthas are very numerous and influential in South Behar including the districts of Monghyr, Patna and Gaya. Raja Ram Narayan, who was Governor of Behar, in the early days of British ascendancy, was an Ambasthi. He has no lineal descendants, but his family is represented by some collaterals, of whom Babu Isri Prasad of Patna is one.

§ 3.—*The Karan Kāyasthas.*

The Karan clan of North Indian Kāyasthas are to be found chiefly in Tirhoot or North Behar where they are usually employed as Patwaris or village accountants.

* Manu, X, 8, 43.

Their position is inferior to that of the Srivastas and Ambastas. The Uttara Rarhi Kāyasthas of Bengal claim to be Karans. The Karans of Orissa have no connection with those of North Behar.

§ 4.—*The Sakya Seni Kāyasthas.*

The Sakya Seni Kāyasthas are very numerous in the District of Etawa in the Doab, and are to be found in every part of the Gangetic valley from Hardwar to Patna. Many of the wealthiest landholders of Etawa, Eta and Fatehpore are Sakya Senis. Like the Srivastas they are divided into three classes, namely, Ail, Dusri and Khore. These do not intermarry, and must be regarded as separate castes. The Sakya Senis have a lower social position than the Srivastas.

Raja Shitab Roy, who was Governor of Behar in the days of what is called the "double Government," was a Sakya Seni. The following account regarding him is to be found in Macaulay's review of the administration of Warren Hastings :—

A chief named Shitab Roy had been intrusted with the government of Behar. His valour and his attachment to the English had more than once been signally proved. On that memorable day on which the people of Patna saw from their walls the whole army of the Mogul scattered by the little band of Captain Knox, the voice of the British conquerors assigned the palm of gallantry to the brave Asiatic. "I never," said Knox, when he introduced Shitab Roy, covered with blood and dust, to the English functionaries assembled in the factory, "I never saw a native fight so before." Shitab Roy was involved in the ruin of Mahomed Reza Khan, was removed from office, and was placed under arrest.

"The revolution completed, the double Government dissolved, the Company installed in the full sovereignty of Bengal, Hastings had no motive to treat the late ministers with rigor. Their trial had been put off on various pleas till the new organization was complete. They were then brought before a committee over which the Governor presided. Shitab Roy was speedily acquitted with honour. A formal apology was made to him for the restraint to which he had been subjected. All the eastern marks of respect were bestowed on him. He was clothed in a robe of state, presented with jewels and with a richly harnessed elephant, and sent back to his Government at Patna. But his health had suffered from confinement; his spirit had been cruelly wounded; and soon after his liberation he died of a broken heart."

The late Raja Bhoop Sen Sing of Patna was the daughter's son of Shitab Roy's son, Kalyan Sing. Bhoop Sen left two sons named Mahipat and Roop Narain. The line of Maharaja Mahipat is now represented by his widowed daughter-in-law, Maharani Tikam Kumari. Kumar Roop Narain is still living, but is a lunatic. The family have their residence in the quarter of Patna called the Dewan Mahallah.

§ 5.—*The Kula Sreshti Kāyasthas.*

The Kula Sreshti Kāyasthas are found chiefly in the districts of Agra and Eta.

§ 6.—*The Bhatnagari.*

The Bhatnagar Kāyasthas derive their name from the town of Bhatnagar or Bhatner in the Hanumangar District on the north of Bikaneer. "They are found in great numbers in almost all the districts inhabited by the Gaur Brahmans, from Sambhal and Moradabad to Agroha and Ajmere. They are also scattered over some of the Eastern provinces. The Bhatnagaris are not considered very pure Hindus, and are more addicted to drinking than other Kāyasthas. But their official position in some places has enabled them to acquire considerable influence. They are the Kanangos of Gwalior and Mahaban in Mathura. The Gaur Bhatnagars are Kanangos of Mariyahu in Jounpore, of Chapra and Monghyr.*

§ 7.—*The Mathuri Kāyasthas.*

The Mathuri Kāyasthas are, as their name indicates, inhabitants of the country round the ancient city of Mathura.

§ 8.—*The Suryadhaja Kāyasthas.*

The Suryadhaja Kāyasthas are to be found in the Districts of Balia and Gazipur. In the Bijnour District the Suryadhajas claim to be Brahmans.

---

* Elliot's *Supplemental Glossary*, p. 86.

§ 9.—*The Balmiki Kāyasthas.*

The Balmiki Kāyasthas are to be found in Gujrat. The late Mr. Justice Nana Bhai Haridas, of the Bombay High Court, was a Balmiki Kāyastha.

§ 10.—*The Ashthana Kāyasthas.*

The Ashthana Kāyasthas are to be found in Agra, Balia and Gazipur.

§ 11.—*The Nigama Kāyasthas.*

The Kāyasthas of Unao claim to be Nigama Kāyasthas.

§ 12.—*The Gaur Kāyasthas.*

Like the Gaur Brahmans, the Gaur Kāyasthas appear to have been originally inhabitants of the tract of country now included in the Delhi Division of the Punjab. The Gaur Kāyasthas are to be found in almost all the Districts lying between Delhi and Patna. The Gaur Kāyasthas of Azimgad are chiefly Sikhs. The Bhatnagaris seem to be a section of the Gaurs.

§ 13.—*The Kāyasthas of Unao.*

The Kāyasthas of Unao are a very important community. They claim to be of the Nigama class. There are many eminent lawyers and high officials among them.

CHAP. IV.—THE WRITER CASTES OF SOUTHERN INDIA.

In the Andhra country, including the north-eastern districts of the Madras Presidency, the work of writers and accountants is done chiefly by the Niyogi Brahmans. The Karnams of the province, whose caste status is similar to that of the Kāyasthas of Northern India, are also employed in similar capacities. The Karnams are, however, a small community, and as very few of them have attained high positions in Government service or in the liberal professions, they cannot be said to be equal to the Kāyasthas of Bengal, either socially or intellectually. The Karnams take the sacred thread, but are regarded by all as Sudras.

In Mysore and in the British districts towards its south and east, the classes that are usually held to be entitled to the designation of writer castes, are the Kanakkans and the Shanbhogs. Intellectually and socially these are more like the Karnams, than like the Kāyasths of Northern India.

In the Dravira country, the Vellalars and some of the Vadugas claim to be Kāyasthas, and though they are generally described as agricultural castes, they seem to have, in many respects, the same position as the writer castes of Northern India. The Vellalars are divided into two classes, the usual surname of one of which is Mudaliar, and that of the other Pillai. The Mudaliars have a higher position than the other Vellalars. The Mudaliars are found chiefly near Arcot and Salem. The

Vellalars, whose surname is Pillai, are found chiefly in the extreme south. Neither the Mudaliars nor the Pillais take the sacred thread ; but they are regarded as very clean Sudras, and the Brahmans accept their gifts without much hesitation.

The Vadugas are not, properly speaking, a separate caste. In Dravira the name is applied to the Sudras of the Telegu country who have migrated, and are domiciled, in the Dravira districts. The high caste Vadugas have the same position as the Vellalars. The usual surname of the Vadugas is Naidu. There are many well-educated men among both the Vadugas and the Vellalars, and members of these castes are as numerous in the public service and the liberal professions in Southern India, as the Kāyasthas are in the same lines of business in Northern India.

CHAP. V.—THE PRABHUS OF THE BOMBAY PRESIDENCY.

THE word Prabhu literally means 'lord.' It is the caste name of a very small but important community found in Western India. Their total number is only 29,559 ; but they are a very intelligent and energetic class. The two main sub-divisions among them are the following :—

1. Chandra Seni Prabhu—found chiefly near Poona.
2. Patani Prabhu—found in Bombay and Gujrat.

There are other classes of Prabhus besides these, as, for instance, the Donna Prabhus, of Goa. The Prabhus wear the sacred thread, and, claiming to be Ksatriyas, perform their poojas and prayers in the same manner as the highest of the twice-born castes. Nevertheless they are usually considered to have only the same footing as that which the Kāyasthas have in Northern India. They held very high offices under the Maratta kings. The great Sivaji's chief secretary was a Chandra Seni Prabhu, named Balaji Auji, whose acuteness and intelligence are recorded by the English Government at Bombay on an occasion of his being sent there on business.* Mulhar Khanderao Chitnavis, Vakil, district Amraoti, is a descendant of Balaji Auji. Two of his other descendants are now receiving their education in England at the expense of the Maharaja Guikwar of Baroda. Sakharam Hari Gupti, who was Minister to

* See Grant Duff's *History of the Marathas*, Vol. I, p. 201.

Raghunâth Rao, Peshwa, and who suffered a cruel death for his fidelity to his master, was a Prabhu also. One of his descendants is employed at present as a General in the army of H. H. the Maharaja Holkar. Rowji Appaji, who was Minister to Govinda Rao Guikwar, and who after the death of his master became the most powerful man in the country and almost a "King maker," was also of the Prabhu caste. Rowji's brother Babaji was the Commander of the Guikwar's Cavalry. Of the same caste were also Mahipat Rao, who was Prime Minister to Madhoji Bhouslay, and Krishna Rao Madhav Chitnavis, who was Prime Minister to Raghuji Bhouslay II, of Nagpore. The Hon'ble Gangadhar Rao Madhav Chitnavis, who is at present on the Legislative Council of India as an Additional Member, is a grandson of the Nagpore premier, Krishna Rao Chitnavis. The Hon'ble G. M. Chitnavis is a young man ; but the ability and moderation which he has displayed on some of the most trying occasions would do credit to many a grey-headed Councillor. His brother, Mr. Shankar Rao Madhav Chitnavis, holds a very high position in the Civil Service of India, being at present a District Magistrate and Collector in the Central Provinces. Of the other conspicuous names among the living members of the Prabhu caste, the following may be mentioned here :—

1. Dewan Bahadoor Luxman Jagannath Vaidya, of Poona, late Dewan of Baroda.
2. Rao Bahadoor Vasudev Mahadeo Somnath, Sir Soobah of Baroda.
3. Raghonath Sheo Rao Tipnavis, Sessions Judge, Bombay Presidency.
4. Rao Bahadoor Kandron Daji Adhicari Huzoor, Accountant, Poona.
5. Rao Bahadoor Anna Gopal Kotwal, Deputy Collector, Surat.

CHAP. VI.—THE KOLITAS OF ASSAM.

THE Kolitas are found not only in Assam, but also in the Southern Tributary States of Chutia Nagpore. Colonel Dalton describes the Kolitas of Chutia Nagpore as of fair complexion, with good features and well-proportioned limbs, and expresses the opinion that they are of Aryan blood with "a slight deterioration arising from intermixture with the less comely aborigines. The same remarks apply to the Kolitas of Assam. They are regarded by the best authorities as genuine Hindus of unmixed descent.*

The highest class Kolitas in Assam, called Bora Kolitas, live chiefly by serving as clerks and accountants. Under the Ahang Rajas almost all the Bora Kolitas were employed in the civil service of their country. Some of the high class Kolitas practise trade. When a Kolita manages to become a big man, he claims to be a Kāyastha and takes the sacred thread. Of the inferior Kolitas, who are mainly agricultural, many serve as menials in the houses of Brahmans. The Kolitas are a pure Sudra caste, and they are almost the only Sudras in Assam who are allowed to enter the cook-room of a Brahman. There are some Kolitas who are artisans, but their status is inferior to that of the agricultural Kolitas. Some of the Kolitas are now the abbots of the monasteries appertaining to a Vaishnava sect founded by an Assamese Brahman in the fifteenth century.

---

* Hunter's *Imperial Gazetteer*, Vol. I, p. 355.

The usual surnames of the Bora Kolitas are Kokatia and Choliha, both of which have the same signification, and are the Assamese and Ahang equivalents of the designation "clerk," their literal meaning being "paper writer." The surname of the inferior Kolitas is Kolita.

The Kolita population is more numerous in Upper and Central Assam than in the Surma Valley. Of the 253,860 Kolitas returned in Assam in 1881, 241,589 were inhabitants of the Bramhaputra Valley. The Kāyastha population of Assam is confined mainly to the Surma Valley.

PART X.

THE MERCANTILE CASTES.

CHAP. I.—THE BANIYAS OF BENGAL.

THE word Baniya is a corruption of the Sanskrit word *banik* which means "merchant." The Baniyas are certainly entitled to be regarded as Vaishyas. But the Baniyas of Bengal do not wear the sacred thread, and the best of them are looked upon as inferior Sudras. The Baniyas proper of Bengal are divided into two classes, namely,—

1. Suvarna Banika—gold merchants.
2. Gandha Banika—spice merchants.

Besides these there are two other classes, namely, the Kansa Banika and the Sankha Banika, whose profession and caste names entitle them to some extent to be regarded as Baniyas, but who are not popularly taken to come under the category. From the point of view of caste, the Gandha Baniks, Kansa Baniks, and Sankha Baniks have all a higher position than Suvarna Baniks ; but in respect of wealth, intelligence and culture, the latter stand on a far higher footing. There are among the Sonar Baniyas a great many who are big capitalists. These have very little enterprise, and generally seek the safest investments. The middle classes among them have generally *poddari* shops in the large towns where they sell and buy gold and silver in the form of ingots, as well as in the shape of plate and jewellery. The Gandha Baniyas form the majority of the grocery shopkeepers of Bengal. The Kansa Baniks and Sankha Baniks also pursue the occupations assigned to their castes. There are many well-to-do people among the Gandha Baniyas and the Kansa Baniyas, but the Sankha Baniyas are, as a class, very poor.

§ 1.—*Suvarna Baniks of Bengal.*

The Suvarna Baniks are popularly called Sonar Baniyas. They are a very intelligent and well-to-do class, but they are treated as a degraded caste. The good Brahmans do not take even a drink of water from their hands. Their spiritual guides are the Chaitanite Gossains, and their religious services are performed by a class of degraded Brahmans called Sonar Baniya Brahmans.

The Sonar Baniyas are believed to be very hard-fisted, and perhaps they are actually so in certain concerns of life; but they never deny themselves any personal comfort consistent with their ideas of economy. Some of them live in palatial mansions, and keep splendid equipages. They do not invest much of their money for the benefit of their souls in the next world, and with the exception of a few of their wealthy members, they very seldom incur any expenditure by way of charity to the poor. As a class the Sonar Baniyas are, by nature, endowed with very strong common sense and sound judgment, and so they seldom fail to prosper in any line of business which they take up. Though traders by caste, they do not take any considerable share in either the internal or the foreign trade of the country. As already stated, there is very little enterprise among them, and a Sonar Baniya who has a long purse generally seeks more to conserve his patrimony than to improve it by risky speculations.

The free admission of all the castes into the English schools and colleges set up in the country, since the commencement of British rule, has enabled many of the Sonar Baniyas to distinguish themselves, more or less, as English scholars. The greatest among these was the late Mr. Lal Behari Dey, the well-known author of the *Govinda Samanta* and the *Folk Tales* of Bengal. Babu Bhola Nath Chandra, the author of *Travels in India*, is also of the Sonar Baniya caste. I do not know any Sonar Baniya who has yet attained much eminence in the Bar; but in the Judicial Service, there are many who hold very high positions. The most notable among them is Babu Brajendra Kumar Seal, who has now the rank of a District Court Judge, and who may one day prove an ornament of the Bengal High Court. In the Medical Service also there are some Sonar Baniyas holding very high positions.

The total Sonar Baniya population of Bengal is according to the last Census 97,540 souls in all. They are divided into two classes called Saptagrami and Bangaja. The usual surnames of the Saptagramis are Mallick, Seal, Dhar, Laha, Baral, Adhya and Sen. Very few of these titles are peculiar to the class. But the leading Mallicks, Seals and Lahas of Calcutta are of the Saptagrami division of the Sonar Baniya caste. Abandoned by the higher classes of Brahmans, the Sonar Baniyas have naturally fallen into the hands of the Chaitanite Gossains. The teachings of their spiritual guides have made them strict abstainers from anmal food and intoxicating drinks. To that extent their religion has had a very wholesome influence on them. The inevitable result of Vishnuvite teachings is, however, to cause a relaxation of the fetters by which the noble religion of the primitive Hindu Rishis sought to enforce sexual fidelity, and it is said that by leading their followers to pander to them in imitating the alleged flirtations of Krishna, the Chaitanite Gossains, and the Ballavachari Maharajas are sometimes able to make them wallow very deep in the mire of the most abominable practices. But, though the religion of the Gossains may be calculated to corrupt the morality of their followers, it must be almost impossible for the teachers to take advantage of their cult for the gratification of their lust, without losing the esteem of their disciples which is their only source of income. Many of the Gossains, whom I know, are themselves very good men, and the *chellas* being also very shrewd men of the world, the stories that are usually retailed about their religious practices must to a great extent be quite without foundation. It is only when the *chella* is a young widow without any near relation to protect her, that the spiritual teacher may find it possible or safe to corrupt her. But even in such cases the Gossain is boycotted by his disciples in a manner which makes him very miserable indeed. Even apart from such checks, no class of men can possibly be so bad as some of their religions tend to make them.

The Sonar Baniyas are very neat and clean in their habits. They dress very decently, and their style of conversation very seldom betrays their low status in caste. Their ladies are generally very handsome.

§ 2.—*The Gandha Baniks of Bengal.*

The Gandha Baniks, though entitled to be regarded as Vaishyas, are treated in Bengal as middle class Sudras, from whom a good Brahman may take a drink of water without any hesitation. A Brahman may even condescend so far as to accept their gifts and officiate at their religious ceremonies, without losing altogether his connection with his caste.

The Gandha Baniks usually live by keeping shops, where they sell spices, sugar, ghi, salt, medicines and food-grains. They retail opium and charas. But they very seldom sell ganja, except through a Mahomedan servant. The majority of the shopkeepers of Bengal are either Gandha Baniks or Telis. There are not, among the

Gandha Baniks, such big capitalists as are to be found among the Sonar Baniyas; nor such big traders as among the Telis. But, generally speaking, the Gandha Baniyas are a well-to-do class. They stick to the profession of their caste, and I do not know any member of the class who has obtained any University distinction, or has held any high office in the service of Government. The Gandha Baniyas are all, however, possessed of sufficient education to be able to keep accounts. Their usual surnames are Sinha, Dhani, Mullik, De, Nag, Sadhu, Datta and Dhar. Their total numerical strength is, according to the last Census, 123,765.

The Gandha Baniyas live in good houses. But they very seldom spend much of their wealth in any other kind of personal comfort. It is very unusual for them to be dressed decently, and even the wealthiest among them generally live in a very shabby style. The Gandha Baniyas spend very considerable amounts in Pujas and marriages. But in other respects, the priestly class have very little influence on them either for good or evil. Their women have a very high character for conjugal fidelity.

CHAP. II.—THE BANIYAS OF NORTHERN INDIA.

To give an exhaustive list of the several Baniya tribes and of their sub-tribes is quite as impossible as the enumeration of the several clans of the Rajputs and the Brahmans. In the *Annals of Rajasthan* it is stated that the author's Jaina teacher, who had for a series of years been engaged in compiling a catalogue of the Baniya tribes, and had at one time included in it the names of not less than 1,800 different clans, was obliged to abandon the pursuit, on obtaining from a brother priest, from a distant province, one hundred and fifty new names.* Colonel Tod's teacher was evidently contemplating the enumeration, not only of the main tribes, but of their sub-divisions in every part of India, including Gujrat, where the sub-divisions among the Baniyas are as numerous as those among the local Brahmans. The main divisions of the Baniyas are not quite so numerous as the statement cited above from the *Annals of Rajasthan* might suggest. The commercial tribes best known and most usually found in Upper India are the following:—

1. Agarwālā.
2. Osswal (including the Srimals and Sir Srimals).
3. Khandelwal.
4. Srimali.
5. Palliwal.
6. Porawal.
7. Bhatiya.
8. Mahesri.
9. Agrahari.
10. Dhusar.
11. Umar.
12. Rastogi.
13. Kesarwani.

---

* Tod's *Annals of Rajasthan*, Vol. II., p. 182.

14. Kesandhan.
15. Lohiya.
16. Soniya.
17. Sura Seni.
18. Bara Seni.
19. Baranwal.
20. Ayodhya Bansi.
21. Jaiswar.
22. Mahobiya.
23. Mahuria.
24. The Bais Baniyas.
25. The Kath Baniyas.
26. The Raoniyas.
27. The Janarya.
28. The Lohana.
39. The Rewari Baniyas.
30. The Kanu.

Of these the first ten are the richest and most enterprising. They claim Rajputana and the adjoining tracts as their original home, but are to be found in every part of Upper India, from the Sutlej to the Brahmaputra. They are, generally speaking, very intelligent, and, although not possessing much of literary culture, their aristocratic appearance, cleanly habits, courteous manners, and capacity for every kind of business, mark them out as men of a superior stamp. They are all strict vegetarians and abstainers from strong drinks.

The above are the chief tribes of Upper India that usually profess to be, and are recognized as, branches of the Baniya or mercantile caste. Among the persons actually connected with the trading business of Hindustan proper, a very large number are of the Kshetri caste, who, as already stated in a previous chapter, claim to be of the military group, but who, as a matter of fact, are mainly cloth merchants. In the Punjab, United Provinces, Behar, and Calcutta, the Kshetris have almost the monopoly for the sale of all kinds of textile fabrics, from Cashmere shawls and Benares brocades to those cheap Manchester dhotis which are now hawked in the streets of towns by the shrill and familiar cry of "three pieces to the rupee; four pieces to the rupee, &c." The majority of the several classes of brokers in Northern India are also of the Kshetri caste. Among the sellers of food-grains, oil-seeds, salt, spices, &c., the several tribes of the Baniyas mentioned above may collectively form the majority. But the number of Telis and Kallwars among them is also very considerable. In fact, the Telis, whose proper avocation is the manufacture of oil, and the Kallwars who are brewers, claim to be Baniyas, though that claim is not admitted by any one outside their own spheres.

§ 1.—*The Agarwāls.*

The Agarwālās, Khandelwals and Ossawals are the most important classes of Baniyas in Upper India, and are to be found in every part of it from the Sutlej to the Brahmaputra, and even outside these limits. The Agarwāls trace their descent from a Ksatriya king, Agra Sen, who reigned in Sirhind, and whose capital was at Agraha, now a small town in the Fatehbad Tahsil of the Hissar District, Punjab. The exact date of Agra Sen is unknown, but some conjecture about it may be made from the tradition that his descendants took an important part in the struggles between Hinduism and Jainaism, and that many of them were led to embrace the Jaina religion at the time. After the capture of Agraha by Sahabuddin Ghori in 1194, and the dispersal of the tribe in consequence of that disaster, they renounced the military profession, and took to trade.

There are a few Jains among the Agarwāls. The majority of the caste are Vishnuvites. Some of them offer worship to the shrines of Siva and Kāli. But there are none among them who can be called Sivites or Saktas. They all profess great reverence for the field of Kurukshetra and the river Ganges. They worship very particularly the goddess Laksmi, and celebrate with great pomp the *Diwali*, or general illumination of their houses, in the night of the new moon in October. The Jain Agarwālās are chiefly of the Digambari order. The Hindu Agarwāls profess great reverence towards snakes, in accordance with their traditional belief that one of their remote female ancestors was a Nag kanya, *i.e.*, the daughter of a serpent king. In Delhi the Vaishnava Agarwāls paint pictures of the snake on either side of the outside doors of their houses, and make offering of fruits and flowers before them. A great many of the

Agarwâls take the sacred thread; but they consider the practice as optional, and not desirable for those whose pursuits or habits of life render it impossible to observe the rules and ceremonies prescribed to the twice-born by the Shastras. According to the last Census, the numerical strength of the Agarwâls is as shown in the following table:—

N.-W. Provinces	311,517
Bengal	19,297
Central Provinces	14,726
Total, including the figures of other Provinces where they are found ...	354,177

There are about 18 Gotras among the Agarwâls, and they observe the rule of the Shastras forbidding marriage within the Gotra. Intermarriage is allowed between the Jainas and Hindus in their caste. Their widows are not allowed to re-marry. The Gauda Brahmans usually minister to them as priests. They are all strict vegetarians and teetotalers. The illegitimate offspring of the Agarwâls are not altogether without a caste status. They are called Dasa, while those of legitimate birth are called Bisa.

The Agarwâls claim to be the only true representatives of the Aryan Vaishyas, and their occupations have throughout been in keeping with the tradition. "After the dispersion of the tribe by Sahabuddin Ghori their talent for business brought individual members to the front under the Mahomedan Emperors of Delhi. Two of Akbar's Ministers—Madhu Sah and Todar Mal—are said to have been Agarwâls."* But the majority of the caste have from remote times been, and still are, employed in banking, trade, petty money-lending, and similar pursuits. A few are zemindars and holders of large tenures; but in most cases their connection with the land may be traced to a profitable mortgage on the estate of an hereditary landholder, so that landholding

* Tod's *Annals of Rajasthan*, Vol. I, p. 548.

cannot properly be reckoned among the characteristic pursuits of the caste. The poorer members of the caste find employment as brokers, book-keepers, touts, workers in gold and silver embroidery, and take to any respectable pursuit except cultivation.*

§ 2.—*The Ossawals, Srimals and Sri Srimals.*

Though bearing different designations according to the names of their original abodes, the Ossawals, Srimals and Sri Srimals are all members of the same caste. They are, however, not to be confounded with the Srimalis who form a distinct caste, and with whom they cannot intermarry. A very considerable number of the great Indian bankers and jewellers are Ossawals, and Colonel Tod cannot be very far from the mark in observing that half the mercantile wealth of India passes through their hands. In Rajputana they hold also very high offices in the service of the local chiefs. But in British India, where only the subordinate appointments are open to the natives of the country, there are scarcely half-a-dozen Ossawals connected with the public service. The late Raja Siva Prasad, who was an Ossawal, held the post of Inspector of Schools in the North-Western Provinces. Among the living officials of the Ossawal caste, the only name generally known is that of Mr. Bishen Chand, who is a Deputy Collector in the United Provinces. In Rajputana the services of the Ossawals are better appreciated. From time immemorial they have held there the highest offices connected with finance and the administration of civil justice; and even at present many of the leading officials there are of the Ossawali clan. The present Dewan of Udaipore, Babu Panna Lal, is of that tribe; so is also Mr. Nath Malji, the chief fiscal officer of Jaipore.

It is said that there are a few Vishnuvites among the Ossawals. But the majority of them are Jains, and

* Risley's *Tribes and Castes of Bengal*, Vol. I, p. 7.

they spend vast sums of money in building and furnishing temples dedicated to their saints. The best and most ancient of these shrines are at Palitana and Girnar. There are also a few recently-built Jain temples in Calcutta which are well worth visiting. The Ossawals are to be found in almost all the great towns of Northern India. The Jagat Setts of Moorshedabad, whose political support mainly paved the way of the English to the acquisition of the sovereignty of Bengal, were Ossawals. That family is well-nigh ruined now, but there is a large colony of Ossawals at Azimgunge near Moorshedabad, who are all very wealthy bankers and landholders. The greatest of these are Ray Dhanpat Sing and his nephew Ray Chatrapat Sing. The members of this family have all been very remarkable men as bankers and zemindars. Ray Latchmipat, the father of Chatrapat, was at one time involved in difficulties which threatened his ruin; but his reputation for strict honesty, and his skill in the management of his business, enabled him to tide over the crisis with success, and to pay his creditors in full with interest. His creditors themselves offered to forego the interest, but he declined to avail himself of the concession even in the darkest hours of his peril, and now the credit of the family is established all the more. There was lately a run on the bank of Ray Dhanpat also. Some of his creditors tried to have him declared an insolvent. But he contested their proceedings, and instead of taking advantage of the law for the relief of insolvent debtors, he is, like his brother, about to pay the last farthing that he owed to his creditors. Such integrity in actual practice has certainly far greater value than the *olla podrida* of copy-book ethics and Machiavelism for which the priestly class claim to be worshipped by their followers.

The great defect in the Baniyas of Northern India is, as already observed, their incapacity to march in advance of, or even with, the times. With all their wealth and capacity for business they have done nothing whatever to introduce those new industries which the country now sadly needs, and which, after the experimental stage is over, are sure to be profitable. They work in the old grooves, or in lines presented to them ready-made, and they have not yet given any evidence of an aptitude for organising new spheres of commercial activity. In this respect they are far surpassed by the Parsis and the Nagar Baniyas of Gujrat. Among our Ossawals, Āgarwāls, Khandelwals, Mahesris or Sonar Baniyas there is not a single name that, in respect of enterprise, can be compared with that of Sir Mangal Das Nathu Bhai or Sir Dinshaw Manikjee Petit.

The Bhojak Brahmans minister to the Ossawals as priests in the performance of those Brahmanical ceremonies that are not eschewed by the Jains. The social rank of the Ossawals is the same as that of the Āgarwāls, and their gifts would be accepted without hesitation by Brahmans of all classes.

Like the Āgarwāls, the Ossawals give a recognised status to their illegitimate progeny calling them Dasa, while those of legitimate birth are called Bisa.

The usual surnames of the Ossawals are Chand, Das, Dosi, Lal, Singh, Golecha, Doogar and Nalaka.

§ 3.—*The Khandelwal Baniyas.*

The Khandelwal Baniyas are not inferior to any of the other divisions of the caste, either in wealth or in respect of refinement. They derive their name from the town of Khandela in the Jaipore State, which at one time was the chief city of the Shekhawati Confederation.* There are both Vishnuvites and Jains among them. The Vishnuvite Khandelwals take the sacred thread. The millionaire Setts of Mathura are Khandelwals and of the Jain persuasion, with the exception of one branch only that has lately adopted the Vishnu-

* See Tod's *Annals of Rajasthan*, Vol. II, p. 434.

vite faith, through the influence of an Achari monk of the Ramanuja sect, named Rangachari Swami. Mulchand Soni of Ajmere is a Jain Khandelwal.

§ 4.—*The Srimali Baniyas.*

Like the Srimali Brahmans, the Srimali Baniyas trace their name to the town of Srimal now called Bhinal, near Jhalore in Marwar. With regard to Bhinal and Sanchore, Colonel Tod says :—

> These towns are on the high road to Cutch and Gujrat, which has given them from the most remote times a commercial celebrity. Bhinal is said to contain fifteen hundred houses, and Sanchore about half that number. Very wealthy *mohajans* or 'merchants' used to reside here, but insecurity both within and without has much injured these cities, the first of which has its name *mál*, from its wealth as a mart.—Tod's *Annals of Rajasthan*, Vol. II, p. 332.

Like the Āgarwāls, the Srimalis give a recognised status to their illegitimate offspring, and call them Dasa Srimalis, while those of legitimate birth are called Bisa. The latter are all Jains. But among the Dasa Srimalis there are both Jains and Vishnuvites. There are many rich men among the Srimali Baniyas, as, for instance, Panna Lal Johori, the leading jeweller of Bombay, and Makhan Lal Karam Chand, the leading banker of Ahmedabad. Like the Ossawals and the Khandelwals, the Srimali Baniyas generally stick to their caste profession, and keep aloof from the public services, and the practice of the liberal professions. There are, however, some exceptions. Dr. Tri Bhuvan Das, of Junagar, is a Srimali.

§ 5.—*The Palliwal Baniyas.*

The Palliwal Baniyas derive their name from the ancient commercial mart of Marwar, about which an account has been already given in connection with the Palliwal Bramhans.* Among the Palliwal Baniyas there are both Jains and Vishnuvites. They are very numerous in Agra and Jaunpur.

---

* See page 68, *ante*.

§ 6.—*The Porawal Baniyas.*

The Porawal Baniyas seem to derive their name from Pore Bunder in Gujrat, and, if so then, they are Gujrati Baniyas. They are strong in Lalitpur, Jhansi, Cawnpur, Agra, Hamirpur, and Banda. They do not take the sacred thread. The Srimali Brahmans minister to them as priests. Mr. Bhagu Bhai, one of the wealthiest bankers of Ahmedabad, is a Porawal.

§ 7.—*The Bhatiyas.*

Like most of the other Baniya castes of Rajputana, the Bhatiyas claim to be Rajputs. But whatever ground there may be for such pretension, this much is certain, that they have no connection whatever with the Bhatti clan of the Rajput tribe. The Bhatiyas deal very largely in the cotton piece-goods imported into this country from Manchester. The last Census gives the following figures regarding their numerical strength :—

Bombay	22,663
Punjab	23,649
Scinde	8,491

There is a large colony of Bhatiyas at Karachi in Scinde.

§ 8.—*The Mahesri Baniyas.*

The Mahesris are a numerous tribe found in almost every part of the N.-W. Provinces, Rajputana and Behar. They are to be found in large numbers in Nagpore also. The majority of them are Vishnuvites, and take the sacred thread. The number of Jains among them is not very considerable. Their name is probably derived from that of the ancient town of Maheshwar near Indore. But some say that their original home is Bikanir, while the Mahesris of Mozufferpore trace their name from the town of Mahesha near Bhurtpore The well-known banker, Bansi Lal Abirchand, of Bikanir, who has agencies in almost every part of India, is a Mahesri. So is Sheva Ram Khosal Chand, of Jubbulpore.

§ 9.—*The Agrahari Baniyas.*

The Agraharis are found chiefly in the districts round Benares. Their numerical strength is slightly in excess of one hundred thousand. There are not many wealthy men among them. They take the sacred thread, and, like the other leading Baniya clans, are strict vegetarians and teetotalers. There are many Agraharis who have embraced the Sikh faith. There is a large colony of such Agraharis in the district of Arrah.

§ 10.—*The Dhunsar Baniyas.*

The Dhunsars are found chiefly in the Gangetic Doab, between Delhi on the west and Mirzapore on the east. There are many big landholders among them. They take their name from Dhusi, a flat-topped hill, near Rewari, in Gurgaon. They are all Vishnuvites, and there are no Jains among them. They do not devote themselves entirely to trade. In fact their chief profession is penmanship, and they combine in themselves the office-aptitude of the Kāyasth, with the Baniya's capacity for mercantile business. Under Mahomedan rule, they occasionally filled many high offices of State. Under the present *régime* a good many of them hold such appointments in the public service as are open to the natives of this country now.

§ 11.—*The Umar Baniyas.*

The Umars are very numerous in the tract of country between Agra on the west and Gorakhpur on the east. The Baniyas of the districts adjoining Cawnpur are chiefly Umars. The tribe has very few representatives in Behar. They are usually recognised as good Vaishyas, and their caste status is not regarded as inferior to that of any other Baniya tribe. They take the sacred thread after the death of their fathers, but not before.

§ 12.—*The Rastogi Baniyas.*

The Rastogis are very numerous in the Upper Doab, and in almost all the chief towns of the United Provinces, as, for instance, Lucknow, Fatehpur, Farakkabad, Meerut, and Azamgarh. The tribe has a few representatives also in Patna and Calcutta. All the Rastogis are Vaishnavas of the Ballava sect. Like the Umars they take the sacred thread after the death of their fathers, and not before. There are some wealthy bankers among them. Even the poorest among them are generally found well clad. They have the following sub-divisions :—

1. Amethi—probably from the Pergunnah of that name, in the Sultanpore District, Oudh.
2. Indrapati—from Indrapat, the ancient name of Delhi.
3. Manhariya—probably from Maihar in Baghelkhand.

§§ 13, 14.—*The Kasarwani and the Kasanadhan Baniyas.*

These two tribes seem to derive their names from the Sanskrit word *kansa*, which means "bell-metal." If that be the correct derivation of their caste designation, then their original occupation was the keeping of shops for the sale of those brass and bell-metal utensils which are a necessity in every Hindu household. But as, in practice, they generally keep shops for the sale of food-grains and oil-seeds, it does not seem impossible that their names are corrupted forms of *Krishana Vanik* and *Krishana Dhani*, both meaning the "husbandman's banker." They are pretty numerous in every part of the United Provinces and Behar. The last Census gives the following figures relating to their numerical strength :—

Kasandhan, 97,741—most numerous in the districts of Banda and Basti.

Kasarwani, 65,625—most numerous in Benares.

The majority of these two tribes are petty shopkeepers, and the number of wealthy men among them is not very considerable. Most of them are quite illiterate.

A few have education enough to serve as book-keepers and clerks in the offices of the Hindu bankers. The Kasarwanis allow their widows to re-marry, but do not recognise the possibility of divorce. Shopkeeping is their regular occupation. But there are a few among them who practise agriculture. The Kasarwanis of the districts round Benares are chiefly Ram worshippers, and are generally strict vegetarians and teetotalers. They, however, offer worship to the Sakti goddess Bindhya Basini, of Mirzapore, releasing the animal which they offer, without slaughtering it. They do not take the sacred thread.

§ 15.—*The Lohiya Baniyas.*

As their name indicates, the caste occupation of the Lohiyas is the sale of ironware. The numerical strength of the class is not very considerable. The majority of them are Vishnuvites; but there are among them some Jains also. The taking of the sacred thread is very rare among them.

§ 16.—*The Soniyas.*

The Soniyas are dealers in gold. But the Soniyas of Upper India are not a very wealthy class like the Sonar Baniyas of Bengal. There are many Sonis in Allahabad. Those of Benares profess to have migrated there from Gujrat.

§ 17.—*The Sura Seni Baniyas.*

The Sura Seni Baniyas evidently derive their designation from the ancient name of the Mathura District.

§ 18.—*The Bara Seni Baniyas.*

The Bara Senis are an important community. There are many rich bankers among them. They seem to derive their name from Barshana in the suburbs of Mathura. At any rate, the clan is very strong in Mathura and the adjoining districts.

§ 19.—*The Baranwal Baniyas.*

The Baranwals are a numerous but not a very wealthy class. They take their name from *Baran*, the old name* of Bulandshahar. They were driven away from their original home by the oppressions of Mahomed Toglak, and are now to be found chiefly in Etawah, Azamgarh, Gorakhpur, Moradabad, Jaunpore, Gazipur, Behar and Tirhoot. They are orthodox Hindus, and allow neither divorce nor the re-marriage of widows. Wherever possible they employ Gaur Brahmans as their priests. In Tirhoot they employ Maithili Brahmans also. They are mostly shopkeepers. A few have taken to agriculture. There are a few big landholders and bankers among them ; as, for instance, Babu Bolaki Lal, of Monghyr. Some of the Baranwals take the sacred thread.

§ 20.—*The Ayodhya Basi Baniyas.*

Like many other castes the Baniyas have a clan deriving their name from the ancient kingdom of Oudh. The Ayodhya Basi Baniyas are to be found in every part of the United Provinces and Behar.

§ 21.—*The Jaiswar Baniyas.*

The Jaiswar Baniyas seem to derive their name from Perganah Jais in the Salon Division of the Rae Bareilly District, Oudh. They are very numerous in the eastern districts of the United Provinces. They do not take the sacred thread. There is a branch of the tribe of brewers called Kallwars in Northern India who pretend to be Jaiswar Baniyas. The Jaiswars are usually to be found among the petty shopkeepers and pedlars.

§ 22.—*The Mahobiya Baniyas.*

The Mahobiya Baniyas derive their name from the town of Mahob in the Hamirpur District.

* See Hunter's *Imperial Gazetteer*, Vol. III, p. 133.

§ 23.—*The Mahuria Baniyas.*

A clan very strong in Behar and in the Doab. In Behar they are the richest of all the local Baniya tribes. There are many big landholders and rural bankers among them. They finance the cultivators of sugar-cane, and have almost the monopoly of the local trade in sugar. They do not take the sacred thread, but are regarded as good Hindus of the Vaishya class. Tika Sahu, of Hansua Noagong, in Gaya, who was one of the biggest zemindars of the district, was a Mahuria. Like the Sikhs the Mahuris are strictly forbidden the use of tobacco, and a man detected smoking would be expelled from the community. In all probability the Mahurias are a section of the Rastogis.

§ 24.—*The Bais Baniyas.*

These Baniyas are found chiefly in Behar. Like the other high caste Baniyas, they allow neither divorce nor the re-marriage of widows. A great many of them keep shops for the sale of brass and bell-metal vessels. Some of them practise agriculture. The Bais of Kumaon are a different clan, having the same status.

§ 25.—*The Kath Baniyas.*

The Kath Baniyas are found in Behar. The majority of them are shopkeepers and money-lenders ; but many have taken to agriculture, and work even as landless day labourers. Some members of the caste have of late become zemindars. The Maithila Brahmans minister to them as priests. They allow the re-marriage of widows, but not of divorced wives. They burn their dead, and perform *sradh* on the thirty-first day.

§ 26.—*The Raoniyar Baniyas.*

The Raoniyars are found in Gorakhpur, Tirhoot and Behar. The local Brahmans minister to them as priests. They allow the re-marriage of their widows ; but not of divorced wives, except with the permission of the Panchait. The Raoniyars are not Vishnuvites like most of the other Baniya tribes. They regard Siva as their tutelary deity, and like the Āgarwāls pay special reverence to Laksmi, the goddess of Fortune. The majority of them are petty traders and money-lenders. They are called also Nonia.

§ 27.—*The Jameya Baniyas.*

These are found chiefly in the Etawa District. They claim to be descendants of Pralhad, who, according to the Vishnuvite legends, was the son of the monster Hiranya Kasyapa, and was saved by Krishna himself from the persecutions to which he was subjected by his father.

§ 28.—*The Lohana Baniyas.*

The Lohanas seem to be allied to the Bhatya. They are found chiefly in Scind. The total Lohana population of India exceeds half a million.

§ 29.—*The Rewari Baniyas.*

The Rewari Baniyas are a very small clan. They evidently derive their name from Rewari in Gurgaon. Their usual occupation is the keeping of cloth shops. There is a small colony of Rewari Baniyas in Gaya.

§ 30.—*The Kanu Baniyas.*

The Kanus are petty shopkeepers dealing chiefly in food-grains and supplying travellers with the requisites for cooking their meals.

CHAP. III.—THE BANIYAS OF GUJRAT.

THE barren deserts of Rajputana are the principal home of the Baniyas. In the contiguous province of Gujrat also the Baniyas are very numerous, wealthy and enterprising. The Srimalis, Ossawals and Khandelwals, who are to be found in large numbers in Gujrat, as in almost every other part of Northern India, are, properly speaking, Baniyas of Rajputana, and have been described already. The main divisions among the Baniyas of Gujrat proper are the following :—

1. Nagar { 1. Dasa. 2. Bisa.
2. Disawal.
3. Porawal { 1. Dasa. 2. Bisa.
4. Gujar.
5. Modh.
6. Lad.
7. Jharola.
8. Sorathiya.
9. Khadaita.
10. Harsora.
11. Kapola.
12. Urvala.
13. Patolia.
14. Vayada.

Each of these sections has a corresponding Brahmanical caste who usually minister to them, and to them only, as priests. For instance, the Nagar Brahmans minister to the Nagar Baniyas ; the Modh Brahmans minister to the Modh Baniyas ; and the case is the same with the others.

The majority of the Gujrati Baniyas are Vishnuvites and followers of Ballabhachari. The number of Jains among them is also very considerable. The Vishnuvite Baniyas take the sacred thread.

CHAP. IV.—THE TRADING CASTES OF THE SOUTHERN DECCAN.

The chief trading castes of the Madras Presidency are the Chettis, Komatis, Nagartas and Lingait Banijigas.

The word Chetti is probably allied to the Sanskrit word *Sreshthi*, which means a banker or a big merchant. The Chettis of the Madras Presidency correspond to the Baniyas of Northern India. The Chettis are divided into numerous clans between whom intermarriage is impossible. Like the Baniyas of Northern India, some of the clans of Chettis take the sacred thread. A few of the Chettis are vegetarians ; but the majority of them eat fish as well as such flesh as is not forbidden by the Shastras.

The Chettis claim to be of the Vaishya caste, and those of them who take the sacred thread are certainly entitled to be regarded as such. But the Brahmans of their Province look upon them as Sudras, and an orthodox Draviri Vaidika will neither accept their gifts nor officiate as a priest for them. The original home of the Natkutai Chettis, who form one of the most important clans in the caste, is Madura. They do not care for English education or for service under Government.

The majority of the Chettis practise trade. They have all a knowledge of the three R's, and some of their clans stand next to only the Brahmans and the Vellalars in respect of literary culture. Some members of these Chetti clans hold very high positions in the service of Government, and in the liberal professions. The total Chetti population is as stated below :—

Madras	...	...	...	693,552
Burma	...	...	...	5,723
Mysore	...	...	...	2,702

The Chettis are very numerous in the town of Madras, and in the Districts of Krishna, Nellore, Cuddapah, Kornool, Madura and Coimbatore. There are very few members of the clan in Malabar or South Kanara. The trade of the Malabar coast is carried on chiefly by the local Brahmans and Mussulmans. The usual profession of the few Chettis there is agricultural banking. "They advance money on growing crops of pepper, ginger, turmeric and other produce, superintend the cultivation themselves, and ultimately obtain possession of the land."*

In Mysore the Lingait Banijigas preponderate over all the other trading castes. The Komatis and Nagartas are usually found only in the towns and practising trade. But of the Lingait Banijigas and Telegu Banijigas a considerable number practise agriculture, and are residents of rural villages.

---

* *Madras Census Report for* 1871, Vol. I, p. 143.

CHAP. V.—THE MERCANTILE CASTES OF THE TELUGU COUNTRY.

THE mercantile castes of the Telugu country are called Komatis. They claim to be Vaishyas, and take the sacred thread. They are an educated class, and count among their number many who have obtained high University distinctions, and hold respectable positions in the liberal professions or in the service of Government. Upon the whole, the Komatis have almost exactly the same position in Telingana, that the Baniyas have in Upper India. The Komatis have many divisions among them, of which the following are the most important :—

1. Gavuri.
2. Kalinga Komati.
3. Beri Komati.
4. Balji Komati.
5. Nagar Komati.

The Gavuri Komatis have the highest position. They are strict vegetarians and teetotalers. The other Komatis are said to be in the habit of eating flesh meat. In matters relating to religion, the majority of the Gavuri and Kalinga Komatis are Sankarites, and only a small fraction are either Lingaits or followers of Ramanuja. Among the Beri Komatis the majority are Lingaits. In matters relating to social discipline, the Komatis acknowledge the authority of the spiritual successors of Bhaskarachari, who have their chief monastry at Gooti in the Bellary District. The Brahmans minister to the Komatis as priests without reciting the Vedic mantras. The Komatis now claim that they are entitled to such recitation. The practice of marrying the maternal uncle's daughter not only prevails among the Komatis as among the other castes of Southern India ; but where there is a maternal uncle's daughter, a Komati has no option, and it is obligatory on him to take her in marriage. The Komatis sell confectioneries, and there is no separate caste in Telingana corresponding to the *Mayara* or the *Halwai*. The total Komati population of India is as stated below :—

Madras	287,983
Hydrabad	212,865
Mysore	29,053
Total ...	545,206

CHAP. VI.—THE BANIYAS OF ORISSA.

As in Bengal so in Orissa there are only two classes of Baniyas, namely, the Sonar Baniya and the Putli Baniya. The Putli or packet Baniyas correspond to the Gandha Baniya of Bengal. The Sonar Baniyas and the Putli Baniyas of Orissa have the very same position there that the corresponding castes have in Bengal—the Putli Baniyas being regarded as a clean caste, and the Sonar Baniyas an unclean caste. As in Bengal, so in Orissa also, the Sonar Baniyas are richer than the spice-selling caste. Like all the other castes of the province the Baniyas of Orissa are generally in a far more backward condition than the corresponding classes of the Hindu community in other parts of India. The Baniyas of Orissa are sadly wanting in both capital and enterprise, and what little wholesale trade there is in the province is almost entirely in the hands of foreigners.

PART XI.

THE ARTISAN CASTES GENERALLY RECOGNIZED AS CLEAN SUDRAS.

CHAP. I.—GENERAL OBSERVATIONS.

THOUGH in practice many of the Banick or Baniya clans, spoken of in the preceding chapters, are treated as having no higher status than that of clean Sudras, and though one of them, namely, that of the Sonar Baniyas is regarded as actually unclean, yet their claim to be reckoned in the third group of the four main Hindu castes being undeniable, they are not included among Sudras in any Shastra, ancient or modern. The cultivating and the manufacturing castes are equally entitled to be looked upon as Vaishya according to the Shastric definition of the term ; but as they do not generally take the sacred thread, they are all regarded as Sudras, and, according to a modern text, only nine of them, namely, the following, are entitled to be treated as clean :—

Artisan castes.	1. Tanti	... ...	Weaver.
	2. Modakakara	... ...	Confectioner.
	3. Kulala	... ...	Potter.
	4. Karmakara	... ...	Ironsmith.
	5. Teli	... ...	Oil manufacturer.
	6. Gopa	... ...	Cowherd.
	7. Barui	... ...	Grower of betel leaf.
	8. Mali	... ...	Florists.
	9. Napita	... ...	Barber.

This list does not include any of the chief agricultural classes, and omits also such clean artisans as the goldsmith and the carpenter. In practice a few of the other artisan classes, not included in the list of Nava Sayakas, are regarded as clean Sudras, as also the majority of the cultivating tribes; while the Telis, though included in it, are regarded as more or less unclean in practice. The manufacturing castes that are actually regarded as more or less clean are the following :—

1.	Tanti ...	... Weaver.
2.	Modakakar ...	... Confectioner.
3.	Kulala ...	... Potter.
4.	Karmakara ...	... Ironsmith.
5.	Svarnakara ...	... Goldsmith.
6.	Sutradhar, Sutar or Barhi ...	Carpenter.
7.	Kasera and Thathera ...	Braziers and coppersmiths.
8.	Kandu and Bhad Bhunja ...	Grain parchers.
9.	Dirji ...	... Tailors.

To form an idea of the exact status of these and other clean Sudras, the reader should bear in mind the following rules of the Hindu caste system :—

1. A man of any of the superior castes may drink such water as is fetched or touched by a clean Sudra, whether the water be of the river Ganges or from any other source.

2. The water of the river Ganges, though fetched by an unclean Sudra, is not thereby rendered unfit for the high caste Hindu's drinking purposes. But every other kind of water is polluted by the touch of an unclean Sudra.

3. Even the water of the sacred Ganges is rendered useless to a Hindu by the touch of a non-Hindu.

4. The touch of non-Hindus and unclean Sudras being contaminating, it is only the clean Sudras that can render the necessary personal service to the high caste Hindus like the Brahmans, Rajputs, Vaidyas, and Kāyasthas.

5. The twice-born castes cannot, without rendering themselves liable to expiation, eat any cooked food

touched by a Sudra. The result of this rule is that a Sudra menial, whether clean or unclean, can be of no use to a high caste Hindu for the actual cooking of his food, or the serving of it. In fact, in the absence of a Brahman cook, the high caste Hindu has himself to cook the food of his servant. For the actual *cuisine* work, the clean and the unclean Sudras stand on the same footing. But while the clean Sudra can assist in the process in various ways, the unclean Sudra is not allowed even to enter the cook-room. It is for this reason that the clean Sudras alone are usually appointed as menials in Hindu households.

6. Another important difference between the clean and the unclean Sudras lies in the fact, that while a Brahman can minister to the former without losing his Brahmanism, he cannot show such honour to the latter without being degraded for ever.

7. Further, though the Shastras forbid the acceptance of the Sudra's gifts without any reference to his status, yet in practice the best Brahmans do not hesitate to accept the bounty of the Nava Sayakas, when the amount offered is a large one. Most of the great Pandits of the country accept, more or less openly, the gifts of Maharani Svarnamayi, who is a Teli by caste. But, with the exception of the Chaitanite Gossains, even the poorest and most illiterate Brahmans will not usually accept the gifts of a washerman, fisherman, vintner or courtesan.

CHAP. II.—THE WEAVERS.

§ 1.—*The Weavers Generally.*

THE weaving industry of India was, until recently, a very lucrative one, and it, therefore, happens that it is not the monopoly of any particular caste. The most important classes engaged in it are :—

In Bengal	1. Tanti	Population in Bengal			472,798.
	2. Tatwa	Do.		Do.	328,778.
	3. Julaha	Do.		Do.	726,781.
	4. Kapali	Do.		Do.	134,002.
	5. Jugi *	Do.		Do.	406,473.
In Assam	1. Tanti	Population in Assam			11,002.
	2. Jugi	Do.		Do.	177,746.
In N.-W. P.	1. Kori	Population in N.-W. Provinces			924,795.
	2. Julaha	Do.		Do.	902,125.
	3. Chipa	Do.		Do.	36,245.
In Western India	1. Koshti	Population in the Bombay Presidency			70,274.
	2. Sali	Do.		Do.	59,161.
	3. Khatri	Do.		Do.	51,740.
	4. Thakerda	Do.		Do.	63,232.
	5. Rawalia	Do.		Do.	53,688.
	6. Devang	Do.		Do.	38,275.
In Southern India	1. Kai Koia	Total population in the Madras Presidency			316,620.
	2. Sali	Do.		Do.	308,285.
	3. Patwa	Do.		Do.	74,374.
	4. Togata	Do.		Do.	59,208.
	5. Domba	Do.		Do.	74,249.

The total population of the several classes of weavers in India is 9,369,902 souls. But all these classes are

* As to this caste, *see* p. 236, *post*.

not Hindus. The Julahas, who form one-fourth of the entire population, may have been at one time low caste Hindus, but are now all Mahomedans. Even among those classes of weavers that are Hindus, the caste status of many is very low, and they certainly do not belong to the group called *Nava Sayakas* or the nine Sudra castes.

The weavers of India were, until recently, a very prosperous class; but the importation of machine-made piece-goods* from Manchester has, of late, thrown many thousands of them out of employ. These dragged on a life of poverty for some years, and at last either died of semi-starvation, or were forced by necessity to become menial servants or tillers of the soil. As the hand-looms of India are now constructed, the best weaver, with the assistance of his whole family to dress and card the yarn, cannot turn out more than five yards of cloth in a day; but the motive power required to work such a loom is very slight, and the machinery might certainly be so improved as to enable one man to work at least half-a-dozen similar looms. It is said by some that if the weaving industry of India has ceased

---

* With regard to the effect of the importation of machine-made piece-goods on the condition of the Indian weavers, Mr. Risley makes the following observations: "Although the Tantis admit weaving to be their immemorial profession, many of them have of late years been driven by the influx of cheap machine-made goods to betake themselves to agriculture. It is difficult or impossible to say with any approach to accuracy what proportion of the caste have abandoned their original craft in favour of trade or agriculture. The Uttara Kula Tantis of Western Bengal have, on the whole, adhered to weaving, and it is popularly believed that their comparative poverty is mainly due to their attachment to the traditional occupation of the caste. Among the Aswini or Moriali about one-third are supposed to have given up weaving and settled down as regular cultivators.—Risley's *Tribes and Castes of Bengal*, Vol. II, p. 301.

It must be exceedingly difficult for a foreigner to appreciate exactly the story of human misery *implied* in the above. If thirty-three per cent. of any class of Tantis have reconciled themselves, by hard necessity, to the handling of the plough, perhaps another thirty-three per cent. died of sheer starvation, before the survivors in the struggle could think of giving up their ancestral looms and shuttles, and adopting such a plebeian occupation as agriculture.

to be paying in consequence of the competition of foreign piece-goods, the Indian weavers should, despite their caste prejudices, take up some other line of business. The principle of Free Trade has been invoked in order to justify our indifference, and that of our Government, to the sufferings brought on the millions of our weavers by the import of Manchester piece-goods. But neither the science of Political Economy nor the principle of Free Trade requires that when foreign goods make their way into the markets of a country, the people of it should make no efforts to save the sinking vessel of their own industries. The principle of Free Trade insists only upon absolute freedom being left to the consumer to buy his goods from the cheapest and best market according to his own judgment.

In this country domestic industry alone suits the genius of the people, and, so far as the weaving industry is concerned, it is certainly not desirable, even from the point of view of Political Economy, that the hand-looms should be superseded by steam-power looms. Domestic industry does not involve any expenditure on account of supervision, mill buildings, or brokerage to company promoters. Domestic industry cannot render it necessary to collect raw materials or manufactured goods in one place to such an extent as to involve the risk of any heavy loss by fire, shipwreck or damp. The skill possessed by the people of a country in any art being, according to the science of Political Economy, an important part of its capital, India is at present suffering a prodigious loss, through allowing the skill acquired by her weavers by generations of practice to remain unemployed and become deteriorated. A very little improvement in the hand-looms might not only enable them yet to hold their own against foreign competition, but save the heavy loss to the Indian people and to the world which now takes place in freight, insurance, warehousing and other charges incurred unnecessarily for the benefit of Manchester. The weavers of India are themselves too ignorant of the mechanical sciences, and too poor at present, to make the necessary improvements in their looms, by their own capital and exertions. The matter is one which deserves the earnest attention of our publicists.

§ 2.—*The Tantis of Bengal.*

The Tantis of Bengal are Sudras of the Nava Sayaka or Upper nine group. They are divided into many sub-castes, which, however, need not be mentioned here. The Brahmans who minister to the clean Sudra castes like the Tantis are not, as already observed, degraded for ever, though as Sudra Yajakas (priests of Sudras) they are looked down upon by the Asudra Pratigrahis, *i.e.*, those who never take any gifts from Sudras. The Tantis being a clean caste their men and women are eligible for domestic service in the houses of the Brahmans. The following are the usual surnames of the Tantis of Bengal :—

1. Basaka—Surname of the higher class Tantis of Dacca, some of whom are now settled in Calcutta.

2. Guin ...	5. Bhar ...	Surnames peculiar to the Tantis of Bengal.
3. Nan ...	6. Radhi ...	
4. Ash ...	7. Bit ...	

8. Seal—A surname of both Tantis and Sonar Baniyas.
9. Nandi—A surname of the Kāyasthas, Telis and Tantis.
10. Datta—A surname of the Kāyasthas, Tantis, Sonar Baniyas, &c.
11. Pal—A surname of the Kāyasthas, Telis, Goalas and Tantis.
12. Shah—A Mahomedan title which is the usual surname of the wine-selling caste called *Sunri;* some of the Dacca Tantis have also this surname.
13. Aitch—A surname of the Kāyasthas and the Tantis.
14. Pramanik—A surname of many of the middle class and inferior Sudras such as the Teli, Napit, Tanti, Tura, &c.
15. Chandra—A surname of the Kāyasthas, Sonar Baniyas and Tantis.

Generally speaking, all the Tantis of Bengal are Vishnuvites and teetotalers. Like the other superior Sudra castes of Bengal, they do not allow divorce or the re-marriage of widows. It is, however, said that some of the Tantis openly live in their houses with widowed females of different castes. The admission of concubines in the dwelling-house and their treatment as wives are common enough among the unclean castes. But such instances among the superior classes are very rare—the discipline of caste being among them still powerful enough to keep under a wholesome check any tendency towards such defiance of public opinion.

The weavers of Calcutta are its earliest settlers, and being still in possession of a considerable portion of its land, they are, generally speaking, a well-to-do class. But the condition of their castemen in the interior has in recent times become indeed deplorable, as stated already. The only places in the interior of Bengal where a few well-to-do Tantis may still be found are Dacca and Santipore. The fine muslins for which these places are famous still command very high prices in the market, and the weavers employed in the industry have not yet been materially affected by the cheap and coarse products of the Manchester mills.

According to the traditional belief of the people of this country, the weavers are as a class very dull-headed. But, as a matter of fact, the weavers of Calcutta have attained very high University distinctions, and are not very inferior to the Brahmans and Kāyasthas in culture and refinement. In the interior the weavers are generally quite illiterate; but the common sense of the majority of the class must be held to be very strong. The religious teachers of the country do not usually find them quite so pliable as the Baniyas. In fact the lamentations of the Gossain, about the indifference of the weavers towards religious sermons and recitations, have passed into a proverb. It is only at Dacca and Kutwa that the Gossains possess any considerable influence over the Tantis. With regard to the weavers of Kutwa a doggerel verse is recited by the other classes of people in the locality which ironically observes that the greatness of a Vaishnava cannot be exactly apprehended even by the gods, and that the Tantis of Kutwa alone can appreciate it.

The weavers of Bengal are very industrious, thrifty and sober. The only luxuries in which they indulge are fish, curry, and a porridge of black kidney beans. They never waste one moment of their time in idle talk or amusement. Their adult males are always at their looms, while their females devote themselves to dressing and carding the yarn whenever they are not occupied with household work. The weavers do not manufacture the yarn. In former times, it was spun by old women of all the classes, including high caste Brahman ladies. But mule twist has now silenced the primeval *charka*, and the sound of the spinning wheel can seldom be heard now even in the remotest villages. The yarn now used by the Indian weavers is mainly imported from England, and is supplied to them by some capitalist who advances also money and food-grains to his constituents, and generally has them completely under his power. They have to give him the products of their looms at a fixed price, and he never allows them to sell a yard of their cloth to any other person. It is only where there is a competition among the capitalists that the poor weavers find a little relief.

§ 3.—*The Tatwas of Behar.*

The Tatwas of Behar have not the same position in the Hindu caste system that the Tantis have in Bengal. The two names are corrupted forms of the same Sanskrit word *Tantubaya*, which means a weaver. But the Tatwas of Behar are in the habit of eating flesh and drinking strong liquors, and so they are regarded as an unclean caste. The existence of such clans as Chamar Tanti and Kahar Tanti among the weavers of Behar points also to the conclusion that their status was lowered partly at least by the admission of low castes among them. Besides the indigenous Tirhutia Tantis, there are in Behar many colonies of Tantis from other provinces as is indicated by the names of Kanojia, Baiswara, &c., by which they are known. The Tatwas being an unclean caste, the Brahmans do not take even a drink of water from their hands, and if a Brahman officiates as their priest he becomes very nearly a degraded person. The priestly work of the Tatwas is sometimes performed by such of their castemen as have enlisted as members of one or other of the modern Hindu sects.

§ 4.—*The Kori and Koli of Northern India.*

The Kori and Koli of Northern India are weavers professing the Hindu faith; but they are very low castes, and a member of any of the higher castes will not take even a drink of water from their hands.

§ 5.—*The Tantis of Orissa.*

The Tantis of Orissa are divided into the following clans :—

1. Gola Tanti—These weave fine cloth.
2. Hans Tanti—These make coloured cloth of various patterns.
3. Moti Bans Tanti—These weave coarse cloth from thread of English or local manufacture.

Many of Moti Bans Tantis of Orissa have of late deserted their ancestral profession, and have become teachers in village schools. The Tantis are regarded as an unclean caste in Orissa.

§ 6.—*The Koshti of the Central Provinces.*

The weavers of the Central Provinces are called Koshti. They are a semi-clean caste. The Mahars of the Province weave coarse cloths.

§ 7.—*The Weavers of Gujrat.*

There is a class of Kshettris in Gujrat whose profession is weaving. They are good Hindus. But there is not in Gujrat any caste that can be said to correspond to the Tantis of Bengal.

§ 8.—*Weavers of the Dravirà country.*

The cotton weavers of Southern India are called Kaikalar. It is said that they are addicted to drinking spirits, and that their habits are similar to those of the aboriginal tribes. But the Sudra Yajak Brahmans minister to them as priests, and there is one class among them called Saliyar, who take the sacred thread. The silk weavers of Southern India are called Patnulkar. Ethnologically they are a superior race, and their caste status is also higher than that of the Kaikalars. According to the traditions of the Patnulkars of Southern India, their original home was Gujrat. Both the Kaikalars and Patnulkars are generally quite illiterate.

§ 9.—*The Weaving Castes of Mysore.*

The general name of the weaving castes of Mysore is Neyige. The following description of the several sections to whom the designation is applicable is taken from the last Census report of Mysore :—

Under the generic name of Neyige (weaving) sixteen sub-castes appear with an aggregate population of 86,986 persons in almost equal numbers for the two sexes, bearing a ratio of 1·76 per cent. to the total population. The sixteen divisions may be condensed into eight distinct sub-orders as below—

Devanga	49,006
Togata	13,300
Sale or Saliga...	10,255
Bilimagga	9,946
Seniga	105
Patvegar	3,174
Khatri	946
Saurashtrika	254
Total ...	86,986

These sub-divisions do not intermarry with one another or have any social intercourse. In numerical strength the Devangas, subdivided into Kannada and Telegu Devangas, hold the first place. The former are Lingaits, but have no intercourse with the Lingait Banijiks; whereas Telegu Devangas are both Vishnuvites and Sivaites. There is no intermarriage, however, between this and the other clan.

The next in order of strength are the Togatas who are Sivite weavers, and produce the coarse kinds of cloth that are worn only by the poorer classes. Their language is Telegu.

Sales or Saligas comprise two clans,—the Padmasale and the Sakunasale. Between them there is no intermarriage. Like the Togatas, they are of Telegu origin. The former are Sivaites, while the latter are worshippers of Vishnu.

Then comes the Bilimagga sub-division, also called *Kuruvina* Banajigaru, the former term being considered a nickname. They are an indigenous caste like the Devangas, and speak Kannada.

Sanigas.—Though a small number, they are a wealthy caste of weavers. They are immigrants from the Lower Karnatic, and manufacture female cloths of superior kind and high value. They are Lingaits by religion, but are not friendly with the Lingait Banajigas, &c.

Patvegars are silk weavers and speak a corrupt Marathi conglomerate of the Gujrati and Hindi. They worship all the Hindu deities, especially the female energy under the name of Sakti, to which a goat is sacrificed on the night of the Dasara festival, a Mussulman slaughtering the animal. After the sacrifice, the family of the Patvegar partake of the flesh. Many of their females are naturally fair and handsome. The Khatri are also silk-weavers, and, in manners, customs and language, are akin to the Patvegars, but do not intermarry with them, although the two castes eat together. The Khatris claim to be Ksatriyas.

Saurashtrika.—The only other ingredient of the class of weavers deserving of special mention is the Saurashtrika, commonly known as the Patnuli or Jam Khanvalla. They manufacture superior kinds of cotton and woollen carpets and an imitation shawl of cotton and silk mixture, and of green colour called *khes*.

These people were originally immigrants from Northern India, and settled in the Madras Presidency where they are known as Patnulis, *i.e.*, weavers of silk and cotton. With silk they manufacture a fine stuff called Kutni, which no other weavers are said to be able to prepare. It is largely used by Mussulmans for trousers and lungas (gown). It is said that Haider Ali, while returning from his expedition against Madras, forcibly brought with him some twenty-five families of these weavers who were living in the Tanjore district, and established them at Ganjam near Seringapatam; and in order to encourage silk and velvet weaving, exempted them from certain taxes. The industry flourished till the fall of Seringapatam, when most of the clan fled from the country, a few only having survived those troublous times. At present there are only 254 souls returned of these people, employed in making carpets in Bangalore city. They speak a dialect peculiar to themselves; it is a mixture of Maharashtra Gujrati, Kannada and Tamil; their written language is Kannada. They are Vishnuvites and wear trident marks. Their hereditary Gurus are the Srivaishnava Brahmans of the Tatachar and Bhattrachar families. In Bangalore the Smarta Brahmans act as their *Purohits* for conducting marriage and other ceremonies. In religious observances, they imitate the Brahmans and perform Upanayana (investiture of the sacred thread) on their boys before the tenth or twelfth year. They do not intermarry with any other class of weavers.—*Mysore Census Report*, pp. 246-247.

Besides the above there is a caste in Mysore called Ganigar. They are sack weavers and makers of gunny bags. Some of them are agriculturists.

§ 10.—*The Weavers of the Telegu country.*

The weavers are called Niyata Kam in the Telegu country. The profession is practised by the following castes :—

1. Pattasali—strict vegetarians.
2. Devangala or Deyandra } These eat fish, but do not in-
3. Saliyar } dulge in intoxicating drinks.

These are all clean castes. The Devangalas and the Saliyars are mostly Lingaits, wearing the Linga Sutra and regarding the Jangamas as their spiritual superiors. Those who are not Lingaits wear the Yajna Sutra of a twice-born Hindu.

§ 11.—*The Jugis.*

Besides the above there is a caste called Jugis who are weavers and who are found in many parts of India. The Jugis are Hindus, and of late years they have been claiming to have the right of taking the sacred thread ; but they are generally regarded as very inferior Sudras, and in all probability they are the illegitimate and semi-legitimate descendants of the mendicants called Jogis* who, with Gorakhpur as their head-quarters, were at one time perhaps as numerous in every part of India, as the Sankarite Sanyasis and Vishnuvite Vairagis are now. The name of the caste, their usual surname of Nath, their practice of burying their dead, and the profession of lace and apron string selling practised by them point to the conclusion that they are connected with the ancient Jogis in the same way as the Ghar Bari Sanyasis and the Grihasthi Vairagis are with the true Sanyasis and Vairagis. Like the Jugis, some of the Jogi mendicants are still found engaged in the making and selling of apron strings and other things of the same kind. These are called Duri Har Jogis.

---

* As the Jugis in some places serve as priests to idols called Dharma Raj, it is quite possible also that they are the descendants of the ancient Buddhist monks.

CHAP. III.—THE MAYARAS, HALWIS AND GURIAS.

THE Mayaras and the Halwis of India make those confections which form very important items in the daily food of the majority of well-to-do Hindus and Mahomedans. These delicacies are highly prized by all classes of the people of India, and the demand of the poorer families for them is limited only by their means. The dainties manufactured and sold by the Halwis are of various kinds, and some of them, as, for instance, the preparations of cream made at Kishnagar, require very considerable skill, and are very costly. Some of the Hindu confectioneries are made of only sugar, curd and fine chips of cocoanut. These, though prepared by a Mayara or Halwi, may be offered to the gods, and are eaten without any objection by orthodox Brahmans, as well as by the widows of the higher castes who are required by the Shastras to be, and, in practice, usually are, quite as puritanic in respect of their diet, as the students of the Vedas are enjoined, and ought to be. Some of the Mayaras and Halwis make other kinds of confections which are called *pakki methai*, and which usually consist of flour, pease meal, pulverised rice, cream, &c., fried in *ghi* or baked in strong solutions of sugar. The *pakki methais* prepared by the Sudra confectioners are eaten by Hindu children, married ladies, and Babus of "liberal views," but never by orthodox Hindus or their widows. In the towns, the Mayaras and the Halwis now make and sell even some kinds of vegetable curries which are eaten by the classes who eat their *pakki methai*. Some of the confectioners in the towns are Brahmans. But even their *methais* are not eaten by the strictly orthodox, or the widows of the higher castes. With regard to the Mahomedans it is hardly necessary to say that as they do not recognize the Hindu caste system, they eat every kind of sweetmeat whether *kachi* or *pakki* and by whatever caste manufactured. Some Mahomedans have learnt to practise the art. But considering the very small number of the Mahomedan Halwis, as they are called, it does not seem that they have been able to secure a very large share of the patronage of even their own co-religionists. In fact they are generally quite unable to manufacture the nicer varieties, and that is, perhaps, the reason why the Hindu-made confectionery finds great favour even with the Mahomedan aristocracy of the country.

The word Mayara is a corrupt form of the Sanskrit compound *Modaka-kara*, which means a confectioner. The word Halwi means primarily a kind of pudding made by frying flour in *ghi*, and then boiling the whole in a solution of milk and sugar. The word *Halwi* is also used as the designation of the confectioner caste in Upper India. The Halwis and Mayaras are divided into a large number of sub-castes, an enumeration of which does not seem to be necessary in this book. Some members of these classes possess a little knowledge of book-keeping. But the majority are quite illiterate. The usual surnames of the Mayaras of Bengal are Manna, Modak, Laha, Nag, Nandi, and Rakshit.

The figures given by the several Censuses as to the total population of the Mayaras and the Halwis do not seem to be quite reliable. According to the Census of 1881, the total number of Mayaras in the Lower Provinces, including perhaps the Halwis, was, at that time, 308,821 souls. According to the last Census, the total Halwi population of Bengal, Behar and Orissa, including perhaps the Mayaras, is 160,859. The Halwi population of the N.-W. Provinces is, according to the last Census, 96,492.

In Panjab, the profession of the Halwi is practised by the Kambohs and also by* the caste called Rora or Arora spoken of at p. 211, *ante*. The class that make sweetmeats in Orissa are called Guria, from the word *Gur*, which means unrefined sugar. In Southern India, there are neither Halwis nor Mayaras, and confections are there usually made and sold by the Brahmans and the Komatis.

---

* See p. 285, *post*.

CHAP. IV.—THE KUMAR OR POTTER.

THE Sanskrit names for the potter are Kulal and Kumbhakara. In Southern India the potters are called Kusaven. The word Kumbhakar literally means a 'maker of earthen jars.' In practice, the Kumars make many other kinds of earthen vessels. As the poorer classes of India use only earthen vessels as their cooking pots and waterpots, and as earthen pots are used even by the rich for cooking purposes, the Kumar is indispensable in every village of importance. The Kumar's services are required also for making those clay images that in Bengal are set up at stated times in the houses of the rich and in public places, and which, after being worshipped for a few days, are thrown into some river or tank with great pomp. Such being the functions of the Kumars, the caste is found in every part of India, and their total numerical strength is, according to the last Census, 3,346,488. Some of the Kumars, as for instance, those of Nadiya and Ghurni, possess very considerable skill in painting and making clay statues. In most parts of the country the Kumars are regarded as a clean caste. In Gujrat they are regarded as exceptionally clean, but in the Central Provinces and Orissa they are regarded as unclean. It is said that in some parts of N.-W. Provinces also they are regarded as an unclean caste.

The Kumars are an illiterate caste, and there are very few among them who can sign their own name. Their usual surname is Pāl.

CHAP. V.—THE KARMAKARS AND LOHARS.

THE Hindu ironsmith is called Karmakar in Bengal, and Lohar in all the other Provinces of Northern India, including Behar and Chutia Nagpur. The Kamars are in Bengal included among the upper nine of the Sudra castes. In Behar the corresponding caste of Lohars have the same position, and there also a Brahman will take a drink of water from the hands of an ironsmith without any hesitation. It is only the Lohars of Chutia Nagpur and Central Provinces who are regarded as an unclean caste. That is, however, not on account of their profession, but their practice of eating fowls.

The Kamars of Bengal are unacquainted with iron smelting, and now-a-days they generally work on pig-iron imported from Europe, and sold by the wholesale dealers of Calcutta. The import of hardware from Europe has led to the absolute neglect of the excellent sources of iron ores which are to be found in many parts of India, and especially in the western districts of Bengal and in Mysore. Iron smelting is, however, still practised to some extent in the Central Provinces and Chutia Nagpur by the local Lohars.* In every village throughout India there is generally a Kamar or Lohar, whose function is to manufacture and repair the agricultural implements of the local people.

---

* For an account of the indigenous process of iron smelting, see Mr. P. N. Bose's *Hindu Civilisation*, Vol. II, p. 308.

In the vicinity of the large towns, Kamars and Lohars are generally to be found who display great skill in the manufacture of cutlery, padlocks, swords, nails, hooks, &c. The name of Prem Chand Kamar, of Kanchan Nagar in Burdwan, is on the way towards becoming almost as famous in connection with cutlery as that of Rogers of Sheffield. The padlocks made by Das & Co. bid fair to supersede those of Chubb, and in respect of the manufacture of swords, the superiority of the Indian Kamar's work has been proved, over and over again, by the experiences of English soldiers in the field.* If in spite of their skill the Indian Kamars are not able to hold their own in the local markets, their failure is not to be attributed to any fault on their part. The products of a domestic industry must necessarily be more costly than machine-made wares. Then, again, the outturn of the small manufactories to be found in the remote villages cannot be so easily collected together in a commercial focus for distribution, and exchange, as the produce of large foundries. The result of these causes is very strikingly illustrated by the fact that while the worthless padlocks turned out by the factories in Birmingham are to be had in every hardware shop in India, and sell in millions, the Kamaria padlocks of the ancient types, which are considered by all to be the best and safest mechanisms of the kind, cannot generally be had either for love or money, and can be procured only by special order to some workmen whose very names are generally unknown,—the advantages of the modern art of advertisement being as yet quite unknown to them.

Circumstanced as India now is, the revival and improvement of the iron industry of the country seems to be well-nigh beyond the bounds of immediate

* See the remarks of Mr. Forbes-Mitchell in his *Reminiscences of the Indian Mutiny.*

possibility. It is only the patronage of the railways that can render large foundries pecuniarily successful. But the Indian railways are all practically in the hands of the Indian Government, and knowing well how our rulers are handicapped by the party politics of the Home Government, no reasonable man can expect them to deny their patronage to the English manufacturers for the sake of benefiting an Indian industry.

The village Kamars and Lohars are generally very poor, their income very seldom exceeding that of an unskilled labourer. In the docks and railway workshops which have lately come into existence in certain parts of the country, the Kamars and Lohars not only find employment readily, but generally earn very high wages. The most well-to-do persons among the Kamars are those who have given up their caste profession, and practise the art of the goldsmith.

The Kamars are generally Sakti worshippers, and are usually employed in slaughtering the animals offered in sacrifice to the bloodthirsty gods and goddesses that receive the adoration of the "energy worshippers." For his services, on such occasions, the Kamar receives the head of the slaughtered goat, or a money gratuity, amounting to about half a shilling. The rich goldsmith Kamars of Dacca are mainly Vishnuvites.

In Southern India there is a caste called variously Kammallars, Panchanam Varlu and Panchval, who combine in them the functions of the goldsmith, coppersmith, brazier, ironsmith, carpenter and sculptor. The Kamars and Lohars are generally quite illiterate. Their total number is, according to the last Census, 2,625,103 souls.

CHAP. VI.—THE GOLDSMITHS.

§ 1.—*The Sonar and Shakra of Northern India.*

THE position of the goldsmith in the Hindu caste system is not the same in all the provinces. Not being expressly included in the Navasayaka group, he is, in Northern India, generally regarded as somewhat unclean. But it is suggested that he comes within the division called Karmakar, and the best Brahmans will not sometimes hesitate to take a drink of water from his hands. The position of the Sonar in Behar, N.-W. Provinces and Panjab is similar to that of the Shakra or Swarnakara of Bengal. In the Panjab, the Hindu Sonars take the sacred thread, just as most of the other Sudra castes there do. In the extreme south of the Indian Peninsula, the goldsmiths do not form a separate caste, but are included in the group called Kammallar, whose sub-sections practise five different kinds of handicraft, *viz.*, work (1) in gold and silver, (2) brass and copper, (3) iron, (4) carpentry, (5) sculpture. The corresponding group of castes in Mysore is called Panchvala. The goldsmith sections in Mysore are called Akkasala or (Arkasala) Agasala. The Agasalas are recognised by the other Panchsalars as the head of the clan. In Telingana there is a similar group of castes called Panchanam Varlu, an account of which is given in § 2 of this chapter. In the Central Provinces there are two classes of goldsmiths called Sonar and Panchallar. They take the sacred thread at the time of marriage, and are regarded as clean castes. The goldsmiths are a very intelligent class—perhaps a little too sharp. They usually practise their hereditary profession, and, as it is very lucrative, they very seldom give a liberal education to their children in order to qualify them for a more ambitious career.

§ 2.—*The Panchanam Varlu of the Telegu country and the Kammallar of Dravira.*

It has been already stated that the artisan castes working on metal, wood or stone are called Panchanam Varlu in the Telegu country, Panchval in Mysore and Kammallar in Dravira. The Panchanams of Telingana trace their origin from the five faces of the god Siva. They take the sacred thread and claim to have a higher status than the priestly Brahmans. But the other castes regard them as very unclean. In fact, not even a Paria will take a drink of water from the hands of a Panchanam. Formerly the Panchanams were not allowed to wear shoes, or to carry umbrellas with them, or to ride in a *palki* even at the time of marriage. They have four subcastes, with five different occupations as stated below :—

1. The profession of the goldsmith is practised by the Kansali.
2. That of the blacksmith by the Kamari.
3. Do. carpenter by the Wadronga.
4. Do. brazier by the Kanshari.
5. Do. sculptor by all the above-mentioned castes.

The Kansalis, or the goldsmiths, have generally a little education, but the others are usually quite illiterate. The Kammallars of Dravira have the same divisions among them, but perhaps a higher status than the Panchanams of the Telegu country. The corresponding group of castes in Mysore is, as already stated, called Panchval. They profess to be descended from the celestial architect Visvakarma and wear the Brahmanical triple cord. They claim to be equal to the Brahmans, but their pretensions are not admitted by any one not of their caste.

CHAP. VII.—THE SUTAR AND THE BARHI.

In Bengal and Western India the carpenters are called Sutra Dhar or Sutar, from the Sanskrit word *Sutra*, the thread, with which the course of the saw is marked. Though their profession is a clean one, they, like the Sonars, are regarded as a semi-clean caste. Good Brahmans do not usually take drinking water from their hands, and they are ministered by a special class of Brahmans who are treated as degraded persons, and whose status is inferior to that of even the Sudra Yajakas. Some of the Sutars of Bengal practise the art of painting pictures of the Hindu gods. The female members of some of the Sutars make an article of food for the middle classes called *chipitaka* or *chira*. It is prepared by boiling unhusked rice, and husking it, while yet slightly soft, by placing it in a wooden mortar, and beating it with a wooden hammer attached to the end of a beam which is worked like a lever. While the motive power is supplied by the foot of one of the females engaged in the manufacture, another female feeds the mortar, and takes out from it the flattened grains mixed with the loose husk which is afterwards winnowed off. The *chira*, when it is first brought out of the mortar, is very sweet. But generally it is eaten long afterwards when it is completely dry. When soaked in milk and mango juice, and mixed with sugar and plantain, it becomes a highly enjoyable delicacy. The making of *chira* is not the monopoly of the Sutars. There is another caste called Ganrariya whose females take a considerable share in the business. The Sutar population of India is, according to the last Census, as stated below :—

Bengal	...	...	...	175,554
Bombay	...	...	...	196,246
Central India	...	...	...	127,776
Hyderabad	...	...	...	103,419

The Barhis have a somewhat higher status than the Sutars. Good Brahmans will take drinking water from their hands, and those who officiate as their priests are not degraded altogether. The Barhi population of India is nearly one million, and is distributed as stated below :—

N.-W. Provinces	...	...	...	568,630
Bengal	...	...	...	293,553
Central Provinces	...	...	...	69,833

The Badigas of Northern Deccan seem to be the same as the Barhis. But they were separately enumerated at the last Census, and their population is stated to be as follows :—

Madras	...	...	...	376,434
Bombay	...	...	...	65,916
Mysore	...	...	...	9,408

The Tarkhans of the Panjab and the Khatis of Rajputana are also carpenters by caste. The total population of the carpenter castes in India exceeds three millions, and yet the demand for their services at present is such that they get very high wages in every part of the country. While a weaver can hardly earn two annas in a day, and an agricultural labourer gets not more than three annas,—the average daily income of a carpenter does not fall short of ten annas. Such being the case, many Mahomedans and low caste Hindus are now taking to the profession.

The carpenters of Bombay are, like those of Bengal, called Sutar. In Western India the Sutars are regarded as a clean caste, and have many educated men among them. The late Dr. Sakharam Arjoon, who had the largest medical practice in his time, was a Sutar. The Sutars of Bengal are generally quite illiterate.

CHAP. VIII.—THE BRAZIERS AND COPPER-SMITHS.

§ 1.—*The Kansa Baniks of Bengal.*

THE Kansa Baniks or Kansaris of Bengal are both manufacturers and sellers of brass, copper and bronze vessels. In the other provinces of Northern India, the corresponding castes are called Kasera, Thathera and Tamhera. The caste status of the Kansa Baniks is exactly similar to that of the Gandha Baniks. The ordinary Sudra Yajaka Brahmans minister to both as priests, and even the best Brahmans will take a drink of water from their hands. Many good Brahmans accept even the Kansaris' gifts openly and without any hesitation. The Kansaris are a well-to-do class, and there are among them a few who are reckoned among the richest men of the country. Such is Babu Kali Krishna Pramanik of Calcutta, and such was the late Babu Guru Das Das of Nadiya. The late Babu Tarak Nath Pramanik, the father of the former, used to spend enormous sums of money every year in charity to the poor, and in the performance of religious ceremonies. But so vast were his resources, that the prosperity of his family continues undiminished to the present day; while the family of Guru Das has been ruined by similar extravagance, combined with injudicious speculations and the bad counsel of his legal advisers.

The total Kansari population of Bengal is, according to the last Census, 55,833 souls in all. There are several sub-classes among them, of which the most important are the Saptagrami and Mohmadabadi.

The usual surnames of the Kansaris are Das, Pramanik and Pal. Generally speaking, the Kansaris are an illiterate class, though some of them are able to keep their own accounts. Kansari boys are sometimes found in the English schools of the country. But they never make much progress. Most of the Kansaris are Devi worshippers and eat flesh meat. Like the Kamars, the Kansaris are sometimes employed to slaughter animals for sacrificial purposes.

§ 2.—*The Kasaras and Thatheras of Northern India.*

The Kasaras and Thatheras of Northern India have, generally speaking, the same characteristics and social status as the Kansaris of Bengal. Some of the Kasaras of Behar worship the Mahomedan saints called Panch Piriya.

§ 3.—*The Gejjegora and Kanchugora of Southern India.*

The Gejjegoras are the makers of the small bells worn by dancing women round their ankles. The Kanchugoras are also called Bogaras. They are the braziers and coppersmiths.

CHAP. IX.—THE SANKHA BANIKS OF BENGAL.

THE designation Sankha Banik literally signifies a "conch shell merchant." The Sankha Baniks are popularly called Sankaris. Their chief business is the manufacture of the shell bracelets which the poorer Hindu women of East Bengal wear for ornamental purposes, and which even the richest Hindu ladies have to wear at the time of their marriage and certain other auspicious occasions. The Sankaris make also those shell bugles which the Hindu warriors of ancient times used on the battle-field, and which are now used only in connection with religious ceremonies. The caste position of the Sankaris is exactly the same as that of the Gandha Baniks and Kansa Baniks. The Sankaris are to be found in only a few of the large towns of Bengal. Their numerical strength is very small, and, generally speaking, they are very poor, and quite illiterate. The profession of the Sankha Banik was never a very lucrative one, and it has of late been injuriously affected by the introduction of glass bracelets which are now in fashion among all classes of Indian women. The glass bracelets are very cheap, and they do not lose their lustre by use like the shell ornaments.

CHAP. X.—THE GRAIN PARCHERS.

THE Kandus derive their name from the Sanskrit word *kandu*, which means a frying-pan or oven. Their caste profession is grain parching, though they not only sell parched grain but many kinds of sweatmeats also. Parched rice, maize or pea is not in itself *kachi* food, and may, though prepared or touched by a Sudra, be eaten by a Brahman. But when put into the mouth such food, by being mixed with the saliva, becomes *kachi khana*, and so orthodox Brahmans and the widows of the Brahmans, Käyasthas and Rajputs cannot eat it, except at dinner-time. In practice the aristocratic widows and the puritanic Brahmans very seldom eat fried rice or any other kind of parched grain, and these things are usually eaten by only little boys, married ladies, and the lower castes, as part of their tiffin. When Brahmans think of eating fried rice they do not evince much hesitation to procure it from a Kandu's shop. Such being the case, it is hardly necessary to add that the Kandus are a clean Sudra caste from whose hands a Brahman may take a drink of water. The total Kandu population of the country is numbered at 524,155 souls. The Kandus are quite illiterate.

The Bhad Bhunjas practise the same profession, and have the same status, as the Kandus. The last Census gives the following figures relating to the numerical strength of the Bhad Bhunjas :—

N.-W. Provinces	...	...	...	**316,368**
Central India	...	...	...	**7,248**
Rajputana	...	...	...	**4,977**

There are two classes of Kahars called Dhimar and Gond, who are also grain parchers. The grain parching castes, mentioned above, are to be found chiefly in the United Provinces and Behar. In Bengal proper the Mayaras act both as grain parchers and sweetmeat makers.

CHAP. XI.—THE DIRJIS OR THE TAILORS.

THERE is a caste in some parts of the Panjab, N.-W. Provinces, Rajputana and Deccan who are called Dirji. They usually live by working as tailors. The Dirjis of the Panjab take the sacred thread. In Bengal the tailors are all Mahomedans. With regard to the Dirjis of Mysore, the following account is given in the last Census Report of the State :—

"The order is divided into two sub-divisions, *viz.*, Dirji, Chippiga or Nam Dev and Rangare. The first three, known by the collective name of Dirji, are professional tailors, while the Rangares are also dyers. The Dirjis are immigrants from the Maharatta country and worship Vitthoba or Krishna."—*Mysore Census Report*, p. 246.

PART XII.

THE MANUFACTURING AND ARTISAN CASTES THAT ARE REGARDED AS UNCLEAN SUDRAS.

CHAP. I.—THE BREWERS, TADI-DRAWERS AND SELLERS OF SPIRITUOUS LIQUORS.

Of the several unclean castes, the most important are those connected with the manufacture and sale of spirituous liquors. Of these the following deserve special notice :—

1. *Brewers.*
   1. Sunri (Found in Bengal, Assam, Madras and Central Provinces. Total population 525,698).
   2. Kalwar (Found in every part of Northern India. Total population 1,195,097).

2. *Tadi or palm juice drawers.*
   3. Shanar and Illawar (Found in Southern India only). Total population :

Shanar	...	... 690,434
Illawar	...	... 703,215
Billawa	...	... 127,037

   4. Bhandari (Found only in the Bombay Presidency. Total population, 70,014).
   5. Pasi (Palm juice drawers; found chiefly in Behar).
   6. Tiyan ... 538,075 } Found in the Deccan.
   7. Idiga ... 196,901 } Found in the Deccan.
   8. Gaundla ... 235,902 } Found in the Deccan.

All these occupy a very low position in the Hindu caste system, and although a great many of them have in recent times become very wealthy, through the encouragement given to the liquor traffic for fiscal purposes, yet their caste status has not improved very materially. They have been, for more than half a century, struggling hard to be recognised as a clean caste. But the only classes who openly hold any communication with them, for purposes other than business, are those followers of the latter-day prophets that fatten on the rejected elements of pure Hinduism. An orthodox Brahman, Rajput, Vaidya or Kāyasth, professing any of the aristocratic forms of ancient Hinduism, would not allow a brewer to enter even his parlour, and if obliged, for the sake of business, to visit a publican in his house, he would after coming home put off his clothes, and put on another suite after regularly bathing, or sprinkling his body with the holy water of the Ganges. In Southern India a Brahman considers himself contaminated by the approach of a Shanar within twenty-four paces. In the other parts of India there is no such hard-and-fast rule. But the practice in this respect is much the same throughout the country. In East Bengal and Orissa, even the ordinary washermen and the barbers refuse to render their usual services to the Sunris, and the very *palki* bearers decline to carry them on their litters.

§ 1.—*The Sunris of Bengal and Behar.*

The Sunris of Bengal and Behar are perhaps the richest of the several clans of brewers. Many of them are now among the leading traders and bankers of the country, and have given up altogether the practice of their caste profession. The Sunris of Bengal proper are all Vishnuvites of the sect founded by Chaitanya, and some of them may be found among the Chaitanite monks called Babajis or Reverend Fathers. Although the Sunris are by nature somewhat hard-fisted, yet they patronise the Chaitanite ministers and shrines with such liberality that, within the last few years, many of the aristocratic Brahmans of the Tāntric cult have espoused the Vishnuvite faith in order to have a share of their largesses, albeit the condition on which they are given is said to be that the donee must partake of the hospitality of the donor. To comply with such a *sine quâ non* must be very humiliating to every Brahman, and it is hard to believe that love of lucre has sufficed in any case yet to overcome Brahmanical pride to such an extent. With regard to the religion of the Sunris, Mr. Risley, on the authority of the late Dr. Wise, makes the following observations which are remarkably in accordance with the actual facts :—

According to Dr. Wise almost every member of the caste is a follower of Chaitaniya, and the rich are celebrated for the ostentatious observance of the Sankirtana chants in honour of Krishna after the decease of any relative. The chief rites observed in Eastern Bengal are the worship of Ganesa on the 1st Baisakh (April—May), and the 1st of Aghan (November—December); of Gandeshwari on the 10th of Asin (September—October); of Durga at the time of the Durga Puja in October; and of Ganga whenever their boats are starting on a trading voyage. The majority being Vaishnavas, animals are rarely offered to any deity; but when this is done, the victim is afterwards released. Shahas are very fond of pigeons, and in the courtyard of almost every house a dovecot is fixed, as they believe that the air fanned by pigeons' wings wafts good luck. They are also devoted worshippers of Kartikeya, the Hindu god of war, constructing annually in November a life-size effigy of the god, and keeping it within the female enclosure for a year. Other Hindu castes throw the image into the river immediately after the Kartik Puja, but the Shahas allege that their special veneration of the god is often rewarded, the barren rejoicing and the husband becoming the joyful father of children. It is easy to understand in what way this figure gives rise to scandalous stories among Bengalis, and how the Shaha becomes a butt for the wit and sarcasm of his neighbours.

The Behar Sunris follow the average Hinduism of that part of the country, and worship most of the regular gods as occasion offers. Their minor gods are very numerous. Dharam Raj, Bandi Goraiya, Govindji, Hanuman, Kasi Panjiar, Joti Panjiyar, Apurba Panjiar, Mira, Saiyed, Julpa, Sokha, Hosan Khan, and Panch Pir. Rice cooked in milk and sugar, cakes of *ghi* (*puri*), and various kinds of fruit are offered to them, and afterwards eaten by the worshippers. Kids are sacrificed to Bandi. On Sundays milk and flowers are offered to the Sun. In Bengal, says Dr. Wise, the Brahman, peculiar to the caste, boasts that he never accepts alms from anyone not a Sunri, but it is quite certain that none of the clean castes would present him with charity. These Brahmans, who assume the bombastic titles of Vidyasagar, Vidyalankar, Chakravarti and Pāthak, like the Purohits of the other low castes, read the funeral service at the burning ghât, and are looked down upon by other members of the sacred order. The Sunris of Behar are served by a low class of Maithila Brahmans, who also minister to the religious necessities of the Teli caste. No other Brahmans will eat and drink with these men, who are known by the contemptuous epithet of Telia Babhan. In Chutia Nagpur the Brahmans who serve the Sunris call themselves Kanojias, but they have no right to the name, and no other Brahmans will have anything to do with them.—Risley's *Tribes and Castes of Bengal*, Vol. II, pp. 278-279.

The Sunris of Bengal being Vishnuvites are strict vegetarians and teetotalers. There are a few Vishnuvite Bhagats among those of Behar also. But the majority of the Behar Sunris eat mutton, goat's flesh and fish. Some eat even field rats. Most of them indulge freely in strong drink. The total number of Sunris in the different provinces is as shown in the following table:—

Bengal	423,466
Assam	51,970
Central Provinces	15,420
Madras	34,842
Total ...	525,698

The usual family names of the Sunris are Saha, Roy, Das, &c.

§ 2.—*The Kalwars of Northern India.*

The Kalwars of Northern India have the same caste status as the Sunris of Bengal, and like them have many rich men among them, as, for instance, Babu Ram Prasad Chowdry, of Monghyr, and Babu Tejnarain, of Bhagalpur, the founder and endower of the Tejnarain College, Bhagalpur. The Kalwars are more numerous than the Sunris, and the majority of them are now petty shopkeepers having nothing to do with their ancestral profession. A very large portion of the Behari grocers and pedlars of Calcutta are Kalwars. On being first questioned they generally profess to be Baniyas, and they confess their real caste status only when sufficiently pressed. The Kalwars are divided into many sections, as, for instance, the following:—

1. Biyahut.
2. Jaiswar or Ajodhyabasi.
3. Banodhya.
4. Khalsa.
5. Khoridaha.
6. Diswár.

The Biyahuts and the Jaiswars have now no concern with the manufacture or sale of spirituous liquors, and as the Biyahuts do not allow their widows to re-marry, they are generally treated as a semi-clean caste. The Jaiswar's profession is similarly unexceptionable, but they worship the Mahomedan saints called Panch Piriya, and chiefly on that account, but partly also on account of their marrying their widows, they are regarded as having a lower status than the Biyahuts. As the Jaiswars worship some of the Mahomedan saints the Biyahuts and Khoridahas take a delight in going directly against the fundamental points of the Islamic faith, by offering pigs and wine to a local divinity called Goriya.* The Banodhyas worship the Brahma Deo, *i.e.*, the spirits of Brahmans dying in the unmarried condition.

The Kalwar population of India is 1,195,097 souls.

In the Central Provinces, the Kalwars are the brewers, and the Mahars are the tadi-drawers. The Kalwars are there generally very rich as in other parts of the country.

In the Punjab the majority of the brewers are Kallals. Some members of the scavenger caste, called Choorha, also practise the some profession.

§ 3.—*The Shanars and Illavars of Dravira.*

The Shanars and Illavars are identical in caste. They are a very rich community, and are very numerous in the southern districts of the Indian Peninsula. The caste is called Illavar in the northern part of the tract where they are found, and Shanar in the extreme south. In South Kanara the Illavars are called Billavars.

---

* The Goriya is worshipped in the form of little mounds or platforms of clay to be found in many Behar villages. The precise nature of the Goriya's claim to worship is not generally known. He seems to be the presiding deity of *gors* or tombs. The pigs and wine which are offered to the Goriya are not eaten or drunk by the votaries, but given to the low caste Dosadhas whose god he is.

The Shanars eat flesh and fish, and drink strong tadi. "The peculiar marriage customs of the Nairs, together with their singular rules of inheritance, are practised by many Illavars and by a few Shanars. Husband and wife easily separate and contract other alliances. All inherited property descends to maternal nephews, while other kinds of property are shared equally by nephews and sons. Socially, these tribes are treat-with great ignominy. Their women were until recently not permitted to wear clothing above their waist. They were not allowed to carry umbrellas, to wear shoes or golden ornaments, to build houses above one story in height, to milk cows, or even to use the ordinary language of the country. Even now their position is one of great humiliation."* The treatment which the Shanars receive from the Hindu community being as stated above, many of them have been easily led by the British missionaries to embrace the faith of Christ.

With regard to the origin, occupation and social position of the Shanars, the Rev. Dr. Caldwell gives the following interesting account :—

There is reason to suppose that the Shanars are immigrants from the northern coast of Ceylon, where the same or a similar caste still exists, bearing a grammatical and intelligible form of the same name 'Shandrar,' of which 'Shanar' is etymologically a corruption. It is also tolerably certain that the Illavars and Teers (*i.e.*, Singhalese and Islanders), who cultivate the cocoanut palm in Travancore, are descendants of Shandrar colonists from Ceylon. There are traces of a common origin among them all; 'Shanar,' for instance, being a title of honour among the Travaucore Illavars. It is traditionally reported that the Shanars who inhabit Tinneveli came from the neighbourhood of Jaffna in Ceylon; that one portion of them, the class now called Nadans (lords of the soil), entered Tinneveli by way of Ramnad, bringing with them the seed nuts of the Jaffna palmyra, the best in the East, and appropriating or obtaining from the ancient Pandya princes, as the most suitable region for the cultivation of the palmyra, the sandy waste lands of Manad in the south-east of Tinneveli, over which to the present day, they claim rights of seignorage, and that the other portion of the immigrants, esteemed a lower division of the caste, came by the sea to the south of Travancore, where vast numbers of them are still found, and whence, having but little land of their own, they have gradually

* *See* Sherring, Vol. III, pp. 184-185.

spread themselves over Tinneveli on the invitation of the Nadans and other proprietors of land, who, without the help of their poorer neighbours, as climbers, could derive but little profit from their immense forests of palmyra. Some of these immigrations have probably taken place since the Christian era; and it is asserted by the Syrian Christians of Travancore, that one portion of the tribe, the Illavars, were brought over from Ceylon by *their* ancestors for the cultivation of the cocoanut palm. The Shanars, though probably immigrants from Ceylon, are Hindus, not of the Brahmanical but of the Tamil or aboriginal race.

The caste of Shanars occupies a middle position between the Vellalars and their Pariah slaves. The majority of the Shanar confine themselves to the hard and weary labour appointed to their race. But a considerable number have become cultivators of the soil, as landowners or farmers, or are engaged in trade.—Dr. Caldwell's *Essay on the Tinneveli Shanars*, pp. 4—7.

Good Brahmans never minister to the Shanars as priests, and their religious ceremonies are usually performed by the Pandarams.

§ 4.—*The Bhandaris of Western India.*

The tadi-drawers of the Kankan and Bombay are called Bhandari. Their total number is about one hundred and seventy thousand souls. They themselves do not drink the juice of the palm in the fermented state.

§ 5.—*The Pasis of Behar.*

The Pasis are the tadi-drawers of Behar. They eat fowls and field rats, and indulge freely in spirituous and fermented liquors. Many of them have taken to cultivation, and hold lands as occupancy or non-occupancy ryots. Others are employed as day labourers, porters and coolies. The good Brahmans never officiate at their religious ceremonies, and at their sacrifices, funerals and marriages, they get either a degraded Brahman, or a member of their own caste, to act as the priest. They allow their widows to re-marry in the *sagai* form. They allow also divorce and the re-marriage of divorced wives. The Pasis worship all the minor gods of Behar, as, for instance, Bandi Goriya and Sokha. In the month of Jeth the sickle (*hansuli*) used for cutting the palm tree is regularly worshipped by them with flowers and grain.

§ 6.—*The Tiyans of Southern India.*

The Tiyans of Malabar and Travancore are palm cultivators and tadi-drawers like the Shanars and Illavars. The Tiyans, however, are regarded as even more unclean. They are generally very handsome, but they are treated as Pariahs. They practise polyandry. The total number of the Tiyans exceeds five hundred thousand souls.

§ 7.—*The Idigas of Mysore and the Telugu country.*

The tadi-drawers of Mysore and the Telugu country are called Idigas. They do not seem to be regarded as a very unclean caste, as they are now freely employed in domestic service. They were formerly employed as soldiers under the local Palligars. The number of persons returned as Idigas by the last Census is 196,901.

§ 8.—*The Gaundla and the Gamalla of the Telugu country.*

The Gaundlas of Hyderabad are a numerous community. They number 235,902 persons. The Gamallas of the Telugu country are the same as the Gaundlas. There are no Shanars or Kalwars in the Telugu country. The Idigas and the Gamallas are the tadi-drawers, while the Sunris are the brewers. There is in the Telugu country another caste named Sittigadu, who have the same occupation as the Idigas.

CHAP. II.—THE OIL MANUFACTURERS.

THE oil manufacturing castes are called Teli, Kalu and Ghanchi in Northern India. In the northern parts of the Deccan the oil-makers are called Ganigas and Tel Kalu Varlu. In the extreme south the name of the caste is Vanikan. They are all regarded as more or less unclean everywhere.*

§ 1.—*The Telis of Bengal.*

The Telis of Bengal have now nothing to do with the manufacture of oil, and they claim to derive their name from Tula, which means the shopman's scale, instead of from Taila, which means oil. But the derivation of Teli from Tula is grammatically impossible, and the suggestion is strongly contradicted by the fact that the Telis in other parts of the country are actually oil-pressers. However that may be, the Telis of Bengal are, as stated in a previous chapter, included among Nava Sayakas, and regarded as clean Sudras.

---

* In speaking of the Telis of Bengal, Mr. Risley says :—

"Their original profession was probably oil-pressing, and the caste may be regarded as a functional group recruited from the respectable middle class of Hindu society. Oil is used by all Hindus for domestic and ceremonial purposes, and its manufacture could only be carried on by men whose social purity was beyond dispute."—Risley's *Tribes and Castes of Bengal*, Vol. II, pp. 305, 306.

The above shows how difficult it is for an English author to give a correct view of the mechanism of our society. The fact is that *ghi* and oil are not contaminated or rendered unfit for a Hindu's use by the touch of even the lowest castes.

The Telis of Bengal are a very important caste. The majority of them being shopkeepers and grain merchants, they are a very well-to-do class. Some of them as, for instance, the family of the celebrated Rani Svarnamayi of Moorshedabad, and the Rajas of Digapatiya have become very rich landholders under British rule. The usual family names of the Telis are—

1. Kundu, peculiar to the class.
2. Pal Chowdry. An aristocratic surname assumed by the big Teli zemindars.
3. Pal }
4. Nandy } not peculiar to the class.
5. Dey }
6. Chowdry }
7. Mallick } not peculiar to any class.
8. Ray }

There are very few among the Telis of Bengal who are quite illiterate, while, under British rule, some of them have attained great eminence as scholars. The most distinguished among them was the late Rai Kisto Das Pal, Bahadoor, whose name is sure to be remembered for a long time as one of India's greatest journalists and public men. The late Babu Rasik Krishna Mallick, who was one of the distinguished batch of scholars turned out by the Hindu College of Calcutta at a very early period of its existence, was also a Teli. Among the living celebrities of the caste, the name of Srinath Pal may be specially mentioned here. He is a nephew of the Maharani Svarnamayi, and is treated by her as her own son. As a student he attained some of the highest honours that the University of Calcutta can confer. For the last ten years he has been managing the Maharani's vast estates with great ability.

The Telis of Bengal have many sub-divisions among them, as, for instance, Ekadasa, Dwadasa, Betna, Tush Kota and Saptagrami.

§ 2.—*The Kalus of Bengal.*

The caste that actually manufactures oil in Bengal is called Kalu, and is regarded as an unclean caste having a somewhat higher status than that of the brewers. The Kalus are all illiterate, and though there are very few wealthy men among them, they are generally quite above want. In the Nadiya district there is at Tihatta a Kalu landholder of the class called Talukdars. The usual surnames of the Kalu are Gorai, Sagari, Sadhu, Khan and Set.

The Kalus number 191,355 persons in Bengal. They are chiefly Vishnuvites. A special class of degraded Brahmans minister to them as priests. Their spiritual guides are the Chaitanite Gossains.

§ 3.—*The Telis and Ghanchis of Upper India.*

In Upper India the oil-pressers are called Teli and also Ghanchi. Their position is nowhere higher than that of the Kalus of Bengal.

§ 4.—*The Tel Kulu Varlu of the Telugu country.*

The oilmen of the Telugu country are called Tel Kulu Varlu. They take the sacred thread.

§ 5.—*The Ganigas and Vanikans of Southern India.*

The oil-pressers are called Vanikan in the Dravira country. In Mysore the name of the caste is Ganiga. In the Kanarase country they are called also Jotiphana or Jotinagora, *i.e.*, the tribe of light. They have also in some localities different names according to peculiarities of their machines, or the method of working them. For instance, those whose mills are made of stone and worked by yoking pairs of oxen are called Hegganigas ; Kiru-Ganigas is the name of those who work with wooden mills ; while those who yoke only one bull to the mill are called Vantiyettu Ganigas. The Linga-wearing Ganigas called Sajjanas, hold no social intercourse with the other sections. There are both Vishnuvites and Sivites among the other Ganigas.

CHAP. III.—THE SALT MANUFACTURERS.

THE Luniyas or Nunias of Northern India are, as their names indicate, primarily salt manufacturers. The salt industry of Bengal being very nearly ruined by the fiscal regulations which give greater facilities to the importation of Cheshire salt than to indigenous manufacture, the practice of their caste profession by the Luniyas has become well-nigh impossible. The majority of them are now saltpetre makers and navvies like the Beldars and the Koras. They are a numerous community as will appear from the following table :—

N.-W. Provinces	412,822
Bengal	318,441
Bombay	14,599

In some parts of Behar the Luniyas are treated as clean Sudras. But the practice is not uniform, and generally they are regarded as semi-clean Sudras. The inferiority of their caste status is due, not to their profession which is a clean one, but to the fact of their being a non-Aryan race, and to their habit of eating pork and drinking spirituous liquors. They are chiefly Saktas, and there are very few Vishnuvite Bhakats among them. They allow divorce, and the re-marriage of widows and divorced wives.

The salt manufacturing caste of the Madras Presidency are called Uppilian, Uppara and Upaliga. The salt-petre-making caste of Northern India are called Rehgar and Shoragar.

CHAP. IV.—THE LEATHER WORKERS.

§ 1.—*The Chamars and Muchis of Northern India.*

The Chamars and Muchis are generally regarded as identical in caste. The name Chamar is derived from the Sanskrit word *Charmakar*, which means "a maker of leather." The meaning of the name Muchi is not very clear. The suggestion that the name is connected with the Sanskrit word *Matsya* is contradicted by the fact that the Muchis have nothing to do with the catching of fish. The Chamar population of Northern India is very large, and exceeds eleven million persons as will appear from the following table :—

N.-W. Provinces	5,855,208
Punjab	1,206,837
Bengal	1,101,253
Central India	888,018
Central Provinces	880,108
Rajputana	846,675

The Muchis are less numerous and number about one million persons. They are distributed as shewn below :—

Bengal	406,333
Punjab	407,634
Bombay	63,051

The Chamars and the Muchis have a variety of occupations. Primarily, they are skinners, tanners, shoemakers, and musical instrument makers. They practise also the weaving of coarse cotton cloths and mats of reed. In Northern India, the Chamars serve for hire as agricultural labourers and workers. In

Bengal they generally supply the bands of instrumental musicians who are a necessity to every Hindu at the time of religious ceremonies of a joyful nature. After the Sepoy Mutiny an attempt was made to recruit the native army from the ranks of the Chamars instead of from the higher castes like the Brahmans and Rajputs. But the experiment did not, it is said, prove successful.

The Chamars and Muchis are very unclean castes. Their very touch renders it necessary for a good Hindu to bathe with all his clothes on. In the villages they generally live in a distinct quarter. When their services are required by a high caste Hindu, he will allow them to enter the outer enclosure of his house, but not into the interior of any building used as a dwelling-house or chapel. For the Muchi and Mahomedan musicians who are a necessity on festive occasions, there is generally special accommodation in the mansions of the rich and in the big temples. Those who play on the kettledrum and the pipe called *sanai*, and who are generally Mahomedans, are perched on the top of the main entrance, while the Muchi bands entertain the bye-standers from the Nat-Mandir or dancing hall in front of the puja *dalan* or chapel.

§ 2.—*The Chakilians and Madigs of Southern India.*

The professions and caste status of the Chakilians and Madigs are the same as those of the Muchis and Chamars of Northern India. The Chakilians number 445,366 persons. The Madig population is nearly double that of the Chakilians. With regard to the Madigs, the following observations are made in the last Census Report of Mysore :—

The Madig is the village cobbler ; he removes the carcases of the village cattle, skins them, and is bound to supply the village community with agricultural articles made of skin or leather, such as thongs of the bullocks, buckets for lifting water, &c. The Madig caste is 239,575 strong. The Madigs are by religion Vishnuvites, Sivites and Saktas. The caste is divided into two independent sub-divisions, the

Desbhaga and *Others*, between whom there is no intermarriage. The former acknowledge the Sri Vaishnava Brahmans as their Gurus, to whom they pay extraordinary homage on all ceremonial occasions. The Madigs in the province are decidedly an indigenous class. They are mostly field labourers, but some of them till land, either leased or their own. In urban localities, on account of the rise in the value of skins, the Madigs have attained to considerable affluence.—*Mysore Census Report for* 1891, pp. 254-55.

§ 3.—*The Leather-working Castes of Rajputana and Central India.*

Besides the Chamars and Muchis there are some other leather-working classes in Rajputana having the following names :—

1. Bambi.	2. Jatia.	3. Sargara.

In Bikanir the Chamars are called Balai. The Bambis are workers in leather, weavers, and village servants, and receive the skins of all unclaimed dead animals. The Jatias, like the Muchis of Bengal, eat the flesh of dead animals. The Sargaras are cultivators and drum-beaters. The worship of the snake goddess *Manasha* is considered by the Muchis in some parts of the country as their speciality. Some Muchis regularly beg from door to door with an image or emblem of either the snake goddess or of the small-pox goddess. A Muchi of Bikanir who lived in the early part of the present century, founded a religious sect.

CHAP. V.—THE MAT-MAKERS AND BASKET-MAKERS.

§ 1.—*The Mat-makers.*

MAT-MAKING and basket-making are clean arts. But they are generally practised by the aboriginal castes, whose low social status is due more to their non-Aryan blood and their non-observance of the Shastric restrictions regarding diet and drink, than to the nature of their professions. The celebrated Sitalpatis (Lit. cool mats) of East Bengal are manufactured by a caste called Patiyals.

The Masnudpatis of Cossijarah are not made by any particular caste, and the art is said to be practised by even the local Brahmans. The nicer varieties of these and the Sitalpatis are very costly ; but they are very cool, and in summer they are considered as a necessity by the Indian aristocracy. I am not aware whether there is any demand for them in foreign countries.

§ 2.—*The Basket-makers.*

The following are the castes that usually make baskets :— ... .

1.	Dom, 1,257,826	... Found everywhere in Northern India.
2.	Baiti	... Found in Bengal.
3.	Metha Koran	... Found in the Madras Presidency.
4.	Bansphor, 89,955	A branch of the Dom tribe, found chiefly in Northern India.
5.	Turi, 50,020	... Found in Bengal and Assam.
6.	Bind	... Found in almost every part of the United Provinces. The Binds not only make mats, but are tadi-drawers, boatmen and fishermen also.

PART XIII.

THE CLEAN AGRICULTURAL CASTES.

CHAP. I.—THE KURMIS AND THE KUNBIS.

THE most important agricultural castes of Northern India are those called Kurmis and Kunbis. They are divided into many sections, which, for practical purposes, are independent castes. But the status of these sections is, generally speaking, the same, and as they all designate themselves as Kurmis or Kunbis, they may be treated as a single caste. The derivation of their name is not very clear. It may be traceable to some aboriginal language, or to an abbreviated form of the Sanskrit compound *Krishi Karmi*, which means an agriculturist.

The Kurmi population of India is very large, the total exceeding ten millions. They are distributed as follows :—

Bombay	3,577,873
N.-W. Provinces	2,035,768
Bengal	1,321,628
Hyderabad	1,233,930
Berar	834,432
Central Provinces	805,766

There are no Kurmis in Bengal proper or Punjab. Taking a bird's-eye view of the ethnology of Northern India, it would appear that the principal elements in the rural population of the country are the Kurmis, Gopas,

Kaibartas and Chamars, and that the Brahmans, Rajputs, Kāyasthas and Baniyas, though numerically very strong, constitute only its town population. From this fact, and from the ethnological difference between the two groups,* the conclusion seems reasonable that the Kurmis, Gopas, Kaibartas and Chamars had occupied the country at a very early period; and that the higher castes subsequently settled among them as conquerors, merchants or priests. The Kurmis, Gopas and Kaibartas are neither pure non-Aryans nor pure Aryans. But their features clearly show that they are a mixed race, having a very large share of Aryan blood. There are the following sub-divisions among the Kurmis :—

In Behar	1. Ghamela. 2. Kochaisa. 3. Sanswar. 4. Chandani (found also in the Central Provinces). 5. Banodhiya (originally of the Banodha country, including the modern districts of Rae Bareilly and Unao). 6. Fasfasia. 7. Jaiswar (found in almost every part of Northern India).
In Gorakpur and Benares.	1. Saithwar. 2. Atharya. 3. Chunorwar. 4. Akorwar. 5. Patnawar. 6. Kewat.
In Rohilkhand ...	1. Rowat. 2. Jadan. 3. Bharti. 4. Kattiar. 5. Gungwari.
Lower Doab ...	1. Singraon. 2. Chaporya.
Central Doab ...	1. Kanojia.
Upper Doab ...	1. Jhunia. 2. Ghorchora.
In Saugor and Bandelkhand.	1. Jaiswar.
In Nagpore ...	1. Jhari.

* See Dalton's *Ethnology of Bengal*, p. 320; see also Campbell's *Ethnology of India*.

In Hoshangabad ...	**1. Chauria.**
In Raipore ...	**1. Manohas.** **2. Charnaos.** **3. Deriesias.** **4. Singrowlo.** **5. Tirola.** **6. Chandariya.**

The religion of the Kurmis in Behar is the same as that of the other local Sudra castes. They offer worship to the gods of the Hindu pantheon, and also to such local deities as Sokha, Sambhu Nath, Goriya, &c. The majority of them are, however, mainly followers of Kabir and Ramanand. Some of the Kurmis worship also the Mahomedan saints called Panch Piriya.

The altar of the Panch Piriya consisting of a platform of earth, is erected outside the dwelling-house. A Mahomedan priest officiates at the worship, and the animal offered is sacrificed in the usual method of the Mahomedans. If a fowl is sacrificed, it is taken away by the priest. Sometimes castrated goats and pigeons are offered, and these, after their *jabai* or ceremonial slaughter, according to Mahomedan ritual, are eaten by the votaries. In accordance with vows previously made for the health of children or some other similar object, the Kurmis of Behar sometimes celebrate also the Mahomedan Maharam festival.

Some of the Kurmis eat fowls and field rats ; but they do not eat pork or beef, and are generally regarded as clean Sudras. The ordinary Sudra Yajaka Brahmans minister to them as priests, and they are deemed by the highest castes as eligible for domestic service.

The Kurmis are an illiterate class. But they make good soldiers, and there are many big landholders among them. The poor and landless members of the caste live chiefly by domestic service.

The Kurmis have no peculiar surnames. But when any one of them attains such wealth or position as to be respected by the local people, he would add to his name one or other of the following adjuncts :—

1. Chowdry.
2. Mahanto.
3. Maharai.
4. Mahto.
5. Manto.
6. Morar.
7. Mukhya.
8. Pramanika.
9. Rout.
10. Sarkar.
11. Sing.

In almost all the sub-castes of the Kurmis, excepting the Ayodhya Bansi, Ghamela and Kochaisa, a widow is allowed to re-marry. If she marry a younger brother or cousin of her late husband, she cannot forfeit her claim to a share of her husband's estate, or her right to the guardianship of her children. If she marry an outsider, these rights are forfeited. Divorce is permitted among the Kurmis, and a divorced wife may marry again in the same manner as a widow. The Kurmis of Northern India usually employ a Brahman to officiate as priest at their marriages. In Chota Nagpore and Orissa, the practice is different. There the work of the priest, on such occasions, is done by some elderly member of the house or by the Laya of the village.

The Kurmis burn their dead, and perform their *shrads* in the same manner as other high caste Sudras. The period for which they observe mourning varies according to local practice, from ten days to thirty days.

CHAP. II.—THE KOERIS OF NORTHERN INDIA.

THE Kurmis and Koeris differ in nothing except that the former are producers of the agricultural staples, while kitchen gardening is the speciality of the latter. In the vicinity of the large towns in Northern India, the Koeris raise the fruits and kitchen vegetables required for local consumption. They take a part also in rearing tobacco, opium, and other agricultural stuffs requiring more care and skill than the staple crops. They never serve in a menial capacity.

The caste status of the Koeris is similar to that of the Kurmis. In the matter of food, the majority of both these castes conform to the rules laid down in the Shastras. But it is said that, like some classes of the Kurmis, fowls and field rats are eaten by some of the Koeris also.

The Sudra Yajaka Brahmans of all classes minister to the Koeris as priests. The majority of the Koeris are Sivites and Saktas, and there are not many Vaishnavas among them. They are regarded as a clean Sudra caste, and the Brahmans will take drinking water from their hands without any hesitation. The Koeris will eat both *kachi* and *pakki* food cooked by a Brahman ; but will not eat the leavings of a Brahman's plate as the Shastras inculcate the Sudras to do, and is practically done by many of the better Sudra clans.

The Koeris are quite as illiterate as the Kurmis. The Koeris are very numerous in Behar, and are found also in the N.-W. Provinces. Their total numerical strength is nearly one and three-quarters of a million.

CHAP. III.—THE MALIS.

In almost every part of Northern and Western India there are tribes called Malis who are devoted mainly to the kind of agriculture practised by the Koeris. Their numerical strength is very considerable, as will appear from the following figures taken from the last Census report:—

Bombay	313,084
Rajputana	381,164
N.-W. Provinces	270,719
Panjab	201,189
Berar	202,488
Bengal	151,962
Central Provinces	141,086

The Malis are supposed to derive their name from the Sanskrit word "mala" which means garland. But there does not appear any reason why the name of the agricultural Malis should have had such an origin. The flower-supplying Malis form a vary small community, and it does not seem probable that the agricultural Malis were originally flower-suppliers. It seems more probable that the florists, who are called Phul Mali in the N.-W. Provinces, are a section of the great Mali tribe whose primary occupation is agriculture. The flower-supplying Malis are found chiefly in the large towns, and in the vicinity of the leading public shrines. Flowers of various kinds, and the leaves of the basil and the wood-apple being indispensable to every Hindu for the worship of his gods, every member of the higher castes has generally a garden attached to his dwelling-house. If he have no such garden, he has to buy the requisites from a Mali, or to procure them from the garden of a neighbour. In the vicinity of the sacred shrines the demand for flowers, garlands and the sacred leaves enables the Mali to carry on a brisk and profitable trade. The Malis of Bengal are also the manufacturers of the tinsel with which the clay idols are usually decorated. They are likewise suppliers of pyrotechnic works, and the tinsel crown which a Hindu has to wear at the time of marriage. The Malis are an illiterate class. They are a clean caste. The Malis of the Central Provinces and Berar are very skilful cultivators. They eat flesh and drink spirits.

CHAP. IV.—THE KACHIS.

THE Kachis are found chiefly in the central districts of Northern India. They are very much like the Koeris. They are very good cultivators. There are many sub-divisions among them, as, for instance, the following :—

1. **Kanojia ... ... From Kanoj.**
2. **Sakya Seni ... ... From the ancient town of Sankisa in Farakkabad.**
3. **Hardiya ... ... Said to derive their name from the fact of their cultivating *huldi* or turmeric).**
4. **Murao ... ... Said to be so named from the fact of their cultivating *mula* or radish.**
5. **Kachchwaba.**
6. **Salloria.**
7. **Anwar.**

The Kachis number 1,384,222 persons distributed as stated in the following table :—

N.-W. Provinces	**706,530**
Central Provinces	**122,646**
Central India	**472,134**

These figures do not, it seems, include the Muraos who were separately enumerated at the last Census. The Muraos number 677,982 persons, and are found only in the United Provinces. The Kachis are very numerous between Rai Bareli and Kanoj.

CHAP. V.—THE LODHAS AND THE LODHIS.

LIKE the Kachis, the Lodhas are found chiefly in the central districts of Northern India. They are distributed as shown in the following table :—

N.-W. Provinces	**1,065,025**
Central Provinces	**293,110**
Central India	**252,658**

The caste status of the Lodhas is somewhat lower than that of the Kurmis. Like the other agricultural castes they are mostly illiterate. There are a few landholders among them. The following are the names of their principal sub-divisions :—

1. Patoria, found chiefly in the districts of Delhi, Alighar and Etah.
2. Mathuria, so named from the ancient town of Mathuria.
3. Sankallajaria.
4. Lakhia.
5. Khoria.
6. Pania.

The Lodhis are a different tribe. They are to be found in Jhansi, Lalitpore Sagor, Damoh, and Hosungabad. The Lodhis are very turbulent and revengeful and are very unlike the peaceable Kurmis. The principal landowners of the district of Damoh are Lodhis.

CHAP. VI.—THE AGRICULTURAL KAIBARTAS OF BENGAL.

THE Chasa Kaibartas of Bengal form an important section of its rural population. In the district of Midnapore they may be reckoned among the local aristocracy. In the other districts where they are found their position is only next to that of the Kāyasthas. The designation of Kaibarta is applicable to four distinct classes having different occupations. Of these the Chasas and the Lakhinarayans of Midnapore are the most numerous, and have the highest position. The Jalias who are fishermen, and the Tutias who are mulberry growers, and devoted chiefly to sericulture, are treated as unclean castes. The Chasa and Lakhinarayan Kaibartas are regarded as very nearly clean.

In the Tumlok and Contai sub-divisions of the Midnapore District, where the number of high caste Brahmans and Kāyasthas is very small, the Kaibartas may be said to form the upper layer of the local population. A great many of them are zemindars and holders of substantial tenures. They were a very well-to-do class until recently, but they have become very much depressed by the abolition of the manufacture of salt in the district since the year 1861. This measure, which has brought about the ruin of one of the most ancient industries in the country, was adopted in accordance with the demands of an agitation which had been got up in England by English ship-owners and merchants. They represented that the East India Company were shamefully oppressing the people by making a monopoly of such a necessity of human life as salt. The word 'monopoly' being a bugbear to English people, they were easily deceived, and the agitationists, finding sympathy from the Press and the Church, could not fail to secure their object. As a matter of fact, the monopoly system on which salt was manufactured by the East India Company, since the days of Clive whose genius first adopted it, was a boon to the country; and its abolition has not been productive of any good to any class of Indian people, though it has been highly beneficial to English ship-owners and salt merchants. Now that the principle of Free Trade is about to divert the salt trade of Bengal so as to mainly benefit Germany and Arabia, it is to be hoped that the question may be reconsidered, and the monopoly re-established on its ancient footing.

In the Metropolitan districts of Nadiya and Twenty-Four Pergunnahs, the Kaibartas form the lower layer of the middle classes. In the former district they may be now said to have even a higher position. In the palmy days of indigo cultivation there, many of the local Kaibartas obtained those ministerial employments in the factories of the English planters which were very lucrative, but were too risky to have much attraction for Brahmans and Kāyasthas. By the practice of every kind of oppression to compel the ryots to cultivate indigo, the Kaibarta employés of the English factors made themselves the greatest favourites with their masters. To such an extent was this the case that in the drama called *Indigo Mirror*—for the translation of which the philanthrophic English missionary, Mr. Long, was sentenced to suffer incarceration as a criminal—a Kāyastha Dewan of an indigo planter is made to brag before his master by saying that, although of the writer caste by birth, he was qualified and prepared to render the very same kind of service as a Kewat. The planters have been ruined chiefly by the litigation in which they involved themselves. But the descendants of their employés are generally in very easy circumstances. Some of them are now big landholders, while, with their ancestral reputation for oppressing the people, and their willingness to run the risk of criminal prosecutions, a good many of them are able to secure high offices in the service of those parvenu zemindars who seek to improve their rent-rolls by the simple method of forcibly evicting the freeholders and permanent tenants from their lands. Some of the Kaibartas of Nadiya have of late been competing for University distinctions, and have attained also high offices in the service of Government. In Calcutta the millionaire Marh family of Jaun Bazar are of the Kaibarta caste. They possess very valuable house property in the town, and also extensive zemindaries in the interior of the country.

The Kaibarta population of India is very large, the total being more than three millions. The Midnapore Kaibartas have the following surnames:—

1. Myti.	6. Gholooi.
2. Bera.	7. Patra.
3. Jana.	8. Pandit.
4. Giri.	9. Das.
5. Bhumya.	10. Maji.

11. Kayal.

The usual surnames of the Nadiya Kaibartas are Das, Biswas, and Bhaumik. Marh, as a surname, is not very common either in Midnapore or in Nadiya. In the Census reports and in Mr. Risley's *Tribes and Castes of Bengal* a distinction is made between Kaibartas and Kewats. As a matter of fact, the name Kewat is only a corrupted form of Kaibarta, and is applied to designate them only when the speaker's contempt for them is meant to be implied.

Though regarded as somewhat unclean, yet in Bengal and in Tirhoot also, the poorer Kaibartas are now and then to be found employed as domestic servants in the households of the higher castes. The Kaibartas have special Brahmans, but in Midnapore the ordinary Sudra Yajaka Brahmans minister to them as priests in all ceremonies excepting *Sradha*.

CHAP. VII.—THE SADGOPAS.

THE majority of the actual tillers of the soil in Bengal are Mahomedans. The only Hindu castes in Bengal proper that are chiefly devoted to agriculture are the following :—

1. Kaibarta.
2. Sadgopa.
3. Koch.
4. Aguri.

Of these, the Aguris and the Koch have been spoken of already in the chapters devoted to the military castes. The Sadgopas are a small community, their total population being slightly above half a million. They are found chiefly in the districts of Burdwan, Midnapore, Hooghly, Nadiya, Twenty-Four Pergunnahs and Bankoora. The majority of them live by agriculture or menial service, but there are among them many big landholders and men of culture. Among the Sadgopa zemindars the names best known are the following :—

1. The Rajas of Narjole in Midnapore.
2. The Sarkars of Peosara in Hooghly.
3. The Roys of Madhavpore near Tumlok.
4. The Haldars of Badla in Midnapore.
5. The Panjas of Jala Bindu in Pergunnah Sabong, Midnapore.

Of the Sadgopas who have attained high offices in the service of Government, the following may be mentioned here :—

1. Babu Grish Chunder Chowdhry, Subordinate Judge, Bengal.
2. The late Roy Sharat Chandra Ghose, Bahadoor, Executive Engineer.

The most distinguished member of the Sadgopa community is the well-known Dr. Mahendra Lall Sarkar of Calcutta, the founder of the Indian Science Association. He is not only one of the best physicians in India, but stands in the foremost rank of Indian scholars and publicists. For several years he has been a member of the Bengal Legislative Council, and a leading member of the Syndicate of the Calcutta University. The Sadgopas have representatives also in what may be called the prophetic trade, which requires neither learning nor culture, but only a little shrewdness. Next to Chaitanya, the most successful of the latter-day prophets of Bengal was a Sadgopa of Ghoshpara. An account of the sect founded by him is given in another part of this work. As usual the Sadgopas are divided into Kulins and Maulika. Their sub-sections and surnames are as stated below :—

1. Kulin ...	1. Poorba kooliya or inhabitants of the eastern side of the Hooghly river.	1. Soor. 2. Newgy. 3. Biswas.
	2. Paschim kooliya or inhabitants of the western side of the river Hooghly.	1. Koowar. 2. Hazra. 3. Roy.
2. Maulika ...	1. Ghosh. 2. Pal. 3. Sirkar. 4. Haldar. 5. Pan. 6. Chowdry. 7. Karfa.	

CHAP. VIII.—THE CHIEF AGRICULTURAL CASTES OF THE CENTRAL PROVINCES.

The chief agricultural castes of the Central Provinces are the following :—

1. Kunbi.
2. Puar.
3. Teli.
4. Mali.
5. Kirat.
6. Lodha.
7. Lodhi.
8. Kolta.

The biggest tenure-holders are the Kunbis, Telis and Malis. The Puars are celebrated for their skill in the construction of reservoirs of water and aqueducts. The Telis are the best agriculturists.

In the Central Provinces the Lodhas are found chiefly in Hosungabad. The Lodhis are a distinct caste. They are very good agriculturists and are found chiefly in Jabbalpore, Saugor, Narsingpore, Hosungabad, Bhandara, Chindwara, and Damoh. The population of the principal agricultural tribe of the Central Provinces is as stated below :—

Kunbi	805,766
Mali	141,086
Lodha	293,110
Teli	731,756

The Teli's proper profession is the manufacture of oil. But the majority of the Telis of the Central Province are engaged in agricultural pursuits. There are many big Teli landholders in the districts near Nagpore and Raipore. The Koltas are found chiefly near Sambalpore.

CHAP. IX.—THE AGRICULTURAL CASTES OF THE PANJAB.

THE chief agricultural castes of the Panjab are the Jats and the Kambohs. An account of the Jats has been given already. The Kambohs have two divisions among them : one practising agriculture, and the other making and selling confectionery. The latter take the sacred thread, but the former do not.

In the Census Reports, the Arrains, Sainis and Ghiraths are included among the agricultural castes of the Panjab. The Arrains are mainly kitchen gardeners like the Koeris and Kachis of Northern India. Most of the Arrains are now Mahomedans. The Sainis are sellers of fodder, and the Ghiraths are a mountain tribe who are employed generally as domestic servants. In the Panjab some of the Sarswat Brahmans till the soil with their own hands. Among the agricultural classes of the province must be included also the Tagus who profess to be a section of the Gour Brahmans. For an account of these Tagus see p. 53, *ante*. The total population of each of the chief agricultural castes in the Panjab is as stated below :—

Jat	**4,625,523**
Kumboh	**151,160**
Arrain	**896,314**
Saini	**125,352**
Ghirath	**173,673**
Tagu	**11,966**

CHAP. X.—THE AGRICULTURAL CASTES OF THE TELEGU COUNTRY.

The agricultural castes of the Telegu country* are the following :—

1. Telega.
2. Vellama Varu.
3. Kamma Varu.
4. Reddi Varu.
5. Kapu.
6. Nagas.

These are all high caste Sudras. They enlist in the army as common soldiers. The Reddis at one time were the rulers of the country. Most of the Paligars belong to one or other of the agricultural castes mentioned above. Bam Dev Rao Nagama Naidu, zemindar of Vallura in the Krishna District, is a Telega. Yarlagada Unkinira, zemindar of Salla Palli in the same district, is a Kamma Varu. The zemindars of Vanaparti and Yadwal in the Nizam's Dominions are Reddi Varus. The zemindars of Venkatagiri, Noozbid, Pittapur and Bobili belong to the Vellamma caste.

The agricultural Sudra castes mentioned above follow the local Ksatriyas in all matters relating to religion and diet. They eat almost every kind of meat excepting beef. They also drink spirituous liquors, though in privacy, and with great moderation.

* As to the geographical boundaries of the Telegu country, see p. 98, *ante*.

CHAP. XI.—THE AGRICULTURAL CASTES OF MYSORE.

THE most important of the agricultural castes of Mysore are the Vakkaligas and the Tigals. The Vakkaligas have many sub-divisions among them, of which the following are the most important :—

1. Gangadhikara.	5. Halli Kara.
2. Kunchitiga.	6. Dasa.
3. Morasu.	7. Halu.
4. Reddi.	10. Musaku.

11. Telegu Vakaliga.

The Tigalas are of Tamil origin. Besides these there are some classes of cultivators called Lingaits, though they are not all followers of the Basavite faith, but have among them Vaishnavas, Saivas and Jains.

The classes that serve as agricultural labourers in Mysore are called Halaya, Huttalu and Mannalu. The Halayas of Mysore correspond to the Parias of the Dravira country. The status of the Huttalu and Mannalu is very much like that of slaves, the former being the hereditary servitors of their masters, and the latter being serfs attached to the soil, and changing hands with it. The total number of Vakkaligas in Mysore is 1,286,217, and that of the agricultural Lingaits in the State 291,857.

CHAP. XII.—THE AGRICULTURAL CASTES OF THE DRAVIRA COUNTRY.

In the Dravira country agriculture is practised chiefly by the Vellalars, Vadugas, Maravans and Ahamudians. These have been described already, the first two as writer castes, and the last two as semi-military castes. Besides these there are many other castes whose principal occupation is agriculture. Of these the most important are the following :—

1. Kavarai { 1. The Baligi. 2. The Totiyar or Kambalatters.
2. Kappilian.
3. Vunnia or Pulli.
4. Oddar or Waddava.
5. Upparava.
6. Pallan.
7. Padeyatchi.
8. Nathambadayan.
9. Urali.

With regard to the Kavaris, Mr. Sherring gives the following account :—

This is a very extensive tribe with at least eighteen branches, some of which are so important and numerous as to deserve to rank as separate tribes. The Kavaris were originally devoted entirely to agriculture, in the capacity of landowners, while their lands were cultivated by inferior races; but, although most are still engaged in their hereditary callings, uniting with it the tilling of the soil, there are several clans which pursue other avocations, and are sailors, small traders, pedlars and the like. They are properly a Telegu people, which language nearly all of them speak, yet some having settled in the 'Tamil' country, now carry on the business of life in the latter tongue. Two branches of the Kavari tribe are the following :—

1. The Baligis—chiefly petty traders, hawkers, and so forth.
2. The Tottiyars—Tottiyans or Kambalattars.

The Tottiyars are said to be split up into nine clans, differing considerably from one another. They are very industrious and energetic as cultivators, and in other pursuits many of them occupy an important position in the city of Madras.

Several clans of Tottiyars entered the District of Madura as colonists four or five hundred years ago, where they have distinguished themselves as agriculturists, especially in reclaiming waste lands. They are fond of cock-fighting and hunting, and have a character for dissoluteness beyond that of other castes. The worship of Vishnu is popular among them, and they have great reverence for relics, are very superstitious, and are peculiarly addicted to the practice of magic. The people generally regard them with awe, because of their mystical rites, which are said to be singularly successful in curing snake-bites. In feature, the Tottiyars have a distinctiveness of their own, separating them in a marked manner from neighbouring tribes. The men wear a bright coloured head-dress, and the women cover themselves with ornaments, neglecting to cover the upper part of their persons. The marriage ceremonies of the Tottiyars are curious. Polyandry in reality, though not professedly, is practised by them. They never consult Brahmans, as they have their own spiritual guides, called Kodangi Nayakkans, who direct their religious ceremonies, preside at their feasts, cast their horoscopes, and enjoy many privileges in return, some of which are not of the most reputable character.

The Kapilians are a respectable class of Canarese cultivators. With regard to the Vannias or Pullis, the following observations are to be found in the Madras Census Report for 1871 :—

Before the British occupation of the country, they were slaves to the Vellalar and Brahman cultivators; but a large number of them are now cultivators on their own account, or else work the lands of the higher castes on a system of sharing half the net produce with the proprietors. Others are simply labourers; and many of them by taking advances from their employers, are still practically serfs of the soil, and unable to extricate themselves from the bondage of the landlord. In all respects, these people have the characteristics of aboriginal tribes. As a rule, they are a very dark-skinned race, but good field labourers, excellent farm servants and cultivators. They abound largely in the Tamil Districts of Trichnapoli and Tanjore.—*The Madras Census Report* for 1871, Vol. I, p. 157.

Of the several classes of agricultural labourers in the Dravira country, the most important are the Pallans. Regarding these the following description is given in Nelson's *Madura Manual* :—

Their principal occupation is ploughing the lands of more fortunate Tamils. Though nominally free, they are usually slaves in almost every sense of the word, earning by the sweat of their brow a bare handful of grain to stay the pangs of hunger, and a rag with which to partly cover their nakedness. They are to be found in almost every village, toiling and moiling for the benefit of Vellalars and others, and with the Pariahs doing patiently nearly all the hard and dirty work that has to be done. Personal contact with them is carefully avoided by all respectable men; and they are never permitted to dwell within the limits of a village; but their huts form a small detached hamlet, removed to a considerable distance from the houses of the respectable inhabitants, and barely separated from that of the Pariahs.—Nelson's *Madura Manual*, Part II, p. 58.

The palm cultivators of the Dravira country are the tadi-drawing castes, namely, the Shanars, Illavars, Billawars and Tiyans. For an account of them see page 259 *et seq.*

The Oddars are an aboriginal race. They serve as agricultural labourers and also as navvies. They profess to be worshippers of Vishnu and bear upon their breasts the trident marks of that deity. But they drink spirits and eat pork and field rats. They are very industrious, and work readily with their wives. Polygamy is largely practised by them. Divorces are very frequent in their community. The Upparavas are properly cultivators, but are employed in the manufacture of salt and saltpetre.

CHAP. XIII.—THE PAN-GROWERS.

§ 1.—*Barui.*

THE Baruji or Barui grow the aromatic betel leaf which Indians of all classes, including both Hindus and Mahomedans, chew in combination with certain spices. The leaves are made into little packets, the inside being painted with slaked lime mixed with catechu, and filled with chips of areca nut, coriander seeds, cardamom, mace and cinnamon. When filled the open end of the packet is fastened with a clove. When chewed in this form the lime and the catechu serve to give a red colour to the lips, while the spices give fragrance to the mouth. The price of the betel leaf varies, according to quality, from half-a-dozen to more than a hundred to the pice. The price of ready-made packets is usually five to the pice. Every native of India who can afford to do so will chew at least half-a-dozen pan packets every day, while some are so fond of this little luxury that they cannot do without at least one hundred in a day. The largest number are chewed after meals and at bed-time. In ceremonial assemblies held by the Indian princes and high functionaries, pan and attar are given to the guests at the end of such meetings. When a relative or familiar friend pays a visit to the house of a Hindu or Mahomedan, the pan salver and the smoking pipe are indispensable for showing due courtesy. When the visit is of a very formal nature, or when the host is a

Mahomedan and the guest a Hindu, then spices are offered instead of pan.

In some parts of India, as, for instance, Upper Assam and the southern parts of the Madras Presidency, the betel leaf grows in the open air as a creeper to the areca nut palm, or to bamboo posts set up in their midst. In these parts of the country, there is no such caste as Baruji ; but throughout the greater part of India, the pan creeper requires very considerable care, and the pan-growers, who have to devote their whole time to their gardens called Baroja, have become a separate caste with the designation of Baruji. The exterior of pan gardens may be seen very often by the Indian Railway traveller, when, through the window of his carriage, he takes a view of the aspect of the country through which he may be passing. The outside is not very attractive, but the scenery inside is very picturesque, and well worth the trouble of visiting.

The Baruis are a clean caste, and the ordinary Sudra Yajaka Brahmans minister to them as priests. Their total population is, according to the last Census, as stated below :—

Bengal	249,841
N.-W. Provinces	153,459
Central Provinces	24,614
Assam	22,797

The Baruis are, generally speaking, quite illiterate and the few among them who have lately attained some degree of culture are trying their best to pass as Kāyasthas.

§ 2.—*The Tambulis.*

The Tambulis derive their name from the Sanskrit word *Tambul*, which means betel leaf. The proper profession of the caste is the sale of the betel leaf, and in some parts of the country the Tambulis still practise their hereditary avocation. But the Tambulis of Bengal are a well-to-do class, and, like the Telis, have long since given up their ancestral business.

They now carry on either wholesale or retail trade in food-grains and oil-seeds, and at present they neither know, nor would admit, that their caste status is the same as that of the Barui. As both Telis and Tambulis generally carry on the same kind of business, the popular idea in Bengal is that the two are sub-divisions of the same caste, if not quite identical. In fact there are reasons for supposing that some Tambuli families have got themselves admitted into the Teli caste, and have given up their connection with their own caste. For instance, it is well known that the founder of the Pal Chowdry family of Ranaghat was one Krishna Panti, who had been originally a pan-seller, but subsequently became a big merchant, and still later a big zemindar, by purchasing, at the time of confusion which followed what is called the Permanent Settlement of Bengal by Cornwallis, the extensive estates belonging to the Nadiya Raj. Krishna Panti was not only a pan-seller originally, but his surname also indicates that he was of the pan-selling caste. The family, however, profess to be Telis, and have, since becoming landholders, created and assumed the aristocratic Teli surname of Pal Chowdry.

The last Census gives the following figures regarding the Tambuli population of India :—

Bengal	**105,416**
N.-W. Provinces	**74,134**
Central India	**24,398**

The Tambulis of Behar, N.-W. Provinces and Central India are generally quite illiterate. In Bengal, their more aristocratic castemen stand on almost the same footing with the Telis in point of culture and refinement. The usual surnames of the Tambulis of Bengal are Pal, Panti, Chail and Rakshit, and those of the Behar Tambulis are Khiliwala and Panti.

PART XIV.

THE COWHERDS AND SHEPHERDS.

CHAP. I.—GENERAL OBSERVATIONS.

THE total population of the several castes whose primary occupation is cattle breeding is very large, amounting to nearly twenty millions in all. About three-fourths of the number are cowherds. They are variously called Goala, Goli, Golla, &c., which designations are all colloquial forms of the Sanskrit word Gopala (lit. keeper of cows).

The majority of the cowherd castes live on the income of the dairy produce of the flocks they keep, supplemented by that of agriculture which they also practise to a very considerable extent. With the exception of the Ahirs, almost all the other cowherd castes are more or less notorious for their thieving propensities. Although the Gopas or cowherds are included among the upper nine of the Sudra castes, yet, with the exception of the Ahirs, they are regarded as somewhat unclean. They have special priests, and a good Brahman cannot minister to any of them without being degraded for ever. Their low status in the caste system is due partly to their being suspected as criminal tribes, and partly also to the fact that they are in the habit of castrating their bull-calves, and branding their cattle with red-hot iron. In the modern towns of British India, some Goalas are suspected to be in the habit of secretly selling their bull-calves and old cows to butchers; but in the interior no Goala can do so knowingly without running the risk of severe persecution by the caste.

Generally speaking the Goalas are a poor and illiterate class. They celebrate their marriages and shradhs in accordance with the Brahmanical shastras; but they are not a priest ridden class, and they do not devote much of their time or money to any religious rite or ceremony beyond those mentioned above. In some parts of the country, the Goalas wear a necklace of beads like the other Nava Shayakas. But it is very unusual for a man or woman of the cowherd caste to be initiated in the mantra of any sect, and that being the case they neither say any prayers nor count beads.

CHAP. II.—THE ABHIRS OR AHIRS.

THE Abhirs are the most numerous and the cleanest of the several castes of cowherds. Their total number exceeds eight millions, and they are to be found in almost every part of India to the north of the river Narmada. From the extent of country over which they are spread, and from the references to them in the most ancient Sanskrit works, it seems very probable that they had been settled in the country long before the Brahmans and the Ksatriyas found their way into it. There is abundant evidence also as to the ancient Abhiras having been capable of wielding the sword as well as the crook. Krishna, the great hero and statesman of ancient India, who is now worshipped by the majority of the Hindus as their chief god, was, if not actually an Abhira himself, at least bred up from his infancy in the house of an Abhira cowherd. The Narayni army which he organised, and which made him so powerful that his friendship was eagerly sought by the greatest kings of his time, is described in the *Mahābhārat* as being all of the Abhira caste. The story of the Sanskrit drama "Mrichakatika" may be taken to warrant the conclusion that for a man of the cowherd caste to be a king, was not an uncommon event in ancient India. Further, it is established by authentic history, that a dynasty of Ahir kings ruled over Nepal at the beginning of the Christian era. But whatever the political importance or the military prowess of the Abhiras may have been in ancient times, they are now simple cattle breeders and tillers of the soil. There are a few landholders among them, but the majority of them are very poor and illiterate. The three main divisions among the Ahirs are the following :—

1. Nand Bans—found chiefly in the Central Doab.
2. Yadu Bans—found chiefly in the Upper Doab and to the west of the river Yamuna.
3. Gwal Bans—found chiefly in the Lower Doab and in the districts adjoining Benares.

The practice of marrying the widows of an elder brother prevails among some of the Ahir tribes in the Upper Doab, as among the Jats and Gujars of the locality. In the neighbourhood of Delhi, the Ahirs eat, drink and smoke with the Jats and the Gujars. The Rajputs generally repudiate all connection with the Ahirs, though it seems very probable that the Yadu Bansi Ksatriyas were originally Ahirs.

The Ahars, who are found chiefly in Rohilkhand, seem to be a sub-class of the Ahirs, though they disclaim such connection.

CHAP. III.—THE GUJARS.

The Gujars are a pastoral tribe of Western India, the majority of whom have in recent times espoused the Mahomedan faith. With the Jats they form the backbone of the rural population of the Panjab, though inferior to them in civilization, industry, and agricultural skill. The Gujars possessed at one time great importance, as appears from the fact that they gave their name to the peninsula of Gujrat, and also to the district of the same name in the Panjab. As the Gujars are at present, they are believed to be one of the criminal classes, there being among them many who are said to be cattle-lifters and gang robbers. The name of the tribe seems to be derived from the compound Gouchor which might mean a "grazier of cows." In Scinde the Gujars keep cows, while the Gowars sell milk and its preparations. The Gujar population of India exceeds two millions, and is distributed as follows :—

Panjab	**711,800**
N.-W. Provinces	**345,978**
Rajputana	**573,003**
Kashmir	**248,789**
Central India	**204,511**

The Gujars are an illiterate caste. There are very few big men among them. It is quite possible that among the minor chiefs and landholders there are a few who were originally Gujars. But as these now claim to be Ksatriyas, it is very rare to find any one even among the barons who will admit his being of the Gujar caste. The higher classes of Brahmans do not minister to the Gujars as priests. They have a special class of ecclesiastic scalled Gujar Gour Brahmans.

It is a noticeable fact that the religion of Guru Nanak, which was eagerly embraced by the Jats and Roras, and gave them a new political life, failed to make any impression on the Gujars. They seem to be quite as indifferent to all forms of religion as the other cowherd castes. A great many of them have, no doubt, espoused the Mahomedan faith, but that must be due to compulsion. In the last Census Report the Gujars are included among the military and agricultural castes; but their proper place seems to be among the pastoral tribes.

CHAP. IV.—THE GOALAS OF THE LOWER PROVINCES.

§ 1.—*The Goalas of Bengal.*

THE common name of the several cowherd castes is Goala. Even the Ahirs and the Gujars are spoken of generally as only sub-divisions of the Goala caste. It is, however, not to be supposed that the Goalas of the different provinces are completely identical in caste. Even in the same province there are generally as many different sections among them as among the higher castes. The Goala population of Bengal is very large. According to the last Census their number exceeds four millions.

The Goalas form the principal Hindu element in the agricultural population of Bengal proper. The majority of the cultivators in the eastern and central districts of Bengal are Mahomedans. Of the Hindu ryots by far the largest number are Goalas among whom may be included the Sadgopas. The only other Hindu castes that usually earn their living by agriculture are the Kaibartas, Aguris, Kapalis and the Paliyas. The Goalas are generally illiterate and poor. There are, however, some among them who hold possession of valuable tenures, and there are a few zemindars also among them. Instances are known also of Goalas having attained University distinctions, and holding such high offices as are now usually allowed to be filled by the natives of this country.

The usual surnames of the Goalas of Bengal are the following :—

1. Ghosh.
2. Pal.
3. Barik.
4. Babui.
5. Dhali.

The Goalas of Bengal are divided into the following classes :—

1. Pallava—found chiefly in Calcutta and its vicinity.
2. Bagri or Ujaini—these are believed to castrate bull-calves, and are therefore treated as somewhat unclean.
3. Bārendra Goalas—the Goalas of North Bengal.
4. Rārhi Goalas—the Goalas of Burdwan.
5. Maghai—Goalas of Maghadha or Behar. These are said to extract butter from unboiled milk, and are therefore regarded as somewhat unclean.
6. Godos—found chiefly in the Nadiya District.
7. Sadgopa—found chiefly in the Burdwan Division.

An account of the Sadgopa tribe has been given already in connection with the agricultural castes of Bengal. Of the other sections of the Bengal Goalas only the Godos require special notice.

The Godos of Bengal.

The name of this class seems to be derived from the *Gada*, which means a fort. From their very name, and from what other facts are known relating to them, it seems probable that formerly they served in the armies of the Hindu and Mahomedan kings of the country. Their services are still utilised by the landholders of Bengal for those little boundary warfares which usually involve them in the most ruinous litigations, civil and criminal. The Godos of the tract of country to the east of the famous field of Plassy are a criminal tribe of the worst type. They are hereditary gang robbers, assassins and free lances. After more than a century of British rule, highway robberies are still so frequent in the locality, that no one can, even now, safely travel alone through the pergunnah inhabited by them. Some of the Godos practise agriculture ; but, like the Irish peasants, they never pay any "rint" to their landlords, and have brought about the ruin of many capitalists who had invested their money in taking perpetual leases of the pergunnah from its zemindar.

Like the other criminal tribes, some of the Godos give regular training to their children in the arts of thieving and gang robbery. On occasions of festivity in the houses of the local nobility, they sometimes exhibit their skill in their art, and amuse and astonish the spectators by their feats. Reclining on a bamboo stick, about six feet long, one would get to the top of a house, while another with a similar weapon would ward off any number of brickbats that might be hurled against him. The importance of such gymnastic skill to a burglar must be obvious.

§ 2.—*The Goalas of Behar.*

Like the Goalas of Bengal, those of Behar also are divided into a large number of sub-tribes. They all appear to be looked upon as good Sudras, and the ordinary Sudra Yajaka priests of Behar minister to them as priests. As in other parts of India, the Goalas of Behar are, generally speaking, an illiterate class. There is, however, among them a section who usually acquire a sufficient knowledge of the three R.'s to be qualified for book-keeping in the vernacular. The Separis, as they are called, are employed by the landholders as Putwaris or village accountants. They are looked upon as an inferior class by the other Goala sub-castes. The Goalas of Behar allow their widows to re-marry.

The usual family names of the Behar Goalas are the following :—

1. Bhandari.
2. Bhagata.
3. Mahato.
4. Majhi.

§ 3.—*The Goalas of Orissa.*

Among the Goalas of Orissa there are three main divisions, namely, the Krishnaut, the Mathura Bansi and the Gaura Bansi. They are all generally very poor. The

Oriya litter-carriers of Calcutta are mostly of the Goala caste. A very large number of them are employed by the European residents of Calcutta as orderlies, punka-pullers, furniture cleaners and gardeners. Being Hindus they cannot serve as cooks or table-servants. But, apart from their caste prejudices, they are very serviceable and obedient, and they are sometimes employed as personal servants by the Hindu residents of Calcutta. The only reason why they are not more largely employed by the Hindu aristocracy of Bengal is the fact that they would never eat any food cooked by a Bengali, and in the household of a Hindu of moderate means, it is considered very inconvenient to have a servant who would cook his own food, instead of eating the preparations of the family cook. The Oriya domestics are generally very trustworthy like the Kahars of Northern India. The master's goods, however valuable, are always safe in their custody. It is only when deputed to make any purchases that an Oriya servant is tempted to act dishonestly, and to appropriate a part of the money by giving a false account. Like the Goalas of Behar those of Orissa allow the re-marriage of their widows.

CHAP. V.—THE COWHERDS OF SOUTHERN INDIA.

In the Telegu country the cowherds are called Gollalu, in Mysore Golla, and in the Tamil country Mattu Edia. Among the Gollalus there are many sub-divisions, one of which is called Yathavas. The Yadava clan of Ksatriyas in Northern India is probably an offshoot of these pastoral Yathavas. Among the Mattu Edias there are two classes, one of which profess the Vaishnava faith, and the others are Sivites. There can be no marriage alliance between these two sub-divisions of the Mattu Edias, and practically they are separate castes. The Gollas of Mysore are divided into two sub-orders called Uru Golla and Kadu Golla, who neither eat together nor intermarry. They are mostly Krishna worshippers. There are some very odd customs among the Kadu Gollas of Mysore. "It is said that on the occurrence of a childbirth, the mother with the babe remains unattended in a small shed outside the village from 7 to 30 days when she is taken back to her home. In the event of her illness, none of the caste will attend on her, but a Nayak (Beda) woman is engaged to do so. Marriages among them are likewise performed in a temporary shed erected outside the village, and the attendant festivities continue for five days when the married couple are brought into the village. Their females do not, on the death of the husband, remove or break the bangles worn at the wrists." *

* *Mysore Census Report*, p. 248.

CHAP. VI.—THE SHEPHERD CASTES.

The following table gives the names of the several shepherd castes of India, together with the figures relating to their numerical strength :—

Gadaria, 1,294,830 (found in Northern India).
Dangar, 1,305,583 (found chiefly in the vicinity of the Marattha country).
Attu Ediyar, 665,232 (found chiefly in Southern India).

The shepherds have a lower caste status than the cowherds. The family of the Maharaja Holkar are said by some to be of the Dangar caste ; but they take the sacred thread, and the Brahmans accept their gifts without any hesitation.

There are many Gadarias in and near some of the old towns of Bengal such as Nadiya and Dacca. These do not practise their caste profession, but live chiefly by working as bricklayers. Their females make the preparation of rice called *chira* described in page 246. The shepherd castes are regarded as somewhat unclean everywhere.

PART XV.

THE CLEAN AND THE UNCLEAN CASTES EMPLOYED IN PERSONAL AND DOMESTIC SERVICE.

CHAP. I.—THE BARBERS.

THOUGH the text referred to at p. 224, *ante*, includes the barbers among the upper nine classes of Sudras, yet as they pare the nails of all the classes, the higher castes do not, in many parts of the country, take even drinking water from their hands. In Bengal, Behar and Orissa the *napit* is regarded as a clean caste. In the Telugu country, the corresponding caste of Mangli is regarded as clean also. In almost all the other provinces, the barber is regarded as unclean. In Orissa the barber caste is called Bhandari ; in the Tamil country the name of the caste is Ambatta ; in Mysore the designation of the class is Nayinda ; in Telingana the caste name of barbers is Mangali ; and in Northern India their most common names are Nai, Nain and Hajam. In the Panjab there are two classes of barbers. The ordinary barbers are regarded as an unclean caste. But there is a class who do only such work as is required of the *napit* on occasions of marriage. These take the sacred thread, and are regarded as a clean caste, from whose hands a Brahman will not only take drinking water, but even *pakki* food.

As a Hindu cannot celebrate any religious ceremony without first shaving, the barber is an important functionary of Hindu society. Every Hindu has his family *napit*, as he has his family Guru, priest and washerman. The *napit* shaves him and all the male members of his family; while the *napit's* wife or mother pares the nails of the ladies, and paints their feet with lac-dye. Besides his regular pay, the *napit* has claims to various kinds of perquisites on every birth, death, marriage and *puja* in the families of his constituents. When a birth takes place the family barber acts as the errand boy to convey the happy news to all the relatives of the babe; and on such occasions the kith and kin are expected to present to the barber a shawl, or a piece of silk cloth, or a brass vessel of some kind, together with some money, according to their means. As a Hindu lady upon her first pregnancy is usually taken to her father's house, the parents of her husband have to pay heavy fees to the family barber of her father, if a male child is born.

In Behar the *napit* acts also as an assistant on the staff of match-making embassies, and makes a handsome extra income by that kind of business. In the remote villages, the Hindu *napits*, like the European barbers of the seventeenth century, practise also surgery and open boils and abscesses. Some *napits* serve as domestic servants in the houses of the higher castes; but a Hindu of the barber caste will never till the soil with his own hands. The *napits* are reputed as very acute people, but as a class they are quite illiterate, and there are very few rich men among them. No *napit* has yet attained any University distinctions, nor has any member of the class been able to attain a high position in the service of Government by dint of ability.

The usual surname of the *napit* in Bengal is Paramanik. A member of the caste is at present in the Subordinate Executive Service of Bengal; but with a few solitary exceptions the *napits* are quite illiterate.

CHAP. II.—THE WASHERMEN.

The Washermen are called Dhopa in Bengal, Dhobi in Northern India, Warthi and Pont in the Central Provinces, Vaunan and Agasia in Southern India and Chakli in the Telugu country. On account of the unclean nature of their occupation, they are regarded as an unclean caste in almost every part of India excepting the Telugu country where the Chakli are held eligible for being employed as domestic servants. They are, generally speaking, quite illiterate. But a few of them have recently managed to get themselves appointed to some very high offices in the service of Government.

Like the *napit*, the Dhobi has not only a regular salary, but has claims to various perquisites on occasions of birth, death and marriage in Hindu families. The Dhobi's personal expenses are not very considerable. He expects and gets a dish of rice at least once every month from each of his constituents, and for purposes of clothing, he freely uses the clothes given to him for washing. The sight of a Dhobi's face is, like that of an oilman, considered as a bad omen at the commencement of a journey, and is avoided.

CHAP. III.—THE CASTES USUALLY EMPLOYED AS DOMESTIC SERVANTS IN HINDU FAMILIES.

§ 1.—*Bengal.*

THE Dakshin Radhi Kāyasthas of Bengal claim, as a matter of honor, to have the right of serving as menials to Brahmans. As a matter of fact, the Kāyasthas are very well-to-do people, and have too much pride to stoop to domestic service. Even the slave Kāyasthas of Eastern Bengal are now trying to give up such service, and to be on the same level with the other Kāyasthas. In Bengal the nine clean Sudra castes mentioned in page 224, *ante*, are generally considered by the aristocratic Hindus as most eligible for domestic service. The Kansaris and the Sankharis who, properly speaking, belong to the mercantile caste, are held eligible also for similar employment. The Sadgopas, being included among the clean Gopas, are regarded as clean Sudras, and are held to be entitled to the same honor. The Shekra, Sutar, and Kaibarta are regarded as clean castes in some places, and unclean in others. The Teli and the Goala, though included among the Nava Sayakas, are not in practice regarded as clean everywhere. However, generally speaking, the Navasayakas with the Kansari, Sankhari, Sadgopa, Shekra, Sutar and Kaibarta may be, and are usually, employed as domestic servants in all Hindu families in Bengal.

§ 2.—*N.-W. Provinces and Behar.*

Kahar.—This caste derives its name from the Sanskrit word *Skandhakara*, which means one who carries things on his shoulders. The primary occupation of this caste is carrying litters. But there are several sub-castes among them, and while some of these practise their proper profession, the others are either boatmen, fishermen, grain parchers, basket-makers, or weavers. The most important sub-castes of the Kahars are the Rawani and the Turah. The Rawanis are to be found in large numbers in every town of Northern India. They serve as litter carriers, punka-pullers, scullions, water-carriers and personal attendants. In every well-to-do family there is at least one Rawani to serve as the "maid of all work." The Turahs, who are boatmen and fishermen, are to be found chiefly in Behar and N.-W. Provinces. They have some colonies in Bengal, in the ancient towns of Dacca and Nadiya, and in the market town of Shah Ganj near Hooghly, founded by Azim Oshan, the grandson of Aurangzebe, who was for some years the Governor of Bengal. The Turahs of Bengal have, however, formed themselves into a separate caste, and the fact that they are a branch of the Kahar caste is not even known to them. Of the Rawanis very few are domiciled in Bengal. Those found in this part of the country are chiefly natives of Gaya, who come every year in the beginning of the winter season, and go back to their native home in June or July, or when they deem it convenient.

No class of Kahars can be said to have the right of being regarded as clean Sudras. The fishing classes are certainly unclean, and they are treated as such. Although the Rawanis do not catch fish, yet even they ought not to stand in a better position. A great many of them are in the habit of drinking spirits, and eating field rats and even pork. But it is difficult to get more trustworthy and obedient servants, and the necessity of Hindu families has made them a clean caste. No good Brahman, however, officiates as a priest for the performance of a religious ceremony in which a Kahar is concerned. The Kahar's priest is treated as a degraded Brahman, and his Guru or spiritual guide is usually an ascetic. Most of the Rawanis are worshippers of Siva and Kāli, and there are very few Vishnuvites among them. They have great reverence for the shrine of Kāli near Calcutta. Those of them who come to Calcutta never fail to give a *puja* there, and even in the districts remote from Calcutta, their usual cry, when they take a litter on their shoulders or drop it, is, *Jai Kali Calcuttawali.** The Kahar population of India is as stated below :—

N.-W. Provinces	1,208,530
Bengal	621,176

Dhanuk.—The Dhanuks are a clean Sudra caste found chiefly in Behar. In all probability they were originally slaves. The superior castes will take a drink of water from their hands, and the Maithila Brahmans minister to them as priests. They are usually employed as domestic servants.

Amat.—The Amats are a clean caste. They are divided into two sections, one of which is called Gharbait, and the other Biahut. The Gharbaits live by practising agriculture, while the Biahuts usually serve as

* The name of Calcutta is supposed by many to be derived from the shrine of Kāli. But there can be very little doubt as to its having a very different derivation. The word Kol, which literally means 'lap,' is usually used to denote the open ends of the alluvial formations which are formed on the sides of the rivers of Bengal by the deflection of their currents. The Kols, so long as they exist, are used as natural harbours. But the peninsulas surrounding them are, after some years, cut through by changes in the course of the river. The place is then called Kata Kol or Kolkata, literally "a lap cut open." There are many riparian villages in Bengal which are called Katakol. The name of Calcutta is clearly formed by the union of the same component words in a different way.

domestic servants. The two sections do not intermarry. The Maithila Brahmans minister to both as priests.

§ 3.—*The Servant Castes of the Panjab.*

The castes that in the Panjab are usually employed by the Hindu aristocracy as domestic servants are the following :—

1. Jhiwar.	4. Kambo.
2. Kirat.	5. Rora.
3. Jat.	6. Salariya.

The proper profession of the Jhiwar is the catching of fish ; but in the Panjab they are not on that account regarded as unclean, and, in fact, are generally the only men in their country who serve as water-carriers. The Hindu Kambos claim to have come from Afghanistan. The Mahomedan Kambos call themselves the descendants of the old Kai sovereigns of Persia.

§ 4.—*The Servant Castes of the Telugu country.*

The castes held eligible in the Telugu country for employment as domestic servants are the following :—

1. Mangli	...	Barber.
2. Chakli	...	Washerman.
3. Idiya	...	Brewer.
4. Golla	...	Cowherd.

§ 5.—*The Servant Castes of Maharashtra and Central Provinces.*

The castes usually employed by the higher classes of the Hindus in the Maharatta country and in the Central Provinces are the inferior Maharattas and the Kunbis. In the Central Provinces the aboriginal Gonds, though they eat beef and are regarded as unclean, are yet employed as domestic servants for such kinds of work as do not require the touching of drinking water.

CHAP. IV.—THE CASTE OF THE DOMESTICS IN ANGLO-INDIAN HOUSEHOLDS.

THE domestics who do menial work in Anglo-Indian households are recruited from low class Mahomedans and the very lowest class Hindus. An up-country Brahman or Ksatriya may be found to do the work of a gate-keeper or orderly in the house of an Englishman, but will never do any work that must compel him to touch his master's plates, dining table, clothes or shoes. If a high caste and orthodox Hindu accidentally touch any of these things, he will neither enter his cook-room nor eat any food without washing away the contamination by bathing. The plates containing cooked meat are an absolute abomination to a good Hindu, and the very sight is shocking to him. According to orthodox Hindu notions, the dining table itself remains unfit to be touched even when the plates are taken off. But in this respect the prejudices of all classes of Hindus are fast wearing off, and not only Hindu officials but independent Hindu gentlemen may in these days often be found sitting by the side of an Englishman's dining table, and afterwards drinking water or chewing *pan* without bathing or change of dress. Such being the case, the high caste Hindu peons and orderlies have not at present the same amount of objection to touch their master's furniture that they had formerly. But even at the present they will not, either for love or money, touch their master's shoes or clothes, or have anything to do with the arrangement of his furniture and bedding.

In Hindu households, a poor Brahman may do the work of a cook; but under no circumstances will a Brahman or a Rajput do such menial service as is fit only for Sudras and low castes. Almost the only kind of work which a high caste Hindu will do in an English household is that of a letter carrier or door attendant for announcing the presence of visitors.

With regard to the caste of the other classes of domestics in Anglo-Indian households, it may be observed, generally, that the Mahomedans have the monopoly of such as appertain to the stable. Even in Hindu households, the coachmen and the footmen are always followers of Islam. The cooks, scullions and butlers are either Mahomedans (or Aracanese) or Madrasis of the low castes called Paria and Tiyan. The punka-pullers are either Goalas of Orissa or Kahars of Behar. Oriyas and Kahars are employed also as *farashes* for wiping off the dust from the furniture, and for cleansing and lighting the lamps. The washerman is the Hindu Dhobi, Vannan or Agasia; while the scavengers and the nightsoil men are all usually of such aboriginal tribes as are called Hāri, Methar, Churha, &c.

In Calcutta the Oriya is the maid of all work in European households in every department except the kitchen and the stable; but it is said that the Madrasi Paria and Tiyan are still more pliant and useful than the cowherds of the land of Jaganath.

PART XVI.

MISCELLANEOUS CASTES.

CHAP. I.—THE FISHERMEN AND BOATMEN.

§ 1.—*The Fishermen and Boatmen of Bengal.*

THE same castes are usually both fishermen and boatmen. They have all a very low caste status. In Bengal the following castes earn their living chiefly by plying boats for the conveyance of goods and passengers, and by catching and selling fish :—

1.	Malo	both boatmen and fishermen.		
2.	Turaha	"	"	"
3.	Chandral	"	"	"
4.	Jelia Kaibart	"	"	"
5.	Tiyar	"	"	"

The Nikaris of Bengal, who are fishermen, are all Musalmans.

§ 2.—*The Fishermen and Boatmen of Northern India.*

The most important classes of boatmen in Northern India are Dhiwars of the United Provinces, and the Jhiwars of Panjab and Scinde. These names are derived from the Sanskrit word *Dhivar*, signifying a fisherman. The boatmen of Northern India are called Mallah. They are closely connected with the caste called Kahar. The Mallahs of Cawnpore are called Kadhar. The

Mallahs are divided into many sections of which the following are the best known :—

1. Gaure.	4. Kanojia.
2. Banar.	5. Saroriya.
3. Tirhutia.	6. Mariyari.

7. Kewat.

The Jhiwars who are found in Panjab and Scinde are considered there as a clean caste. They are not only fishermen, but serve also as water-carriers to high caste Hindu families. The boatmen of the Panjab are mostly Mahomedans.

§ 3.—*The Fishermen of Gujrat.*

The fishermen of Gujrat are called Machi.

§ 4.—*The Fishermen of the Malabar Coast.*

The following are the fishermen castes of the Malabar Coast :—

1. Vellamar, live by fresh water fishing.
2. Marakan, enjoy the monopoly of the sea-fisheries.
3. Shembadan, fishermen of Malabar.

§ 5.—*The Fishermen, Boatmen and Litter-carriers of Mysore.*

The caste that generally work as fishermen, boatmen and litter-carriers in Mysore are there called *Besta.* With reference to these, the following account is given in the last Census Report of Mysore :—

These (the *Besta*) are fishermen, boatmen and palanquin-bearers. Their number is 99,897, or a little short of one hundred thousand persons, absorbing a little over two per cent. of the total and are more than 5 per cent. of the class. These are known by different names according to localities. In the Eastern districts, they are called *Besta* (fishermen); in the Southern *Toraya*, *Ambica* and *Gange Makkalu.* The Telugu-speaking population call them Parivora (boatmen); while in the Western parts their names are Kalyara and *Bhais.* There are a few other sub-divisions returned, with insignificant numbers, under the names of Belli, Chammadi, Rayaravuta and Surmakalu. These are acknowledged to be of a lower rank. Their chief occupations are fishing, palanquin-bearing and lime-burning. Some of them are employed by Government as peons, &c., whilst a large number is engaged in agricultural pursuits.

CHAP. II.—THE CRIMINAL TRIBES.

AMONG the Goalas who are cowherds by caste, and are to be found in almost every part of India, there are many bad characters, but the class as a whole cannot be called a criminal tribe. The Gujars, who are to be found chiefly in Rajputana and Scinde, and who are also cowherds by caste, are believed to be addicted to thieving. Besides these there are particular castes and tribes in every province of India who are believed to be professional thieves and gang robbers. In Bengal the following castes furnish by far the largest number of criminals :—

1. **Bagdi** ... **An aboriginal caste, generally employed as navvies and wood-cutters.**
2. **Baori** ... **An aboriginal caste, found in large number in West Burdwan.**
3. **Kaora** } **Found chiefly in the tracts to the South**
4. **Pod** } **and South-East of Calcutta.**
5. **Dome** } **Aboriginal tribes whose ostensible occupa-**
   Nolo } **tion is basket and mat-making.**
6. **Hari** ... **Sweepers.**
7. **Bedia** ... **Herbalists and snake-catchers.**

The criminal tribes of Behar are the following :—

1. **Dome.** | 2. **Bind.**

The following are the criminal tribes of the Upper Gangetic Doab :—

1. **Gujar.**
2. **Jat.**
3. **Sansi.**
4. **Marasi.**
5. **Mehter.**
6. **Meo (mostly Mahomedans now, though observing Hindu festivals and rites).**
7. **Bahelya.**
8. **Haibora.**

The undermentioned are the criminal tribes of Rajputana : —

1. Thori.
2. Chura.
3. Sansi.
4. Bauria.
5. Maghaya.
6. Mewa.
7. Grassia.
8. Bheel.

The following are the criminal tribes of the Madras Presidency :—

1. Kallau (found in the Dravira).
2. Koravar (Do. do.)
3. Gerakalas (found in Telingana).
4. Chaphon (found chiefly in the valley of the Krishna river).

The following are the criminal tribes of the Bombay Presidency :—

1. Ramusi (found chiefly in Maharashtra).
2. Katha Kavi (found in Northern Konkan).
3. Katori (found in Northern Konkan).
4. Banjari.
5. Lambanis.
6. Waddar.
7. Bedar (found in the Southern Maharatta country).
8. Pardhi (found in Khandesh and Berar).
9. Bheels (found in Khandesh).
10. Bompti (found in the Maharatta country).
11. Pindari (found everywhere in the Deccan. Not a separate caste, but originally an association of vagabonds and robbers).

HINDU SECTS.

—:o:—

PART I.

INTRODUCTION.

CHAP I.—THE PROPER METHOD OF ENQUIRY REGARDING RELIGIONS.

To give an intelligible account of the Hindu sects and to fix their precise place relatively to other religious systems, it seems to me absolutely necessary, at the outset, to say something about the essential nature of religions generally, and the usual course of their development. It is only by the light of such a disquisition that the study of the origin and growth of the several religious sects to be found in this country can be made interesting and profitable. In what I am going to say the reader will, I fear, find a great deal that is not in accordance with the prevailing ideas on the subject; and, in order that there may be no mistake in weighing and appraising the opinions I express, I must at the very threshold explain the method on which I propose to proceed.

In theology, as in astronomy, physiology, geology and many other sciences, we cannot, by mere observation, carry our investigations to the required point. As the functions of the internal organs of the human body or the manner in which the rocks have been formed cannot be known by direct observation, so it is impossible, by the same means, to give a satisfactory answer to many of the vexed questions of theology. We cannot depute anyone to any place beyond this earth to ascertain whether our so-called prophets were in fact what they professed to be, or whether they were not mere men like ourselves though possessed of greater shrewdness. The only way open in such cases to arrive at the truth is to start with a hypothesis which is based on probability. If the hypothesis which is adopted suffice to explain all the known facts connected with the subject, no scientific mind can hesitate to accept it. At any rate when an hypothesis fails to explain the phenomena which it is meant to account for, it must be rejected at once.

The belief of every orthodox person that his own religion was brought direct from heaven by an incarnation of God Almighty, or by a trusted agent specially deputed by the Most High, has *primâ facie* the same element of improbability as the Ptolemaic theory of astronomy. It is perhaps much more reasonable to suppose that the sun and the planets revolve round our poor earth, than to believe that although this little orb of ours, is as a speck compared with the entirety of the universe, yet it is the place where God Almighty delights to make long sojourns in human form.

To a man whose common sense has not been perverted by early training, and who knows the ways of the world, the assertion that any particular religion has had its origin in a special message of Divine favour to any race or nation, might appear to be open to question. When a stock-broker or company promoter issues a rose-coloured prospectus regarding the present condition or probable future of a commercial concern, no man who understands business thinks of buying its shares without satisfying himself by proper in quiriesthat the persons recommending it to the public are competent to form a correct forecast, and are not interested in misrepresenting the facts. When a quack advertises a medicine as having the power to cure every kind of malady that the human system is heir to, he is always looked upon with suspicion, though he may dupe many poor sufferers who, in their hopelessness, may be disposed to rely upon him. The alchemists and Sanyasis, who claim to have the power of converting the baser metals into gold, very seldom find in these days anyone foolish enough to be taken in by them. When a cute loafer appears in a native court, and pretends to be a near relative or secret agent of the Viceroy, he is seldom trusted even by the weakest of our Princes. If then it is a wise policy in other departments of life to look with suspicion upon the men who promise too much and profess to possess extraordinary powers, it must be difficult to see any reason why we should make an exception in favour of the professors of the theocratic art, who apparently lived and died in exactly the same manner as any ordinary mortal, and yet claimed to be the incarnations, representatives or trusted agents of the Most High. *Primâ facie* they stand on no better footing than the alchemist, the company promoter, the quack medicine vendor, and the loafer without credentials.

To those who have had opportunities for studying the ways of sharpers, the man of religion must appear to be even more unreliable than those who practise on the credulity of the people in other spheres. The honesty of the latter can be tested in various ways, and as they know well that if they fail to achieve what they promise they might become legally punishable, none but the most reckless among them can feel inclined to cheat men by alchemy or a commercial bubble. But the priests of modern times very seldom make any promise which they can be called upon to fulfil in this world. They deal in salvation and the spiritual happiness of the soul after death, and, for the purpose of avoiding an audit, they have a far safer vantage ground than even the engineers of the Indian Public Works Department, and the mooktears or attorneys of the Indian county courts. The P. W. D. official who attempts to enrich himself by the pretence that the embankment which he had been commissioned to build on the sea-coast has been washed away by a storm-wave, or the mooktear of the old type who attempts to cheat his master by pretending to have bribed the Police for him, runs a chance of detection which might lead to his utter ruin. But such fears need not disturb the priest's deep repose.

Such being the case, and the profession of the priest being calculated to bring far more honour, power and wealth than any other calling, his temptations are great. So he cannot reasonably claim from men even that amount of confidence which can be reposed on the quack or the alchemist. It is true that the curers of our souls very often affect to be quite indifferent to wealth and worldly comforts, and from this fact it is argued that the motive to cheat men being wanting, they may be treated with confidence. But to every one who has studied the ways of the priests, it must be evident that they have all a morbid craving, for, at least, being honoured by men, and that though, at the outset, they may profess to be above the vulgar love of lucre, yet as soon as their power is sufficiently established, they betray an amount of avarice and craving for luxurious living that is not to be found in the greatest secular rulers. While the latter are satisfied with a small fraction of the income of their subjects, the priest will bring complete ruin on his victims, if by doing so he can turn an extra penny. Even the lawyer's fees have a limit. But there is no limit whatever to the demand of a priest. He pretends to have the power of enriching his followers. But the actual result of his operations is only to impoverish them.

Like some unscrupulous loan brokers the man of religion does not hesitate the least to break even a bruised reed. In fact the greater the embarrassment of the victim, the greater is the opportunity of both. A big landowner is heavily in debt. A broker comes to him, and offers to raise the loan required by him at a very moderate rate of interest. The proposal is very tempting to him, and when it is accepted, the broker finds little difficulty in getting out of him a few hundred rupees for alleged preliminary expenses. With that money he goes away, never to turn up again. The same experiment is tried by every one of the birds of the same feather, and the result of their combined operations is to make their victim sink deeper and deeper in the mire. The *modus operandi* of the priest is exactly the same, the only difference being that he never finds it necessary to abscond or decamp. When his rites and incantations are proved by the event to be ineffective, he will throw the responsibility on a malignant star, or account for the failure by attributing it to want of faith in his dupe.

At an early stage of their career, the spiritual teachers, no doubt, deal in a little genuine milk of wholesome morality. But that fact cannot entitle them to be implicitly trusted, for as soon as they find that they are blindly followed by the mob, they hesitate not the least to adulterate their ethical stock-in-trade with the most powerful anæsthetics, intoxicants and narcotics, so as to dispose their followers to submit to their operations with alacrity. The priests ask us to have faith in them, and we are too much accustomed to the demand to perceive its absurdity. But if an alchemist, quack or company promoter were to press upon us such advice, surely we would not blindly yield to it.

So far I have been speaking of only the natural presumption which there ought to be against the claims to extraordinary powers put forward by, or on behalf of, the so-called prophets and incarnations. That presumption may or may not be rebutted by the evidence adduced to support their case. That is not the question which I am going to deal with just now. But in order to discuss it properly, I must first of all try to analyse the way in which, according to the evidence afforded by history, religious systems have been actually developed. I shall then show that their course is consistent only with the doctrine that they have their origin in the policy of men, and not in any extraordinary measure adopted by the Most High through His mercy towards us.

CHAP. II.—THE EVOLUTION OF THE THEOCRATIC ART.

On the supposition that our religions have been given to us by God Almighty, they cannot possibly have any course of development. They must have existed, at the beginning, in the same state as now. As the speculations of Laplace, Lyell and Darwin are shut out altogether on the supposition that the universe was created in the manner described in the ancient scriptures and codes of law, so a faith in divine revelation precludes all inquiry as to the origin and evolution of the theocratic art. But the evidence afforded by history shows that religions have had a regular course of evolution, and I propose first of all to trace its successive steps.

With reference to the subject which I purpose to deal with here, there are at present two quite opposite theories which, for want of better names, I may call the orthodox theory and the modern theory. According to the orthodox theory, religion was in its highest state of purity in the beginning of creation, and, through the growing wickedness of men, it is becoming more and more corrupt, as the world is advancing in age. According to the other theory, which is favoured by the philosophers of modern Europe, and by those of our countrymen who blindly follow them, religious ideas were extremely crude in the primitive times, and, as civilisation has advanced, its inevitable progress has been from fetichism, idolatry and polytheism to monotheism pure and simple. With regard to the orthodox theory,

I need not say anything. But with regard to the modern theory it must be observed that it is open to exception on more grounds than one. It assumes that, as in other departments, the progress of religion is determined solely by the advancement of men in philosophical thoughtfulness. This view is directly contradicted by one of the greatest of English historians. Macaulay says :—

> There are branches of knowledge with respect to which the law of the human mind is progress. In mathematics, when once a proposition has been demonstrated, it is never afterwards contested. Every fresh story is as solid a basis for a new superstructure as the original foundation was. Here, therefore, is a constant addition to the stock of truth. In the inductive sciences again, the law is progress. Every day furnishes new facts, and thus brings theory nearer and nearer to perfection. There is no chance that, either in the purely demonstrative, or in the purely experimental sciences, the world will ever go back or even remain stationary. Nobody ever heard of a reaction against Taylor's theorem, or of a reaction against Harvey's doctrine of the circulation of the blood.
>
> But with theology the case is very different. As respects natural religion—revelation being for the present altogether left out of the question—it is not easy to see that a philosopher of the present day is more favourably situated than Thales or Simmonides. He has before him just the same evidences of design in the structure of the universe which the early Greeks had. We say just the same, for the discoveries of modern astronomers and anatomists have really added nothing to the force of that argument which a reflecting mind finds in every beast, bird, insect, fish, leaf, flower and shale. The reasoning by which Socrates, in Zenophon's hearing, confuted the little atheist Aristodemus, is exactly the reasoning of Paley's Natural Theology. As to the other great questions, the question, what becomes of man after death? we do not see that a highly educated European, left to his unassisted reason, is more likely to be in the right than a Blackfoot Indian. Not a single one of the many sciences in which we surpass the Blackfoot Indians throws the smallest light on the state of the soul after the animal life is extinct. In truth, all the philosophers, ancient and modern, who have attempted, without the help of revelation, to prove the immortality of man, from Plato down to Franklin, appear to us to have failed deplorably.

The great English historian, in his usual way, goes here a little too far. There are clearly marks of progressive development in the theocratic art. However, the historian is certainly right in the view that the progress of theology has not been in the same lines as that of the physical or the mathematical sciences. The reason of this is not far to seek. The progress of the sciences depends upon the progress of the human intellect, and not upon any other circumstance. A scientific discovery cannot, in most cases, affect the pecuniary or political interest of any class. And even where it has a prejudicial effect on such interests, the arguments and experiments by which it is proved render it quite impossible to ignore it. But the changes in the *modus operandi* of the priests depend upon, not one, but three different factors, namely, their increasing shrewdness, the increasing boldness engendered in them by their success, and the state of society with which they have to deal. Hence, in theology there are those complicated movements which puzzle the superficial thinkers, and are characterised by them as backward or forward according to their peculiar ideas of progress or retrogression.

When other circumstances do not offer any impediment, the theocratic art certainly becomes more and more developed according to a law of its own, and the view propounded by Macaulay that it has remained stationary cannot be accepted, consistently with the facts recorded in history and the sacred Scriptures. The now generally accepted doctrine of the European philosophers who hold that the natural progress of religion is from fetichism, polytheism and idolatry to monotheism seems to be equally undeserving of acceptance. It no doubt embodies a fraction of the truth. The theocratic art begins indeed with fetichism. But the highest development it is capable of, is not monotheism,—which represents only an usual concomitant* of one of its intermediate states,—but abomination-worship, which is the climax that it can attain. This is proved by the undeniable evidence of history, and it must be so according to the hypothesis that religion has its origin in the policy of the priests, and not in divine grace.

There is by nature a groundwork for superstitious belief in the human mind. So long as the fortunes of

* See page 323.

men depend to a great extent on chance, so long as the medical science is not sufficiently advanced, and so long again as we are unable to predict or control meteorological phenomena, the human mind must be prepared more or less to submit to the exactions of the priest, the quack and the fortune-teller. The jurisdiction of these is becoming more and more narrowed with the progress of the sciences, and of the arts of shipbuilding, navigation and canal irrigation, coupled with such institutions of modern civilization as insurance offices, fire brigades, poor-houses and hospitals. When anyone gets fever now, whatever may be his orthodoxy, he depends more upon quinine than upon the Batuka Vairaba or the Aparajita incantations of his priests. There was a time when, in order to avoid the visitation of heaven's wrath in the form of the thunderbolt, every Hindu caused a label to be stuck up on the upper parts of the door frames in his house, containing a few Sanskrit verses. But the science of electricity has of late been teaching the people to depend more upon the lightning rod, than on the names of the five thunder-preventing saints. In order to prevent loss by fire or boatwreck, Indian traders, in many places, still spend very large sums of money to secure the favour of Bramha, Ganga and Vallabhachari. But the advantages of brick buildings and insurance are being understood more and more, and, in Bengal at least, the rage for Bramha Puja and Ganga Puja has diminished very materially. Whether the clearances of the Vallabhachari shrine at Nathdowra from marine policies, vowed to it by the traders of Gujrat and Bombay, have diminished or not, is a matter as to which I have not been able to get any reliable information. In any case, the sphere of the priests' operations is becoming more and more circumscribed. However, his domain is still wide enough.

But because there was, and still is, a natural inclination in men to believe in, and rely on, the supernatural, it does not follow that their religious beliefs have a spontaneous course as the European thinkers seem to assume. History proves that the empires of the priests are established in the very same manner as those of the secular monarchs. However much a settled Government may be desired by men, yet history does not furnish a single instance in which the blessing of a strong ruler at the head has not been more or less forced upon the people who are placed under his sway. Similarly, however much a religion may be valued by those who profess it, it had never been wanted until it was forced upon them by the literary genius or political tact of some great teacher. In fact, in religion and politics, as in every other sphere, it is the artist that creates the demand for the inventions of his art.

Upon a careful survey of the religious systems of the world, it appears that all the primitive religions inculcate the worship of either the friendly powers of nature or of demons. Generally speaking, the priest cannot approach the savage, who lives by hunting, fishing or cattle breeding, except by the most merciless bullying. The savage can have no scope or ambition for acquiring wealth or high office, and as he has *en hypothisie* no idea of any kind of luxury, the promise of heaven can have no influence on him, and he can have no motive to worship friendly gods. The only way to make him amenable to priestly discipline, lies in leading him to believe that diseases and deaths are caused by a set of fierce and bloodthirsty gods who can be propitiated only by the sacrifice of goats, pigs, sheep, &c. His cattle being his principal, if not his sole, wealth that is the only method of worship which his priest can turn to account. Hence the demon-worship and the sacrifice of animals in the pre-agricultural stage of civilization.

With the development of society, men become subject to hopes, influences and fears which had been unknown to them before. When agriculture begins to be practised, the tillers of the soil find that rain is necessary for their operations, and that it does not take place in all years when most wanted. At this stage the shrewder members of society, who hate manual labour and desire nothing so much as to live on the fruits of other people's industry, can easily persuade the primitive ploughman to believe that rainfall depends upon the will or caprice of a deity who, like most mortals, has his price. The belief being impressed, the primitive priest has only to invent a plausible and attractive programme. The expedient which he has usually recourse to is the kindling of a fire, and the burning of butter or incense on the altar. These are the least bulky goods that the primitive agriculturist could be called upon to supply to his priest. The process is somewhat wasteful if carried out under too much vigilance. But in the operations of the priest, as in those of the political adventurer, wastefulness is inevitable.

The primitive priest is compelled by the necessity of his position to promise tangible good service, such as rainfall to the tillers of the soil, health to the sick, and children to barren women. His constituents cannot appreciate the value of salvation, Moksha, Nirvana or spiritual happiness of the soul after death, and in order to make them venerate him and submit to his exactions, he is obliged to promise more substantial services. In doing so he has to tread upon very treacherous ground. But rainfall may take place at the required time in the course of nature; the sick man may be restored to health by nature; and a woman believed to be barren may also bear a child in the course of nature. If the event be such as to support the priest's pretensions, he knows how to take the credit. If there be disappointment, he knows how to transfer the responsibility to a malignant star, or to want of faith on the part of his dupe.

Nevertheless the priest cannot but be conscious that it is not safe to promise the rendering of worldly service. He therefore takes the earliest opportunity to shift his ground. By promising Nirvan, Moksha or salvation he runs no risk whatever. He therefore sets himself to *educate* the people to value these principalities in Utopia. That seems to be the true origin of the Upanishads and the metaphysics of the ancients.

In the primitive stage of agriculture, the powers supposed to be concerned in sending rain to earth receive the largest share of worship. When the priest finds how easy it is to dupe the majority of men, he goes on adding more and more gods to his pantheon, inventing at the same time the most complicated and attractive programmes, so as to win the esteem and confidence of the people, and to make himself a necessity to them. Nothing comes amiss to him at this stage. Allegorical divinities, the souls of deceased persons, nay, rivers, hot springs, trees, birds, beasts and serpents suffice to serve as the bases of elaborate rites. The votary is called upon to supply not merely butter, mutton, goats, wine and scents, but everything else that might add dignity to, or put a decent veil on, the priest's operations. Some of the things required by him to give cover to his spoliations are quite useless, and withal very difficult to procure. But, as I have already said, wastefulness is inevitable in priestcraft as in the *modus operandi* of the other classes who live by their wits. Neither the priests nor any other class of sharp men can afford to abide by the principles of taxation laid down by Adam Smith. The secular rulers may be called upon to be satisfied with only such sources of revenue as enable them to get almost the whole of what is paid by those who are made liable to the tax. But the priest, the mooktear and the engineer will very seldom hesitate to set their weapons in motion for fear that they might not get more than a fraction of what their victims must lose.

The nature-worshipping priests have, in some countries, been able to maintain their empire for ages. But it is simply impossible that they should be allowed to reign unmolested for ever, and, sooner or later, their success leads others to play a bolder game. These autocratic and ambitious teachers generally succeed in giving a rude shock to the fabric built by the nature-worshippers. They claim to be worshipped as gods themselves, and cannot tolerate the practice of according any homage to the dumb material objects and powers. So they proclaim, more or less directly, that men must worship them, and not Indra or Woden, Jupiter or Thor, who might serve as convenient shams in the beginning, but are, like the Bahadoor Shahs and the Wajid Alis, quite useless when the adventurer's power is completely established. Whether this view of the origin of the man-worshipping religions, and of the process by which they supersede the nature-worshipping cults, be accepted or not, this much at least is established beyond doubt, by the evidence of history, that the former have always followed the latter, and that there is not a single instance in which they have appeared in the contrary order.

According to the ideas generally favoured by the modern thinkers, monotheism is the highest development that religion is capable of. This view is quite natural in those who are more conversant with Christianity and Mahomedanism than with any of the other religions. The Mahomedans never take the trouble to study other religions, and Europeans are placed amidst such surroundings, that, with all their inquisitiveness and industry, it is well-nigh impossible for them to make an accurate estimate of the several systems, or to arrive at a correct determination regarding their relative position. Europe knows only one form of faith, and that cult is an exotic plant so stunted and dwarfed by the Lutheran Reformation, that it has never found scope for developing all its potentialities. Europe is, in fact, no more the place for the study of religions than the desert of Sahara is for thestudy of botany.

The evidence afforded by history goes very far to prove that monotheism is only the usual appendage of the man-worshipping religions. The apostle of monotheism says :—"There is but one God and I am his viceroy." On the supposition that such preaching is not based upon genuine revelation, it must be admitted to have for its object the creation of a strict monopoly. The truth seems to be that monotheism is no more an advanced idea in theology than the absolute monarchies set up by Julius Cæsar and Cromwell were institutions in advance of the Roman Senate, and the British Long Parliament.

In our experience of every-day life, we see that when too much power is acquired by any individual, its abuse is inevitable, and priestly power is no exception to the rule. The success with which the nature-worshipping and the man-worshipping priests are able to ply their trade, emboldens some adventurers to play still more daring games, and to inculcate the worship of such abominations as enable them to create every possible opportunity for gratifying their depraved lust by corrupting the morals of their dupes. The cults invented by them are, generally speaking, of very recent origin, and cannot but be taken to be the highest developments that the theocratic art is capable of.

From what is stated above, it will appear that the usual transition of all religions is from nature-worship to man-worship, and from man-worship to abomination-worship. In India all these forms of faith are to be found in the living condition. In Europe nature-worship has been since long suppressed altogether, and the Lutheran Reformation, combined with the common sense of the laity, has smothered the inevitable tendency to abomination-worship. Perhaps it was rendered unnecessary by the confessional rites of the Roman Catholic Church. But the fact of there having been such tendencies even in Europe is abundantly proved by history. Perhaps no class of priests have been more prone to abuse their power than the Popes and their lieutenants. In speaking of the See of Rome Macaulay says :—

During the generation which preceded the Reformation that Court had been a scandal to the Christian name. Its annals are black with treason, murder and incest. Even its more respectable members were utterly unfit to be ministers of religion. Their years glided by in a soft dream of sensual and intellectual voluptuousness. Choice cookery, delicious wines, lovely women, hounds, falcons, horses, newly-discovered manuscripts of the classics and burlesque romances in the sweetest Tuscan, just as licentious as a fine sense of the graceful would permit, these things were the delight and even the serious business of their lives. * * * *

When these circumstances, and the history of such early sects as the Marcionites and the Carpocratians* are taken into consideration, it seems that Europe has had a very narrow escape from abomination-worship of the aggravated type with which we are unfortunately too familiar in this country. However that may be, the existence of the abomination-worshipping sects in the world cannot be ignored, and, if their origin and history be studied, it would appear that they have, in all cases, followed the man-worshipping cults, as they must do on the hypothesis that the religions have had their origin in human policy.

---

* See Gibbons' *Decline and Fall of the Roman Empire.*

CHAP III.—THE CLASSIFICATION OF THE RELIGIOUS SYSTEMS.

THE religious systems existing in the world can be classified in various ways, in accordance with different principles. From the point of view of their usual course of evolution, they are, as stated in the last chapter, capable of being divided into the following classes :—

1.	1. DEMON-WORSHIP	Found chiefly among savages.
	2. NATURE-WORSHIP (including the worship of allegorical divinities, trees, rivers, hot springs, birds, beasts, &c.).	Found chiefly among the agricultural nations of primitive times.
2.	1. MAN-WORSHIP	Found in almost every civilized country.
	(a) Religions inculcating the worship of an imaginary god of such a type as to dispose men to worship of the mendicant beggars.	The Siva-worshipping religion is of this class, though there is in it an element of abomination-worship.
	(b) Religions inculcating the worship of some great teachers believed to have attained a higher condition than that of the gods, by austerities or any other means.	Buddhism and Jainism.
	(c) Religions inculcating the worship of some great men believed to be the agents of the Most High.	Christianity, Mahomedanism and Sikhism.
	(d) Religions inculcating the worship of an ancient hero as a god, or an incarnation of a god.	Ram-worship, Krishna-worship.
	3. IDEA-WORSHIP	Found among cultured people in civilized countries.

4. ABOMINATION-WORSHIP	Found only in countries that have an ancient civilization combined with the ignorance of the masses.
5. MIXED RELIGIONS.	

Viewing the religions in connection with their influence on the morality of men, they fall under the following groups :—

1. Religions having little or nothing to do with the preaching of morality.
2. Religions encouraging chiefly pure morality according to the lights of their teachers.
3. Religions encouraging immorality more or less, while inculcating some morality also.
4. Religions directly inculcating the grossest immoralities.
5. Religions indirectly encouraging immorality.

Looked at from the point of view of the services which the priests offer to perform, their faiths may be classified as follows :—

1. Tangible-service-promising religions.
2. Intangible-service-promising religions.
3. Mischief-making religions.

Looked at from the point of view of the subsidies and services claimed by the priests, the religions may be classified as follows :—

1. Ghi, incense, meat and wine-demanding religions.	Almost all the ancient religions are of this character, and favour indirect taxation.
2. Religions demanding the building of monasteries and temples in addition to other votive offerings.	Most of the man-worshipping and abomination-worshipping religions are of this character.
3. Mere alms-taking religions.	These may be said to favour direct taxation.
4. Religions demanding military service.	The religions of the Mahomedans, the Sikhs, and the Nagas are more or less of this character.

Looked at from the point of view of church government, the religions may be grouped in many different ways, as, for instance, the following :—

1. Aristocratic religions, of which the ministers are hereditary priests.
2. Republican religions, of which the ministers are ordained by nomination or election.
3. Religions that profess to have no priests.

If the attitude of the several religions towards each other be taken into consideration, then they may be classified as follows :—

1. Federal religions shewing due toleration to every form of faith.
2. Autocratic religions teaching their followers to hate every cult, not their own, as false superstition.

The man-worshipping religions are generally the most autocratic, though founded by teachers who push up the lower classes in order to destroy the power of the nature-worshipping priests. Like the Turk the prophets who claim adoration for themselves cannot bear a brother near their throne.

Having regard to the visible objects and symbols to which worship is offered, the most important forms of faith are the following :—

1. Tree, bird, beast and serpent-worshipping religions.
2. Sun, moon and planet-worshipping religions.
3. River, hot spring, lake and sea-worshipping religions.
4. Mound-worshipping religions.
5. Fire-worshipping religions.
6. Children-worshipping religions.
7. Decent image-worshipping religions.
8. Obscene symbol-worshipping religions.
9. Altar-worshipping, book-worshipping and monastery subsidising religions.
10. Guru-worshipping religions.

Of these, the first four are found chiefly among half civilized and savage nations. The fifth form, namely, fire-worship, finds great favour among some of the most advanced races of men in the world. Its only drawbacks are :—

1. It involves great waste.
2. It is not a convenient way for appropriating bulky and identifiable goods.
3. It cannot enable the priest to make unlimited demands on public charity.

The sixth form is not well suited for purposes of priestcraft, and is very rare. The seventh and the eighth forms enable the priesthood not only to acquire every kind of property, but also to corrupt the morals of their female votaries. The abuse which the image-worshipping priests make of their powers and opportunities leads, however, very often to revolts that threaten to make a clean sweep of idolatry. But the so-called reformations are, generally more apparent than real, the operations of the iconoclasts serving, in nine cases out of ten, to establish only altar-worship, book-worship, monastery-worship, or guru-worship, which are, in many respects, worse than idolatry.

Quite recently some very earnest attempts have been made by teachers like the late Pundit Dayanand to replace idolatry by the ancient Vedic cult. But idol-worship is a much more effective and useful weapon to the priest than fire-worship, and is no more likely to be superseded by it than railways of modern times by the ancient means of locomotion like the dak palki, the postchaise and the bullock-cart. Idol-worship may give way only to monasteries and churches claiming endowments of property and State subsidies while like idolatrous shrines, serving also as permanent contrivances for drawing towards them the small charities of the public.

CHAP. IV.—DEFINITIONS OF RELIGION.

WE all possess a vague notion of what is called religion which suffices for all practical purposes. But the least attempt to define the term shows that our ideas on the subject are very far from being clear and definite. In fact, like the juridical terms:—"law," "legal right," and "possession" the word religion, though appearing to be a very simple one, cannot possibly be defined except by a very careful analysis. The reader who may be curious to study the definitions proposed by the thinkers of Europe, ancient and modern, may refer to Professor Max Müller's treatise on the *Origin of Religion.* In his *Science of Religion*, the eminent philosopher himself gives the following definition of the term :—

"Religion is a mental faculty or disposition which, independent of, nay, in spite of sense and reason, enables man to apprehend the Infinite under different names and under varying disguises."

This definition has been condemned by the author himself. In one of his later works, he says :—

"Religion consists in the perception of the Infinite under such manifestations as are able to influence the moral character of man. —*The Gifford Lectures*, 1888, p. 188.

These definitions might be taken to embody their author's ideas as to what religion ought to be. But very few of the religions actually existing in this world can be said to have anything to do with the apprehension of the Infinite.

To me it seems that the word religion has two different meanings. According to one of its aspects, it is the art of bringing men under priestly discipline, by means of threats and hopes held out in the names of superior and unseen powers. In its other aspect, it can be defined only as the sum total of the beliefs, sentiments and practices to which the laity are led by priestly influence and art. In fact, religion is to a great extent the same thing as politics, the only difference being that the rewards and punishments by which the politician acquires and maintains his power are all of an earthly nature, whereas the priest terrorises and consoles men by implanting in their minds a belief in supernatural influences for good and evil. Where the priests have for their object the improvement of the morality of men, or of their social and domestic virtues, they are generally able to do great good to society. But, like most worldly men, they usually seek more to aggrandise themselves than to do any good to mankind, and they not only do very little to improve the morality of men, but sometimes encourage the grossest immorality, either to gratify their own carnal appetites, or simply to attract followers. They profess to make men happy, and, by the hopes of future bliss which they hold out, they no doubt actually impart a ray of light in the darkest hours of our woes. But, generally speaking, they take a delight in wanton cruelty, and, like some of the greatest political tyrants, do more to increase the stock of our miseries than to alleviate them. Fasting, hook-swinging, bathing in cold water in winter mornings, living on half rations, eating the most unpalatable food, roasting under a midday sun or amidst artificial fires, standing erect on one leg, keeping one arm constantly uplifted—these are some of the tortures to which the dupes of the priest are subjected. He has the satisfaction of finding that the discipline imposed on society by him is being conformed to. But, in practising such cruelty, he betrays a kind of hard-heartedness which is not to be found even in the worst of secular rulers. Sometimes, as in encouraging indiscriminate charity and restricting usury, the authors of the religions may be credited with philanthropic motives. But the practical result of their legislation is that they do a great deal of mischief, though with the best of intentions. For such teachings we cannot blame them. But they certainly prove that either the modern sciences are fraught with errors, or that the so-called prophets were only ordinary men, and very far from possessing that omniscience which they claimed. In fact there is hardly a single religion in the world which is based on infallible knowledge or unexceptionable morality. Considering the forms of faith with which we are acquainted, it seems impossible to define religion in any other way than as mentioned above. It has certainly nothing to do with the perception of the Infinite.

CHAP. V.—THE TRUE ORIGIN OF RELIGIONS.

It is believed by most men that religion has its origin in the will of Divine Providence; but a careful examination of the tenets of the several religions would lead inevitably to the conclusion that our faiths have had their source in human policy, and not in Divine will. At any rate, the theory deriving it from human policy can alone give a satisfactory explanation of such theological questions as the following :—

1. Why is it that the nature-worshipping religions precede the man-worshipping faiths, and that man-worship precedes abomination-worship?
2. Why is there such progressive development at all?
3. Why is it that the tangible-service-promising religions precede the cults that value only spiritual bliss?
4. Why is it that there are such differences between the several religions as are to be found in them now?
5. Why is it that some religions actually encourage immorality?
6. Why is it that the ancient religions recommended the sacrifice of animals and of even human beings?
7. Why is it that the modern religions do not, generally speaking, encourage the sacrifice of animals?
8. Why is it that the ancient religions insisted upon the burning of *ghi* and incense?
9. Why is it that the Hindus believe in ten Avatars or successive incarnations?
10. Why is it that even when actuated by the best of motives the so-called prophets and incarnations have not been able to give any indication of their knowing even the most elementary principles of the economical and the physical sciences?

On the theory that the religions have their origin in human policy, there cannot possibly be any difficulty in explaining these questions; but on any other supposition they are quite insoluble.

Admitting, as we must do, that all the religions have their origin in human policy, the question next arises whether they are the outcome of true philanthrophy, or of selfishness, pure and simple. The fact is, that while there is an element of genuine philanthropy in some of the religions, there is a great deal of the foulest selfishness in the majority of them. If our religions be admitted to be the outcome of human policy, then the doctrine that the founders of the several systems of faith were actuated by purely unselfish zeal would be quite as absurd as the supposition that the object which Alexander, Mahomed Ghori, Sultan Baber, William the Conqueror, and Napoleon had in their view was only to give the blessing of good government to the countries which they conquered. The religious sect founders are in fact neither better nor worse men than our political rulers. To outbid a powerful rival, or to avoid losing the confidence of the public, both the politician and the prophet may profess very high principles. Bu,t in the absence of an Opposition and an intelligent public opinion, it is very unusual for a religious or secular ruler to keep to the path of duty and rectitude.

CHAP. VI.—THE ALLEGED NECESSITY OF RELIGION FOR THE ATTAINMENT OF THE HIGHEST STANDARD OF MORALS.

Is religion necessary for giving to men the highest ideal of moral life? This question is very often asked, but the answers given regarding it are extremely conflicting. There is no doubt that no system of law, however cleverly devised or efficiently administered, can go far enough to elevate the moral nature of man beyond a very limited range. But it does not follow that there ever has been any religion which enables man to attain anything like the highest moral altitude. On the contrary, many of the so-called religions of men tend more to corrupt their morality, than to purify it. There are in fact some religions as, for instance, those of the Tāntrics, Kauls, Karta Bhajas, Bija Margis, Jalaliyas, Aghoris, &c., which have perhaps not one redeeming feature in them, and which tend only to make their followers wallow in the mire of abominations. There are no doubt some religions which sincerely aim at improving the character of men in all their relations. But even the best of these fall far short of the ideal of good citizenship taught by the exigencies of modern social life. A man may not violate the ten commandments of Moses or the Panch Sila of Buddha, and still his character may be such as to make him a sore spot in the commonwealth.

Upon a careful examination of the foundation of ethics, it must appear to every reasonable and unbiased mind that the principle of utility is the only source of morality, and that the character of men is regulated more by public opinion, than by the rules imposed on society by any revealed scripture. By threats of future evil or promises of future bliss, religion can no doubt go a great way to enforce the rules of morality on men. But experience shows that public opinion, when it is wide awake and is of a healthy nature, has far greater influence than any terror or hope that a priest may hold out. Religion may do good by moulding the views of men ; but, apart from public opinion, it is never productive of any important result. According to the religion of both Hindus and Mahomedans there is not a greater sin than the drinking of spirituous liquors. But public opinion treats the vice more leniently than the Koran and the Smritis enjoin, and it is certainly not quite so rare as it ought to be. Take, however, the case of beef-eating by a Hindu. The sin involved in the act is, according to the Shastras, not at all of a serious nature. But popular feeling is strong on the subject, and till lately there was perhaps not a single beef-eating Hindu in the country. Among the Mahomedans there is perhaps still not a single pork-eater. These facts clearly show that it is public opinion,, and not any religious code, that has the greatest influence in building up what is called the conscience of men. Whatever influence religion has, is due chiefly to its being an important factor in moulding the opinions of men. The proper authorities to regulate public opinion on the subject are the philosophers, historians, statesmen and publicists. The sooner the priests cease to meddle in the matter, the better for the world. It is not at all desirable that morality should be based on false hopes and false terrors, however effective they may prove to be at times. The experience of the whole world shows that men who can invent falsehoods for the good of the world, are never slow to have recourse to the same means for attaining their own selfish objects. At any rate there is not a single religion in the world whose moral standard is sufficiently high for the exigencies of civilized life.

To be a good citizen the most important thing is to have a deep sense of moral responsibility for all our acts and omissions. A man may not be an actual thief, liar or murderer, but the result is all the same if he has not sufficient firmness and sense of duty. A ship surveyor gives a certificate of seaworthiness to a ship, without carefully examining her condition. The vessel springs a leak while on a voyage, and is wrecked with all her crew, cargo and passengers. If the real cause of the disaster be ascertainable by any evidence, the surveyor may be legally punished. But, whether he pays the penalty for his negligence, or is able to escape scot-free, his delinquency hardly comes within the purview of any revealed code of morals.

Then, again, suppose that an engineer in charge of the construction of a bridge fails to supervise the work of the contractors properly. The piers are not sunk to the required depth, or are built with unsuitable materials. The structure is finished, and is somehow able to go through a test. But, lo! when one day the river is in high flood through abnormal rainfall, and a heavily laden train passes over the bridge, it gives way, and there is one of those disasters which cast a gloom over the whole country. Yet the engineer may be reckoned as a highly moral man, if judged by the standard of the so-called religious teachers of the world.

If a king or political minister needlessly declares war against an unoffending nation, and wastes the resources of his own country in spreading misery and desolation on his neighbours, he yet may be regarded as a good man, and the priest may not find anything in the religious codes to justify even a proposal for the punishment of excommunication which perhaps no one deserves more than he. He ought certainly to be boycotted and execrated by society while alive, and to die, unwept, unhonoured and unknown. But the whole history of the world does not perhaps afford one single instance in which the priesthood have so punished a bloodthirsty destroyer of nations, except when the interest of the priestly class itself is served or affected. In fact there is no authority in any scripture for the condign punishment of such monsters in purple.

Take, again, the case of a man in power who, out of jealousy, causes the ruin of a rival or subordinate, and, by vetoing his measures or handicapping him, subjects his country to an irreparable loss. The little man, dressed in brief authority, may be the model of a good Hindu or Christian ; but it must be admitted by every one that he deserves only to be hated and cursed.

Suppose again, for instance, that a man of prayers organises and floats a commercial, mining or railway enterprise. His learning and reputation for piety serve to attract capital from every quarter. But either the scheme itself is quite unpractical, or the promoter is quite incapable of placing it on a sound footing. Whatever be the cause, it fails, and thousands of families are ruined altogether by the crash. The promoter may be given credit for honesty in the usual narrow sense of the term. He may even continue to be regarded as a man of piety, according to the standard of the priestly class. But, from the point of view of that elevated morality which is understood and valued only by practical men of the world, he cannot be regarded as a man of a very high moral sense.

The prophets who affect to teach us morality, and claim to be worshipped on that account, are generally the men who betray the greatest disregard of that sense of moral responsibility which is the essence of good citizenship. To begin with, they generally teach their followers to lead an idle life, and to live by begging, bullying or cheating. The latter-day prophets of India, at least, are, in fact, so many givers of licenses to beg, and to corrupt the morality of the people. The mischief done by encouraging able-bodied men to neglect the proper work of life, and live as drones on public charity, is simply incalculable. It is not like the act of a thief or murderer which affects only a limited number of victims. Its effects are far-reaching, and its baneful influence continues, from generation to generation, very often increasing in momentum in the course of its progress. That is, however, not the only way in which the so-called religious teachers of mankind have made their condition far worse than it would otherwise have been. They profess to make men happy. But, as a matter of fact, their teachings serve only to increase the sum total of human misery. As if our natural afflictions were not enough for us, the priests have invented methods of self-torture—like fasts, hook-swinging, cold baths in winter, and exposure for whole days under an Indian sun—which, on account of their fiendish character, surpass everything that the imagination of the worst of secular tyrants has ever devised.

The worst result of the teachings of the so-called prophets is, perhaps, the bad blood which they excite against those who refuse to be their followers. It is easy enough for a shrewd man to create bitter feelings between different nations and classes of men. But the prophets who affect to bring tidings of joy and peace from heaven, ought certainly to have a better sense of moral responsibility than that which they show by kindling the hell-fire of sectarian bigotry.

As are the prophets, so are their ministers and tools. The persecution to which the great philosopher Galileo was subjected by the authorities of the Roman Catholic Church is one of the typical cases that reflect everlasting disgrace on the spiritual rulers of men. The mischief may be all the same even without the practice of any kind of positive tyranny. A play-wright, publicist or temple promoter, who, for the sake of money or mere popularity, encourages any of the forms of abomination-worship, may succeed in securing popular praise or reverence. But, whether he simply gives countenance to Yoni worship, Linga worship and Radha worship, or actually recommends them by some ingenious plea put forward on their behalf, he deserves to be stigmatised as only an evil genius of mankind. When we find many of our educated countrymen now-a-days patrolling the streets in connection with Sankirtan parties, or offering puja to those emblems of obscenity and immodesty called Kāli and Siva, it ought to be obvious to every thoughtful mind how little there is of common sense, or of a consciousness of responsibility among our public men. If only in order to be on the safe side they, at least, ought to keep themselves aloof from Kāli, Siva and Radha. *Primâ facie* there can be nothing in them to deserve the devotion of the pious. That fact alone ought to place every one on his guard. No doubt many esoteric explanations are suggested to whitewash the things. But no one can, I suppose, honestly say that he is so satisfied with those pleas, as not to entertain any misgivings in his heart of hearts. And if he have any misgivings, the proper course for him certainly is to be not too enthusiastic. But he takes up a different line, and by his zeal proves only that religion can very seldom impress on men the value of a proper sense of moral responsibility. Religion teaches blind faith and blind fervour, the result being that it is very seldom conducive towards the development of a capacity for discrimination between good and evil.

CHAP. VII.—GENERAL OBSERVATIONS ABOUT THE SECT FOUNDERS.

THE religious sects founded and existing in India are too numerous to be catalogued with anything like completeness in a book like this. India is pre-eminently the land of prophets and "gods in disguise." In Europe the autocratic and overshadowing power of the Popes of Imperial Rome kept under a wholesome check the would-be vicegerents of the Divinity. While punishing with merciless severity every tendency towards heresy, the rulers of the Vatican, with their usual wisdom, conferred high offices and honours on such persons as appeared to possess the necessary ability and energy to organize a successful schism. Thus was the empire of the Popes maintained in undiminished glory for more than a thousand years, and the hold which the Christian religion thus acquired on the European mind has been, even after the Reformation, so strong that no power has yet arisen that has applied itself to the task of shaking it off or setting up in its place a new cult. The position of Christianity in Europe still is what that of the Emperors of Delhi was during the last century. As the Maharattas, the Nabobs of Oudh and the English, with all their powers at the time, recognized the supremacy of the Mogul, so the sect founders of modern Europe, while setting at defiance the authority of the Popes, have never been able to claim divine worship for themselves instead of for Christ.

In India the case has been very different, especially since the commencement of Mahomedan rule. Here the absence of a strong central authority recognized by all as supreme in ecclesiastical matters, and the ignorance of the masses, have enabled many a clever adventurer to play the rôle of "incarnations," and to carve out independent religious principalities. The profession does not require much preliminary training or expenditure of capital. It is unattended with most of those risks that beset the secular politician, and to those who possess the necessary tact, steadiness, histrionic skill, debating power, and genius for inventing unexplodable legends, it brings not only power, money, fame, and honour, but everything else that the most wicked lust of the most depraved of human beings can have a craving for. Such being the case, the number of persons that are found to be actually engaged in the game, is generally limited only by the resources of the society to feed the idlers.

The part which the "incarnation" has to play is a very difficult one. Without material resources of any kind, he has to collect round him an army of disciples who must be at least as devoted to him as the followers of any secular prince. He must, through his disciples, circulate the most extravagant stories about his miraculous powers; but, at the same time, must avoid their exhibition. He must avoid debates. But if he is ever compelled to take a part in any controversy, he must contrive to be victorious. He must have also histrionic powers of a very superior type, and be able to swoon and shed tears whenever necessary. He must lead a life of celibacy, and maintain a character for being above the vulgar appetites of human beings though like Siva he might, in order to oblige the gods, enjoy the delights of conjugal life, or like Vallabhāchari, might take a wife in fulfilment of the commands of some deity. The most difficult part of his work is the exercise of due discrimination in the choice of his immediate disciples. He should be very careful never to have a traitor or malcontent in his camp. The fabric built by him after years of arduous labour may be demolished in the course of a single day by a Madame Coulomb.

The sect founders generally claim to derive their inspiration from some invisible teachers. The Kut Humis and Aulia Gossains are so very useful that they are almost indispensable to the prophets in the beginning of their careers. When the young Avatar's power is sufficiently established, then alone he can shake off the fiction of such subordinate alliance.

The event which the biographers of the prophet find it most difficult to explain, and account for, is his death. There is certainly nothing which hard swearing and combined action cannot accomplish in this world. But the prophet must leave some friends surviving him, who would undertake for his sake, or for promoting their own interest, the task of inventing and circulating legends about his miraculous disappearance from earth.

The difficulty of playing the rôle of a prophet being great, and the number of the competitors being many, the careers of those who attempt the game are very seldom attended with more than partial success. Even when a great religious kingdom is successfully established, on an apparently sound footing, it usually proves quite as ephemeral as the secular monarchies founded in the last century by political adventurers of the type of Hyder Ali. But in spite of all the checks on the overgrowth of the sects, their number at the present time is not at all inconsiderable. In fact so numerous are they, and so complicated is the history of their growth, that I cannot hope to give in this book more than a brief account of the most important among them.

CHAP. VIII.—THE INDUCEMENTS HELD OUT BY SECT FOUNDERS TO ATTRACT FOLLOWERS

The sect founders of our country attract followers chiefly by relaxing the discipline of the ancient Shastras, and by throwing open to them the rejected elements of pure Hinduism. The Brahmanical codes lay down that the acceptance of a gift from a degraded person or a member of a low caste is a very sinful act. The Brahmans accordingly refuse their ministrations to the vintners and the courtesans, and treat them as beyond the pale of humanity. But the Tāntric and Vishnuvite prophets have, in different ways, supplied the much-needed pretexts for overcoming such scruples. The Tāntrics actually enjoin the worship of courtesans, and lay down also that when sitting together for the practice of the Bacchanalian rites which they inculcate, the members of their orgies have all a higher position than even that of the Brahmans. In the same manner the Vishnuvite teachers profess the most large-hearted philanthropy, and declare that, with such a potent remedy as the name of Hari for curing the souls of men, they have no right to refuse their ministrations to any class, however low or degraded. The wealth of the sinners, which is rejected by the Brahmans, being thus made lawful prize, almost all the sect founders, from Buddha to Chaitanya, have been able to attract very large numbers of followers. Buddha himself accepted the hospitality and the gifts of a courtesan, just as some of the Chaitanite Gossains of Calcutta are known to do at present.

The rich pastures and virgin fields opened by our prophets to their disciples, were in themselves sufficient to attract followers. But with a view to remove all possible difficulties from the way, and to hold out other inducements, almost all our sect founders have admitted females into their ecclesiastical orders, and have done their utmost to promote the building of monasteries which might serve as barracks and recruiting camps for their followers. The Brahmanical Shastras lay down that a married woman has no right to practise any religious rite, except in the company of her husband, and that the highest duties of a widow are the preservation of her chastity, and the performance of such rites as benefit the soul of her deceased husband in the next world. The great Hindu legislators strictly prohibit the association of females, on familiar terms, with even such males as are very near relatives. The sect founders set aside these wholesome ordinances, and admitted nuns into their monasteries. What the result has been is well known.

With a view to render the cultivation of learning possible, our ancient law-givers laid down that it was proper for a Vedic student to live by begging. That was good and noble indeed. But the sect founders could not have any justification in letting loose on the world their armies of mendicants whose only functions are to advertise and glorify them, and to misappropriate the fund which properly belongs to the aged, the infirm and the helpless.

The sect founders are, at the present time, regarded by many as entitled to great credit for having elevated the lower castes. But caste distinctions among the laity are recognized by the modern sects in the same manner as by the Brahmans professing the ancient forms of Hinduism. It is only among the monks and nuns that caste distinctions are ignored to a great extent; but they can have no legitimate children, and their illegitimate and semi-legitimate progeny have necessarily a very low status. Thus, in practice, the low castes are still in the same position as before, in spite of the so-called reformations of the latter-day prophets.

CHAP IX.—THE METHODS OF PRIESTLY OPERATIONS.

The means which the priests and the prophets adopt in order to establish their power are not the same in every age and country. On the supposition that they do not derive their systems from genuine revelation, it must be admitted that they are all obliged to have recourse to hard swearing to a very large extent; but that alone cannot suffice to enable them to gain their end. At the beginning they have necessarily to profess that they possess the power of working miracles. That is a dangerous game. A living prophet of Bengal made a great sensation, some years ago, by promising to bring back to life, after six months, all the deceased relatives of his followers. A large number of widows and bereaved mothers eagerly took the bait, and paid handsomely for his good graces. He made some money. But the day of reckoning soon arrived, and he has been discredited for ever. Such men are desperate gamblers who may make some noise for a time, but are sure to end their days in disgrace. The true master of the art may allow his disciples to retail such stories about his miraculous powers as they can invent. But as soon as he is called upon to give an exhibition, he turns round indignantly and asks: "Am I a juggler?" After his death, the stories of his miracles might serve important purposes, through the manipulations of his literary disciples. The latter find it advantageous also to give the most extravagant accounts relating to the birth, death and outward appearance of their master.

From professing to have the power of working miracles, the next step is to invent legends for frightening men, and for leading them to fool's paradise. But even these cannot directly serve the purposes of priestcraft in a material degree. What is most important to the priest is to invent incantations and complicated rituals. By means of the latter, he is enabled to demand heavy payments in advance. He is placed in a position to say :—"I may not be given any fee for my services, but I cannot be expected to make bricks without straw." By such representations, he manages to have himself remunerated indirectly in anticipation, and he does not lose much if the rite fails to be productive of any good to the party celebrating it. At an early stage the laity are made to believe that the ceremonies and formulas of the priest are capable of yielding the result which his so-called sacred books promise. But soon he shifts his ground, and begins to recommend them as useful for their own sake. The Vedic hymns and the Tāntric formulas were evidently valued at first as means to an end. But it is now very seldom pretended that the mystical words, phrases or syllables, in any book of ritual, can cause the destruction of an hostile army, or add one pice to the wealth of the votary. The Hindu is led now-a-days to receive the sacrament of the mantra from his Guru, not by any hope that the meaningless syllables whispered into his ears would be productive of any worldly good, but by the belief that they are useful for spiritual purposes. The transition that is thus made to take place in the popular view regarding their utility, is very similar to what commonly happens in secular spheres in the courts of the Indian princes. A high official has a favourite to provide for. He is represented as having great influence on the refractory subjects of the State, and on persons having the ears of the British Resident. He is appointed, and when it becomes apparent that it is quite beyond his power to redeem his promises, his retention is justified by some such plea as that he is a member of a very respectable family, and that, though unable through bad luck to render any tangible good work, yet the very fact of his being in the service of the State adds dignity to it.

Closely allied to the power of working miracles is the healing art. Incantations may fail to cure a disease, but with good medicines the man of religion might achieve better success. The kind of medicine, however, that can serve the purpose of the prophet is, or at least was, very rare before the days of Hahnemann. An homœopathic drop might be administered as consecrated water, but not so any other drug. From miracles, incantations and medicines, the man of religion therefore shifts his ground to asceticism, gymnastics and pantomimic exhibitions. By professing absolute indifference towards worldly happiness, he puts a decent veil on his poverty, and, at the same time, secures the confidence of men as to his being disinterested in cheating them. The attitude of silent contemplation in which he is always seen serves the same purposes, and also impresses the spectators with awe and faith. But these methods have great disadvantages. To begin with, they are very irksome, and it is quite impossible for most ordinary men to go through the tortures of such semi-starvation and "solitary imprisonment" *suo moto* for any length of time. The ascetic may, when he has established a character for superior sanctity, give up his self-imposed restraints, and try to enjoy a little of worldly pleasures. But as soon as he puts off his harness, he is lowered in the estimation of his followers. Moreover, the Shastric canon, once an ascetic always an ascetic, renders it very difficult for him to be readmitted to society or to get married. He may pass the remaining years of his life as a member of the class called householder ascetics. But they are a disreputable order, and he feels great reluctance to associate with them. At any rate, he is precluded forever from enjoying that respect of his fellow-castemen and fellow-villagers which is the ambition of every Hindu. Such being the case, absolute asceticism, with all its advantages, cannot have much attraction to the man of religion.

Fine speeches are sometimes as effective as the pantomimic exhibitions of Yoga and the practice of asceticism. But the gift of oratory is a rare one, and the man who has the ambition to be a leader of the mob, and yet does not possess the fair-spoken tongue of a demagogue, must seek for other weapons. Moreover, for the proper display of oratorical powers, town halls and expensive furnitures are absolutely necessary. And these are very rare in India. It is also to be borne in mind that while speech is silver, silence is often equivalent to gold. The Tāntrics therefore adopted some mystical syllables and gestures which serve as the ingredients of an imposing and awe-inspiring liturgy. But their laconic syllables and silent gesticulations cannot stir the fervour of the mob. So the later Hindu prophets invented other weapons which are far more effective, and, at the same time, are capable of being easily wielded. One of these consists in attaching great importance to the constant repetition of the name of some deity. The other, which has been of late very successfully imitated, in a modified form, by "General" Booth, is the kind of religious procession called Sankirtan. There cannot possibly be any difficulty in organising such a party of musicians to patrol the streets with flags, drums and bugles. The music of the Sankirtan has itself an attraction, and when combined with the frequent repetition of the names of the cherished Hindu gods, its effect on the people is simply maddening. It generates an irresistible mania in them for joining the procession. It acts like a great ocean wave which dissolves in its progress the most refractory elements.

CHAP. X.—GENERAL CHARACTER OF THE HINDU SECTS.

It is the fashion now-a-days to speak of the Hindu sect founders as so many religious reformers,

> As if religion were intended
> For nothing else but to be mended.

Looked at with the light of sober common sense and unbiased judgment, the net result of their so-called reformations is that they let loose on society an army of able-bodied beggars, with the most preposterous claims on the charity and the reverence of the laity. Moral teaching of any kind very seldom forms a part of the programmes of our prophets. They teach their followers to sing some songs which tend either to corrupt their morality, or to make them indifferent to work for the production of wealth. The most important part of the discipline imposed by our "incarnations" on their lay followers consists in requiring them to paint or brand their bodies in some particular manner, and to show every possible honour to their spiritual guides and to the begging mendicants. The monks and the nuns of every sect are only so many licensed beggars. To be distinguishable from the followers of other sects, they are required not only to brand or paint their bodies in the same manner as the laity, but to dress and toilet in some particular manner. Each sect has also a peculiar method of begging for its monks and nuns—the distinguishing feature being either in the alms bowl, or in the time and mode of applying for alms, or in the shape in which alms would be taken. The alms bowl is either an earthen or a brass pot, or a hemispherical portion of a cocoanut shell, or a basket, or a cooking pot, or a bag of cotton cloth. Some have a staff and a water pot in addition to the alms bowl, while there are others who do not encumber themselves with any of these things, but will receive in the palm of their hand the food that is offered to them. The mendicants of most of the sects take uncooked rice, or pice, or whatever else of value is offered to them excepting cooked food. But there are some sects the monks and nuns of which will accept only a spoonful of cooked rice, while there are others whose ecclesiastics will not, in order to show their indifference to wealth, take either pice or rice, but will only eat cooked food if offered by a Brahman with due honour. Some of the religious mendicants rove about for alms during daytime only; while with others night is the favourite time for such excursions. Some pass through the streets repeating the name of some god or that of the founder of their sect or only some queer phrase, and the people give them alms without any further solicitation on their part. Some carry about their person small bells by the tinkling of which the people are apprised of their presence. But generally they stop at every door on the road side, and use one or other of the following means to induce or compel the inmates of the tenements to submit to their demands :—

1. Singing songs impressing upon men the uselessness of wealth to its owner after his death.
2. Singing, in the names of the gods and goddesses, amorous songs which are necessarily very agreeable to the ears of young men and women, and for which they gladly give alms.
3. Singing songs relating to Rama's exile, Durgā's marriage with Siva, and Krishna's neglect of his foster parents—such songs being calculated to awaken the tenderest sentiments in the matrons.
4. Singing songs calculated to impress upon men the idea that great danger might arise by slighting the mendicants.
5. Parading an idol representing one of the mischief-making gods or goddesses, as, for instance, those that are believed to have the power of causing the death of their scoffers by means of cholera, small-pox or snake-bite.

6. By simply lavishing good wishes.
7. By offering holy water or consecrated food brought from some sacred place.
8. Playing on the credulity of the people by fortune-telling and palmistry.
9. By professing to be only collectors of subscriptions for the feeding of poor pilgrims.
10. By professing to be *en route* to, or from, a place of pilgrimage.
11. Terrifying the people by threatening to commit suicide in their presence.
12. Carrying snakes, carrion and ordure to disgust and horrify the people.

The last two methods are not very common. Some of the Sankarite monks are well versed in Sanskrit lore. But the mendicants of most of the other sects are generally quite illiterate. There are a few good and harmless men among them. But the majority of them are men of very low morals. They have among them ex-convicts, criminals "wanted" by the Police, and persons outcasted for making illicit loves. The teaching of morality by such men is out of the question. Their sect marks and uniforms serve to rehabilitate them to some extent, and, in their new character, they are very often able to become the heads of monasteries with harems full of so-called "nuns."

A good many of the mendicants have to pass their lives in great misery. Those who lack the required amount of shrewdness can never rise above the condition of beggars, and when age or infirmity overtakes them their condition becomes very deplorable. Some find an asylum in the monasteries of their sects. Some get a still more precarious shelter in the public rest-houses and temples. But the majority, being without friends and relatives, die in great misery. In the places of pilgrimage, and by the sides of the roads leading to them, may very often be seen the ghastly spectacle of the body of some mendicant being torn and devoured by jackals and vultures. Sometimes the feast is commenced even before death.

In spite, however, of the sad fate of a great many of the monks and nuns, the profession has had great attractions in every age. In former times, the heads of the mendicants became, in some cases, recognised as important powers in the country. They acted as the spies of the kings, and very often supplied recruits to them in times of war. Under British rule their political importance is well-nigh gone. But in their own spheres, they still flourish as before. Some attain almost princely positions by becoming the abbots of the existing monasteries. Some establish new monasteries and place themselves in charge. They all begin their career as beggars. Some of them succeed in ingratiating themselves in the favour of the superiors of their sects, and become their successors sooner or later. A few of the monks and nuns manage to attain a high position by means of fortune-telling, or by developing the curious power of swooning on the mere mention of the name of some god. When a mendicant has acquired a character for sanctity by any one of the usual processes, he has only to give out that he has found an idol by miracle, with injunctions to erect a temple to it. The necessary funds for the purpose being never supplied miraculously to the devotee, he invites subscriptions from the pious; and when the temple is built, a part of it naturally becomes his dwelling-house. With the further contributions made by the visitors to the shrine, he is enabled to live in comfort. When a shrine is in the struggling stage, the high priest generally leads a pure life, and spends a large part of his income in feeding the poor pilgrims. But the high priests of the temples that have a well-established character for sanctity are usually just the kind of men that they ought not to be. There are thus five stages in the careers of the successful monks and nuns. First, the beggar; then the charlatan; then the temple promoter; then the princely high priest; and last of all the debauchee. The theme is one to which justice could be done only by the genius of a Shakespeare.

Some of the mendicants attain the highest developments possible for their class by shorter cuts. Whenever a monk manages to become the favourite of some weak prince, nothing else is necessary to make him wealthy and to establish his character for sanctity. The people naturally worship the man who is worshipped by their king.

CHAP. XI.—CLASSIFICATION OF THE SECTS.

BEFORE enumerating the classes under which the several sects now existing may be grouped, I must warn the reader against supposing that every Hindu is necessarily a member of some particular brotherhood. As a matter of fact the majority of the high caste Hindus in Northern India do not belong to any of the modern sects, but worship all the gods of their pantheon, giving special importance either to Siva or to one of his consorts, or to Vishnu. The aristocratic Brahman usually keeps in his private chapel an ammonite Salagram representing Vishnu, and a pair of phallic emblems representing Siva and his wife. He worships these every day after bathing, and before breakfast. When he goes to any place of pilgrimage, like Benares, Brindaban or Puri, he pays his homage both to the Sivite and the Vishnuvite shrines there. He does not admit the pretensions of the latter-day prophets like Chaitanya and Vallabhāchari. But, whatever deity may be entitled to special adoration by his family, he does not hesitate to worship any of the other gods of the ancient Hindu pantheon. In fact, it is very common for Vishnuvites to celebrate the Durgā Puja, and for Sivites and Saktas to have images of Krishna in their private chapels.

Sectarian bigotry and exclusiveness are to be found chiefly among the professional leaders of the modern brotherhoods, and among their low caste disciples who are taught to believe that theirs are the only true gods, and that the rest do not deserve any reverence whatever. Some sectarians avoid even the utterance of the names of the deities worshipped by their opponents, and this kind of bigotry is carried so far by the Chaitanites of Bengal that, when they have to use an equivalent for the word 'ink,' they use the Persian word *sihai*, and would never speak of it by its Bengali name *kāli*, that word being also the name for the goddess worshipped by the Saktas. A Chaitanite would rather starve than eat any food that has been offered to Kāli or Durgā. The Vira Saivas or Lingaits of Southern India carry their bigotry to the same extent. They would on no account repeat the name of Hari, and would avoid every form of Vishnu worship as the greatest of abominations in the world.

The existing Hindu and quasi-Hindu sects may be divided into the following principal groups :—

1. Worshippers of Siva.
2. Worshippers of Siva's consorts.
3. Worshippers of Rama.
4. Worshippers of Krishna and his wives and sweethearts.
5. Worshippers of modern incarnations of Krishna.
6. Worshippers of great teachers, ancient and modern.

The Rama-worshipping religion, and some of the faiths falling under the last mentioned group, are pure man-worshipping religions. The others are man-worshipping cults also. But they are more or less combined with abomination-worship.

CHAP. XII.—THE MODE OF ASCERTAINING THE SECT TO WHICH A MONK BELONGS.

According to our social etiquette, any Hindu householder may be asked to mention his name, his father's name, his Gotra, his Vedas, and his caste. But a religious mendicant cannot be properly asked any question about his name, or his family, or his caste. A monk may, however, be asked to give such information regarding his sect as may be required of him. Generally the sect may be ascertained from the marks on his forehead and from his dress. The proper forms of the questions that might be asked with a view to elicit the necessary information are not the same for all the sects. A Chaitanite monk or nun of Bengal may be interrogated in the following manner :—

1. Who is the Lord of the family to which you belong?
2. Where is your Sripat?

To a Sankarite, the following queries may be put without any breach of decorum :—

What is your Kshettra?
What is your Deva?
What is your Devi?
What is your Tirtha?
What is your Vedas?
What is your Maha Bakya?
What is your Marhi?

PART II.

THE SIVITE AND SEMI-SIVITE SECTS.

CHAP. I.—THE NATURE OF THE SIVITE RELIGION AND ITS GREAT PREVALENCE.

THE three deities composing the Hindu Triad bear, as is well-known, the names of Brahma, Vishnu and Siva. According to the view usually taken of their functions, Brahma is the creator of the universe, Vishnu is its preserver, and Siva is its destroyer. The creating god being *functus officio*, has very few worshippers. The preserving god is daily worshipped by every Brahman, he being represented among the penates by an ammonite pebble of the kind found at the source of the river Gandak, and called Salgram. Some Brahmans and Sanyasis carry about their person a Salgram, and there are some public temples in which the presiding deity has that form. In the majority of the Vishnuvite shrines, however, the god is represented by an image of stone, wood or metal, having the cowherd boy's form that he assumed when he incarnated as Krishna. The god Siva is described in the Purâns as a mendicant dressed in tiger skin, with matted locks, and snakes serving the purpose of ribbons and apron strings. He is represented also with watery half-shut eyes, and with the garb and demeanour of a person under the influence of wine and *bhang*. Images of Siva having these characteristics are sometimes met with. But they seldom receive any worship, and the Sivites usually offer their adoration to only the images of the Linga. These are cylindrical pieces of stone, mounted in most cases on a perforated circular piece representing the Yoni.

The Sivite cult is the most common and ancient form of abomination-worship.* It has been established by the researches of antiquarians that the worship of Siva, in the form of Linga, prevailed in India long before the commencement of the era of Christ. In all probability the worship of the phallic emblems of the grim god was one of the common institutions of the Aryan nations in their original home. The Greek god Bacchus and the Egyptian god Osiris were worshipped in the very same form. From the account which Megasthenes has given of the Hindu pantheon, it is evident that in speaking of the worship of Bacchus in India, he meant only Siva's Linga.† This much at least is certain that Siva-worship was in a very flourishing condition at the time of the invasions of Mahmud of Ghazni.‡

---

* The nomenclature that I have used here is somewhat offensive. But in the English language there does not seem to be any other term that might express what I mean, without wounding the feelings of any class.

† See *Ancient India as described by Megasthenes and Arrian*, p. 111. By J. W. McCrindle, M.A.

‡ The Sivite shrine of Somnath destroyed by Mahmud was, and in its restored condition is, reckoned as one of the twelve chief Sivite shrines in India. The following are the other eleven :—

2. Mallikarjuna of Sri Saila, in the District of Kurnool, in the Madras Presidency.
3. Mahakala in Ujiayin.
4. Omkara Nath on the banks of the Narmada.
5. Amareshwara near Ujiayin.
6. Vaidyanath on the Chord Line, E. I. Railway.
7. Rameshwara, an island between Ceylon and the Southern end of the Indian Peninsula.
8. Bhima Sankara at Dakini or Dracharam near Raj Mahindri.
9. Tryambaka on the Gomati.
10. Goutamesha.
11. Kedarnatha on the Himalayan slopes, in the District of Gharwal.
12. Bishweshwar in Benares.

The worship of Siva is still the most prevailing element in the religion of all classes of Hindus, excepting the Banias. Every high caste Brahman has an image of the Linga among his penates, and there is hardly a single Hindu village in the country that has not a Sivite shrine. In connection with these village idols of Siva, it may be mentioned here that, for some days in the year, they are touched and worshipped by such members of the low castes as dedicate themselves, for the time being, to their service. The season for their saturnalia is the second week of April. During that period the low caste men, who take the vow, are required to observe the discipline of the Sanyasis or ascetics; and to subject themselves to a variety of self-inflicted tortures. The hook-swinging, which was the most cruel feature of the programme, has been happily stopped by the British Government. But walking upon heaps of live charcoal and rolling upon "cushions" of thorns are still allowed to be practised. The Sivite low castes who enlist themselves as Sanyasis in the last week of the Bengali year subject themselves to various other tortures, as, for instance, piercing the tongue and the sides with heavy javelins. The higher castes are accustomed from infancy to enjoy such spectacles as a fun.

CHAP. II.—THE PROBABLE ORIGIN OF THE SIVITE RELIGION.

THE Sivite religion being the one most prevalent among the Hindus in every part of India, the time and manner in which it first came into existence are questions of very considerable interest to the theological student. Siva worship is beyond doubt an ancient cult, and, considering some of the* characters in which the deity is represented, it does not seem impossible that the recognition of his godhead is a survival of some ancient form of demon-worship directly degenerating into abomination-worship. Destruction is still held to be the principal function of the god, and, although in some places he is described as having been an ascetic and a contemplative philosopher, the very opposite character is given to him quite as often in the Hindu mythologies. "He is a wild and jovial mountaineer (Kirata), addicted to hunting and wine drinking, fond of dancing (Nritya Priya, also called Natesvara, 'lord of dancers'), often dancing with his wife the Tandava dance, and surrounded by dwarfish, buffoon-like troops (Gana) of attendants, who, like their master, are fond of good living and occasionally inebriated by intoxicating liquors." Such conceptions of the deity, and his robe of tiger skin, as also the snakes used by him as apron strings and ribbons, are clearly of the demon-

* See *Brahmanism and Hinduism*, by Sir Monier Williams, pp. 82—85. See also the Batuku Bhairava hymn in the *Tantra Sara*, p. 209, Battola Edition.

worshipping stage. But the Purānic stories have, it seems, a very different and a very recent origin. These represent him as the greatest of *yogis* or contemplative saints, and also as a mendicant who, in respect of dress and demeanour, resembled very much the begging Sanyasis that are to be found in all the large towns and places of pilgrimage in India. In the Purāns it is stated also that Siva's first wife, Sati, was the daughter of the patriarch Daksha ; that as Siva and his wife were not invited by Daksha to a feast celebrated in his house, they felt themselves so insulted that Sati actually committed suicide, and that Siva caused the festivities to be completely spoilt through the instrumentality of the ghosts and demons that are his devoted attendants ; that after the death of Sati, Siva became so rapt in contemplation that he became quite unmindful of every thing else ; that the other gods were in great distress at the time, having been turned out from heaven by a great monster ; that they applied to Brahma for the necessary remedy ; that Brahma told them that their enemy could be vanquished only by a son of Siva ; that the god of love (Kama) was accordingly deputed to awaken Siva from his trance, and to give rise in his mind to a desire for taking a second wife and procreating a child ; that the great god was so offended by the disturbance that he at once caused the death of Kama ; that nevertheless he was successfully courted by his future consort Parvati, the daughter of the Himalayan King ; that when he agreed to meet the wishes of his would-be bride her father gave her in marriage to him with great *éclat ;* that the issue of that marriage, Kartika, fought the battles of the gods and restored them to their proper power and positions ; and, finally, that Kartika never married, but set his whole heart on fine dresses, sweetmeats, and boyish games.

To those who are wanting in faith, all this must at first sight appear as quite puerile. But it seems to me that, even without the enchanting colour that faith can lend, the stories summarised above have a deep meaning. They can certainly be made very intelligible by the theory that they are the inventions of a mendicant. The story of Sati is clearly meant to secure for the Sanyasis the sympathy of the matrons. The story of Daksha and the agencies that marred his festive preparations, are meant to bully the kings and the aristocracy, and to secure for the mendicants a proper invitation to their feasts. The story of Kama, trying to excite a desire for marriage in Siva, is evidently intended to make the people believe that ordinarily the Sanyasis are quite above the vulgar appetites of ordinary men. The story of the courting of Siva by Parvati gives an audible expression to a wish which perhaps lurks in the minds of all classes of men, from the greatest of kings to the poorest of beggars. Considering the amount of worry and trouble which most men have to go through in order to secure the favour of their future partners, it is impossible for any one of the sterner sex not to wish that the order of things were reversed. To the beggars who cannot possibly hope to secure their object by any kind of attention or humiliation, the mere dream of such joy cannot but be a source of ecstasy. The story of the Himalayan King, feeling himself honoured by being allowed to give his daughter to Siva, is clearly meant to imply that other kings should follow his example by making the mendicants their sons-in-law. The legend about Kartik fighting the battles of the gods, and never taking a wife, suggests that if the kings would give their daughters in marriage to the mendicants, they might expect to have, by the issue of such marriage, very able generals for their armies who would never be a source of danger to them or to their successors in the male lines. If the meaning of the Sivite legends be not as stated above, they must, it seems, be said to be incapable of any rational explanation.

The form in which Siva is usually worshipped, combined with the *mahabakya* of the Sivite mendicants, points also to the conclusion that their cult is the invention of some clever beggar of their brotherhood. The Sivite is required by his religion to assert every now and then that he is Siva. His *mahabakya*, "I am Siva," when taken in connection with Linga worship, renders the object of repeating the formula intelligible enough. But looked at separately, and from the point of view of those who regard the religion as a pure and noble one, neither the phallic worship nor the *mahabakya* can have any rational meaning.

CHAP. III.—THE SIVITE FOLLOWERS OF SANKARACHARYA.

FROM the literature of the Sankarite sects, it appears that even before the time of the great champion of Brahmanism, there were several Sivite sects embracing within their folds a very large portion of the Hindu population of the country. Sankara did not found any Sivite sects properly so-called. His primary object was to root out Buddhism* from the country, and, in order to attain that end, he countenanced every form of Hinduism, including the worship of Siva, Sakti, Vishnu, Sun and Ganesh. He himself had great faith in the Vedantic doctrine of one God, manifesting himself by the creation of the universe, without the help of *prakriti* or material basis. But he did not discard the gods and goddesses of the Hindu pantheon, and it seems very probable that either he himself or his disciples gave great encouragement to Siva worship in order to render Buddha worship obsolete. Nowhere is Sankara represented as a destroyer of Buddhistic temples and images. In all probability he and his disciples took those shrines under their protection, and found it much safer to represent the idols worshipped therein as images of the Hindu god Siva, than to throw them away into the streets, or to destroy them. Even now there are many shrines bearing the designation of Dharma Raj, where the Hindus daily offer worship, in

* See *Brihat Dharma Purān.*

the belief that their presiding deity is Siva, and without entertaining the least suspicion that the idols receiving their homage as such were in fact Buddhistic images.

The fact that Sankara directly encouraged the worship of the gods and goddesses of the Hindu pantheon is proved by other evidences also. In the monastery of Sringeri,* which is the chief of the four *maths* set up by him, the presiding deity is Sarswati, the goddess of learning. In the Joshi *math* on the Himalayan slopes the principal shrine is the Vishnuvite temple of Badari Nath. But the most conclusive evidence, as to Sankara having countenanced the worship of the personal gods of the Hindu pantheon, is afforded by the *Sankara Digvijaya*, or the History of Sankara's controversial victories, by his disciple Ananda Giri. In that work, the authority of which is reckoned by the sect as unquestionable, it is distinctly stated that by Sankara's order his apostles Lakmanacharya and Hasta Malaka converted the east and the west to Vaishnavism, and that another of his disciples named Paramata Kalanala visited various places in India, and everywhere initiated the people in the Sivite faith.

Whatever Sankara's own faith may have been, his followers are practically Sivites. The Smarta Brahmans of the Deccan, who acknowledge him as their principal teacher, are all professed Sivites. The grim god is regarded by them all as the chief object of worship, and they paint on their foreheads the Sivite Tripundra, consisting of three horizontal lines of Bibhuti or sacred ashes. The mendicants of the several orders founded by Sankara theoretically claim to be the worshippers of an invisible god. But the Sivite Tripundras

* Sringeri is at the source of the Tunga Bhadra within the territories of the Mysore Raj. The head of the Sringeri *math* has great power throughout the Deccan. He can by his fiat excommunicate any non-Vishnuvite Hindu of the Deccan. The Sankarite monastery at Puri is called Goverdhan *math*, and that at Dwarika is called Sharada *math*. The superiors of these or of the Joshi *math* have not much influence.

which they paint on their foreheads, and the Sivite hymns which they recite, point to the conclusion that they are in reality worshippers of Siva. Sankara did not admit any nuns into his monasteries. The monks of the orders founded by him are called Dasnamis from their using one or other of the following surnames:—

1.	Sarswati	The name of the goddess of learning.
2.	Bharati	Another name of the goddess of learning.
3.	Puri	Lit. Town.
4.	Tirtha	Lit. Place of pilgrimage.
5.	Asram	Lit. Refuge.
6.	Bana	Lit. Forest.
7.	Giri	Lit. Hill.
8.	Aranya	Lit. Forest.
9.	Parvata	Lit. Mountain.
10.	Sagara	Lit. Sea.

These surnames are derived from the names or academic titles of the ten disciples of Sankara's immediate pupils. The first three, namely, Sarswati, Bharati and Puri are supposed to be attached to the Sringeri monastery. The Tirthas and the Asrams look up to the Sharoda *Math* of Dwarika as their chief monastery; the Bans and Aranyas profess to be connected with the Goverdhan *Math* of Puri ; and the Joshi *Math* on the Himalaya is the chief centre of monks bearing the surnames Giri, Parvata and Sagara. Monks bearing the titles of Aranya, Sagara and Parvata are not usually to be found now-a-days.

These different surnames do not imply any difference of religion or religious practice. The classification of the Sankarite monks which is based on a difference of observances, is as follows:—

1. Dandi.
2. Sanyasi.
3. Parama Hansa.
4. Brahmachari.
5. Grihastha Gossains.

The actual differences between the first four of the above orders are very trivial. They are only slightly modified forms of the Asramas, or modes of passing life, which the ancient Hindu legislators recommended, but under conditions that checked every possible tendency towards vagrancy. In our holy codes it is laid down that every member of the three superior castes should pass through the following conditions :—

1. As a Brahmachari or Vedic student living on alms.	Generally speaking from the 8th to the 26th year.
2. As a Grihastha or householder with wife.	During the entire period of youthful vigour.
3. As a Banaprastha or forest recluse with or without wife, living on the spontaneous products of the earth collected by his own industry.	During what is called the third part of life.
4. As a Sanyasi or begging mendicant.	During the closing years of life.

From the ordinances on the subject contained in our ancient codes, it might seem at first sight that our Rishis encouraged vagrancy *pro tanto.* But reading their texts between the lines, it would appear that what they really intended was to encourage men to marry and live as peaceful householders, instead of observing celibacy and running the risk of drifting into a disreputable course of life. Asceticism has naturally a great attraction for such adventurous men as have a craving for being venerated by the mob for their holy character. But it is impossible to fight against nature, and these men generally fail most miserably in maintaining their original vows. It was not, however, consistent with the policy of our holy law-givers to declare that there was no merit whatever in the life of an ascetic. They knew too well how to maintain the dignity of the holy orders, to expose even the impostors to infamy. So instead of discrediting asceticism, they actually recommended it, though at a period of life when it can have no attraction even to the most adventurous spirits. Manu says :—

1. When the father of a family perceives his muscles become flaccid and his hair grey, and sees the child of his child, let him then seek refuge in a forest.
2. Abandoning all food eaten in towns and all his household utensils let him repair to the lonely wood.
16. Let him not eat the produce of ploughed land though abandoned by any man, nor fruits and roots produced in a town, even though hunger oppresses him.
29. For the purpose of uniting his soul with the divine spirit, let him study the various Upanishads.

33. Having thus performed religious acts in a forest during the third portion of life, let him become a *Sanyasi* for the fourth portion of it, abandoning all sensual affections.

37. If a Brahman have not read the Veda, if he have not begotten a son, and if he have not performed sacrifices, yet shall aim at final beatitude, he shall sink to a place of degradation.—*Manu* VI, vs. 2, 3, 16, 29, 33.

These ordinances clearly show that the real object of the law-giver was not to encourage the practice of asceticism, but to check it to the utmost extent possible. The sage distinctly gives preference to the life of a householder. He says :—

77. As all creatures subsist by receiving support from air, thus all orders of men exist by receiving support from house-keepers.

78. And since men of the three other orders are each day nourished by them, a house-keeper is for this reason of the most eminent order—*Manu* III, 77, 78.

The Grihastha Gossains represent, it seems, the second stage of life spoken of and recommended in the ancient Hindu codes. They marry and live as householders. They act as Gurus to the lay members of their sect, administering the sacrament of the mantra to their disciples. They never serve as purohits or priests. In fact, in the religious ceremonies celebrated in their own houses, the functions of the purohit are performed by Brahmans who are not of their order. Unlike the mendicants, the Grihasthas wear the sacred thread, and dress like householders. Generally speaking, their pujas and prayers are the same as those of other Sivite Brahmans, and their only peculiarity lies in the fact that they do not perform the Sandhya prayer. They keep among their penates a Sivite Linga and a Salgram, and worship these emblems of Siva and Vishnu in the same manner as most of the high caste Brahmans do. They do not worship Krishna, Radhika or Kāli in their own houses, but show due honour to the idols representing them in the public shrines. The only female divinity that receives their special adoration is Sarswati, the goddess of learning. They wear garlands of Rudraksha, and like the mendicants, utter every now and then the formula, Sivoham, signifying "I am Siva." They are, or ought to be, like the mendicants, strict vegetarians and teetotalers. They marry within their own order, but cannot take a wife from a family bearing the same surname. They do not throw their dead into a river, as the mendicants do, but burn or bury their deceased relatives as they think fit. If buried, the corpse is placed in the sitting posture of religious contemplation. A Grihastha may, before marriage, become a mendicant, but not afterwards. The Grihasthas show great reverence to the mendicants. A Grihastha Gossain may eat twice in twenty-four hours. Among the Sankarite monks, there are a few who devote themselves more or less to the cultivation of learning; but the rest have no justification whatever for the kind of life that they lead.

CHAP. IV.—THE DANDIS.

THE Sankarite ascetics called Dandis are so designated on account of their bearing a *Danda* or wand, like the ancient Vedic students. None but a fatherless, motherless, wifeless and childless Brahman can be initiated as a Dandi. The process of initiation to the sect is an elaborate one, of which the burning of the neophyte's sacred thread, and the eating of the ashes thereof by him, are the most important parts. By these and certain other ceremonies indicative of a new birth, he is supposed to pass into the condition of a god, and he himself constantly expresses his belief in such transformation by repeating the Soham formula. After his baptism, he takes a new name with one of the following surnames :—

1. Tirtha.
2. Asrama.
3. Bharati.
4. Sarswati.

The usual dress of a Dandi consists of five pieces of cotton cloth dyed red with ochre. Of these one small piece serves as a cover for the loins, and another of the same size as a girdle to keep the other in position. The other three pieces are of larger size, being each about two yards in length, and a yard in breadth. One of these is tied round the waist, and serves to cover the thighs and the legs ; another is tied round the breast and hangs down like a barrister's gown ; the third piece is wrapped round the head to serve the purpose of a turban.

The Dandis are not required by their religion to worship any god. But, in actual practice, they carry about them either an image of Vishnu in the form of a Salgram, or a phallic emblem of Siva. The Dandis are found in large numbers in Benares, where they are fed with great honour by the pilgrims. But it is said that a great many of the so-called Dandis of Benares are pure shams, being in fact the poorest of beggars whom the local lodging house-keepers and guides palm off as Dandis to partake of the hospitality and the largesses of the pilgrims. What is eaten by them becomes theirs irrevocably as a matter of course ; but the new clothes, water-pots, and other things which are given to them by their hosts fall to the share of the party acting as broker in securing them invitations.

The Dandis affect that they do not accept pecuniary gratuities. But they have usually with them such companions as would readily accept, on their behalf, any coins that might be offered to them by any one. With a view to strengthen their claim to the hospitality of the laity, the Dandis pretend also that they do not touch fire on any account, not even for cooking their food. But when they fail to procure dressed food by begging, their spiritual companions dress their food for them. Like most of the several classes of mendicants, the Dandis are allowed to have only one meal in twenty-four hours.

CHAP. V.—THE SANYASIS.

A BRAHMAN alone can become a Dandi properly so-called. But the order called Sanyasi is open not only to the three superior castes, but to some extent to even Sudras. Some persons take up the garb of the Sanyasi without being initiated to the order. A person who has a wife or an infant son or aged parents cannot be admitted to be a mendicant of any class. When a man duly qualified desires to be a Sanyasi, the proper course for him is to apply to a Guru or superior of the sect, and to go through a ceremony in the course of which he has to put off his sacred thread, if he have any, and to shave off the tuft of hair which every orthodox Hindu keeps at the central part of his head. The Guru whispers into the ears of the neophyte the words *Namah Sivaya* or *Om Namah Sivaya*, and a Sanskrit couplet, the purport of which is as follows :—

O thou wise man! Please contemplate yourself and myself as identical with the Divine essence, and roam about without pride or affection according to your inclination.

The formula which the neophyte has to recite, at the time of saluting the Guru, is still more curious. Its purport is as follows :—

Salutation to you and salutation to me. Salutation again to both you and my ownself. Thou art thou, and I am identical with the great soul pervading the Universe. Therefore I salute thee.

At the conclusion of these ceremonies, the neophyte receives a new name with one of the following surnames :—

1. Giri.
2. Puri.
3. Bharati.
4. Ban.
5. Aranya.
6. Parvata.
7. Ságara.

The neophyte is then enjoined to go through a course of probation during which he has to visit some places of pilgrimage, according to the directions of his spiritual superior, and to conform also to the routine prescribed by him for his daily prayers.

When the period of apprenticeship is completed, then the following ceremonies have to be gone through :—

1. Ceremonies for pleasing the gods, the saints, and the ancestors of the neophyte.
2. His Sradha or rites performable after his death.
3. The taking up of the sacred thread for the purpose of again abandoning it.

The Sivite Sanyasis smear their bodies with ashes, and have generally a tiger skin wrapped round their waist or carried underneath their armpit when travelling, but used as a cushion or bed whenever seated. They do not, like the Dandis, shave their heads or their beards, but allow their hirsute appendages to grow without limit, the hair of their heads being generally matted and formed into coils by the accumulation of dirt. Some of the Sivite Sanyasis paint an eye on their forehead in order to be like the god Siva as much as possible. They carry either a conch shell or a pair of pincers in their hands. They are usually found in towns, by the sides of the busy thoroughfares, or within the enclosures of the principal Sivite shrines. Wherever seated they usually kindle a fire before them, and pass their time in the continual smoking of *ganja*. They carry about their person various articles indicative of their having visited the great Hindu shrines in the different parts of India. One of these is an arm ring of iron, brass or copper having the images of various Hindu gods carved on its sides, and indicating that the wearer has visited one or other of the great shrines of Pasupatinath, Kedarnath and Badarinath on the Himalayan slopes. A smaller ring obtainable at the same places would be worn by the Sivite Sanyasi as a part of his Rudraksha garland. Those who have visited the shrine of Kāli at Hingalaj in Beluchistan wear necklaces of little stone beads called Thumra, and adorn their hair by a metallic substance called Swarna Makshi (lit. golden fly). Similar beads are obtainable also at the hot springs of Manikarnika on the Himalayan slopes, and are worn by Sanyasis who have visited that shrine. A pilgrimage to Rameshwara in the extreme south is indicated by a ring of conch shell worn on the wrist. There are various other odds and ends of the same kind which are used similarly by the class of mendicants that are being spoken of here.

As the Sivite Sanyasis have no objection to touch fire, they generally cook their own food. They would, without any hesitation eat cooked food offered to them by a Brahmana. In fact, some of them profess that they are prepared to eat any kind of food offered to them by anyone. Whatever the theoretical injunctions may be, the Sivite Sanyasis accept both coins and uncooked eatables. Generally speaking, they are quite illiterate. Some of them have a little knowledge of therapeutics, and there are among them a few who have perhaps the best medicines for some of the most obstinate diseases that man is heir to. Unfortunately they never divulge the secrets of their healing art for the benefit of the public.

The Dandis and Param Hansas are mostly Sankarites. But among the Sanyasis there are many Vishnuvites and Tāntrics. Those who become Sanyasis in an irregular manner are called Abadhuta Sanyasis.

CHAP. VI.—THE PARAMA HANSA.

AFTER a period of probation which properly ought to extend to twelve years, the Dandi and the Sanyasi become qualified to be a Parama Hansa. The word Hansa ordinarily means a "goose." But it is also one of the names of Vishnu, and the expression "Parama Hansa" evidently means the "Supreme Vishnu." Properly speaking, the Parama Hansa is neither a Sivite nor a Vishnuvite. He is in fact a self-worshipper. The Sivite prayers, which form a part of the Dandi's ritual, are omitted by the Parama Hansa. The latter has only to repeat constantly the mystic syllable *Om*. Like the Dandis, the Parama Hansas are required also to assert, every now and then, their identity with the Divine Spirit.

The Parama Hansas are of two kinds. Those who enter the order after having been Dandis are called Dandi Parama Hansas, while those who are promoted from the ranks of the Abadhuta Sanyasis are called Abadhuta Parama Hansas. A few of the Parama Hansas go about naked. But the majority of them are to be found gracefully clad in the same manner as the Dandis. With reference to the class of ascetics under notice, Professor Wilson in his *Hindu Sects* makes the following observations :—

According to the introduction of the *Dwadasa Mahabakya* by a *Dandi* author, Vaikantha Puri, the Sanyasi is of four kinds, the *Kutichaka*, *Bahudaka*, *Hansa* and *Parama Hansa ;* the difference between whom, however, is only the graduated intensity of their self-mortification and profound abstraction. The *Parama Hansa* is the most eminent of these gradations and is the ascetic who is solely occupied with the investigation of Brahma, or spirit, and who is equally indifferent to pleasure or pain, insensible of heat or cold, and incapable of satiety or want.

Agreeably to this definition, individuals are sometimes met with who pretend to have attained such a degree of perfection: in proof of it they go naked in all weathers, never speak, and never indicate any natural want: what is brought to them as alms or food, by any person, is received by his attendants, whom their supposed sanctity or confederation of interest attaches to them, and by these attendants they are fed and served on all occasions, as if they were as helpless as infants. It may be supposed that there is much knavery in their helplessness, but there are many Hindus whose simple enthusiasm induces them honestly to practise such self-denial, and there is little risk in the attempt, as the credulity of their countrymen, or rather countrywomen, will, in most places, take care that their wants are amply supplied.

Some of the Sanyasis and Parama Hansas pretend that they do not eat any kind of food. One of this class visited the late Babu Ram Ratan Roy of Narail, about the year 1854, with a large number of companions. Babu Roy kept him under close surveillance for more than a month, and was ultimately so satisfied as to his miraculous powers that he gave his followers a bonus of one thousand rupees. Some years later when the Babu was proceeding to Benares, and his boats were anchored off some place near Monghyr, one of his attendants who went on shore found the *quondam* Parama Hansa, and some members of his party, engaged in ploughing some adjacent fields. When questioned, one of them not only admitted his identity, but made a clean breast of the whole secret. He confessed that the man had sustained himself on food vomited by his companions.*

Like the Dandis, the Parama Hansas are found in large numbers in and near Benares. They live in convents, and some of them are very learned men. The head of a Parama Hansa convent is called Swamiji. By courtesy, even the juniors are sometimes called

* I believe there are still some men living who can vouch to the authenticity of the story narrated above. I heard it from several officers connected with the service of the Narail Babus, and also from one of the old Vakils of Jessore who was the chief legal adviser of Babu Ram Ratan.

Swamiji. Dandis, Sanyasis and Parama Hansas accost each other by the formula *Namo Narayana.* Householders address them in the same manner. But they respond by only uttering the name of Narayana. For inviting them to dinner the proper formula is the question: "Will Narayan accept alms here?" The Parama Hansas do not burn their dead, but will dispose of a corpse by either burying it, or throwing it in a river.

CHAP. VII.—THE BRAHMACHARIS.

CLOSELY allied to the several orders noticed in the last three chapters is that of the Sivite Brahmacharis. Properly speaking, a Brahmachari is a Vedic student who, after his initiation with the sacred thread, has to observe certain rules as to diet and dress, and to live by begging, until he has mastered the Vedas. In actual practice Brahmanical policy has very nearly suppressed the study of the Vedas, and neither the few Vedic students to be found at present, nor the Brahman boys who devote their scholastic years to the study of the far more difficult sciences of grammar, philosophy, logic and theology, are now required to observe the rules as to diet and dress prescribed for the Brahmachari or the reader of our holy scriptures. The long observance of Brahmacharya discipline is actually prohibited by the later codes of the Hindus as unsuited to the present age, and at the present time the form is gone through, after the thread ceremony, for a period varying from only three to eleven days. In Calcutta, some of the Brahmana boys are initiated with the thread in the local shrine of Kāli, and those who go through the ceremony in that way are made to throw away their staff and Brahmachari's garb on the very day of their initiation. Such being the case, Brahmacharis, properly so-called, are very rare in these days. But the fertile genius of Sankara created four new orders of Brahmacharis, one to be attached to each of his four principal monasteries. These Brahmacharis are theoretically personal assistants and companions to the Dandis and the Parama Hansas. As the latter are not allowed to touch fire or coin, the Brahmacharis serve as their cooks and as receivers of alms for them. In actual practice, the line of demarcation between the two classes is not very broad, and many of the Brahmacharis live by begging independently. The usual surnames of the Sivite Brahmacharis are Anand, Chaitanya, Prakash and Swarupa. They dress like the Dandis and Parama Hansas in red robes.

The Tāntric Brahmacharis are a different order altogether, and will be spoken of in their proper place.

CHAP. VIII.—THE HOUSEHOLDER SANYASIS.

THE word Sanyasi denotes a person who has cut off his connection with the world and his family, and the expression "Householder Sanyasi" is a contradiction in terms. But in Benares and in other places also there are persons called Dandis and Sanyasis who marry, or live with female associates, like other men of the world. The fact is that in the days of youthful enthusiasm some men are led to take the vow of mendicancy which they soon find themselves quite unable to maintain. When such a person attains a character for sanctity, or otherwise becomes able to afford the cost, he tries to get a female, for constant association, either as a professed wife, or as a pious sister. The progeny of such unions multiply fast, and the ultimate tendency of each monkish order is to become a separate caste and endogamous group; such castes have generally a very low position. The householder Sanyasis are not to be confounded with the Grihastha Gossains spoken of on page 378. The latter are a very respectable class.

CHAP. IX.—THE AGHORIS.

THE Aghoris are a very small community. They are said to worship a deity called Aghori Mata. But, properly speaking, they have no religion, unless the name be taken to include even that misguided fanaticism which degrades them to a lower level than that of the filthiest of beasts. They profess to carry the pantheistic philosophy of the Vedanta to its logical consequence, and to look upon even fæcal matter in the same light as the fragrant paste prepared by the trituration of sandal-wood.

The Aghoris used in former times to offer human sacrifices and to eat human flesh. The number of Aghoris in the country was perhaps never very large. At any rate, at the present time, an Aghori is very seldom met with. The race, however, is not yet quite extinct. "The head-quarters of the Aghori Panthis appear to have been always at Mount Abu and Girnar. They have such an evil reputation at Girnar that the authorities do not like Europeans to go there without an escort. The country people have a great horror of the Aghori Panthis or the Aghoris who are believed to kidnap and murder children and weak and defenceless persons. At Benares these objectionable people live at both the burning ghâts, and are supposed to number between one hundred and two hundred. The greater number of them are rapacious, shameless mendicants who, by the terror of their attributes, horrible appearance and threats of eating human flesh and filth, if their demands are not complied with, still continue to prey on the credulity of the ignorant or timid. They are believed to hold converse with all the evil spirits frequenting the burning ghâts; and a funeral party must be poorly off or very strong-minded which refuses them something."*

"The various meanings of the term Aghori are held to be, one who is solitary, separate, distinct from other men. All castes can become Aghori Panthis. Notwithstanding the astounding wickedness of their teachings, they claim for them that they are the doctrines of equality and humanity. Indifference to all that is should be the all-in-all of existence. No one really has a father or mother; 'it is all mere accident.' If a well comes in one's way, he should walk into it. Celibacy is strictly enjoined, but the Census returns of 1881 for the Central Provinces and the N.-W. Provinces show that in this respect discipline must be very lax."*

The Aghoris are a very ancient sect. There is a clear reference to it in the Sanskrit drama called *Malati Madhava*, the hero of which rescues his mistress from being offered as a sacrifice by one named Aghori Ghanta. The French writer M. d'Anville alludes to the Aghori as "*une espece de monstre*." The author of that extraordinary Persian work, the *Dabistan, or School of Manners*, writing probably about the middle of the 16th century, gives a brief but clear description of the Aghoris who practised acts of "atilia" or "Aghori," says that the sect originated with Gorakshanath, and that he saw one of them "singing the customary song" and seated upon a corpse, which he ate when it became putrid. M. Thevenot, whose travels were republished in London in 1687, alludes apparently to a community of these cannibals, established at a place called Debea, in the Broach district, and Kazi Sahabadin, C.I.E., formerly Dewan of Baroda, ascertained that there is a tradition still extant among the people that a colony of cannibals did exist in the village of Walwad, on the

* *Statesman*, March 7, 1893.

Mahi river, a century or two ago. In the early part of this century there were several Aghori Panthis in Baroda, and the remains of a temple dedicated to the Aghoreshwari Mata, their tutelary goddess. At the present day there is an Aghori Sthan between Ahmedabad and Kadu. In his *Travels in Western India* Colonel Todd came across some Aghoris, "the jackal" of their species, and his account of the superstitious dread with which the Kalika shrine on Girnar and the Aghori Panthis were regarded, exactly coincides with the statements made to the late Mr. Leith by Gossains of the present day.

The initiation ceremony of the Aghori Panthis is said to be very terrible and only practised in lonely spots; but the professors of the sect in Benares, Allahabad and other places, now-a-days seem to have to content themselves with making the neophyte go through a ceremonial that is made as filthy and loathsome as possible. In Benares many old men state that they have seen Aghori Panthis eating dead men's flesh, and affirm that the custom yet prevails, especially among drunken men, who will seize upon corpses floating in the water and bite off the flesh. One Aghori Panthi boldly admitted to Mr. Leith in that city that this is a fact, and offered to swallow man's flesh himself. On the 29th December 1884, one Krishna Das Babaji was fined Rs. 15 by Mr. Ishan Chandra Sen, Deputy Magistrate of Berhampore, Moorshedabad district, for committing a public nuisance, namely, devouring part of a woman's corpse before a number of people at Khagra cremation ghât. Some Aghori Panthis say that their religion prompts them to the act, and, moreover, that if at initiation they refused to eat dead men's flesh, they would be dismissed by the Guru as unfit for their calling. One excuse sometimes offered by an Aghori Panthi is that by the taste of such flesh, he can acquire the knowledge of *jadu* or magic. The fact is that as Brahmanism inculcated cleanliness and the eating of wholesome food, the Aghoris, who formed one of the sects setting up "opposition shops" as it were, insisted on the utmost degree of filth, and hoped to get alms by horrifying the people, and not by gaining their respect.

Some of the Aghoris have associated with them female Aghorinis, and these people are extremely shameless. The doctrine enunciated by Burke in one of his famous speeches that the quality of modesty was the attribute which, more than reason, distinguished men from beasts, is certainly not applicable to some of the Indian sects. They are the pest of society, and it is much to be regretted that of late they have been receiving very considerable encouragement from some educated men of the country. The pure morals and the noble discipline, imposed on the society by the Brahmanic Shastras, are things of which the Hindus may be justly proud. But the beastly Aghori, the Bacchanalian Tāntric and the dissolute Vaishnava are a disgrace to the Hindu name. With all his cleanliness, vegetarianism and teetotalism, the Vaishnava is perhaps the most dangerous in the whole list. He has done great good service in civilizing the lower classes to some extent, and in suppressing the horrors of the Tāntric worship. But the moral laxity which the Vaishnava encourages by the stories of the illicit loves between his gods and goddesses, and by the strong tendency to imitate them which his teachings generate, outweighs the good done by him. Every man of common sense naturally feels a horror at the Tāntric and the Aghori. But the Vaishnava insinuates himself in a manner which is irresistible.

CHAP. X—THE LINGAITS OF SOUTHERN INDIA.

A VERY large part of the population of Southern India are Lingaits or Vira Saivas. These alone are perhaps entitled to be regarded as a strictly Sivite sect. The Sankarite sects spoken of in the preceding chapters are more or less Sivites also. But they pay due homage to the other ancient gods of the Hindu pantheon, and they cannot be said to be exclusively Siva worshippers.

The common accounts relating to the origin of the Lingait sect trace it to a renegade Brahman who had been excommunicated by his caste men for some offence, and who thereupon revenged himself by starting the new cult. In all probability Linga worship had been the prevailing form of idolatry in the Deccan long before Sankara's time. The champion of Brahmanism countenanced it in a manner, without actually encouraging it. But his followers became practically Sivites, and this led to a very successful movement for the spread of the Vishnuvite cult by Ramanuja, who lived in the eleventh century of the Christian era. This innovation paved the way towards a reaction in favour of the Sivite religion. Basava, the renegade Brahman, who was the leader of this counter-movement, was born in the village of Bhagwan, in the Belgaum district of the Southern Maratta country, and lived in the twelfth century of the Christian era. The historical facts or myths about this remarkable man are recorded in a Sanakrit work called the *Basava Purān*, and in several Kanarese works. At a very early period of his life he repaired to Kalyan, the metropolis of the Chalukya Empire, and there married the daughter of the *Dandanayaka* or the chief magistrate of police. He succeeded to the post himself after the death of his father-in-law, and made use of his official position to attract round him a crowd of followers. His chief disciple Machaya had been condemned by the king to suffer death for having killed a child. But Basava refused to carry out the order on the plea that it would be unavailing to offer any harm to a worshipper of Siva. The king thereupon ordered some of his other officers to execute the sentence, and the legend as usual goes on to state that Machaya saved himself miraculously. Two other Sivite citizens were condemned by the king to have their eyes plucked out. This led to the departure of Basava from Kalyan, and the fixing of his residence at Sangameshwar, on the Shastri river, in the modern district of Ratnagiri. Basava's exile, whether it was voluntary or enforced, was followed by an insurrection in the course of which the king was killed, and the city of Kalyan was finally destroyed.

The founder of the Lingait sect directed his attacks against both the Hindus and the Jains. The *Basava Purān* contains several dialogues between Jangamas and Jainas in which every effort is made to convince the latter of the superiority of the Saiva religion. Basava did not believe in any god besides Siva; he denied the superiority of the Brahmans, and tried his best to abolish the distinction of caste. He had no faith whatever in penance, or in the feeding of Brahmans for the benefit of the souls of deceased persons. Pilgrimages and fasts were declared by him to be quite useless, and he rejected altogether the doctrine of the transmigration of souls. But with all these "atheistic views," as they would be called by a Brahman, he insisted on one of the least attractive forms of Hindu idolatry, and in his zeal for the phallic emblem went so far as to enjoin that his followers should always carry about their person some lingas by fastening them on the neck and the arms with what is called the Linga Sutram, as opposed to Yajna Sutram or sacred thread of the Brahman. The object of the founder was no doubt to create a new badge to place his low caste followers on a footing of equality or rivalry to the Brahmans. The Vishnuvite sect founders have also given similarly new badges to their followers. But neither the Linga Sutram of the Lingaits, nor the necklace of basil beads worn by the Vaishnavas, nor the Sheli of the Kanfat Yogis have been able to command the veneration that the Yajna Sutram of the Brahmans enjoys.

The Lingaits, like most other sects, have an order of mendicants among them. The Lingait monks called Vaders (lit. master or lord) have, in addition to the lingas, some small bells attached to their arms, so that when they pass through the streets the people are apprised of their being in the neighbourhood, and enabled to bestow their alms to them without any solicitation on their part. The lay Lingaits carry their veneration for the Vaders to an extent which is very unusual, and would hardly be believed by the Hindus of Northern India. Guru-worship is naturally favoured by the priest-ridden Hindu everywhere. But it is only among the Lingaits that an image of a god would be humiliated for the glorification of the Guru. The drinking of such water as has been touched by the feet of a Guru, or used to wash his feet, is common enough. But the Lingaits go much further. Before their holy men called the Vaders, they not only humiliate themseives, but their very idols. The Vaders are feasted by the laymen on all important occasions, and when there is a guest of that class in the house, the host places his own linga on a metal tray, and the guest's feet being placed on the vessel are washed by the host, the water contained in the same being ultimately swallowed by the host and his family with great reverence.

The Jangamas are the Gurus of the Lingaits. They are married men, but have charge of *maths* or monasteries. There are some learned men among them. The Aradhyas are Brahmans who minister to the Lingaits as Gurus.

With regard to the Lingait community of Mysore, Mr. Narasimmayengar makes the following remarks in his report on the last Census :—

As a community the Lingaits are intelligent, sober, industrious, thrifty and clannish. They have brought some departments of Kanara literature to a high degree of culture, and as tradesmen their place is in the van of Hindu society. As a race some of their divisions are unmistakably Aryan in descent, their women being, as a rule, object lessons in female loveliness and grace. To them as a body also belongs the credit of maintaining the strictest sobriety and non-alcoholism.—*Mysore Census Report for* 1891, Vol. XXV, p. 238.

The bitterness of the Lingaits is still as great as ever towards the Brahmans. But curiously enough, they claimed at the last Census to be included among Brahmans. They made some desperate efforts to secure that honour. But in the end they had to be satisfied with being separately enumerated as Lingaits.

There are very few Lingaits among the regular population of Northern India. The Rawal or high priest of the shrine of Kedarnath, on the Himalayan slopes in the district of Garwal, is a Jangama. So are the priests of the temple of Kedarnath in Benares. A Lingait may now and then be seen in Bengal and Behar leading a neatly caparisoned bull, and begging for alms by making the animal perform many curious feats, and representing it as the favouritec harger of Siva. These Lingait beggars are taken by the people of Bengal to be Pandas of the shrine of Vaidyanath.

CHAP. XI.—THE SIVITE YOGIS.

LITERALLY the word Yogi means an "unionist." What kind of union the Yogis claim to bring about, it is difficult to say. According to one version, which is very far from being intelligible to ordinary men, a Yogi is so-called on account of his being able, by his prayers and exercises, to get his individual soul united with the supreme soul. In the *Bhagavatgita*, which is the most popular work on theology in Sanskrit, the word yoga seems to be used throughout in the sense of "means." At any rate, the expressions Karma Yoga, Jnana Yoga and Bhakti Yoga cannot otherwise have any rational meaning. Whatever difficulty there may however be in the way of comprehending the exact nature of the intellectual or spiritual part of the practice called yoga, there can be no doubt that it is one of our most ancient forms of religious exercise. The great law-giver Yajnavalkya refers to it in his Code and says :—

> Of all acts, such as sacrifices, ceremonial observances, repression of sensual desires, harmlessness, gifts, and the study of the Vedas, this is the source of highest religions, namely, viewing one's self by means of the Yoga.—Yajnavalkya I, 8.

The most important physical exercises involved in Yoga are as described below :—

(*a*) The Yogi has to sit with his right leg on his left thigh, and his left leg on his right thigh, and in that uncomfortable position to point his eyes towards the tip of his nose.

(*b*) He must, while so seated, shut up one of his nostrils by the tips of two of his right-hand fingers, and while repeating certain formulæ mentally, he should with his open nostril inhale as much air as possible.

(*c*) When the lungs are inflated to the utmost degree possible, the Yogi is required to shut up both the nostrils, the open one being closed by pressing the thumb of his right hand.

(*d*) In the condition mentioned above, the Yogi has to repeat the prescribed formula a certain number of times again.

(*e*) When the recitation mentioned above is completed, then the Yogi must remove his fingers from the nostril first closed, and go on repeating the mystic formula a certain number of times again.

The whole operation is very simple and at the same time very imposing. It does not require any extraordinary quality of either the head or the heart, and yet the man, who can go through it with a little pantomimic skill and seriousness, can, at a very little cost, acquire a character for superior sanctity. The rules relating to the exercise require that it should be gone through in a secluded place. But in practice many men may be found engaged in the exercise in the most open places on the banks of the holy rivers, and in the premises of the great shrines. Such persons, however, never attain a very high place in the estimation of their co-religionists. It is those who are believed to practise Yoga in privacy that are usually credited with the possession of miraculous powers. Some of them are supposed to have the power of floating in the air, and of being able, if so inclined, to become immortal or to die at such time and place as they deem fit, death being a matter of option with them. "The Yogi is liberated in his living body from the clog of material incumbrance, and acquires an entire command over all worldly desires. He can make himself lighter than the lightest substances, heavier than the heaviest, can become as vast or as minute as he pleases, can traverse all space, can animate any dead body by transferring his spirit into it from his own frame, can render himself invisible, can attain all objects, becomes equally acquainted with the past, present and future; and is finally united with Siva."* To pretend that some particular Yogis have achieved immortality, and are living on the Himalayan slopes from a remote period of antiquity, is easy and convenient enough. It is very difficult, if not absolutely impossible, to explode such legends, and the charlatan who seeks to exact some money from credulous persons by pretending to have seen their great-great-great-grandfathers in Thibet cannot be prevented from plying his trade. As to the other powers claimed by the Yogis, they do not enjoy any similar vantage ground for maintaining their credit. At any rate, even among the most revered Yogis, there is not, I fear, one single individual who has ever, by actual performance, proved his possession of the power of aërial navigation to a greater extent than is exhibited by the jugglers of the country. With regard to the Yogis and their art Professor Wilson makes the following remarks :—

> They specially practise the various gesticulations and postures of which it consists, and labour assiduously to suppress their breath and fix their thoughts until the effect does somewhat realise expectation, and the brain, in a state of overwrought excitement, bodies forth a host of crude and wild conceptions, and gives to airy nothingness a local habitation and a name.—Wilson's *Hindu Sects*, p. 132.

There must be a great deal of truth in these observations, though the case of Ranjit Sing's famous Yogi must remain a mystery in the present state of the science of physiology. As to the case of the Madras Yogi† who floated in the air with the help of a rod fixed to the earth, suffice it to say that similar feats are daily exhibited by the poor jugglers of the country who do not lay claim to any supernatural powers. Even Ranjit Sing's Yogi is said to have been more a mercenary caterer than a holy saint, and similar performances, though for

---

* See Wilson's *Hindu Sects*, p. 131.

† See Akshoy Kumar Datta's *Hindu Religious Sects*, Vol II, p. 123; Wilson's *Hindu Sects*, p. 133.

shorter periods, are given now and then by the rustic magicians. Upon the whole, it seems that the so-called Yoga, even in its most astonishing aspects, is only a form of gymnastics and magic, and that it has as little connection with religion as the feats of Vaneck, Maskelyn, Hossain Khan or Anderson. As for the Yoga of the ordinary charlatans, it may, like "gravity," be defined as a "mysterious carriage of the body for hiding the defects of the mind."

The exercise of Yoga is allowed not only to mendicants, but to householders and family men as well. According to some authorities, Yoga cannot be effective in this Kâli Yuga or age of sin. The majority of the so-called Yogis are regarded as mere charlatans, and they neither claim to be, nor are looked upon as, men of superior sanctity.

CHAP. XII.—THE INFERIOR YOGIS.

THE inferior Yogi mendicants are divided into various orders, among whom the following are the most important:—

1. **Kanfat Yogis.**
2. **Aghore Panthi Yogis.**
3. **Kanipa Yogis.**

Kanfat Yogis.—The sect was founded by one Guru Gorakshanath, who is believed by his followers to have been an incarnation of the god Siva. The Kanfats are Sivites, and may be of any caste. They are so named because their ears are bored at the time of their initiation. They paint their body with ashes, and they have the usual transverse lines on the forehead which are the peculiarity of the Sivites. Like the Abadhutas, they allow their hair and nails to grow without pruning. Their dress also resembles that of the Abadhutas, excepting so far that many of them wear a patchwork skull cap instead of a turban. The distinguishing marks of the sect are their earrings, and the phallic emblems called *nad* which are tied to their neck by woollen threads.

The principal shrine of this sect is in the district of Gorakpore. There are places sacred to the sect also in Peshawar, Hardwar and Gujrat. The temple of Pasuputinath in Nepal and that of Eklinga in Mewar appertain to this sect. There are two small Kanfat shrines in Bengal, one at Mahanad in the district of Hooghly, and the other near the cantonment of Dum-Dum in the suburbs of Calcutta.

Large numbers of Kanfat Yogis are often met with in many parts of Northern India. They profess to have renounced the world. But many of them carry on trading business on a very extensive scale. The Kanfats sometimes enlisted in the army under the Hindu kings.

The Kanfats say that some of their saints are immortal, and are in existence in this world for thousands of years. The names of some of these immortal saints roaming on the Himalayan slopes are given in the *Hatha Pradipika*. Madame Blavatsky's *Kut Humi* is not expressly mentioned in this list, nor does it include the name of King Bhartri Hari, whom every Kanfat pretends to have seen.

The usual surname of the male Kanfats is Nath, and of the females, who are admitted to the order, Nathini. There is reason to suppose that the Yugi caste of Bengal and Assam are the progeny of the Kanfats.

Aghore Panthi Yogis.—The Aghore Panthi Yogis are exactly like the Aghoris, the only difference being that the former wear rings on their ears like the Kanfats.

Kanipa Yogis.—Some of the snake-charmers dress exactly like the Kanfats, and call themselves Kanipa Yogis. These are family men, and they earn the means of their livelihood chiefly by the exhibition of their skill in managing snakes.

CHAP. XIII.—THE SECTS THAT PRACTISE SEVERE AUSTERITIES.

The adult males among the inferior castes enlist themselves as Sivite ascetics in the middle of April every year, and during the week that they remain under the vow, they practise the most severe self-tortures and privations. See p. 369.

Besides the above who are householders there are some permanent ascetics who subject themselves to peculiar kinds of self-torture in order to be revered by the people. The practice of austerities, and not the worship of any particular deity, forms the most important part of their religious discipline. Upon the whole, however, they seem to be more addicted to the worship of Siva than to that of any other god or goddess. The most important classes of permanent ascetics professing the Sivite faith and practising the severe austerities are the following :—

1. **Urdha Bahu** ... Ascetics with uplifted hands.
2. **Tharasri** ... Ascetics who always remain in a standing posture.
3. **Urdhamukhi** .. Ascetics who with their feet attached to the bough of a tree, keep their heads hanging downwards.
4. **Panchadhuni** ... Ascetics who keep themselves in all seasons constantly surrounded by five fires.
5. **Jalashayi** ... Ascetics who keep themselves in all seasons immersed in water from sunset to sunrise.
6. **Jaladhara Tapashi.** Ascetics who keep themselves in all seasons under a jet of water from sunset to sunrise.

7. Farari ... Ascetics who live only on fruits.
8. Dudhahari ... Ascetics who live only on milk.
9. Aluna ... Ascetics who never eat salt with their food.

The number of such ascetics is very small; and of the few that profess to practice the terrible austerities of their respective orders, a great many are suspected to be mere pretenders. But there are many misguided simpletons who are genuine ascetics, and who actually observe their vow even at times when they are not watched by outsiders. The tortures to which such fanatics must subject themselves are terrible indeed. The penance of Simon Stylites was child's play compared with, for instance, the sufferings of the Tharasri. It is bad enough to be perched on the top of a pillar for thirty years and exposed to

Rain, wind, frost, heat, hail, damp and sleet and snow.

But to remain in a standing posture for years together without enjoying for a moment the delight of sleeping on a bed, or of even sitting down, is a kind of refinement in cruelty which, perhaps, has never been surpassed by the greatest of secular tyrants, ancient or modern. Bad as the record may be of the Indian Police and the Indian Jails, they allow even the greatest criminals the privilege of enjoying

Tired Nature's sweet restorer, balmy sleep.

A suspected person may now and then be subjected by a zealous thief-catching official to the same kind of operations as those to which the Panchadhuni, the Jalashayi, and the Jaladhara Tapashi voluntarily subject themselves. But if a single instance of such cruelty, though practised for an hour or two, ever becomes known to the outside world, the complaint is heard in everybody's mouth, and not only the Police but the British Government of India would be abused as a curse to the country. The far worse and quite gratuitous tyrannies of religion are, however, not only condoned, but actually admired.

PART III.

THE SAKTAS.

CHAP. I.—THE NATURE OF SAKTI WORSHIP.

THE religion of the Saktas may be regarded as a counterpart of Siva worship, for while the latter inculcates the adoration of the male organ of generation, the former attaches greater importance to the worship of the female organ. Some of the Sivites and Saktas worship the two organs in a state of combination.

The word Sakti literally means 'energy' or 'power'; and, taking into consideration what is said about it in the Tāntric scriptures, it seems to be used therein in the sense in which the word power is used in English, when a person is spoken of as a political or spiritual power. Some of the modern exponents of the Hindu religion profess to entertain the view that the Sakti of the Tāntrics denotes the same things as the terms 'energy' and 'force' of Natural Philosophy. Such abuse of scientific terms by men of religion has been common enough in India from a remote period of antiquity.

The essence of the Sakta cult is, as stated above, the worship of the female organ of generation. According to a text of the Tāntras the best form of Sakti worship is to adore a naked woman, and it is said that some Tāntrics actually perform their daily service in their private chapels by placing before them a female completely divested of her clothing. The following are used as substitutes :—

1. The Yantra or triangular plate of brass or copper kept among the penates of every Tāntric Brahman.
2. A triangle painted on a copper dish. The painting is made and worshipped only in the absence of a regular plate among the household penates.

The naked female, the Yantra, and the painted triangle are worshipped only in private services. In public the Tāntric offers his adoration to the naked image of a female deity called by various names such as Kāli, Tara, &c., and usually made to stand erect on the breast of a half-sleeping image of Siva in a similar state of nudity. The true nature of such images is not generally known, though it is defined in unmistakable terms in the Dhyan or formula for contemplating the goddess Kāli. The popular ideas on the subject are as stated below :—

She (the goddess Kāli) is represented as a woman, with four arms. In one hand she has a weapon, in another hand the head of the giant she has slain,—with the two others she is encouraging her worshippers. For earrings she has two dead bodies; she wears a necklace of skulls, her only clothing is a garland made of men's skulls. After her victory over the giants she danced so furiously that the earth trembled beneath her weight. At the request of the gods Siva asked her to stop; but, as owing to the excitement, she did not notice him, he lay down among the slain. She continued dancing till she caught sight of her husband under her feet; upon which, in Hindu fashion, she thrust out her tongue to express surprise and regret.—Murdoch on *Swami Vivekananda*, p. 40.

As a matter of fact, the image of Kāli, that Mr. Murdoch, of the Madras Mission, has attempted to hold up to ridicule in the above passage, is a thing far worse than he has taken it to be. What its real meaning is cannot possibly be explained here. Those inclined to dive into such filth must study the ritual for Kāli worship.

CHAP. II.—THE DIFFERENT CLASSES OF SAKTAS AND THEIR METHODS OF WORSHIP.

THE Saktas are chiefly householders, and there are very few mendicants among them. They are divided into various classes according to the extent to which they allow drinking, debauchery and slaughter of animals as parts of their ritual. The classes of Saktas best known in the country are the following :—

1. **Dakshinachari or the Right-handed Saktas.**
2. **Bamachari or the Left-handed Saktas.**
3. **Kowls or the Extreme Saktas.**

Some of the Saktas perform their worship in exactly the same manner as the Vaishnavas. They do not offer wine to their goddess, and, to avoid even the semblance of bloodshed, they conduct their ritual without any kind of red flower, or any stuff of blood colour like red sandal-wood. The majority of the respectable Saktas are Dakshinacharis, and though they do not avoid red flowers and red sandal-wood, they offer neither wine nor flesh meat to the deity. The number of Bamacharis in the country is not very large, and even among those who are so by family custom, the majority are so moderate that, instead of offering wine to their goddess, they use, as its substitute, cocoanut water in a copper vessel, such liquor being, according to the Shastras, equivalent to wine, for puja purposes. The extreme Bamacharis offer wine to their goddess, and when it is consecrated they sprinkle it on every kind of cooked and uncooked food brought before her. The quantity actually drunk by the worshipper and his family very seldom exceeds a few drops. Bamacharis of all classes generally offer some kind of sacrifice to their goddess. It is usually a kid. Some offer a large number of kids, with or without a buffalo in addition. In all cases the head of the slaughtered animal is placed before the grim deity with an earthen lamp fed by *ghi* burning above it. In the case of a buffalo being sacrificed, the body is given to the Muchi musicians. If the animal sacrificed is a goat, then the body is skinned and chopped, and when the flesh is cooked, it is consecrated again before the goddess. The meat is ultimately served to the invited guests, along with the other delicacies consecrated to the goddess. Some of the Bamacharis do not offer any animal, and instead of slaughtering kids and buffaloes, as they are required to do by their Shastras, they cut with due ceremony a pumpkin, a cocoanut or a sugarcane. This substitution may in some cases be due to compassion for the poor animals, but is generally owing to the superstitious fear entertained by all Hindus as to the result that must follow the executioner's failing to sever the head of the animal at one stroke. The sacrifice of an animal before a goddess is an occasion of great rejoicing to some young folks ; but to the votary, it is a sore trial. As a preliminary, special services are held supplicating the goddess that the ceremony might pass off without any hitch. Even at the time of the sacrifice, when the arena before the puja hall is filled with the shouts of the bye-standers, and the discordant music of the village Muchi band, the head of the house may be found standing in one corner muttering prayers with an air of deep devotion, if not actually with tears.

If, in spite of such prayers and supplications, the wrath of the deity is indicated by the failure of the executioner to make a clean cut through the neck of the animal by his first stroke, then the whole family is thrown into a deep gloom by the apprehension of a great catastrophe within the year following. Like the inmates of a sinking ship, they await in terrible agony the Divine visitation. The fear thus engendered gives rise to a plentiful harvest of expiatory ceremonies which benefit the priests. If a death or other misfortune happen to the family in the course of the year, it is attributed by all to the hitch in the sacrifice at the preceding puja. If no such disaster happen, the priest has all the credit. After such an occurrence the family generally determine never to offer sacrifices again; and in this way the slaughter of animals, as a part of puja ceremonies in private houses, is becoming more and more rare.

The Shastras of the Sakti worshippers recommend homicide before their goddesses as the best and most acceptable offering. But there are texts also which interdict such fiendish demonstration of piety; and as the killing of a human being, for puja purposes, might serve as a dangerous precedent, and recoil one day upon the priests themselves, the practice has never prevailed to any considerable extent in India. It is recommended in the Shastras only to make the votary ready to offer a goat, the flesh of which is an acceptable luxury to the Tāntric Brahmans. See p. 88, *ante*.

The Bamacharis slaughter kids and buffaloes openly; but even their most zealous bigots do not offer wine publicly. The Kowls or Extreme Saktas themselves conceal as much as possible their habit of indulging in intoxicating drinks. Their very Shastras enjoin hypocrisy, it being laid down therein that they must conduct themselves as Sivites and Vishnuvites in public. In actual practice some of the Kowls and Bamacharis are sometimes found in a tipsy condition. The Kowls usually betray their cult by painting their foreheads with vermilion dissolved in oil. The tint of blood being their favourite colour, they wear either scarlet silk, or cotton cloth dyed with ochre. The mark on the forehead of a Bamachari consists of three transverse lines painted with the charcoal of the sacred fire, dissolved in *ghi*. The Dakhinacharis have generally an Urdhapundra, or perpendicular streak, in the central part of the forehead, the colouring material being either a paste of sandal-wood, or a solution in *ghi* of charcoal obtained from a Hom fire. All classes of Saktas wear a necklace of Rudraksha seeds like the Sivites.

The extreme Kowls are almost quite as fiendish as the Aghoris, though in public they appear to be more clean and respectable in their habits. The Kowls do not eat carrion or ordure. It is, however, said of them that, in the hope of attaining supernatural powers, some of them practise what they call Sava Sadhan, or devotional exercise with a dead body. But, as the ceremony must be held at midnight, and at a burial or cremation yard far removed from the habitations of men, very few have, it is supposed, the hardihood to undertake it. The belief that those who undertake it, and fail to go through the programme to the end, become insane from that moment, also serves to deter novices, and to heighten the glory of those who claim to have accomplished the feat. The Kowls are, however, well-known to be in the habit of holding those bacchanalian orgies which are spoken of in their Shastras as Bhairavichakra and Lata Sadhan. These ceremonies are of such a beastly character that it is impossible even to think of them without horror. It is impossible in this book to give their details. Suffice it to state that they admit such females as are available for the purpose, and begin with the exhibition of every form of indecency that both the males and females are capable of. In the beginning some so-called religious rites are also seriously performed which, to any ordinary man, must appear highly comic. What follows may well be imagined, and, strange to say, that all this passes under the name of religion.

The Tāntric cult prevails to a greater extent in Bengal, Behar and Assam than perhaps in any other part of India. In Southern India, the Hindus are either Sivites or Vishnuvites. In the North-Western parts of India, the majority of the Brahmans are either Sivites or Vishnuvites. The few Saktas that there are in North-Western India are generally of an extreme type not usually to be found in any other part of India. In the Maharatta country the Karhadis, who are the only Saktas, are generally now of a moderate type. Among the higher Sudra castes the Kāyasthas are generally extreme Saktas in Upper India, and moderate Saktas in Bengal. The Baniyas are generally Vishnuvites throughout India. The Tāntric religion is a modern institution, but it is certainly more ancient than the Vishnuvite sects.

About the motive that brought such a horrible religion as that of the Tāntrics into existence, the good and respectable Brahmans say that it was devised by the gods for bringing about the destruction of the oppressors of men. There is a great deal of truth in this view. To me it seems that the Tāntric cult was invented partly to justify the habit of drinking which prevailed among the Brahmans even after the prohibition of it by their great law-givers, but chiefly to enable the Brahmanical courtiers of the beastly kings to compete with the secular courtiers in the struggle for becoming favourites, and causing the ruin of their royal masters.

PART IV.

THE VISHNUVITE SECTS.

CHAP. I.—THE TEN INCARNATIONS OF VISHNU.

It has been already stated that the Vaishnava sects are all of more recent date than the Sivite religion, and that the worship of Krishna has been gradually supplanting all the other cults in almost every part of India. According to the Shastras the great god Vishnu has, from time to time, appeared in this world in various shapes. Almost every one of the latter-day prophets have claimed the honour, with more or less success; but the right of Chaitanya, Vallabhāchari, &c., to be regarded as incarnations of Vishnu, is admitted by very few outside the sects founded by them. There is, however, no dispute as to the following being the true incarnations of Vishnu :—

1. As a fish.	It is believed that Vishnu assumed this shape in order to save Manu, the progenitor of the human race, from the universal deluge. On account of his piety in an age of sin he was apprised of the approach of submergence and commanded to build a ship and go on board with the seven Rishis or patriarchs, and the seeds of all existing things. When the flood came Vishnu took the form of a fish with a horn on its head to which the ship's cable was fastened.

2. As a tortoise.	To serve as a pivot for churning the ocean with the Mandara mountain as a churning rod and the Shesha serpent as the string for turning the same. The things recovered by this process were many, including the Amrita or the nectar of immortality; Laksmi the consort of Vishnu; the jewel Kaustava supposed to be the same as the Kohinoor which now adorns the diadem of Her Majesty, and a deadly poison swallowed or rather kept in his neck by Siva.
3. As a boar.	To rescue the earth from a deluge by which it was completely submerged.
4. As Nara Sinha or Man Lion.	To deliver the world from the tyrant Hiranya Kasipu, and to save his pious son, Pralhad, from being killed by the father for his devotion to Vishnu. When the sentence was about to be executed against the boy, Vishnu appeared suddenly from the midst of a pillar, and in the man-lion form tore Hiranya Kasipu to pieces.
5. As a dwarf.	The demon Bali having become very powerful, and having offered to give to every one what he wanted, the god Vishnu appeared before him as a dwarf and asked him to give as much ground as could be covered by three paces. No sooner was his request granted, than the god in disguise began to expand his form till both heaven and earth were occupied by his feet. To complete the promised gift, Bali placed his head at the third foot of the deity, and the god was satisfied.
6. As Parushu Rama.	Parushu Ram is said to have been a Brahman who caused the annihilation of the Ksatriya race twenty-one times.
7. As Ram Chandra.	See the account in the next chapter.
8. As Balaram.	The elder brother of Krishna.
9. As Buddha.	See the account in Pt. VII, *post*.
10. As Kalki.	The future incarnation whose appearance is promised at the end of the present age of sin for rescuing the land of the Aryas from the oppressors.

Krishna is regarded by some as the eighth incarnation, but according to the more orthodox view he was Vishnu himself, and was not a mere incarnation. Accordingly Krishna receives the largest share of worship from the Vishnuvites, while of the other nine incarnations it is only Ram who has regular votaries among those who are regarded as Hindus. Buddha has a much larger number of worshippers, but the Buddhists are not, strictly speaking, Hindus. The other eight incarnations have a few shrines in India, but they have no votaries specially devoted to their worship. Such being the case, the question naturally arises, why are they regarded as incarnations at all? The fact that the great god Vishnu is believed to have appeared in the form of a fish, a tortoise, or a boar, seems at first sight to be incapable of any rational explanation. The Hindu student of the European sciences might say that, in his descents on this world, the shapes assumed by God have been in accordance with the evolution of the species. But, admitting the correctness of the Darwinian theory, it is difficult to see why the god Vishnu should have appeared on earth in the forms of such animals as the fish, the tortoise and the boar. The orthodox might say that it is not proper to attempt at fathoming the depth of Divine Wisdom, but that amounts only to begging the question to some extent. If it be admitted that the Purāns are eternal, and that they have been sent to us direct from heaven, then alone the student of Hindu theology can be called upon not to be too inquisitive about the ways of Providence; but the probability as to the Purāns being human creations being very strong, it is certainly worth while to enquire whether they contain or not any internal evidence of their human authorship? If it can be shown that their framework is of such a nature as to be favourable to Brahmanical policy, then the inherent probability of their being the works of our ancient Pandits, becomes too strong to be rejected lightly by any reasonable man. The stories about the ten incarnations do not at first sight seem to favour anybody. But, with a little careful study, it must appear that the whole is one of the cleverest devices that have given to the Brahmans the position of almost gods on earth, in the estimation of other Hindus. Upon going through the list of the incarnations, the student cannot fail to notice that of the four historical and human forms among them, only Parushurama was a Brahman, and that while Ram and Buddha were beyond doubt Ksatriyas by birth, Balaram's claim to the rank of even the military caste is doubtful. In matters relating to the political affairs of the country, the Brahmans had pushed up the Ksatriyas to the utmost extent possible. When, therefore, Ksatriyas, like Buddha, tried to acquire spiritual supremacy also, the problem that presented itself before the Brahmans was how to make them powerless in their new sphere, without actually quarrelling with them. So the authors of the Purāns raised not only Buddha, but Rama and Krishna with him, to the rank of the god Vishnu himself. The Brahmans could not admit a Ksatriya to their own ranks. That would have been a dangerous precedent. The safest and the most convenient course was to promote the ambitious Buddha to the rank of a god, together with some other great Ksatriya heroes. The object of the whole evidently was to represent that, although Buddha did not admit Brahmanical pretensions, far greater members of the military caste had paid their homage to the descendants of the Rishis. The admission of Rama and Krishna to the rank of the gods not only took the shine out of Buddha, but served as an excellent basis for the invention of stories calculated to glorify the Brahmans, and to strengthen their position still more. In the *Mahābhārat* it is stated that, at the Rajshuya sacrifice celebrated by Yudhisthira, Krishna accepted the menial office * of washing the feet of the Brahman guests. In the Purāns it is stated again that the Rishi Bhrigu kicked at the breast of Krishna, but that, instead of resenting at the violence, the god meekly inquired of the Rishi whether his foot had not been hurt in the process. In fact, the Ksatriya Avatars served only to heighten the glory of the Brahmans in the same manner as the semi-independent Rajas and Nabobs of India serve to add lustre to British supremacy.

* Sabhu Parva, Chap. XXXV.

The admission of Krishna, Ram and Buddha to the rank of gods might have enabled the Ksatriyas and the Goalas to claim at least a reflected glory, and to aspire to a higher position than that of the Brahmans. In fact the Ksatriyas of Oudh and the Goalas of Mathura do sometimes actually claim such honour. The story of the ten Avatars therefore seems to have been invented by the Brahmans to be provided with a ready answer to such pretensions of the Ksatriyas and Goalas as are mentioned above. When a Ksatriya boasts of Ram Chundra having been born in his clan, or when a Goala boasts that Krishna was a member of the community to which he belongs, the Brahman, with his legends about the fish, the tortoise, and the boar, is easily able to silence his adversary by saying that God can have no caste, and that, if the fact of Vishnu having been born in Ksatriya families could be claimed as a source of glory by the Ksatriyas, then the very boars, which they daily killed and ate, would also be entitled to be reverenced in the same way. The story of the sixth Avatar, Parushurama, is evidently intended to make the Ksatriyas entertain a wholesome fear regarding the latent military powers of the Brahmans. Parushurama was, in all probability, a historical character. But in giving him the credit of having twenty-one times annihilated the Ksatriyas, the Brahmans evidently magnified his prowess and his achievements to an extent which was neither necessary nor very rational. Annihilation can take place only once, and not twenty-one times. The orthodox Brahmans are themselves obliged to admit, when hard pressed, that the twenty-one annihilations mean only so many massacres on a large scale.

CHAP. II.—THE LEGENDS ABOUT RAMA.

As most of the Vishnuvite sects are either Ram worshippers or Krishna worshippers, it seems necessary to give a brief account of the historical facts and legends connected with the names of the two great hero gods of the Hindu pantheon. The story of Rama is contained chiefly in the epic called *Ramayan*, which is one of the best works of the kind to be found in any language It breathes throughout a high moral tone, and furnishes models of conjugal fidelity and fraternal affection which have perhaps contributed in much greater degree to the happiness of Hindu family life than even Manu's Code. The hero who forms the central character of the epic, was the eldest son of King Dasarath of Ayodhya. His father had three wives, named Kausalya, Sumitra and Kaikayi. The two first were on very friendly terms, but Kaikayi entertained against them all the bitterness that a female heart is capable of bearing against a rival. Ram was the eldest son of Dasarath, and had three younger brothers, namely, Laksman, Bharat and Satrughna. Rama was the son of Kausalya; Laksman's mother was Sumitra; and the other two brothers were the sons of Kaikayi. When the brothers arrived at the proper age for marriage, they attended a tournament in the court of King Janaka of Mithila, and the success of Rama in satisfying the required condition of stringing a big bow, enabled him and his brothers to secure for each of them one of the daughters of King Janaka. After the return of the brothers, with their newly-married wives, to their home, King Dasarath announced his intention to recognise Ram, the eldest, as the heir-apparent. The necessary preparations were made for a great festivity; but when everything was ready for the due performance of the ceremony, all the arrangements were upset by an intriguing chambermaid who excited Kaikayi's jealousy, and prevailed upon her to stand in the way of the wishes of the old king. In a fit of excessive love, he had once promised to Kaikayi to grant her any favour that she might ask at any time. The artful queen, instigated by her still more artful maid, now insisted that her son Bharat should be made king, and that Ram should be banished from the country for twelve years. The prayer came like a thunderbolt on the old king. But he was helpless. As a true Ksatriya, he could not refuse to give effect to his promise. On the other hand, it simply broke his heart even to think of banishing his eldest and beloved son. He was completely in a fix, and could not arrive at any decision. But Ram insisted upon going into exile, in order that his father might not incur the guilt of a breach of promise. The great hero was followed not only by his wife Sita, but also by his loving brother Laksman. Bharat and Satrughna loved him with the same ardour, but they were obliged to remain at home for the sake of their mother. The old king did not long survive this sad turn of affairs. After his death Bharat went in search of Ram, and finding him on the Chitrakuta mountain, near the modern city of Allahabad, besought him, with great fervour, to return to the metropolis of their kingdom, and to assume the reins of Government as the rightful successor. Rama performed the funeral rites of his father, but, for the sake of giving effect to his promise, he refused to comply with the prayer of Bharat. The loving step-brother returned home with a sad heart; but instead of setting himself up as the king, he ruled the country as regent, placing the sandals of his absent brother on the throne.

In their exile Ram, Laksman and Sita passed through various places in Central India, and ultimately fixed their residence at Pancha Bati, near the modern town of Nasik at the source of the Godaveri. Here, during a short absence of the brothers from their cottage, the demon king Ravana of Ceylon carried away Sita by force. Ram secured the friendship of Hanuman, Sugriva and certain other heroes, represented in the *Ramayan* as monkey chiefs, and with their help invaded Ceylon. There was a long and sanguinary war, the upshot of which was that Ravana was killed, and Sita was recovered. She was then made to undergo a trial by ordeal which established her purity. The period of Rama's exile having expired, he then returned to Ayodhya, with Laksman, Sita, and some of his allies, notably his monkey general Hanuman. The joy of the whole royal family and of the people of Oudh knew no bounds upon their getting their rightful king. Even Kaikayi, whose bitterness had worn off, was obliged to apologise, and everything went on happily. But just at the time when Sita was about to be a mother, Ram was obliged, by the pressure of public opinion among his subjects, to abandon his loving queen, and to send her to exile. The episode is a heart-rending one, and forms the theme of the drama called *Uttara Ram Charita*. In her second exile she was taken care of by the Rishi Valmiki. She gave birth to the twins, who afterwards became distinguished under the names of Lab and Kush, and are claimed as progenitors by most of the Rajput Kings of India. After the banishment of Sita, Rama could have taken another wife; but such was his love for her that he preferred to live the life of a virtual widower. To perform those religious ceremonies that require the association of the wife as a *sine quâ non*, he caused a golden image of Sita to be used as her substitute. The sons, Lab and Kush, grew up to manhood under the care of their mother and the Rishi Valmiki. Ram admitted them into his house; but when the Rishi asked him to re-admit Sita into his palace, he proposed that she should go through a second ordeal before an assembly of the chief nobles and prelates of the realm. As a dutiful wife, Sita agreed to the condition insisted upon by Rama. But when she appeared before the court of her lord, she refrained from doing anything to be re-admitted into her position as queen, and instead, asked her mother-earth* to testify to her purity by opening up her bosom for giving her a final resting-place. The story of the *Ramayan* virtually closes with the miraculous but pathetic disappearance of Sita underground amidst a shower of flowers sent down by the gods. The concluding chapters of the *Ramayan* are apt to rouse a feeling of indignation in the reader such as a child might feel at seeing his mother ill-treated by his father. But whatever the first impulse may be to charge Rama with cruelty and weakness, it is impossible not to take into consideration the long war that he waged for Sita's sake, and the miserable life that he led during her exile. Even the verdict of the Hindu matrons, as evidenced by the indirect expressions of their highest aspirations, is in favour of Rama having been the model of a loving husband. When an unmarried girl salutes an elderly Hindu lady, the latter, in pronouncing her benediction, will say, "May your husband be like Rama, your mother-in-law like Kausalya, and your brothers-in-law like Laksman."

---

* Sita is described in the Ramayan as having been found by King Janak in the furrow of a field. Ramayan, Adi Kanda Chap. 67, v. 14.

CHAP. III.—THE HERO GOD KRISHNA AS A HISTORICAL CHARACTER.

THE majority of the Vishnuvite Hindus are worshippers of the hero god Krishna. He is, in the belief of his votaries, the Supreme God, while the other incarnations, such as Rama and Buddha, represented only a part of the great spirit pervading the universe. Krishna was not born in the purple, and never assumed the position of a *de jure* king in any of the countries which he virtually ruled ; but, by his ability as a political minister, combined with his military resources, he came to be recognised as the greatest power in the country in his time, and his friendship was eagerly sought by the mightiest of the kings in Northern India. According to the *Mahābhārat* and the earlier Purāns, Krishna was the model of a great Ksatriya hero and counsellor. But the later Purāns, while representing him as God Himself in human form, have connected his name with a large number of legends, depicting him as the worst type of a shameless sensualist, faithless lover, and undutiful son. These stories, though they have served the purposes of priestcraft in more ways than one, have not, in all probability, any foundation in truth, and might well be rejected by the historian not only as palpable myths, but as utterly unwarrantable defamations on the character of one of the greatest men that India has ever produced. In this work, however, some of these stories will have to be referred to, in order to enable the reader to form an exact idea of the doctrines and practices of our most important religious sects.

The *Mahābhārat* is very nearly silent as to the early life of Krishna, but the Purāns are unanimous as to the following particulars :—

1. That he was a true Ksatriya of the Yadu race.
2. That his father was Basudeva, and that his mother, Devaki, was one of the sisters of King Kansa of Mathura.
3. That his brother Balaram was the son of Basudeva by another wife named Rohini.
4. That, in consequence of a prediction that one of the sons of Devaki would kill Kansa, most of her children were killed by him.
5. That Krishna and Balaram were surreptitiously removed from Mathura by their father, to the house of a cow-herd chief, named Nanda Ghosh, who lived in the village of Gokula in the neighbourhood.
6. That Krishna and Balaram were treated by Nanda's wife Jashoda as her own sons, and that, in their earlier years, they tended Nanda's cattle.
7. That when they grew up to manhood, they invaded Mathura, and having killed Kansa, restored his father Ugra Sena to the throne.
8. That, as Kansa was the son-in-law and a vassal of Jara Sandha, the Emperor of Magadha sent several expeditions to chastise those who took the lead in dethroning and killing him.
9. That though Krishna successfully resisted these invasions, he ultimately thought it prudent to remove to Gujrat with all his relatives, and that he founded there the city of Dwarika which was made the metropolis of his new kingdom.
10. That Krishna married several wives, the chief of whom were Rukmini, Kubja and Satya Bhama.

The facts which make the life of Krishna particularly interesting are those that have reference to his connection with the Pandava brothers. They were the sons of his father's sister, Kunti, and of King Pandu of Hastinapore. Pandu died while they were all very young, and after his demise they remained for some time under the guardianship of their blind uncle, Dhrita Rastra, who was the elder brother of their father, but had been excluded from the throne, on account of the law of the Hindu Shastras which renders blind, deaf and dumb persons incapable of taking any property by inheritance. At first Dhrita Rastra sincerely loved his nephews, and did not entertain any intention to have their claims overlooked for the benefit of his own progeny. But his eldest son Duryodhana persistently urged him to banish them from the kingdom, and after a great deal of hesitation, he gave effect to his son's evil counsels. On some plausible pretexts they were sent to a country-house at a place called Baranabat. The building, which was given to them there for their residence, was, by Duryodhana's order, constructed with highly combustible materials, and it was planned that the house should be set on fire at night. Yudhisthira was apprised of these wicked intentions on the part of his cousins, but instead of betraying any reluctance to comply with the orders of his uncle, he quietly went to Baranabat with his brothers and his mother, as Dhrita Rastra wished him to do. In due course the agents of the wicked Duryodhana set fire to the Baranabat villa. But the Pandava brothers effected their exit from it through a subterranean passage which they had caused to be excavated in order to be able to escape from destruction. The whole building was reduced to ashes within a very short time, and when the news reached Duryodhana he was filled with joy at the quiet removal of the obstacles to his ambition. The situation of the Pandava brothers was now a perilous one. They apprehended that their enemies having failed to bring about their destruction by meanness and treachery, would now have recourse to actual violence, and that, as they were in possession of all the resources of the empire, they had only to order what they wished. Yudhisthira with his brothers and mother, therefore, determined to remain concealed in the wilderness, and not to let anyone know who they were. For years they lived a very miserable life, roaming through the forests, and eking out the means of their subsistence by various shifts and expedients. At last it came to their notice that the great King of Panchala, whose power and resources were almost equal to those of the Hastinapore monarchy, was about to give his daughter in marriage by the Swayamvara ceremony, the condition being that she was to be wedded to the person who would prove his superiority in archery by a public test. All the great princes of India were invited to attend and compete. The Pandava brothers saw their opportunity to emerge from their obscurity. They hastened towards Kampilya, the capital of Panchala, and on the appointed day and hour presented themselves among the assembled guests, in the guise of Brahmans. The feat of archery which was made the test was, if not actually impossible, a very difficult one. Many of the most renowned princes present on the occasion wisely abstained from making the attempt, and the few who risked their fame, for the sake of the prize, made themselves simply ridiculous by their failure. At last one of the Pandava brothers, the renowned Arjuna, advanced to the centre of the arena, and his success in satisfying the condition was soon followed by the decking of his neck with the garland that the daughter of the Panchala King held in her hand. The Ksatriya princes assembled on the spot were greatly enraged at first at the triumph of a person whom they supposed to be a Brahman. But they were pacified by the wise counsels of Krishna, and Arjuna with his bride, and all his brothers repaired to the lodgings they had taken up.

Krishna, the hero god, was present on the occasion. He had never before seen the Pandava brothers ; but he could easily make out who the winner of the fair prize, and the persons accompanying him, were. He surmised that, with the help of the Panchala King, they would, before long, be able to recover their ancestral kingdom. So he followed them, and introduced himself to them in the usual way. He prostrated himself before Kunti, and also before Yudhisthira, who was older than he. The other brothers were accosted as younger cousins. The Pandavas were still in a very miserable plight. Arjuna had secured the hand of the daughter of the Panchala King, but the five brothers with their mother were still in the condition of poor beggars. Krishna saw their situation, and immediately after the marriage, sent them very valuable presents. These were highly welcome to them at the time, and Krishna thus laid the foundation of a lifelong friendship with them.

The powerful alliance of the Panchala King, soon enabled the Pandavas to secure a moiety of their ancestral kingdom, with Indraprastha (modern Delhi) as their capital. Arjuna was then led to visit Dwarika, the capital of the kingdom founded by Krishna in Gujrat, and the opportunity was made use of to cement the friendship already formed by the marriage of Krishna's sister Subhadra with the great Pandava hero.

Up to this time Krishna did not seek to derive any direct advantage from his friendship with the Pandavas. But the policy which led him to seek their powerful alliance, and through them that of the Panchala Kings, soon unfolded itself. It has been already seen that Krishna was compelled by Jara Sandha to leave his native kingdom of Mathura, and naturally he was seeking for an opportunity to crush the mighty Emperor of Magadha. That opportunity presented itself when Yudhisthira announced his intention to celebrate the Rajshuya sacrifice. According to the *Mahābhārat*, the idea originated in a communication which the Rishi Narada was deputed, by the spirit of Pandu, to make to Yudhisthira. The nature of the message that Narada brought may be gathered from the following passages in the conversation that took place between him and Yudhisthira :—

Yudhisthira said:—"O great *Muni*, thou hast mentioned one only earthly monarch—*viz.*, the royal *Rishi* Harish Chundra as being a member of the council of the king of the gods! What act was performed by that celebrated king, or what ascetic penances with steady vows, in consequence of which he hath been equal to Indra himself? O Brahmana, how didst thou also meet with my father, the exalted Pandu, now a guest of the region assigned for the residence of departed souls. O exalted one of excellent vows, hath he told thee anything? O tell me all. I am exceedingly curious to hear all this from thee!"

Narada said :—"O King of Kings, I shall tell thee all that thou askest me about Harish Chundra. He was a powerful king, in fact an emperor over all the kings of the earth. And O monarch, having subjugated the whole earth, he made preparations for the great sacrifice called Rajshuya. And all the kings of the earth brought at his command wealth unto the sacrifice. * * * The powerful Harish Chundra, having concluded his great sacrifice, became installed in the sovereignty of the earth and looked resplendent on his throne. O bull of the Bharata race, all those monarchs that perform the great sacrifice of Rajshuya are able to attain the region of Indra and to pass their time in felicity in Indra's company. O King of Kings, O son of Kunti, thy father Pandu, beholding the good fortune of Harish Chundra and wondering much thereat, hath told me something. Knowing that I was coming to the world of men, he bowed unto me and said: 'Thou shouldst tell Yudhisthira, O *Rishi*, that he can subjugate the whole earth, inasmuch as his brothers are all obedient to him. And having done this, let him commence the great sacrifice called Rajshuya. He is my son. If he performeth that sacrifice, I may, like Harish Chundra, soon attain to the mansion of Indra, and there in his Sabha pass countless years in continuous joy.' I have now answered in detail all that thou hast asked me. With thy leave I will now go to the city of Dwaravati."—*Mahābhārat, Sabha Parva*, sec. 12.

If the allegation of the deputation by Pandu's spirit be left out of consideration, as, on account of its supernatural character, it deserves to be, then the message must have had its origin either in priestcraft on the part of Narada, or in statecraft on the part of Krishna, with whom Narada seems to have had some mysterious connection as principal and agent. At any rate, when Krishna was sent for and consulted about the matter, he did not fail to take the utmost advantage of the desire which was awakened in the mind of Yudhisthira to celebrate the Rajshuya sacrifice. Krishna drew the attention of his cousin to the fact that so long as Jara Sandha reigned supreme throughout the greater part of the north-eastern provinces of India, the King of Indraprastha, with all his wealth and resources, could have no right to perform the Rajshuya. To fight with Jara Sandha and bring him under subjection was out of the question. On the other hand, as a dutiful son, Yudhisthira could not give up altogether the idea of fulfilling the wishes of his departed father. He was therefore in a dilemma from which Krishna proposed to extricate him, by offering to effect the death of Jara

Sandha with only the help of the two brothers Bhima and Arjuna. They set out on their mission in the disguise of Brahmans, and having arrived at the city of Giri Braja, the metropolis of the Magadha empire, they easily managed to have an interview with the king. In the course of the conversation that took place, Krishna charged Jara Sandha with tyranny, and challenged him to fight a duel. The great emperor denied that he had ever been guilty of oppressing his subjects; but he was, for the sake of vindicating his Ksatriya honour, obliged to accept the challenge, and the result was that he was killed by Bhima. Thereupon the princes who had been held captive by Jara Sandha, were released, and not only they, but the emperor's son, Sahadeva, paid homage to Krishna and to the Pandavas. Thus Krishna's triumph over his great enemy was complete, and at the same time he laid Yudhisthira under a fresh obligation.

After these events, the Rajshuya sacrifice was duly celebrated by the Pandava King, and for a time he was in the zenith of imperial glory. But, before long, he was led by the wily courtiers of his cousin Duryodhana, to stake everything that he possessed, in a game of chance. The result was that he not only lost his kingdom and his crown, but was obliged to seek refuge in the woods again with his brothers, and the queen Draupadi. At the time of their exile, Krishna does not appear to have maintained any communication with them. But when the period of thirteen years, during which Yudhisthira was bound by his gambling vow to rove in the forests with his brothers, expired, Krishna appeared in their midst again, and urged them to declare war against their cousin unless he consented to make over at least a moiety of the kingdom of Hastinapore to them. Krishna himself accepted the office of ambassador to bring about peace. But whether his real object was peace, or whether he used his influence and opportunities only to involve the parties in war, are questions as to which there may be considerable difference of opinion. Even the bigoted Vishnuvites are sometimes obliged to admit that there was a little too much of diplomacy in the part that Krishna took on the occasion.

I need not refer to the other important events in the political life of Krishna. However interesting they may be, they do not come within the scope of this work. So I conclude this part of the sketch with some passages cited from the *Mahābhārat*, showing how exalted his position in the political horizon was in his time. The following is from the Udyoga Parva of the great epic:—

Yudhisthira said:—"Without doubt, O Sanjaya, it is true that righteous deeds are the foremost of all our acts, as thou sayest. Thou shouldst, however, censure me *after* you have first ascertained whether it is virtue or vice that I practise * * * Here is Krishna, the giver of virtue's fruits, who is clever, politic, intelligent, who is devoted to the service of the Brahmans, who knows everything and counsels various mighty kings! Let the celebrated Krishna say whether I should be censurable if I dismiss all idea of peace, or whether if I fight, I should be abandoning the duties of my caste, for Krishna seeketh the welfare of both sides! This Satyaki, these Chedis, the Andhakas, the Vrishnis, the Bhojas, the Kukuras, the Srinijoyas, adopting the counsels of Krishna, slay their foes and delight their friends. The Vrishnis and the Andhakas, at whose head stands Ugra Sena, led by Krishna, have become like Indra, high spirited, devoted to truth, mighty and happy. Vabhru, the King of Kasi, having obtained Krishna, hath attained the highest prosperity. O sire, so great is this Krishna. I never disregard what Krishna sayeth."

That the friendship of Krishna was valued also by the enemies of the Pandavas would appear clear from the following extracts:—

After Krishna and Valrama had both departed for Dwarika, the royal son of Dhritarastra went there by means of fine horses having the speed of wind. On that very day, the son of Kunti and Pandu also arrived at the beautiful city of the Anarata land. And the two scions of the Kuru race, on arriving there, saw that Krishna was asleep, and drew near him as he lay down. And as Krishna was sleeping, Duryodhana entered the room and sat down on a fine seat at the head of the bed, and after him entered the magnanimous Arjuna, and he stood at the back of the bed, bowing and joining hands, and when Krishna awoke, he first cast his eyes on Arjuna * * * Then Duryodhana addressed Krishna saying:—It behoveth you to lend me your help in the impending war. Arjuna and myself are both equally your friends, you also bear the same relationship to both of us. I have been the first to come to you. Right-minded persons take up the cause of him who comes first to them. This is how the ancients acted. And, O Krishna, you stand at the top of all right-minded persons in the world and are always respected.

CHAP. IV.—KRISHNA AS THE GOD OF THE MODERN VISHNUVITE SECTS.

IN the *Mahābhārat*, Krishna is depicted as a great warrior and statesman, and as a sincere reverer of the Brahmans. In some places he is spoken of as a god, but most of these passages are open to the suspicion of being interpolations. At any rate, the main burden of the story, so far as Krishna is concerned, is to establish that he was a human being of a superior type whose example every Ksatriya king ought to follow. That was enough for the political purposes of the Brahmans at the time when the religion of the Ksatriya Buddha threatened to supersede the Vedic faith and practices. The teachings of the *Mahābhārat* and the *Ramayan* virtually asked the Ksatriya rulers of the country to follow their great ancestors Ram, Krishna and Yudhisthira, and not to attach any importance to the revolutionary doctrines of the son of a petty chieftain of the Himalayan Terai. The plan of campaign was eminently successful, and it is only natural that the victorious party, or at least their camp-followers, should have taken some undue advantage. The manner in which, in the case of Krishna, man-worship has degenerated into abomination-worship, may be traced step by step. In the *Mahābhārat* it is pure man-worship. In the *Vishnu Purān* and the *Hari Vansa*, a tendency to make use of the great name of Krishna for corrupting the morals of men is clearly visible, though under more or less decent veils. But the *Bhagvat* and the *Bramha Vai-*

varta, throw aside every kind of mask, and, in the most shameless manner, attempt to sanctify every form of debauchery, so as to enable the priestly class to gratify their lust.

The Krishna of the latter-day Purāns mentioned above has very little in common with the great hero of the *Mahābhārat*. In the *Bhagvat* and the *Bramha Bibarta* the reader is called upon to admire and worship Krishna, not on account of his having been a great warrior and political minister, but on account of his having seduced the milkmaids of Brindavan, by every kind of trick that the most wicked of human beings could invent. The chief object of his love was one Radha, who, according to some of the authorities, was the wife of the brother of his foster-mother. The very name of this Radha is not to be found even in the *Bhagvat*. But, by an abuse of scientific terms which was as common in ancient times as it is now, she is represented by the latter-day Vishnuvites as the Prakriti or the material basis of the Yoga philosophy, while Krishna is represented as the Purush or the Supreme Spirit by whose union with the Prakriti this universe was created. In almost all the modern Vishnuvite shrines, an image of Radha is associated with that of Krishna, and in Northern India there are very few temples in which Rukmini or any of the other married wives of Krishna are worshipped with him. The tales and songs connected with Radha and Krishna cannot, for the sake of decency, be referred to here. The reader unacquainted with them, and curious to know their details, must take the trouble to read the two modern Purāns mentioned above, and also *Jayadev*, *Vidyapati*, *Chandidas*, &c. According to the legends contained in these works, when Krishna, by killing Kansa, became the virtual ruler of Mathura, he forsook not only Radha and the other cowherd women of Brindavan whom he had seduced, but, in the most heartless manner, disowned even his foster-parents.

These stories form the theme of the most heart-rending songs and odes, and being much more intelligible to all classes of women, both young and old, than the wars and intrigues of the *Mahābhārat*, are much better calculated than anything else to enable the priest to acquire a hold on their hearts by awakening their tenderest sentiments.

CHAP. V.—THE SRI VAISHNAVAS OF SOUTHERN INDIA.

Of the existing Vishnuvite sects, one of the earliest and purest is that founded by Ramanuja, who lived in the eleventh century of the Christian era, and was born at a place called Sri Perambudur, 25 miles to the west of Madras. The Sivite religion, which had been flourishing since the effacement of Buddhism in the eighth century, through the teachings of Sankara, was then in undisputed possession of the field, and, with perhaps a very laudable object, Ramanuja directed all his efforts to abolish the worship of the phallic Linga, and to set up Vishnu as the only true god. Ramanuja recommended the adoration of Vishnu, Krishna and Ram together with their lawfully married wives Laksmi, Rukmini and Sita. Radha worship is unknown in Southern India. Images of Ramanuja, and of some of his leading followers, are provided with special niches in the Vishnuvite shrines appertaining to this sect. At Sri Perambudor the birth-place of Ramanuja there is a temple in which an image of the prophet is worshipped as the principal deity.

The personal history of Ramanuja does not fall within the scope of this work. According to the Kanarese account of his life, called the *Dibya Charitra*, his father's name was Kesava Acharya, and his mother was Bhumi Devi. He studied the Shastras at Kanchi, and it was there also that he first commenced to teach his religion. At a later period, he fixed his residence at Sri Rangam, an island formed by the bifurcation of the river Kaveri near the town of Trichinapali. Here Ramanuja composed his principal works, namely, the *Sri Bhashya*, the *Gita Bhasya*, the *Vedartha Sangraha*, *Vedanta Pradipa*, and the *Vedanta Sara*. After completing these works, the author performed a tour through various parts of India, vanquishing the champions of the Sivite creed, and converting many Sivite shrines into temples for the worship of Vishnuvite deities. But by these proceedings, he created many enemies, and, through their instigation, he was threatened with such persecution by the king of his native country, that he was obliged to seek refuge in the court of Vetaldeva, King of Karnata. Vetaldeva himself was a Jaina, but his queen was a believer in Vishnu, and partly through her influence, and partly by curing the king's daughter from a malady which threatened her life, Ramanuja was able to convert him to Vaishnavism, The Raja built a Vishnuvite temple at Yadavagiri. now called Mailkoti, about twelve miles to the north of Seringapatam. Here Ramanuja lived for twelve years; but on the death of his persecutor, the Chola King, he returned to Sri Rangam, where he passed the remaining years of his life, and where his tomb is still in existence.

The philosophy of Ramanuja is popularly called *Vishishtadwaita Vada* or qualified non-duality. But, as a matter of fact, he believed in three distinct original principles, namely,—

1. The Supreme Spirit 'Parabramha or Ishwara'.
2. The separate spirits of men 'Chit'.
3. Non-spirit 'Achit'.

Ramanuja was not altogether against self-worship as practised by the Sankarites. But, for the common people, he recommended the worship of images of Vishnu, Krishna and Rama.

The most important shrines of the Ramanuja sect are at Sri Rangam and Mailkoti. The shrines of Badari

Nath on the Himalayan slopes, of Jagannath in Orissa, of Dwarika in Gujrat, and of Tirupati in North Arcot, are also said to be connected with the Ramanujite order.

The Ramanujites are called Sri Vaishnavas, and they derive their designation from the fact that they worship Sri or Laksmi as the consort of their god. They are divided into two sects, called the Vadagala and the Tengala. The word Vadagala means the language of the North, and the word Tengala is a corrupted form of the expression "Tri-Yumulaya," which means the language of the blessed saints. The Vadagalas, as their name indicates, give preference to the Sanskrit, while the Tengalas regard their Tamil translations as equal to the original scriptures of the Hindus. Among the Vadagala exegetes the most renowned name is that of Desika, who was a Brahman of Kanjivaram. The chief authority of the Tengala, or the Southern School, is Manavala Mahamuni. The doctrinal differences between the two sects may, to an outsider, seem to be too trivial to account for the bitterness between them. According to the Vadagalas, the human spirit lays hold of the Supreme Being by its own will, acts and efforts, just as the young monkey clings to its mother. According to the Tengalas, the human spirit has no independent will, and is led by the Supreme Spirit, just as kittens are taken from place to place by the mother cat. Another difference between the tenets of the two sects lies in the views they take of the position of Vishnu's consort. The Vadagalas regard Laksmi as equal to Vishnu himself in every respect, but the Tengalas maintain that Laksmi is a created and finite being, and that she is to be worshipped only as a mediator.

The Vadagalas are the more aristocratic of the two sects, and have among them very few Sudras. Among the Tengalas, the plebeians are the predominating element, and they use the vernacular Tamil as the language of their ritual, very nearly eschewing Sanskrit, which is favoured by the Vadagalas. The Tamil book of rituals compiled by the Tengalas is regarded by them as not inferior to the Sanskrit Veda. These circumstances may partially explain the bitter feud existing between the two sects. But the chief cause of their quarrels seems to be the fact that a former King of Madura placed all the Vishnuvite shrines within his dominions in the charge of Tengala priests, excluding altogether the Vadagalas from the profits and perquisites of the ecclesiastical service.

The two sects have different forehead marks by which they can be distinguished without any difficulty. The *Tilak* of the Vadagalas is like the letter U, and that of the Tengalas like the letter Y. In both a perpendicular red or yellow streak, representing Sri or Laksmi the consort of Vishnu, bisects the space between the arms, which are painted with the white magnesian or calcareous clay called Tiruman. In addition to the mark painted on the forehead, the Ramanujites, both male and female, brand themselves like the Madhavas, with the marks of Krishna's emblems, namely, conch shell, and discus. Boys are branded after thread ceremony, at the age of seven or upwards, and girls are subjected to the rite after marriage. The branding is done by the family Guru with a red-hot metallic stamp, and forms a part of the rites which are performed by him when he communicates to his disciple the sacred formula that is supposed to cause his regeneration. In Northern India, branding is never practised, and the sacred formula consists of a few meaningless syllables. But among the Vishnuvites of Southern and Western India, the branding is the most important part of the ceremony and the sacred formula is either the eight syllabled *mantra* "Om namah Narayanaya" or the well-known verse of Gita wherein Krishna calls upon Arjoon to follow him implicitly in all things, and not to act according to his own sense of right and wrong. The Acharya clears a very handsome amount from the fees which are paid to him for his fiendish ministrations.

Of the Acharyas who have the privilege of practising the profession of Guru among the Ramanujites, some are the descendants of the chief disciples of the prophet. Gurus of this class are married men, and they live and dress like householders. The same privilege is enjoyed also by the superiors of the monasteries appertaining to the sect as, for instance, those of Ahobalam in the Karnool district, and Vanomamula in Tinnevelli. These spiritual superiors are Brahmans, and they minister only to Brahmans and the Satanis. The latter are said to have been originally Sudras. But they minister to the low castes as priests, and sometimes claim to have the same rank as the Brahmans. The derivation of the name is not well known. Some say that it is a corrupted form of the Sanskrit word *Sanatan*, which means "primeval." Some of the lower class Satanis themselves say that they are so called because they are Sat Ani or $\frac{7}{16}$ of a god. The following remarks are made with reference to them in the last *Census Report of Mysore* :—

> What the Brahman Gurus are to themselves, they are to the non-Brahmans of their own persuasion. A certain number among them have taken to agriculture, but, as a rule, they are employed in the Vishnu temples as Pujaris, flower-gatherers, torch-bearers, &c.

The Satanis have their own *maths*. But they are all married men, and it is said that in worshipping their gods they use wine, which is an abomination to all Vishnuvites.

There are among the followers of Ramanuja a class called Dasa or Dasari. Like the Satanis, these are of non-Brahmanical castes. They call themselves *Dasas* or servants of God, in fulfilment of vows made either by themselves or their kinsmen in times of illness, pain or distress. "They are of various castes, and exhibit rather conspicuously certain of the externals of the Vaishnava faith, and are much honoured by non-Brahmanic people on religious and festive occasions. The approach of the Vaishnava Brahman Gurus is heralded by them, and they head certain funeral and car processions, sounding their peculiar drums and trumpets. It is also stated that they are active in converting to the tenets of Ramanuja the people of the inferior castes."*

The formula for accosting a clerical member of the Ramanuja sect is *Dasoshmi* or Dasoham literally, "I am your slave." The *mantra* communicated by a Guru at the time of admitting anyone to his *chellaship* is a formula signifying "salutation to Narayana."

The usual surnames of the Ramanujite Brahmans are Ayangar, Acharya, Charlu and Acharlu. The last two are corrupted forms of the Sanskrit word Acharya.

There are many big men among the Vadagala section of the Sri Vaishnavas. The late Mr. Ranga Charlu, who was the Prime Minister of Mysore for many years, was a Vadagala. The sect is represented in the Bar of the Madras High Court by such eminent Advocates as Messrs. Bhashyam Ayangar and Ananda Charlu.

In the observance of caste rules, as to the cooking and eating of cooked food, both the Vadagala and the Tengala Brahmans are more puritanic than the most orthodox members of other communities. Sankar Acharya required his mendicant followers not to touch fire, and enjoined that they should live only by partaking of the hospitality of Brahman householders. Ramanuja, who first set up an opposition, allowed his disciples not only to touch fire, but prohibited their eating any food that had been cooked or even seen by a stranger. Like the Sankarite monks, the Ramanujite ascetics wear cotton clothes dyed red with ochre. The householders wear silk and woollen clothes after bathing, and at the time of taking their midday meal. The Ramanujites use necklaces and rosaries of basil wood, though not to the same extent as the other Vishnuvites. Among the ascetic followers of Ramanuja there is a class who carry staffs, and are called Dandis. But they wear the sacred thread, and do not throw it off like the Sankarite Dandis.

---

* *Mysore Census Report*, 1891, p. 238.

CHAP. VI.—MADHWACHARI.

RAMANUJA was a bitter opponent of the Sivite cult, and tried to suppress it altogether. The next great Vishnuvite teacher of Southern India, whose name was Madhwacharya, and who was born in Kanara in the year 1199 A.C., was less intolerant of the phallic Linga. The worship of Krishna forms the predominating element in Madhwa's cult, but images of Siva and Parvati are to be found in the temples set up by him, and it is said that his chief object was to reconcile the Sivites and the Vishnuvites. The principal shrine set up by him is that at Udipi in the South Kanara District, Madras Presidency. Subordinate to the temple at Udipi, there are eight monasteries in and near Kanara. The management of the Udipi temple, which is very ancient and largely endowed, is held by the heads of these eight monasteries in rotation for two years each. The Madhwas give the designation of heretic to both the Ramanujites and the Lingaits, the former being called Vishnu Pashandas, and the latter Shaiva Pashandas.

According to the philosophical tenets of the Madhwas the essence of the human soul is quite different from that of the divine soul, and they are, therefore, called Dwaitavadi or Dualists. They admit the existence of difference between the Divine Soul and the Universe, and between the human soul and the material world. Consistently with their doctrine of Dualism, they do not admit the possibility of the kind of *liberation* called

Nirvan, which is held by the Adwaitavadis to take place by the extinction of the human soul, and its absorption in the Divine Essence.

The Madhwas paint their foreheads in almost the same manner as the Sri Vaishnavas of the Vadagala class, the only difference being that the former have their central line painted black, and not in red or yellow as the Ramanujites. It has been already stated that the followers of Ramanuja are, when young, branded by their teachers with red-hot metallic stamps, having the figures of Krishna's conch shell and discus engraved on them. The Madhwas are subjected to this kind of torture and degradation, whenever they are visited by their Gurus. A member of any caste may be a Madhwa ; but only a Brahman can be a Guru or ecclesiastic. The Madhwa mendicants resemble the Saiva Dandis in every respect. Like the latter, they destroy their sacred thread at the time of their initiation, and shave off their hair at very short intervals. They put on also red garments like the Sivites, instead of the yellow and white garments usually worn by the other Vishnuvites. They imitate the Dandis to the extent also of carrying a staff and a water-pot.

Like the Ramanujites, the Madhwas are divided into two classes called the Vyaskuta and the Dasakuta. With regard to the latter, the following account is given by Mr. Narsimayangar in his report on the last Census of Mysore :—

This sect (the Dasakuta) has been gaining some notoriety of late years, and its followers protest that they believe and practise the truths and philosophy inculcated by Madhava, and that they are not different from the main body of their fellow-Dwaitas, or believers in Dualism. It is asserted, moreover, by them that as nearly all their religious literature was in Sanskrit, which was unknown to, and unintelligible by, the majority of the sect, certain devout personages had several centuries ago, in order to benefit the more ignorant of their countrymen, rendered into Kanarese hymns, songs, prayers, &c., in verse as well as prose, the tenets taught by Madhavacharya and amplified by his commentators. Their Kanarese religious literature is of considerable proportions, and among the authors are the well-known Purandar Das, Kanaka Das, Vijaya Das, &c. The word Dasa or servant is espoused by them as pre-eminently the servants

God. This body of the Madhvas is styled Dasakuta, in contradistinction to Vyaskuta, of which the members follow the Sanskritic style of rituals, &c.

Many of the Dasas are at the present day in the habit of going about with the tambourine and other musical instruments, singing Kanarase songs and hymns in honour of the Divine Being, and His manifestations in the Hindu Avatars. The sect presents much that is akin to the Tengali division of the Sri Vaishnavas, especially in the pre-eminence that is given to the vernacular versions of the Sanskrit sacred writings, which remain a sealed book to the majority of the congregation.—*Mysore Census Report*, 1891, Vol. XXV, p. 61.

CHAP. VII.—THE RAMANANDIS OR THE RAMATS OF NORTHERN INDIA.

THE success of Ramanuja and Madhava in the South led to similar experiments in the North. Ramanand, who organised the earliest of the Vishnuvite sects of Northern India, was very probably a Ramanujite in his early life. He is expressly described as having been so in the works of his school, and the story is confirmed very materially by several important coincidences between the doctrines and practices of the two sects. Both the sects call themselves Sri Vaishnavas, and the Ramats paint their foreheads in the very same manner as the Vadagala section of the Ramanujites. The most important point of difference between the two sects lies in the fact that the Ramats devote their worship mainly to Ram and Sita, and not to Vishnu or Laksmi. The Ramats do not attach any importance to the observance of seclusion in the cooking and eating of food. They have also some other distinguishing features which are of a minor character. For instance, while the initiatory *mantra* of a Ramanujite is *Sri Ramaya Namah,* that of the Ramats is only *Sri Ram.*

Regarding the personal history of Ramanand very little is known for certain, excepting that, during the latter years of his life, he lived in Benares at a place near the Panch Ganga Ghat. Formerly there was a monastery on the spot, but it is now marked only by a terrace built of stone.

Unlike Ramanuja, Ramanand directly admitted the lowest castes among his followers. Of his chief disciples Kabir was a Jolaha or Mahomedan weaver, and Rai Das* was a Chamar or shoemaker. The religion of Ramanand, though originally adopted by only the plebeian classes, has now within its fold many high caste Kanojia and Saroria Brahmans. The Ramats are very numerous in every part of the Gangetic valley from Hardwar to Rajmahal. The deity, who has the largest share of their devotions, is, as already stated, Ramchandra. Some worship Rama alone; but most of them pay equal homage to him and to his wife Sita. They have very large and richly endowed monasteries in almost every part of Northern India. In Bengal the majority of the Vaishnavas are Chaitanites. But there are, in this part of the country, many Ramat convents too, and the Vaishnavas, who are to be found in or near Calcutta with the Trifala† painted on their foreheads, are mainly Ramats. The clerical followers of Ramanand are divided into the following four classes :—

1. Achari.
2. Sanyasi.
3. Bairagi.
4. Khaki.

All these are supposed to lead a life of celibacy. The Acharis are Brahmans, and they enlist only Brahmans among their disciples. A man of any caste may be a Ramat Sanyasi, Bairagi or Khaki. The lower castes among the followers of Ramanand receive their initiatory *mantra* from these Sanyasis and Bairagis, and also from clerical Brahmans living the life of householders. There is considerable difference between the dresses usually worn by the three classes of celibates mentioned above. While silk and woollen garments

* From the name of this great disciple of Ramanand, the shoemaking caste generally designate themselves as Rui Das or Ui Das.

† Trifala is the popular name among the Hindustanis for the forehead mark of the Ramats consisting of three perpendicular lines, the central one of which is of red colour, and the two outer ones of white.

alone are considered as appropriate for the sacred person of an Achari, a Ramat Sanyasi will wear only cotton clothes stained red with ochre. The uniform of the latter is not very expensive, but he shaves and dresses himself very decently like the Sankarite Dandis. Among the Ramats there is a class called Khaki. These go about almost naked, smearing their bodies with ashes, and allowing their hair and nails to grow without limit. There is another class of Ramats called Bairagis who dress in the same manner as the Vaishnavas of Bengal, putting on a small piece of rag to cover the loins, and having an outer piece called Bahir Bas worn round the waist. The Ramat monks of this order have generally a large number of nuns attached to their convents, with whom they openly live as man and wife. The Ramat Sanyasis and Bairagis are not very strict about the caste rules, and they will usually eat cooked food given to them by a clean Sudra of any caste. The Ramats use necklaces and rosaries of basil beads like most of the other Vishnuvite sects. The non-Brahmanical Ramats accost each other by pronouncing "Rama, Rama." But when they have to address a Brahman, they use the usual expression "Paun Lagi," signifying "Thy feet are touched."

CHAP. VIII.—OTHER RAM-WORSHIPPING SECTS.

Mulluk Dasi.—The Mulluk Dasis are also worshippers of Ram and Sita. Their sect mark is a single red line on the forehead. Their principal monastery is at the village called Kara Manikpore on the river Ganges in the vicinity of Allahabad. Monasteries appertaining to the sect are to be found also at Benares, Allahabad, Lucknow, Ayodhya, Brindavan and Puri. Mulluk Das, the founder of this sect, lived in the seventeenth century. He was born at Kara, and he died at Puri.

Dadu Panthi.—This sect was founded by a man of a very low caste, named Dadu, who was originally a native of Ahmedabad, but who subsequently settled himself at a place called Naraina, about 40 miles towards the west of Jeypore. The followers of Dadu do not worship any image or any visible emblem of any deity. The repetition of the name of Rama is the only ritual that they have to observe. The Dadu Panthis do not paint their forehead, neither do they wear necklaces of any kind. The only peculiarity in their outfit is a four-cornered or round skull cap, with a tuft hanging behind. They are divided into three classes, namely, householders, mendicants and Naga soldiers. The Jeypore Raj had at one time a very large Naga army. The Nagas make very good soldiers.

The chief monastery of the Dadu Panthis is at the place called Naraina mentioned above. According to the authority of the *Dabistan*, Dadu was a contemporary of Akbar. The followers of Dadu believe that he did not die like ordinary men, but disappeared from the world in accordance with a message that he received from heaven. There is a small house on the hill of Naraina which marks the spot from which he ascended to heaven. The Dadu Panthis ordinarily burn their dead, but the more devout express a wish at the time of their death that their bodies might be kept exposed in some lonely place in order to afford a meal to the jackals and vultures.

Ram Sanehi.—This also is an offshoot of the Ramat sect. The founder of this order was one Ram Charan, who was born in the year 1718 at a village named Sura Sena within the territories of the Jeypore Raj. He was at first a Ramat, but he soon became a staunch opponent of idol worship, and the persecution to which he was, on that account, subjected by the local Brahmans, compelled him to leave the place of his birth. After travelling through various parts of India, he ultimately settled at Shahapur, the chief town of the Tributary State of Shahapur in Rajputana.

The Ram Sanehis do not worship images. Their religious services are to some extent similar to those of the Mahomedans. Five services are held every day in their shrines. In the morning the monks assemble first, then the male members of the laity, and last of all the females. Men and women are not allowed to worship at the same time. Of the two other services, one is held in the afternoon, and the other in the evening. Females are not allowed to attend on these occasions.

The Ram Sanehi mendicants are divided into two classes, called the Bidehi and the Mohini. The Bidehis go about completely naked. The Mohinis wear two pieces of cotton cloth dyed red in ochre. The mendicant's water-pot is made of wood, and he dines from off a stone or an earthen plate. The monks, who lead a life of celibacy, are the men who usually officiate as the priests of the sect; but householders and females are eligible for the service. The Ram Sanehis are not only strict vegetarians and teetotalers, but they have to abstain from every kind of intoxicating liquor and drug, including tobacco and opium.

A Hindu of any caste may be admitted to the Ram Sanehi sect. The baptism is effected by the chief of the monastery at Shahapur. The Ram Sanehis paint their forehead with a white perpendicular line. They shave their heads and wear necklaces of basil beads. When a man is admitted to the holy order, his name is changed, and his head is so shaved as to leave only a tuft of hair in the centre.

The moral discipline of the Ram Sanehis is said to be very strict. There are regular officers, attached to the chief monastery of the sect at Shahapur, who exercise supreme ecclesiastical jurisdiction over both the clergy and the laity, and who, when necessary, hold special courts for the trial of the delinquents. For controlling the morals of the laity, there are monks in every village who have jurisdiction to decide all petty cases. In cases of a serious nature, the accused person, whether he is a monk or a householder, is taken to Shahapur, and if found guilty by the ecclesiastical court there, then he is excommunicated, his necklace of basil beads being torn off and his head being shaved clean. Thenceforward the convict becomes incapable of worshipping in any temple appertaining to the sect, or of joining any dinner-party given by any member of it.

The Ram Sanehi sect has the largest following in Mewar and Alwar. Members of the sect are to be found also in Bombay, Gujrat, Surat, Haidrabad, Poona, Ahmedabad and Benares.

CHAP. IX.—THE NIMATS.

ACCORDING to a popular classification, the Vishnuvites are divided into the following four sects :—

1. **Sri Samprodaya, lit., the order of the goddess of wealth, who, according to Hindu mythology, is the consort of Vishnu, the creating god of the Hindu Triad. The founder of the Sri sect was Ramanuja.**
2. **Bramha Sampradaya, founded by Madhava.**
3. **Rudra Sampradaya, founded by Vallabha or some previous teacher of the same school.**
4. **Sanakadi Sampradaya, lit., the order of the saint named Sanaka. Nimat, the other name of this sect, is given to it from the fact of its having been founded by one Nimbaditya.**

An account of the first two sects has been given already. The Nimats have their head-quarters at Muttra, and have a considerable following in the districts round that town ; but they have no literature which they can call as their own, excepting, perhaps, the poems of Jayadev ; and they are fast being thrown into the shade by the Chaitanites and the Vallabhites.

The Nimats were apparently the first to insist upon the worship of Radha conjointly with that of Krishna. To this cult the Chaitanites and the Radha Vallabhites have given such impetus that there are very few Vishnuvite shrines now in Northern India in which an image of Radha is not associated with that of Krishna. The only Vishnuvite temple in Bengal in which Krishna's married wife Rukmini is associated with him on the altar, is perhaps that of *Rukmini Kanta Ji* or *Kantaji* in Dinajpur.

The superior of the Nimat monastery at Dhruva Kshetra near Mathura claims to be a descendant of

Nimbaditya. The Nimats, like some of the other Vaishnava sects, paint their foreheads with two perpendicular lines of Gopi Chandan; but instead of having red lines in the interior like a Sri Vaishnava or Ramat, the Nimat has a circular mark of black colour within the space enclosed by the white lines of Gopi Chandana. Jayadev, the author of the lascivious pastoral poem in Sanskrit called Gita Govind, was, it is said, a Nimat.

CHAP. X.—THE BALLAVACHARYA SECT.

The early Vishnuvite teachers inculcated the worship of Vishnu, either in his original form, or in the forms of Krishna and Ram, in which the preserving god of the Hindu Triad had incarnated among men in past ages. In paying homage to these, the earlier teachers associated with them their married wives Laksmi, Rukmini and Sita, respectively; and so the cults of the Ramanujas, Madhwas and Ramats were calculated to elevate the morality of their followers. Their systems could not, therefore, suit the policy of the later Vishnuvites, who were led by their success to play bolder games. They had apparently the same objects in view as the Sivites and the Tāntrics; but the phallic cults inculcated by the latter, though they became widespread, have very seldom yielded the particular result which they were meant to bring about. In any case, the Vishnuvites of the modern schools saw that they must invent some new machinery, if they were to encompass the same object. The Sivites called upon their followers to worship the male organ of generation. The Tāntrics inculcated the adoration of the female organ. The plan of campaigning prescribed for the Saiva ecclesiastic requires him to maintain an attitude of passiveness and indifference. He may assert every now and then that he is Siva. But he cannot go any further. The Tāntrics, who inculcate the worship of the female organ, may proceed in a more aggressive spirit. But in their essential nature the Tāntric and the

Sivite cults being both equally indecent, their ecclesiastics cannot ordinarily dare to explain their true nature or claim worship for themselves as living Sivas. Their religions, being thus very imperfectly understood by the people, have very seldom served the purposes for which they were meant. They have led men to worship stone and clay emblems, but nothing more real. The Vishnuvites avoided all material indecencies, and sought to corrupt the morals of men and women, not by obscene exhibitions, or by claiming undue familiarity on the plea of performing religious rites, but by legends and songs which might prove effective even from a distance by appealing to the imitative spirit of both men and women. The idea was first conceived by the authors of the *Bhagvat* and the *Bramha Vaivarta;* but it was perhaps either Nimbaditya or Chaitanya who first made organised attempts to reduce it to practice.

According to the chronological data obtainable from the literature of the Vishnuvite sects, Ballavacharya was the contemporary of Chaitanya. Both of them evidently followed some earlier teachers. Chaitanya was admittedly a Nimat, while with regard to the Ballavite sect, it is said that its original founder was a Brahman named Vishnu Swami, who communicated his doctrines to only Brahmanical ascetics. Vishnu Swami was succeeded by Jnana Deva, who was followed by Nama Deva and Trilochana, and they by Ballabha. The Ballabhites worship Krishna in the character and form of Bala Gopala, or cowherd boy. In consonance with this method of worship, they originally fixed their headquarters at Gokoola, the place where Krishna passed the years of his boyhood as the foster son of the cowherd Nand Ghosh. The Nimats and the Chaitanites exclude from their altar the married wives of Krishna, and, for the purposes of their adoration, associate with him the milkwoman Radha, who, according to the *Bramha Vaivarta* and the later Purāns, was the chief object of his attentions during his bachelorhood when he tended the cattle of his foster-parents at Brindavan. The Ballabhites worship Krishna as a cowherd boy, and do not usually associate with him any of his consorts married or unmarried.

The Bala Gopala worship practised by the Ballabhites seems to be of an earlier date than the Radha worship favoured by the Nimats and Chaitanites. It is true that Ballava and Chaitanya were contemporaries; but the historical facts referred to above go very far to show that the faiths connected with their names did not actually originate with them, and if Radha worship originated with Nimbaditya, and Bala Gopala worship with Vishnu Swami, there can be no chronological objection to the view that the latter preceded the former. The positive evidence in favour of this view of their sequence is afforded by their very nature. The Bala Gopala worship is an innocent cult, the proclamation of which required no preliminary preparation of the ground. But Radha worship, though sanctioned by some of the Purāns, could not have possibly been floated without very serious misgivings as to its ultimate success, and it seems more reasonable to suppose that Bala Gopala worship prepared the way for the introduction of Radha worship, than that this last phase of the Vishnuvite cult had come into existence at an earlier period.

Ballabha was born in the year 1479 A.D. His father, Lakman Bhatta, was a Velnad Brahman of Telingana, whose original home was Kankarkam, near Raipore, but who had settled in Benares some time before the birth of Ballabha. The prophet had his education in the holy city where his father lived, and, as a matter of course, became a great Sanskrit scholar at a very early age. At that time almost the whole of Northern India was under the rule of the Mahomedans, and the kingdom of Vizianagaram in the Deccan was perhaps the most powerful Hindu monarchy then in existence. Ballabha had a near relative in the service of King Krishna Dev, of Vizianagram, and was naturally attracted to the court of that great monarch. In all probability, the adventure did not prove very successful. At any rate, Ballabha could not make a permanent impression on the king or his courtiers, though, if we are to believe the accounts given of the prophet's life by his followers, he vanquished in argumentative contest all the Sankarite courtiers of Krishna Dev, and made the king himself one of his followers. In the course of his peregrinations, Ballabha visited Ujin, Muttra and Chunar, and the spots where he rested, in or near these towns, are still pointed out as his *Baithak*. During the course of his travels, he was on more than one occasion visited by the great god Krishna, *in propria persona*, and directed by him to marry and to set up a shrine for him at Gokool. He complied with both these injunctions, and his descendants for some generations remained at Gokool in charge of the temples founded by him. At a later period, the persecutions of Arungzebe compelled the then representatives of his family to leave Gokool for good with their idols, and seek for refuge in the Hindu kingdom of Udaipura.

"When Arungzebe proscribed Kanai, and rendered his shrines impure throughout Vrij, Rana Raj Sing offered the heads of one hundred thousand Rajputs for his service," and the god was conducted by the route of Kotah and Rampurah to Mewar. An omen decided the spot of his future residence. As he journeyed to go in the capital of the Sesodia the charriot wheel sunk deep into the earth and defied extrication: upon which the *Sookuni* (augur) interpreted the pleasure of the god, that he desired to dwell there. This circumstance occurred at an inconsiderable village called Siarh, in the fief of Dailwara, one of the sixteen nobles of Mewar. Rejoiced at this decided manifestation of favour, the chief hastened to make a perpetual gift of the village and its lands, which was speedily confirmed by the patent of the Rana. Nathji (the god) was removed from his car, and, in due time, a temple was erected for his reception, when the hamlet of Siarh became the town of Nathdwara, which now contains many thousand inhabitants, who, reposing under the especial protection of the god, are exempt from every mortal tribunal. The site is not uninteresting, nor devoid of the means of defence. To the east it is shut in by a cluster of hills, and to the westward flows the Bunas, which nearly bathes the extreme points of the hills. Within these bounds is the sanctuary (sirna) of Kuniya where the criminal is free from pursuit; nor dare the rod of justice appear on the mount, or the foot of the pursuer pass the stream; neither within it can blood be spilt, for the pastoral Kanai delights not in offerings of this kind. The territory contains within its precincts abundant space for the town, the temple and the establishments of the priests, as well as for the numerous resident worshippers and the constant influx of votaries from the most distant regions who find abundant shelter from the noontide blaze in the grooves of tamarind, peepul and simal where they listen to the mystic hymns of Joyadeva. Here those whom ambition has cloyed, superstition unsettled, satiety disgusted, commerce ruined, or crime disquieted, may be found as ascetic attendants on the mildest of the gods of India.

The dead stock of Krishna's shrine is augmented chiefly by those who are happy to barter "the wealth of Ormus and of Ind" for the intercessional prayers of the high priest and his passport to Haripur, the heaven of Hari. From the banks of the Indus to the mouth of the Ganges, from the coasts of the Peninsula to the shores of the Red Sea, the gifts of gratitude or of fear are lavishly poured in. The safe arrival of a galleon from Safala or Arabia produced as much to the shrine as to the insurance office, for Kanai is the St. Nicholas of the Hindu navigator, as was Apollo to the Greek and Celtic sailors. A storm yields in proportion to its violence, or to the nerve of the owner of the vessel. The appearance of a long-denied heir might deprive him of half his patrimony, and force him to lament his parent's distrust in natural causes; while the accidental mistake of touching forbidden food on particular fasts requires expiation, not by flagellation or seclusion, but by the penance of the purse.—Tod's *Rajasthan*, Vol. I, p. 553 *et seq.*

The shrine of Srinath at Nath Dwara is the principal shrine of the Ballabhite sect. Besides this, which may be regarded as their head-quarters station, they have seven other shrines within the territories of the Hindu Rajas of Rajputana, and in the adjacent British districts. The names and local habitations of these idols* are given below:—

1. Nanita ... Natha Dwara.
2. Mathura Nath ... Kotah.
3. Dwarka Nath ... Kankerwoli.
4. Gokool Nath ... Jeypur.
5. Yadu Nath ... Surat.
6. Vithal Nath ... Kotah.
7. Madanamohan ... Jeypur.

All these idols are said to have been originally discovered by Ballava by some kind of miracle or other, and to have been set up for worship by him in or near Mathura and Gokool, from whence they were removed

* See Tod's *Rajasthan*, Vol. I, p. 529.

to Rajputana, at or about the same time as Nathji. They are all in the possession of the descendants of Ballabha, who are venerated as gods by their followers, and usually called Maharajas. They are called also Gokoolastha Gossains from the fact of their having been residents of Gokool before their migration to Rajputana. Of the five great Vishnuvite prophets of modern times, namely, Ramanuja, Madhava, Ramanand, Ballabha and Chaitanya, the first two are in possession of the Deccan. The faith of the third prevails throughout the greater part of Northern India, and while Ballabha has undisputed mastery over the western provinces of India, Chaitanya has very nearly the same position in Bengal. Of the shrines appertaining to their sects, the Ramanujite temple at Sri Rangam and the Ballabhite temple at Nath Dwara are perhaps the wealthiest. Ramanuja and Madhava have the highest castes among their followers. Ramanand admitted within his fold both the high castes and the low castes ; and while Ballabha, with an eye to the main chance, enrolled chiefly the mercantile castes, the Chaitanites never refuse their ministration to any one, however low or degraded.

The Ballabhites do not admit to their order such low castes as the Dhobi, Mochi, Darzi and the Napit. The clean Sudra castes, such as the Kāyasthas, the Kunbi, the Abhir, and the Malis are admitted as disciples by the Ballabhite Maharajas.

The Bala Gopala worship practised by the Ballabhites is apparently innocent enough. But its inevitable tendency, where conjoined with recitations from *Bhagavat* and *Jayadev*, is to develop into all the immoralities of the Radha worship. At any rate, serious charges of that nature are usually brought against the Ballabhacharya Gossains, and were proved to some extent in the celebrated case of the Bombay Maharajas, which came before the Supreme Court of Bombay on the 26th January 1862. The following is an extract from the judgment of Sir Matthew Sausse in the above case :—

> The Maharajas have been sedulous in identifying themselves with the god Krishna by means of their own writings and teachings and by the similarity of ceremonies of worship and addresses which they require to be offered to themselves by their followers. All songs connected with the god Krishna, which were brought before us, were of an amorous character, and it appeared that songs of a corrupting and licentious tendency, both in ideas and expressions, are sung by young females to the Maharaja, upon festive occasions, in which they are identified with the god in his most licentious aspect. In these songs, as well as stories, both written and traditional, which latter are treated as of a religious character in the sect, the subject of sexual intercourse is most prominent. Adultery is made familiar to the minds of all ; it is nowhere discouraged or denounced ; but, on the contrary, in some of the stories, those persons who have committed that great moral and social offence are commended.
> *History of the Bombay Maharajas*, p. 142.

The observations made in the above must, I fear, be admitted to be well grounded. But they do not prove that there is any immorality in actual practice. The corrupting influence of a religion, that can make its female votaries address amorous songs to their spiritual guides, must be very great. But the weapon, though devised with diabolical cleverness, must generally fall short of the mark. For the sake of maintaining his character for sanctity, and to avoid making himself too cheap, the Maharaja has to keep himself at a distance and to be in a dignified attitude. For every act of condescension the Maharajas expect a regular fee, and that they could not have exacted if they mixed too freely with their worshippers. Their tariff is as given below:—

For homage by sight, Rs. 5.
For homage by touch, Rs. 20.
For the honor of washing the Maharaja's foot, Rs. 35.
For swinging him, Rs. 40.
For rubbing sweet ungents on his body, Rs. 42.
For being allowed to sit with him on the same couch, Rs. 60.
For being closeted with him in the same room, from Rs. 50 to Rs. 500.
For eating pan from the mouth of the Maharaja, Rs. 17.
For the privilege of dancing with him, Rs. 100 to Rs. 200.
For drinking the water in which he has bathed, Rs. 17.

Whether the privileges of sitting with the Maharaja, or of being closeted with him, are ever sought by any one is a matter as to which I have no definite information. But this much is well known—that, in order to maintain their dignity, the Maharajas usually keep their followers at more than arm's length. In fact, a careful survey of the religions of the Hindus on the one hand, and their practices on the other, would lead any impartial and unbiased enquirer to the conclusion that the moral nature of the Hindus, as a nation, is, generally speaking, far superior to most of their religions. The cleverest devices of their prophets have therefore fallen flat upon them.

The Ballabhite method of worship is called Pushni Marga, or the road of nourishing food. This name is given to the faith on account of its forbidding ascetism, and insisting upon the doctrine that the spiritual progress of the soul is possible only by keeping the body and its powers in a sound condition.

CHAP. XI.—THE CHAITANITE SECT OF BENGAL.

CHAITANYA, the founder of the Vishnuvite sect of Bengal, which is now spreading in every direction, was a high caste Vaidika Brahman of Nadiya, the chief seat of Sanskrit learning in Bengal, and at one time its metropolis. He was born in the year 1484 of the Christian era. His father, Jagannath Misra, was originally a native of Sylhet, and probably came to Nadiya, at a very early age, as a student. Jagannath was of the Bharadwaj Gotra, and his family professed the Sama Veda. Being a high caste Kulin of his clan, and a very eligible bridegroom, a resident Vaidika Brahman of Nadiya gave him in marriage his daughter Sachi. After his marriage Jagannath permanently settled in Nadiya, and was before long blessed with two male children, the eldest of whom was named Bishwarup, and the younger, who subsequently became the famous Vishnuvite prophet of Bengal, received the names of Nimai and Bishwambhar from his parents. Bishwarup went away from home at a very early age, and died somewhere near Sri Rangam on the Kaveri. Jagannath did not long survive the mendicancy of his eldest son, and Nimai, the younger, was for some time the only source of solace to his bereaved mother. It is said that he became a great Sanskrit scholar at a very early age, and his admirers go so far as to assert that he became the rival of the famous Ragunath Siromani, the founder of the Nya philosophy of Nadiya.

That he was a very clever scholar may certainly be admitted. But there are very strong grounds for questioning the assertion that he was superior to, or even the equal of, the great giants of Sanskrit scholarship that lived in his time. The ambition of every successful student of Nadiya is to be a professor of his own special branch of learning in his native town, and one who has the least chance of attaining any distinction as a teacher at Nadiya will never go to another part of the country to set up a grammar school. But, in the biographies of Chaitanya, it is distinctly stated that he left home after his first marriage, and for a time set up a school somewhere in East Bengal. Whether this adventure proved successful or not is a matter as to which it is not necessary to hazard any conjecture. Suffice it to state that he returned home within about two years, and that he never thought of going back to his place of sojourn. At the time when Chaitanya left Nadiya for East Bengal he was only twenty years old. That was certainly not the age at which any one, in the ordinary course of things, ever has been, or ever can be, a great Pandit. When he came back to Nadiya, his age was only twenty-two, and, as from that time he gave up his studies, the story that he became the rival of Raghunath and Raghunandan cannot be accepted as having any element of probability in it. As the most intelligent students of Nadiya are not able to finish their scholastic career before the age of thirty, it seems that Chaitanya never attempted to study law or philosophy, and that his learning was confined to Sanskrit grammar only. In fact, in his biographies, it is distinctly stated, in some places, that his fame as a Sanskrit scholar rested only upon his knowledge of grammar.

During his absence in East Bengal, his first wife Laksmi Priya died of snake-bite, and he took a second wife named Vishnu Priya. Up to this time he had evidently no intention of leaving home as a mendicant. In his twenty-third year, he went to Gaya in order to discharge the duties which, as a pious Hindu son, he owed to the soul of his deceased father. This pilgrimage shows again that, at the time of its performance, the son of Jagannath and Sachi had no idea of his being the great god Vishnu himself, for if he knew himself to be so, he could have no business to go to Gaya for offering pindas at the footprints of Gadādhar. At Gaya the pilgrim became the disciple of a Sankarite mendicant, and from that time a great change came over him.

After his return to Nadiya, he very nearly gave up study and teaching, and organised the kind of religious exercise and singing called Sankirtan which was the main secret of the rapid spread of his faith. The Sakti worshippers then predominated in Nadiya, as they do still to some extent. For fear of them, and of the Mahomedan Governor of the town, Chaitanya's Sankirtans were at first performed *in camera*, in the house of one of his collaborateurs named Sri Vasha. At a later period Chaitanya ordered every one of his followers to celebrate the Sankirtan in his own house. The Sakti worshippers could not tolerate such uproar, and upon their complaining to the Kazi, he not only caused the musical instruments in one of the houses to be broken, but strictly prohibited the repetition of the nuisance. Chaitanya determined to set at defiance the order of the Governor. He organised three strong Sankirtan parties, and, at the head of one of them, marched to the very door of the Kazi's house. The gate had been shut up. But, in response to Chaitanya's message, the Kazi came out, and, before long, they became staunch friends. Chaitanya took the Kazi to task for his un-Mahomedan conduct in not properly receiving a guest at his door. The Kazi, thus put to shame, was obliged to apologise. The result was a sweet reconciliation between the parties which their co-religionists might now-a-days study and imitate with advantage to all. After securing the friendship of the

Mahomedan Governor of the town, Chaitanya carried on his Sankirtans with redoubled vigour. His mania for Krishna worship was now fast developing. He not only held Sankirtans, but organised an amateur theatrical party in which he himself played the part of Rukmini, the chief of the married wives of Krishna. These proceedings made the condition of his young and impressionable mind akin to madness. As he was one day uttering, in a theatrical mood, the words, "O the milkmaids! O the milkmaids!" a Sanskrit student of the town took him to task for his eccentricity. At this his irritation was such that he actually pursued his critic with a stick. Thereupon the Sakti worshipping Pandits of Nadiya and their pupils got that pretext for persecuting him, which they wanted. When the young prophet thus made his native town too hot for him, he determined to leave it for good, and to enter one of the monastic orders founded by Sankara Acharya. At this time he was visited by a Sankarite monk, named Keshav Bharati, who, after taking him to Katwa, caused him to be duly initiated as a member of the holy order to which he belonged.

The account of Chaitanya's early life given above includes all the material facts, excepting only the miraculous portions. The circumstances that are referred to in his biographies, as the causes of his becoming a mendicant, are intelligible enough. Whether there were other causes or not to lead him in the same direction, is a matter as to which history does not furnish the necessary materials for a satisfactory answer. Admitting that his personal character was blameless, and that the only motive which actuated him was the supersession of the beastly cult of the Tāntrics by Krishna worship, it is still difficult to regard him in the light of a great reformer. What he sought to abolish was bad indeed. But it cannot be said that what he gave in lieu of it was unexceptionable. We may well be grateful to him for enforcing teetotalism and vegetarianism among his followers. But to persons unbiased by sectarian feelings, there can be little to choose between a Tāntric's orgies, and a Vaishnava's imitations of Krishna's flirtations. The utmost that can be said in favour of Chaitanya is that he looked upon the illicit amours of Krishna in a spiritual sense, and that he never meant that they should be imitated by his followers for the gratification of their sensuality. But his whole life shows that though he was apparently mad at times, yet there was in him a statesmanlike genius which is very rare in this world. To suppose that he never could anticipate the results which are now found to arise out of the cult that he inculcated, is the height of absurdity. The veriest tyro ought to be able to foresee what the fruits of a tree must be that owes its existence to seeds supplied by the *Bhagvat* and the *Brahma Vaivarta*. Admitting that Chaitanya's own character was a pure one, and that he could have no motives to reap any benefit for himself, it does not necessarily follow that he was not actuated by a reckless ambition to spite, at any cost, his rivals and persecutors among his fellow-castemen of Nadiya. For attracting followers, it was certainly quite as necessary then as now to hold out some inducements. And is there anything in the life of Chaitanya to show that his standard of morality was much higher than that of the secular rulers, statesmen and generals who are known to have sacrificed their principles for the sake of their party? If some of the greatest of generals have been capable of giving direct encouragement to immorality, in order to keep Tommy Atkins in good humour, a similar trick practised by a sect founder need not cause any surprise at all. The safest and most reasonable view seems to be that the prophets and incarnations that we have had were neither better nor worse men than political adventurers. When forced by necessity, both are capable of doing a great many things that cannot be justified on any principle of morality.

Chaitanya admitted not only the lowest castes, but even Mahomedans, among his followers. Three of his principal disciples, namely, Rup, Sanatan and Haridas, were Islamites. Rup and Sanatan were originally Brahmans, but were apparently compelled to espouse Mahomedanism against their will. They held very high offices in the service of Hossain Shah, the then King of Bengal. They quitted the service of their king, and became followers of Chaitanya, with the view apparently of being re-admitted into Hindu society. Haridas was a poor Mahomedan who had suffered much by his heresy, and whom Chaitanya had to keep near him at all times for the purpose of protecting him from the persecutions of his co-religionists. To avoid offending the prejudices of his other followers, he kept Haridas at a slight distance. But there are various incidents in the life of Chaitanya which prove conclusively that he dearly loved the Yavana. At the present time, the Chaitanite teachers are never found to minister to any Mahomedan. But they do not deny the benefit of their services to any of the low castes that can pay them adequately. Even Chamars, Doms, Bauris and Bagdis are sometimes admitted within their fold. Such action on their part may by some be regarded as evidence of a liberal spirit. But the same view cannot certainly be taken of their enrolling the unfortunates of the towns among their spiritual constituents.

Among the Chaitanites, as among almost all the other sects, there are both mendicants and regular householders. The leading men among the Chaitanite householders are the descendants of the immediate disciples and apostles of the prophet. They are looked down upon by the aristocratic Hindus as persons who live by trading on the rejected elements of pure Brahmanism. But some of them have almost princely incomes from the contributions of their disciples and the emoluments of the shrines of which they are the owners. The majority of the Gossains of Nadiya are descendants of the father of Vishnupria, the second wife of Chaitanya. These so-called Gossains are not recognised as such in any authoritative work of the sect, and in fact they are Sakta Brahmans partially converted to the Chaitanite faith on account of its lucrativeness, but yet conducting themselves now and then as Sakti worshippers, except when taking their parts in the service of the great Chaitanite shrine, of which they are the hereditary proprietors. Among the followers of Chaitanya, the highest positions were held by Adwaita and Nityananda. They were called the two Prabhus or Lords, while Chaitanya himself was called the Maha Prabhu or the Great Lord. Adwaita was a Bārendra Brahman of Santipore, where a large number of his descendants are still living. Nityananda was a Brahman of Rarhiya clan. He was a native of the district of Birbhoom, and was, it seems, a Nimat Vaishnava of the school of Jayadev, who had his head-quarters in the villages of Kenduvilla, in the same district. It was perhaps Nityanand's influence that made Chaitanya a Radha-worshipping Vishnuvite. Nityanand's descendants are to be found chiefly in Calcutta and in a village called Khardaha, near Barrackpore. Next to that of the two Prabhus mentioned above, there was a grade which consisted of six members called Gossains. These were not all Brahmans. But their descendants are highly revered.

Among the so-called mendicants (Vairagis) of the Chaitanite sect, there are both males and females. The males are called Babaji, and the females Mataji. The number of real ascetics among them is very small, if not actually *nil*. The majority of the Babajis and the Matajis openly live as husbands and wives, the only difference being that the former dress like ascetics, and the latter like widows. Some of the Babajis pretend to be Brikat, or men disgusted with the world. But these are generally the men who are most notorious for profligacy. They live in monasteries, and affect such hatred of the female class that they cook their food with their own hands, and do not allow any member of the softer sex to enter their kitchens. But the vow of celibacy is against nature, and it need hardly be observed that very few are able to maintain it.

The Chaitanites are teetotalers and very inoffensive people. The poorer among the mendicants live by begging a handful of rice from door to door. There are a few among the ascetics who have rich disciples, and have incomes on which they can manage to live decently. These men spend a large part of what they earn in building and improving monasteries, and in feeding pilgrims. Sometimes they happen to have very rich men among their guests, and these not unoften make very liberal contributions to their monasteries. In Nadiya, the birthplace of Chaitanya, there are several very flourishing monasteries where the Vishnuvite pilgrims and sojourners are treated as honoured guests, and provided with both food and shelter. The Superiors of these establishments have a very high position in their sect, though the alien rulers of the country have been led somehow to treat them as lodging house-keepers, and to subject them to a tax as such. The humiliation is felt by them very keenly, and it is much to be regretted that these leading Divines of one of the most important sects in India should be so treated for a paltry revenue of about £40 per annum.

The majority of the Chaitanite Babajis are of the clean Sudra castes, the Kāyasthas among them having generally the highest position, however much they may profess equality. The male element of the monastic orders consist to some extent of childless persons and persons who have suffered such bereavements as to make their life a burden to them. These are generally the most respectable members in their community. There are among them many bad characters too. If proper enquiries be made, it may appear that they have in their society many ex-convicts, criminals who have eluded the pursuit of the police, and persons who have been excommunicated by their castemen for unholy love-making. The ranks of the Chaitanites, as of many other sects, are swelled also by bachelors and widowers unable to get a bride for marriage in orthodox form.

The Chaitanite nuns are recruited chiefly from the superannuated unfortunates of the towns. The order is joined also by some of the unchaste widows of the lower classes.

The dress of the Chaitanite monks consists of the usual *lenguti* and girdle, with a *bahir bas* or outer garment, which is a piece of cotton cloth without border and about two yards in length. The *bahir bas* is sometimes dyed yellow by means of turmeric. But generally the garments of the Chaitanite monks are of white colour. Their dress, however, does not give to them the respectable appearance that is imparted by the red garments of the Sankarite Dandis and Parama Hansas. The Chaitanites have great regard for the basil plant, and not only are their necklaces and rosaries made of basil beads, but they eat basil leaves with every article of food and drink.

The Chaitanites paint their foreheads, in different manners, according to the directions of their teachers. There are always the usual perpendicular lines of the Vishnuvite. But at the bottom there is something like a bamboo leaf or basil leaf. The usual painting material is the faint yellow of Gopi Chandan. The Chaitanites paint not only their foreheads, but several other parts of their body. They do not brand themselves like the Ramanujites or the Madhavites. But by means of engraved metallic stamps immersed in a solution of Gopi Chandan, they imprint daily on their arms and breasts the names of their deities. By such odd demonstrations of their devoutness, and especially by painting the name "Gora" on their arms and body, they make themselves the butt of a great deal of ridicule. The word Gora is a corrupted form of the Sanskrit word "goura," which means yellow, and is not only one of the many names of Chaitanya, but is applied also to the English soldiers of the British Indian Army, as contra-distinguished from the Kala or the black sepoy soldiers. From this double sense of the word Gora, the point of the joke that is usually cracked, at the cost of a painted Chaitanite, may be easily understood. As the Highland regiments are called *Nangta Gora* in India, a Brahman wag would ask the Babaji to paint that expression on his body, instead of having on it the word Gora alone unqualified by the adjective *Nangta* or naked.

Of all the great teachers of the world no one has done more to popularize religion than Chaitanya. As, on the one hand, a Chaitanite teacher need not either be a scholar or an eloquent speaker, so, on the other, anybody may at any time, and at any place, practise the cult. The operation is simplicity itself. The devout Chaitanite need not have a priest by his side for performing his worship. He has only to paint his body and to count his beads. The business does not require any elaborate preparation, or knowledge of Sanskrit liturgy. The painting materials and the rosary of the Chaitanite are all his stock-in-trade, and these are so cheap and so handy that the poorest can afford to have them by his side at all times. The most potent engine invented by Chaitanya for spreading his religion is the musical procession called Sankirtan. The Hindu temples are places for silently offering flowers, money and other acceptable presents to the presiding deities. In no Hindu town is there any such place as a Christian church, or a Mahomedan mosque, where a priest might deliver a sermon. Then, again, to attract an audience by an impressive speech requires a kind of power which is very rare. But a Sankirtan party for patrolling the streets may be organised without any difficulty, and is generally far more effective than a sermon, however eloquent.

Chaitanya's object, like that of Buddha, was to attract an army of followers anyhow. But the prophet of Nadiya adopted a method which was far better calculated to serve his purpose than that of any other religious leader, ancient or modern. Buddha neglected the laity, and preached a religion which was very far from being intelligible to ordinary men. Chaitanya taught that Bhakti, or fervent devotion, was the only road towards God, and that Bhakti was of the following kinds :—

1. The devotion of a servant to his master.
2. Do. friend to a friend.
3. Do. parent to a child.
4. Do. lady to her lover.

Chaitanya recommended Radha worship, and taught that the best form of devotion was that which Radha, as the beloved mistress of Krishna, felt for him. Chaitanya's cult is therefore called the Bhakti marga, or the road of fervent devotion, as contra-distinguished from the Jnan marga of the learned Sanskritists, the Yoga marga of the poor illiterate Yogis, the Karma marga of the priestly Brahmans, and the Pushni * marga of the Ballavites. To persons incapable of cherishing such feelings, Chaitanya recommended the repeated utterance of the names of Krishna and Radha. Such practice gives an occupation to votaries not inclined to think or work hard, and enables them to obtain a high character for piety at a very little cost.

The most important feature in Chaitanya's cult is the rejection of esoteric methods. The great Vishnuvite prophet of Bengal does not ask his followers to conceal anything, or to pretend to be what they are not. In these respects the Chaitanite cult differs very materially from the Tāntric faith.

Before the time of Chaitanya, Mathura was the chief centre of Krishna worship, and Brindavan, the scene

* See p. 458, *ante*.

of Krishna's flirtations with the milk-maids, was actually a forest. Chaitanya, with his followers Rup and Sanatan, not only reclaimed that place, but after identifying the sacred spots in it which are specially named in the Purāns, caused those big shrines to be built which formed the nucleus for the town that the place has now developed into.

In the birthplace of Chaitanya, a temple for worshipping his image was set up, it is said, in his lifetime, by his second wife, Vishnu Priya Devi. The temple itself was washed away, at the end of the last century, by the adjoining river Bhagirathi. But the image had perhaps become valuable property, and was preserved by the descendants of Vishnu Priya's father, although they were then staunch Saktas. During the palmy days of the Sakta Rajas of Nadiya, the idol had, however, to be kept concealed. But when the celebrated Ganga Govind Sing became, by the favour of Hastings, the most powerful man in the country, he successfully prevented the Nadiya Rajas from persecuting the Chaitanites. A splendid shrine was built for the old image which had been, for a long time, kept concealed by the Gossains. Other shrines sprang up rapidly, and the Chaitanites are now about to be numerically the predominating element in the population of Nadiya. Ganga Govind himself built some splendid temples in the suburban village of Ram Chandrapore to the north-west of the present town. But these temples were washed away by the Bhagirathi in the time of Lala Babu, the grandson of Ganga Govinda. Lala Babu made himself famous by becoming a Chaitanite mendicant. But instead of attempting to build new temples in or near Nadiya, he adopted the more ambitious programme of making Brindavan his head-quarters. He built a magnificent temple there, and, by affecting a zeal for restoring to the locality its primeval condition, he managed to acquire, free of charge, almost all the villages which formed the scene of Krishna's sports. Nadiya has since then been neglected by the descendants of Ganga Govind. But, even without their patronage, the Chaitanite cult is now, under the ægis of British rule, flourishing in its birthplace. The saying that a prophet is never honoured in his own country enshrines an eternal truth, although it sounds somewhat paradoxical. But it is only a particular case of the obvious truth embodied in the adage which says that no man can be a hero to his *valet de chambre*. Nearly four hundred years have passed since Chaitanya left Nadiya for good. His highest ambition at that time was, according to his biographers, to make himself entitled to be treated with respect by the Brahmans of his native town. The Nadiya people, from generation to generation, continued to hate him. But just now there is a turn in the tide. The large incomes cleared by the owners of the Chaitanite shrines, have opened the eyes of the Sakta Brahmans of the town to the advantages of the new cult, and already a good many of them are to be found with necklaces of basil wood on their necks to denote that they are Chaitanites in faith. Some of these new converts have already opened Chaitanite shrines, and if these become successful, as they now promise to be, there are likely to be more converts and more Chaitanite shrines. If the great prophet could now visit his birthplace, he might not yet receive that homage from his fellow-castemen which was the highest object of his ambition at the beginning of his ministry. But what he would find would far exceed his most sanguine expectations. The sect that he organised has developed into a gigantic body which threatens to throw into shade the representatives of his old enemies, if not to make them all humble followers.

CHAP. XII.—THE SWAMI NARAYAN SECT OF GUJRAT.

THE Swami Narayan sect, which is fast gaining ground in Gujrat, was founded by a Brahman of Rohilkhand, who was apparently a Sankarite ascetic in his youth. His monastic name was Sahajanand, but he is now known by the name of Swami Narayan, which he took up when he set himself up as a Vishnuvite teacher. He left his home in the year 1800, and, in the course of his peregrinations, repaired to Gujrat, with the object apparently of visiting the places of pilgrimage in the province. While there, he was led to place himself under a Guru, named Ramanand Swami, with whom he resided for some time in Junagarh, and afterwards at Ahmedabad. At the latter place, Sahajanand, by his learning and fascinating manners, drew round himself such a large army of disciples as to excite the jealousy of the local Brahmans and magnates. To avoid being persecuted by them, he removed to the village of Jetalpur, twelve miles to the south of Ahmedabad. Even here he was not allowed to remain in peace. On the pretence that there might be a collision between his followers and the other Hindus of the locality, he was arrested by the officials of the Gaikwar and thrown into prison. This unjust and cruel treatment roused popular sympathy in his favour, and served only to increase his influence. Verses were published extolling his merits, and pronouncing curses against his persecutors. The result was that they were before long obliged to release him. Thereupon he retired with his followers to Wartal, then a small village, now a town, in the Kaira District of the Bombay Presidency. He had now arrived at the stage in his prophetic career, when it was necessary for him to build some temples and convents for giving a local habitation and footing to his cult. His popularity and fame were then at their height, and there could not be any difficulty in raising the necessary funds.

The religion of Swami Narayan is a mixture of Laksmi worship and Radha worship, as would appear from the fact that of his two principal temples at Wartal, one is dedicated to Narayan and Laksmi, and the other to Radha and Krishna. The worship of Krishna, in his character of Ranchor or fight-quitter, being very common in Gujrat, an image of the deity, representing the part that he played in quitting Mathura is associated with those of Laksmi and Narayan in the principal shrine. An image of Swami Narayan himself is similarly associated with those of Krishna and Radha in the second temple. The town of Ahmedabad has also similar shrines of the Swami sect. In the Vallabhite sect, the Swami had very powerful enemies to deal with. Their power was so firmly established that it was no easy work to oust them, or even to attain a position of rivalry by their side. The Swami, therefore, proceeded very cautiously, and the same spirit still characterises not only his representatives at Wartal and Ahmedabad, but also his monks. The result is that though the Vallabhacharis have not yet lost much of the ground appropriated by them, and are yet in full possession of the middle classes, including the Baniyas, the Kunbis, the Ahirs and the Kāyasths, yet the superior morality of the Swami Narayan has seriously undermined the power of the Maharajas, and there are signs that their influence is waning. The Swami Narayan sect is, on the contrary, in the full vigour of youthful growth. The middle classes being in the possession of the Vallabhites, the Swami, from the necessity of his position, was obliged to admit to his faith the low castes such as the Dhobi, the Mochi, the Darzi and the Napit, who were rejected by the Vallabhites. But the Swami did not, on that account, fall very low in the estimation of his countrymen. He maintained his dignity by keeping the unclean castes at arm's length, and by ordaining that nowhere, except in Jagannath, shall cooked food or water be accepted from them, though it be the remains of an offering to Krishna. Thus, while the Swami secured for his sect the adhesion of the low castes, he succeeded in maintaining for it a character for respectability that rendered it possible to attract followers from even the highest castes. The total strength of the sect is at present about 200,000 souls. But the rule being that every person admitted to it should try to bring in at least six others, its number is fast increasing. As in almost every other Hindu sect, there are among the followers of Swami two classes of men, namely, mendicants and householders. The number of mendicants exceeds 1,000. They are bound by their vows to live a life of celibacy. They serve as missionaries, and, in their proselytizing work, usually itinerate in pairs to cheer, support and watch each other. While at head-quarters they live in the convents attached to their shrines. They have a regular manual of instructions and moral precepts which they distribute among the people in the manner of the Christian missionaries.

The Swami Narayanis are required to wear two rosaries made of basil stems, one for Krishna and the other for Radha. The forehead mark of the sect is like the letter U with a circular spot in the centre representing *Teeka*. The females have to paint a circular mark with red powder of saffron. The mendicants of the sect wear the salmon-coloured dress of ascetics.

Bishop Heber, in the course of one of his tours in Western India, had an interview with Swami Narayan, and the following is an extract from the interesting account that he has left of it :—

About eleven o'clock, I had the expected visit from Svami-Narayana. The holy man was a middle-sized, thin, plain-looking person, about my own age, with a mild and diffident expression of countenance, but nothing about him indicative of any extraordinary talent. He came in somewhat different style from all I had expected, having with him nearly two hundred horsemen. When I considered that I had myself an escort of more than fifty horse I could not help smiling, though my sensations were in some degree painful and humiliating at the idea of two religious teachers meeting at the head of little armies, and filling the city which was the scene of this interview with the rattling of quivers, the clash of shields, and the tramp of the war-horse. Had our troops been opposed to each other, mine, though less numerous, would have been doubtless far more effective, from the superiority of arms and discipline. But in moral grandeur what a difference there was between his troops and mine! Mine neither knew me nor cared for me, though they escorted me faithfully. The guards of Svami-Narayana were his own disciples and enthusiastic admirers, men who had voluntarily repaired to hear his lessons, who now took a pride in doing him honour, and who would cheerfully fight to the last drop of blood rather than suffer a fringe of his garment to be handled roughly. In my own parish of Hodnet there were once, perhaps, a few honest countrymen who felt something like this for me, but how long a time must elapse before a Christian Minister in India can hope to be thus loved and honoured? —Chap. XXV.

CHAP. XIII—MIRA BAI.

THE name of Mira Bai is highly revered among the Vishnuvites of Western India, and especially among the Vallabhites. She cannot be said to have been the founder of any sect. But the author of the *Bhakta Mala*, or biographical sketches of the Vishnuvite saints, gives a very prominent place to her in his book, and connects with her name a large number of legends of a more or less miraculous character. The following account of her life is taken from Wilson's *Hindu Sects*:—

Mira was the daughter of a petty Raja, the sovereign of a place called Merta; she was married to the Rana of Udayapur, but soon after being taken home by him, quarrelled with her mother-in-law, a worshipper of Devi, respecting compliance with the family adoration of that goddess, and was, in consequence of her persevering refusal to desert the worship of Krishna, expelled the Rana's bed and palace: she appears to have been treated, however, with consideration, and to have been allowed an independent establishment, owing, probably, rather to the respect paid to her abilities, than a notion of her personal sanctity, although the latter was attested, if we may believe our guides, by her drinking unhesitatingly a draught of poison presented to her by her husband, and without its having the power to do her harm. In her uncontrolled station, she adopted the worship of Ranachhor, a form of the youthful Krishna; she became the patroness of the vagrant Vaishnavas, and visited, in pilgrimage, Brindaban and Dwaraka. Whilst at the latter, some persecution of the Vaishnavas, at Udayapur, appears to have been instituted, and Brahmans were sent to bring her home from Dwaraka; previously to departing, she visited the temple of her tutelary deity, to take leave of him, when, on the completion of her adorations, the image opened, and Mira leaping into the fissure, it closed, and she finally disappeared. In memory of this miracle it is said, that the image of Mira Bai is worshipped at Udayapur, in conjunction with that of Ranachhor. The Padas that induced this marvel, and which are current as the compositions of Mira Bai are the two following:—

Pada I.—Oh, Sovereign Ranachhor, give me to make Dwaraka my abode: with thy shell, discus, mace, and lotus, dispel the fear of

Yama : eternal rest is visiting thy sacred shrines ; supreme delight is the clash of thy shell and cymbals : I have abandoned my love, my possessions, my principality, my husband. Mira, thy servant, comes to thee for refuge : oh, take her wholly to thee.

Pada 2.—If thou knowest me free from stain, so accept me : save thee, there is none other that will show me compassion : do thou, then, have mercy on me : let not weariness, hunger, anxiety, and restlessness, consume this frame with momentary decay. Lord of Mira, Girdhara her beloved, accept her, and never let her be separated from thee.

There may be a substratum of truth in the account of Mira's life summarised in the above. But as the greater part of it is well calculated to make the inmates of royal zenanas unduly favourable towards the Vishnuvite religion and the Vishnuvite mendicants, the miraculous features of the story cannot but be attributed to the inventive genius of some clever Krishna-worshipping monks. It involves a phase of clerical politics which is well worth studying. To the sharp man nothing is impossible. His ambition knows no bounds, and of him it may be truly said that

Stone walls do not a prison make,
Nor iron bars a cage.

The Ranas of Udaipore should have given an emphatic denial to the whole story. But the bait of reflected glory was made too alluring, and they could not avoid falling into the trap.

CHAP. XIV.--THE MAHAPURUSHIA SECT OF ASSAM.

THE Mahapurushia is the most important of the Vishnuvite sects in Upper Assam. It was founded by a Kāyastha bearing the name of Sankar Dev. It is said that his father was a native of Upper India, and that he himself was born at a place called Alipukhori in Assam in the year 1448 A.D. He received a sound education in Sanskrit in his boyhood, and, in the course of his peregrinations as a pilgrim, is said to have visited Nadiya, and to have been initiated in the Vaishnava faith there by Chaitanya. Sankara wrote some original works on the Vaishnava faith, besides translating into Assamese the *Bhagavat* and some other important Vishnuvite Purāns. In Assam there are several monasteries appertaining to the sect. These are called Satra, and are usually presided over by a Superior of the Kalita caste. The most important parts of a Satra are the Nam Ghar and the Bhaona Ghar. The Nam Ghar is the chapel where the followers of the faith meet together for recitations and songs involving frequent mentions of the several names of Vishnu. Sankara was opposed to idolatry. But in the Nam Ghar there is always a copy of the *Bhagavat* enthroned on a dais. Every Satra has also, among its objects of worship, a block of stone with the footprint of Sankara engraved thereon. The followers of the faith reverentially offer their adoration to these footprints. The Bhaona Ghar corresponds to the Nat Mandir or dancing-hall of the Hindu shrines in Bengal. Sankar wrote some dramatic works of a religious nature, and the Bhaona Ghar serves the purpose of theatres for exhibiting these.

The most important of the Satras are at Bardowa, in the District of Nowgong, and at Barpeta in the District of Gowhati. The mendicants of the Mahapurushia sect are called Kevalia. For the accommodation of these there are large convents attached to most of the Satras. Female devotees are allowed to live in the Satras, but are not allowed to mix with the other sex at the time of worship. The tombs of Sankar Deva and his principal disciple, Madhav Deva, are to be found in the Barpeta Satra.

PART V.

THE SEMI-VISHNUVITE AND GURU-WORSHIPPING SECTS.

CHAP. I.—THE DISREPUTABLE CHAITANITE SECTS OF BENGAL.

FROM what has been already said about the Chaitanite sect, it would appear that its respectable members are of the following classes :—

1. The Gossains, who are the descendants of the disciples of Chaitanya.
2. The Vrikats, who are celibates.
3. The lay followers of the faith.

The position of the lay followers depends upon their secular condition and caste status, and the fact of their professing the Chaitanite faith does not elevate or lower them in public estimation. The Gossains, who are Brahmans, are generally looked down upon by the non-Chaitanites on account of their being in the habit of administering the sacrament of the *mantra* to the low castes, and accepting their hospitality. The aristocratic Brahmans generally avoid eating any cooked food in the house of a Chaitanite Brahman. But alliances by marriage between the two classes take place very frequently, and the Gossains have, generally speaking, a respectable position in Hindu society. They dress and live like householders.

The majority of the Vrikats are men of the clean Sudra castes. They are bound to a life of celibacy, and, theoretically at least, they hate female society to such an extent that they cannot allow a woman to cook their food. They are mostly cenobites, living in monasteries which are supported by their disciples, and by the lay members of their sect. Very few of them have to beg for food from door to door. Some of them have a little education, and pass some portion of their time in studying the religious literature of their sect, and in giving recitations which are attended by their co-religionists in the neighbourhood. The majority of them are quite illiterate, and fritter away their time in a weary round of ablutions, body painting and counting of beads. They have a peculiar but not very graceful uniform. Their position in their sect is very high, but in Hindu society generally they are looked down upon, more or less, as charlatans.

Besides the Vrikats, who never marry, and do not admit having any connection with any female, there are some classes of Chaitanites who dress and make their toilet like monks, but have some females regularly and openly associated with them. All these have, generally speaking, a very low position in society. They are divided into the following classes:—

1. **Sanjogi.**
2. **Spashta Dayaka.**
3. **Sahajia.**
4. **Nara.**
5. **Baul.**

Sanjogis.—The Sanjogis, as their name implies, are married men. They live, work and dress like householders. They are mostly descended from the unfortunates of the towns.

Spashta Dayakas.—The Spashta Dayakas are a semi-monastic order. They assume the garb of mendicants. But their monks and nuns live together in the same monastery, and it is hardly necessary to say what their mutual relationship is understood to be. It is only the low castes that get themselves admitted to the order.

The so-called monks of this sect may be recognised at once by the single string of basil bead necklace which they wear. The nuns of the sect shave their heads clean, with only a tuft in the centre. The forehead mark of the Spashta Dayaka is slightly smaller than that of the other Chaitanites. The Spashta Dayaka monks and nuns openly join together in dancing and singing.

The Sahajias.—The Sahajias represent the most developed form of Radha worship. They inculcate that every man is Krishna, and that every woman is Radha. They also profess that no man or woman need be attached to a single Guru. The result of these doctrines is the utter absence of any bar to promiscuous intercourse, and the full play of the inclinations and impulses of the parties.

Nara Neri.—The Nara Neris are very low class Chaitanites. A Nara is a male; and a Neri is his female associate. Their peculiarity is that the husband and wife sing and beg together, and not separately. They generally wear a coat of Kantha or rags patched together. The following is a translation of a Bengali song giving a very comic description of the duties of the female associate :—

> If you want Gour, you must be prepared to carry on your shoulder my Kantha (bed sheet of rags.)
> You must carry my Kantha and accompany me in my eleemosynary tours.
> You must sleep at night under the shade of some tree, and prepare every now and then my pipe of hemp.
> If you want Gour, you must carry on your shoulders my Kantha.

In the original the song is very amusing.

The Bauls.—The name of this sect is derived from the Sanskrit word "Batul," which means a madman. The Bauls are low class men, and make it a point to appear as dirty as possible. They have a regular uniform, which consists of a cone-shaped skull cap and a long jacket of dirty rags patched together, extending from the shoulders to the lower parts of the legs. Not only their dress, but their musical instruments, their dancing, and their songs are all characterised by a kind of queerness which makes them very amusing. The quaint allegories and the rustic philosophy of their songs are highly appreciated by the low classes. Their exhibitions are upon the whole so enjoyable that, in most of the important towns of Bengal, amateur parties of Bauls have been organised who cause great merriment, on festive occasions, by their mimicry.

The Bauls are spoken of as Vaishnavas; but, properly speaking, they are a godless sect. They do not worship any idols, and, on that account, their religion may be regarded as a very advanced one. But according to their tenets, sexual indulgence is the most approved form of religious exercise, and it is said that they have been known to drink a solution made from human excretions. The moral condition of these and some of the other sects, such as the Karta Bhajas, Margis, Bija Margis, Paltu Dasis, Apapanthis and the Satnamis, is deplorable indeed, and the more so as there is no sign of any effort in any quarter to rescue them. Aristocratic Brahmanism can only punish them by keeping them excluded from the pale of humanity. The modern religions can afford to give them better treatment. But they seem to be considered as too low or incorrigible by even the proselytising religions. If the Chaitanite Gossains, Christian Missionaries or Mahomedan Mullas could reclaim these they would be entitled to the everlasting gratitude of mankind.

CHAP. II.—THE DISREPUTABLE VISHNUVITE SECTS OF UPPER INDIA.

§ 1.—*The Radha Ballabhis.*

IT has been seen already that the earlier Krishna-worshipping sects associated with him his married wives, and that they do not even now offer any adoration to his mistress Radha. The neglect of the worship of Lakshmi, and the adoration of Radha as the consort of Krishna, originated probably in the fifteenth century, and it seems that it was either Nimbaditya or Chaitanya who introduced it. The Radha Ballabhi sect, which gives greater importance to the worship of Radha than to that of Krishna himself, was founded, it is said, by one Hari Vans, who lived at the end of the sixteenth century. Some say that the Radha Ballabhi is a sub-sect of the Vallavabites. The Radha Vallabhis have their head-quarters in Vrindaban. Radha Vallabhite Gossains and shrines are to be found in every part of Upper India.

§ 2.—*The Sākhi Bhavas.*

The Sākhi Bhava sect acquired some importance about half a century ago, and at that time included in it a few of the best men of the country. But it seems to be now nearly extinct. Its members were taught to regard themselves as Sākhis or the female companions of Radha, and, in order to approach that character to the utmost extent possible, some of the Sākhi Bhavas went the length of assuming the female dress and wearing female ornaments. They also feigned some physical conditions which are possible only to women.

CHAP. III.—THE DISREPUTABLE GURU-WORSHIPPING SECTS OF BENGAL.

§ 1.—*The Kartabhajas.*

THE word Karta literally means a "doer." In the vernacular of Bengal it is used as the designation of the executive head of a joint family. The expression Kartabhaja may be translated into English as the "adorers of the headman." The Kartabhaja sect is the most important of the class that may be called as Guru-worshippers in Bengal. It was founded by a man of the Sadgopa caste, named Ram Sarana Pal, who was an inhabitant of the village of Ghoshpara, in the vicinity of the Kanchrapara Station of the Eastern Bengal Railway. Like most of the other latter-day prophets, he professed to have derived his powers from an invisible teacher. The Aulia Gossain, whom he acknowledged as the source of his inspiration, was in all probability a pure myth, invented by him for being better able to impress upon his followers the importance of having a Guru. After Ram Saran's death, he was succeeded by his widow, generally known by the name of Sachi Mayi. After her death the *gaddi* of the Guru was occupied by his son Ram Dulal Pal, and he was succeeded by his son Ishwar Pal. The sect seems to be still flourishing as in the time of the original founder.

Like most other sect founders, Ram Saran was a man of great originality. To be ready with a pretext for exacting money from his followers, he declared that he was the proprietor of every human body, and that he was entitled to claim rent from every human being for allowing his soul to occupy his body. The idea is very similar to that involved in the Mahratta claim of *chouth*, and has, though on a much smaller scale, served very similar purposes. To enforce his right, and to give a pecuniary interest to his followers, the Karta appoints the chief men among the latter as his bailiffs and agents for collecting his revenue. The majority of the dupes of the sect are women who readily pay the small tax that is demanded of them, for the sake of securing long life to their husbands and children. Each agent of the Karta is generally on very intimate terms with a childless and friendless widow in the village or group of villages entrusted to his charge, and through the instrumentality of this woman he is able to hold secret meetings which are attended by all the female votaries within his jurisdiction, and in which he plays the part of Krishna.

The agents of the Karta are required to pay over their collections to him, at a grand levee held by him at his family residence in the month of March. At this time the Karta performs the most astounding miracles. Leprosy, blindness, deafness and every kind of malady which the medical science deems as incurable, are said to be cured by the Guru of the Kartabhajas in the course of a few moments. When a very large number of persons are interested in propping up a myth, it is no wonder that it should find ready believers. To give to the reader an idea of the process by which miracles are achieved by the Karta, I may relate here what I once heard about the experiences of a blind man at one of the annual levees at Ghoshpara. The crowd was great, but somehow he managed to elbow his way through it, and to bring his case to the notice of the Karta. Quite suddenly he was seized by some attendants, and taken to the side of a tank within the premises. He was there laid on the ground, and, while holding him fast to it, some of them commenced to rub the sockets of his eyes with sand, in the most violent manner. While the process was going on, they vociferously enquired every now and then whether his eyesight was restored or not. Finding no other way of escape from the excruciating torture to which he was being subjected, the man, after a while, gave an answer in the affirmative, and then there was a shout of "Sachi Mayi-ki-Jai," which resounded through the whole village. He was made to bathe in the tank for washing away the sand, and being clad in a new *dhooti* he was given something like the honour of a Roman triumph. He was borne aloft on the air, and taken through the crowd with the same vociferous shouts, and the same declarations to the effect that the blind man was restored his eyesight through the mercy of Sachí Mayi. After this advertisement of the miracle, the subject of it was deported from the village in such manner as to render it impossible for anyone among the crowd of pilgrims to make any independent enquiry about the matter. Perhaps the sequel was that one of the attendants represented himself as the blind man restored to his eyesight.

The Kartabhajas have no distinguishing marks, nor have they any sacred literature which they can call their own. They have no monasteries or mendicants.

The formula for the first initiation of a person to the Kartabhaja sect is : "The spiritual teacher alone has real existence." When the neophyte has made sufficient progress in spirituality then the teacher whispers in his ears another formula, of which the following is a translation ;—

> The great lord Aulia is the head of all. I move about according to your pleasure. I do not live apart from you for a moment. I am always with you, O great lord.

The exhibition of fervid love is the only form of religious exercise practised by the Kartabhajas. They do not worship any god or goddess. At their secret nocturnal meetings they sing some songs regarding Aulia Gossain, Krishna or Gouranga, and while some of the party become so affected as to fall in a swoon, the rest anxiously repeat the name of Hāri in their ears in order ostensibly to restore them to their senses, but in reality to render undue familiarity justifiable. What the results of such practices are may be easily imagined.

§ 2.—*The Pratap Chandi Sect.*

The Pratap Chandi sect is said to have been founded by the unfortunate Raja Pratap Chand of Burdwan. He was the only son of Maharaja Tej Chand by his first wife. Pratap's mother died when he was very young, and his father took another wife named Rani Kamal Kumari. From his boyhood Pratapa showed great favour to the mendicants that visited Burdwan, and passed a considerable portion of his time in their company. As he was by caste a Punjabi Kshettri, it is quite possible that, among the mendicants that paid him court, there were some spies from Lahore. However that may have been, he became very much disgusted with the kind of life that his father led, and the amount of power that was given in the management of affairs to Paran Babu, the brother of Rani Kamal Kumari. Things had become intolerable enough, and when Tej Chandra, in his old age, married a daughter of Paran Babu, Pratap made one desperate effort to bring his father to his senses. Leaving the palace of Burdwan, he repaired to Kalna, and after living there for some time gave out that he was seriously ill.

His object in doing so was to test his father's affection for him, and also to extricate him from the surroundings by which Rani Kamal Kumari and her brother, Paran, kept him enmeshed. Maharaja Tej Chand actually started from Burdwan with a view to see his son at Kalna. But the intrigues of the Rani and her brother led him to discontinue his journey, and to trace his steps back to his palace. To please his son, the old Raja sent two lacs of rupees to him for his death-bed expenses, but that served only to provoke him all the more. It was given out in Kalna one evening that he was dead. A part of the foreshore of the river Bhagirathi at Kalna was enclosed by screens, and while a funeral pyre was made to burn within it, the Raja effected his escape in a boat which had been brought for him. It is believed that he went directly to Lahore, and that he left Lahore only when he heard of the death of his father. In the meantime Paran had managed to get one of his sons adopted by Maharaja Tej Chand, and when Pratapa arrived at Burdwan, Paran had so managed matters that the real heir-at-law found it impossible to get admission to his palace. Pratapa then tried to take possession of Kalna. But the Collector of Burdwan befriended Paran and his son, and while the Raja and his men were sleeping in a steamer, they were taken by surprise by the troops sent against them. Several members of the Raja's retinue were killed by the musketry fire which was opened against them. The Rajah effected his escape by throwing himself overboard, and swimming across the river. He was arrested afterwards and hauled up before a criminal court on a charge of rioting. The best men among the witnessės deposed in favour of his identity, and the only men that swore against him were either the relatives of Paran, or persons well known as being capable of perjury. However, the evidence in his favor was disbelieved, and he was sentenced to suffer incarceration for six months. After his release, he was still the idol of the people, and, at this time, he organised the sect which bears his name. Like that of the Kartabhajas, it favoured esoteric worship, and it very seldom came prominently to public notice. Nevertheless it flourished all the same at one time. Its ramifications extended to the remotest villages in the province. It seems to be dying out now.

CHAP. IV.—THE GURU-WORSHIPPING AND DISREPUTABLE SECTS OF UPPER INDIA.

§ 1.—*The Satnami Sect of Oude.*

THE Satnami sect of Oude was founded by one Jagjivandas, a Ksatriya who lived about a century ago, and was an inhabitant of the village of Sardaha on the bank of the Saruju. He died at Kotwa, a place lying midway between Ajodhya and Lucknow. He wrote several tracts inculcating, like the other sect founders, absolute indifference to the world and implicit obedience to the spiritual guide. Among his followers there are both householders and mendicants. The former recognise the distinctions based on caste; but, like the mendicants of the other Indian sects, the Satnami monks, though recruited from different castes, stand on the same footing. The Satnami mendicants do not beg from door to door, but are supported by the lay members of their sect. They have several convents, the chief one being at Kotwa where Jagjiwan's tomb is still in existence. The heads of the Satnami convents are addressed as Saheb. The inferior mendicants use the surname of Das or slave. A Satnami mendicant may be known at once by his red coat, his skull cap of red colour, his perforated mantle, and the perpendicular mark painted with ashes or Shama Bindi clay, and extending from the tip of the nose to the uppermost part of the forehead.

The lay members of the sect are initiated in the Ram-worshipping cult, and are taught to repeat a long formula giving pre-eminence to the great hero god of Oude. The mendicants are also initiated in the same mantra, and to that extent their creed is unexceptionable. But like the Bauls of Bengal they are said to practise the horrible rite called the Gayatri Kriya, which is nothing more or less than the drinking of a solution of the secretions and excreta of the human body.

The Satnamis do not worship any idol. They are strict vegetarians and teetotalers.

§ 2.—*The Paltu Dasi Sect.*

The Paltu Dasi sect is essentially of the same character as the Satnamis. The Paltu Dasis have their chief monastery in Ajodhya. The mendicants of the sect wear yellow garments and cap. Some of them allow their hirsute appendages to grow without limit, while others shave their heads and moustaches clean. They accost each other saying "Satyaram." They are found chiefly in Ajodhya, Lucknow and Nepal. They are said to perform the Gayatri Kriya like the Satnamis. The sect was founded by one Paltu Das about the same time as that of the Satnamis.

§ 3.—*The Appa Panthis.*

The Appa Pantha sect was founded by one Munna Das, who was a goldsmith by caste, and who was an inhabitant of a place called Marwa to the west of Ajodhya. The Appa Panthis are practically semen worshippers. They dress like the Paltu Dasis.

§ 4.—*The Bija Margis and Margis.*

The Bija Margis and Margis are found chiefly in Kathiwar. The monks of the sect have each a nun associated with him, whom he would place at the disposal of any male member of the Hindu community, on payment of a reasonable fee, and on condition of observing certain rites. The monks practically serve as panders of their wives. This is the peculiar and the most extraordinary feature of the Bija Margi cult. There are many religions which sanction murder, rapine, drinking, debauchery and adultery. But the sect under notice is perhaps the only one in the world which expressly sanctifies pandering of the worst kind. The Bij Margis have, it is said, many other horrible practices.

CHAP. V.—THE MINOR GURU-WORSHIPPING SECTS OF BENGAL.

§ 1.—*The Bala Hari Sect.*

THIS sect was founded about half a century ago by a man of the sweeper caste named Bala Hari. He was in his youth employed as a watchman in the service of a local family of zemindars, and being very cruelly treated for alleged neglect of duty he severed his connection with them. After wandering about for some years, he set himself up as a religious teacher, and attracted round him more than twenty thousand disciples. The most important feature of his cult was the hatred that he taught his followers to entertain towards Brahmans. He was quite illiterate, but he had a power of inventing puns by which he could astonish his audience whenever he talked or debated. His widow inherited not only his position, but all his powers. I met her in the year 1872. Her first question to me was about my caste. I knew well about the hatred of the sect towards Brahmans, and instead of mentioning that I was a Brahman, I used a pun to say that I was a human being. She was very much pleased, and after offering me a seat she went on propounding the tenets of her sect. The greater part of her utterances was meaningless jargon, but she talked very fluently and with the dignity of a person accustomed to command. Though a Hari by caste, she did not hesitate to offer me her hospitality. I declined it as politely as I could, but considering the courtesy that she showed to me, I could not but feel some regret that the barrier of caste rendered it quite impossible for me to comply with her request.

The followers of Bala Hari have no peculiar sect marks or uniform. Some members of the sect are in the habit of begging for food from door to door. They are known not only by the absence of sect marks on their person, but also by their refraining from mentioning the name of any god or goddess at the time of asking for alms.

§ 2.—*The Kali Kumari Sect of East Bengal.*

The following account of the Kali Kumari sect of East Bengal is taken from Babu Guru Prasad Sen's *Introduction to the Study of Hinduism*:—

In the district of Dacca one Kali Kumar Tagore became the centre of a religion, the like of which sways the masses every now and then. Kali Kumar knew only the ordinary Bengali, which fitted him to be the *gomashta* of a rich widow, of the Kâyastha caste of his village. Beyond the *Gayatri*, he did not know anything of the *Vedas*, and, as for the *Purânas*, he knew as much as a Bengali Brahman, or a *Bhadralog* would know from recitations thereof by others, and not by reading them in the original for himself. Nor was there any peculiar sanctity in his life, as the mode of business which he followed shows. Yet it came to be known that he had cured some cases of incurable diseases. His fame spread, and, within a short time, his home became something like a splendid fair, where a vast mass of people congregated every day from all parts of the district, some to get themselves treated for diseases, and others to have a look at a real live god. The prescribed mode of treatment which is said to have been very successful was nothing else than bathing three times a day, believing in the divinity of Kali Kumar Tagore, taking in a little ball of earth from Kali Kumar's house, and giving a Hari-loot. A warrant of arrest was issued by the Sub-divisional Officer, in connection with something which Kali Kumar did with regard to his business as a *gomashta*, and before it could be executed, he died, and the religion of which he became the temporary centre died with him. At one time his followers could be counted by lacs.

PART VI.

RELIGIONS INTENDED TO BRING ABOUT UNION BETWEEN THE HINDUS AND THE MAHOMEDANS.

CHAP. I.—THE KABIR PANTHIS.

THE Mahomedans established their empire in India in the thirteenth century, and within less than two hundred years, sects began to be organised with the avowed object of bringing about a fusion of the creeds professed by the rulers and the ruled. The experiments that were made did not prove very successful. But their moral effect was great, and they tended at least to soften the bitterness between the Hindus and the Mahomedans, and to establish greater harmony than would otherwise have been possible. Among the noble teachers who undertook to bridge over the gulf, the van was led by a low caste poet named Kabir who lived at the end of the fifteenth century. Chaitanya admitted some Mahomedan disciples. But the Radha-worshipping religion which he inculcated had nothing in common with the pure monotheism of the Arabian prophet. Kabir sought to create a new platform on which both Hindus and Mahomedans could meet without departing very considerably from the fundamental tenets of their original creeds.

Kabir is usually said to have been a Jolaha or Mahomedan weaver. His Mahomedan followers believe him to have been a Mahomedan. But, according to his Hindu biographers, he was the child of a Brahman widow, and having been abandoned by his mother, was taken possession of and brought up by a Jolaha. Kabir is said to have been a disciple of Ramanand, and his religion is in fact a form of the Ramait cult. Kabir did not deny the existence of the Hindu deities ; but he declared that their worship, and the performance of the rites prescribed by the Shastras, were quite unnecessary. Kabir admitted Mahomedans among his followers, and strongly criticised the faith and practices of both Hindus and Mahomedans. Kabir recommended the adoration of the Divinity under the name of Rama, and his followers generally worship Rama as the supreme god. The Kabirite monks worship the spirit of Kabir. The priests of the sect do not administer any mantra to their followers. The latter accost the former by saying either "Dandpat" or "Bandgi" or "Ram Ram." The spiritual superiors respond to the salute by uttering the formula "Guru ki Daya," which means "the mercy of the preceptor."

The followers of Kabir have no peculiar dress. Some of them wear necklaces of basil beads, and paint their foreheads in the same manner as the Ramats. But they do not admit the necessity of these symbols. Kabir was a great controversialist himself. But to his followers, he recommended the practice of hypocrisy in order to avoid polemics. His advice to them was—

Shab se hiliye shab se miliye shab ka lijiye nam
Han Ji Han Ji shabse kijiye wosa apna gam.

Translation:—Associate and mix with all, and take the names of all; say to every one, yes sir, yes sir. Abide in your own abode.

A large part of the low caste population of Central and Western India are followers of Kabir. In Bengal and Southern India there are very few resident Kabirites. But there is hardly a town in India where strolling beggars may not be found singing songs of Kabir in original, or as translated in the local dialects.

CHAP. II.—HISTORY OF THE SIKH FAITH.

§ 1.—*Nanak, the first Sikh Guru.*

THE religion of the Sikhs, like that of Kabir, was originally meant to bring about union between the Hindus and the Mahomedans. But the actual result was very different from what had been contemplated. Nanak, the founder of the Sikh religion, was a contemporary of Kabir, Chaitanya, Ballavachari and Martin Luther. In all probability Nanak was a disciple of Kabir. At any rate, the ethics and theology of the great poet and moral teacher made a profound impression upon him. The programme that he chalked out for himself was to bring about that much-desired peace between the Hindus and the Mahomedans, which was impossible, while the latter were under the belief that there was great merit in spreading their religion by means of the sword.

Nanak was a Kshettri of the Bedi clan. His father Kalloo was a resident of the village of Tilwandi, a place about sixty miles to the north of Lahore. Nanak himself was not born there. When pregnant, his mother, in accordance with the time-honoured custom of the country, was taken to her father's house; and the honour of being the birthplace of the first Sikh Guru belongs to the village of Maru near Kot Katchwa, where his maternal grandfather had his residence. Nanak was married at a very early age, and his father tried hard to set him up in some kind of business. But he had an irresistible ambition for the position of a religious teacher; and neither the remonstrances of his father, nor the blisses of domestic life that awaited him at home, could dissuade him from the line that he was bent upon adopting. He travelled to many distant places, and, in the course of his peregrinations, is said to have visited Mecca.

Nanak's religion may be described briefly as a Hinduised form of Mahomedanism or a Mahomedanised form of Hinduism. He admitted the mission of Mahomet, and regarded himself as a successor to the Arabian prophet. But with this attitude towards the Mahomedan faith, Nanak did not deny the existence of the Hindu gods and goddesses, and he only deprecated their worship. Like Mahomet, Nanak inculcated the worship of a Supreme Deity. The exact nature of his views on the subject may be gathered from the following:—

> A hundred thousand of Mahomeds, a million of Brahmas, Vishnus, and a hundred thousand Ramas, stand at the gate of the Most High; these all perish, God alone is immortal. Yet men who unite in the praise of God, are not ashamed of living in contention with each other. He alone is a true Hindu whose heart is just, and he only is a good Mussulman whose life is pure.

Whatever might have been his views about the other prophets that lived before him, Nanak believed in his own mission and called upon his followers to have faith in him. It is said of him:—

> One day Nanak heard a voice from above, exclaiming, 'Nanak approach!' He replied 'Oh God! what power have I to stand in Thy presence?' The voice said, 'close thine eyes.' Nanak shut his eyes and advanced: he was told to look up: he did so, and heard the word, 'wa'! or '*well done!*' pronounced five times, and then '*wa! Guruji*, or *well done! Teacher*.' After this God said 'Nanak! I have sent thee into the world in the Kaliyuga (or depraved age)—go and bear my name!' Nanak said, Oh God! how can I bear the mighty burthen? If my age was extended to tens of millions of years, if I drank of immortality, and my eyes were formed of the sun and moon, and were never closed, still Oh God! I could not presume to take charge of Thy wonderful name! 'I will be thy Guru' Teacher, said God, and thou shalt be a Guru to all mankind, thy sect shall be great in the world, and thy word "Puri Puri!" the word of the Bairagi is "Ram! Ram!" that of the Sanyasi, "Om Nama Narayan!" and the word of the Yogis "Ades! Ades!" and the salutation of the Mahomedans is "Salam Alikum" and that of the

Hindus "Ram! Ram!" but the word of thy sect shall be "Guru" and I will forgive the crimes of thy disciples. The place of worship of the Bairagis is called Ram Sala; that of Yogis, Asan; that of the Sanyas is Mat; but that of thy tribe shall be Dharma Sala. Thou must teach unto thy followers three lessons —the first, to worship my name; the second, charity; the third, ablution. They must not abandon the world, and they must do ill to no being; for into every being have I infused breath; and whatever I am, thou art, for between us there is no difference. It is a blessing that thou art sent into the Kaliyuga. After this 'wa! Guru' or '*well done! Teacher,*' was pronounced from the mouth of the Most High Guru or teacher (God) and Nanak came to give light and freedom to the universe.

Thus like Mahomet and Christ, Nanak professed to be the representative of the Most High, the only difference being that while Christ called himself the son of God, and Mahomet made his followers believe that he was the trusted agent or ambassador of the Almighty, Nanak assumed a relationship which, though not identical with any affected by any one before him, was equally intelligible to both the Hindus and Mahomedans of India. Nanak declared that he had the honour of having God Almighty for his own Guru, and that he was appointed by the Deity himself to be the Guru of mankind. By adopting this attitude Nanak not only showed great originality, but struck a chord in the hearts of his countrymen which could not fail to secure him their reverence and affection. As a disciple has not necessarily all the powers of the Guru, Nanak, in the above legend, takes care to attribute to God Almighty the observation that there was no difference between Him and His duly appointed disciple.

As Nanak took the name of Guru, his disciples call themselves Sikhs, the designation being a corrupted form of the Sanskrit word *Shishya*, which means a disciple. Nanak had a large number of followers from an early period of his ministry. One of them was Mardana, who was a Mussulman by birth. Of the other followers of the first Sikh Guru, the two most celebrated were Boodha and Lehna, the former a Jat, and the latter a Kshettri of the Tihan clan. Nanak set aside the claims of his own sons, and appointed Lehna, to whom he gave the name of Angat, to be his successor. Nanak died at Kirtiporo on the bank of the Ravi in the year 1539 A.D. The village is now one of the principal places of Sikh pilgrimage, though the tomb has been washed away by the river. Nanak had two sons named Lutchmi Das and Sreechand. The Honorable Baba Khem Sing is descended from one of them.

Nanak's precepts for the guidance of his followers are contained in the Adi Granth or First Holy Book of the Sikhs. The second part of their scripture, called the Dasam Padsha ki Granth, or Book of the Tenth King, was composed by Guru Govind, the tenth and last of the Sikh pontiffs. The Adi Granth has been translated into English by Professor Trumpp, of Munich. As the religion of Mahomet had served to give rise to war and rapine, Nanak was fortunate enough in being able to take upon himself the function of a peacemaker. The life of every living being was sacred in his eyes. The breath that was given by the Almighty was to be taken away only by Him. Nanak denounced war which involved murder and discord. We shall see further on how the Sikhs were led, at a subsequent period, to adopt the very opposite doctrines and practices.

§ 2.—*Angat, the second Sikh Guru.*

It has been already stated that Nanak set aside the claims of his own sons, and appointed one of his disciples, to whom he gave the name of Angat, to be his successor. Angat was naturally hated by the sons of Nanak, and to avoid their persecutions, he removed to a place called Kudoor, on the bank of the Beas. He there lived in obscurity with only one attendant named Amar Das. His death took place in the year 1552 A.D.

§ 3.—*Amar Das, the third Sikh Guru.*

Angat had no children, and was succeeded by his attendant Amar Das, who was a Kshettri of the Bhalle clan. Amar Das attracted a large number of disciples, and resided at his native village of Govindwal, where he died in the year 1575 A.D.

§ 4.—*Ram Das, the fourth Sikh Guru.*

The fourth Sikh Guru was Ram Das, who was the son-in-law of his predecessor Amar Das. Ram Das and his successors were all of the Sodi clan. He obtained from Akbar a freehold grant of the land on which now stands the town of Amritsar, that, since its foundation, has been the metropolis of the Sikh religion. The political importance that Ram Das acquired through the favour of the great monarch was of far greater consequence than the actual bounties of the Crown. When it came to be known that Ram Das stood high in the favour of the Emperor, many of the local barons enlisted themselves among his disciples.

§ 5.—*Arjoon, the fifth Sikh Guru.*

Ram Das died in 1582 A.D., and was succeeded by his youngest son Arjoon. The fifth Sikh Guru kept great state and lived in splendour. The four preceding Gurus used to dress themselves as *fakirs* or beggars, but Arjoon was clothed in costly raiments, and kept fine horses. Towards the latter part of his reign, he removed to Amritsar, where he built his dwelling-house, and the temple in the midst of a tank which still forms the chief shrine of the Sikhs. The Adi Granth or the Sikh old testament was commenced by Nanak, and after being finished by Arjoon was deposited in the temple built by him. Guru Arjoon drowned himself in the river Ravi to avoid the persecutions threatened by the Hindu Governor of Lahore named Chandashah, who was a member of the same caste as the Guru, and whom the Guru had mortally offended by refusing an offer of matrimonial alliance.

§ 6.—*Har Govind, the sixth Sikh Guru.*

The sixth Sikh Guru Har Govind was the son of Arjoon. Har Govind possessed the talents of a great general, and was the first to entertain a standing army. Dara, the eldest son of Shah Jehan, who was the Governor of the Panjab at the time, was a man of catholic views like Akbar, and did not at first give any trouble to Har Govind. But a very unjust and high-handed act on the part of the Governor's attendants led Har Govind to retaliate and right himself in a manner which gave great provocation to the Governor. The result was that an expedition was sent against the Guru. The latter succeeded in defeating and driving off the Imperial army, but knowing well the resources of the Mogal Empire, he left Amritsar, and took refuge for a time in the jangals of Bhatinda in the District of Hissar. While there a second army was sent against him, which was repulsed in the same manner as the first. The Guru was equally successful in repelling a third attack by a large detachment of the Imperial army. After this Har Govind retired to a mountain fastness, called Hiratpore, on the bank of the Sutlej. He died there in the year 1639 A.D. He had five sons of whom the eldest died in his lifetime, leaving a son named Har Rao. Teg Bahadoor, the ninth Guru of the Sikhs, was the second son of Har Govind.

§ 7.—*Har Rao, the seventh Sikh Guru.*

Har Govind was succeeded by his grandson Har Rao. The seventh Guru assisted Dara in his struggle for the throne of Delhi, and by doing so incurred the wrath of Aurengzebe. When the latter had established his power, he sent a threatening message to Har Rao. The Guru pacified him by sending his eldest son, Ram Rao, to the Imperial Court, with a message to the effect that he was only a *fakir*, and that his only employment was to pray for the prosperity of His Majesty.

§ 8.—*Har Kisen, the eighth Sikh Guru.*

Har Rao died in 1663 A.D., and was succeeded by his youngest son Har Kisen. Ram Rao, the eldest son of Har Rao, was then at Delhi, and, upon hearing of his exclusion from the succession, appealed to the Emperor in order to have the nomination made by his father set aside, and to be recognised as the lawful Guru of the sect. Aurengzebe summoned Har Kisen to show cause against the claim made by Ram Rao. Har Kisen obeyed the summons, but on arriving at Delhi died there of small-pox in the year 1666 A.D.

§ 9.—*Teg Bahadoor, the ninth Sikh Guru.*

By the death of Har Kisen, Ram Rao derived no advantage whatever. The Sikhs on this occasion elected Teg Bahadoor, the second son of Har Govind, as their Guru, and Ram Rao was sorely disappointed again. Teg Bahadoor lived at Bukala, and, attracting numerous followers, became a greater Guru than most of his predecessors. The members of his own family were, however, not friendly to him, and, through the advice of one of his followers, he removed to Delhi with the view perhaps of settling there permanently, and acquiring the vantage ground which residence in a metropolis never fails to give to a religious teacher. But, unfortunately for him, his grand-nephew Ram Rao was still at the Imperial Court, and tried to injure him by poisoning the mind of the Emperor against him. The Emperor saw through the artifice, and allowed him at first to depart in peace. After leaving Delhi he travelled towards the east, and, arriving at Patna, lived there for some years. Guru Govind was born here. After that Teg Bahadoor, with his family, returned to Delhi. But no sooner had Ram Rao heard of his arrival than he began to intrigue for his ruin again. The Emperor was led to summon him for answering the charges that were brought against him. Teg Bahadoor was alarmed, and he again left Delhi, settling himself ultimately at a place called Mukhwal in the territories of the Raja of Kuhloor. When Ram Rao came to know his whereabouts, he managed to get him summoned again before the

Imperial Court. Knowing the danger of refusing compliance with the order of the Great Mogal, the Guru sent for his youthful son, and addressing him said:—"My son, they have sent for me for the purpose of taking away my life, but though they kill me, do not lament my death; you will be my successor, and do not forget to avenge my blood." Having thus appointed Govind Rao his successor, the Guru departed from Mukhwal. On his arrival in Delhi, he was thrown into prison. Some days afterwards he was sent for to the Emperor's presence. Aurengzebe had apparently no intention to injure him. But, out of a kind of weakness which was very unusual in him, he allowed Ram Rao to have his own way in the matter. Ram Rao demanded an explanation from his grand-uncle in the presence of the Emperor. The Guru was not, it seems, actually ordered to be executed. When Ram Rao persisted in calling upon him to state what he had to say by way of defence, he wrapped a piece of paper round his neck, and challenged his adversary to cut the same with a sword. This gave Ram Rao the opportunity he wanted. The executioner upon being ordered to deal the blow, cut off the head of the Guru, without being able to cut the paper. When taken up and read, it was found to contain a few words in Hindi signifying 'I give my head but not my secret.' Aurengzebe is generally blamed by historians for this act of cold-blooded murder. But considering the manner in which the Emperor was led to countenance the act, it seems that it must have been due more to the malice of Ram Rao than to religious bigotry on the part of the Emperor.

§10.—*Govind, the tenth Guru of the Sikhs.*

Teg Bahadoor was succeeded by his son Govind. By the injunction of his father he was pledged to avenge his death. The new Guru therefore lost no time to assemble together the followers of the faith. Messengers were sent to every part of the

Panjab to invite the faithful to Mukhwal, and in a short time crowds began to pour into the city of the Sikh Guru from every direction. When they were assembled, Govind stood up in their midst and addressed them as follows :—

> My father Teg Bahadoor ordered me to avenge his blood, and with this view I have collected a large army, but money is required for its maintenance. Now, my friends, every one of you must prepare to obey my orders and contribute money.
>
> In the next place you must be all of one mind, and adopt the same manners and have the same religious belief. There must be no castes among you as exist among the Hindus. You must be all equal, and no man greater than another. You must place no belief in the Shastras, or religious books of the Hindus. You must abstain from visiting any of the places of religious worship, such as the Ganges, Budreenath, and pay no respect to any of their gods : pay respect to Guru Nanak and to none else. The four castes of the Hindus are to be dissolved from henceforth.

At the conclusion of the above speech, most of the Brahmans and Kshettris among the audience openly declared that they would not accept Nanak or any other Guru as their guide. They were thereupon allowed to depart in peace ; but a large number remained behind who were mostly low caste men, and they expressed their willingness to follow the Guru. Next day Govind collected them all, and formally initiated them in the faith by the Sikh ceremony of baptism, called *pahooldi* and also *Amrita Diksha*, which was invented and made use of on this occasion for the first time. An account of the nature of this ceremony is given in the next chapter.

With the military resources which Govind acquired in the manner described above, he proceeded to conquer the territories of some of the local chiefs. He attained some success at first. But they applied to the Emperor for help, and the Governors of Lahore and Sirhind were ordered to give them due protection. The Imperial troops, combined with those of the Rajas, marched against Govind, and closely besieged the Fort of Mukhwal where he had his residence. His cause becoming hopeless, he was deserted by most of his followers, and with the few that remained faithful to him, he effected his escape. The miseries and privations that he suffered for some time afterwards were great. But he again managed to organise an army, and inflicted a signal defeat on the Imperial troops in a battle which was fought at a place called Moogatsir. The place which Govind had at this time made his head-quarters was in the midst of an arid desert, where no water was procurable, except from a few tanks which he held in his possession. The Imperial troops, unable to obtain any water, dispersed, and, being pursued by the Sikhs, numbers of them perished.

The news of Govinda's victory spread like wildfire, and large crowds resorted to him every day to swell his army. When Aurengzebe heard of the ill success that had attended the expedition sent against Govinda, he sent a messenger summoning him to answer for his conduct. The Guru not only showed great honour to the Imperial messenger, but professed great humility, and softened the bitterness of the Emperor also by submitting a versified statement of his grievances in Persian. Aurengzebe was then having enough of trouble from the Marattas, and was not inclined to exasperate any other class of his Hindu subjects. Whether on that account, or because he was satisfied that Govind had been unjustly persecuted, the order summoning the Guru was cancelled, and Govind was politely invited to visit the Emperor. Govind, after some hesitation proceeded to the south in order to have the honour of an interview with the Great Mogal. But while Govind was on his way to the Deccan, Aurengzebe died there. The Guru, however, was received with great honours by Bahadoor Shah, the son and successor of Aurengzebe, and was prevailed upon to accept service under the Mogal as a commander of five thousand. Govind, after these events, might have lived for a long time in peace ; but the great ambition of his life was frustrated. The four sons that he had, and who all promised to be his worthy successors, had met with sad deaths during the period of trouble that followed the siege of Mukhwal. There was no tie now to bind him to the world, and being weary of life he schemed to bring about his death. The son of a man whom he had murdered in the course of a quarrel, was invited to take his revenge by killing him. The young man had received such kind treatment from the Guru that he was quite inclined to forgive him. But the youth was taunted as a coward for not retaliating for the death of his father, and was ultimately so provoked as to inflict a mortal wound on the Guru. Govind's death took place in the year 1708 at a place called Nandser in the dominions of the Nizam.

§ 11.—*Govinda's successor Banda.*

Govinda's sons had pre-deceased him, and he appointed none formally to be his successor as Guru. So the title ended with him. Before his death, he however charged his disciple Banda with the task of avenging the blood of his father and grandfather. Banda, though a Byragi (a religious ascetic unconcerned with the world), was a very ambitious man, and he did not fail to utilise to the utmost the opportunities and resources that the dying injunction of the last Guru placed within his reach. He aimed at nothing less than the conquest and sovereignty of the Panjab, and he began his operations by the siege and destruction of Sirhind where the two youngest sons of Govind had been murdered in cold blood, at the time when the Guru himself was shut up within the walls of Mukhwal. Banda set fire to Sirhind, and murdered all the inhabitants, sparing none on account of either age or sex. The fury of the Sikhs being now excited to the utmost extent possible, and they being made to advance too far to recede, Banda crossed the Sutlej, and employed fire and sword wherever he went. He destroyed the town of Wattala, and proceeded to Lahore. After having burned and pillaged that city, he massacred its inhabitants. After these operations, the Byragi crossed the Ravi, and marched towards Jammu. When the Emperor Ferokshere heard of the desolation caused by the bloodthirsty fanatic, he appointed one of his best generals, named Abdool Samad, to be the Governor of the Panjab. On reaching Lahore, the new Governor pursued Banda closely, and succeeded in bringing about an engagement in which the Byragi was signally defeated. For a time, the Sikh leader obtained refuge in a hill fort, but the place was closely invested by the Imperial general, and captured by him within a short time. Banda was made a prisoner and taken to Delhi, where he was first of all compelled to be the silent and helpless spectator of the execution of 740 of his companions. Their discipline was such that not one of them winced under the excruciating tortures to which they were subjected. In the closing scene of this horrible drama, Banda's son was placed in his lap, and the father was ordered to cut the son's throat. Banda did what he was ordered to do, without uttering a word. As if that was not enough, the son's heart was taken out of his body, and thrown in Banda's face. Banda himself then had his life tortured out of him, his flesh being torn out with red-hot pincers. The savage slaughter of Banda and his companions in Delhi, and the strong measures adopted by Abdool Samad in the Panjab, annihilated the Sikh faction for a time. Abdool Samad died during the reign of Mahomed Shah, and was succeeded by his son Zukeera Khan, who proved to be a very weak administrator. During his viceroyalty, the zemindars of the Panjab threw off their allegiance to the Mussulmans, refused to pay their revenue, and oppressed the ryots. The latter, who were mostly Jats, embraced the Sikh faith in order to have that protection which the *de jure* ruler of the country was unable to afford. About this time Ahmed Shah Durani attempted to hold possession of the Panjab;

but the Sikhs collected in large numbers round Lahore, and inflicted a signal defeat on the Afghan General Jehan Khan. Upon the death of the Durani King, which took place shortly afterwards, the Sikh leaders parcelled out the territories of the Panjab among themselves, and established something like a federal government over the whole extent of country between the Jamna and the Indus. The independent principalities thus formed were called Missuls, and at the beginning these Missuls never came into collision with one another. But this state of things could not possibly last long, and ultimately the whole of the Panjab came under the sway of the powerful Ranjit Sing.

CHAP. III.—NATURE OF THE SIKH RELIGION AND ITS PRESENT CONDITION.

It has been already stated that the religion of the Sikhs is a mixture of Hinduism and Mahomedanism. The followers of Guru Nanak, like those of Mahomet, profess for theoretical purposes to be monotheists. But in practice, while the Mahomedans revere their prophet as the trusted friend and agent of the Most High, the Sikhs in a similar manner regard Nanak and his successors as Gurus or teachers duly initiated and appointed by the Deity himself. So far as belief in superior powers is concerned, the only difference between the Sikhs and the Mahomedans lies in the fact that while the former recognise the existence of the Hindu gods, the latter deny altogether the divinity of the heathen deities. Broadly speaking, Sikhism may be described as Mahomedanism, *minus* circumcision and cow-killing, and *plus* faith in the Gurus.

Even in outward appearance, a Sikh, with his short trousers, flowing beard, forehead free from paint, and neck without beads, looks more like a Mahomedan than a Hindu. The only visible sign by which he may be distinguished is the iron ring which he wears on the wrist. According to the strict tenets of their faith, the followers of the Gurus are precluded from performing any fasts, pilgrimages or rites enjoined by the Hindu Shastras. In practice many of the Sikhs not only visit the places held sacred by the Hindus,* but perform many of the ceremonies prescribed for the orthodox. The few Brahmans and Kshettris that there are among the Sikhs, take even the sacred thread which the last Guru ordered to be put off. Under British rule Sikhism is fast losing its vitality, and drifting towards amalgamation with the Hindu faith properly so-called. During the decaying period of the Mogal power, when lawlessness and anarchy prevailed in almost all the distant provinces of the Empire, the Sikh faith became very popular in the Panjab, as it not only gave that protection to the people which the officers of the Crown were incapable of affording, but opened out to the Jat cultivators a career of ambition which, according to the orthodox, is deserved only by the aristocratic Rajputs. "The quiet and industrious Jat, so long as he remained a cultivator of the field, never concerned himself with his neighbours' affairs or prospects ; but when he saw a lawless set of Sikh robbers, with numerous followers, and apparently in the enjoyment of every luxury of life, which he found it impossible, with every exertion of himself and his family, to procure, it is no wonder that he was often tempted to renounce his life of toil and trouble for the less irksome pursuits of a robber."†

At the present time the acquisition of wealth or political power by robbery or brigandage has been rendered well-nigh impossible by the *pax Britannica* which reigns over the whole country, and the religion of the Sikhs has therefore lost its chief attraction. In the course of a few more generations Sikhism is likely to be superseded by one of those forms of Vaishnavism which alone have the best chance of success among a subject nation in times of profound and undisturbable peace.

---

* The Sikhs perform religious ablutions in the holy rivers in the same manner as the Hindus. Ranjit Sing came to British territory in 1804 to bathe in the Ganges.—McGregor's *History of the Sikhs*, Vol. I, p. 156.

† McGregor's *History of the Sikhs*, Vol. I, p. 157.

The total Sikh population of India is less than two millions. Of these the majority are Jats and Churahas. There are a few Brahmans and Kshettris in the sect, but their number is very small. The Sikh Gurus tried to abolish the distinction of caste altogether. But that institution is naturally dear to those to whom it gives an elevated status by hereditary right, and it is no wonder that the Brahmans and Kshettris held aloof from the confederacy in spite of its political advantages. The castes that eagerly joined the standard of the Sikh Gurus were the agricultural Jats, the trading Roras, and the tribe of scavengers called Churaha. The Jats, like the Marattas, are a fighting nation by instinct. Perhaps the iron rule of the Rajputs repressed the martial ardour of both for ages. But when the Rajputs were subverted by the Mahomedans, and the Mahomedans themselves became too weak to wield the sword with success, the Jats in the north, like the Marattas in the south, required only competent leaders at their head to urge them on to "the paths of glory that lead but to the grave." The Jats are looked down upon by the Rajputs, and that was perhaps one of the great motives why the former willingly submitted to the leadership of the Sikh Gurus, and discarded the authority of the Brahmans who supported the pretensions of the "king's sons." The Roras were similarly looked down upon by the Kshettris and had a similar motive to attain to a position higher than theirs. Whatever was the cause, the Jats and the Roras formed the backbone of the Sikh brotherhood. The low caste of scavengers, called the Churaha, were also eager to embrace the new faith, as it alone gave them a chance of abandoning their filthy profession, and attaining a position of respectability, with the title of Sing. The Churahas were admitted to the faith by the baptism of *pahooldi*; but the high caste Sikhs refused to be placed on the same footing with them. The result was the formation of something like a new caste under the name of Mazabi Sikhs. The Churaha Sikhs, called Mazabi, are not allowed to eat or drink with the high caste Sikhs. In the Sikh wars the Mazabis greatly distinguished themselves. They were remorselessly cruel in battle.

The Sikhs have no regular priesthood, and no religious ceremonies besides the baptism of *pahooldi* called also *Amrita Diksha*. Even this baptismal rite was unknown during the time of the first nine Gurus, and was first invented by the tenth pontiff, Govind. As neither the Hindus nor the Mahomedans have any ceremony corresponding with it, it is quite possible that Guru Govind derived the idea from the practice of the Christian Church. The ceremony itself is a very simple and rude one, and has nothing of the grandeur or complicacy of a Hindu rite. As stated already, the Sikhs have no regular priesthood, and it is therefore ordained that the *pahooldi* or *Amrita Diksha* may be conducted by any five persons duly initiated in the faith. When there is a candidate for baptism, a meeting of the initiated members residing in the locality is held. The prayer of the applicant is brought to the notice of the assembly, and, if they decide in favour of admitting him, a stone cup containing a solution of sugar in water is brought before them. The liquid is stirred with a double-edged sword by at least five of the elders present. When this is done a portion of the solution is sprinkled over the eyes, ears and head of the neophyte, and the rest is drunk by all present including him.

The Sikhs denounce idolatry, but at the same time worship the Granth or the Bible of their sect in the very same manner as the Hindus worship the images of their gods. In speaking of the Granth in the shrine of Amritsar, Sir Monier Williams says :—

> The Granth is, in fact, the real divinity of the shrine, and is treated as if it had a veritable personal existence. Every morning it is dressed out in costly brocade, and reverently placed on a low throne under a jewelled canopy, said to have been constructed

by Ranjit Sing at a cost of 50,000 rupees. All day long chowries are waved over the sacred volume, and every evening it is transported to the second temple on the edge of the lake opposite the causeway, where it is made to repose for the night in a golden bed within a consecrated chamber, railed off and protected from all profane intrusion by bolts and bars.—Sir Monier Williams' *Hinduism and Brahmanism*, p. 177.

The Holy Book is treated as a living personality, also by the dedication, before it, of a pan of Halwa called Kara Prasad. After being kept before the Granth for some time, the Halwa is distributed among all persons present in the temple at the time. Even good Hindus are said to accept the dole* reverentially. The Sikhs do not usually offer any other kind of food before the object of their adoration.

For an idea of the contents of the Granth, the following passages may be referred to :—

At the beginning is the True One.

Know that there are two ways (that of Hindus and t at of Mussalmans), but only one Lord.

By thyself all the creation is produced; by thyself, having created, the whole is caused to disappear.

Thou O Hari! alone art inside and outside; thou knowest the secrets of the heart.

Mutter the name of Hari, Hari, O my heart, by which comfort is brought about, by which all sins and vice disappear, by which poverty and pain cease.

Thou art I, I am thou, of what kind is the difference? Like gold and the bracelet, like water and a wave.

By the perfect Guru the name of Hari is made firm in me. Hari is my beloved, my king. If some one bring and unite (him with me), my life is revived.

Thou art my father, my mother, my cousin, my protector in all places. Then what fear and grief can there be in me? By thy mercy I have known thee. Thou art my support, my trust. Without thee there is none other; all is thy play and thy arena, O Lord!

The Lord is my dear friend. He is sweeter to me than mother and father, sister, brother and all friends; like thee there is none other, O Lord!

Be united with the Lord of the Universe. After a long time this (human) body was obtained. In some births thou wast made a rock and mountain. In some births thou wast produced as pot herb. In the eighty-four lakhs of existence thou wast caused to

* This practice clearly shews that the Sikhs are regarded as Hindus by the *members* of the orthodox faith. It may be also mentioned here that the name of Guru Nanak is actually invoked by many orthodox Brahmans of Northern India, along with those of some other Hindu gods.

wander about. No hot wind touches those who are protected by the true Guru. The Guru is the true creator.

Protected by the Guru he is admitted to the true house and palace of Hari. Death cannot eat him.

I am continually a sacrifice to my own Guru.

I am become a sacrifice to my own Lord. From the Veda, from the book of the Koran, from the whole world he is conspicuous. The King of Nanak is openly seen.

Having forgotten all things meditate on the One! Drop false conceit, offer up thy mind and body.—Sir Monier Williams' *Hinduism and Brahmanism*, p. 171.

The doctrines and sentiments contained in the above are such as are favoured by every Hindu. The good words put in at every step for securing to the Guru the love and regard of his followers, are the usual characteristic of the sacred literature of modern Hinduism.

The Sikh Gurus never encouraged celibacy or mendicancy, and declared that marriage and the acquisition of wealth were necessities of human life. The class of Sikh fanatics called Akalis, or 'men for times of danger,' do however, in practice, generally remain unmarried. They usually live in the Sikh monasteries called Dharmasala, and they are easily known by their blue turbans with iron discs. They are regular desperadoes, and it is a very dangerous thing to provoke them. During the days of Sikh rule, they were generally treated with great indulgence, and were kept as a reserve for great emergencies.

The Sikhs have several sub-sects, among which the Udasis, the Nirmailis and the Govind Shahis are the most important. The first two are followers of Nanak. The last belong to the order founded by Guru Govind.

The Sikhs reverence the descendants of Guru Nanak and the representatives of the family of Govind. But no one has priestly authority in the sect either by birth or by appointment. The *pahooldi* of the Sodis and the Bedis themselves has to be conducted in the same manner as that of the other Sikhs. The chief shrines of the Sikhs are those of Amritsar, Patna, Nander, Tarantara, Moogatsar, Kartarpore and Panja Shah. The name of the first of these places literally means "the tank of nectar." It is the site of the tank, the dry bed of which was by Nanak miraculously filled with water. The fourth Guru Arjoon first built the temple, and at a later period the town became the rendezvous of the Sikh leaders. Patna is held to be a sacred town on account of its being the birthplace of Guru Govind. Nander is the name of the place in the Nizam's dominions where Guru Govind died. Tarantara, in the Amritsar district, is held sacred by the Sikhs on account of its having a tank the water of which is believed to be a cure for leprosy. Moogatsar is in the Ferozepore district, and is held sacred on account of its being the site of the famous battle by which Guru Govind re-established his power. Panja Shah is near Rawal Pindi, and is celebrated as the place where Guru Nanak performed certain very extraordinary miracles. He drew out water from the rocky base of a hill, and when a rival saint tried to crush him and his followers by hurling the hill upon them, Nanak kept it in position by stretching out his right hand for its support. The hill has on its sides some finger-marks which are taken by the devout to be conclusive evidence of the truth of the legends.

PART VII.

BUDDHISM.

CHAP. I.—PERSONAL HISTORY OF BUDDHA.

ALTHOUGH the religion of Buddha is not usually regarded as a form of the Hindu faith, and although it has disappeared almost entirely from India proper, the land of its origin, yet, for many reasons, it seems to me necessary to say something in this book about its history and character. Buddha rejected the authority of the Vedas, and strictly prohibited the performance of the Vedic rites, which involved the killing of animals and the drinking of strong liquor. But his own system was founded entirely upon Hindu philosophy, and as it recognized the gods of the Hindu pantheon, it cannot be said to have the same relation to Hinduism as Christianity or Mahomedanism. In fact, Buddhism is not more antagonistic to orthodox Hinduism than the cults of the Jangamites or the Vaishnavas. The latter, though they reject the authority of the Vedas and deny the spiritual supremacy of the Brahmans, are yet regarded as Hindus, and there is no reason why Buddhism should be assigned a different footing.

The religion of Buddha was, if not the first, at least one of the earliest, of the man-worshipping and morality-preaching faiths. The Vedic singers who preceded them never claimed to be superior to, or identical with, the gods of their pantheon. Their highest ambition was only to be recognised as men of extraordinary powers. Their religion offered chiefly tangible good service, and had not much to do with either the improvement or the corruption of morality. Their success in securing the reverence of men naturally led those who followed them to aim at attaining higher altitudes. Buddha did not, like the later prophets, claim to be an incarnation or agent of the Most High. Ideas of that kind were perhaps unknown to him, and, at any rate, did not originate with him. However, he tried to attain the same goal by a different route. He, in a manner, denied the existence of a Supreme Brahma, and spoke of the lesser gods of the Hindus pantheon as his inferiors. According to his elaboration of the Hindu doctrine of metempsychosis, the condition of a god is the highest stage* which every sentient being is capable of attaining before becoming a Buddha or Bodhisatwa.† In the Buddhistic scripture we read of a certain frog ‡ that from simply listening to the Buddha's voice, while reciting the law, was born as a god in the Trayastriusa heaven. In some of the stories of Buddha's miracles, as, for instance, in the one relating to his descent§ from heaven to Sankisa, it is stated that the gods acted as his personal attendants. It is also stated in some places that the gods reverenced him as a superior being, and, when allowed, congregated together to hear his preachings. His policy with regard to the lesser deities of the Hindu pantheon was, in fact, the same as that of the British Government of the present time towards the Indian princes, and not that of Dalhousie. He did not, like some of the later prophets, aim at being in the position of a "lonesome tower" in the midst of a level plain. Such being the case, his religion must be said to be a form of Hinduism, and not wholly antagonistic to it.

---

* See Sir Monier Williams on *Buddhism*, p. 121.
† See Glossary.
‡ See Sir Monier Williams on *Buddhism*, p. 122.
§ Rockhill's *Life of Buddha*, p. 81; Sir Monier Williams' *Buddhism*, p. 414, *et seq.*; Legge's *Fa Hian*, p. 48.

The main facts relating to the personal history of Buddha* are well-known, and I refer to them only for the purpose of marshalling them in such a manner as to render their historical bearing and value clear enough. The great prophet was the son of a Ksatriya chief named Suddhodana, who ruled over a small kingdom at the foot of the Himalayas, between the rivers Rapti and Rohini. The chief town of the State was Kapilavastu, which has been identified with a village named Bhuila, in the Basti district, about 25 miles to the north-east of Fyzabad, and 12 miles to the north-west of the town of Basti. Buddha's mother, Maha Maya, died on the seventh day after his birth, and although he was taken care of by his mother's sister, Maya *alias* Gautami Mahaprajapati, who was also one of his father's wives, his childhood was in all probability not a very happy one. In his early years, he received some education under a teacher named Kaucika,† and it was perhaps this teacher who awakened in his young mind that craving for the study of the Hindu philosophical systems which was very strong in his mind at the time that he left his paternal roof. He married three wives, and, according to some of the accounts relating to his life, he was blessed with a child when he was himself twenty-nine years old. According to other accounts, his wife Yasodhara gave birth to Rahula long after his departure from home. In any case, with such intellectual and physical activity as he possessed, the monotony of home-life was perhaps extremely irksome to him. Possibly the fact of his

---

* I shall in this chapter speak of the prophet everywhere by the name of Buddha, though that designation is applicable to him only in the condition which he attained when he was about thirty-seven years old. His other names were :—

1. Sakya Sinha, Lion of the Sakya race.
2. Siddhartha, one who has attained the object of his religious practices.
3. Tathagata } A person in the path of enlightenment.
4. Sugata }

† Rockhill on the *Life of Buddha*, p. 19.

being motherless, and his father having other wives, made him very miserable. That he was not a great favourite with the family appears pretty clear from the fact that, after his voluntary exile, his father did nothing whatever to bring him back to his palace. If, like the late Raja Pratapa Chand,* of Burdwan, Buddha wanted to test the affection of his father for a motherless child, he was doomed to a sad disappointment, though, for the sake of the good name of his father, or in order to uphold his own prophetic pretensions, he never expressed his feelings on the subject. What the real cause of Buddha's renunciation of home was, cannot possibly be known. But there cannot be much doubt that the stories to be found on the subject in the Budhistic scriptures are mere myths.

According to these legends Buddha grew up to manhood without having any idea of death, disease or the decay caused by old age, and that when in his twenty-ninth year he first saw a dead body, an old man and a diseased person, he was so impressed with the miseries of human life, as to determine at once to leave his home in the search after a remedy. The stories on the subject are very dramatic no doubt; but they cannot be taken to have any element of probability consistently with what is known to all men regarding the usual course of human affairs. Even supposing that Buddha's domestic life was a happy one, and that the only motive which led him to adopt the garb of a mendicant was his philanthropic zeal for the good of mankind, it does not seem reasonable to suppose that his determination was the result of a sudden impulse. Cases of renunciation like his are not of rare occurrence among Indian princes. In our own days Lala Babu and Rajas Protab Chand and Ram Krishna have perhaps made far greater sacrifices than the son of Suddhodana. In every case of Sanyas in high life that has taken place in recent times,

---

* For an account of the Raja, see page 488, *ante*.

the determination is more or less known to have been caused by domestic unhappiness, or by the undue influence of some religious teacher on the enthusiastic neophyte. It seems likely, therefore, that Buddha was influenced in the same way. At any rate, the steadiness which he evinced in the course of life that he adopted, goes very far to show that his determination was not the result of a sudden impulse, but of long and careful deliberation. If he had been led by only an accidental flash of enthusiasm, his zeal would have cooled down as quickly, and he would have come back to his father within a few days. But he had evidently gone through a long course of mental preparation, and the realities of a mendicant's life did not frighten him.

After leaving home Buddha repaired to Raj Giri, the metropolis of the Magadha Empire at the time. This line of action on his part, at the very outset, does not seem to be consistent with the view that it was only the miseries which he had found existing in the world that led him to leave his paternal roof. Surely he could have no reason whatever to suppose that Raj Giri was the place where the necessary remedy was obtainable. It seems much more probable that, like other men of ability and ambition, he was naturally attracted to the metropolis of the Empire in a search after adventure. According to his biographers, his soothsayers had predicted that he was to be either a mighty Emperor or a Buddha. This may be taken to show what the goals of his ambition originally were. Evidently he saw no way to be an Emperor, and therefore adopted the safer but more ambitious career that ultimately led to his being worshipped as a god by all classes, including both princes and peasants.

It is said that the princely mendicant of Kapilavastu attracted the notice of King Bimbasara on the occasion of his very first entrance into Raj Giri. That is not impossible. But it seems more probable that he became known to the king either through his preceptor

Ram Putra Rudraka, or through Amba Pali of Vaisali, who was Bimbasara's mistress, and who subsequently became one of the leading Buddhistic nuns. Ram Putra Rudraka was evidently one of the favoured Pandits of the Court of Bimbasara, and as such Pandits, when they visit the kings who patronise them, are generally accompanied by their leading pupils, it seems highly probable that the Buddha's first introduction to Bimbasara was the result of his having enlisted himself as a pupil of the great philosophical teacher of Raj Giri at the time. Whatever the origin of the acquaintance may have been, the great prophet knew that to establish a high position in the country, or in the estimation of the king, by dint of Sanskrit scholarship alone was a very difficult task, and was quite impossible during the lifetime of his preceptor. So after passing some time at Raj Giri as a pupil of Ram Putra Rudraka, and acquiring some reputation there as a scholar of great promise, he retired to an adjoining forest on the banks of the river Niranjan, and there for a time gave himself up to the practice of the most severe austerities. The discipline to which he was believed to have subjected himself at the time raised him considerably in the veneration of King Bimbasara and the people of the country. But the practice of asceticism, though highly useful at the beginning of a religious man's career, cannot be continued by him forever, if he has a secular ambition. At any rate, after six years of self-mortification, the Incarnation of Enlightenment discovered that penances and fasts were not the road to heaven. His reputation for superior sanctity had been then completely established, and so he emerged from his seclusion, giving out that he had discovered the true remedy for the miseries of this world. The panacea that he professed to have discovered was neither very original nor of any use for practical purposes. His doctrines were exactly the same as those of many orthodox Hindus, namely, that our miseries are caused by desires, and that, in order to get rid of the miseries, we must learn to overcome the desires. Sir Monier Williams* gives Buddha the credit of having had the power to clothe old ideas in new and more attractive dresses. But, in this instance, the great anti-Brahmanical prophet adopted the ideas of Brahmanical philosophy, without any modification whatever. Cessation of desires was the panacea prescribed by both, as if it were possible for any human being to feel happy without food, drink, health, and the joys of conjugal association. From the point of view of common sense, the true remedies for the miseries of life are the sciences of medicine, agriculture, &c., the arts of weaving, road-making, navigation, &c., properly managed political governments, and such institutions as hospitals, poor-houses, insurance offices, light houses, fire brigades, &c. A spiritual teacher may be believed to have the power of saving the soul from perdition after death. But so far as the miseries of this world are concerned, it is impossible to give either Buddha, or any other prophet, the credit of having given us a satisfactory remedy.

However that may be, Buddha was so convinced of the value of his discovery, that he at first felt inclined to keep it to himself† instead of giving the benefit of it to the world. Even the gods were distressed at this determination on his part, and he was led to abandon it only for the sake of the repeated remonstrances addressed to him by the great deity‡ Brahma. This legend affords a typical instance of the manner in which Buddha utilised the agency of the gods to serve his political purposes. In secular spheres such tactics would hardly be of any use even with the weakest of Asiatic princes. But the faith of men in the saints and prophets is unbounded.

When Buddha at length made up his mind to give men the benefit of his discovery, he thought of making

* See Sir Monier's *Buddhism*, p. 104.
† *Mahavagga*, I, 3, 4.
‡ *Ib.*, I, 5, 6.

his former teachers Ruddaka and Allada* his first pupils. If this had been possible his name and fame could have been made at once. But the idea, though a very clever one, could not possibly be given effect to. As soon as it arose in his mind, a god, who was in waiting, informed him that his old teachers had passed away from the earth. He then proceeded to Benares with a view to preach the new faith to the five men who had been deputed by his father to attend him when he was studying philosophy at Raj Giri. They attended him also when he practised austerities on the banks of the Niranjana river. But when he gave up asceticism, and became mindful of worldly comforts, these men left him and went to Benares. According to the Buddhistic scriptures, the cause of their leaving his company was his abandonment of asceticism. But the fact that they did not return to their native country, but proceeded to Benares, seems to point to the conclusion that they had been sent thither by Buddha in order to prepare the ground for him. However that may be, the five attendants were not, according to the Buddhist chronicles, at first inclined to recognise the Buddhahood of their former master. But they were soon overpowered by his commanding bearing, and the sermon that he delivered to them. They had addressed him familiarly as a 'friend,' and he spoke as follows :—

Do not address, O Bhikshus, the Tathagata by his name, and with appellation "Friend." The Tathagata, O Bhikshus, is the holy absolute Sambudha. Give ear, O Bhikshu! The immortal (Amata) has been won (by me): I will teach you: to you I preach the doctrine. If you walk in the way I show you, you will ere long have penetrated to the truth, having yourselves known it and seen it face to face; and you will live in the possession of that highest goal of the holy life for the sake of which noble youths fully give up the world and go forth into the homeless state."—*Mahavagga*, I, 6, 12.

The five quondam attendants to whom Buddha spoke as above were all under the belief that there was

* *Mahavagga*, I, 6, 2—4.

great merit in asceticism, and, addressing him again in the same familiar style as before, they said :—

> By those observances, Friend Gautama, by those practices, by those austerities, you have not been able to obtain power surpassing that of men, nor the superiority of full and holy knowledge and insight. How will you now, living in abundance, having given up your exertions, having turned to an abundant life, be able to obtain power surpassing that of men and the superiority of full and holy knowledge and insight ?—*Mahavagga*, I, 6, 13.

The reply which Buddha gave to this embodies a doctrine which would have entitled him to be regarded as one of the greatest benefactors of mankind, if he had not insisted upon his followers to give up their connection with the world, and to become monks and nuns. He said :—

> There are two extremes, O Bhikshus, which he who has given up the world ought to avoid. What are these two extremes ! A life given to pleasures, devoted to pleasures and lusts : this is degrading, sensual, vulgar, ignoble, and profitless : and a life given to mortifications, this is painful, ignoble and profitless. By avoiding these two extremes, O Bhikshus, the Tathagata has gained the knowledge of the Middle Path which leads to insight, which leads to wisdom, which conduces to calm, to knowledge, to the Sambodhi, to Nirvana. —*Mahavagga*, I, 6, 17.

A nobler doctrine, no doubt, than that of those who taught their followers to practise self-mortification in every possible form. But as Buddha insisted upon renunciation of home life, it is impossible to give him even the negative credit of having done nothing to make men more miserable than they are by nature. That compliment is due to Manu and Yajnyavalkya, and not to any of the latter day prophets.

To return to the story of the first conversions made by Buddha. The sermons which the prophet addressed to his attendants did not at first make any impression. The same questions and the same answers had to be repeated thrice, and, if we are to believe the Buddhist scriptures, the prophet had to struggle hard in order to convince them of the truth of his doctrines.

Buddha's sixth convert was a young man* of Benares named Yasa. He was followed by his parents. While

* *Mahavagga*, I, 7, 4—10.

the neophyte was passing the first night after his conversion in the hermitage of his teacher, his father searched for him in every part of the town. The son had left his slippers on the banks of the Varuna, and the father upon seeing them was led to apprehend that he had been killed by some wild beast. When thus in a state of terrible anxiety he met with Buddha, who, upon being questioned, offered him the information he wanted on condition of his accepting the new faith. Yasa himself became a Bhikshu, while his father, mother and wife remained at home as lay disciples. Fifty-four other men of Benares were led to follow the example of Yasa, so that there were sixty Bhikshus in all at the end of the first year. Buddha deputed these, two by two, to preach his faith in other parts of the country. He himself returned to the vicinity of Gaya, where, before long, he succeeded in converting some of the greatest of the local Pandits, together with their disciples. The prophet had now a very large number of followers, and had acquired such importance that he was invited by King Bimbasara to revisit Raj Giri. A large and commodious garden house, called the Venuvana, or the Bamboo grove, was presented to him by the king. Bimbasara supplied also everything that Buddha and his followers required for food, drink and clothing. Being thus able to keep his followers well-housed and well-fed, Buddha was able to add to the number of his disciples every day. These disciples spent nine months in the year in preaching the new faith, and passed the three months of the rainy season in one of those monasteries that either the kings or the people of the country built in different places for their accommodation.

Buddha passed the second year of his ministry in Raj Giri. It was at this period that Sudatta, a rich merchant of Sravasti,* became his disciple, and invited

* For an account of this city, see p. 188, *ante*.

him to visit the chief city of Kosala. Buddha suggested to him the building of a Vihara for his reception. Sudatta built the monastery of Jetavana, and when everything was ready he sent word to Buddha asking him to take possession. When Buddha arrived at Sravasti he was received with great honour, and a formal gift of the Jetavana was made to him. Buddha passed the *woos* or rainy season of the third year of his ministry in Sravasti. During his residence there King Prasnajit of Kosala was converted to his faith.

Shortly after his conversion the King of Kosala sent a message to Suddhodana, congratulating him for having such a great son as the Buddha. Thereupon the King of Kapilavastu sent several messengers to Buddha asking him to visit his parents and relatives.

After avoiding compliance for a long time, Buddha at last consented to meet the wishes of his aged father on condition of his building a monastery for the holy order at Kapilavastu. Suddhodana agreed to the condition, and built a Vihara, to which was given the name of Nyagrodhvana or Banyan grove. When Buddha arrived at Kapilavastu, his father and his other relatives gave him a warm reception. They all embraced his faith, and a great many of them entered the monastic order. Some of these Sakya monks gave great trouble to him afterwards.

From the Buddhistic histories it appears that no teacher before Buddha had ever allowed women to enter any monastic order. Buddha himself had, it is said, some misgivings on the subject. It is represented that he regarded women with great distrust, and that he was ultimately obliged to grant them the privilege, for the sake of his favourite disciple Ananda, who pleaded their cause, and for meeting the wishes of his old maternal aunt and step-mother, Mahaprajapati Gautami. At the council held at Raj Giri after Buddha's death, his first *locum tenens*, Maha Kasyapa, severely censured Ananda for the part that he had taken to get women admitted to the holy order.* But when Mahaprajapati Gautami and her companions were admitted as nuns, Ananda's age cannot have been more than ten years, and it is therefore difficult to see how he could be responsible for enrolling them in the holy orders. The entreaties of Gautami Mahaprajapati, if the story be based upon truth, were certainly irresistible to Buddha. But it seems very probable that he wanted to admit females, more for the sake of adding to the attractions of monastic life, than for the sake of obliging either Ananda or his aged aunt. Some of the rules laid down for the guidance† of the Bhikshus point to the above conclusion.

Buddha, like many other mendicants, was a great favourite with the softer sex. While yet engaged in his meditations at Gaya, he was attended by a girl named Sujata. Later on he went one day to a neighbouring village named Senika, the headman of which had two unmarried daughters named Nanda and Nanda Bala. These ladies prepared a nice pudding for Buddha, and after putting the same into his alms-bowl, asked him to marry them. Their guest rejected their prayer. But he visited them again when on his way from Benares to Raj Giri, and on this occasion admitted them into his sect as lay disciples. Another of his devoted female disciple was the lady of Vaisali called "Visakha, the mother of Mrigadhara," in the Buddhistic annals.

The precise time when Amba Pali, the mistress of Bimbasara, became a disciple of Buddha, is not known. Most likely the acquaintance began at the time when Buddha was a student at Raj Giri. At any rate, when he began to preach his new faith, Amba became one of his most devoted disciples, and he not only accepted the gift of a garden house made by her to him, but actually partook of her hospitality‡ with all the monks

---

* See Rockhill on the *Life of Buddha*, p. 152.

† See *ib.*, pp. 61, 62; Cullanvagga X, 1.

‡ See *ib.*, p. 129; Legge's *Travels of Fa Hian*, p. 72.

accompanying him. The example thus set by the teacher was perhaps very largely followed by his disciples. What the result was may be easily imagined.

After the conversion of the Sakya ladies, Buddha went to the town of Vaisali, now identified with a village called Bisarah, in the vicinity of Bakhra, in the Muzafferpur district. Vaisali was a sort of free city governed by an oligarchy consisting of its leading residents called the Lichavis. At Vaisali Buddha vanquished in argument Purna Kacyap and many other philosophical teachers. After these feats Buddha went to the Trayastrinsat* heaven, and there preached his faith to his mother and a host of gods. During the period that he was away from earth his disciples were oppressed with grief on account of his absence. He felt compassion for them, and after about three months came down to earth again by a Vaidurya (*lapis lazuli*) staircase, the foot of which was fixed near an Udumbar tree in the town of Sankisa near Canouj.

A few years before Buddha's death there was a great schism in his camp, headed by his cousin, Deva Datta. He had been made to enter the holy order by a stratagem, and was never a very sincere follower of Buddha. As Buddha had the confidence of the old King Bimbasara, Deva Datta somehow managed to make himself a favourite with Ajata Satru, the heir-apparent to the throne of Magadha. Ajata Satru brought about the death of his affectionate father in a very cruel manner ; but Deva Datta's attempts to put an end to the life of his great cousin were frustrated by some kind of miracle or other. After the death of Bimbasara, the inevitable reaction came on in the mind of Ajata Satru. He was sorely oppressed with remorse, and, through the influence of his step-brother and physician Jivan Kumara Bhand, he soon took steps to be reconciled to Buddha. In Kosala also there took place a revolution similar to that in Magadha. King

* See Glossary.

Prasnajit's son, Virudhaka, was led by Ambarisha, a son of the royal chaplain, to dethrone his father, and to compel him to leave the kingdom. The Prime Minister of the State at first refused to help Virudhaka. But the ultimate success of the heir-apparent in attaining the object of his guilty ambition was mainly due to the co-operation of the premier. After his dethronement, Prasnajit repaired to Raj Giri in order to seek for refuge. But he died of hunger and thirst before Ajata Satru could do anything for his relief.

The success of the revolution that took place in Kosala was in all probability due to the support that Virudhaka received from the orthodox faction, and not to that of any schism among the followers of Buddha. At any rate, Virudhaka, after ascending the throne of Kosala, never showed any sympathy for the new faith. On the contrary, he immediately declared war against the Sakyas of Kapilavastu, and, after conquering them, effected their complete destruction.

Buddha was, it seems, made an eye-witness of the ruin of his race. After the completion of the conquest of Kapilavastu by Virudhaka, Buddha repaired to Raj Giri and lived there for some time. He had been reconciled to Ajata Satru. But after his humiliation at Kosala, the young king of Magadha apparently refused to treat him and his followers with the liberality that they had been accustomed to before. According to the Buddhistic histories there was a great famine in the country about a year before the prophet's death, and he was obliged to confess to his army of monks that he was not in position to support them, and that they must shift for themselves. Apparently the prophet felt very much distressed at the collapse of his ambitious schemes, and so he left Raj Giri for good. He had now very nearly completed the usual span of human life, and yet did not think of dying in peace in the city which he had made his head-quarters, and where alone he could expect to have a large number of his followers round him during his last moments. On his way to Kushinara, on the Gondah, where he intended to die, the prophet sojourned for a few days at Patali Putra, and the Buddhist chronicles take care to record that he was there respectfully entertained by Varshakar, the Brahman Minister of King Ajata Satru. The biographers of the prophet are, however, silent as to the kind of treatment that he received from King Ajata Satru when leaving Raj Giri for good. The omission seems to be significant.

After leaving Patna, Buddha made a halt at Vaisali, living there for a few days in the garden house presented to him by Amba Pali, and partaking of the hospitality of the old courtezan.

The event in the life of a prophet which causes the greatest strain on the ingenuity of his loyal biographer, is his death. For an exact idea of the manner in which the Buddhistic annalists acquitted themselves in this difficult task, the reader must refer to the original works. The biographers of Buddha sometimes state the facts without any kind of colouring. But this is not the case throughout. For instance, in many places the favourite disciple Ananda is charged with the responsibility of his master's death, because of his not asking him to prolong his life.* It is stated also that while at Beluva, a dire illness fell upon Buddha,† but he thought that it would not be right for him to pass away while the congregation of Bhikshus was scattered. So he determined to retain hold on his body until it had accomplished its task.

Divested of the coating of legendary colouring, the plain fact was that Buddha recovered from the illness which seized him while he was at Beluva. After passing the rainy season there, he went back to Vaisali and stayed there for a short time. He made

---

* Rockhill's *Life of Buddha*, p. 152.
† *Ib.*, p. 130.

up his mind to die at Kushinara, and with that object left Vaisali for good before long. On his way to his intended place of death, he halted at various places, and at one of these, then called Jalauka, he was invited by one Kundu, a worker in metal, to partake of his hospitality. The host put some pork in Buddha's alms-bowl, and that was the cause of the malady that brought about his death. His demise caused the earth to shake and thunderbolts to fall. His funeral was performed by the Mallas of Kushinara, in accordance with the directions which he gave before his death, and which were as stated in the following report of the conversation he had with Ananda on the subject :—

"*Ananda.*—How then, Lord, must the Brahmans and householders who are believers honour the Blessed One's remains.

Buddha.—Ananda, they must treat them as those of a King of Kings.

Ananda.—Lord, how do they treat the remains of a King of Kings?

Buddha.—Ananda, the body of a King of Kings is wrapped in bands of cotton, and when it has thus been wrapped, it is covered with five hundred layers. After that it is put in an iron-case filled with oil, and it is covered with a double cover of iron; then a funeral pile of all kinds of odoriferous woods is built; the remains are burnt, and the fire is put out with milk. Then they put his bones in a golden casket and in the cross road they build a chaitya over his remains, and with baldachins, flags and streamers, perfumes, garlands, incense and sweet powders, with sounds of music, they honour, praise, venerate and revere him, and celebrate a feast in his honour. So likewise, Ananda, must they treat the Tathagata's remains."*

These directions may be taken to show what kind of ambition lurked in the heart of the great mendicant. As instances of suicide in high life are not quite unknown, so there are many cases on record of men in affluent circumstances renouncing home, either for domestic unhappiness, or for love of adventure, or out of a craving for variety. But Sannyash for such causes deserves no more admiration or honour than *felo de se.* The monarch who sacrifices his personal comfort for the happiness of his subjects has certainly far better claims to be adored by them, than a thought-

* Rockhill's *Life of Buddha*, p. 137.

less heir-apparent who voluntarily sacrifices his prospects with a view to sink into a position of obscurity. A love of physical comforts and worldly honour is inherent in human nature, and whatever indifference an ascetic may profess towards such things, it must be impossible for him to smother altogether his natural craving for them.

The late Lala Babu voluntarily left home in the garb of a mendicant, leaving his princely estate in the hands of his wife. But a close study of the methods by which he afterwards acquired the valuable zemindaris in Mathura, Aligar and Bulandshahar that he dedicated to his idol at Brindaban, renders it impossible to give him credit for being even then free from the usual Kāyastha instincts. The case with Buddha was apparently the same. He gave up, it is true, the certain prospect of inheriting the petty principality ruled by his father. But every act done, and almost every word uttered, by him show that he was actuated by a deep-rooted ambition for a far higher position.

CHAP. II.—THE RAPID SPREAD OF BUDDHISM AND ITS SUBSEQUENT DISAPPEARANCE FROM INDIA.

The instruments and measures which contributed most to the rapid spread of Buddha's religion were (1) the army of monks that he succeeded in raising; (2) the admission of Sudras and women to the holy orders; and (3) the rage for building monasteries that he managed to create. The Hindu law-givers had declared that it was lawful for the Vedic students to live by begging. The inevitable result was that many pretenders assumed the garb of Vedic scholars. At a subsequent time, ascetics like the Nigranthis, without even any pretension of learning, swelled the ranks of beggars. When Buddha commenced his preachings, the number of such mendicants was apparently very considerable. But they never had any organisation, and although, in years of plenty, they could procure their food by begging, they had no friend or patron to see that they were well-housed and well-clad, or properly fed in seasons of scarcity. Buddha was able to attract such men by offering them better prospects. There was generally no difficulty about their commissariat. That was managed by leaving them to billet themselves on the people. The most important thing was to provide them with barracks. *Ex hypothesi*, they had voluntarily renounced home, and the public could not well be asked to find for them what they professed to have abandoned *suo moto*, in their indifference to worldly comfort. The genius of Buddha, however, was ready with a pretext for the new requisition on the laity. The monks were themselves quite indifferent to physical comforts and discomforts; but the practice of severe austerities, and the passing of the rainy season in an uncovered place, were strictly prohibited by their master. By travelling in the rainy season, a monk might unwittingly cause the destruction of insects. That was to be avoided anyhow.

As a specimen of the preaching by which kings and rich men were led to build Viharas and Sangaramas, the following may be referred to :—

> To give houses to the order, a place of refuge and joy, so that we may there exercise concentration and holy intuition, has been commanded by Buddha as the most noble gift. Therefore let a wise man, who understands what is best for himself, build beautiful houses, and receive into them the knowers of the doctrine. He may give food and drink, clothes and lodging to such the upright with cheerful heart. These preach to him the doctrine which drives away all suffering; if he apprehends the doctrine here below, he goes sinless into Nirvana.—*Cullavogga*, VI, 15.

From the beginning of his career as a prophet, Buddha saw the importance of having for his army of monks suitable habitations. In the second year of his ministry, he managed to get the Venuvana garden house at Raj Giri from King Bimbasara. The next year the merchant prince Sudatta Anatha Pindada was led to build the Jetavanavihara at Sravasti. In the sixth year Suddhodan built, at his son's request, a monastery at Kapilavastu. The date when Amba Pali presented to Buddha her garden house at Vaisali is not known. In all probability the gift was made at an early period. Sometimes the rich were induced, or compelled by adverse circumstances, to make over all their property to the Sanga. A notable instance was Jyotiska, a merchant of Raj Giri, whose wealth had excited the jealousy of King Ajata Satru, and led to his persecution in various ways. To avoid further molestation, he made over all his estates to Buddha, and enrolled himself a Bhikshu.

Theoretically, the Buddhist monks were entitled to live in their Vihars only during the rains. But, as Sir Monier Williams* rightly observes, such restrictions were soon ignored, and a residence in covered houses became usual at all seasons. Thus homeless beggars were provided with comfortable habitations at the expense of the toiling classes.

Through the liberality of the pious men and women among his lay disciples, Buddha was generally able to keep his followers well-housed and well-fed. But there were times when neither the charity of the rich, nor the miraculous powers of the prophet, sufficed to provide his monks with the means of sustenance. Just before his death, when there was a famine in the land, he advised them to billet themselves on their friends and relatives. The occasions for such shifts and expedients, however, were rare. As a general rule, his followers were better housed and better fed than the majority of people. As Buddhism spread, kings, princes and the rich vied with each other for the privilege of endowing monasteries. The result was that not only were the monks enabled to live in comfort, but a career of ambition was opened to a great many of them. Each of the monasteries became a centre of power. The monk who could manage to become the head of one of them, generally acquired princely wealth and influence. Neither orthodox Hinduism nor any of the pre-Buddhist sects had such attractions for poor men of ambition. Each monastery in the frontier stations became a fresh centre of power, and thus the new religion spread by gigantic strides.

To Buddha is given the credit of doing away with caste. He, however, never interfered with the state of things he found among the laity. He ignored caste only so far as to admit all classes to his Sanga, and to allow his monks to take cooked food from even the

---

* See Sir Monier William's *Buddhism*, p. 428.

lowest castes. One of his greatest disciples, Upali, was a barber, and he made the junior monks, drawn from the higher castes, bow to him. This innovation may be regarded as praiseworthy by many. Buddha however was no reformer. When it suited his policy, he talked of morality, to discredit the Vedic rituals. But his chief aim in all that he did and said was to attract a swarm of followers, and to that end he sacrificed everything else. He set at nought some of the noblest rules of discipline imposed on society by the Hindu Shastras. To keep his army well-fed, he made it lawful for them to accept the hospitality of even the degraded.

What led Buddha to admit women to holy orders, it is not possible to say. This much seems probable, that they proved one of the chief attractions to the new faith. As the orthodox Hindu religion does not favour the re-marriage of widows, and as in Hindu society an old widower cannot possibly get a bride of such an age as to be a proper mate for him, aged men and women, among the lower castes, are sometimes obliged to embrace one of the modern Vishnuvite faiths for the sake of marriage. It is chiefly by the operation of this cause that fresh recruits are now-a-days secured for the existing monastic orders, and their practice is apparently based on that of the ancient Buddhists, whose place they now occupy.

By the orthodox faith, no Hindu lady is permitted to perform any religious rite except in the company, or for the benefit, of her husband. In fact, according to the Hindu Shastras, the only religious duties of a woman are, to obey her husband in his lifetime, and, after his death, to live an abstemious life under the guardianship of her sons or some relative of her deceased lord. Whatever conflicts there may be in our ancient codes as to other points, they all agree in not allowing a woman to go out of the protection of her husband or guardian, for joining any class of mendicants. Buddha himself had adopted the same policy at first. The innovation he sanctioned later on has been productive of a deal of mischief. The circumstances which had induced him to the step have been referred to already. It is said that he evinced great reluctance in enrolling among his followers the Bhikshunis or nuns. It is said also that the regulations originally framed were such as to keep the two sexes completely separate. They were not allowed to live in the same monastery like the *matajis* and *babajis* of the present day. The Buddhist nuns were not to reside in forest hermitages, but within the walls of a village or town "in huts or nunneries, by twos or in greater number, for a sister was not allowed to live alone."* "To make a journey with a nun, to go aboard the same boat with her or to sit with her alone and without a witness, was strictly forbidden."* These were wholesome regulations no doubt. But it is to be feared that the confessional invitations and observances neutralised them altogether. The nuns were required every half month to "betake themselves to the monk, who had been named to them, by a resolution of the brotherhood, to receive his spiritual instruction and admonition. In the presence of another monk, that monk sits waiting the nuns, and when they have made their appearance, bowed themselves to the ground, and sat down before him he speaks to them of the eight high ordinances, and expounds to them, either by way of sermon or by question and answer, what he deems profitable of the teaching and maxims of Buddha."*

These rules and regulations may at first sight seem unobjectionable. But such opportunities as they created for contact between the monks and the nuns were tempting enough to celibates.

As among the modern Vaishnavas, so among the Buddhists, the female devotees proved the source of

* Oldenberg's *Life of Buddha*, translated by Mr. W. Hoey, pp. 380, 381.

both their strength and weakness. Buddha himself, as we have seen, had admitted a courtezan. In their old age the fallen women become anxious to be restored to society. But an orthodox Brahman cannot minister to any of them, without being himself degraded. It is only the followers of the latter-day prophets that can elevate their social status.

The rapid spread of Buddhism at first was perhaps due more to the monastic system, the admission of Sudras into the holy orders, and the enrolment of nuns, than to any intrinsic merit of its own. The monasteries in the beginning served like military cantonments and recruiting camps. The wealth of the fallen women served as an attraction to the beggars. But the admission of such women necessarily brought discredit on the faith, and rendered the continuance of the higher classes in it quite impossible. And when the monasteries themselves became hot-beds of immorality, the whole system melted away under the fierce rays of public opinion among the Brahmans and other higher classes.

CHAP. III.—THE RELIGION OF BUDDHA.

Buddha never recommended the worship of any deity, visible or invisible, and his religion is therefore usually regarded as godless. To form, however, an exact idea of his faith, it is necessary to examine his tenets in connection with those of the Vedic priests and the Nigranthi ascetics whom he sought to discredit. The Brahmans were interested in upholding the importance of the great Vedic sacrifices. To make their agency indispensable, the exegetes of the Mimansa school went so far as to declare that the gods had no real existence, and that it was only by the performance of the sacrifices in the manner prescribed by their Shastras, and not by independent prayers, that men could hope to derive the benefit they sought from the invisible powers. The weakest points in the Vedic cult were the denial of the real existence of the gods, and the encouragement it gave to the slaughter of animals, and the drinking of strong liquors. The Nigranthis were the first to protest against these doctrines and practices, and Buddha adopted their tenets with certain modifications so as to suit his policy. The object of the Nigranthis was to discredit Brahmanism, and to secure at least the respect of the mercantile castes. The Ksatriyas, whose proper profession was war, could not feel much aversion towards the bloody and bacchanalian rites of the Brahmans. To keep the fighting classes in good humour, the Vedic priests had to neglect and lower the manufacturing and mercantile castes.

To secure the veneration of these classes, who are interested in peace, the Nigranthis made their religion as inoffensive as possible. Buddha wanted to make his religion equally acceptable to both the Ksatriyas and the Vaishyas. He prohibited the killing of animals, but allowed his followers to eat the flesh of animals killed by others. Buddha himself ate flesh meat when given to him as alms. In fact, his death was caused by the eating of pork.

The great bugbear of the Hindu theologians of all classes is the necessity of transmigration, and the consequent difficulty of avoiding the pains of birth, diseases, decay and death. The Vedic priests, with their ritualistic learning, professed the doctrine that the desired liberation from the bonds of flesh was obtainable either by Vedic knowledge, or by the performance of the Vedic sacrifices. The Nigranthis, who were poor and illiterate beggars, found it more convenient to parade their poverty, and to inculcate that the practice of asceticism was the only way to attain salvation and superior wisdom. Buddha's object was to organise a large army of monks. He therefore condemned both luxury and asceticism, and recommended moderate living, avoiding both over-indulgence and excessive self-mortification. The way to attain wisdom and beatitude lies, in his opinion, in religious contemplation and the practice of the rules of morality, and not in asceticism. The Vedic priests of Jaimini's school denied the real existence of the gods. Buddha not only admitted their reality, but emphasized his belief in them, by assigning to them separate and well-defined heavens. He was, however, quite as interested in declaring them powerless as Jaimini himself. The latter taught that the only way to attain happiness and avoid misery was the performance of sacrifices, and that, as the gods had no real existence, prayers addressed to them, in any other form, were useless. Buddha taught (1) that there was nothing but misery in the world;

(2) that to get rid of this misery men must cease to have desires; (3) and that cessation of desires could be brought about by every man,—whether Brahman, Ksatriya, Vaishya or Sudra,—by deep meditation, and the observance of certain rules of diet and discipline. The ultimate object of the Vedic priests was to exact as much ghi, meat and wine as possible, by indirect taxation on the Ksatriya princes. The ambition of the Nigranthi beggars did not extend beyond securing for the benefit of the class the small charities of the niggardly Baniyas. The purpose which Buddha evidently had in view was to collect round him a cheap and large army of followers, and to be in a position to keep them well-housed and well-fed by the method of direct taxation involved in the claims of the mendicants for alms.

Buddha admitted the existence of the gods, but maintained that they were subordinate to the man of enlightenment, and powerless for good and evil. He did not prescribe any form of liturgy or worship. His object was to make himself a power in the country, and to make men honour him as a god. So he prescribed for recitation the following formula :—

Buddham Saranam Gachami; Dharmam Saranam Gachami; Sangam Saranam Gachami.

Translation :—I go for refuge to the Buddha; I go for refuge to the law; I go for refuge to the order.

The deification of Dharma or law in a personified form is certainly free from any taint of selfishness. But as Buddha inculcated the same reverence to himself and to the order founded by him, it cannot be said that his teachings were the outcome of pure philanthropy. The inevitable result of the direction was to lead to the regular worship of Buddha with his Dharma and his Sanga. These three, called the Tri Ratna, or the three jewels, afterwards became the Buddhist Triad. Images representing them were set up in the Vihars, and became regular objects of worship. The way being opened, other gods and saints were soon admitted to the pantheon, and the religion of the great iconoclast became one of the most idolatrous and superstitious faiths in the world. Buddha may not be responsible for all the later accretions. But there cannot be much doubt as to his having struggled hard to be worshipped as a god. He put an end to the old dynasty of kings, not for giving liberty to the people, but only to step into the throne himself under a new name.

For an account of the later phases of Buddhism and the development of abomination worship in connection with it, the reader must refer to treatises expressly devoted to the subject.

CHAP. IV.—THE MORALITY OF THE RELIGION OF BUDDHA.

It has been already observed that Buddhism was perhaps one of the earliest of the morality-preaching religions. The early Vedic faith was more concerned with rainfall and other worldly matters, than with the inculcation of ethical principles. Buddha and his principal disciples professed to have miraculous powers for controlling the course of natural phenomena. But they performed miracles by the mere exercise of their will, and not, like the Brahmans, by incantations—by burning of ghi, libation of wine, or the slaughtering of animals. It must, however, be mentioned here that Buddha never encouraged the performance of miracles by his followers. On the contrary, he censured them severely whenever they displayed their powers in violation of his orders. Thus the Buddhistic scriptures countenance the pretensions of the monks, and at the same time supply them with a pretext for avoiding requisitions for exhibiting their powers.

So far as Buddha preached such rules of morality as the Pancha Sila, his religion deserves every praise. The fundamental principles of his moral code were—(1) kill no living creature; (2) steal not; (3) commit not adultery; (4) lie not; (5) drink not strong drink. For teaching such ethics, he is entitled to the heart-felt gratitude of the world. But there is nothing in his cult to show that the teaching of morality was his sole or his principal object. The Vedic religion, which prevailed in his time, encouraged, for sacrificial purposes, the killing of animals, and the drinking of strong liquors. The abuse had, at one time, become very great, as appears from the Mimansa and the Brahmana literature. The first to raise the voice of protest were the Nigranthis. However, Buddha also deserves due credit for holding up to ridicule the Vedic sacrifices.

Buddha was digging for the foundations of a new religion, and he naturally treated without mercy the weak points of the ancient faith. But the religion and practices that he inculcated were very far from being unalloyed blessings. The Brahmanical Shastras caused no doubt a great waste of the resources of the country, for the cultivation of a kind of learning the value of the greater part of which might certainly be questioned. But while the exactions of the Vedic priests were occasional and justifiable to some extent, Buddha imposed on his countrymen the burden of a standing army of idlers. It may be alleged that some of the Buddhist monks were men of true piety, and did good to society by earnest efforts to improve its morality. But it is difficult to suppose that the Buddhist monks and nuns were of a better type than the Vishnuvite Babajis, Matajis or Mohants that we see at the present day. The fact seems to be that the wifeless and childless cenobites—and especially those who hold charge of the rich monasteries or are otherwise well provided—cannot have any regard for public opinion, and their inevitable tendency, in most cases, is to drift into a disreputable course of life. The preaching of morality by such men is out of the question.

In his zeal for the success of his own religion, Buddha tried to upset even the best and most unexceptionable sides of Brahmanism. The Shastric laws relating to social discipline are based upon an express recognition of the natural wants, necessities and appetites of men. For instance, the orthodox codes not only regard marriage as allowable, but make it imperative on every man and woman. Such legislation is beyond all praise and, at any rate, is intelligible. But it does not seem possible to view in the same light the laws imposed by Buddha on his followers. His injunctions were that all able-bodied and healthy men, not in the service of the king, should sever their connection with the world, should lead a life of celibacy, and should live on the charity of the public. If universally accepted, such legislation would tend to the total extirpation of the human race. Surely that was not the object of the great prophet. What then was it?

A careful review of his life and teachings leads to the conclusion that his sole object was to make himself a power in the country, by organising an army of monks. He professed to have found a remedy for the miseries of this world. He professed to be a teacher of morality. But the actual result of his teachings was to increase, rather than diminish, the sum total of human misery and immorality. By following him, some of his monks and nuns derived no doubt certain advantages. But their gains were like those of the comrades of a Nadir Shah or a Mahmood of Ghazni. They contributed nothing, either directly or indirectly, to the production of wealth, and whatever they gained was only so much loss to the world. The demoralisation that was caused by Buddha's teachings may be gathered from the following account of the circumstances under which he ruled that minors, under the age of twenty, were not to be ordained as monks:—

1. At that time there was in Rajgraha a company of seventeen boys, friends of each other: young Upali* was first among them. Now Upali's father and mother thought: How will Upali after our death live a life of ease and without pain? Then Upali's father and mother said to themselves: 'If Upali could learn writing, he would after our death live a life of ease and without pain.' But then Upali's father and mother thought again: If Upali learns writing, his fingers will become sore; but if Upali could learn arithmetic, he would, after our death, live a life of ease without pain.

* This Upali is different from the famous Upali who was one of the chief disciples of Buddha; the latter came not from Raj Griha, but from the Sakya ountry.

2. But then Upali's father and mother thought again: 'If Upali learns arithmetic, his breast will become diseased.' But if Upali could learn money-changing, he would, after our death, live a life of ease and comfort, and without pain. But then Upali's father and mother said to themselves: 'If Upali learns money-changing, his eyes will suffer. Now here are the Sakka Puttiya Samanas who keep commodious precepts and live a commodious life; they have good meals and lie down on beds protected from the wind. If Upali could be ordained with the Sakkya Puttiya Samanas, he would, after our death, live a life of ease and without pain.'—*Mahavagga*, I, 49, 1-2.

From the above, it would appear that the Buddha's monks were, in his time, believed to live in greater comfort than even clerks, accountants and money-changers. If this was actually so, the economical demoralisation caused by him must have been very serious, and such as could be rectified only by bitter experience. Whatever the case may have been in Buddha's lifetime, there cannot be any doubt that after his death the majority of the monks had to pass their lives in great misery. If they had been left free to marry and to work for bread, they might have become happier and more useful members of society. The fact that they often broke their vows* shows how galling the restraints were to which they subjected themselves. No doubt, they acted with their eyes wide open. But the majority of men in this world are utterly incapable of guiding themselves by their own judgment. They allow themselves to be fascinated by fine words and clever jugglery. When their guides lead them rightly, they deserve to be worshipped as benefactors of mankind. It is, however, impossible to accord that credit to a teacher who gave the utmost encouragement to all classes to become monks and nuns.

* A great many of such cases formed the occasions for fresh legislation. See *Mahavagga*.

PART VIII.

THE JAINS.

CHAP. I.—THE RELATIVE ANTIQUITY OF JAINISM AND BUDDHISM.

FROM what has been already stated in connection with the religions of the mercantile castes, it will have appeared clear that Jainism is one of the most important of the living cults among the Hindus. It is professed by at least a million men, and some of those are among the wealthiest and most refined in the Hindu community. It seems to be a very ancient religion, having apparently a more hoary antiquity than even Buddhism.

The Buddhist scriptures speak of certain hostile sects called the Nigranthis and the Tirthikas. In all probability these were the very sects that, at a subsequent period, came to be designated Jains. The Nigranthis were evidently so-called, in early times, on account of their having no written scriptures. They secured the veneration of the public by the practice of austerities, by pretending to work miracles, and by professing tenderness for every form of animal life. To them written scriptures were unnecessary, and even if their early teachers possessed sufficient learning and capacity for recording the tenets and legends of their cult, it was perhaps more to their interest to deny the utility of all written scriptures than to give countenance to bookish blind faith. However, their success soon brought literary men to the field, and the example of the Buddhists led them to compile canonical treatises on the model of those of Buddha. It was not until then that the members of the sect began to evince a preference for the designation of Jain. They never disavowed their identity with the old Nigranthis. In fact, there are passages in the Jain scriptures where their authors speak of themselves and their sect as the Nigranthis. But the word is now interpreted as denotative of persons who are not bound to this world by any tie. This interpretation is rendered necessary by the fact that, if taken in its true and natural sense, the old designation of the sect might serve to discredit the authenticity of its modern scriptures. As to the sect called the Tirthikas in Buddha's time, it is hardly necessary to observe that its very name goes a great way to establish its identity with the Jains who worship the Tirthankaras.

The existence of the Jain religion before Buddha's time, is rendered probable by a great many other facts. The Jains believe in twenty-four deified saints called by them Jinas and also Tirthankaras, of whom at least the last two, namely, Paresanath and Mahavira *alias* Vardhamana, were historical personages. In the Jain Kalpa Sutras it is stated that Kumara Pal will found Anhilwara Patan and become a disciple of Hem Chandra 1,669 years after the death of Mahavira. There is independent evidence to shew that the conversion of Kumar Pal took place about 1174 A.D., and consequently the last Jina had passed away about 500 years before Christ. The Jains of Bengal reckon Vardhamana to have lived 580 years before Vikramaditya, *i.e.*, in the seventh century B.C. According to the Jain histories, Mahavira lived in the sixth century B.C. This date being given by authors who evidently lived at a much later period, and who were interested in a hoary antiquity for their prophets, may not be regarded as thoroughly reliable. But it is corroborated to some extent by Buddhist books. According to the sacred history of the Jains, Mahavira had many disciples, among whom was Gosala, who headed a schism which led to the formation of a sect called the Ajivakas. This sect, and the name of its founder, are distinctly referred to in the earliest of the Buddhist scriptures.

The Buddhist sacred writings frequently speak of a hostile teacher bearing the name of Nigantha Nataputra, who went about naked in the streets, and whom Buddha vanquished in argument. The Jain Kalpa Sutras also speak of Mahavira by the name of Nataputra. There is, therefore, good reason for holding that Buddha and Mahavira were contemporaries. In the Jain scriptures, a Gautama is spoken of as one of the disciples of Mahavira. But the Gautama of the Jains was a Brahman, and the account of his life, as given in their sacred books, does not tally in any way with what is known regarding the personal history of Buddha. However, as Buddha himself is called a Jina, and as he at one time sought to attain wisdom by the practice of austerities, like the Nigranthis, it is not impossible that he was a disciple of Mahavira. This view receives material support from the fact that the Sakyamuni is sometimes spoken of in the sacred books of his cult as the twenty-fifth Buddha or Jina. As according to the Jains, Mahavira was the twenty-fourth Jina, it may be that Buddha was originally a disciple of Mahavira, and that, after organising a new schism, he proclaimed himself as the twenty-fifth Jina.

If the Jains are not the same as the Nigranthis and the Tirthikas, they are, at any rate, followers of a similar faith. The Vedic Brahmans indulged in animal food, intoxicating drinks and other luxuries. The Nigranthis were perhaps the first to protest against these practices in the most uncompromising manner. The Jains profess the same tenderness for every living creature, and the same aversion from flesh meat. The Nigranthis practised asceticism for the attainment of beatitude. The Jain monks do the same. The Nigranthis went about without any garment. The Digambara Jains are, according to their name, naked ascetics. We do not know what gods or saints the ancient Nigranthis worshipped. To that extent alone there is room for doubt as to the identity of the Jains with the pre-Buddhist Nigranthis.

Whatever doubts there may be as to the period when the Jain religion, as we find it now, first originated, there cannot be any question as to its appertaining to an earlier stratum of religious thought than Buddhism. This is proved historically by the Jain's identity with the pre-Buddhist Nigranthis and also by an examination of their ascetic nature. Their asceticism, and extreme tenderness for every form of animal life, are the outcome of a spirit of bitter hostility to the Vedic religion. Buddha steered a middle course. He preached that "unkindness cannot purify a mortal who has not overcome desires." He forbade the killing of animals, but allowed his followers to eat flesh meat. In fact, even to the last, he never sought to overcome his Rajput predilection for pork. It seems reasonable then to conclude that Buddhism arose in India at a later period than Jainism. In all probability the Jain faith had been established among the mercantile classes long before Buddha, and when Buddha preached his new faith he did not find it possible to secure any class as a whole among his followers. The Ksatriyas were from time immemorial in the hands of the Brahmans. The peaceful religion of the Nigranthis had greater attraction for the mercantile Banyas. Buddha found both the fields occupied, and addressed himself more to organise monasteries and missionaries, than to secure, among his lay disciples, any particular class of citizens.

If the Jain faith is not the same as that of the pre-Buddhist Nigranthis, then it must be held to have had its origin at a much later period than Buddhism. It is true that the Jain scriptures place the last of their Tirthankaras before Buddha. But there is no reliable proof that any religion bearing the name of Jainism existed before the era of Christ.

CHAP. II.—THE NATURE OF THE JAINA RELIGION.

LIKE the Buddhists, the Jains reject the authority of the Vedas, and deny the spiritual supremacy of the Brahmans. But they do so more in theory than for practical purposes. In actual practice, they celebrate most of the purificatory rites prescribed by the Brahmanical Shastras, and employ Brahmans as priests for the performance of these, as well as for offering worship to their deified saints. They show greater respect to their *yatis* or monks than to the Brahmans who serve as their priests. The *yatis* are recruited from all the higher castes. They live in monasteries, where, at stated times, they recite their holy books before the audience of lay visitors that assemble on such occasions. They also deliver extempore sermons and lectures before their co-religionists. They never do any priestly service in connection with the worship of any deity or saint, or for the performance of any domestic rite. The middle class *yatis* cast horoscopes, and give astrological advice to their constituents. But the higher class *yatis* refuse to do even that kind of work.

There are two principal sub-sects among the Jains. One of these bears the name of Digambara ; and the other Swetambara. The word Digambara means *sky clad*, i.e., naked, and the Digambari Jains are so called because some of their monks go about in the streets naked, and because their images are never dressed or ornamented. The Swetambars are so called because their monks wear white robes. A Swetambari monk may carry an alms bowl in his hand. A Digbambar *yati* is not allowed to do so, and has to receive his food in the palm of his hands. The Swetambaris carry with them a brush and a handkerchief for preventing flies from entering the mouth or the nose. The Digambaras do not attach any importance to the Chamar or the Puttika.

The Ossawalis are all Swetambari Jains. In Southern India, Jaypore and Behar, the Digambaris are more numerous than the Swetambaris. The majority of the Agarwals are Vishnuvites. Of those among them who profess the Jain faith, the greater number are Digambaras. In Northern India, there are no Jains outside the mercantile Baniya classes. In Southern India, there are Jains having a higher or lower caste status. In Punjab there is a caste called Pabra who are all said to be Jains.

The Jaina monks are not allowed to marry. A man of any caste may be a Jaina *yati*. The Jaina monks beg cooked food, taking a spoonful from each house. They do not take coins. They have no regular monasteries, and usually live in Dharmasalas, or guest houses, founded by the lay Jains. When they do so they do not take any kind of alms from the proprietor of the establishment. They always travel on foot, and are not allowed by the rules of their order to ride on a palki, carriage or horse. Formerly they were divided into a large number of Gachas or brotherhoods. Most of these have ceased to exist since long. The only Gachas existing now are the following :—

1. Khartar Gacha.
2. Tapa Gacha.
3. Kamala Gacha.
4. Lonka Gacha.
5. Pachani Gacha.

Each Gacha forms a distinct brotherhood. But a difference of Gacha does not imply any difference of religion. There are, however, sub-divisions among both the Digambaris and the Swetambaris which originated in doctrinal differences. The Digambaris have the following sub-orders among them :—

1. **Mula Sangi** ... These use brushes of peacock's feathers, wear red garments and receive alms in their hands.
2. **Kashta Sangis**... These worship wooden images and employ brushes of the tail of yak.
3. **The Tera Panthis** The Tera Panthis do not worship images, and have neither temples nor *yatis*. Their lay presbyters recite their sacred books and serve as teachers of the faith for the benefit of younger generations.
4. **Bis Panthis** ... These worship images, but make their offerings in front of them and not on them.

There are similar sub-sects among the Swetambaris. They are as follow :—

1. **Lumpaka** ... Founded by Jinendra Suri in the 16th century. These do not worship images.
2. **Bais Tala** ... Founded by a teacher named Raghunath.
3. **Tera Panthi** ... Founded by a teacher named Bhikan Nath, and hence called also Bhikan Panthi. These discard images, and keep their mouths veiled when they go out.
4. **Dhoondias** ... These keep their mouths veiled at all times, and affect to conform strictly to all the moral rules of their religion. They do not worship images. They have nuns among them called Dhoondis.

The Jain laity are called Sravaks (*vulg.* Soragi). The word Sravak literally means hearer, and the designation is applied to the laity, because it is their duty to hear the sermons and recitations delivered by the *yatis*. The Jain's daily routine of prayers is neither long nor complicated. The *yatis* are not bound by any rules at all, and the Sravak is only required to visit a temple, to walk round the images within it three times, to make an obeisance to the idols with an offering, and pronounce some such mantra or salutation formula as the following :—

Namo Arhatanam ; Namo Siddhanam ; Namo Aryanam; Namo Upadhyanam ; Nama Loe Sabba Sahunam.

***Translation*.—Salutation to the Arhats ; salutation to the Saints who have attained the supreme objects of their religious life ; salutation to the Sages ; salutation to the Teachers ; salutation to all the Devout in the world.**

The Jain Sravaks wear neither the sacred thread, nor any necklace of wooden beads to denote their religion. They do not paint any kind of mark on their foreheads like the Hindus properly so called. The chief festivals of the Jains take place on the days consecrated by the birth and death of their last two Tirthankars.

The Jains observe some of the Hindu festivals also, as for instance the following :—

1. **Sri Panchami, or the worship of the goddess of learning in the month of Magh (January—February).**
2. **Vasanta Yatra, or the spring festival popularly called *Holi*.**
3. **Aksaya Tritiya, or the day of the commencement of the Satya Yuga.**

The chief places of Jaina pilgrimage are the following :—

1.	Girnar	... In Gujrat.
2.	Abu.	... In Rajputana.
3.	Benares	... The place where Parswanath was born.
4.	Pareshnath	... A hill in the district of Hazaribag, Bengal, where Parswanath attained enlightenment.
5.	Kundalgrama	... The birthplace of Mahavira. It is in the vicinity of the Laksmi Sarai Station, E. I. Railway.
6.	Papapuri	... The place where Mahavira died. It is near Raj Giri.

INDEX AND GLOSSARY.

Calcutta, July 1896.

THACKER, SPINK AND CO.'S

PUBLICATIONS.

—CONTENTS—

A HANDBOOK OF PHOTOGRAPHY for Amateurs in India. By George Ewing. With Illustrations. 1 Volume. Crown 8vo. 623 pages. Rs. 7.

"This excellently prepared Handbook will probably find a large public. It is conceived on a capital scheme, and is provided with an intelligent index. All obscure points are illustrated by diagrams. A most useful and practical Handbook."—*Indian Daily News.*

"The Indian amateur is to be congratulated in having now a book that will give him all the information he is likely to require. Mr. Ewing's *Handbook* will obviate the necessity for collecting a number of works—it is a library in itself . . . . Excellently planned, it is full of valuable information conveyed in the most happy and lucid language."—*Journal of the Photographic Society of India.*

"All amateurs who procure it will find this Handbook an ever, useful and reliable companion; for it is a book which can be turned to for information and guidance on all points connected with Photography, whilst it is replete with time-saving tables and calculations which only an amateur knows how to value."—*Pioneer.*

"We can confidently recommend it to Indian amateurs."—*Statesman.*

THACKER, SPINK AND CO., CALCUTTA.

2500:—24-7-96.

POETRY, FICTION, ETC.

BURMESE TALES AND SKETCHES. By Mrs. H. Calthrop. Crown 8vo, sewed, Re. 1.

Contents:—A Tale of Old Mandalay—A River Tragedy—Theebaw's Umbrella—At the Avagye Mission.

"The Sketches are singularly well written, and hit off some Burmese characteristics with wonderful fidelity. . . . . The Tales are all written in a light vein, and are well calculated to while away an idle hour or two."—*Indian Daily News.*

"The stories are all well worth reading, and we are sure to hear of Mrs. Calthrop again."—*Ceylon Observer.*

"A group of exceedingly graphic and life-like sketches."—*Englishman.*

THE SPOILT CHILD. A Tale of Hindu Domestic Life. A Translation by G. D. Oswell, M.A., of the Bengali Novel, *Alaler Gharer Dulal*, by Peary Chand Mitter (Tek Chand Thakur). Crown 8vo. cloth, Rs. 3; paper, Rs. 2-8.

"Interesting as throwing a fairly vivid light upon the intimate life of a Hindu household."—*Daily Chronicle.*

"May be heartily commended both for its literary qualities and for the vivid picture it gives of Bengali manners and customs."—*Scotsman.*

SONG OF SHORUNJUNG & OTHER POEMS. Crown 8vo, cloth. Rs. 2-8.

Contents:—Darjeeling: Summer—The Song of Shorunjung—The Tsari Reed—To the Uplands—A Pastoral—The Jessamine—The Fakir—The Fisher's Supper—A Son—Two Moods—Farewell to Devon—Song—The London Maid—Infancy—A Lullaby—There are Words—Borodino—The Lone Night—The Captive—Cossack Cradle Song—Gifts of the Terek—The Cup of Life—Scenes from Eugene Onyegin.

"Full of tastefully conceived description. . . . Some of the single verses are very tuneful. . . A number of translations from the Russian form a noteworthy part of it. The poems have been admirably done into English, the translator having not only retained the sense of the original but the distinctive Russian character of expression and metre."—*Englishman.*

SQUIBS FROM THE "PIG": being a Series of Nonsensical Lays, compiled from the *Indian Planters' Gazette.* By H. E. Abbott. Crown 8vo, sewed. Rs. 3.

"They have not a little humour and smartness, and they are very fearless indeed. Sport, politics, journalism and society all come under the poetical lash, and are laughed at not unskilfully."—*Indian Daily News.*

STRAY STRAWS: BEING A COLLECTION OF SKETCHES AND STORIES. By "MIGNON." Crown 8vo. Re. 1-8.

"It is a capital book to take up when one has a few spare moments on hand."—*Englishman.*

"A very interesting collection of short stories and sketches."—*Morning Post* (Allahabad).

RHYMING LEGENDS OF IND. BY H. KIRKWOOD GRACEY, B.A., C.S. Crown 8vo, cloth. Rs. 3-8.

CONTENTS:—The City of Gore—A Mother's Vengeance—The Blue Cow—Famine—A Terrible Tiger—The Legend of Somnath—Treasure Trove—The Idol of Kalinga—Mind *vs.* Matter—*Vultur in partibus.*

"A collection of bright little poems. Keen satirical touches are introduced here and there throughout the volume. . . The clever little book."—*Morning Post.*

ELSIE ELLERTON. A NOVELETTE OF ANGLO-INDIAN LIFE. BY MAY EDWOOD, Author of "Stray Straws," "Autobiography of a Spin," etc. Crown 8vo. Re. 1-8.

"This novel is amusing, pure in tone, and distinguished by much local colouring."—*Athenæum.*

"Rudyard Kipling has taken the most becoming phase of Anglo-Indian life and in the main made the worst of it. Miss Edwood takes the pleasantest, and makes the most of it."—*Home News.*

INDIAN LYRICS. BY W. TREGO WEBB, M.A., PROFESSOR OF ENGLISH Literature, Presidency College. Fcap. 8vo, cloth, Rs. 2-8; sewed, Rs. 2.

"Vivacious and clever . . . He presents the various sorts and conditions of humanity that comprise the round of life in Bengal in a series of vivid vignettes . . He writes with scholarly directness and finish."—*Saturday Review.*

"A volume of poems of more than ordinary interest and undoubted ability."—*Oxford and Cambridge Undergraduates' Journal.*

LIGHT AND SHADE. BY HERBERT SHERRING. A COLLECTION OF Tales and Poems. Crown 8vo, cloth. Rs. 3.

"Piquant and humorous—decidedly original—not unworthy of Sterne."—*Spectator* (London).

POPPIED SLEEP. A CHRISTMAS STORY OF AN UP-COUNTRY STATION. By Mrs. H. A. FLETCHER, author of "Here's Rue for You." Crown 8vo, sewed. Re. 1-8.

A QUEER ASSORTMENT. A COLLECTION OF SKETCHES. BY A. HARVEY JAMES. Crown 8vo. Re. 1.

INDIAN IDYLLS. By an Idle Exile (Mrs. Cuthell), Author of "In Tent and Bungalow" and "By a Himalayan Lake." Crown 8vo, cloth. Rs. 2-8.

Contents:—The Maharajah's Guest—The Major's Mess Clothes—In a Haunted Grove—How we got rid of Hunks—My Wedding Day—Mrs. Caramel's Bow-Wow—The Tables Turned—A Polo Smash—After the Wily Boar—In the Rajah's Palace—Two Strings—A Modern Lochinvar—My First Snipe—Mrs. Dimple's Victim—Lizzie; a Shipwreck—How the Convalescent Depôt killed a Tiger—Faithful unto Death—The Haunted Bungalow—Christmas with the Crimson Cuirassiers—In Death they were not Divided.

"A pleasant little book of short stories and sketches, bright and light for the most part, dealing with frays and feasting, polo and pigsticking, with a ghost story thrown in by way of relief."—*Saturday Review.*

"All these are thoroughly Indian in colour and tone, but are not the less amusing and sprightly matter for reading in idle half hours."—*Daily Telegraph.*

THE TRIBES ON MY FRONTIER. An Indian Naturalist's Foreign Policy. By Eha. With 50 Illustrations by F. C. Macrae. Imp. 16mo. Uniform with "Lays of Ind." Fourth Edition. Rs. 7.

"We have only to thank our Anglo-Indian naturalist for the delightful book which he has sent home to his countrymen in Britain. May he live to give us another such."—*Chambers' Journal.*

"A most charming series of sprightly and entertaining essays on what may be termed the fauna of the Indian Bungalow. . . . . . We have no doubt that this amusing book will find its way into every Anglo-Indian's library."—*Allen's Indian Mail.*

"This is a delightful book, irresistibly funny in description and illustration, but full of genuine science too. . . . . . . There is not a dull or uninstructive page in the whole book."—*Knowledge.*

INDIA IN 1983. A Reprint of this celebrated Prophesy of Native Rule in India. Fcap. 8vo. Re. 1.

"Instructive as well as amusing."—*Indian Daily News.*

"There is not a dull page in the hundred and thirty-seven pages of which it consists."—*Times of India.*

LALU, THE CHILD-WIDOW. A Poem in seven parts: Proem—The Zemindar—The Farm—The Betrothal—The Lovers—Widowhood—The Pyre—Rest. By Lt.-Col. W. L. Greenstreet. Crown 8vo. Rs. 2.

AUTOBIOGRAPHY OF A SPIN. BY MAY EDWOOD, AUTHOR OF "Elsie Ellerton," "Stray Straws," &c. Re. 1-8.

"Undeniably a clever and not unaffecting study of the natural history of flirtation."—*Saturday Review.*

BEHIND THE BUNGALOW. BY EHA, Author of "THE TRIBES ON MY FRONTIER," With Illustrations by F. C. MACRAE. Fourth Edition. Imp. 16mo. Rs. 5.

"Of this book it may conscientiously be said that it does not contain a dull page, while it contains very many which sparkle with a bright and fascinating humour, refined by the unmistakable evidences of culture."—*Home News.*

"The author of 'Behind the Bungalow' has an excellent sense of humour combined with a kindliness of heart which makes his little book delightful reading."—*Saturday Review.*

"There is plenty of fun in 'Behind the Bungalow.'"—*World.*

"A series of sketches of Indian servants, the humour and acute observation of which will appeal to every Anglo-Indian."—*Englishman.*

"Drawn with delightful humour and keen observation."—*Athenæum.*

"Every variety of native character, the individual as well as the nation caste, trade, or class, is cleverly portrayed in these diverting sketches."—*Illustrated London News.*

INDIAN ENGLISH AND INDIAN CHARACTER. BY ELLIS UNDERWOOD. Fcap. 8vo. As. 12.

LAYS OF IND. BY ALIPH CHEEM. COMIC, SATIRICAL, AND Descriptive Poems illustrative of Anglo-Indian Life. Ninth Edition. Enlarged. With 70 Illustrations. Cloth, elegant gilt edges. Rs. 7-8.

"There is no mistaking the humour, and at times, indeed, the fun is both 'fast and furious.' One can readily imagine the merriment created round the camp fire by the recitation of 'The Two Thumpers,' which is irresistibly droll."—*Liverpool Mercury.*

"The verses are characterised by high animal spirits, great cleverness, and most excellent fooling."—*World.*

THE CAPTAIN'S DAUGHTER. A NOVEL. BY A. C. POOSHKIN. Literally translated from the Russian by STUART H. GODFREY, Captain, Bo. S.C. Crown 8vo. Rs. 2.

"Possesses the charm of giving vividly, in about an hour's reading, a conception of Russian life and manners which many persons desire to possess."—*Englishman.*

"The story will interest keenly any English reader."—*Overland Mail.*

A NATURALIST ON THE PROWL. BY EHA, Author of "Tribes on My Frontier," "Behind the Bungalow." Imp. 16mo. Rs. 8.

Profusely illustrated by Photographs of Animals in their habitat and at work; and Sketches by R. A. STERNDALE.

"The Author is a keen observer of nature, and his descriptions are felicitous and apt. He is entirely at home amid the Indian fauna, and writes of things which he knows and loves."—*Glasgow Herald.*

"A charming record of wild life in the jungle."—*Saturday Review.*

"Attractive alike in subject, treatment and appearance."—*Literary World.*

"Very easy and delightful reading."—*The Field.*

"We have not for a long time come across so readable a volume as this." —*Admiralty and Horse Guards Gazette.*

"Anyone who takes up this book will follow our example and not leave his chair until he has read it through. It is one of the most interesting books upon natural history that we have read for a long time."—*Daily Chronicle.*

"HERE'S RUE FOR YOU." NOVELETTES, ENGLISH AND ANGLO-Indian. By Mrs. H. A. FLETCHER. Crown 8vo, sewed. Rs. 2.

CONTENTS:—A Summer Madness—Whom the Gods Love—Nemesis—A Gathered Rose—At Sea: a P. and O. Story—Esther: an Episode.

ONOOCOOL CHUNDER MOOKERJEE. A MEMOIR OF THE LATE JUSTICE ONOOCOOL CHUNDER MOOKERJEE. By M. MOOKERJEE. Fifth Edition. 12mo. Re. 1.

"The reader is earnestly advised to procure the life of this gentleman, written by his nephew, and read it."—*The Tribes on My Frontier.*

DEPARTMENTAL DITTIES AND OTHER VERSES. By RUDYARD KIPLING. Eighth Edition. With additional Poems. Cloth. Rs. 3.

"This tiny volume will not be undeserving of a place on the bookshelf that holds 'Twenty-one Days in India.' Its contents, indeed, are not unlike the sort of verse we might have expected from poor 'Ali Baba' if he had been spared to give it us. Mr. Kipling resembles him in lightness of touch, quaintness of fancy, and unexpected humour."—*Pioneer.*

"The verses are all written in a light style, which is very attractive, and no one with the slightest appreciation of humour will fail to indulge in many a hearty laugh before turning over the last page."—*Times of India.*

"Mr. Kipling's rhymes are rhymes to some purpose. He calls them Departmental Ditties: but they are in reality social sketches of Indian officialism from a single view point, that of the satirist, though the satire is of the mildest and most delightful sort."—*Indian Planters' Gazette.*

THE INSPECTOR. A COMEDY. BY GOGOL. TRANSLATED FROM THE Russian by T. HART-DAVIES, Bombay Civil Service. Crown 8vo. Rs. 2.

"His translation, we may add, is a very good one."—*The Academy.*

A MIDSUMMER NIGHT'S DREAM (SHAKESPEARE). **Adapted to Pastoral** Representation. By N. NEWNHAM-DAVIS. Crown 8vo. Re. 1.

HISTORY, CUSTOMS, TRAVELS, ETC.

THE EARLY ANNALS OF THE ENGLISH IN BENGAL: BEING THE Bengal Public Consultations for the first half—the 18th Century. Summarised, Extracted and Edited, Introduction and Illustrative Addenda. By C. R. WILSON, M.A. Volume I. Royal 8vo, cloth. Rs. 12.

"The work is most excellently done, combining historical value with literary merit, and it is certain to command a large sale amongst those who are interested in the problem which in Mr. Wilson's view remains to be solved: How is it the English conquered India, and not the Portuguese French or Dutch?"—*Bombay Gazette.*

HINDU CASTES AND SECTS; AN EXPOSITION OF THE ORIGIN OF the Hindu Caste System and the bearing of the Sects towards each other and towards other Religious Systems. By Pandit JOGENDRA NATH BHATTACHARYA, M.A. D.L. Crown 8vo, cloth. Rs. 12.

CONTENTS:—The Brahmans—The Military Castes—The Scientific Castes—The Writer Castes—The Mercantile Castes—The Manufacturing and Artisan Castes—The Agricultural Castes—The Cowherds and Shepherds—Miscellaneous Castes—The Sivites—The Vishnuvites—The Semi-Vishnuvites and Guru-Worshippers—Modern Religions intended to bring about Union between Hindus and Mahomedans.

THE ORIGIN OF THE MAHOMEDANS IN BENGAL. BY MOULVIE FUZL RUBBEE. Crown 8vo. Rs. 3-8.

THE HINDOOS AS THEY ARE. A DESCRIPTION OF THE MANNERS, Customs and Inner Life of Hindoo Society, Bengal. By SHIB CHUNDER BOSE. Second Edition, Revised. Crown 8vo, cloth. Rs. 5.

HINDU MYTHOLOGY. VEDIC AND PURANIC. BY W. J. WILKINS, of the London Missionary Society, Calcutta. Profusely Illustrated. Imp. 16mo, cloth, gilt elegant. Rs. 7-8.

"His aim has been to give a faithful account of the Hindu deities such as an intelligent native would himself give, and he has endeavoured, in order to achieve his purpose, to keep his mind free from prejudice or theological bias. The author has attempted a work of no little ambition and has succeeded in his attempt, the volume being one of great interest and usefulness."—*Home News.*

"Mr. Wilkins has done his work well, with an honest desire to state facts apart from all theological prepossession, and his volume is likely to be a useful book of reference."—*Guardian.*

MODERN HINDUISM: BEING AN ACCOUNT OF THE RELIGION AND Life of the Hindus in Northern India. By W. J. WILKINS, Author of "Hindu Mythology, Vedic and Puranic." Demy 8vo. Rs. 8.

"He writes in a liberal and comprehensive spirit."—*Saturday Review.*

THE SOVEREIGN PRINCES AND CHIEFS OF CENTRAL INDIA. BY G. R. ABERIGH-MACKAY. Volume I—The House of Holkar. Imp. 8vo, cloth Rs. 12.

THE DHAMMAPADA; OR, SCRIPTURAL TEXTS. A BOOK OF BUDdhist Precepts and Maxims. Translated from the Pali on the Basis of Burmese Manuscripts. By JAMES GRAY. Second Edition. 8vo, boards. Rs. 2.

THE ETHICS OF ISLAM. A LECTURE BY THE HON'BLE AMEER ALI, C.I.E., Author of "The Spirit of Islam," "The Personal Law of the Mahomedans," etc. Crown 8vo, cloth gilt. Rs. 2-8.

An attempt towards the exposition of Islâmic Ethics in the English language. Besides most of the Koranic Ordinances, a number of the precepts and sayings of the Prophet, the Caliph Ali, and of 'Our Lady,' are translated and given.

THE LIFE AND TEACHING OF KESHUB CHUNDER SEN. BY P. C. MAZUMDAR. Second and Cheaper Edition. Rs. 2.

THEOSOPHICAL CHRISTIANITY. AN ADDRESS BY L. S. SECOND Edition, Revised and Enlarged. Small 4to. As. 8.

KASHGARIA (EASTERN OR CHINESE TURKESTAN). HISTORICAL, Geographical, Military, and Industrial. By Col. KUROPATKIN, Russian Army. Translated by Maj. GOWAN, H. M.'s Indian Army. 8vo. Rs. 2.

ANCIENT INDIA AS DESCRIBED BY PTOLEMY. WITH INTRODUCtion, Commentary, Map of India. By J. W. McCRINDLE, M.A. 8vo, cloth, lettered. Rs. 4-4.

ANCIENT INDIA AS DESCRIBED BY MEGASTHENES AND ARRIAN. With Introduction, Notes, and a Map of Ancient India. By J. W. McCRINDLE, M.A. 8vo. Rs. 2-8.

THE COMMERCE AND NAVIGATION OF THE ERYTHRÆAN SEA; Periplus Maris Erythræi; and of Arrian's Account of the Voyage of Nearkhos. With Introduction, Commentary, Notes, and Index. By J. W. McCRINDLE, M.A. 8vo. Rs. 3.

ANCIENT INDIA AS DESCRIBED BY KTESIAS THE KNIDIAN. A Translation of the Abridgment of his 'Indika,' by Photios. With Introduction, Notes, Index. By J. W. McCRINDLE, M.A. 8vo. Rs. 3.

A MEMOIR OF CENTRAL INDIA, INCLUDING MALWA AND ADJOINING Provinces, with the History, and copious Illustrations, of the Past and Present Condition of that Country. By Maj.-Gen. S. J. MALCOLM, G.C.B., &c. *Reprinted from Third Edition.* 2 vols. Crown 8vo, cloth. Rs. 5.

BOOK OF INDIAN ERAS. WITH TABLES FOR CALCULATING INDIAN Dates. By ALEXANDER CUNNINGHAM, C.S.I., C.I.E., Major-General, Royal Engineers. Royal 8vo, cloth. Rs. 12.

TALES FROM INDIAN HISTORY: BEING THE ANNALS OF INDIA re-told in Narratives. By J. TALBOYS WHEELER. Crown 8vo, cloth. Rs. 3. School Edition, cloth, limp. Re. 1-8.

"The history of our great dependency made extremely attractive reading. Altogether, this is a work of rare merit."—*Broad Arrow.*

"Will absorb the attention of all who delight in drilling records of adventure and daring. It is no mere compilation, but an earnest and brightly written book."—*Daily Chronicle.*

A CRITICAL EXPOSITION OF THE POPULAR "JIHAD." SHOWING that all the Wars of Mahammad were defensive, and that Aggressive War or Compulsory Conversion is not allowed in the Koran, &c. By Moulavi CHERAGH ALI, Author of "Reforms under Moslem Rule," "Hyderabad under Sir Salar Jung." 8vo. Rs. 6.

MAYAM-MA: THE HOME OF THE BURMAN. BY TSAYA (REV. H. POWELL). Crown 8vo. Rs. 2.

AN INTRODUCTION TO THE STUDY OF HINDUISM. BY GURU PERSHAD SEN. Crown 8vo, cloth, Rs. 3; paper, Rs. 2.

CHIN-LUSHAI LAND. INCLUDING A DESCRIPTION OF THE VARIOUS Expeditions into the Chin-Lushai Hills and the Final Annexation of the Country. By Surgn.-Lieut.-Colonel A. S. REID, M.B., Indian Medical Service. With three Maps and eight Phototint Illustrations. Cloth, gilt. Rs. 12.

Contains a description of the Chin-Lushai Hills and their inhabitants, from the earliest records, with an account of the various expeditions into the country, the last, *viz.*, that of 1889-90, which led to the final annexation of the wild mountainous tract which lies between India and Burma, being given in full detail.

"A valuable contribution to the History of our Indian border."—*Pall Mall Gazette.*

THE EMPEROR AKBAR. A CONTRIBUTION TOWARDS THE HISTORY OF INDIA in the 16th Century. By FREDERICK AUGUSTUS, Count of Noer, Translated from the German by ANNETTE S. BEVERIDGE. 2 vols. 8vo. cloth, gilt. Rs. 5.

THE IMAGE OF WAR; OR SERVICE IN THE CHIN HILLS. A COLLECTION of 34 Full-page Collotypes of Instantaneous Photographs and 160 interspersed in the reading. By Surgeon-Captain A. G. NEWLAND. With Introductory Notes by J. D. MACNABB, Esq., B.C.S. 4to, cloth, gilt elegant. Rs. 32.

"It would be difficult to give a more graphic picture of an Indian Frontier Expedition."—*The Times.*

"Brings home to us the Chins themselves, their ways and homes, the nature of the country marched through, method of campaign, and daily social habits and experiences of the campaigners. The letter-press, bright and simple, is worthy of the photographs."—*Broad Arrow.*

AN INDIAN JOURNALIST: BEING THE LIFE, LETTERS AND CORRESPONDENCE of Dr. SAMBHU CH. MOOKERJEE, late Editor of *Reis and Rayyet*. By F. H. SKRINE, I.C.S. With Portrait. Crown 8vo, cloth. Rs. 5.

THE RACES OF AFGHANISTAN: BEING A BRIEF ACCOUNT OF THE principal Nations inhabiting that Country. By Surgn.-Maj. H. W. BELLEW, C.S.I., late on Special Political Duty at Kabul. 8vo, cloth Rs. 2.

THE POVERTY PROBLEM IN INDIA: BEING A DISSERTATION ON THE Causes and Remedies of Indian Poverty. By PRITHWIS CHANDRA RAY. Crown 8vo, cloth. Rs. 3.

KURRACHEE: ITS PAST, PRESENT, AND FUTURE. BY ALEXANDER F. BAILLIE, F.R.G.S., Author of "A Paraguayan Treasure," &c. With Maps, Plans, and Photographs, showing the most recent Improvements. Super-royal 8vo, cloth. Rs. 15.

THE TRIAL OF MAHARAJA NANDA KUMAR. A NARRATIVE OF A Judical Murder. By H. BEVERIDGE, B.C.S. Demy 8vo. Rs. 5.

"Mr. Beveridge has given a great amount of thought, labour, and research to the marshalling of his facts, and he has done his utmost to put the exceedingly complicated and contradicting evidence in a clear and intelligible form." —*Home News.*

ECHOES FROM OLD CALCUTTA: BEING CHIEFLY REMINISCENCES of the days of Warren Hastings, Francis, and Impey. By H. E. BUSTEED. Second Edition, Enlarged and Illustrated. Post 8vo. Rs. 6.

"The book will be read by all interested in India."—*Army & Navy Magazine*

"Dr. Busteed's valuable and entertaining 'Echoes from Old Calcutta' has arrived at a second edition, revised, enlarged and illustrated with portraits and other plates rare or quaint. It is a pleasure to reiterate the warm commendation of this instructive and lively volume which its appearance called forth some years since."—*Saturday Review.*

"A series of illustrations which are highly entertaining and instructive of the life and manners of Anglo-Indian society a hundred years ago . . . The book from first to last has not a dull page in it, and it is a work of the kind of which the value will increase with years."—*Englishman.*

CAPT. HAYES' WORKS ON HORSES.

ILLUSTRATED HORSE BREAKING. By CAPTAIN M. H. HAYES. Second Edition. Numerous Illustrations by J. H. OSWALD-BROWN. Square. Rs. 21.

SUMMARY OF CONTENTS:—Mental Qualities of the Horse—Theory of Horse Control—Theory of Mouthing—Methods of Horse Control—Breaking on Foot—Ordinary Mounted Breaking—Teaching Horses to Jump—Breaking to Harness—School Breaking—Breaking for Special Work—Faults of Mouth—Faults of Temper—Circus Tricks—Index.

"One great merit of the book is its simplicity."—*Indian Daily News.*

"A work which is entitled to high praise as being far and away the best reasoned-out one on breaking under a new system we have seen."—*Field.*

"Clearly written."—*Saturday Review.*

"The best and most instructive book of its class that has appeared for many years."—*Times of India.*

RIDING: ON THE FLAT AND ACROSS COUNTRY. A GUIDE TO Practical Horsemanship. By Captain M. H. HAYES. With 70 Illustrations by STURGESS and J. H. OSWALD-BROWN. Third Edition, Revised and Enlarged. Rs. 7-8.

The whole text has been so revised or re-written as to make the work the most perfect in existence, essential to all who wish to attain the art of riding correctly.

"One of the most valuable additions to modern literature on the subject."—*Civil and Military Gazette.*

"A very instructive and readable book."—*Sport.*

"This useful and eminently practical book."—*Freeman's Journal.*

THE POINTS OF THE HORSE. A FAMILIAR TREATISE ON EQUINE CONFORMATION. Describing the points in which the perfection of each class of horses consists. By Captain M. H. HAYES. Illustrated.

[*New Edition in the Press.*

INDIAN RACING REMINISCENCES: BEING ENTERTAINING NARRATIVES and Anecdotes of Men, Horses, and Sport. By Captain M. H. HAYES. Illustrated with 42 Portraits and Engravings. Imp. 16mo. Rs. 6.

"Captain Hayes has done wisely in publishing these lively sketches of life in India. The book is full of racy anecdote."—*Bell's Life.*

"All sportsmen who can appreciate a book on racing, written in a chatty style, and full of anecdote, will like Captain Hayes' latest work."—*Field.*

"Many a racing anecdote and many a curious character our readers will find in the book, which is very well got up, and embellished with many portraits."—*Bailey's Magazine.*

VETERINARY NOTES FOR HORSE-OWNERS. A POPULAR GUIDE to Horse Medicine and Surgery. By Captain M. H. HAYES. Fifth Edition, Enlarged and Revised to the latest Science of the Day. With many New Illustrations by J. H. OSWALD-BROWN. Crown 8vo, buckram.

[*In the Press.*

The chief new matter in this Edition is—Articles on Contracted Heels, Donkey's Foot Disease, Forging or Clicking, Rheumatic Joint Disease, Abscess, Dislocation of the Shoulder Joint, Inflammation of the Mouth and Tongue, Flatulent Distension of the Stomach, Twist of the Intestines, Relapsing Fever, Cape Horse Sickness, Horse Syphilis, Rabies, Megrims, Staggers, Epilepsy, Sunstroke, Poisoning, Castration by the Ecraseur, and Mechanism of the Foot (in Chapter on Shoeing).

"Of the many popular veterinary books which have come under our notice, this is certainly one of the most scientific and reliable. . . . . The description of symptoms and the directions for the application of remedies are given in perfectly plain terms, which the tyro will find no difficulty in comprehending."—*Field.*

"Simplicity is one of the most commendable features in the book."—*Illustrated Sporting and Dramatic News.*

"Captain Hayes, in the new edition of 'Veterinary Notes,' has added considerably to its value, and rendered the book more useful to those non-professional people who may be inclined or compelled to treat their own horses when sick or injured."—*Veterinary Journal.*

"We do not think that horse-owners in general are likely to find a more reliable and useful book for guidance in an emergency."—*Field.*

TRAINING AND HORSE MANAGEMENT IN INDIA. BY CAPTAIN M. H. HAYES, Author of "Veterinary Notes for Horse-Owners," "Riding," &c. Fifth Edition. Crown 8vo. Rs. 6.

"No better guide could be placed in the hands of either amateur horseman or veterinary surgeon."—*Veterinary Journal.*

"A useful guide in regard to horses anywhere. . . . Concise, practical, and portable."—*Saturday Review.*

SOUNDNESS AND AGE OF HORSES. A VETERINARY AND LEGAL Guide to the Examination of Horses for Soundness. By Captain M. H. HAYES, M.R.C.V.S. With 100 Illustrations. Crown 8vo. Rs. 6.

"Captain Hayes is entitled to much credit for the explicit and sensible manner in which he has discussed the many questions—some of them extremely vexed ones—which pertain to soundness and unsoundness in horses." —*Veterinary Journal.*

"All who have horses to buy, sell, or keep will find plenty to interest them in this manual, which is full of illustrations, and still fuller of hints and wrinkles."—*Referee.*

"Captain Hayes' work is evidently the result of much careful research, and the horseman, as well as the veterinarian, will find in it much that is interesting and instructive."—*Field.*

THE HORSE WOMAN. A PRACTICAL GUIDE TO SIDE-SADDLE RIDING. By Mrs. HAYES, and Edited by Captain M. H. HAYES. Illustrated by 48 Drawings by J. OSWALD-BROWN and 4 Photographs. Uniform with "Riding: on the Flat and Across Country." Imp. 16mo. Rs. 7-8.

"This is the first occasion on which a practical horseman and a practical horsewoman have collaborated in bringing out a book on riding for ladies. The result is in every way satisfactory."—*Field.*

"A large amount of sound practical instruction, very judiciously and pleasantly imparted."—*Times.*

"We have seldom come across a brighter book than 'The Horsewoman.'"—*Athenæum.*

"Eminently sensible and practical."—*Daily Chronicle.*

SPORT AND VETERINARY WORKS.

NOTES ON STABLE MANAGEMENT. BY VETY.-SURG. J. A. NUNN, F.R.C.V.S., C.I.E., D.S.O. Crown 8vo, sewed. Re. 1.

"The notes are eminently practical, and give sound advice on everything pertaining to the proper care of horses, such as can be utilized by the uninitated to the best advantage."—*Indian Daily News.*

HIGHLANDS OF CENTRAL INDIA. NOTES ON THEIR FORESTS and Wild Tribes, Natural History, and Sports. By Capt. J. FORSYTH, B.S.C. New Edition. With Map and Tinted Illustrations. Rs. 7-8.

CALCUTTA TURF CLUB RULES OF RACING, TOGETHER WITH THE Rules relating to Lotteries, Betting, Defaulters, and the Rules of the Calcutta Turf Club. Revised May 1892. Authorized Edition. Rs. 2.

THE RACING CALENDAR, VOL. VII, FROM MAY 1895 TO APRIL 1896, Races Past. Published by the Calcutta Turf Club. CONTENTS:—Rules of Racing, Lotteries, C. T. C., etc., Registered Colours; Licensed Trainers and Jockeys; Assumed Names; List of Horses Aged, Classed and Measured by C. T. C. and W. I. T. C.; Races Run under C. T. C. Rules; Performances of Horses; Appendix and Index. Rs. 4.

THE RACING CALENDAR FROM 1ST AUGUST 1888 TO 30TH APRIL 1889, Races Past. 12mo, cloth. Vol. I, Rs. 4. Vol. II, to April 1890, Rs. 4. Vol. III, to April 1891, Rs. 4. Vol. IV, to April 1892, Rs. 4. Vol. V, to April 1893, Rs. 4. Vol. VI, to April 1894, Rs. 4. Vol. VII to April 1895, Rs. 4. Vol. VIII, to April 1896, Rs. 4.

CALCUTTA RACING CALENDAR. PUBLISHED EVERY FORTNIGHT. Annual Subscription, Rs. 12.

THE SPORTSMAN'S MANUAL. IN QUEST OF GAME IN KULLU, Lahoul, and Ladak to the Tso Morari Lake, with Notes on Shooting in Spiti, Bara Bagahal, Chamba, and Kashmir, and a detailed description of Sport in more than 100 Nalas. With 9 Maps. By Lt.-Col. R. H. TYACKE, late H. M.'s 98th and 84th Regiments. Fcap. 8vo, cloth. Rs. 3-8.

SEONEE: OR, CAMP LIFE ON THE SATPURA RANGE. A TALE OF Indian Adventure. By R. A. STERNDALE, Author of "Mammalia of India," "Denizens of the Jungles." Illustrated by the Author. With a Map and an Appendix containing a brief Topographical and Historical Account of the District of Seonee in the Central Provinces of India. Crown 8vo, cloth. Rs. 7.

LARGE GAME SHOOTING IN THIBET, THE HIMALAYAS, NORTHERN and Central India. By Brig.-General ALEXANDER A. KINLOCH. Containing Descriptions of the Country and of the various Animals to be found; together with Extracts from a journal of several years' standing. With 36 Illustrations from Photographs and a Map. Third Edition, Revised and Enlarged. Demy 4to, elegantly bound. Rs. 25.

"This splendidly illustrated record of sport, the photogravures, especially the heads of the various antelopes, are life-like; and the letter-press is very pleasant reading."—*Graphic.*

"The book is capitally got up, the type is better than in former editions, and the excellent photogravures give an exceptional value to the work."—*Asian.*

DENIZENS OF THE JUNGLES. A SERIES OF SKETCHES OF WILD Animals, illustrating their form and natural attitude. With Letter-press Description of each Plate. By R. A. STERNDALE, F.R.G.S., F.Z.S., Author of "Natural History of the Mammalia of India," "Seonee," &c. Oblong folio. Rs. 10.

LORD WILLIAM BERESFORD: SOLDIER, STATESMAN AND SPORTS-man: being a Record of his Eighteen Years in India and a full *Résumé* of his Racing Career. By H. E. ABBOTT. Crown 8vo, sewed. Re. 1.

REMINISCENCES OF TWENTY YEARS' PIG-STICKING IN BENGAL. By RAOUL. Illustrated with 6 Portraits. Crown 8vo, cloth gilt. Rs. 6-12.

HORSE BREEDING AND REARING IN INDIA. WITH NOTES ON Training for the Flat, and Across Country, and on Purchase, Breaking in and General Management. By Major JOHN HUMFREY, B.S.C., F.Z.S. Crown 8vo, cloth. Rs. 3-8.

INDIAN HORSE NOTES. AN EPITOME OF USEFUL INFORMATION arranged for ready reference on Emergencies, and specially adapted for Officers and Mofussil Residents. All Technical Terms explained and Simplest Remedies selected. By Major C——, Author of "Indian Notes about Dogs." Third Edition, Revised and considerably Enlarged. Fcap. 8vo, cloth. Rs. 2.

DOGS FOR HOT CLIMATES. A GUIDE FOR RESIDENTS IN TROPICAL Countries as to suitable Breeds, their Respective Uses, Management and Doctoring. By VERO SHAW and Captain M. H. HAYES. With Illustrations. Crown 8vo, cloth. Rs. 8.

"The authors of 'Dogs for Hot Climates' show in a concise practical way how to treat dogs out here, and what breeds best stand the climate. The book should be on every one's table, for sensible treatment will save the life of many a valuable and much-loved pet."—*Indian Planters' Gazette.*

A BOBBERY PACK IN INDIA. WITH AN APPENDIX CONTAINING A short *Excursus* on Banting and an Interview with Mr. Pickwick. By Captain JULIAN. Crown 8vo, sewed. Re. 1-8.

GUIDE TO EXAMINATION OF HORSES, FOR SOUNDNESS FOR STUdents and Beginners. By MOORE, F.R.C.V.S., Army Vety. Dept., Vety. Officer, Remount Depôt, Calcutta. Fcap. 8vo, limp cloth. Re. 1.

RIDING FOR LADIES, WITH HINTS ON THE STABLE. A LADY'S Horse Book. By MRS. POWER O'DONOGHUE. With 75 Illustrations by A. CHANTREY CORBOULD. Elegantly printed and bound. Imp. 16mo, gilt. Rs. 7-8.

INDIAN NOTES ABOUT DOGS. THEIR DISEASES AND TREATMENT. By Major C——. Fourth Edition. Fcap. 8vo, cloth. Re. 1-8.

ANGLING ON THE KUMAON LAKES. WITH A MAP OF THE KUMAON Lake Country and Plan of each Lake. By Depy. Surgeon-General W. WALKER. Crown 8vo, cloth. Rs. 4.

"Written with all the tenderness and attention to detail which characterist the followers of the gentle art."—*Hayes' Sporting News.*

THE ARMS ACT (XI OF 1878). WITH ALL THE NOTICES OF THE GOVERNMENT OF INDIA, the Bengal, North-Western Provinces and Punjab Governments, and High Court Decisions and Rulings. By W. HAWKINS. Second Edition. 8vo, cloth. Rs. 7-8.

THACKER, SPINK AND CO., CALCUTTA.

MODERN POLO. A GUIDE TO THE GAME, WITH INSTRUCTIONS ON THE Selection and Training of the Ponies. By E. D. MILLER (late 17th Lancers). Edited by Capt. M. H. HAYES. Illustrated from Photographs. Imp. 16mo, cloth. Rs. 12-8.

"A book which beginners and veterans alike may study with pleasure and profit."—*Asian.*

"Should be a text-book on the subject."—*Star.*

"Polo players owe a debt of gratitude to Mr. Miller for producing what will probably be recognised as the best book on the subject."—*Scotsman.*

"That Mr. Miller has suceeded admirably in his task there can be no doubt."—*Glasgow Herald.*

"Both in the matter of polo playing and in that of choosing or breeding polo ponies the volume is of a certain authority."—*Times.*

"Everything that has to do with the game is explained, and the chapters on polo ponies.........are excellent."—*Sporting Life.*

POLO RULES. RULES OF THE CALCUTTA POLO CLUB AND OF THE Indian Polo Association, with the Article on Polo by "An Old Hand." Reprinted from *Hayes' Sporting News.* Fcap. 8vo. Re. 1.

THE POLO CALENDAR. COMPILED BY THE INDIAN POLO ASSOCIATION. CONTENTS:—Committee of Stewards, Rules for the Regulation of Tournaments, &c.—Rules of the Game—Station Polo—List of Members—List of Existing Polo Ponies, names and description, with Alphabetical List—Records of Tournaments.—Previous Winners. VOL. I, 1892-93. VOL. II, 1893-94. Each Re. 1-8. Vol. III, 1894-95, Rs. 2. Vol. IV, 1895.96. Rs. 2. RULES OF POLO.—From the Polo Calendar. Revised 1895. As. 8.

MEDICINE, HYGIENE, ETC.

AIDS TO PRACTICAL HYGIENE. By J. C. BATTERSBY, B.A., M.B., B.CH., Univ. Dublin. Fcap. 8vo, cloth. Rs. 2.

"A valuable handbook to the layman interested in sanitation."—*Morning Post.*

"To the busy practitioner or the medical student it will serve the purposes of a correct and intelligent guide."—*Medical Record.*

HINTS FOR THE MANAGEMENT AND MEDICAL TREATMENT OF Children in India. By EDWARD A. BIRCH, M.D., Late Principal, Medical College, Calcutta. Third Edition, Revised. Being the Ninth Edition of "Goodeve's Hints for the Management of Children in India." Crown 8vo, cloth. Rs. 7.

The Medical Times and Gazette, in an article upon this work and Moore's "Family Medicine for India," says:—"The two works before us are in themselves probably about the best examples of medical works written for non-professional readers. The style of each is simple, and as free as possible from technical expressions. The modes of treatment recommended are generally those most likely to yield good results in the hands of laymen; and throughout each volume the important fact is kept constantly before the mind of the reader, that the volume he is using is but a poor substitute for personal professional advice, for which it must be discarded whenever there is the opportunity."

"It is a book which ought to be found in every household."—*Pioneer.*

THE INDIGENOUS DRUGS OF INDIA. SHORT DESCRIPTIVE NOTICES of the principal Medicinal Products met with in British India. By RAI BAHADUR KANNY LALL DEY, C.I.E. Second Edition. Revised and entirely Re-written. Demy 8vo. Rs. 12.

QUERIES AT A MESS TABLE. WHAT SHALL WE EAT? WHAT SHALL we Drink? By Surgn.-Lieut.-Col. JOSHUA DUKE. Fcap. 8vo, cloth, gilt. Rs. 2-4.

BANTING IN INDIA. WITH SOME REMARKS ON DIET AND THINGS in General. By Surg.-Lieut.-Col. JOSHUA DUKE. Third Edition. Cloth. Re. 1-8.

OUTLINES OF MEDICAL JURISPRUDENCE FOR INDIA. BY J. D. B. GRIBBLE, M.C.S. (Retired), and PATRICK HEHIR, M.D., F.R.C.S.E. Third Edition, Revised, Enlarged, and Annotated. Demy 8vo. Rs. 5-8.

RUDIMENTS OF SANITATION. FOR INDIAN SCHOOLS. BY PATRICK HEHIR, M.D. Second Edition. 12mo, cloth. Re. 1-4.

THE TEETH: THEIR STRUCTURE, DISEASE, AND PRESERVATION. With some Notes on Conservative and Prosthetic Dentistry. Nine Plates. By JOS. MILLER, L.D.S., R.C.S.E. Second Edition. 8vo, cloth. Rs. 2-8.

THE BABY. NOTES ON THE FEEDING, REARING AND DISEASES OF Infants. By S. O. MOSES, Licentiate of the Royal College of Physicians, Edinburgh, &c. 18mo, cloth. Rs. 2.

MY LEPER FRIENDS. AN ACCOUNT OF PERSONAL WORK AMONG Lepers, and their Daily Life in India. By MRS. HAYES. With Illustrations from Photographs, and a Chapter on Leprosy by Dr. G. G. MACLAREN. Imp. square 32mo. Rs. 2-8.

HYGIENE OF WATER AND WATER SUPPLIES. BY PATRICK HEHIR, M.D., Lecturer on Hygiene, Hyderabad Med. School. 8vo, cloth, flush. Rs. 2.

CHOLERA EPIDEMIC IN KASHMIR, 1892. BY A. MITRA, L.R.C.P. L.R.C.S., Principal Medical Officer in Kashmir. With Map and Tables. 4to, sewed. Re. 1.

A RECORD OF THREE YEARS' WORK OF THE NATIONAL ASSOCIATION for Supplying Female Medical Aid to the Women of India, August 1885 to August 1888. By H. E. THE COUNTESS OF DUFFERIN. Crown 8vo. Re. 1.

THE NATIONAL ASSOCIATION FOR SUPPLYING FEMALE MEDICAL AID to the Women of India. By H. E. THE COUNTESS OF DUFFERIN. Reprinted from the *Asiatic Quarterly Review*, by permission. As. 8.

THE INDIAN MEDICAL SERVICE. A GUIDE FOR INTENDED CANDIDATES for Commissions and for the Junior Officers of the Service. By WILLIAM WEBB, M.B., Surgeon, Bengal Army, late Agency Surgeon at the Court of Bikanir, Superintendent of Dispensaries, Jails, and Vaccination in the Bikanir State, and for some time Guardian to H. H. the Maharajah. Crown 8vo. Rs. 4.

"We recommend the book to all who think of competing for admission into the Indian Medical Service."—*Lancet.*

AGUE; OR, INTERMITTENT FEVER. BY M. D. O'CONNEL, M.D. 8vo, sewed. Rs. 2.

THE LANDMARKS OF SNAKE-POISON LITERATURE: BEING A Review of the more important Researches into the Nature of Snake-Poisons. By VINCENT RICHARDS, F.R.C.S. ED., &c., Civil Medical Officer of Goalundo, Bengal. Rs. 2-8.

THE CARLSBAD TREATMENT FOR TROPICAL AILMENTS, AND HOW to carry it out in India. By Surgn.-Major L. TARLETON YOUNG. Ex. fcap. 8vo. Rs. 4.

"A book not only most useful and most instructive, but very readable and interesting. It is short . . . . . . because it is pithy. The subjects are thoroughly and fully treated: we feel no lack, nothing unexplained: but it is done in a clear and concise style, every word to the point."— *Pioneer.*

"The book is of a most useful nature, and inspires confidence by the candour and fulness of its information and points of guidance."—*Irish Times.*

"The book contains the result of six years' practical experience, and should be of as much advantage to medical men as to sufferers."—*Home News.*

"We may venture to express the great pleasure we have derived from reading Dr. Young's book. Its lucidity and pithiness are indeed refreshing. There is no verbal plethora here: everything is to the point."—*Civil and Military Gazette.*

PERSONAL AND DOMESTIC HYGIENE FOR THE SCHOOL AND HOME: being a Text-book on Elementary Physiology, Hygiene, Home Nursing, and First Aid to the Injured; for Senior Schools and Family Reference. By Mrs. HAROLD HENDLEY, Medallist, National Health Society, England. 36 Illustrations. Ex. fcap. 8vo, cloth. Rs. 2; or cloth, gilt, Rs. 2-8.

"We are decidedly of opinion that it is the most practical and useful book of its kind which has been published in India. We trust it will gain a large circulation in the schools and homes of India."—*Indian Medical Gazette.*

"We can recommend this volume without hesitation. In the absence of the doctor one might obtain hints from any page of it on Hygiene, Nursing, Accidents and Emergencies. So far as we can see nothing is omitted, and every direction is given in simple intelligible language."—*Statesman.*

MALARIA; its Cause and Effects; Malaria and the Spleen; Injuries of the Spleen; An Analysis of 39 cases. By E. G. Russell, m.b., b.sc. 8vo, cloth. Rs. 8.

MEDICAL JURISPRUDENCE FOR INDIA. By J. B. Lyon, f.c.s., f.c., Brigade-Surgeon, Professor of Medical Jurisprudence, Grant Medical College, Bombay. The Legal Matter revised by J. D. Inverarity, Bar.-at-law. Second Edition. Illustrated. 8vo. Rs. 16.

INDIAN MEDICAL GAZETTE. Published Monthly. Subscription Rs. 18 yearly.

DOMESTIC BOOKS.

THE INDIAN COOKERY BOOK. A Practical Handbook to the Kitchen in India adapted to the Three Presidencies. Containing Original and Approved Recipes in every department of Indian Cookery; Recipes for Summer Beverages and Home-made Liqueurs; Medicinal and other Recipes; together with a variety of things worth knowing. By a Thirty-five Years' Resident. Rs. 8.

INDIAN DOMESTIC ECONOMY AND RECEIPT BOOK, WITH HINDUSTANEE romanized names. Comprising numerous directions for plain wholesome Cookery, both Oriental and English; with much miscellaneous matter, answering all general purposes of reference connected with Household affairs likely to be immediately required by Families, Messes and private individuals residing at the Presidencies or Out-Stations. By Dr. R. Riddell. Eighth Edition. Revised. Post 8vo, cloth. Rs. 6.

FIRMINGER'S MANUAL OF GARDENING FOR INDIA. A New Edition (the fourth) thoroughly Revised and Re-written. With many Illustrations. By H. St. J. Jackson. Imp. 16mo, cloth, gilt. Rs. 10.

POULTRY-KEEPING IN INDIA. A Simple and Practical Book on their care and treatment, their various Breeds, and the means of rendering them profitable. By Isa Tweed, Author of "Cow-Keeping in India." With Illustrations. Crown 8vo, cloth, gilt. Rs. [illegible]

"A book which will be found of great use by all those who keep a poultry-yard."—*Madras Mail.*

"We can recommend it to all who either keep poultry from a liking for fowls, or because they desire something better for the table than bazaar eggs and bazaar murghis."—*Civil and Military Gazette.*

COW-KEEPING IN INDIA. A SIMPLE AND PRACTICAL BOOK ON THEIR care and treatment, their various Breeds, and the means of rendering them profitable. By ISA TWEED. With 37 Illustrations of the various Breeds, &c. Crown 8vo, cloth, gilt. Rs. 4-8.

"A most useful contribution to a very important subject, and we can strongly recommend it."—*Madras Mail.*

"A valuable contribution to Agricultural Literature in the East."—*Ceylon Observer.*

ENGLISH ETIQUETTE FOR INDIAN GENTLEMEN. BY W. TREGO WEBB, Bengal Educational Department. Third Edition. Fcap. 8vo, cloth, Re. 1-4; paper, Re. 1.

The book comprises chapters on General Conduct, Calls, Dining-out, Levées, Balls, Garden-parties, Railway-travelling, &c. It also contains a chapter on Letter-writing, proper Modes of Address, &c., together with Hints on how to draw up Applications for Appointments, with Examples.

PERSONAL AND DOMESTIC HYGIENE FOR THE SCHOOL AND HOME: being a Text-book on Elementary Physiology, Hygiene, Home Nursing, and First Aid to the Injured; for Senior Schools and Family Reference. By MRS. HAROLD HENDLEY. Ex. fcap. 8vo, cloth, Rs. 2; or cloth gilt, Rs. 2-8.

THE AMATEUR GARDENER IN THE HILLS. WITH A FEW HINTS on Fowls, Pigeons, and Rabbits. By an Amateur. Second Edition, Revised and Enlarged. Crown 8vo. Rs. 2-8.

THE MEM-SAHIB'S BOOK OF CAKES, BISCUITS, ETC. WITH REMAKES on Ovens, and Hindustani Vocabulary, Weights and Measures. 18mo, cloth. Rs. 2.

FLOWERS AND GARDENS IN INDIA. A MANUAL FOR BEGINNERS. By MRS. R. TEMPLE-WRIGHT. Third Edition. Post 8vo, boards. Rs. 2.

......"A most useful little book which we cannot too strongly recommend. We can recommend it to our readers with the utmost confidence, as being not only instructive, but extremely interesting, and written in a delightfully easy, chatty strain."—*Civil and Military Gazette.*

"Very practical throughout. There could not be better advice than this and the way it is given shows the enthusiasm of Mrs. Temple-Wright." —*Pioneer.*

"It is written in a light conversational style, and it imparts instruction very clearly."—*Englishman.*

THACKER'S INDIAN DIRECTORIES AND MAPS.

MAP OF THE CIVIL DIVISIONS OF INDIA. INCLUDING GOVERNMENT, Divisions and Districts, Political Agencies, and Native States; also the Cities and Towns with 10,000 Inhabitants and upwards. Coloured. 20 in. × 36 in. Folded, Re. 1. On linen, Rs. 2.

CALCUTTA.—PLANS OF THE OFFICIAL AND BUSINESS PORTION, WITH Houses numbered, and Index of Government Offices and Houses of Business on the Map. Plan of the Residence portion of Calcutta with Houses numbered so that their position may easily be found. Two Maps in pocket case. The Maps are on a large scale. Re. 1.

1896.—THACKER'S INDIAN DIRECTORY. OFFICIAL, LEGAL, EDUCAtional, Professional and Commercial Directories of the whole of India; General Information; Holidays, &c.; Stamp Duties, Customs Tariff, Tonnage Schedules; Post Offices in India, forming a Gazetteer; List of Governors-General and Administrators of India from beginning of British Rule; Orders of the Star of India, Indian Empire, &c.; Warrant of Precedence, Table of Salutes, &c.; The Civil Service of India; An Army List of the Three Presidencies; A Railway Directory; A Newspaper and Periodical Directory; A Conveyance Directory; a Directory of the Chief Industries of India; Tea, Indigo, Silk, and Coffee, Cotton, Jute, Mines, Flour Mills, Rice Mills, Dairies, etc., etc., also a separate list of Tea and Coffee Estates in Ceylon. List of Clubs in India; Alphabetical List of Residents, European and Native, and a List of British and Foreign Manufacturers with their Indian Agents. With 5 Maps. A Railway Map of India. A Map of the Tea Districts. A Map of the Coal and Iron Mines. A Map of the Official and Business portion of Calcutta and a Map of the European Residence portion of Calcutta. Thick Royal 8vo, leather bound. Rs. 24.

THE CHIEF INDUSTRIES OF INDIA: A LIST OF INDIAN AND CEYLON TEA GARDENS, Indigo Concerns, Silk Filatures, Sugar Factories, Cinchona Concerns, Coffee Estates, Cotton, Jute, Rice and Flour Mills, Collieries, Mines, etc. With their Capital, Directors, Proprietors, Agents, Managers, Assistants, &c., and their Factory Marks with a Map of the Tea Districts and a Map of the Coal and Iron Fields. [1896.] Rs. 4.

THACKER'S MAP OF INDIA, WITH INSET MAPS, OF THE VARIOUS PRODUCTS OF INDIA AND OF THE TEA DISTRICTS, SKETCH PLANS of Calcutta, Bombay, and Madras. Edited by J. G. BARTHOLOMEW. Corrected to date. With Railways, Political Changes, and an Index of 10,000 Names, being every place mentioned in "Hunter's Imperial Gazetteer." [*Nearly ready.*

"An excellent map."—*Glasgow Herald.*

"This is a really splendid map of India, produced with the greatest skill and care."—*Army and Navy Gazette.*

"For compactness and completeness of information few works surpassing or approaching it have been seen in cartography."—*Scotsman.*

THACKER, SPINK AND CO., CALCUTTA.

SCIENTIFIC WORKS.

ANTHROPOMETRY IN BENGAL; OR IDENTIFICATION OF CRIMINALS by Anthropometric Measurements and Thumb Impressions. By Col. H. M. RAMSAY, District Superintendent of Police. Royal 8vo, sewed. As. 8.

"An interesting and instructive treatise."—*Englishman.*

THE FUTURE OF THE DATE PALM IN INDIA (PHŒNIX DACTYLIPTERA). By E. BONAVIA, M.D., Brigade-Surgeon, Indian Medical Department. Crown 8vo, cloth. Rs. 2-8.

GAME, SHORE, AND WATER BIRDS OF INDIA. BY COL. A. LE MESSURIER, R.E. A *vade mecum* for Sportsmen. With 121 Illustrations. 8vo. Rs. 10.

HANDBOOK TO THE FERNS OF INDIA, CEYLON, AND THE MALAY PENINSULA. By Colonel R. H. BEDDOME, Author of the "Ferns of British India." With 300 Illustrations by the Author. Imp. 16mo. Rs. 10.

"A most valuable work of reference."—*Garden.*

"It is the first special book of portable size and moderate price which has been devoted to Indian Ferns, and is in every way deserving."—*Nature.*

SUPPLEMENT TO THE FERNS OF BRITISH INDIA, CEYLON AND THE Malay Peninsula, containing Ferns which have been discovered since the publication of the "Handbook to the Ferns of British India," &c. By Col. R. H. BEDDOME, F.L.S. Crown 8vo, sewed. Rs. 2-12.

GOLD, COPPER, AND LEAD IN CHOTA-NAGPORE. COMPILED BY W. KING, D.SC., Director of the Geological Survey of India, and T. A. POPE, Deputy Superintendent, Survey of India. With Map showing the Geological Formation and the Areas taken up by the various Prospecting and Mining Companies. Crown 8vo, cloth. Rs. 5.

ON INDIGO MANUFACTURE. A PRACTICAL AND THEORETICAL GUIDE to the Production of the Dye. With numerous Illustrative Experiments. By J. BRIDGES LEE, M.A., F.G.S. Crown 8vo, cloth. Rs. 4.

"The book is thoroughly practical, and is as free from technicalities as such a work can well be, and it gives as much information as could well be imparted in so small a compass."—*Indian Daily News.*

"Instructive and useful alike to planter and proprietor . . . A very clear and undoubtedly valuable treatise for the use of practical planters, and one which every planter would do well to have always at hand during his manufacturing season. For the rest, a planter has only to open the book for it to commend itself to him."—*Pioneer.*

COMPOSITÆ INDICÆ DESCRIPTÆ ET SECUS GENERA BENTHAMII ordinatæ. By C. B. CLARKE. 8vo, boards. Rs. 1-8.

MANUAL OF AGRICULTURE FOR INDIA. By LIEUT. FREDERICK POGSON. Illustrated. Crown 8vo, cloth, gilt. Rs. 5.

ROXBURGH'S FLORA INDICA; OR, DESCRIPTION OF INDIAN PLANTS. Reprinted *literatim* from Cary's Edition. 8vo, cloth. Rs. 5.

THE CULTURE AND MANUFACTURE OF INDIGO. WWITH A DEscription of a Planter's Life and Resources. By WALTER MACLAGAN REID. Crown 8vo. With 19 Full-page Illustrations. Rs. 5.

"It is proposed in the following Sketches of Indigo Life in Tirhoot and Lower Bengal to give those who have never witnessed the manufacture of Indigo, or seen an Indigo Factory in this country, an idea of how the finished marketable article is produced: together with other phases and incidents of an Indigo Planter's life, such as may be interesting and amusing to friends at home."—*Introduction.*

A NATURAL HISTORY OF THE MAMMALIA OF INDIA, BURMAH AND CEYLON. By R. A. STERNDALE, F.R.G.S., F.Z.S., &c., Author of "Seonee," "The Denizens of the Jungle." With 170 Illustrations by the Author and others. Imp. 16mo. Rs. 10.

"The very model of what a popular natural history should be."—*Knowledge.*

"The book will, no doubt, be specially useful to the sportsman, and, indeed, has been extended so as to include all territories likely to be reached by the sportsman from India."—*Times.*

A TEA PLANTER'S LIFE IN ASSAM. By GEORGE M. BARKER. With 75 Illustrations by the Author. Crown 8vo. Rs. 6-8.

"Mr. Barker has supplied us with a very good and readable description accompanied by numerous illustrations drawn by himself. What may be called the business parts of the book are of most value."—*Contemporary Review.*

"Cheery, well-written little book."—*Graphic.*

"A very interesting and amusing book, artistically illustrated from sketches drawn by the author."—*Mark Lane Express.*

A TEXT-BOOK OF INDIAN BOTANY: MORPHOLOGICAL, PHYSIOLOGICAL, and SYSTEMATIC. By W. H. GREGG, B.M.S., Lecturer on Botany at the Hugli Government College. Profusely Illustrated. Crown 8vo. Rs. 5.

THE INLAND EMIGRATION ACT, AS AMENDED BY ACT VII OF 1893. The Health Act; Sanitation of Emigrants; The Artificer's Act; Land Rules of Assam, etc. Crown 8vo, cloth. Rs. 2.

ENGINEERING, SURVEYING, ETC.

STATISTICS OF HYDRAULIC WORKS, AND HYDROLOGY OF ENGland, Cnaada, Egypt, and India. Collected and reduced by LOWIS D'A. JACKSON, C.E. Royal 8vo. Rs. 10.

PERMANENT WAY POCKET-BOOK. CONTAINING COMPLETE FORmulæ for Laying Points, Crossings, Cross-over Roads, Through Roads, Diversions, Curves, etc., suitable for any Gauge. With Illustrations. By T. W. JONES. Pocket-Book Form, cloth. Rs. 3.

A HANDBOOK OF PRACTICAL SURVEYING FOR INDIA. Illustrated with Plans, Diagrams, etc. Fourth Edition, Revised. By F. W. KELLY, late of the Indian Survey. With 24 Plates. 8vo. Rs. 8.

PROJECTION OF MAPS. By R. SINCLAIR. With Diagrams. Foolscap 8vo, boards. Rs. 2.

IRRIGATED INDIA. AN AUSTRALIAN VIEW OF INDIA AND CEYLON: their Irrigation and Agriculture. By the Hon. ALFRED DEAKIN, M.L.A., formerly Chief Secretary and Minister of Water-Supply of Victoria, Australia. With a Map. 8vo, cloth. Rs. 7-8.

AN EXPLANATION OF QUADRUPLEX TELEGRAPHY. With 2 Diagrams. By BEN. J. STOW, Telegraph Master. Fcap. 4to. Rs. 2.

AN EXPLANATION ON DUPLEX, QUADRUPLEX, OPEN AND TRANSLATION WORKING AND OTHER CIRCUITS. Testing of Currents, Batteries, Instruments, Earths, and Line, with the Tangent Galvanometer. With 12 Plates. By E. H. NELTHROPP, Telegraph Master. Crown 8vo, sewed. Rs. 2.

MANUAL OF SURVEYING FOR INDIA. DETAILING THE MODE OF Operations on the Trigonometrical, Topographical, and Revenue Surveys of India. By Col. H. L. THUILLIER and Lieut.-Col. H. SMYTH. Third Edition, Revised and Enlarged. Royal 8vo, cloth. Rs. 12.

FIRE INSURANCE IN INDIA. A Short Account of the Principles and Practice of Fire Insurance, Settlement of Losses, Extinction and Prevention of Fire, &c. By BREMAWALLAH. Crown 8vo, sewed. Re. 1-8.

COLEBROOKE'S TRANSLATION OF THE LILAVATI. WITH NOTES By HARAN CHANDRA BANERJI, M.A., B.L. 8vo, cloth. Rs. 4.

This edition includes the Text in Sanskrit. The Lilavati is a standard work on Hindu Mathematics written by Bháskarácháya, a celebrated mathematician of the twelfth century.

RAILWAY CURVES. PRACTICAL HINT ON SETTING OUT CURVES, WITH a Table of Tangents for a 1° Curve for all angles from 2° to 135° increasing by minutes: and other useful Tables. With a Working Plan and Section of Two miles of Railway. By A. G. WATSON, Assistant Engineer. Rs. 4.

A HANDBOOK OF PHOTOGRAPHY FOR AMATEURS IN INDIA. By By GEORGE EWING. Illustrated. Crown 8vo. Cloth. Rs. 7.

EXPOSURE TABLES FOR PHOTOGRAPHERS IN INDIA AND THE EAST. By GEORGE EWING, Author of "A Handbook of Photography." 12mo, cloth, pocket shape. Re. 1.

THE JOURNAL OF THE PHOTOGRAPHIC SOCIETY. Published Monthly. With Illustrations. Subscription Rs. 6 yearly.

MILITARY WORKS.

THE RECONNOITRER'S GUIDE AND FIELD BOOK. ADAPTED FOR India. By Colonel M. J. KING-HARMAN, B.S.C. Fourth Edition, Revised and Enlarged.

It contains all that is required for the guidance of the Military Reconnoitrer in India: it can be used as an ordinary Pocket Note Book, or as a Field Message Book; the pages are ruled as a Field Book, and in sections, for written description or sketch.

The book has been highly approved by Lord Roberts, who regards it as a most valuable and practical composition.

"To Officers serving in India the Guide will be invaluable."—*Broad Arrow.*

"It appears to contain all that is absolutely required by the Military Reconnoitrer in India, and will thus dispense with many bulky works. In fact it contains just what is wanted and nothing not likely to be wanted."—*Naval and Military Gazette.*

"It has been found invaluable to many a Staff Officer and Commandant of a Regiment, as well as of the greatest possible assistance to officers studying for the Garrison Course Examination."—*Madras Mail.*

THE QUARTERMASTER'S ALMANAC. A DIARY OF THE DUTIES, with other information. By Lieut. HARRINGTON BUSH. 8vo. Re. 1-8.

THACKER, SPINK AND CO., CALCUTTA.

LETTERS ON TACTICS AND ORGANIZATION BY CAPT. F.N. MAUDE, R.E. (Papers reprinted from the *Pioneer* and *Civil and Military Gazette.*) Crown 8vo, cloth. Rs. 5.

"The author displays considerable knowledge of the subjects with which he deals, and has evidently thought much on them. His views are broad and advanced. Every soldier should read this book."—*Athenæum.*

THE INVASION AND DEFENCE OF ENGLAND. BY CAPT. F. N. MAUDE R.E. Crown 8vo, cloth. Re. 1-8.

THE SEPOY OFFICER'S MANUAL. BY CAPT. E. G. BARROW. THIRD Edition, Entirely Re-written, and brought up to date. By CAPT. E. H. BINGLEY, 7th Bengal Infantry. 12mo, cloth. Rs. 2-8.

"It seems to contain almost everything required in one of the modern type of Civilian Soldiers . . . . In the most interesting part of the book is an account of the composition of the Bengal Army with descriptive note on the Brahmans, Rajputs, Sikhs, Goorkhas, Pathans and other races."—*Englishman.*

"A vast amount of technical and historical data of which no Anglo-Indian Officer should be ignorant."—*Broad Arrow.*

"The notes are brief and well digested, and contain all that it is necessary for a candidate to know."—*Army and Navy Gazette.*

A TEXT-BOOK OF INDIAN MILITARY LAW. COMPRISING THE Indian Articles of War fully annotated, the Indian Penal Code and the Indian Evidence Act, and has, in the form of Appendices, all existing Regulations with regard to the Procedure of Courts-martial and Forms of Charges. With Tables shewing the Powers and Jurisdiction of different Courts-martial and the difference in Procedure and Evidence between English Military Law and Indian Military Law. By Captain E. H. BERNARD, Cantonment Magistrate, Mandalay. Crown 8vo, cloth. Rs. 8.

INDIAN ARTICLES OF WAR, REVISED TO DATE. WITH AN APPENDIX containing Definitions, Rules of Procedure, Forms of Charges, Statement of Objects and Reasons and an Index. Crown 8vo. Rs. 3-8.

THE INDIAN FIELD MESSAGE BOOK FOR MILITARY OFFICERS. INTERLEAVED FOR KEEPING COPIES. With 12 Authorised Pattern Envelopes. Re. 1-4.

NOTES ON THE COURSE OF GARRISON INSTRUCTION, TACTICS Topography, Fortifications, condensed from the Text-Books, with explanations and additional matter. With Diagrams. By Major E. LLOYD, Garrison Instructor. Crown 8vo, cloth. Rs. 2-8.

PAPER SIGHTS FOR TARGET PRACTICE. White, Blue, Green and Red lines, or assorted colours. Packets of 100, annas Four.

HINDUSTANI, PERSIAN, ETC.

GLOSSARY OF MEDICAL AND MEDICO-LEGAL TERMS, INCLUDING those most frequently met with in the Law Courts. By R. F. HUTCHISON, M.D., Surgeon-Major. Second Edition. Fcap. 8vo, cloth. Rs. 2.

THE DIVAN-I-HAFIZ. THE DIVAN WRITTEN IN THE FOURTEENTH Century by Khwaja-Shams-ud-din Mohammad-i-Hafiz-i-Shirazi, translated for the first time out of the Persian into English Prose, with Critical and Explanatory Remarks, with an Introductory Preface, a Note on Sufi'ism, and Life of the Author. By Lieut.-Col. H. WILBERFORCE CLARKE, author of "The Persian Manual," translator of "The Bustan-i-Sa'di," "The Sekandar Namah-i-Nizami," etc. 2 vols. 4to. Rs. 25.

THE 'AWARIFU-L-MA'ARIF. WRITTEN IN THE THIRTEENTH CENtury by Shaikh Shahab-ud-din—'Umar bin Muhammad-i-Sahrwardi translated (out of the Arabic into Persian) by Mamud bin 'Ali al Kashani. Companion in Sufi'ism to the Divan-i-Khwaja Hafiz; translated for the first time (out of the Persian into English) by Lieut.-Col. H. WILBERFORCE CLARKE. 4to. Rs. 18.

INTRODUCTORY EXERCISES IN URDU PROSE COMPOSITION. A Collection of 50 Exercises with Idiomatic Phrases and Grammatical Notes, accompanied by a full Vocabulary and Translation of each passage. By Surg.-Lieut.-Col. G. S. A. RANKING, B.A., M.D., Secretary to the Board of Examiners. Crown 8vo, cloth. Rs. 5.

"One of the best works on the Urdu language that we have yet seen . . . . , the student will find in Dr. Ranking's work a really valuable aid . . . . . . The work is a thoroughly practical one, and explains all the various phrases and intricacies of a language the acquirement of which is too often neglected by Anglo-Indians from mere prejudice.—*Indian Daily News.*

THE RUSSIAN CONVERSATION GRAMMAR. By ALEX. KINLOCH, late Interpreter to H. B. M. Consulate and British Consul in the Russian Law Courts; Instructor for Official Examinations. Crown 8vo, cloth. Rs. 6-8.

This work is constructed on the excellent system of Otto in his "German Conversation Grammar," with illustrations accompanying every rule, in the form of usual phrases and idioms, thus leading the student by easy but rapid gradations to a colloquial attainment of the language.

TRANSLATIONS INTO PERSIAN. SELECTIONS FROM *Murray's History of India, Foliorum Centuria—Gibbon's Roman Empire—Our Faithful Ally the Nizam.* By Major Sir A. C. TALBOT. Part I, English. Part II, Persian. 2 vols. 8vo. Rs. 10.

GRAMMAR OF THE URDU OR HINDUSTANI LANGUAGE IN ITS ROMANIZED CHARACTER. By GEORGE SMALL, M.A. Crown 8vo, cloth limp. Rs. 5.

"We recommend it to those who wish to gain a more scientific knowledge of Urdu than the ordinary primers afford."—*Indian Churchman.*

"His exposition of idiom and construction is exceedingly lucid."—*Indian Daily News.*

"The manual altogether deserves high commendation for the lucidity with which it explains the essentials of Urdu."—*Athenæum.*

ANGLO-URDU MEDICAL HANDBOOK OR HINDUSTANI GUIDE. For the use of Medical Practitioners (male and female) in Northern India. By Revd. GEORGE SMALL, M.A. With the aid of Surgn.-General C. R. FRANCIS, M.B., and of Mrs. FRASER NASH, L.R.C.P. Crown 8vo, cloth limp. Rs. 5.

"A very convenient manual . . . . . . we recommend it to the attention not only of Medical Students, but of all who may even accidentally find themselves compelled to act on occasions as amateur doctors."—*Indian Churchman.*

"Capitally arranged and thoroughly inclusive and useful."—*Indian Daily News.*

"This handbook should prove invaluable for use in schools and colleges where surgeons, missionaries and nurses are being trained for work in the East."—*Home News.*

"Ought to find a place on every planter's office shelf. In treating coolies and others employed on gardens it would be invaluable."—*Indian Planters' Gazette.*

A POCKET-BOOK OF COLLOQUIAL URDU FOR MILITARY RECONNAISSANCE. For the use of Officers and Men. For Reference and on Service. By Surgn.-Lieut-Col. G. S. A. RANKING, B.A., M.D., Secretary to the Board of Examiners, Fort William. 16mo, cloth. Rs. 2.

HANDBOOK OF COLLOQUIAL TIBETAN. A PRACTICAL GUIDE TO the Language of Central Tibet. By GRAHAM SANDBERG, B.A. 8vo, cloth. Rs. 14.

MALAVIKAGNIMITRA. A SANSKRIT PLAY BY KALIDASA. LITERALLY translated into English Prose by C. H. TAWNEY, M.A., Principal, Presidency College, Calcutta. Second Edition. Crown 8vo. Re. 1-8.

A HANDBOOK OF THE KAYATHI CHARACTER. By GEORGE A. GRIERSON, I.C.S. Quarto. Rs. 6.

A GUIDE TO HINDUSTANI. SPECIALLY DESIGNED FOR THE USE OF Officers and Men serving in India. Containing Colloquial Sentences in Persian and Roman Character, and in English, also a Series of Arzis in Urdu written character with their transliteration in Roman-Urdu, and English translations. By Surgeon-Lieut.-Col. GEO. S. RANKING, B.A., M.D., Offg. Secretary to the Board of Examiners, Fort William. Third Edition. Revised and Enlarged. Crown 8vo, cloth. Rs. 6.

"The work on the whole, we believe, will meet a want. . . . . . It contains an excellent list of technical military terms and idioms, and will prove especially serviceable to any one who has to act as an interpreter at courts-martial and cognate enquiries."—*Civil and Military Gazette.*

"There can be no question as to the practical utility of the book."—*Pioneer.*

"Surgeon-Major Ranking has undoubtedly rendered good service to the many military men for whom knowledge of Hindustani is essential."—*Athenæum.*

"Has the merit of conciseness and portability, and the selections at the end, of the historical and colloquial style, are well chosen."—*Saturday Review.*

"A well-conceived book, and has much useful matter in it. The sentences are very good, practical and idiomatic."—*Homeward Mail.*

"Supplies a want long felt, by none more than by young Medical Officers of the Army of India. We think the work admirably adapted for its purpose."—*British Medical Journal.*

TWO CENTURIES OF BHARTRIHARI. TRANSLATED INTO ENGLISH Verse by C. H. TAWNEY, M.A. Fcap. 8vo, cloth. Rs. 2.

HINDUSTANI AS IT OUGHT TO BE SPOKEN. BY J. TWEEDIE, BENGAL Civil Service. Second Edition. Crown 8vo, pp. xvi, 350, cloth. Rs. 4-8.

SUPPLEMENT containing Key to the Exercises and Translation of the Reader with Notes. Rs. 2.

The work has been thoroughly Revised and partly Re-Written, and much additional matter added. The VOCABULARIES have been improved, and all words used in the book have been embodied in the GLOSSARIES, ENGLISH-HINDUSTANI—HINDUSTANI-ENGLISH. A READER is also given, and a GENERAL INDEX to the whole book.

"The Young Civilian or Officer, reading for his Examination, could not do better than master this Revised Edition from cover to cover."—*I. Daily News.*

"The book is divided into twelve easy lessons, and there is nothing to prevent the most khansamah-worried *mem-saheb* from mastering one of these a day. At the end of a fortnight she will have acquired a small useful vocabulary, and should be quite certain how to use the words she knows."—*Englishman.*

BOOK-KEEPING AND OFFICE MANUALS.

A GUIDE TO BOOK-KEEPING. BY SINGLE, MIXED AND DOUBLE Entries. Commercial Accounts of the most intricate nature fully illustrated by Examples and Annotations; Answers to Examination Questions, Book-Keeping, for Promotion to Assistant Examiner (1st grade) and to Accountant (2nd grade), from 1880 to 1891. By S. GEORGE, late Chief Accountant, P. W. D., Bengal. Demy 8vo, cloth. Rs. 2-8.

PHONOGRAPHY IN BENGALI. BY DWIJENDRA NATH SHINGHAW, Professor of Phonography in Calcutta. Being a Handbook for the study of Shorthand on the principle of Pitman's System. 12mo. As. 8. With a Key. 12mo. As. 4 extra.

THE INDIAN SERVICE MANUAL; OR, GUIDE TO THE SEVERAL Departments of the Government of India, containing the Rules for Admission, Notes on the working of each Department, &c. By C. R. HARDLESS, Author of "The Clerk's Manual."

THE GOVERNMENT OFFICE MANUAL. A GUIDE TO THE DUTIES, Privileges and Responsibilities of the Government Service in all Grades. By CHARLES HARDLESS. Crown 8vo. Rs. 2.

SPENS' THE INDIAN READY RECKONER. CONTAINING TABLES FOR ascertaining the value of any number of articles, &c., from three pies to five rupees; also Tables of Wages from four annas to twenty-five rupees. By Captain A. T. SPENS. Re. 1-8.

THE INDIAN LETTER-WRITER. CONTAINING AN INTRODUCTION ON Letter Writing, with numerous Examples in the various styles of Correspondence. By H. ANDERSON. Crown 8vo, cloth. Re. 1.

THE CLERK'S MANUAL. A COMPLETE GUIDE TO GENERAL OFFICE Routine (Government and Business). By CHARLES R. HARDLESS. Second Edition, Revised. 12mo, boards. Rs. 2.

EDUCATIONAL BOOKS.

AN ELEMENTARY COURSE OF ETHICS DESIGNED TO COVER THE Syllabus of the Calcutta University for the B. A. Examination. By C. R. WILSON, M.A., and E. M, WHEELER, M.A.

THE ELEMENTS OF ARITHMETIC. BY GOOROO DASS BANERJEE, M.A., D.L. Sixth Edition. Revised and Enlarged. Crown 8vo, cloth. Re. 1-8.

HINTS ON THE STUDY OF ENGLISH. BY F. J. ROWE, M.A., AND W. T. WEBB, M.A., Professors of English Literature, Presidency College, Calcutta. New Edition. (Ninety Seventh Thousand.) With an additional chapter on the Structure and Analysis of Sentences, and Exercises on the Correction of Mistakes commonly made by Students. Crown 8vo, cloth.. Rs. 2-8.

A COMPANION READER TO "HINTS ON THE STUDY OF ENGLISH." (Eighteenth Thousand.) Demy 8vo, Re. 1-4; Key, Rs. 2.

ENTRANCE TEST EXAMINATION QUESTIONS AND ANSWERS IN English, being the Questions appended to "Hints on the Study of English," with their Answers, together with Fifty Supplementary Questions and Answers. By W. T. WEBB, M.A. 12mo, sewed. Re. 1.

PRINCIPAL EVENTS IN INDIAN AND BRITISH HISTORY. WITH their Dates in Suggestive Sentences. In Two Parts. By MISS ADAMS, La Martinière College for Girls, Calcutta. Second Edition. Demy 8vo, boards. Re. 1.

THE STUDENT'S HANDBOOK TO HAMILTON AND MILL. BY W. BELL, M.A., Professor of Philosophy and Logic, Government College, Lahore. 8vo, boards. Rs. 2.

AN ANALYSIS OF HAMILTON'S LECTURES ON METAPHYSICS. With Dissertations and Copious Notes. By W. C. FINK. 8vo, boards. Rs. 2.

PROJECTION OF MAPS. BY R. SINCLAIR. With Diagrams. Foolscap 8vo. Rs. 2.

ENGLISH SELECTIONS APPOINTED BY THE SYNDICATE OF THE CALcutta University for the Entrance Examination. Crown 8vo, cloth. Re. 1-8.

THE LAWS OF WEALTH. A PRIMER ON POLITICAL ECONOMY FOR the Middle Classes in India. By HORACE BELL, C.E. Seventh Thousand. Fcap. 8vo. As. 8.

THE INDIAN LETTER-WRITER. CONTAINING AN INTRODUCTION ON Letter Writing, with numerous Examples in the various styles of Correspondence. By H. ANDERSON. Crown 8vo, cloth. Re. 1.

A CATECHISM ON THE RUDIMENTS OF MUSIC. SIMPLIFIED FOR Beginners. By I. LITTLEPAGE. 12mo, sewed. Re. 1.

CALCUTTA UNIVERSITY CALENDAR FOR THE YEAR 1896. CONtaining Acts, Bye-Laws, Regulations, The University Rules for Examination, Text-Book Endowments, Affiliated Institutions, List of Graduates and Under-Graduates, Examination Papers, 1895. Cloth. Rs. 5.

CALENDAR for previous years. *Each* Rs. 5.

THE PRINCIPLES OF HEAT. FOR THE F. A. EXAMINATION OF THE Calcutta University. By LEONARD HALL, M.A. Crown 8vo. As. 8.

ANALYSIS OF REID'S ENQUIRY INTO THE HUMAN MIND. WITH Copious Notes. By W. C. FINK. Second Edition. Re. 1-12.

FIFTY GRADUATED PAPERS IN ARITHMETIC, ALGEBRA, AND GEOmetry for the use of Students preparing for the Entrance Examinations of the Indian Universities. With Hints on Methods of Shortening Work and on the Writing of Examination Papers. By W. H. WOOD, B.A., F.C.S., Principal, La Martinière College. Re. 1-8.

THE ENGLISH PEOPLE AND THEIR LANGUAGE. Translated from the German of Loth. By C. H. TAWNEY, M.A., Professor in the Presidency College, Calcutta. Stitched. As. 8.

TALES FROM INDIAN HISTORY. BEING THE ANNALS OF INDIA re-told in Narratives. By J. TALBOYS WHEELER. Crown 8vo, cloth. School Edition. Re. 1-8.

A NOTE ON THE DEVANAGARI ALPHABET FOR BENGALI STUDENTS. By GURU DAS BANERJEE, M.A., D.L. Crown 8vo. As. 4.

THE GOVERNMENT OF INDIA. A PRIMER FOR INDIAN SCHOOLS. By HORACE BELL, C.E. Third Edition. Fcap. 8vo, sewed, As. 8; in cloth, Re. 1.

Translated into Bengali. By J. N. BHATTACHARJEE. 8vo. As. 12.

AN INQUIRY INTO THE HUMAN MIND ON THE PRINCIPLES OF Common Sense. By THOMAS REID, D.D. 8vo, cloth. Re. 1-4.

A TEXT-BOOK OF INDIAN BOTANY: MORPHOLOGICAL, PHYSIOLOGICAL, and Systematic. By W. H. GREGG, B.M.S., Lecturer on Botany at Hugli Government College. Profusely Illustrated. Crown 8vo. Rs. 5.

A MORAL READING BOOK FROM ENGLISH AND ORIENTAL SOURCES. By Sir ROPER LETHBRIDGE, C.I.E., M.A. Crown 8vo, cloth. As. 14.

A PRIMER CATECHISM OF SANITATION FOR INDIAN SCHOOLS. Founded on Dr. Cunningham's Sanitary Primer. By L. A. STAPLEY. Second Edition. As. 4.

NOTES ON MILL'S EXAMINATION OF HAMILTON'S PHILOSOPHY. By THOMAS EDWARDS, F.E.I.S. Fcap., sewed. Re. 1.

A SHORT HISTORY OF THE ENGLISH LANGUAGE. BY THOMAS EDWARDS, F.E.I.S. 18mo. Re. 1-4.

LAMB'S TALES FROM SHAKESPEARE. AN EDITION IN GOOD TYPE. Cloth. As. 12.

LAND TENURES AND LAND REVENUE.

AZIZUDDIN AHMED.—THE N.-W. PROVINCES LAND REVENUE Act. Being Act XIX of 1873 as amended by Acts I and VIII of 1879, XII of 1881, XIII and XIV of 1882, XX of 1890, and XII of 1891. With Notes, Government Orders, Board Circulars and Decisions, and Rulings of the Allahabad High Court. By AZIZUDDIN AHMED, Deputy Collector and Magistrate. Demy 8vo, cloth. Rs. 8.

BEVERLEY.—THE LAND ACQUISITION ACTS (ACTS I OF 1894 AND XVIII OF 1885, Mines). With Introduction and Notes. The whole forming a complete Manual of Law and Practice on the subject of Compensation for Lands taken for Public Purposes. Applicable to all India. By H. BEVERLEY, M.A., B.C.S. Third Edition. Cloth gilt. Rs. 6.

FORSYTH.—REVENUE SALE-LAW OF LOWER BENGAL, COMPRIS- Act XI of 1859; Bengal Act VII of 1868; Bengal Act VII of 1880 (Public Demands Recovery Act), and the unrepealed Regulations and the Rules of the Board of Revenue on the subject. With Notes. Edited by WM. E. H. FORSYTH. Demy 8vo, cloth. Rs. 5.

PHILLIPS.—MANUAL OF REVENUE AND COLLECTORATE LAW. With Important Rulings and Annotations. By H. A. D. PHILLIPS, Bengal Civil Service. Crown 8vo, cloth. [1884.] Rs. 10.

CONTENTS:—Alluvion and Diluvian, Certificate, Cesses, Road and Public Works, Collectors, Assistant Collectors, Drainage, Embankment, Evidence, Excise, Lakhiraj Grants and Service Tenures, and Land Acquisition, Land Registration, Legal Practitioners, License Tax, Limitation, Opium, Partition, Public Demands Recovery, Putni Sales, Registration, Revenue Sales, Salt, Settlement, Stamps, Survey and Wards.

REYNOLDS.—THE NORTH-WESTERN PROVINCES RENT ACT. With Notes, &c. By H. W. REYNOLDS, C.S. Demy 8vo. [1886.] Rs. 7.

FIELD.—LANDHOLDING, AND THE RELATION OF LANDLORD AND Tenant in various countries of the world. By C. D. FIELD, M.A., LL.D. Second Edition. 8vo, cloth. Rs. 16.

N.B.—This edition contains "The Bengal Tenancy Act, 1885," with Notes and Observations: and an Index to the whole of the Law of Landlord and Tenant in Bengal.

"We may take it that, as regards Indian laws and customs, Mr. Field shows himself to be at once an able and skilled authority. In order, however, to render his work more complete, he has compiled, chiefly from Blue-books and similar public sources, a mass of information having reference to the land-laws of most European countries, of the United States of America, and our Australasian colonies."—*Field.*

GRIMLEY.—MANUAL OF THE REVENUE SALE LAW AND CERTIFICATE Procedure of Lower Bengal, including the Acts on the Subject and Selections from the Rules and Circular Orders of the Board of Revenue. With Notes. By W. H. GRIMLEY, B.A., C.S. 8vo. Rs. 5-8; interleaved, Rs. 6.

PHILLIPS.—THE LAW RELATING TO THE LAND TENURES OF Lower Bengal. (Tagore Law Lectures, 1875.) By ARTHUR PHILLIPS. Royal 8vo, cloth. Rs. 10.

REGULATIONS OF THE BENGAL CODE. A SELECTION INTENDED chiefly for the use of Candidates for appointments in the Judicial and Revenue Departments. Royal 8vo, stitched. Rs. 4.

PHILLIPS.—OUR ADMINISTRATION OF INDIA: BEING A COMPLETE ACCOUNT of the Revenue and Collectorate Administration in all departments, with special reference to the work and duties of a District Officer in Bengal. By H. A. D. PHILLIPS. Rs. 5.

"In eleven chapters Mr. Phillips gives a complete epitome of the civil, in distinction from the criminal, duties of an Indian Collector."—*London Quarterly Review.*

WHISH.—A DISTRICT OFFICE IN NORTHERN INDIA. WITH SOME suggestions on Administration. By C. W. WHISH, B.C.S. Demy 8vo, cloth. Rs. 4.

"Mr. Whish has produced an extremely useful and thoughtful book, which will pave the way for the junior members of his service. It is above all things practical, and sets forth the whole scheme of district duties in a clear and systematic manner."—*Englishman.*

FIELD.—INTRODUCTION TO THE REGULATIONS OF THE BENGAL CODE. By C. D. FIELD, M.A., LL.D. Crown 8vo. Rs. 8.

CONTENTS:—(I) The Acquisition of Territorial Sovereignty by the English in the Presidency of Bengal. (II) The Tenure of Land in the Bengal Presidency. (III) The Administration of the Land Revenue. (IV) The Administration of Justice.

MARKBY.—LECTURES ON INDIAN LAW. BY WILLIAM MARKBY, M.A. Crown 8vo, cloth. Rs. 8.

CONTENTS:—(I) Resumption of Lands held Rent-free. (II) The Revenue Sale Land of the Permanently Settled Districts. (III) Shekust Pywust, or Alluvion and Diluvian. (IV-V) The Charge of the Person and Property of Minors. (VI) Of the Protection afforded to Purchasers and Mortgagees when their title is impeached. Appendix—The Permanent Settlement—Glossary.

HOUSE.—THE N.-W. PROVINCES RENT ACT: BEING ACT XII of 1881, as amended by subsequent Acts. Edited with Introduction, Commentary and Appendices. By H. F. HOUSE, C.S. 8vo, cloth. Rs. 10.

CIVIL LAW.

HOLMWOOD.—THE LAW AND PRACTICE OF REGISTRATION IN BENGAL: comprising the History, Statute Law, Judicial Rulings, Rules and Circular Orders of Government; Extracts and Rules under the Bengal Tenancy Act regarding Registration; The Stamp Law, with a Digest of Rulings and a List of Registration Districts and Sub-Districts. By H. HOLMWOOD, I.C.S., Recently Registrar-General of Assurances, Bengal. Royal 8vo, cloth. Rs. 12.

ALEXANDER.—INDIAN CASE-LAW ON TORTS. BY THE LATE R. D. ALEXANDER, C.S. An entirely new Edition, Re-written and Enlarged by R. F. RAMPINI, C.S. 8vo, cloth. *Reprinting.*

BELCHAMBERS.—RULES AND ORDERS OF THE HIGH COURT OF Judicature at Fort William in Bengal in its several Jurisdictions. By R. BELCHAMBERS, Registrar. Royal 8vo, cloth. Rs. 16.

CHALMERS.—THE NEGOTIABLE INSTRUMENTS ACT, 1881. Being an Act to define and amend the Law relating to Promissory Notes, Bills of Exchange, and Cheques. Edited by M. D. CHALMERS, M.A., Barrister-at-law, Author of "A Digest of the Law of Bills of Exchange," &c.; and Editor of Wilson's "Judicature Acts." 8vo, cloth.

COLLETT.—THE LAW OF SPECIFIC RELIEF IN INDIA. BEING a Commentary on Act I of 1877. By CHARLES COLLETT, late of the Madras Civil Service, of Lincoln's Inn, Barrister-at-Law, and formerly a Judge of the High Court at Madras. Second Edition. Revised and brought up to date. By H. N. MORISON, Barrister-at-Law. 8vo, cloth. [*In the Press.*

KELLEHER.—PRINCIPLES OF SPECIFIC PERFORMANCE AND MISTAKE. By J. KELLEHER, C.S. 8vo, cloth. Rs. 8.

KELLEHER.—MORTGAGE IN THE CIVIL LAW. BEING AN OUTLINE of the Principles of the Law of Security, followed by the text of the Digest of Justinian, with Translation and Notes; and a Translation of the corresponding titles of the Indian Code. By J. KELLEHER, B.C.S., Author of "Possession in the Civil Law." Royal 8vo. Rs. 10.

KELLEHER.—POSSESSION IN THE CIVIL LAW. Abridged from the Treatise of Von Savigny, to which is added the Text of the Title on Possession from the Digest. By J. KELLEHER, C.S. 8vo, cloth. Rs. 8.

GASPERSZ.—THE LAW OF ESTOPPEL IN INDIA. Part I—Estoppel by Representation. Part II—Estoppel by Judgment. Being the Tagore Law Lectures, 1893. By A. CASPERSZ, Bar.-at-Law. Second Edition. Roy 8vo, cloth.

THE TRANSFER OF PROPERTY ACT. WITH NOTES AND LEADING CASES. By A. C. MITRA, Barrister-at-Law. Second Edition. Revised.

THE INDIAN INSOLVENCY ACT. BEING A REPRINT OF THE LAW AS to Insolvent Debtors in India, 11 and 12 Vict. Cap. 21 (June 1848). Royal 8vo, sewed. (Uniform with Acts of the Legislative Council.) Re. 1-8.

THE LAW OF FRAUD, MISREPRESENTATION AND MISTAKE IN BRITISH INDIA. By SIR FREDERICK POLLOCK, Bart., Barrister-at-Law Professor of Jurisprudence, Oxford. Being the Tagore Law Lectures, 1894 Royal 8vo, cloth gilt. Rs. 10.

A TREATISE ON THE LAW OF RES JUDICATA: INCLUDING THE Doctrines of Jurisdiction, Bar by Suit and Lis Pendens. By HUKM CHAND, M.A. Royal 8vo, cloth. Rs. 24.

"This is an enormous and exhaustive work. It deals most thoroughly with subjects which in ordinary books are not sufficiently dealt with, and is a perfect mine of decisions on the doctrine it touches. We have but tasted at this fountain-head of learning. We congratulate the author on having compiled such a monumental work."—*The Law Notes.*

RIVAZ.—THE INDIAN LIMITATION ACT (ACT XV OF 1877) AS AMENDed to date. With Notes. By the Hon'ble H. T. RIVAZ, Barrister-at-Law. Judge of the High Court of the Punjab. Fourth Edition. Royal 8vo, cloth. Rs. 10.

SUCCESSION, ADMINISTRATION, ETC.

FORSYTH.—THE PROBATE AND ADMINISTRATION ACT. BEING Act V of 1881. With Notes. By W. E. H. FORSYTH. Edited, with Index, by F. J. COLLINSON. Demy 8vo, cloth. Rs. 5.

HENDERSON.—THE LAW OF TESTAMENTARY DEVISE, AS ADministered in India, or the Law relating to Wills in India. With an Appendix, containing:—The Indian Succession Act (X of 1865), the Hindu Wills Act (XXI of 1870), the Probate and Administration Act (V of 1881) with all amendments, the Probate Administration Act (VI of 1889), and the Certificate of Succession Act (VII of 1889). By G. S. HENDERSON, M.A. Barrister-at-Law. (Tagore Law Lectures, 1887.) Royal 8vo, cloth. Rs. 16.

CIVIL PROCEDURE, SMALL CAUSE COURT, ETC.

BROUGHTON.—THE CODE OF CIVIL PROCEDURE. BEING ACT X of 1877. With Notes and Appendix. By the Hon'ble L. P. DELVES BROUGHTON, assisted by W. F. AGNEW and G. S. HENDERSON. Royal 8vo, cloth. Reduced to Rs. 7.

O'KINEALY.—THE CODE OF CIVIL PROCEDURE (ACT XIV OF 1882). With Notes, Appendices, &c. By the Hon'ble J. O'KINEALY. Fourth Edition. Royal 8vo. Rs. 16.

MACEWEN.—THE PRACTICE OF THE PRESIDENCY COURT OF SMALL CAUSES OF CALCUTTA, under the Presidency Small Cause Courts Act (XV of 1882). With Notes and an Appendix. By R. S. T. MACEWEN, of Lincoln's Inn, Barrister-at-Law, one of the Judges of the Presidency Court of Small Causes of Calcutta. Thick 8vo. Rs. 10.

POCKET CODE OF CIVIL LAW. CONTAINING THE CIVIL PROCEDURE Code (Act XIV of 1882), The Court-Fees Act (VII of 1870), The Evidence Act (I of 1872), The Specific Relief Act (I of 1877), The Registration Act (III of 1877), The Limitation Act (XV of 1877), The Stamp Act (I of 1879). With Supplement containing the Amending Act of 1888, and a General Index. Revised, 1891. Fcap. 8vo, cloth. Rs. 4.

LOCAL SELF-GOVERNMENT.

STERNDALE.—MUNICIPAL WORK IN INDIA; OR, HINTS ON SANITATION, General Conservancy and Improvement in Municipalities, Towns, and Villages. By R. C. STERNDALE. Crown 8vo, cloth. Rs. 3.

COLLIER.—THE BENGAL LOCAL SELF-GOVERNMENT HANDBOOK. Being ACT III OF 1885, B. C., and the General Rules framed thereunder. With Notes, Hints regarding Procedure, and References to Leading Cases; an Appendix, containing the principal Acts referred to, &c., &c. By F. R. STANLEY COLLIER, B.C.S. Third Edition, thoroughly revised and brought up to date. Crown 8vo. Rs. 5.

COLLIER.—THE BENGAL MUNICIPAL MANUAL. BEING B. C. ACT III of 1884. With Notes, and an Appendix containing all the Acts and Rules relating to Municipalities. By F. R. STANLEY COLLIER, C.S. Fourth Edition. Crown 8vo. Rs. 6.

CRIMINAL LAW.

HAMILTON.—INDIAN PENAL CODE: WITH A COMMENTARY. BY W. R. HAMILTON, Barrister-at-Law, Presidency Magistrate, Bombay. Royal 8vo, cloth. Rs. 16.

"It is one more valuable contribution to the slowly increasing series of standard commentaries on statute law by authors who have had practical experience in the administration of the law in India."—*Times of India.*

"The main features of Mr. Hamilton's work is that large extracts are given from the different reports of the Law Commissioners, and reference made to the different stages in the history of the enactments . . . . . . An appreciative and praise worthy piece of work, and should commend itself to a large circle of readers, legal as well as lay."—*Indian Daily News.*

"Of the book itself we have a high opinion. It contains, in fact, practically everything of importance that can guide to a knowledge or administration of the Penal Code, while notes on procedure appended to each section that defines an offence, stating briefly whether the offence be cognizable, bailable, compoundable, and so on, enable the reader to gain at a glance all the information he requires."—*Statesman.*

POCKET PENAL, CRIMINAL PROCEDURE, AND POLICE CODES. Also the Whipping Act and the Railway Servants' Act, being Acts XLV of 1860 (with Amendments), X of 1882, V of 1861, VI of 1864, and XXXI of 1867. With a General Index. Revised 1892. Fcap. 8vo, cloth. Rs. 4.

AGNEW AND HENDERSON.—THE CODE OF CRIMINAL PROCEDURE (ACT X OF 1882), together with Rulings, Circular Orders, Notifications, &c., of all the High Courts in India, and Notifications and Orders of the Government of India and the Local Governments. Edited, with Copious Notes and Full Index, by W. F. AGNEW, Bar.-at-Law, Author of "A Treatise on the Law of Trusts in India"; and GILBERT S. HENDERSON, M.A., Bar.-at-Law, Author of "A Treatise on the Law of Testamentary and Intestate Succession in India." Third Edition. Rs. 14.

THE INDIAN CRIMINAL DIGEST. CONTAINING ALL THE IMPORTANT Criminal Rulings of the various High Courts in India, together with many English Cases which bear on the Criminal Law as Administered in India. In Four Parts: I.—Indian Penal Code. II.—Evidence. III.—Criminal Procedure. IV.—Special and Local Acts. Vol. II.—1885 to 1893. By J. T. HUME, Solicitor, High Court, Calcutta, in charge of Government Prosecutions. Royal 8vo, cloth. Rs. 7-8.

PHILLIPS.—MANUAL OF INDIAN CRIMINAL LAW. BEING THE Penal Code, Criminal Procedure Code, Evidence, Whipping, General Clauses, Police, Cattle-Trespass, Extradition Acts, with Penal Clauses of Legal Practitioners' Act, Registration, Arms, Stamp, &c., Acts. Fully Annotated, and containing all Applicable Rulings of all High Courts arranged under the Appropriate Sections up to date; also Circular Orders and Notifications. By H. A. D. PHILLIPS, C.S. Second Edition. Thick crown 8vo. Rs. 10.

PHILLIPS.—COMPARATIVE CRIMINAL JURISPRUDENCE. SHOWING the Law, Procedure, and Case-Law of other Countries, arranged under the corresponding sections of the Indian Codes. By H. A. D. PHILLIPS, B.C.S. Vol. I, Crimes and Punishments. Vol. II, Procedure and Police. Demy 8vo, cloth. Rs. 12.

PRINSEP.—CODE OF CRIMINAL PROCEDURE ACT X OF 1882, AS amended by Acts III of 1884, X of 1886, V and XIV of 1887, I, V and XIII of 1889, III, IV, X and XII of 1891, III and X of 1894 and IV of 1895. With Notes of Judgments and Orders thereon. By the Hon'ble Sir H. T. PRINSEP, Judge, High Court, Calcutta. Eleventh Edition, brought up to 1895. Royal 8vo. Rs. 12.

TOYNBEE.—THE VILLAGE CHAUKIDARI MANUAL. BEING ACT VI (B. C.) of 1870, as amended by Acts I (B. C.) of 1871 and 1886. With Notes, Appendices, &c. By G. TOYNBEE, C.S., Magistrate of Hooghly. Third Edition, Revised. With additions to 1896. Crown 8vo, cloth. Re. 1-8.

SWINHOE.—THE CASE NOTED PENAL CODE, AND OTHER ACTS. Act XLV of 1860 as amended with References to all Reported Cases decided under each section. Crown 8vo, cloth. Rs. 7.

EVIDENCE.

FIELD.—THE LAW OF EVIDENCE IN BRITISH INDIA: BEING A Treatise on the Indian Evidence Act as amended by Act XVIII of 1872. By the Hon'ble C. D. FIELD, M.A., LL.D. Fifth Edition. Rs. 18.

STEPHEN.—THE PRINCIPLES OF JUDICIAL EVIDENCE. AN INTRODUCTION to the Indian Evidence Act, 1872. By SIR JAMES FITZ-JAMES STEPHEN, formerly Legislative Member of the Supreme Council of India. A New Edition. Crown 8vo, cloth. Rs. 3.

AMEER ALI AND WOODROFFE.—THE LAW OF EVIDENCE APPLICABLE TO BRITISH INDIA. By SYED AMEER ALI, M.A., C.I.E. Barrister-at-Law, Judge of the High Court of Judicature, and J. G. WOODROFFE, M.A., B.C.L., Barrister-at-Law. Demy 8vo, cloth. [*In preparation.*

MEDICAL JURISPRUDENCE.

LYON.—MEDICAL JURISPRUDENCE FOR INDIA. BY J. B. LYON, F.C.S., F.C., Brigade-Surgeon, Professor of Medical Jurisprudence, Grant Medical College, Bombay. The Legal Matter revised by J. D. INVERARITY, Barrister-at-Law. Second Edition. Illustrated. 8vo. Rs. 16.

GRIBBLE.—OUTLINES OF MEDICAL JURISPRUDENCE FOR INDIA. By J.D.B.GRIBBLE, M.C.S. (Retired), & PATRICK HEHIR, M.D., F.R.C.S.E. Third Edition, Revised, Enlarged, and Annotated. Demy 8vo. Rs. 5-8.

DIGESTS.

SUTHERLAND.—THE DIGEST OF INDIAN LAW REPORTS. A Compendium of the Rulings of the High Court of Calcutta from 1862, and of the Privy Council from 1831 to 1876. By D. SUTHERLAND, Barrister-at-Law. Imp. 8vo, Rs. 8. Vol. II, 1876 to 1890, thick cloth, imp. 8vo. Rs. 12.

WOODMAN.—A DIGEST OF THE INDIAN LAW REPORTS AND OF THE Reports of the cases heard in Appeal by the Privy Council Vol. VI. 1887 to 1889. Edited by J. V. WOODMAN, Barrister-at-Law. Super-royal 8vo. cloth. Rs. 12.

WOODMAN.—A DIGEST OF THE INDIAN LAW REPORTS AND OF THE Reports of the cases heard in Appeal by the Privy Council, Vol. VII 1890 to 1893. Edited by J. V. WOODMAN. Super-royal 8vo. Rs. 16.

HINDU AND MAHOMMEDAN LAW.

AMEER ALI.—THE STUDENT'S HAND-BOOK OF MAHOMMEDAN LAW. By the Hon'ble SYED AMEER ALI, C.I.E., author of "The Law relating to Gifts, Trusts, &c.," "Personal Law of the Mahommedans," &c., &c. Crown 8vo, Second Edition, Revised. Rs. 3.

AMEER ALI.—MAHOMMEDAN LAW, VOL. I. BY THE HON'BLE SYED AMEER ALI, C.I.E., Barrister-at-Law. Containing the Law relating to Gifts, Wakfs, Wills, Pre-emption, and Bailment. With an Introduction on Mahommedan Jurisprudence and Works on Law. (Being the Second Edition of Tagore Law Lectures, 1884.) Royal 8vo, cloth. Rs. 16.

AMEER ALI.—MAHOMMEDAN LAW, VOL. II. BY THE HON'BLE SYED AMEER ALI, C.I.E., Barrister-at-Law. Containing the Law relating to Succession and Status, according to the Hanafi, Mâliki, Shâfei, Shiah and Mutazala schools, with Explanatory Notes and an Introduction on the Islâmic system of Law. Being a Second Edition of "The Personal Law of the Mahommedans." Revised. Royal 8vo, cloth. Rs. 14.

These two volumes form a complete Digest of the Mahommedan Law.

COWELL.—A SHORT TREATISE ON HINDU LAW as administered in the Courts of British India. By HERBERT COWELL, Barrister-at-Law. Demy 8vo, cloth. Rs. 6.

THE HINDU LAW OF MARRIAGE AND STRIDHAN. BY THE Hon'ble GURUDASS BANERJEE, M.A., D.L. Second Edition. Revised. Royal 8vo, cloth.

JOLLY.—THE HINDU LAW OF INHERITANCE, PARTITION, AND Adoption according to the Smritis. By Prof. JULIUS JOLLY, of Wurtzburg. (Tagore Law Lectures. 1888.) Royal 8vo. Rs. 10.

MITRA.—THE HINDU LAW OF INHERITANCE, PARTITION, STRIDHAN and Wills, with Leading Cases from 1825 to 1895. By A. C. MITRA, Barrister-at-Law. Third Edition. Revised. 8vo, cloth. Rs. 10.

SARASWATI.-THE HINDU LAW OF ENDOWMENTS. BEBING THE Tagore Law Lectures, 1891. By PANDIT PRANNATH SARASWATI. Royal 8vo. cloth.

RUMSEY.—AL SIRAJIYYAH; OR, THE MAHOMMEDAN LAW OF INheritanced, with Notes and Appendix. By ALMARIC RUMSEY. Second Edition, Revised, with Additions. Crown 8vo. Rs. 4-8.

SIROMANI.—A COMMENTARY ON HINDU LAW OF INHERITANCE Succession, Partition, Adoption, Marriage, Stridhan and Testamentary Disposition. By Pundit JOGENDRO NATH BHATTACHARJEE, M.A., B.L. Second Edition. 8vo. Rs. 16.

WILSON.—INTRODUCTION TO THE STUDY OF ANGLO-MAHOMMEDAN LAW. By Sir ROLAND KNYVET WILSON, Bart., M.A., LL.M., late Reader in Indian Law to the University of Cambridge, author of "Modern English Law." 8vo, cloth. Rs. 6.

WILSON.—A DIGEST OF ANGLO-MUHAMMADAN LAW. BEING AN attempt to set forth, in the form of a Code, the rules now actually administered to Muhammadans only by the Civil Courts of British India, with explanatory Notes and full reference to Modern Case-Law, as well as to the ancient authorities. By Sir ROLAND KNYVET WILSON. 8vo, cloth. Rs. 15.

THACKER, SPINK AND CO., CALCUTTA.

LAW MANUALS, ETC.

COWELL.—THE HISTORY AND CONSTITUTION OF THE COURTS AND LEGISLATIVE AUTHORITIES IN INDIA. Second Edition, Revised. By HERBERT COWELL. 8vo, cloth. [1894] Rs. 6.

HANDBOOK OF INDIAN LAW. A POPULAR AND CONCISE STATEment of the Law generally in force in British India, designed for non-legal people, on subjects relating to Person and Property. By a Barrister-at-Law and Advocate of the High Court at Calcutta. Crown 8vo, pp. xxiv, 754. Cloth gilt. Rs. 12.

"This handbook is intended primarily to present to the non-legal public and to students an abridgment of the law, criminal and civil, generally in force throughout British India. It is concise, popularly written, and, so far as we have been able to form an opinion on the point, complete. Lawyers as well as students may find it serviceable at a pinch. A short and excellent historial account of legislation and Courts of Law in British India from the time of the East India Company until the present day is embodied in an introduction. The Index is admirable. This book will be of great use to competition-wallahs."—*The Law Journal, December* 22nd, 1894.

"Presenting in a concise, intelligent, and popular form the law in force in British India it should meet the much, felt want of a 'ready lawyer' for the office table. A clear and accurate presentment of the law is given on more than a hundred subjects arranged alphabetically, and including such subjects as most nearly concern the mercantile community."—*Capital.*

CARNEGY.—KACHAHRI TECHNICALITIES. A GLOSSARY OF TERMS, Rural, Official and General, in daily use in the Courts of Law, and in illustration of the Tenures, Customs, Arts, and Manufactures of Hindustan. By P. CARNEGY. Second Edition. 8vo, cloth. Rs. 9.

CURRIE.—THE INDIAN LAW EXAMINATION MANUAL. BY FENDALL CURRIE, of Lincoln's Inn, Barrister-at-Law. Fourth Edition. Revised. Demy 8vo. [1892.] Rs. 5.

CONTENTS:—Introduction—Hindoo Law—Mahommedan Law—Indian Penal Code—Code of Civil Procedure—Evidence Act—Limitation Act—Succession Act—Contract Act—Registration Act—Stamp and Court-Fees Acts—Mortgage—Code of Criminal Procedure—The Easements Act—The Trust Act—The Transfer of Property Act—The Negotiable Instruments Act.

CHAN TOON.—THE PRINCIPLES OF BUDDHIST LAW, ALSO CONtaining a translation of important portions of the Manu Thara Shwe Myin, with Notes. By CHAN TOON, Barrister-at-Law. 8vo, cloth. Rs. 5.

THE SEA CUSTOMS LAW OF INDIA (ACT VIII OF 1878) WITH NOTES And the Tariff Act of 1894. By W. H. GRIMLEY, I.C.S., late Secretary to the Board of Revenue, Calcutta. 8vo, cloth. Rs. 7-8.

LEGISLATIVE ACTS OF THE GOVERNOR-GENERAL OF INDIA IN COUNCIL 1895. With Table of Contents and Index. Royal 8vo. cloth. Rs. 8-8. *Previous Volumes available.*

DONOGH.—THE STAMP LAW OF BRITISH INDIA. AS CONSTITUTED by the Indian Stamp Act (I of 1879), Rulings and Circular Orders, Notifications, Resolutions, Rules, and Orders, together with Schedules of all the Stamp Duties chargeable on Instruments in India from the earliest times. Edited, with Notes and complete Index, by WALTER R. DONOGH, M.A., of the Inner Temple, Barrister-at-Law. Demy 8vo, cloth, gilt. With Supplements to 1894. Rs. 8.

GRIMLEY.—AN INCOME-TAX MANUAL. BEING ACT II OF 1886, With Notes. By W. H. GRIMLEY, B.A., C.S., Commissioner of Income-Tax, Bengal. Royal 8vo, Rs. 3-8. Interleaved, Rs. 4.

ADVOCACY AND THE EXAMINATION OF WITNESSES. THE WORK treats of matters of practice such as taking instructions, speech, argument, examination-in-chief and cross-examination, and includes a resumé of the duties and liabilities of Pleaders in India. The Legal Practitioners' Act with the Rules of the High Courts relating to the admission of Pleaders and Mookhtars, appears in the form of an Appendix. By H. N. MORISON, Barrister-at-Law. Crown 8vo, cloth. Rs. 6.

"Undoubtedly juniors and, possibly, not a few seniors too, may profit by the sensible and practical hints Mr. Morison gives as to the *finesse* of Counsel, and the treatment of Witnesses . . . . Mr. Morison's book is certainly one that should be bought."—*Statesman.*

"A work which will be of material service to the younger members of the legal profession in India."—*Indian Daily News.*

THACKER, SPINK AND CO, CALCUTTA.

THE JOURNAL OF THE

PHOTOGRAPHIC SOCIETY OF INDIA.

AN ILLUSTRATED MONTHLY JOURNAL.

Invaluable to all lovers of the Art of Photography.

A medium for the earliest information on all discoveries in Photography, Photographic Literature, Experience and News.

The Journal has a large and increasing circulation, is affiliated with Clubs or Amateur Societies all over India, Ceylon, Burma and the Straits Settlements, and has an extensive circulation out of India.

Each number of the Journal is illustrated with a Picture reproduced by a photo-mechanical process.

SUBSCRIPTION—Rs. 6 PER ANNUM.

Single numbers, Re. 1 each.

THE RACING CALENDAR.

A FORTNIGHTLY CALENDAR.

Published in accordance with the Rules of Racing, under the authority of the Stewards of the Calcutta Turf Club.

A Record of all Race Performances in India, Racing Fixtures and Racing information, Meetings of the Calcutta Turf Club, Registration of Colours, Assumed Names of Owners, Jockeys' Licenses, Unpaid Forfeit List, List of Defaulters, Change in Horses' Names, Horses and Ponies classed, aged and measured, and all information relating to Racing.

ANNUAL SUBSCRIPTION, Rs. 12.

THACKER, SPINK AND CO., CALCUTTA.

STANDARD WORKS ON INDIA.

THE JOURNAL OF INDIAN ART. WITH FULL-PAGE COLOURED Illustrations. Folio 15 by 11. Parts 1 to 54 ready. Rs. 2-4 each.

THE SACRED BOOKS OF THE EAST. TRANSLATED BY VARIOUS Oriental Scholars. Edited by F. MAX MULLER. *List of Volumes on application.*

THE FAUNA OF BRITISH INDIA. INCLUDING CEYLON AND BURMA. Published under the authority of the Secretary of State for India. Edited by W. T. BLANFORD, F.R.S., and Illustrated.

Mammalia.	By W. T. BLANFORD, F.R.S.	...	20s.
Fishes, 2 vols.	By Dr. FRANCIS DAY	...	40s.
Birds, 3 vols.	By F. W. OATES	...	50s.
Reptilia and Batrachia.	By G. A. BOULENGER	...	20s.
Moths, 3 vols.	By F. HAMPSON	...	60s.

THE INDIAN MUTINY, 1857-58. SELECTIONS FROM THE LETTERS, Despatches, and other State Papers preserved in the Military Department of the Government of India. Edited by GEORGE W. FORREST, B.A., Director of Records of the Government of India. With a Map and Plans. Vol. I.—Delhi. Royal 8vo. Rs. 10.

WARREN HASTINGS. SELECTION FROM THE LETTERS, DESPATCHES, and other State Papers preserved in the Foreign Department of the Government of India, 1772-1785. Edited by GEORGE W. FORREST, B.A. 3 vols. Fcap., cloth. Rs. 12.

THE ADMINISTRATION OF WARREN HASTINGS, 1772-1785. Reviewed and Illustrated from Original Documents. By G. W. FORREST, B.A. 8vo, cloth. Rs. 4.

THE EARLY ANNALS OF THE ENGLISH IN BENGAL: BEING THE Bengal Public Consultations for the first half of the 18th Century. Summarised, Extracted and Edited, Introduction and Illustrative Addenda. By C. R. WILSON, M.A. Volume 1. Royal 8vo, cloth. Rs. 12.

ANNALS OF RURAL BENGAL. BY Sir W. W. HUNTER, C.I.E., LL.D. 8vo. Rs. 6.

ILLUSTRATION OF SOME OF THE GRASSES OF THE SOUTHERN PUNJAB. Being Photo-Lithograph Illustrations of some of the principal Grasses found at Hissar. With short descriptive Letter-press. By WILLIAM COLDSTREAM, B.A., B.C.S. Illustrated with 39 Plates. Demy folio. Rs. 8.

ILLUSTRATIONS OF INDIAN FIELD SPORTS. SELECTED AND REPRODUCED from the Coloured Engravings first published in 1807 after designs by Captain THOMAS WILLIAMSON. Bengal Army. Small oblong, handsome cloth cover. Printed in colours. Rs. 5.

THACKER, SPINK AND CO., CALCUTTA.

THACKER, SPINK & CO.'S UNIFORM SERIES.

ILLUSTRATED AND ELEGANTLY BOUND.

DEPARTMENTAL DITTIES AND OTHER VERSES. By Rudyard Kipling. Eighth Edition. With additional Poems. Cloth. Rs. 3.

BEHIND THE BUNGALOW. By Eha, Author of "Tribes on my Frontier." With 42 Illustrations by the Illustrator of "The Tribes on My Frontier." Fourth Edition. With Additional Illustrations. Impl. 16mo. Rs. 5.

THE TRIBES ON MY FRONTIER. An Indian Naturalist's Foreign Policy. By Eha. With 50 Illustrations by F. C. Mackak. Impl. 16mo. Fourth Edition. Rs. 7.

HINDU MYTHOLOGY: VEDIC AND PURANIC. By the Rev. W. J. Wilkins, of the London Missionary Society, Calcutta. Profusely Illustrated. Rs. 7-8.

A NATURAL HISTORY OF THE MAMMALIA OF INDIA, BURMA and Ceylon. By R. A. Sterndale, F.R.G.S., F.Z.S., &c. With 170 Illustrations. Impl. 16mo. Rs. 10.

HANDBOOK TO THE FERNS OF INDIA, CEYLON, AND THE MALAY Peninsula. By Colonel R. H. Beddome. With 300 Illustrations by the Author. Impl. 16mo. Rs. 10.

LAYS OF IND. By Aliph Cheem. Comic, Satirical, and Descriptive Poems illustrative of Anglo-Indian Life. Ninth Edition. With 70 Illustrations. Cloth, elegant gilt edges. Rs. 7-8.

RIDING: ON THE FLAT AND ACROSS COUNTRY. A Guide to Practical Horsemanship. By Captain M. H. Hayes. Illustrated by Sturgess and J. H. Oswald-Brown. Third Edition. Revised and Enlarged. Impl. 16mo. Rs. 7-8.

MODERN POLO. A Guide to the Game, with Introductions on the Selection and Training of the Ponies. By E. D. Miller (late 17th Lancers). Edited by Capt. M. H. Hayes. Illustrated from Photographs. Impl. 16mo, cloth. Rs. 12-8.

THE HORSE WOMAN. An Illustrated Guide to Side-Saddle Riding. By Mrs. Hayes, and Edited by Capt. M. H. Hayes. Uniform with "Riding: on the Flat and Across Country." Impl. 16mo. Rs. 7-8.

RIDING FOR LADIES, WITH HINTS ON THE STABLE. A Lady's Horse Book. By Mrs. Power O'Donoghue. With 75 Illustrations by A. Chantrey Corbould. Rs. 7-8.

INDIAN RACING REMINISCENCES: being Entertaining Narrative and Anecdotes of Men, Horses, and Sport. By Captain M. H. Hayes. Illustrated with Portraits and Engravings. Rs. 6.

THACKER, SPINK AND CO., CALCUTTA.

INDEX.